BOTANY
FOR
AGRICULTURAL STUDENTS

BY

JOHN N. MARTIN

*Professor of Botany at the Iowa State College of Agriculture
and Mechanic Arts*

FIRST EDITION

NEW YORK

JOHN WILEY & SONS, Inc.

London: CHAPMAN & HALL, Limited

1919

WINDHAM PRESS
CLASSIC REPRINTS

PREFACE

Although students vary widely in their reasons for studying Botany, the fundamental facts or principles of the subject are not thereby altered. One has considerable freedom, however, in the presentation of the subject to adapt the subject matter to special aims of different classes of students, and especially is this true in courses for agricultural students, since much of the work in Agriculture is based upon the principles of Botany. In the choice of material to illustrate principles and in the presentation of the applications of principles, there is special opportunity to relate courses in Botany to courses in Agriculture.

In any elementary course in Botany, regardless of the kind of education the student desires to obtain, the primary aim should be to give the student a notion of the fundamental principles of Botany. This aim should be the guiding one in both recitation and laboratory, determining the trend of discussions in recitation, and the nature of the material and procedure in the laboratory. The primary aim should be accompanied by a secondary aim to relate the subject to the student's major line of work. When the relation of the subject to major lines of work is obvious, the student is more likely to appreciate the subject and is thereby put in a favorable mood to study the subject. Even for students who take Botany merely as a part of a general education, it in no way detracts from the course or makes botanical training less efficient to present the practical aspects of the subject.

This book is intended for elementary courses in Botany in colleges and universities. In its preparation the aim has been to present the fundamental principles of Botany with emphasis upon the practical application of these principles. The subject matter is presented in two parts, part I being devoted to the study of the structures and functions chiefly of Flowering Plants, and Part II, to the study of the kinds of plants, relationships, Evolution, Heredity, and Plant Breeding.

In the preparation of the book, I had the following objects in view: (1) to present the structures and functions of Flowering

Plants and relate them to such agricultural subjects as Farm Crops, Forestry, and Horticulture, and to the more advanced courses in Botany; (2) to present the kinds of plants with emphasis upon their evolutionary relationships and their economic importance; and (3) to present Evolution, Heredity, and Plant Breeding as related to the improvement of plants.

The topics are arranged in the book in the order in which I usually present them. The presentation of the reproductive structures and processes of Flowering Plants, followed by that of the vegetative organs, has fitted in at Iowa State College with the time of year at which the agricultural students begin the study of Botany and also with the courses in Agriculture. In other schools where conditions are different, other arrangements of the topics are more suitable. In recognition of this fact, most of the chapters have been written so as to be separately understandable, the aim being to make the book adaptable to any arrangement of topics that the teacher may prefer.

In the discussion of a subject the presentation of the general features precedes that of the particular features, and the latter are presented in most cases by the study of type plants chosen on account of their familiarity and economic importance.

The book is intended for an entire year's work in Botany and to be accompanied by laboratory work. Where less time is devoted to the subject, the organization of the chapters so as to be separately understandable permits a selection of topics according to the requirements of the course.

The reproductive structures and processes in Flowering Plants (Chapters III and IV) are dwelt upon more than is necessary for students who have had a good course in Botany in a high school. A large percentage of the students in my elementary classes have had no Botany and have difficulty in understanding sexual reproduction in Flowering Plants. In an effort to thoroughly acquaint the student with this subject, I have dwelt at considerable length upon those phases of the subject that are in my experience difficult for the student to understand. In case students are familiar with this subject, parts of Chapters III and IV can be omitted or read hastily in review.

Usually there are some students in the class that are especially interested in certain topics and desire a more complete discussion of the topics than the text affords. In recognition of this fact, I have added, chiefly as footnotes, many references. Most of the references are bulletins on the special topics, and in addition to giving further information on the special topics, these references introduce the student to that vast source of information contained in the bulletins published by the U. S. Department and the experiment stations of the different states.

Many of the illustrations have been taken from the publications of various authors whose names or the names of their publications appear in connection with the illustrations. To these authors I am much indebted. Most of the original illustrations have been made by Mrs. Edith Martin, who has also given me valuable assistance in other ways in the preparation of the book. Also much credit is due Mr. H. S. Doty and Mr. L. E. Yocum, my assistants, who have given me valuable suggestions. To Dr. L. H. Pammel, who read some of the topics on Fungi and offered valuable suggestions, I am also much indebted.

The book no doubt has many faults, but I hope it has some particular value and that the criticisms which teachers offer will make me a more efficient teacher.

J. N. MARTIN.

AMES, IOWA
Oct. 7, 1918

CONTENTS

INTRODUCTION

PART I

PLANTS (CHIEFLY SEED PLANTS), AS TO STRUCTURES AND FUNCTIONS

Botany for Agricultural Students

CHAPTER I

THE NATURE OF BOTANY

Botany is a branch of *Biology* which includes all of the sciences that deal with living things. Zoology, Bacteriology, Human Anatomy and Physiology are some other biological sciences that are familiar and closely related to Botany.

The word botany comes from a Greek word, *bosko*, meaning, "I eat.' Botany was originally the science of things good to eat, and in its naming the fact was recognized that plants are the source of our food. Of course at the present time Botany studies all kinds of plants which include besides the many useful for food, many useful as medicine, and many that are poisonous. Botany is commonly defined as that science which treats of plants. This definition is not entirely satisfactory because it does not separate Botany from such agricultural subjects as Horticulture, Forestry, and Farm Crops which also treat of plants.

Between Botany and those agricultural subjects which study plants, there is no sharp division line. Much of the work in these agricultural subjects is based upon the principles of Botany. Such features as plant structures, plant functions, and relation of functions to sunlight, air, soil, etc., which are studied in Botany, are features of consideration in Horticulture, Forestry, and Farm Crops. Although Botany and these agricultural subjects study many plant features in common, the latter subjects differ from Botany in studying only special groups of plants, and in limiting the study to the practical and economic phases of plants.

A plant may be studied in a number of different ways. It may be considered in reference to structure, functions, and in relation to other plants. Botany is divided into a number of subjects which consider different phases of plant life.

1

MORPHOLOGY considers the form and structure of plants. It considers the forms of plant bodies and the organs and tissues which compose them. Morphology studies the structure of roots, stem, leaves, buds, and flowers, and establishes the relationships of organs. Morphology not only considers the more complex plants but also the simpler ones, and traces the development of plant structures through the different plant groups. The phase of Morphology in which the development of the more complex plants from the simpler ones is studied, is called *Plant Evolution*. When Morphology is concerned with the microscopical study of the finer structures of plants, then it is called *Anatomy*, and if the study is mainly concerned with the structure of the cell, then it is called *Cytology*. Anatomy and Cytology are often spoken of as *Histology*. Another phase of Morphology is *Embryology* which, as the term suggests, is the study of the embryo, or the study of the plant during its formation in the seed.

PLANT PHYSIOLOGY studies the functions of plant structures and the relation of these functions to light, temperature, air, soil, etc. It treats of how the plant lives, respires, feeds, grows, and reproduces. In the study of Plant Physiology we learn how plant food is made and transported, and how plants grow. As a basis for the study of Plant Physiology, one must have a knowledge of the Morphology of plants and also a knowledge of Chemistry and Physics.

PLANT PATHOLOGY treats of plant diseases. In this subject one learns the disease producing plants and how they affect the plant diseased. In the study of Plant Pathology, in order to know how the diseased plant is injured, one must know the nature and function of the tissues attacked. This means that one should know Morphology and Plant Physiology. Furthermore, in order to know how the disease producing form attacks other plants and propagates itself, one needs to know its Morphology and Physiology.

PLANT ECOLOGY considers plants in relation to the conditions under which they live. Some plants can live on a dry hill top, while others can live only in moist, shady places. Some can live in colder regions than others. Some plants, like many of the weeds, can thrive when crowded among other plants, while some like the Corn plant can not. Marshes, bogs, forests, sandbars, etc., all have their characteristic plants. One set of plants often prepares the way for others. On exposed rocks only very small plants are able to grow at first, but due to their presence soil accumulates and larger plants are able to follow. Such problems as the above are studied in Ecology. Ecology studies plants in relation to the effects of soil, climate, and friendly, or hostile animals and plants. It also studies the effect of the different conditions upon the form and structure of plants.

PLANT GEOGRAPHY is much like Ecology and treats of the distribution of the different kinds of plants over the earth's surface.

TAXONOMY, or SYSTEMATIC BOTANY, treats of the classification of plants. As a result of this kind of study, plants have been arranged in groups, such as Algæ, Bacteria, Fungi, Mosses, Ferns, and Seed Plants. These large groups are further subdivided into smaller groups. Keys have been arranged by which plants unknown to the student may be identified. Through the study of Systematic Botany one can learn the names and some of the characteristics of the different kinds of Grasses, weeds, shrubs, and trees that grow on the farm or in any other region.

ECONOMIC BOTANY treats of the uses of plants to man.

PALEOBOTANY is concerned with the history of plants as shown by their preserved forms, known as fossils, which occur in the different layers of rock composing the earth's crust. Paleobotany is studied in connection with Geology. In the study of this subject much has been learned about the plants which lived millions of years ago, and this knowledge is very useful in understanding the evolution of the plants which now exist.

Subjects treated in this Book.— To become a master in any one of the above subjects would require years of one's time. A study of any of the special subjects of Botany requires a general knowledge of the anatomy and the functions of plant structures This means that one must have a general course in Botany before making a special study of Morphology, Plant Physiology, or any of the special botanical subjects. One purpose of this book is to give a general knowledge of cultivated plants, of plants not cultivated but like the Rusts and Smuts related to Agriculture, and of those plants which one must know in order to understand the evolution of plants. Another purpose is to give such a general knowledge of plant anatomy and the functions of plant structures, that one will have the necessary knowledge for the study of such agricultural subjects as Horticulture, Forestry, and Farm Crops, and also a basis for the study of the special botanical subjects. These special subjects of Botany are not only very important to one who makes a special study of Botany, but some phases of Morphology, Plant Physiology, Plant Pathology, Systematic Botany, and Ecology are important studies for agricultural students in certain agricultural courses. *Part I*, this book, deals mainly with the parts of plants as to structure and function and, therefore, emphasizes the Morphology and Physiology of plants. But structure and function as well as other aspects of plants, accompany and explain each other and can not well be separated in an elementary study of Botany. So the different phases of the plant are studied as they occur in relation to each other and without any designation as to whether or not the fact belongs to Morphology, Physiology, or any other special phase of Botany. *Part II* is devoted chiefly to a study of plants as to kinds, relationships, evolution, and heredity.

CHAPTER II

A GENERAL VIEW OF PLANTS

Abundance and Distribution of Plants. — Plants are so abundant and generally distributed that there are very few regions that do not have plants. Plants occur in the water and in the soil as well as on the surface of the earth. Some plants live in the bodies of animals. Some are able to live where the temperature is intensely cold, while others can live in hot springs where the temperature is not far from the boiling point. Even on rocks that look quite bare, a close examination will show that some plant forms are present. Only in exceptional places, such as volcanic regions, some hot springs, and regions of salt deposits, are plants generally absent.

The abundance or scarcity of plants in a given region depends upon how well the conditions of the region meet the requirements for plant growth. If the soil is dry, as in desert regions, the average number of plants per area is usually quite small, while in regions where there is sufficient moisture and sufficient mineral substances, more than 100,000 plants may occur on an area no larger than an average garden. However, the number of plants which can occur on a given area, is often very different from the number that can do well on this same area. Many more grain plants can be grown per acre than are grown, but agriculturists have learned that only a limited number of plants per acre can do well. Among plants, as among animals, there is competition. Plants must compete with each other for moisture, mineral substances, and sunlight, and when the competition is too great, as occurs when plants are too much crowded, some or all of the plants suffer and fail to produce good yields. By controlling the amount of seed sown and by properly distributing the seed, the farmer is able to raise the greatest number of plants per acre with the least loss from competition among the plants.

Diversity of Plant Forms. — Plants are not only the smallest, but also the largest of living organisms. Many plants are so

5

small that they can be seen only with a microscope. Ranging from these very small plants to the largest trees, plants of all sizes and complexity occur about us. The different plant forms differ very much in structure, methods of getting food, and methods of reproduction. The plants which concern us most are those which have flowers. They are known as the Flowering Plants. Most of the cultivated plants and nearly all weeds belong to this group. They are the plants which furnish nearly all of our food and fibers and much of our lumber. *Part I* of this book is devoted to the study of the Flowering Plants.

Although the Flowering Plants concern us most, it must not be concluded that the simpler plants are of no importance. The simpler plants, even the microscopic forms, not only help and hinder in the cultivation of the Flowering Plants, but affect us in other ways and must receive consideration. Much of *Part II* is devoted to the study of them.

Parts of a Plant. — In plants, as in animals, there is a living body consisting of parts each of which has a special work to perform. The various parts of a plant having their own special work are called *organs*, and the special work of an organ is its *function*. Plants, like animals, being composed of organs, are called *organisms*. In the Flowering Plants, the plant body consists of roots, stem, leaves, buds, flowers, seeds, and fruit. All of these structures are not present at all times, but unless a Flowering Plant develops all of these organs during its life, its development is considered incomplete. Through the special functions of its organs, the plant is able to exist and reproduce itself. The roots hold the plant to the soil and furnish water and salts; the stem supports the leaves, flowers, and fruit in the air and sunlight; the leaves make food; the buds produce new leaves and flowers; and the flowers, seed, and fruit have to do with the production of new plants. But each organ is also composed of parts and to understand an organ one must understand its special groups of cells, known as *tissues*, of which the organ is composed.

Life Cycle of Flowering Plants. — A characteristic of living organisms is their ability to use substances as food, grow, and develop. Living organisms are also much influenced by their surroundings. Plants are much influenced by the nature of the soil, air, sunlight, and plants which grow about them.

To understand a plant one needs to study it in its various

stages of development. The tiny Corn plant, called embryo or
germ, which we find in the Corn kernel, does not look much like
the plant that bears tassel and ears. From the embryo to the
flower and seed stage, many things take place. The series of
events which take place in the development of the embryo to a
mature plant constitutes the *life cycle* of a plant. Starting from

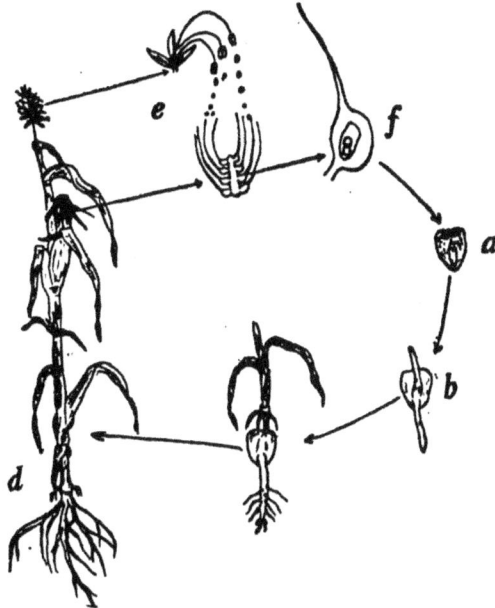

FIG. 1. — Life cycle as illustrated by the Corn plant. *a*, mature kernel;
b, germination; next, seedling; *d*, mature plant composed of roots, stems,
leaves, and flowers, all of which are composed of tissues having special functions to perform; *e*, the two kinds of flowers with pollination indicated;
f, fertilization indicated by the two globular bodies, sperm and egg, on the
inside of the ovary or portion that develops into the kernel. After fertilization the ovary develops into another kernel and thus the life cycle is
completed.

the seed, this series of events consists of germination, development of seedling with its different organs and tissues, development of root, stem bud, and leaf structures of the more mature
plant, development of flowers, pollination and fertilization, and
development of other kernels. The life cycle of any Flowering
Plant is similar to that of the Corn. Thus it is seen that the life

cycle of a plant returns us to the place of starting.   The series of events may be represented as shown in *Figure 1*, and in tracing them one can begin at any point.   The yield of the plant at maturity depends upon how well it has done at the different stages in its life cycle.   The purpose of cultivation is to help the plant to do well at all stages, and it is for this reason that we look after the fertility of the soil, select seed, prepare a seed bed, sow or plant a certain amount of seed and in a certain way, prevent the growth of weeds, etc.   But often methods of cultivation must take into account the structure and function of plant organs as they occur at the different stages in the life cycle of the plant, and unless the peculiar features of the plant are understood, the methods employed in cultivation may not be adapted to secure the best results.

CHAPTER III

FLOWERS

General Characteristics and Structure of Flowers

On account of their colors and odors, flowers very much excel other plant organs in attracting attention. Everybody is interested in flowers on account of their æsthetic charm, if for no other reason. The attractive colors and pleasant odors common to flowers not only interest the scientist but also appeal to the æsthetic sense of people in general. In fact many people would define the flower as the showy part of the plant. However showiness is not an essential feature, for there are many flowers which have no attractive colors or odors and yet they are just as genuine in function as are showy flowers. Most forest and shade trees, the Grasses, and many weeds do not have showy flowers. The flowers of such plants as the Oaks, Elms, Maples, and Pines lack showy parts and are so inconspicuous that most people have not noticed them, yet these flowers are just as genuine in function as those of a Lily or Rose.

On account of their showiness and importance in reproduction, flowers were first to receive careful study; and in the early history of Botany, flowers were about the only plant structures that received much attention. At the present time there are some people who have the erroneous notion that the study of Botany and flowers are still almost identical despite the fact that the study of flowers is now of no more importance than many other phases of plant life, as is well shown by the large amount of space devoted by our present botanical texts to the study of roots, stems, leaves, and other phases of plants.

In *size*, flowers may be almost microscopical as in some of the small floating water plants, such as the Duckweeds, or they may be of huge dimensions as some tropical flowers which are two or more feet across. Even in the ordinary greenhouse, some flowers are so small that they are not conspicuous except in large clusters,

9

while those of Carnations and Roses are conspicuous when single. In Chrysanthemums, Daisies, and Sunflowers the individual flowers, although small, form a cluster so compact that it is often erroneously considered a single flower.

As to *color*, which is the character most closely related to securing pollination by insects, flowers are exceedingly various. Some, especially those that depend upon the wind for pollination, are green like leaves. Some are white, while among others nearly every color imaginable can be found. It is claimed that by means of colors flowers solicit the visitation of insects, which are important agents in pollination.

The *odors* of flowers, usually pleasant, but sometimes repulsive to us, as in case of the Carrion-flower and Skunk Cabbage, probably serve in attracting insects. Furthermore, pleasant odors add to the value of plants for ornamental purposes.

Flowers present various *forms*. When well open, some are wheel-shaped, some funnel-shaped, some tubular, while others depart from these forms with various irregularities, as in the Sweet Pea, where the flower resembles a butter-

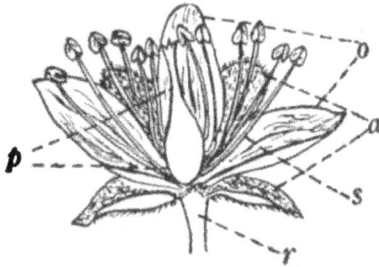

FIG. 2. — Basswood flower with portions removed from one side so that the interior of the flower may be seen. *a*, calyx composed of leaf-like portions or sepals; *o*, corolla composed of leaf-like portions called petals; *s*, stamens; *p*, pistil; *r*, receptacle. Much enlarged.

fly in shape, or in the Orchids where parts of the flower may be so shaped as to resemble a slipper, as the Orchid known as the Lady's-slipper illustrates. The shape of the flower in many cases favors the visitation of only special insects, and, therefore, is closely related to the problem of pollination.

To discover the essential features of a flower, it becomes necessary to determine the function of the flower, and become acquainted with its parts and the use of each part in relation to the work of the flower.

Function of the Flower. — The flower is the plant's principal organ of reproduction, being devoted to the production of seed which is the plant's principal device for producing new plants.

Functionally, the flower may be defined as the organ which has to do with seed production. Flowers which have been so modified through cultivation that they no longer produce seed are not true flowers. However, the true function of the flower is often not the important feature to the plant grower. Many flowers are cultivated entirely for their æsthetic charm. In case of fruit trees, Tomatoes, and many other plants, the structure developing from the flower and known as the fruit is more important to the plant grower than the seed. However, when plants are grown for seed or fruit, the amount of seed or fruit harvested depends very much upon the number of flowers produced. For example, the gardener does not expect to gather many Beans or Peas if the vines produce only a few flowers. Likewise, good crops of Clover and Alfalfa seed depend upon a

FIG. 3. — Apetalous flower of Buckwheat. c, calyx; s, stamens; p, pistil; r, receptacle. Much enlarged. After Marchand.

good crop of flowers; and not much fruit is expected when the flowers in the orchard are few. It is in connection with the function of reproduction, that flowers have developed the various colors, forms, and odors which assist in bringing about fertilization, the central feature of sexual reproduction to which the flower is devoted, and the process upon which the development of seed usually depends.

Despite the multitudinous forms and colors which flowers present, there is much unity and simplicity in structure, all parts being organized to assist in performing the function of seed production.

Parts of the Flower. — The parts of a flower are of two general kinds; those which are directly concerned in the production of seed; and those which act as protective and attractive organs. The former are known as the *essential organs*, and consist of *stamens* and *pistils*. The latter are known as floral *envelopes* or *perianth*, and usually consist of two sets of organs, one called *calyx* and the other, *corolla*. In *Figure 2*, the calyx is the lowest whorl and consists of green leaf-like portions called *sepals*. The second whorl is the corolla and each separate portion is a *petal*. The pistil occupies the central position and is surrounded by the whorl of stamens. The end of the flower stem to which these

FIG. 4. — A flower of Tobacco. *c*, the funnel-shaped corolla made up of united petals; *b*, calyx. The sepals are also united below. Reduced.

FIG. 5. — Flower of Red Clover. *c*, corolla; *b*, cup-like calyx. Much enlarged. After Hayden.

floral parts are attached is called *torus* or *receptacle*. The receptacle may be flat, conical, or cup-shaped, and often forms

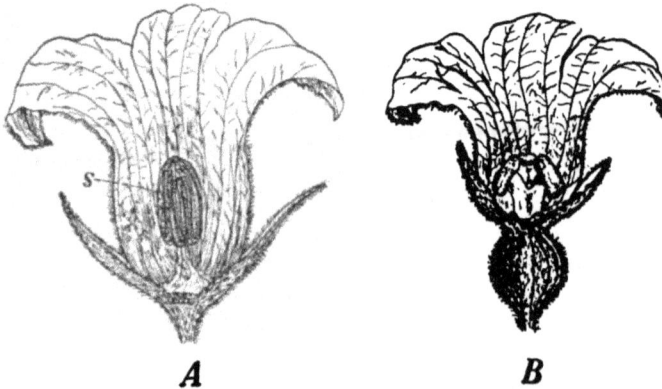

A   *B*

FIG. 6. — The two unisexual flowers of the Pumpkin with a portion of the bell-shaped corollas torn away to show the interior of the flowers.

A, staminate flower; *s*, stamens fitting together, forming a column. *B*, pistillate flower. Less than half natural size.

an important part of the fruit. The corolla is usually bright colored, and, therefore, the conspicuous part of the flower. It is also the fleeting part of the flower, usually lasting only a few days.

Flowers having the four sets of organs, as shown in *Figure 2*, are called *complete* flowers to distinguish them from *incomplete* flowers, that is, flowers in which some of the organs are lacking. The organs are generally arranged in a circular fashion around the receptacle, and are characterized as being in cycles or whorls. In some flowers a part or all of the perianth is lacking. In the Buckwheat, as shown in *Figure 3*, only one whorl surrounds the stamens and pistil, and it is evident that this flower does not have both calyx and corolla. In such cases, the petals are considered missing and the flower is said to be *apetalous* ("without petals"). Often instead of being composed of entirely separate petals (polypetalous), the corolla is a tube or funnel-shaped structure, which appears to be composed of united petals (gamopetalous), separate only at the top. (*Fig. 4.*) The flowers of the Tobacco Plant, Pumpkins, Squashes, and Watermelons are examples of gamopetalous flowers. In some cases, as in the Tobacco, Clover, and some other plants, the sepals seem to have joined into one structure (gamosepalous), forming a tube- or cup-like calyx. (*Fig. 4* and *5*.) Flowers also differ in the essential organs contained.

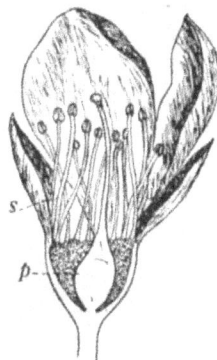

Fig. 7. — Section through a flower of the Peach. There is but one pistil (*p*), but many stamens (*s*). Much enlarged.

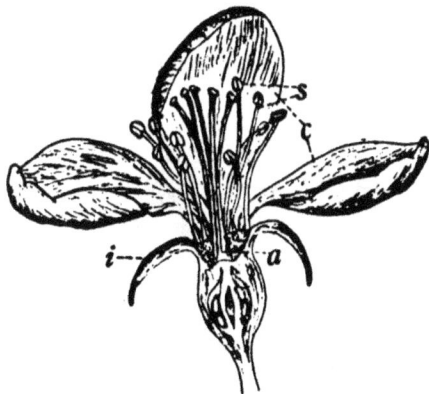

Fig. 8. — Section through an Apple flower showing the compound pistil composed of five carpels. The five carpels (*a*) are free above but joined below. *c*, corolla; *s*, stamens; *i*, calyx. Much enlarged.

Unisexual Flowers. —

Flowers having both stamens and pistils are known as *perfect* or *bisexual* flowers. In some plants, the stamens and pistils occur in different flowers, in which case the flower having stamens only is called a *staminate flower*, while the other having pistils only is called a *pistillate flower*. Such flowers are said to be *unisexual*. Pumpkins, Cucumbers, Corn, Hemp, Willows, and Poplars are some of the familiar plants which have *unisexual flowers*. In *Figure 6* are shown the unisexual flowers of the Pumpkin. In some cases, as in Corn, Cucumbers, and Pumpkins, both staminate and pistillate flowers are borne on the same plant. Such plants are said to be *monœcious* (meaning " of one household "). In other cases, as in Hemp, Willows, and Poplars, the staminate and pistillate flowers are borne on different individuals, that is, one plant has only staminate while another has only pistillate flowers. Such plants are said to be *diœcious* (meaning " of two households ").

FIG. 9.—Section through the flower of Cotton. *s*, stamens joined into a tube which surrounds the pistil; *p*, pistil composed of carpels more united than those of the Apple. Smaller than natural size. After Baillon.

Pistils and Stamens. — As everyone knows, the pistils are the organs in which fertilization occurs and seed is produced, while the stamens furnish the pollen, which is essential for fertilization. Flowers usually have more stamens than pistils, but the number

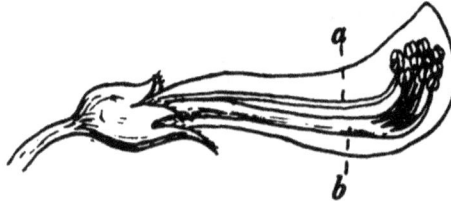

FIG. 10. — A flower of a Legume with petals removed to show the diadelphous stamens. *a*, free stamen; *b*, tube formed by the joining of the other stamens.

of each varies much in the flowers of different plants. Some flowers, as those of the Strawberry, have numerous stamens and pistils, while in some flowers, as in the Peach or Plum, there is only one pistil, but many stamens. (*Fig. 7.*) The Apple flower, which has many stamens, really has five pistils, but the lower parts of the pistils are joined, leaving only the upper parts free.

A pistil like that of the Apple is called a *compound pistil*, and the pistil-like structures which compose it, instead of being called pistils, are called *carpels*. Thus in *Figure 8*, each of the branches in the upper region of the pistil is the upper portion of a carpel. If the enlarged bases of these were separated, then each carpel would resemble the pistil of the Cherry or Plum flower. Pistils like those of the Cherry and Plum consist of only one carpel and are, therefore, called *simple pistils*. In flowers having but one carpel, *pistil* and *carpel* mean the same thing. The flower of the Cotton Plant, shown in *Figure 9*, has a compound pistil in which the carpels are more united than in the Apple.

In most flowers the stamens are separate from one another (polyadelphous), but in some groups of plants they are more or

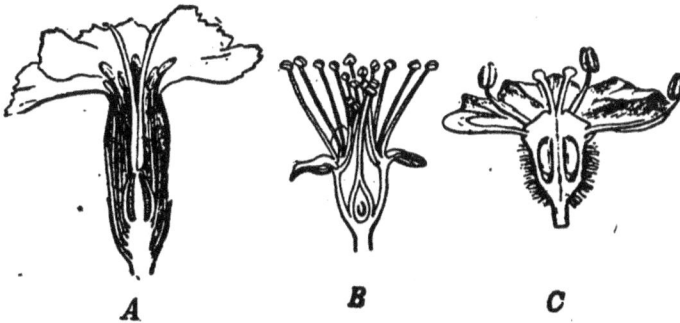

Fig. 11. — *A*, hypogynous flower of Pink; *B*, perigynous flower of Cherry; *C*, epigynous flower of Wild Carrot. Modified from Warming.

less united (monadelphous). In Cotton and other plants of this group, the stamens are joined in such a way as to form a tube around the pistil. (*Fig. 9.*) In Clover, Alfalfa, and some other plants of this family, the ten stamens form two groups (diadelphous), nine being joined and one remaining free.

The relative positions of the different parts of the flower show considerable variation. In some flowers, as those of the Dandelion or Sunflower illustrate, the calyx, corolla, and stamens arise from the top of the ovary. (*Fig. 24.*) Such flowers are *epigynous*, i.e., the floral structures are on the gynous the word "gynous" referring to the ovary, which in this case is described as *inferior*. In the Basswood flower, calyx, corolla, and stamens are attached to the receptacle at the base of the ovary, which is described as *superior*. Such flowers are *hypogynous*. In some flowers, as in the Peach shown in *Figure 7*, the calyx, corolla, and stamens are attached to the rim of a cup-like structure surrounding the ovary. In this case the flower is *perigynous*, and the ovary is described as *half inferior*. To which of the above classes does the Apple flower belong? In *Figure 11* the three positions of the perianth and stamens in reference to the ovary are shown for comparison.

Some Particular Forms of Flowers

That there are numerous differences among flowers is shown by the fact that largely upon differences pertaining to flowers, the Flowering Plants have been divided into many classes, such as orders, which in turn are subdivided into families, then into genera, and finally into species of which there are more than 100,000. The differences are mainly structural, and between flowers of different families they are often quite prominent. For example, when such flowers as those of the Grass, Bean, Sunflower, and Orchid family are compared, that there are peculiar differences in the character of flowers is obvious.

FIG. 12. — Corn plant. *t*, tassel consisting of staminate flowers; *e*, cars on which the pistillate flowers are found.

Grass Flowers. — One of the characteristic features of the Grass flowers is, that there are no showy organs. Grass flowers are usually green like leaves, and their stamens and pistils are enclosed and protected by small leaf-like bodies called *bracts*, which take the place of a calyx and corolla. Although quite inconspicuous, yet in being characteristic of such Grasses as Corn, Wheat, Oats, Barley, Rye, Rice, and Timothy, Grass flowers are so important that they deserve some special attention.

Corn Flowers. — As already stated (page 14) Corn flowers are unisexual. The staminate flowers are produced in the tassel, while the pistillate flowers occur on the ear. (*Fig. 12.*)

The *staminate flowers* bear three stamens and occur in groups of twos, called *spikelets*. The branches of the tassel upon which the spikelets are crowded are known as *spikes*. In *Figure 13* is shown a spike or branch of the Corn tassel so drawn as to show the spikelets.

The two flowers of each spikelet are in such close contact, that in order to identify each flower, the bracts must be spread apart as shown in *Figure 14.* In the older flower, the stamens have elongated and pushed out of the bracts. The boat-shaped bracts are so fitted together as to make a good enclosure for the stamens during their development. The two outer bracts, situated on opposite sides of the spikelet and facing each other, so as to close together and enclose the flowers, are known as *glumes*. Between each glume and set of stamens is the bract called *lemma*. The bract on the opposite side of the stamens, with its concave side turned toward that of the lemma, is known as the *palea*. The palea and lemma, when closed against each other, enclose the stamens. The small bodies at the base of the stamens are called *lodicules*, and may, by their swelling, spread the bracts apart, thus helping the stamens to escape from their enclosure. The structure of the flower will be more easily understood by a study of *Figure 14.* The glume is not considered a part of the flower. The two glumes form a covering for the spikelet.

Fig. 13.—A branch or spike from the Corn tassel. *sp*, spikelets. Only three of the spikelets are pointed out. Slightly enlarged.

Other names are often applied to the glume and lemma. In courses in Agriculture, the glume is often called *outer* or *empty* glume and the lemma, the *flowering glume*.

The *pistillate flowers* are arranged on a cob and enclosed by husks, so that only the outer ends or silks of the pistils are

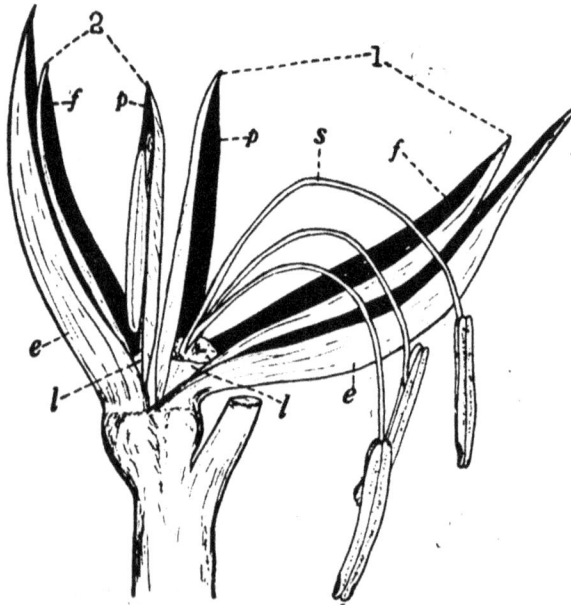

FIG. 14. — A spikelet from the Corn tassel. Much enlarged to show the two staminate flowers

The flowers are numbered (*1*) and (*2*), No. *1* being more mature. *e*, glumes; *f*, lemma; *p*, palea; *s*, stamens; *l*, lodicules.

exposed. When the husks are removed, the flowers are seen arranged on the cob just as the kernels are in the mature ear, for each kernel develops from a flower. Explain what is shown in *Figure 15*. The pistillate flowers occur in groups of two's or spikelets, but only one flower of the spikelet completes its development. The flower which remains rudimentary develops no silk and remains so inconspicuous that one needs a magnifier to see it. Since it has no pistil, its presence is known only by its bracts. In *Figure 16*, point out the rudimentary flower and the one that develops.

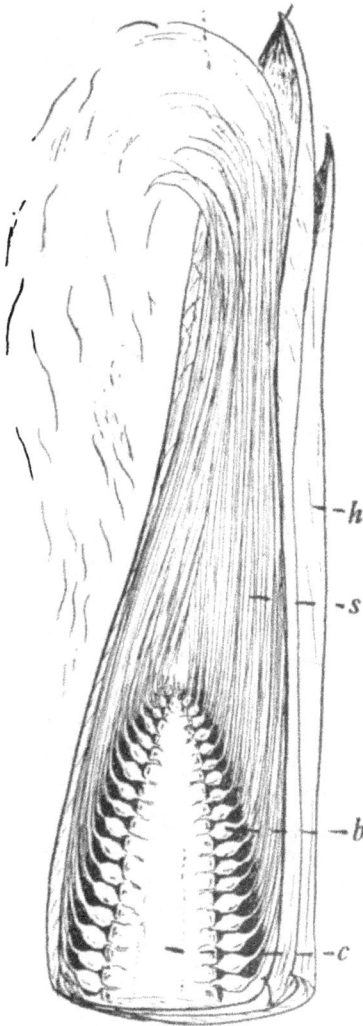

FIG. 15. — Lengthwise section through the end of a young ear of Corn, showing the spikelets containing the pistillate flowers. *h*, husk; *s*, silks of the pistils; *b*, enlarged bases of the pistils enclosed by bracts; *c*, cob. Slightly enlarged.

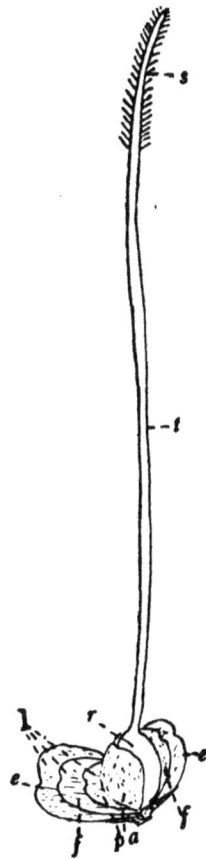

FIG. 16. — A spikelet from a young ear of Corn to show the two pistillate flowers. *l*, the bracts of the flower that develops no pistil. The other bracts belong to the flower having the pistil. *r*, ovary which becomes the kernel; *t*, style of the silk; *s*, the branched stigma; *e*, glumes; *f*, lemmas; *pa*, paleas. The lodicules are very small and are not shown. Very much enlarged.

A study of *Figure 16* shows that the base of the pistil is surrounded by bracts, corresponding to those surrounding the stamens in the staminate flowers. The bracts of the pistillate flowers are small, membranous, and form the chaff of the cob.

Oat Flower. — A head of Oats, as shown in *Figure 17*, is much branched and the spikelets occur at the ends of the branches. Each spikelet consists of two or more flowers, which are well enclosed by the two glumes. When the glumes are spread apart as shown in *Figure 18*, it is seen that the flowers are attached, one above another, to a small slender axis. This axis is known as the *rachilla*. Rachilla means small rachis." Rachis is the name applied to the main axis of the Oat head from which the branches arise. The small branches bearing the spikelets at their ends are called *pedicels*. Thus branches arise from the rachis and end in the rachilla to which the flowers of the spikelets are attached.

Fig. 17. — Head or panicle of the Oat plant. *s*, spikelets; *b*, branches; *r*, rachis; *p*, pedicels. About one-half natural size.

The spikelet shown in *Figure 18* contains three flowers, but the upper one is rudimentary and, therefore, produces no grain. There is one very important difference between the flowers of Oats and those of Corn. In Corn the pistils and stamens occur in different flowers, but in Oats the stamens and pistils occur together in the same flower. The Oat flower is, therefore, a perfect or bisexual flower. In each Oat flower there is one pistil and three stamens enclosed by the lemma and palea. The lodicules, which are two small scale-like bracts at the base of the pistil and stamens, are not easily seen in the Oat flower. The two glumes of the Oat spikelet are so large that when closed together they

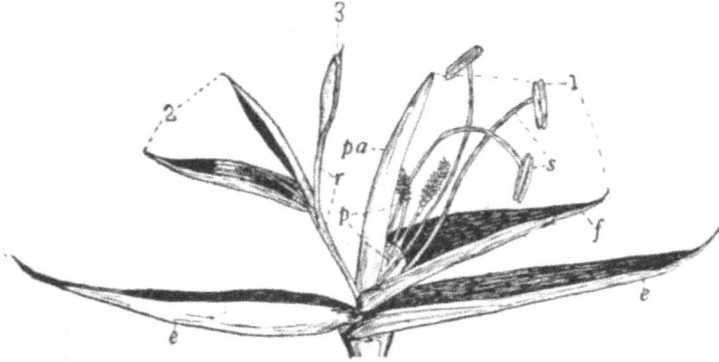

Fig. 18. — Spikelet of the Oat head, with the bracts spread apart to show the flowers. There are three flowers, only (*1*) and (*2*) of which develop and produce kernels. *e*, glumes or empty glumes; *f*, lemma or flowering glume; *pa*, palea; *s*, stamens; *p*, pistil; *r*, rachilla. The parts of flowers (*2*) and (*3*) are not indicated. Many times enlarged.

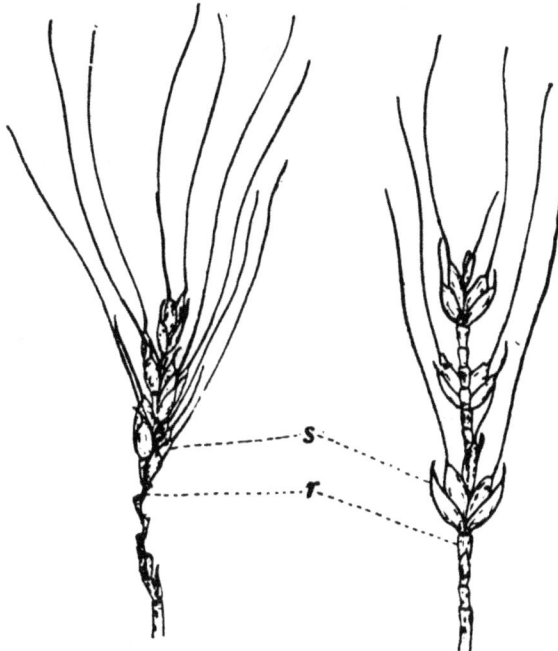

Fig. 19. — Two views of a head of Wheat with some spikelets removed to show the zig-zag rachis. An edge view of the spikelets is shown at the left and a side view at the right. *r*, rachis; *s*, spikelets.

almost completely enclose the flowers of the spikelet. In threshing most varieties of Oats, only the glumes are removed, the
kernel still remaining enclosed by the lemma and palea, which
form the covering known as the hull of the grain. A grain of
Oats, therefore consists of the kernel and its hull; and the
quality of Oats depends much upon the proportion of hull to
kernel. As indicated in *Figure 18*, the lower flower grows

FIG. 20. — Spikelet of Wheat much enlarged and shown with the bracts
spread apart, so that parts of the flower may be seen. The flowers are numbered and the parts of one flower are labelled. *e*, outer glumes; *f*, lemma;
pa, palea; *p*, pistil; *s*, stamens; *l*, lodicule; *a*, awn or beard; *r*, rachis.

more rapidly than the others and forms the larger kernel to
which the smaller one sometimes remains attached after
threshing.

Wheat Flowers. — In Wheat the head, usually called spike,
consists of many spikelets arranged in two rows along the zig-zag
axis of the head. (*Fig. 19.*) This zig-zag axis is the rachis of
the spike. The spikelets are not borne at the ends of branches

as in Oats, but are directly attached to the rachis.   This feature distinguishes the spike from the branching head, called *panicle*, of the Oats.   In the varieties of common Wheat, each spikelet contains three or more flowers arranged one above another on the rachilla, and one or more of the upper flowers are rudimentary. Each fully developed flower, just as in Oats, consists of three stamens and a pistil enclosed by the lemma and palea.   The lodicules, like those of the Oat flower, are small inconspicuous scales at the base of pistil and stamens.   In Wheat, where the spikelets are broad, the spikelet is only partly enclosed by the glumes.   In thresh- ing Wheat the kernel is separated from the bracts — the latter being blown away as chaff.

A study of the spikelet shown in *Figure 20* will aid the student in un- derstanding the s t r u c t u r e of Wheat flowers and their arrange- ment in the spike- let.

Flowers of the Legumes or Bean Family. — The flowers of the Bean Family of which Beans, Peas, Clover, Al- falfa, and Vetch are familiar representatives have a number of peculiar features.   The one most prominent among the cultivated ones of the family is the irregularity in the shape of the parts of the perianth, as the flowers of Peas or Red Clover illustrate.   The calyx is a shallow five-toothed cup.   The corolla is composed of four pieces; the large expanded portion at the back, known as the *standard* or

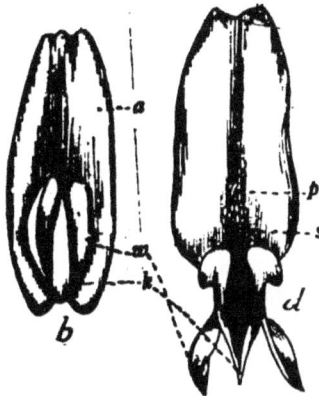

Fig. 22. — End view of an un- tripped and tripped flower of Red Clover.

b, flower untripped. *a*, stand- ard; *w*, wings; *k*, keel. *d*, flower tripped, in which case the keel and wings are bent down, exposing the pistil (*s*) and stamens (*s*).   Much enlarged.   After C. M. King.

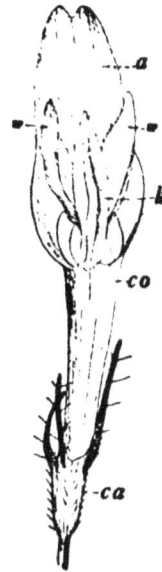

Fig. 21.—Flower of Red Clover. *ca*, calyx; *co*, corolla; *a*, standard; *w*, wings; *k*, keel. Many times en- larged.   After C. M. King.

banner; the two side pieces, known as *wings;* and the single boat-shaped portion beneath the wings, known as the *keel.* In the Red Clover flower shown in *Figure 21,* these parts are pointed out. The stamens and pistil are entirely enclosed by the keel, and when pressure is exerted on the keel, the stamens and pistil spring out of their enclosure with considerable force. (*Fig. 22.*)

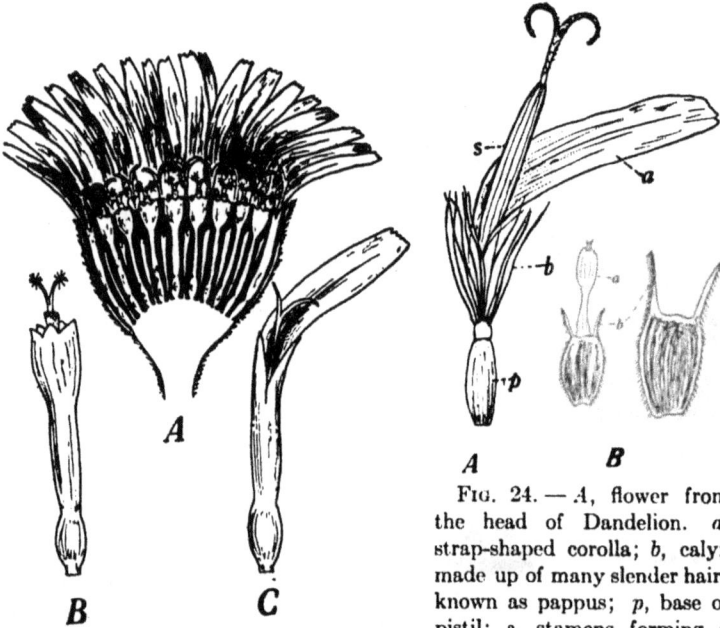

A

B   **C**

FIG. 23. — Flowers of the Yarrow (*Achillea millefolium*), a Composite. *A,* a head of flowers sectioned, showing the strap-shaped flowers around the margin and the tubular flowers occupying the central region of the head. *B* and *C* are tubular and strap-shaped flowers more enlarged

A   **B**

FIG. 24. — *A,* flower from the head of Dandelion. *a,* strap-shaped corolla; *b,* calyx made up of many slender hairs known as pappus; *p,* base of pistil; *s,* stamens forming a tube around the upper part of the pistil. *B,* tubular flower and fruit of Beggar's Tick showing tubular corolla (*a*) and the calyx (*b*) consisting of two spiny teeth which persist and aid in scattering the fruit.

This process of releasing the stamens and pistil, known as " tripping the flower," is mainly the work of insects and is important, because in some of the Legumes the flowers will produce no seed unless tripped.

Composite Flowers. — There is a large group of plants to which Lettuce, Dandelions, Sunflowers, Beggar's Tick, Thistles, and many other plants belong, that have their many small flowers grouped in a compact head as shown at *A* in *Figure 23*. This group of plants is called *Composites*, and includes some of our useful plants as well as some of the most troublesome weeds.

FIG. 25. — A cluster of Lady's-slippers.

Both calyx and corolla are somewhat peculiar. In some cases, as in the Sunflower, the flowers occupying the center of the head have tube-like corollas and are called *tubular* flowers, while those around the margin have strap-shaped and much more showy corollas, and are called *ligulate* flowers. See *A, B*, and *C* of *Figure 23*. In some of the Composites, as in the Dandelion, all of the flowers of the head are ligulate, while in some, like the Thistle, all the flowers are tubular. The calyx is often composed of hair-like structures called *pappus*, as shown in *Figure 24*. In some, as the Dandelion illustrates, the pappus remains after the seed is mature, forming a parachute-like arrangement which assists in floating the seed about. In some of the Composites, the calyx consists of a few teeth, which in the Spanish Needles and Beggar's Tick, become spiny, and thereby assist in seed distribution by catching onto passing objects.

Orchid Flowers. — It is among Orchid flowers, many of which are spectacular, that the most notable irregu'arities occur. Besides the distinguishing feature of having the stamens and pistil joined into one body, known as the *column*, Orchid flowers often have pronounced variations in the shape and size of petals. In some, as in the Lady's-slipper, one of the petals is developed into a great sac or "slipper," while the others have no extraordinary features. These peculiarities in flower structure, which are apparently adjustments for insect pollination, sometimes so closely conform to the shape and habit of certain insects that only one or a few kinds of insects can pollinate a flower. Such highly modified flowers contrast strikingly with the simple, inconspicuous flowers of such plants as the Jack-in-the-pulpit or Indian Turnip and Skunk Cabbage, in which a perianth is either lacking or inconspicuous and the flowers are crowded on a fleshy spike, known as a *spadix*, which is enclosed in or attended by a leaf, called *spathe*. The spathe, by becoming colored, often aids like a corolla in attracting insects. (*Figs. 25* and *26*.)

FIG. 26. — The inconspicuous flowers of the Indian Turnip (*Arisæma triphyllum*). The flowers shown are pistillate and are clustered at the base of the fleshy axis or spadix which is enclosed in the large leaf-like bract or spathe. Reduced about one-half.

Arrangement of Flowers or Inflorescence

The arrangement of flowers on the stem is one of the floral characters much used in the classification of the Flowering Plants. In the arrangement of flowers, a number of things are considered, the principal ones being: (1) the position of the flower on the stem, whether terminal or lateral; (2) whether the flowers are single or in clusters; (3) whether the terminal or lateral flowers of a cluster open first; and (4) the character of the cluster in regard to shape and compactness, which depend upon the elongation of the stem region bearing the flowers and the length of the individual flower stalks. These features taken singly, together, and along with some minor features form the basis upon which floral arrangements are classified.

Flowers develop from buds and buds are either terminal or lateral on the stem. So as to position, flowers are either *terminal* or *lateral* on the flower axis. Flowers borne singly are called *solitary flowers*, and solitary flowers may be terminal, as in some

FIG. 27. — Solitary terminal flower of a Lily. After Andrews.

FIG. 28. — A portion of a Squash plant showing the axillary arrangement of flowers. Much reduced.

Lilies of which the Tulip is an example, or lateral, as Squashes illustrate. (*Figs. 27* and *28*.)

The flower cluster may be regarded as a modification of that lateral arrangement, in which the flowers are scattered on a fully

elongated stem bearing normally developed leaves in the axils
of which the flowers occur. Thus, if a Pumpkin or Gourd vine
should remain short, the flowers instead of being well separated
as they normally are, would be crowded, and, with the reduction
of leaves to bracts, a typical flower cluster would result. Most
small flowers are produced in clusters. For small flowers pollinated by insects, there is considerable advantage in the cluster
habit, since the cluster, being much more conspicuous than the individual flowers, serves well as an attractive device.

Flower clusters are divided into two main classes according to their method of development. In the *corymbose* or *indeterminate* cluster, growth at the tip and the develop-ment of new flowers just behind continues throughout a considerable period, thus producing a cluster in which the older flowers are left farther and farther behind. As the term indeterminate suggests, such a method of development permits a rather indefinite expansion of the cluster. In the *cymose* or *determi-nate* cluster, the oldest flower is formed at the tip, which is thereby closed to further growth, and the new flowers are formed from buds developing lower down. Such a cluster is much limited in its power

Fig. 29. — Raceme of Com-
mon Cabbage (*Brassica*). From
Warming.

to expand. The flower clusters of Apples and Pears, known as
cymes, illustrate the determinate type of cluster.

The simplest form of the indeterminate cluster is the *raceme*,
an unbranched cluster in which the flowers are borne on short
stalks. The racemes of the Shepherd's-purse, Radish, Cabbage,
and others of the Mustard family, in which the flower cluster
may continue its expansion for a long period, producing new
flowers at the tip while pods are maturing at the base, well
illustrate the nature of the raceme. (*Fig. 29.*) The racemes of

the Snap-dragon, Sweet Clover, and Alfalfa are examples of racemes with a short growth period. Racemes may be terminal or lateral, as in case of Sweet Clover.

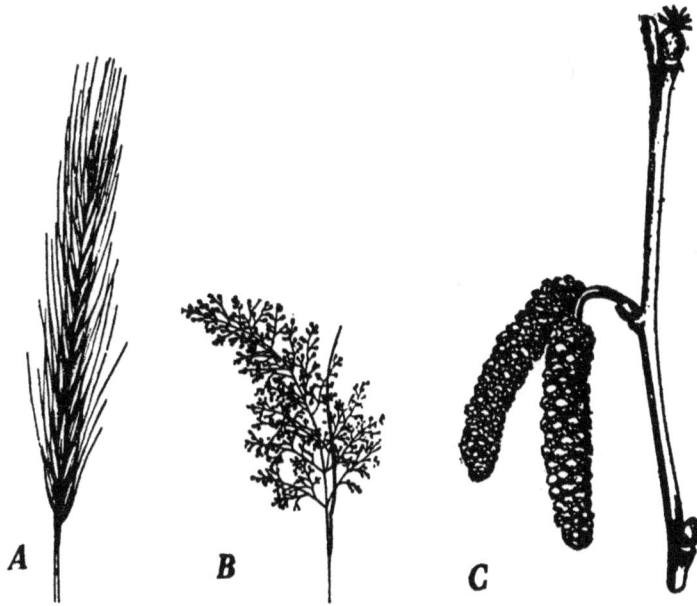

FIG. 30. — *A*, spike of Rye. *B*, panicle of Grass. *C*, flowers of the Hazel with staminate flowers in catkins and the pistillate flowers borne singly.

FIG. 31. — *A*, head of Clover. *B*, close head of Yellow Daisy.

Raceme-like clusters in which the flowers have very snort stalks or none at all are called *spikes* of which the heads of Wheat and Timothy are familiar examples. A special form of the spike is the *catkin* in which the flowers, unisexual in typical cases, usually have scaly bracts instead of a true perianth, and the whole cluster falls after fruiting. Catkins are typical of Poplars, Willows, Hickories, and Birches. When the raceme is so short that the compact mass of flowers form a more or less rounded cluster as in Red Clover, then a *head* is formed. In the Composites there is the special kind of head which is the most highly organized of all flower clusters. The flowers besides often being differentiated into two kinds are so compactly arranged as to form a cluster resembling a single flower and the cluster is surrounded by bracts, which form a structure known as the *involucre*. (*Fig. 31.*)

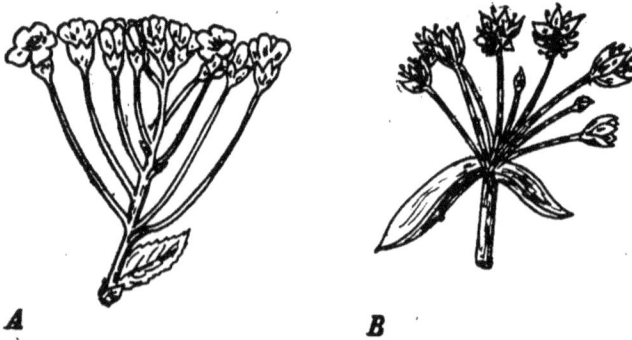

A   **B**

Fig. 32. — *A*, Corymb of one of the Cherries. *B*, umbel of a species of Onion.

In contrast to the spike there are those raceme-like clusters in which the flowers have long stalks, as in the typical *panicle*, where the cluster is loosely branched. When the portion of stem to which the flowers are attached is short and the stalks of all of the flowers are so elongated as to bring all of the flowers to about the same level then a *corymb* results. A further modification in which the portion of stem to which the flowers are attached is so short that the flower stalks appear to be of the same length and attached in a circle around the stem results in the *umbel*, the form of cluster characteristic of the Parsley Family, called *Umbelliferæ*, on account of the character of the flower cluster. Of this family the Parsnips, Carrots, and others are common. The umbel is also common among the Milkweeds. Umbels may be simple or compound, that is, so branched as to be composed of a number of small umbels. (*Fig. 32.*)

Fig. 33. — *A*, cyme of the Apple.   *B*, thyrse of the Lilac.

In complex flower clusters combinations of the simpler types of clusters often occur together. Thus, in the *thyrse*, the complex cluster which is typical of the Lilac and Horse-Chestnut, and, in

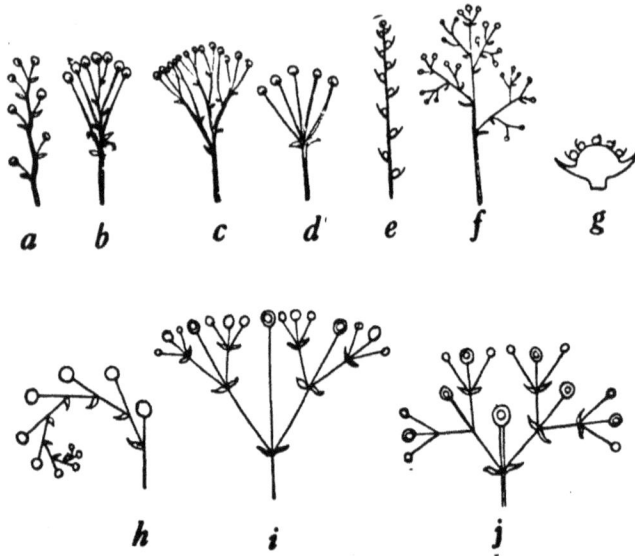

FIG. 34. — Upper diagrams show types of indeterminate inflorescences. *a*, raceme; *b*, corymb; *c*, compound corymb; *d*, umbel; *e*, spike; *f*, panicle; *g*, head.

Lower diagrams show types of determinate inflorescences; *h*, cyme half developed (scorpioid); *i*, flat-topped or corymbose cyme; *j*, typical cyme.

the panicle of the Grasses, the characteristics of both racemes and cymes are present. (*Fig. 33.*)

The diagrams in *Figure 34* show the common types of flower arrangements.

CHAPTER IV

PISTILS AND STAMENS

Structure and Function of Pistils and Stamens

The pistils and stamens are the organs upon which the production of seed depends and for this reason are called the essential parts of the flower. The calyx and corolla protect the essential organs and often assist in seed production, but they are not essential.

In unisexual flowers, seeds appear only in the flowers having pistils. The staminate flowers in the Corn tassel produce no kernels, and in diœcious plants, such as Hemp, Willows, and the Mulberry, seed and fruit are limited to those individuals bearing pistillate flowers. From this it might appear that the stamens take no part in the work of producing the seed; but observations show that unless stamens are close at hand, the pistil will produce no seed. A well isolated Corn plant with tassel removed before the stamens are mature will produce no kernels. Some varieties of Strawberries are diœcious, and unless both kinds of plants are grown in the same bed, there will be no seed or fruit.

Fig. 35. — Flower of the Cherry with parts of the pistil indicated. *o*, ovary; *st*, stigma; *s*, style. Much enlarged.

To understand just how the essential organs function in seed production, a careful study of their parts must be made.

Parts of the Pistil. — The pistil usually consists of three parts: the enlarged base which is the *ovary* and the portion in which the seeds develop; the flattened or expanded surface at the upper extremity, known as the *stigma;* and the stalk-like part connect-

33

ing the ovary and stigma, known as the *style*. In the pistil of the
Cherry shown in *Figure 35* the parts are indicated. The ovary is
at *o*. The stigma is the expanded surface at *st*. The style is at *s*
and is a stalk-like structure projecting from
the ovary and supporting the stigma.

In the Corn the style is extremely long and
the stigma branched. (*Fig. 36.*) In Wheat,
Oats, Barley, and Rice there are two very
short styles and the stigmas are much
branched and plume-like. (*Fig. 37.*) Styles
and stigmas vary much among plants.

Ovary. — The ovary is the most important part of the pistil because within it the
seeds are produced, and often it makes the
edible portion of fruits.

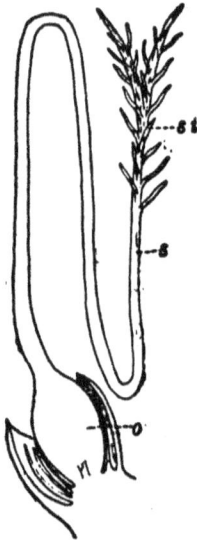

Fig. 36. — Pistillate
flower of Corn, drawn
to show the parts of
the pistil. A portion
of the bracts have
been cut away to give
a view of the ovary.
o, ovary, the portion
that becomes the ker-
nel; *s*, style; *st*, stigma.
Much enlarged.

Fig. 37. — Pistil of
Wheat and the two
lodicules. *o*, ovary; *st*,
stigmas; *s*, styles; *l*,
lodicules. Much en-
larged.

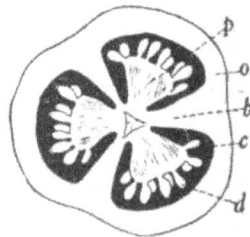

Fig. 38. — Cross section
of the ovary of a Tomato.
o, ovary wall; *b*, partition
walls of the ovary; *c*, locules
or cavities in the ovary; *d*,
ovules; *p*, placentas or parts
of the ovary to which the
ovules are attached. Much
enlarged.

When the ovary is sectioned so that its interior may be studied,
it is seen that it is not a solid body, but consists of a wall
enclosing one or more cavities, called *locules*. (*Fig. 38.*) In
these cavities or locules are the small bodies called *ovules*, each
of which is capable of developing into a seed. Point out the
parts of the ovary shown in *Figure 38*.

The ovary may contain one locule or many and the number of
ovules in a locule also varies in different ovaries. In Beans and

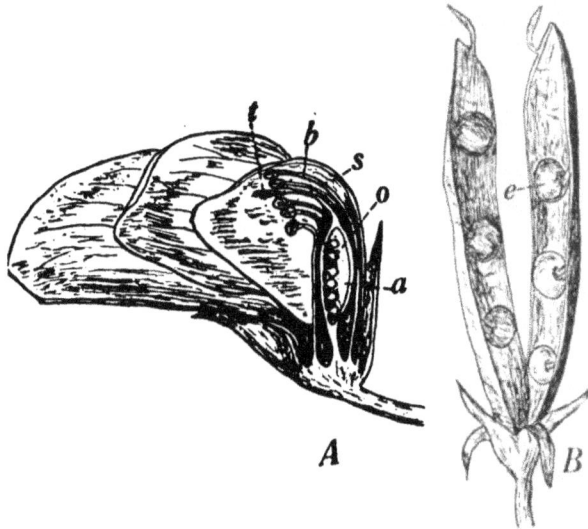

Fig. 39. — Flower and pod of the Garden Pea. *A*, section through the flower to show ovules. *a*, ovary; *o*, ovules; *b*, stamens; *t*, stigma; *s*, style. *B*, the matured ovary, called pod, opened to show the matured ovules or seeds (*e*). Flower enlarged but pod less than natural size.

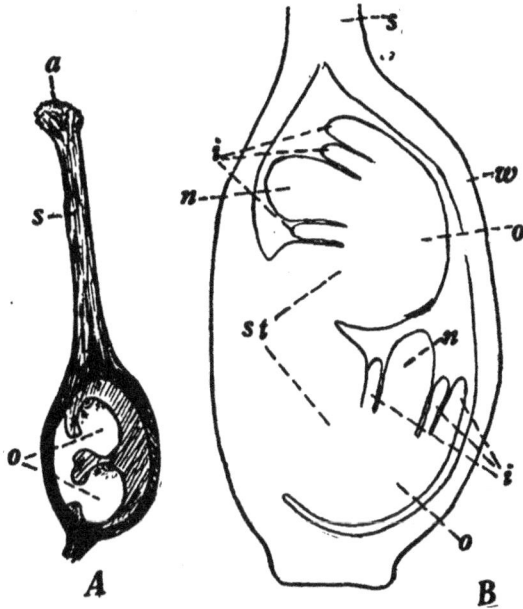

Fig. 40. — *A*, pistil of Red Clover with one side of ovary cut away so that the ovules (*o*) may be seen. *a*, stigma; *s*, style. *B*, lengthwise section through the ovary and ovules of Red Clover and very much enlarged to show the parts of the young ovules. *w*, ovary wall; *o*, ovules; *s*, base of style; *st*, stalk or funiculus of the ovules; *n*, nucellus; *i*, integuments.

Peas, the ovary has one locule enclosing a number of ovules. In *A* of *Figure 39*, showing a lengthwise section through the flower of the Pea, one side of the ovary wall is removed to show the locule with its ovules. In this particular flower of the Pea, there are six ovules, but other flowers might have more or fewer. In *B* of *Figure 39* is shown the ovary after it becomes a mature pod.

The pod is opened to show the seeds. Each seed is a developed ovule and the pod enclosing the seeds is the ovary wall much enlarged. Notice how the ovules and seeds compare in number.

In Red Clover, shown in *Figure 40*, there is one locule and two ovules. The ovaries of Alfalfa have only one locule, but may have as many as eighteen ovules.

In the ovary of Corn, Wheat, Oats, and Grasses in general, there is one locule and a

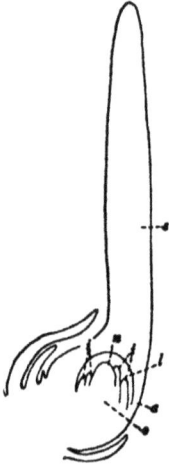

FIG. 41.—Lengthwise section through a young pistil of Corn to show the locule and ovule. *a*, ovary; *s*, style; *o*, ovule consisting of nucellus (*n*) and integuments (*i*); *l*, locule or cavity in which the ovule is located. Much enlarged.

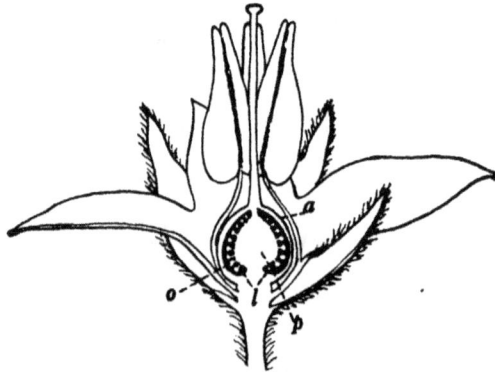

FIG. 42. — Lengthwise section through a Tomato flower to show the interior of the ovary. *a*, ovary; *l*, locules, represented by dark shading; *o*, ovules; *p*, placentas. Much enlarged.

single large ovule. A lengthwise section through the pistil of Corn is shown in *Figure 41*. Notice the ovule at *o* and that it almost fills the locule.

Tomato ovaries have few or many locules which contain a large number of ovules. *Figure 42* shows a lengthwise section of a Tomato ovary showing two locules and many ovules. By counting the ovules shown in *Figure 42* and those shown in *Figure 38* the number of ovules in a Tomato may be roughly estimated.

An examination of the ovaries of many plants would show considerable variation in the number of locules and ovules, but in general, all ovaries consist of an ovary wall enclosing one or more locules which contain one or more ovules.

Ovule. — Since ovules develop into seeds, they have the most to do with seed production and are, therefore, the most directly related to the function of the flower. The process of fertilization, one of the most important events in plant life, takes place in the ovule and a good understanding of fertilization requires a knowledge of the ovule.

Size of Ovules and how their Number Compares with the Number of Seeds. — Although ovules are the chief structures in performing the function of seed-production, in size they are usually very inconspicuous and not much can be learned about them without the aid of the microscope. In many plants the ovules are barely visible to the unaided eye. When ovaries and ovules are shown in drawings, they are usually much enlarged, so that much more is shown than could be seen by cutting sections and studying the ovaries themselves, unless a microscope were used. In *Figure 43*, the pistil of the Tomato is shown natural size. By comparing it with the pistil shown in *Figure 42*, it will be seen that in order to show the structures of the ovary, the pistil in the latter Figure is much enlarged.

FIG. 43. — Pistil of the Tomato taken from the flower and drawn natural size.

Since ovules are small, it is difficult to count them in ovaries where they are numerous. It is possible in many cases to make a rough estimate of the number of ovules by counting the seeds produced. Since each seed is a developed ovule, there must occur in the young ovary as many ovules as there are seeds in the mature ovary. From this it follows that those Tomatoes containing two hundred or more seeds must have had as many ovules in their young ovaries.

If all the ovules became seeds then a count of the seeds would give the exact number of ovules; but in many cases, due to a lack of fertilization, space, or sufficient food supply, only a part of the ovules complete their development and become seeds. In Red Clover, as shown in *Figure 40*, there are two ovules, but when the mature pod is threshed, only one seed is found. In Alfalfa only about one third of the ovules produce seed. In the Apple, Pear, Tomato, and other fruits some of the ovules often fail to develop, and in case of seedless fruits none of the ovules complete their development. In most fruits the production of seed is not an important feature to the plant grower, the seedless fruit in many cases being more desirable; but in case of Clover, Alfalfa, Flax, and other plants valuable for seed, the value of the plant as a seed producer is directly related to the number of ovules which be-

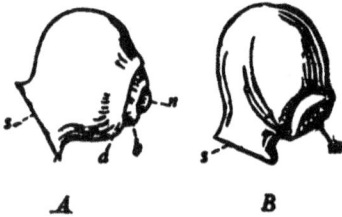

FIG. 44. — Surface view of an ovule at two stages of development. *A*, stage of development showing the integuments (*a, b*) growing up over the nucellus (*n*). *B*, older stage in which the integuments have closed over the nucellus, leaving only a small opening, the micropyle (*m*). *s*, the funiculus. Much enlarged.

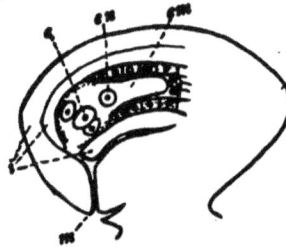

FIG. 45. — Section through the ovule of Red Clover showing the embryo sac. *em*, embryo sac with the egg (*e*) and the primary endosperm nucleus (*en*) indicated; *i*, integuments; *m*, micropyle. Many times enlarged.

come seed. How much could the seed yield of Clover and Alfalfa be increased if they could be made to develop all of their ovules into seed? If clover seed were selling at $10 per bushel, what would be the value of the increased yield on ten acres of average Clover?

Parts of the Ovule. — The ovule consists of a main body and a stalk known as the *funiculus* which connects to the ovary wall. The main body consists of a central (usually rounded) portion called *nucellus*, which is enclosed by one or more coverings called *integuments* that grow up from the funiculus. In *Figure 40*, showing the ovules of Clover, the stalk or funiculus is at *st*; the central portion or nucellus of the main body is at *n*; the coverings or integuments of the nucellus are at *i*. Turn to this *Figure* and point out these parts. In the ovule of the Corn, shown in *Figure 41*, the funiculus is apparently absent. In *Figure 44* is shown a surface view of an ovule at two stages of development. Notice how the nucellus is enclosed by the integuments, leaving only a small opening at *m* known as the *micropyle*.

The pollen tube, a tube-like structure produced by the pollen grain in connection with fertilization, often uses the micropyle as an entrance to the ovule. Some ovules are straight but oftener there is a curving to one side during growth as shown in *Figure 44*. By curving the micropyle is brought near the base of the ovule, a position more favorable for the entrance of the pollen tube.

How the Parts of an Ovule are made up. — The ovule, like all other parts of the plant, is made up of many living units called *cells*. A cell consists of a mass of living matter called *protoplasm*, which is generally enclosed by walls. A very important part of the living matter is the *nucleus*, a globular body commonly occupying a central position in the cell. The ovule, although a very small body, is composed of many hundreds of cells, all of which are in some way related to seed formation.

The cells of the funiculus, integuments, and most of those of the nucellus furnish food and develop a covering for the inner and more vital parts of the seed. In form and structure they are similar to cells composing other parts of the plant. The cells

FIG. 46. — Lengthwise section through the ovary of Corn showing embryo sac. *o*, ovule; *em*, embryo sac; *e*, egg; *en*, the two nuclei which fuse to form the primary endosperm nucleus; *i*, integuments; *w*, ovary wall; *s*, base of style or silk. Much enlarged.

peculiar to the ovule are those forming a special group, usually seven or eight in number and occupying a central position in the nucellus One peculiar feature of these cells is that they usually are not separated by cell walls and their masses of protoplasm lie in contact or closely join with each other. The region which these cells occupy is known as the *embryo sac*, so named because within it the embryo develops. The embryo sac, being deeply buried in the nucellus wh ch is in turn enclosed by the integuments, is well protected and to study it the ovule must be sec-

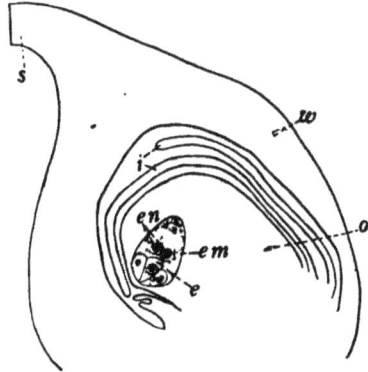

tioned. In some ovules the embryo sac may be seen without the microscope, but in most ovules it is microscopic. There is only one cell and one nucleus in the embryo sac, which have an important function in the formation of the seed. The important cell is the egg. The egg is at the micropylar end and after fertilization produces the embryo of the seed. The important nucleus, referred to as nucleus because it has no definite amount of protoplasm, is the *primary endosperm nucleus.* It is near the center of the embryo sac and is important because upon it the development of the stored food or *endosperm* of the seed depends. The remaining cells and nuclei of the

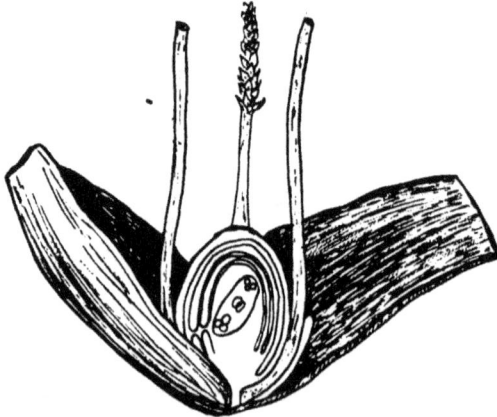

Fig. 47. — A vertical section through an Oat ovary to show the parts of the ovule. Parts of the lemma, palea, and two stamens are shown, and one style and stigma remains. Label the parts of the ovule. Much enlarged.

embryo sac are absorbed and disappear soon after the egg is fertilized. In the ovules of Clover and many other plants, the cells at the inner end (chalazal end) of the embryo sac disappear even before the egg is fertilized.

A section through an ovule of Red Clover is shown in *Figure 45.* Point out the embryo sac. Notice the egg at *e* and the endosperm nucleus at *en.* Point out the embryo sac of Corn in *Figure 46.* Notice that instead of a single primary endosperm nucleus, there are two nuclei lying in contact. These nuclei fuse and form the primary endosperm nucleus. A section through an ovule of Oats is shown n *Figure 47.* Point out the embryo sac, egg, and primary endosperm nucleus. Redraw this figure on a sheet of paper and label the parts.

Although pistils vary much in number of carpels, length of styles, and in number of locules and ovules, there is uniformity in organization and adaptation of parts to special functions. The stigma is especially adapted for receiving pollen, the style supports the stigma in a position suitable for receiving the pollen, and the ovary protects the delicate ovules in which is the embryo sac containing the egg and primary endosperm nucleus, which are the chief structures of the pistil.

The Stamen. — The stamen usually consists of two parts; the enlarged terminal portion, or *anther;* and the stalk, or *filament.* The filament is often so short as to seem to be absent. Point out the parts of the stamen in *A* of *Figure 48.*

The anther is usually four lobed and within each lobe is a cavity, called *locule,* which contains many globular bodies known as *pollen* or *pollen grains.* When the pollen is mature, the walls of the anther

FIG. 48. — *A,* stamen. *a,* anther; *f,* filament. *B,* much enlarged cross section of an anther, showing the locules and pollen grains. The two locules at the left have opened, allowing the pollen to escape.

open and allow the pollen to escape. Notice the cross section of an anther shown in *B* of *Figure 48.* Point out the locules and pollen grains. Notice that two of the locules have opened.

The Pollen Grain and its Work. — The pollen grain is a cell with its living matter enclosed in a heavy protective wall. It needs to be well protected, for during its journey to the pistil, destructive agencies such as cold, heat, and drying are encountered. The transference of the pollen to the stigma is called *pollination.* Pollination is a very important event, for the pollen cannot perform its function except on the stigma.

On the stigma the pollen grain grows a tube which traverses the stigma and style, pierces the ovule, and reaches the embryo sac. Pollen grains, when first formed in the anther, have only one nucleus, but in preparation for the work of fertilization, there is nuclear division and as a result there are three nuclei in a well

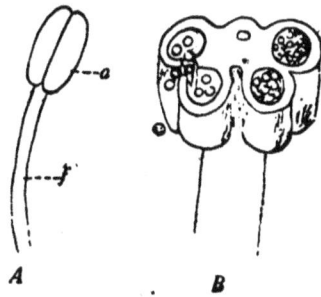

developed pollen tube.   This feature is shown in *Figure 49*.   The
nucleus at the end of the tube and known as *tube nucleus* directs
the growth of the tube and disappears
soon after reaching the embryo sac.
The two nuclei following closely behind the tube nucleus are the *sperms*
or *male nuclei*, the structures which
join with the egg and primary endosperm nucleus in fertilization.   The
pollen tube is a passage way through
which the sperms pass to the embryo
sac.

Fertilization.—After the two sperms
reach the embryo sac, one approaches
the egg and fuses with its nucleus, while

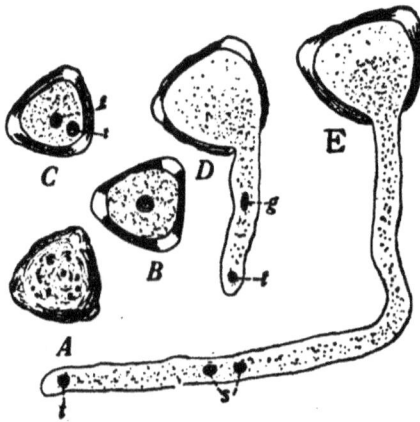

FIG. 49. — Pollen grains in different stages preparatory to fertilization. A, surface view of a pollen grain; B, section through pollen grain in uni-nucleate stage; C, section through pollen grain showing the nucleus divided into the generative (g) and tube nucleus (t); D, pollen tube forming into which the two nuclei have passed; E, tube more developed and generative nucleus divided into two sperms (g). Much enlarged.

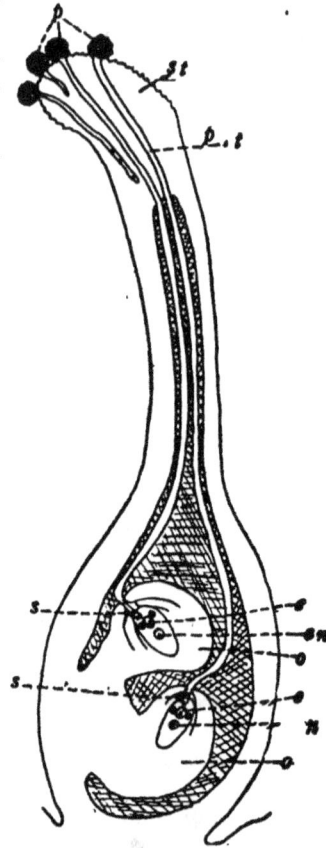

FIG. 50. — A diagram of a length-wise section through the pistil of Red Clover, showing pollen tubes traversing the stigma and style.   Two pollen tubes have reached the embryo sacs. p, pollen grains developing tubes; st, stigma; p.t, pollen tubes; o, ovules; e, egg; en, endosperm nucleus; s, sperms. Much enlarged.

the other approaches the primary endosperm nucleus and fuses with
it. This process of fusion is called *fertilization*. Since there are two

fusions, there are two fertilizations, and the two fertilizations are called "double fertilization." Both egg and primary endosperm nucleus are now said to be fertilized, and the pollen grain has performed its function, which is an important one, for without fertilization the ovule would not develop into a seed. Pollination, the growth of the pollen tube to the embryo sac, and the formation of the two sperms are simply preliminary acts to fertilization, which is the final achievement of the pollen grain. Study the pollen grains shown in *Figure 49*. Notice that the tube has broken through the

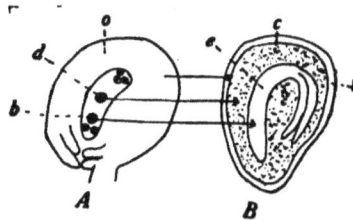

FIG. 52. — *A*, diagrammatic section of an ovule of the Tomato in which the egg (*b*) and primary endosperm nucleus (*d*) have been fertilized. *o*, portion of ovule surrounding and enclosing the embryo sac. *B*, diagrammatic section of the seed of the Tomato. *e*, embryo; *c*, endosperm; *t*, seed coat. The lines drawn from the ovule to the seed indicate the parts of the ovule from which the different parts of the seed have developed. Both are enlarged but the ovule is enlarged much more than the seed.

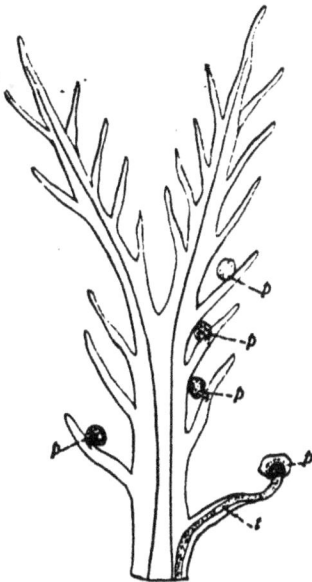

FIG. 51. — Stigma of Corn showing how the pollen grains grow their tubes into the stigma. *p*, pollen grains; *t*, pollen tube. Much enlarged.

pollen wall. How have the two sperms been formed? In *Figure 50* trace the pollen tubes to the embryo sac. How do the pollen tubes make their way through the style? Where do they obtain their food for growth? Notice how the pollen tubes enter the branched stigma of Corn in *Figure 51*.

The Development of the Ovule into a Seed. — After the egg and primary endosperm nucleus have been fertilized, the ovule begins its development, which results in the production of a seed. There

are three main structures involved in this development: (1) the
fertilized egg; (2) the fertilized primary endosperm nucleus;
and (3) the parts of the ovule surrounding the embryo sac.
The development of each of these parts into their respective seed
parts takes place simultaneously. The fertilized egg becomes
the embryo, the endosperm nucleus has to do with the forming
of the endosperm, and a part of the surrounding portion of the
ovule becomes the *seed coat*. *Figure 52* shows a Tomato ovule

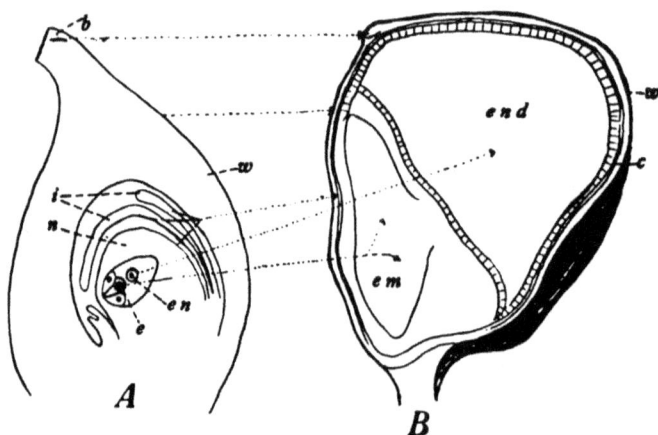

FIG. 53. — A young ovary of Corn just after fertilization and a mature
ovary or kernel, both of which are sectioned lengthwise and the relation of
parts indicated. *A*, lengthwise section of the young ovary showing nucellus
(*n*), egg (*e*), endosperm nucleus (*en*), integuments (*i*), ovary wall (*w*), and
base of style (*b*). *B*, the lengthwise section through the kernel showing the
embryo (*em*), endosperm (*end*), seed coat (*c*), ovary wall (*w*), and the base
of the style (*b*). The dotted lines indicate the parts of the ovule from which
the different parts of the kernel have developed.

in which the egg and endosperm nucleus have just been fertilized
and also shows the seed which develops from the ovule. The lines
indicate the parts of the ovule from which the different parts of
the seed have come. Study *Figure 53* showing the development
of the ovule of Corn into a seed. Point out the different parts of
the kernel and the part of the ovule from which they came.
Notice that the heavy outer covering of the kernel is the ovary
wall, and does not come from the ovule. A kernel of Corn is a
seed closely jacketed by the ovary wall. Copy on a sheet of

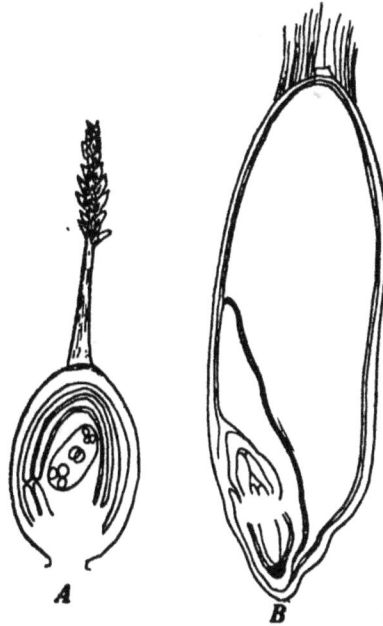

FIG. 54. — *A*, a vertical section through an Oat ovary showing one style and stigma, the ovary wall, and the parts of the ovule. *B*, a vertical section through an Oat kernel showing its parts. After comparing with *Figure 53* label the parts of *A* and *B* and with lines indicate the parts of *A* from which the parts of *B* have developed.

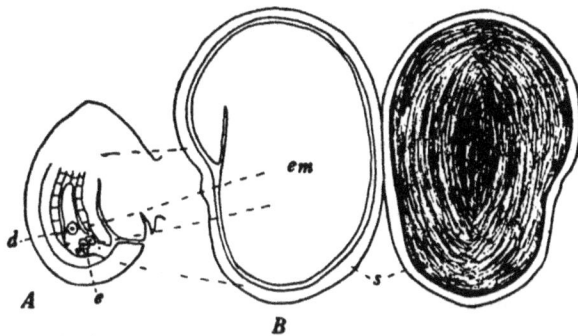

FIG. 55. — A diagram showing the relation of the parts of the ovule to those of the seed in Red Clover. *A*, ovule just after fertilization showing the egg (*e*) and the endosperm nucleus (*d*). *B*, seed with half of the seed coat (*s*) removed to show the large embryo (*em*). The dotted lines indicate the relation of the parts of the ovule to those of the seed.

paper the drawings in *Figure 54* and with lines indicate the parts in *A* from which the different parts shown in *B* have come.

In many plants the endosperm does not remain outside of the embryo as it does in Corn and other grains. If one removes the thin rind-like testa from a soaked Bean, all that remains is the large embryo. The endosperm is stored in the embryo and as a result the embryo is much enlarged and fills the space within the testa. Clover, Alfalfa seed, and many other seeds have the endosperm stored in the embryo. Study the Clover seed in *Figure 55*. Notice that there is apparently no endosperm, and that the much enlarged embryo occupies nearly all the space within the testa.

In some seeds a stored food known as *perisperm* occurs. Usually as the ovule develops into the seed, the nucellus is destroyed and replaced by the developing endosperm, leaving only the integuments from which the seed coat is formed. However, in the formation of a few seeds, some of the nucellus remains, and a portion of its outer region becomes filled with stored food, thus forming the layer of stored food known as perisperm, which surrounds the endosperm and embryo.

Pollination

Nature of Pollination. — Pollination is the transference of pollen to the stigma. After the pollen is on the stigma, it may produce a tube reaching to an ovule and effect fertilization, or it may lie dormant; but in either case the stigma is considered pollinated. Much pollination occurs in nature that does not result in fertilization. Corn pollen, for example, as it is blown about may fall on the stigmas of various other species of plants, but since no fertilization results, the pollination is not effective. Pollen is usually effective only on stigmas of plants similar to the plant which produced the pollen. Thus Apple pollen is effective only on Apple stigmas, Corn pollen only on Corn stigmas, etc.

Pollinating Agents. — The most important pollinating agents are gravity, wind, insects, and man. In some cases, as in Rice, Wheat, and Oats, where the pollen falls from the anthers to the stigma, pollination depends upon gravity. Even in orchards some pollination may be accomplished by pollen falling from the higher branches. In early spring, before there are many insects, many of our trees, such as Willows, Poplars, Oaks, and Pines, depend upon the wind for pollination. The wind is also an important agent in the pollination of Corn and aids some in orchard pollination. Plants having showy flowers depend upon insects for pollination and it is among these plants that attractive colors, secretions of nectar, and various structural arrangements, which are interpreted as adaptations to secure pollination, occur. The pollination of Fruit trees, Clovers, and Alfalfa is done chiefly by insects. (*Fig. 56.*) In experimental work, such as crossing

Fig. 56. — Bumble bee pollinating Red Clover.

Tomatoes, Corn, and Fruit trees, man himself often does the pollinating so as to have it under control.

Kinds of Pollination. — On the basis of the relation of the stamen furnishing the pollen to the pistil pollinated, there can be different kinds of pollination. The transfer of pollen from the stamen to the pistil of the same flower is *self-pollination*, while the transfer to the pistil of another flower is *cross-pollination*. Various relationships may occur in pollination. Thus the pistil of a Ben Davis Apple blossom may be pollinated: (1) with pollen from the same flower; (2) with pollen from another flower in the same cluster; (3) with pollen from a flower on another branch; (4) with pollen from another Ben Davis tree located in the same or a neighboring orchard; or (5) with pollen from a Jonathan or some other different variety. In case of fruit trees horticulturists sometimes consider the pistil of a blossom self-pollinated if the pollen comes from the same flower, from another flower on the same tree, or from another tree of the same kind, and consider the pistil cross-pollinated only when the pollen comes from another variety of fruit tree. Corn breeders speak of *self-*, *close-*, and *cross-pollination*. Pollination resulting from the pollen falling from the tassel to the silks of the same plant is called self-pollination. Pollination in which the pollen from one plant falls on the silks of another plant is called *close-pollination* if both of these plants came from kernels taken from the same ear, but cross-pollination if these plants came from kernels taken from different ears. In case of cross-pollination, the plants may be of the same variety or of different varieties.

The Amount of Pollen Required for Good Pollination. — One pollen grain is required to fertilize each ovule, and, therefore, a pistil with many ovules requires many pollen grains for good pollination. In Corn, Wheat, and Oats where there is only one ovule, one good pollen grain on the stigma is sufficient, although a large number is usually present. Due to the great waste of pollen during transportation, much more is produced than is really needed. A medium-sized plant of Indian Corn produces about 50,000,000 pollen grains or about 7000 for each silk. Many of these never reach a silk, and of the many that do all, except the one that reaches the ovule first with its tube, accomplish nothing. On the stigma of the Red Clover, although each pistil has only two ovules, there are often as many as 25 pollen grains, 23 of which are wasted.

On the other hand, in flowers where the ovaries contain numerous ovules, as in Tomatoes and Melons, it often happens that not enough pollen reaches the stigma to effect fertilization in all the ovules. In the Tomato, for example, an ovary may contain as many as 200 ovules, in some of which fertilization may not occur because of insufficient pollination. Even in Beans, Apples, and Pears, where the ovules are not numerous, one often finds in the mature fruit some undeveloped ovules, which due to the lack of fertilization did not become seeds. Although much of the variation that occurs in the number of seeds in many of the fruits is due to the failure of the pollen to function properly on the stigma or to the insufficient nourishment of the ovules, much of the variation can be attributed to insufficient pollination.

There is good evidence that the imperfect development of fruit is due in some cases to insufficient pollination. By pollinating the stigmas of Tomatoes in such a way that portions of the stigmas received no pollen, one[1] investigator found that no fertilization occurred in some locules, and that the portion of the ovary surrounding these locules developed much less than those portions of the ovary surrounding those locules in which fertilization occurred, thus causing one-sided fruits.

How Pollen is Affected by External Factors. — Pollen is not so specially prepared as seeds are to endure extreme conditions during transportation. During transportation and while on the stigma, pollen may be either killed or rendered functionless by extremes of temperature and moisture. The pollen of most plants is so sensitive to dryness that an exposure to the ordinary dryness of the air cannot be endured more than a few days and in many cases only a few hours.

In the storage of pollen, which is sometimes necessary in experimental work, the main caution is to store the pollen where it will not be dried out too much by evaporation, although the pollen must be kept dry enough that it will not mold. It has been found that Plum and Apple pollen can be kept alive much longer when stored in closed chambers where there is less drying than in laboratory air. One investigator has reported that Corn pollen will die in two or three hours when exposed to the air of the laboratory or living room, but will live two days when stored in a moist chamber. Some investigators think that hot dry weather during the pollination of fruit trees may affect the setting of fruit by destroying some of the pollen.

The pollen of some plants, as in case of Red Clover and Alfalfa, absorbs water so rapidly that it is destroyed by bursting when immersed in water or stored in a saturated air. Consequently these plants are not successfully pollinated when they are wet

[1] Pollination and Reproduction of Lycopersicum esculentum (Tomato). Minnesota *Botanical Studies*, p. 636, Nov. 30, 1896.

with dew or rain.   Apple pollen and the pollen of many other
fruit trees, although not destroyed when immersed in water, will
not function nearly so well and for this reason rain or dew on
a stigma may hinder the pollen in its work.

The pollen of many plants is quite sensitive to a low temperature, showing a decrease in vitality when exposed for a few hours
to a temperature only a little below freezing.   Pollen, if not injured by cold, will not germinate while the temperature is low.
In the Apple, Pear, Plum, Peach, and Cherry[1] a temperature of
$-1°$ C. has been found to interfere with the proper functioning
of the pollen by injuring the stigmas and preventing the germination of the pollen.   Cold during the blooming period may
be responsible for much failure in fruit-setting.

The Results of Pollination. — The most immediate as well as
the most important result of pollination is the fertilization of the
egg cell and primary endosperm nucleus.   Through the process
of fertilization the pollen stimulates the ovule and other structures to develop, and transmits factors by means of which the
embryo and the endosperm of the seed inherit the characters of
the pollen parent.

The importance of the stimulative effect of fertilization in
the development of a seed is obvious, for unless fertilization
occurs, the egg, endosperm nucleus, and other parts of the ovule
rarely develop into their respective seed structures, and consequently the ovule either disappears or remains as a small
withered body as often seen in fruits.   Furthermore, the development of fruit depends upon the stimulative effect of fertilization, as shown in case of fruit trees, Melons, Alfalfa, etc., in which
the flowers wither and fall from the plant unless fertilization
occurs in some of the ovules.   There are, however, a few instances
in which the stimulative effect of fertilization is not necessary,
as in seedless Oranges, seedless Persimmons, Bananas, and a
few other fruits known as *parthenocarpic* fruits, which develop,
although no fertilization occurs.   There are a few plants, the
Dandelion being a common one, in which ovules develop into
seeds *parthenogenetically*, that is, without fertilization, but such
plants as well as those that develop seedless fruits are exceptional.
In most cases our harvest of seed and fruit depends upon the
stimulative effect of fertilization.

[1] *Research Bulletin 4*, Wisconsin Agr. Exp. Sta., 1909.

The effect of fertilization in reference to the influence which the sperms have upon the character of the endosperm of the seed and upon the character of the plant which the embryo of the seed will produce is a subject receiving much attention in plant-breeding. The endosperm nucleus consists of a sperm and a primary endosperm nucleus, each of which is capable of determining the character of the endosperm. Likewise, in the fertilized egg, the contents of both sperm and egg are capable of determining the characteristics of the plant developing from the fertilized egg. But the influence of the sperm is toward the production of both endosperm and plants having the features which are characteristic of the pollen parent, while the egg and primary endosperm nucleus tend to reproduce in the offspring those features characteristic of the mother plant. Thus it follows that if the pollen parent is very different from the mother plant, as is the case when the parents belong to different varieties or species, there will be opposing tendencies in the fertilized egg and endosperm nucleus. Such a fertilized egg develops into a plant known as a *hybrid*. The hybrid character of the endosperm in most seeds is either lost through the absorption of the endosperm by the embryo or obscured by coverings. It is in the Grass type of seeds, as in Corn where the endosperm remains outside of the embryo and can be seen through the pericarp, that the influence of the sperm on the endosperm and known as *xenia* is often noticeable. Notice the ear of Corn shown in *Figure 57*. This was an ear of Sweet Corn which was partly pollinated with pollen from hard Field Corn. Notice the kernels which have the hard plump endosperm and resemble the kernels of Field Corn. In the de-

FIG. 57. — An ear of Sweet Corn showing the effect of the pollen of Yellow Dent Corn. The plump kernels have endosperm like the Yellow Dent Corn, due to the influence of the sperm which fused with the primary endosperm nucleus. After H. J. Webber.

velopment of these kernels, the sperm portion of the endosperm nucleus dominated, and thus the endosperm is like the endosperm of the pollen parent. The sperm may even determine the color and fat content of the endosperm. On the other hand, if Field Corn is pollinated with pollen from Sweet Corn, then usually the primary endosperm nucleus dominates and one sees no effect of the sperm. Thus it is seen that the character of the endosperm of a seed may be determined by either of the members which fused in forming the endosperm nucleus.

The kernels in *Figure 57* which have the endosperm features of Field Corn also have embryos with opposing tendencies.

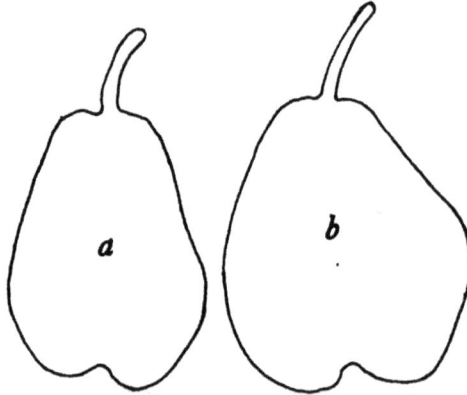

FIG. 58. — Pears showing a difference between the results of self- and cross-pollination. *a*, fruit resulting from self-pollination; *b*, fruit resulting from cross-pollination. After Waite.

These embryos received from the egg tendencies to develop into plants having all of the features of Sweet Corn. They also received from the sperm tendencies to develop plants having all of the features of Field Corn. In the hybrid offspring it is likely that some of the characters of both parents will be present.

The Kind of Pollination Giving the Best Results. — Plants in general seem to favor cross-pollination and often have their flowers so constructed as to prevent self-pollination. In some plants, however, as in the small grains, Beans, Peas, and some other plants, self-pollination is the usual method and gives good results. Red clover, many fruit trees, and many other plants require cross-pollination and will develop very little seed or fruit when self-pollinated. Many of our Pears, such as the Anjou, Bartlett, Pound, Lawrence, Jones, Howell, Sheldon, Wilder, and some others will not produce much fruit unless pollinated with pollen from other varieties, while the Kiefer, Buffum, Seckel, and some others known as self-fertile varieties set fruit well when self-pollinated. Moreover, some trees which are self-fertile develop larger and better fruit when cross-pollinated. (*Fig. 58.*) Many of our Apple trees and Cherry trees are known to require cross-pollination.

Furthermore, some varieties of fruit trees[1] which require cross-

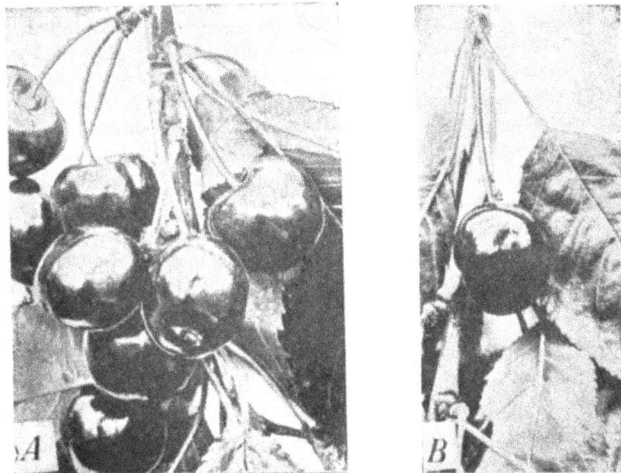

Fig. 59. — Results of cross-pollination with different varieties in the Sweet Cherry. A, fruit obtained by pollinating a cluster of flowers of the Bing with pollen from the Black Republican. B, fruit obtained by pollinating a cluster of flowers of the Bing with pollen from the Knight. After V. R. Gardner.

pollination will not do equally well when crossed with all varieties. In Apples, Pears, and Cherries better results have been obtained

[1] The pollination of pear flowers. *Bulletin 5*, Div. of Veg. Path., U. S. Dept. of Agr., 1894.

Pollination of the apple. *Bulletin 104*, Oregon Agr. College Exp. Sta., 1909.

Pollination of the Sweet Cherry. *Bulletin 116*, Oregon Agr. College Exp. Sta., 1913.

Read Pollination in Orchards. *Bulletin 187*, Cornell University Exp. Sta., 1909. Also Pollination of Bartlett and Kiefer Pear. *Ann. Report*, Virginia Agr. Exp. Sta., 1911.

by crossing with some varieties than with others.   (*Fig. 59.*)   In case of Sweet Cherries, when flowers of the Bing, a variety requiring cross-pollination, were pollinated with pollen from the variety called the Knight, only a few fruits developed; while flowers pollinated with pollen from the Black Republican produced fruit abundantly.   Obviously much of the success in orcharding has to do with securing for each variety of fruits the best kind of pollination.

CHAPTER V

SEEDS AND FRUITS

Nature and Structure of Seeds

The seed is the principal structure by which plants increase in number. The chief function of a seed is to produce a plant like the one that bore it. For plants to increase in number and at the same time thrive well, they must spread to new areas. Seeds are thus so constructed that they can separate from the parent plant and be carried to regions where there is opportunity for new plants to develop. Seeds, being able in a dormant state to live long and endure adverse conditions, are the means by which those plants living only one season are able to perpetuate themselves. As to origin the seed is sometimes defined as a matured ovule, that is, it is an ovule in which three things have taken place: (1) the fertilized egg has developed into an embryo, the miniature plant of the seed; (2) the fertilized primary endosperm nucleus with some adjacent protoplasm has produced a mass of stored food or endosperm; and (3) the outer portions of the ovule have been modified into a testa or seed coat. Despite a wide variation in size, shape, color, and other external features, seeds possess in common an embryo, stored food, and seed coat. In many cases these three parts are not separate, for the endosperm may be absorbed by the embryo during the development of the seed. This is true in the Bean, Pumpkin, and a number of other families, where the seeds consequently have only two distinct parts, embryo and testa.

Each part of the seed has a distinct function to perform. The embryo develops into a new plant, the reserve food nourishes the young plant until roots and leaves are established, and the seed coat protects the embryo and endosperm during the resting stage of the seed. It is due to the embryo that seeds are valuable in the production of new plants, while the stored food makes many seeds valuable food for animals.

The embryo, which is the chief structure of the seed, is the young plant, which after reaching a certain stage of development, varying in different plants, passes into a dormant stage from which it may awake if conditions are favorable and continue its development until it becomes a mature plant. In the development of the embryo from the fertilization of the egg to the dormant stage, certain structures which function in the further development of the young plant are usually more or less developed. In a well formed embryo like that of the Bean, there are four parts, *hypocotyl*, *plumule*, *cotyledons*, and *radicle*. In *Figure 60* of the Bean, *h* is hypocotyl, *p*, plumule, and *c*, cotyledons. The radicle (*r*) is at the lower end of the hypocotyl and is so closely joined with the hypocotyl that it does not appear as a separate structure. The cotyledons of the Bean have absorbed the endosperm and consequently are so much enlarged that they form the bulk of the embryo. The special functions performed by the different parts of the embryo are quite noticeable in the germination of the seed. The cotyledons supply food; the plumule develops stem and leaves; the radicle develops a root; and the hypocotyl in many cases pulls the cotyledons and plumule out of the seed coat and raises them above ground.

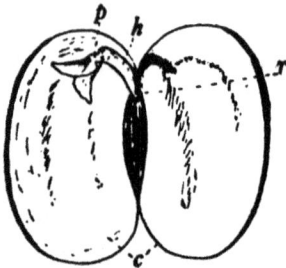

Fig. 60. — Bean with testa removed and cotyledons spread apart. *c*, cotyledons; *h*, hypocotyl; *p*, plumule; *r*, radicle.

The stored food and seed coat are temporary structures. They nourish and protect the young plant in its early stage of development and then disappear. The stored food, consisting chiefly of starch, proteins, and oils, the proportion varying in different seeds, develops in close contact with the embryo and when not absorbed as rapidly as it develops, it forms the storage tissue or endosperm in which the embryo becomes imbedded. The testa, the protective structure of the seed and usually formed from the integuments of the ovule, generally consists of a single covering so much thickened and hardened that it protects the embryo against injuries. Often there is a thin inner covering and in exceptional seeds, like those of the Water Lily, an extra outer covering called the *aril* develops later than the integuments and forms a loose covering about the seed. (*Fig. 62.*)

On the surface of seeds occur certain structures which suggest the structural relation of the seed to the ovule. The *micropyle*, the small opening through which the pollen tube entered the ovule, persists as a tiny pit on the seed coat. Usually near the micropyle there is a much larger scar, called the *hilum*, left where the seed broke away from the funiculus, the stalk-like structure which attached the ovule to the ovary and through which the seed received food and water during its development. (*Fig. 61.*) In case an ovule turns over on its elongated stalk and grows fast to it, the stalk persists on the seed coat as a distinct ridge, called the *raphe*. (*Fig. 62.*) In some seeds, like those of

Fig. 61. — Beans showing the hylum at *h* and the micropyle at *m*.

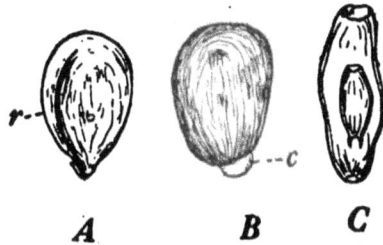

Fig. 62. — *A*, seed of Pansy showing raphe (*r*). *B*, seed of Castor Bean showing caruncle (*c*). *C*, seed of White Water Lily showing the aril or loose jacket around the seed.

the Castor Bean, an enlargement known as the *caruncle* develops near the micropyle.

Structures such as hairs, plumes, hooks, and other appendages which do not occur on ovules, are direct outgrowths of the seed coat and function chiefly in dissemination. Similar appendages occur often on one-seeded ovaries in which case one can tell only by dissection whether the structure is a seed or one-seeded fruit.

Many of the small one-seeded fruits are commonly called seeds. In addition to a seed, they contain the ovary wall which persists as an outer covering over the seed. The so-called seeds of Lettuce, Buckwheat, Ragweed, and the grains such as Corn, Wheat, Barley, Rye, and Oats are familiar examples of one-seeded fruits which are commonly called seeds. While they are not identical with true seeds in structure, they are in function and therefore may be appropriately discussed with seeds. In these one-seeded fruits, the seed is protected by the hardened ovary wall, and consequently, the seed coat is poorly developed, forming only a thin covering, which is usually tightly pressed against the inner side of the ovary wall.

In general structure seeds are similar, all having an embryo, stored food, and seed coat, but in size, shape, and in features which pertain to the structure of the embryo, composition of the stored food, and character of the seed coat, seeds vary widely and can be used in many ways by man. The number of cotyledons developed by the embryo is used as a basis upon which to classify the Flowering Plants into two classes, Monocotyledons and Dicotyledons. From the stored food, whether stored as endosperm or in the embryo, various valuable products, such as starch, protein, fats and oils, are obtained; and from the hairlike outgrowth of the seed coat, as in case of Cotton, various fiber products are made. Although seeds may be divided into many types on the basis of their structure and external features, only those types which include the most common seeds will be studied in this presentation.

Bean Type of Seeds. — Of this type of seeds, those of the Bean, Pea, Peanut, Clover, Vetch, Alfalfa, Cotton, Pumpkin, Squash, Melon, Apple, Peach, Oak, Hickory, and Walnut are examples. The type is so named because it is characteristic of the Bean family (*Leguminosae*), a family notable for its many valuable cultivated forms among which are Clover, Alfalfa, Beans, Peas, Vetch, and Peanuts. The type is also characteristic of the Rose family (*Rosaceae*), the family to which most fruits, such as the Apple, Peach, Pear, Cherry, etc. belong. In this family, however, it is the fruit (rarely the seed) that is important. The seeds of the Bean type are common to a number of plant families and to species and varieties of plants so numerous that a list naming them all would require a page or more. Although many are valuable commercial seeds, some are borne by weeds and hence of interest because of their undesirable features.

These seeds differ from other types in having little or no endosperm. As the seed develops, all or almost all of the food tissue formed by the endosperm nucleus and adjacent cytoplasm is absorbed by the embryo where it is stored in the cotyledons, which, consequently, are so much enlarged that they are much the largest part of the embryo. (*Fig. 63.*) For this reason these seeds are called *exalbuminous* seeds, that is, seeds without endosperm.   Another feature to be noted is that the embryo has two cotyledons.

In external characters they vary so much that their type in most cases can be determined only by an examination of their structure.   In size, those most commonly grown in our region vary from the smallest of the Clover Seeds up to the largest of the Beans.   They are kidney-shaped, globular, oval, or flattened.   Among them various colors such as red, purple, brown, yellow, green, mottled, and black occur. In identifying the different seeds of this type, especially those of the Bean family, size, shape, and color are important aids.

In importance, the seeds of this type rank next to those of the Grass family.   In Beans, Peas, and Peanuts, which are used directly as food, the value depends upon the protein, fats, and starches stored in the embryo.   In the Cotton seed both embryo and seed coat

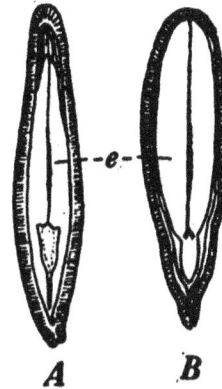

Fig. 63. — A, Squash seed sectioned longitudinally.   B, Apple seed sectioned longitudinally. e, embryo.   B much more enlarged than A.

are valuable structures.   The embryo is rich in oil from which many useful products are made, while the hairs of the seed coat are the Cotton fibers of commerce.   (Fig. 64.)   The seeds of Clover and Alfalfa are important because the plants which bear them increase the soil fertility and are valuable for hay and forage.

Fig. 64. — Section through a Cotton seed showing the embryo with its much folded cotyledons, and the seed coat with the seed hairs.   Enlarged about twice.

Seeds of the Buckwheat and Tomato Type. — Some common seeds of this type are those of the Buckwheat, Beet, Tomato, Potato, Tobacco, Red Pepper, Coffee, Flax, and Castor-oil plant.   The type is common to a number of families, which contain some useful plants and many weeds, such as Nightshades, Spurges, Morning Glories, Bindweeds, Dodders, Milkweeds, Docks, Smartweeds, and Corn Cockle.

In structure these seeds differ from those of the Bean type in that they have three distinct parts, an embryo, endosperm, and seed coat, but in number of cotyledons, which is two, the two types are identical. Since endosperm is present, the seeds of this type are known as *albuminous* seeds. (*Fig. 65.*) Although some endosperm is always present, sometimes, however, much of it is absorbed by the embryo during the development of the seed, and in this case the cotyledons, which are comparatively free from stored food in many of these seeds, assume some importance as storage organs, though not so much as in the Bean type. In the Buckwheat family, represented by Buckwheat, Rhubarb, Docks, and Smartweeds, and also in some plants of the Goosefoot family, the hardened ovary wall, which, when mature resembles a seed coat, persists as an outer covering over the seed, thus forming with the seed a fruit-like structure known as an *achene*, a term which is applied to many hard, usually one-seeded fruits, that do not dehisce or, in other words, that do not open to allow the seed to escape.

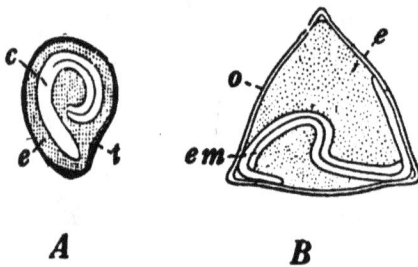

FIG. 65. — *A*, section through a Potato seed. *c*, embryo; *e*, endosperm; *t*, testa. *B*, section through an achene of Buckwheat. *em*, embryo; *e*, endosperm; *o*, ovary wall and testa. Enlarged.

In external characters, seeds of this type present various differences by means of which one can usually identify the family and often the species to which the seed belongs. Those most common in our region range in size from the smallest of the Dodder seeds, which are almost dust fine, to the size of the Castor Bean. The shape, which in many cases is the chief character by which the family and often the species to which the seed belongs is identified, may be globular, oval, flat, or angled. Such colors as red, yellow, brown, and black are common and serve along with shape and size as a means of identifying different seeds. Sometimes the seed coat is much roughened, as in the Cockle, and in some cases, as in the Milkweeds, the seed coat develops hair-like appendages.

In case of Flax, Buckwheat, Coffee, and the Castor-oil plant, the seeds themselves are valuable on account of the oil, protein, starch, or alkaloid-like substances which they contain. From the endosperm and embryo of the Flax seed, linseed oil, the chief solvent for paints, is obtained. After the oil is pressed out of the flax seed, there remains the cake, which has considerable value as a feed for stock. The Castor Bean yields castor-oil which is much used as a medicine and sometimes as a lubricant and illuminant. Buckwheat, which contains much starch and some fat and protein, is much used for food when ground into flour. Often, as in case of the Tomato, Potato, Beet, and Tobacco, the value of the plants depends upon the fruit, tubers, roots, or leaves, and not upon the seed, which in these cases has no value except for growing new plants. Of the weed seeds of this type, some commonly occur as impurities among the seeds of Clover, Alfalfa, Flax, and the small grains and, when present in considerable quantities, they either lower the price or prevent the sale of these agricultural seeds, thus bringing loss to the farmer. In case of Cow Cockle and Corn Cockle, the seeds, which are frequently found among the small grains, are poisonous and when ground with Wheat make the flour unwholesome and when fed with grain to stock often cause injury. Other weed seeds of this type, as those of Dodder, Morning Glories, Black Bindweed, Sheep Sorrel, and others are objectionable because the plants themselves hinder the cultivation and growth of useful plants. Sometimes, as in case of the Black Nightshade and Jimson Weed, the plants are poisonous.

Grass Type of Seeds. — As the name suggests, these are the seeds of the Grass family, the family to which Corn, Wheat, Oats, Rye, Barley, and Rice belong and hence the family most depended upon for food. Many of the Grass seeds, as in case of Timothy, Red Top, Blue Grass, etc., though not used for food, are valuable because the plants themselves are useful for pasture and hay. Some of the Grasses, however, are regarded as weeds and their seeds are often troublesome impurities among agricultural seeds.

As previously noted, in structure the seeds of the Grass type are not true seeds. Besides a seed, they contain the ovary wall, called the *pericarp*, which remains about the seed as a closely fitting jacket. They are one-seeded ovaries and hence structurally they are fruits rather than seeds. Although popularly known as a seed, this fruit-like structure of the Grasses is scientifically called a *cariopsis*, a term which refers to its nut-like character.

The seed itself contains three distinct parts, embryo, endosperm, and seed coat. The seed coat, however, since it is covered by the ovary wall which performs the protective function of an ordinary seed coat, is poorly developed and so closely joined with the ovary wall that it appears to be a part of its structure. In containing three distinct parts, embryo, endosperm, and seed coat, it is seen that the seeds of the Grass type are identical with those of the Flax and Buckwheat type: but in possessing only one cotyledon instead of two, they are clearly distinguished from both of the other types.

In external features, the seeds of the Grasses present many variations, though probably not so many as occur among some other types of seeds. Most of them are small, but various sizes, ranging from that of a Timothy seed and even smaller up to that of a Corn kernel occur. In most cases they are elongated, and have a groove on one side. In most varieties of Oats and Barley, and in many of the Grasses having very small seeds, the cariopsis remains enveloped by the palea and flowering glume, in which case the entire structure may have the appearance of a seed, especially when the barbed awns and other structures developed by the flowering glume function in dissemination. The seeds of most Grasses are white, gray, yellow or brown, but in Corn such colors as red, blue, purple, and black often occur.

The seeds of those Grasses known as the grains are our chief source of food. Although all of the grains contain practically the same food elements, they differ in the proportion of the different elements and consequently are fitted for different uses. Even within a seed, various structures differ so much in composition that they are adapted to special uses as is well shown in the milling of Wheat. Likewise in case of Corn, the oil and protein content are so closely related to structure that one can judge the relative proportion of these substances by observing the relative sizes of certain structures of the kernel.

Corn Kernel. — A study of a section through a kernel of corn, as shown in *Figure 66*, will give a notion of the general structure of the Grass type of seeds. Notice that within the covering (*a*) there are two distinct regions, that to the right and below being the embryo, and that to the left and above being the endosperm.

The location of the embryo at one side of the endosperm, instead of being centrally located and surrounded by the endosperm, is a peculiar feature of the Grass type of seeds.

The embryo consists of two main parts: the large *scutellum* or *cotyledon* (*cot*) which lies in contact with the endosperm, and the embryonic axis which upon germination produces the stem at its upper and roots at its lower end. The axis is attached along its central region to the cotyledon, which supplies it food during growth. At the upper end of the axis is the plumule, a small bud-like structure consisting of a growing point (*gr*) and some small leaves (*l*). The plumule is enclosed in a sheath (*ct*) called *coleoptile*. Between the plumule and the attachment of the cotyledon is a short stem (*st*), which with the plumule is often called *epicotyl* (the portion above the cotyledon). The portion of the axis below the cotyledon consists chiefly of the *radicle* (*r*), the structure which develops the first root.

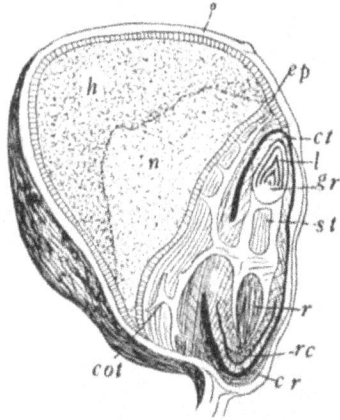

FIG. 66. — Section through a kernel of Corn. *cot*, cotyledon; *ep*, epithelial layer of cotyledon; *ct*, coleoptile; *gr*, growing point of plumule; *l*, young leaves; *st*, epicotyl; *r*, radicle; *rc*, root cap; *cr*, coleorhiza; *n*, soft endosperm; *h*, hard endosperm; *o*, covering called pericarp. Much enlarged.

The radicle bears at its tip the *root cap* (*rc*) and is enclosed by the *coleorhiza* (*cr*).

The hypocotyl, which is all or only a part of the axis between the plumule and radicle (a point in dispute among botanists), is the portion of the axis developing least when the embryo resumes growth. In the Grasses there is very little elongation of the hypocotyl and, consequently, the establishment of the young plant in the soil and light depends mainly upon the growth of the radicle and plumule. The fact that the hypocotyl remains small while the radicle, since it forms the first root, becomes a prominent structure, accounts for the general application of the term radicle to all of the lower portion of the axis, and the rare use of the term hypocotyl in connection with grass embryos.

Concerning the cotyledon of the Grass embryo, there is some dispute. Some morphologists regard the scutellum as the cotyledon, while others think that the cotyledon includes both the scutellum and coleoptile. Although the cotyledon may include other structures, the scutellum, in absorbing and supplying food to the growing parts of the embryo, performs the function of a cotyledon. The scutellum is a boat-shaped structure with its keel-like portion imbedded in the endosperm. Its broad side bearing the axis of the embryo is visible through the testa and ovary wall. The keel-like portion is covered with specialized cells formed into a layer called the *epithelium*. The epithelium secretes soluble substances called *enzymes*, which after diffusing to the endosperm change the foods stored there into soluble forms, which are then absorbed by the cotyledon and carried to the plumule and radicle where they are used for growth.

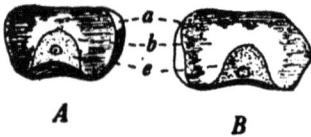

FIG. 67. — Kernels of Corn with high and with low percentages of protein. *A*, kernel with high percentage of protein. *B*, kernel with low percentage of protein. *a*, horny endosperm; *b*, white starchy endosperm; *e*, embryo. After *Bulletin 87*, University of Illinois Agricultural Experiment Station.

The principal food substances, stored in the endosperm are starch, fat, and protein. Although occurring together in most parts of the endosperm, each substance is present in a greater proportion in some regions than in others.

The cells around the border of the endosperm and forming the *aleuron layer* are especially rich in protein, which is present in the form of granules and so abundant that the cells appear as dense granular masses. The remaining endosperm, which is especially rich in starch, consists of two regions. The outer region (more deeply shaded) is the *horny endosperm* (h) and contains much protein in addition to starch. The inner region (n) (with lighter shading) is the *starchy endosperm*, which is not only much softer and more granular than the horny endosperm but also contains less protein. The richness[1] of the kernel in protein depends so much upon the amount of horny endosperm that by cutting across a kernel as shown in *Figure 67*, one may judge the richness of the kernel in protein by observing the relative amount of the two kinds of the endosperm. Likewise, since the embryo of the ker-

[1] See *Bulletins 44, 82,* and *87*, University of Illinois Agricultural Experiment Station.

nel contains most of the oil, the oil content depends largely upon the size of the embryo. (*Fig. 68.*) Sometimes, however, much of the starch of the endosperm is replaced by sugar, as in case of Sweet Corn, which is much used as a vegetable on account of its soft sweet endosperm.

Grain of Wheat. — In structure, a grain of Wheat is similar to a kernel of Corn. In the section through a Wheat grain, shown in *Figure 69*, though the parts are not labelled, they can be determined by referring to the section of the Corn kernel shown in

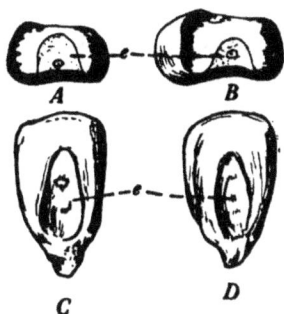

Fig. 68. — Kernels of Corn with high and with low percentage of oil. *A*, kernel with large embryo and hence rich in oil. *B*, kernel with small embryo and low percentage of oil. *C* and *D*, face views of two kernels differing in size of embryos and therefore in oil content. *e*, embryo. After *Bulletin 87*, University of Illinois Agricultural Experiment Station.

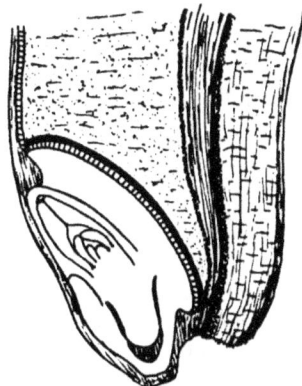

Fig. 69. — Lengthwise section through a Wheat kernel. The embryo is to be compared with the embryo of the Corn kernel (*Fig. 66*) and parts labelled.

Figure 66. In milling[1] a grain of Wheat, a number of special products are obtained. The woody pericarp and seed coat with the aleuron layer and some of the outermost starch cells constitute the bran. When bran is finely ground, it is known as shorts. Middlings differ from shorts only in containing a larger percentage of starchy endosperm. In making the best grades of flour, only the starchy endosperm is used and the quality of the

[1] On Bread. *Bulletin 4*, Ohio Agricultural College. Bread and Bread Making. *Farmers' Bulletin 389*, U. S. Dept. of Agriculture.

flour depends much upon the amount and quality of protein (gluten) which the endosperm contains. When there is a good quality of gluten present, the flour is characterized as being strong and is the kind which bakers prefer. Graham flour is the entire grain finely ground. In making entire wheat flour, after the grain is finely ground, some of the bran is removed. The embryo, which constitutes about eight per cent of the grain, contains much fat and oil, and, if the embryo is ground up with the flour, the oil is apt to become rancid and impair the flavor of the flour. For this reason, the embryo is removed in making high grade flour and sold with the middlings or used in making breakfast foods. (*Fig. 70.*)

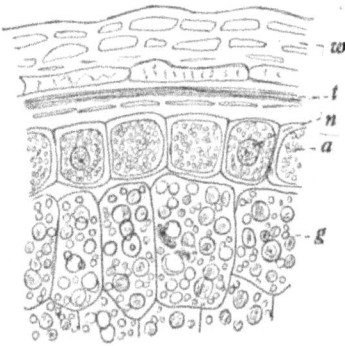

FIG. 70. — Section through the outer portion of a Wheat grain. *w*, ovary wall, often called pericarp; *t*, testa or seed coat; *a*, aleuron layer with cells filled with grains of protein; *g*, starchy endosperm with cells large and filled mainly with starch grains. Some protein grains are present in the starch cells. *n*, nucleus.

Oat Kernel. — In general form and structure the Oat kernel is similar to the grain of Wheat, excepting that it is more elongated and the ovary wall is hairy. The kernel usually remains enclosed in the lemma and palea, and the quality of Oats depends upon the proportion of hull to kernel. The endosperm contains protein, starch, and fat and is a valuable food for both man and live stock.

Comparison of Seed Types. — The three types of seeds differ fundamentally in the number of cotyledons and in the location of the stored food. The difference in the number of cotyledons is probably the more important one because all Flowering Plants have been divided into two classes on the basis of whether or not one or two cotyledons are present.. Plants with seeds having but one cotyledon are called *Monocotyledons* (one cotyledon). Not only the grains and all other Grasses, but also Palms, Lilies, Asparagus, Onions, and many other plants are Monocotyledons. Plants with seeds having two cotyledons, as in case of the Bean, and Buckwheat type, are called *Dicotyledons* (two cotyledons). Besides Beans and Buckwheat, many other common plants, such as Peas, Clover, Alfalfa, Tomatoes, Melons, Cotton, Fruit trees, and many forest trees are Dicotyledons. Each of these classes includes a large number of important cultivated plants as well as many that are regarded as weeds.

Since the classification into Monocotyledons and Dicotyledons applies only to the Flowering Plants, such plants as the Larch, Pine, Spruce, Fir, Hemlock, which belong to the Gymnosperms where there are no true flowers, are omitted in this classification. The seeds of a number of the Gymnosperms commonly have more than two and those of the Pine and Cypress commonly have many cotyledons. (*Fig. 71.*) They are polycotyledonous seeds and the plants may be described as *Polycotyledons*.

The difference in the location of the stored food in seeds serves in distinguishing them but does not affect their function or commercial value. In all types of seeds, the endosperm must be absorbed by the cotyledons before it is available for the growth of the embryo. This absorption occurs before germination in the ex-albuminous seeds but during germination in albu-minous seeds. Among Monocotyledons albumi-nous seeds prevail, while both types are about equally common among Dicotyledons.

FIG. 71. — *a*, Pine seed sectioned lengthwise to show polycot-yledony. *b*, Pine seed germinating, the many cotyle-dons becoming free from the seed coat. Both are enlarged.

Resting Period, Vitality, and Longevity of Seeds

The function of a seed as the plant's organ of dissemination depends upon a number of physi-ological features, of which the chief one is the ability of the seed to remain alive with the ordi-nary life processes so slowed that they seem not to be taking place at all.

Resting Period. — The resting condition is a valuable physio-logical feature to the seed, because in this condition the embryo can endure cold, heat, dryness, intense light, and various other conditions to which the seed is exposed during dissemination. How the resting condition is brought about and how it is main-tained, often many years, are not thoroughly understood. The resting condition is associated with dryness, a condition obtained in the seed by allowing the greater part of the water to escape during the process of maturing. Since the life processes depend upon water for dissolving and transporting the necessary substances, they are naturally slowed down when water is withdrawn and apparently without injury even when so checked that no action can be detected by ordinary laboratory methods. Some investigators have maintained that these life processes actually stop, but the evidence sustains the view that these processes never stop so long as the seed remains capable of germinating. There are various factors involved in maintaining the rest period, but chiefly they have to do with keeping water and oxygen from the embryo.

The ability of seeds to endure extreme conditions while in the resting stage is well shown in the case of temperature. In liquid air, seeds of Alfalfa, Mustard, and Wheat have been kept at a temperature of $-250°$ C. for three days and afterwards successfully germinated, though their embryos when active are quickly killed by a temperature a little below freezing. The ability of dry seeds to endure heat is also surprising. Some in the resting stage, if kept dry, can endure a temperature of $100°$ C., the temperature of boiling water, without having their vitality impaired, while their embryos, if active, would perish at $60°$ C.

The length of the resting period varies much for different kinds of seeds and for seeds of the same kind. In a sample of Clover seed, for example, many of the seeds may germinate in two or three days, and some may not germinate for a month or a year. Although the seeds of some wild plants will germinate as soon as mature, if given favorable conditions of moisture and warmth, most of them, however, have a rest period which extends over days, weeks, months, or even years, and often saves the young plants from getting started at a time when they would soon be caught by unfavorable conditions. Excepting some seeds like those of the Clovers and Alfalfa, the seeds of cultivated plants will usually germinate about as soon as mature. Although a desirable feature, it sometimes results in loss, in that Corn, Wheat, Oats, and other crops germinate in the field if the weather following harvest is warm and wet. The resting period, which is retained by Wild Oats and some other wild plants kindred to cultivated ones, has been lost from our cultivated plants through many years of selection.

In preventing the absorption of water and oxygen, which are the elements upon which germination in most cases depends, the seed coat and other protective structures are important factors.

Seed coats that prevent the escape of water and thus protect the embryo against excessive drying also prevent the entrance of water, and, if the seed coat is too impervious to water and air, the germination of the seed is delayed. Seeds which have very hard coats, unless they are treated artificially, must be exposed to the weather until the seed coat is decayed sufficiently to allow the entrance of water and air to the embryo before germination can take place. In a sample of Red Clover, Sweet Clover, and Alfalfa seed, often there are many seeds, known as *hard seeds*, with coats so hard that germination is delayed or prevented. When sown, they either lie in the ground too long before germination or do not germinate at all. By scratching or pricking their seed coats, so that water and air can enter more readily, they germinate more promptly. Experiments[1] have shown that Clover seed which has been thrashed through a huller where it is scratched by the spikes germinates much better than seed hulled by hand. This principle is so well recognized that machines especially devised for scratching or pricking the coats of Clover seed have been invented. The opening of the seed coats of the Sweet Pea and Canna with a file and Peach pits with a hammer are other instances in which the rest period is broken by artificial means.

In some cases, as in the Hawthorne, delayed germination depends upon the embryo, which must undergo a process known as "after-ripening" in which acids, enzymes, or other essential substances are formed. In some weed seeds, delayed germination has been found to depend upon the toughness of the seed coat, which allows water and air to enter, but is so resistant to pressure that it will not allow the embryo to expand until its resistance is weakened by decay.

Vitality and Vigor of Seeds. — Seeds are worthless for planting unless they have life, or vitality. Not only the vitality, but also the amount of life or vigor the seed has is an important feature. If the embryo of a seed is dead, the seed will not germinate. If the embryo is lacking in energy, though it may germinate, the plant which it produces will be weak. Only seeds with vigorous embryos are fit for planting.

[1] See, *Bulletin 177*, Vermont Agricultural Experiment Station.

The vitality and vigor of seeds depend upon the following factors: (1) the vigor of the plant which produced the seeds; (2) external conditions which affect seeds during their development; (3) maturity of seeds; (4) weight and size of seeds; (5) methods of storing; and (6) age of seeds.

The seeds of vigorous plants are preferable to those of weak plants, for the sperms and eggs of vigorous plants are likely to be more vigorous than those of weak plants, and, therefore, more capable of producing vigorous embryos. Furthermore, seeds of vigorous plants may have more stored food for the embryo to feed upon during germination and the seedling stage. Plants having a stunted growth, due to drought, lack of food, or attacks of enemies, are likely to produce small and often shriveled seeds which are lacking in stored food and usually have weak embryos.

Seeds are often injured by frosts occurring while the seeds are immature and full of water. The embryos of Corn and other seeds are sometimes killed by early frosts. Even seeds which have reached maturity cannot endure hard freezing unless they are dry. For this reason most seeds should be collected from the field before they have been exposed to a hard freeze.

Abnormal seeds have a low vitality or will not germinate at all. Kernels of Corn produced on the tassel usually give a low percentage of germination. Sometimes, as in case of Sweet Clover and Alfalfa, when the conditions are unfavorable, seeds are produced with imperfect embryos which are not capable of developing plants. There are some plants in which seeds sometimes develop without embryos and of course will not germinate at all. This sometimes occurs in the Apple and Pear. When seeds are mutilated their vitality is usually impaired. Larbaletrier asserts that 15 per cent of the Wheat crop in France is injured by the threshing machine. He cut the kernels with a knife so as to represent the injury from the machine and compared their germinative power with that of sound kernels, obtaining a much lower percentage of germination as the results given in the table below

Sound kernels, per cent of germination.	Cut kernels, per cent of germination.
68	34
74	3
99	38

show. Sturtevant mutilated the kernels of a Flint Corn and the seeds of Beans and found the percentage of germination much reduced in each case.

Seeds collected while immature usually show a low percentage of germination and their embryos grow slowly. In the case of Rye, seeds have been harvested at different stages of their development and, after similar treatment in respect to drying and storage, the percentage of germination and vigor of embryos determined. In the milk stage five per cent germinated, while in the dry ripe stage eighty-four per cent germinated. The embryos of the dry ripe seeds were much more vigorous in growth than those of the immature seeds. Tomato seeds, while still green and not more than two-thirds the weight of mature seeds, may be germinated, if properly cured, but the plants produced are likely to be weak. The germination of unripe seeds has been given considerable attention by Sturtevant, Arthur, and Golf.[1]

Experiments[2] with seeds of the Radish, Sweet Pea, Cane, Rye, Oats, and Cotton have shown that better stands in the field and more vigorous and better yielding plants are secured by using only the heavier seeds.

The vitality and vigor of seeds depend very much upon the methods of storing. Seeds are more easily killed by extremes of temperature when wet. Seeds stored where there is considerable moisture may start to germinate, and then die. Seeds, massed together before they are well dried, become moist and often so warm that the embryos are injured. On the other hand, when stored in rooms where the air is warm and extremely dry, seeds may lose moisture so rapidly that the embryos are killed. A storage room should be cool but above freezing, and dry, although not excessively dry. Until the seeds are well dried, they should not be massed together, but so arranged that the air can circulate about them. Thus methods of storing seed Corn and other seeds must reckon with a number of factors which affect the vitality and vigor of seeds under storage conditions.

Longevity. — The vitality and vigor of seeds depend much upon their age. Seeds in excellent condition and stored by the best methods finally lose their vitality, due to the coagulation of their protoplasms, too much drying, or some other factor not under-

---

[1] *American Naturalist*, pp. 806 and 904. 1895.

[2] *Farmers' Bulletin 676*, U. S. Dept. of Agriculture.

stood. Some seeds may retain their vitality for centuries, but most seeds lose it in a few years. The length of time during which seeds retain their vitality is called their *longevity*. Most agricultural seeds can be stored two or three years without much loss of vitality, and some, when stored a much longer period, may contain a large number of live seeds. One investigator found that 50 per cent of samples of Red Clover seeds germinated after being stored in bottles for 12 years; and in samples of the seeds of Pigweed, Sheep Sorrel, Black Mustard, and Pepper Grass, stored in the same way, a large percentage germinated after a storage of 25 years. In samples of White Sweet Clover seeds, which have well modified seed coats, 18 per cent have germinated after a storage of 50 years. There is good evidence that some of the leguminous seeds may retain their vitality for more than a century. Many of the weed seeds when buried in the soil can retain their vitality for many years and then germinate when conditions become favorable.

The longevity of seeds depends so much upon the conditions under which the seeds were grown, maturity when collected, and methods of storing, that statements as to how old any kind of seeds may be and still be safe for planting are not reliable. Old seeds are often preferable to new ones grown under unfavorable conditions. Seeds from poorly developed plants, although similar in appearance to those produced under favorable conditions and giving a high percentage of germination soon after harvest, decline rapidly in vitality, often being worthless at the next planting season. For example, Cabbage seeds eight years old may germinate 70 or 80 per cent, while some only three years of age but grown in an unfavorable year may germinate less than 40 per cent. Seeds collected green may germinate well after proper curing but they have a short longevity.

The longevity of seeds depends probably more upon dryness than any other factor. For this reason the place of storage should be dry and the seeds should be cured before they are stored by placing them in a dry airy place. Experiments show that Corn collected soon after maturity and properly cured and stored gives a much higher percentage of germination the next season than Corn allowed to stand in the shock, or taken from the crib. Comparative [1] germinative tests of seeds stored in different

[1] *Bulletin 58*, Bureau of Plant Industry, U. S. Dept. of Agriculture.

parts of the United States have shown that seeds do not live as long in the warm moist air of the Southern states as they do in the cool dry air of the Northern states.

In the following table compiled from various sources is given the time beyond which it is not advisable to use the seeds mentioned unless the contrary is shown by germinative tests.

	Years.		Years.
Corn...............	2	Mustard...........	3 to 4
Wheat.............	2	Cabbage...........	3 to 4
Oats..............	2	Turnips............	3 to 4
Barley............	2	Swede............	3 to 4
Rye...............	2	Pumpkin...........	5
Buckwheat.........	2	Melon (musk)......	5
Beans (common).....	4 to 5	Melon (water)......	5
Peas..............	4 to 5	Squash............	3
Clovers............	2 to 3	Tomato............	6
Alfalfa............	3 to 4	Timothy...........	1 to 2
Onion.............	1	Celery.............	1

In some cases perfect seeds well stored may have more than double the longevity given in the above table. Thus Sturtevant obtained 100 per cent germination of various varieties of Corn after being stored 5 years. Tomato seeds 14 years old have been known to give a high percentage of germination. On the other hand, using the same seeds as an example, both Corn and Tomato seeds are sometimes unfit for use when only 1 year of age. These varying results emphasize the importance of testing the germinative power of seeds before use.

The variation in the longevity of the seeds of a given lot is obvious when the percentages of germination for different periods of storage are compared. The decrease in the percentage of germination as the length of the storage period increases shows that some seeds die early and others later until finally all are dead.

Fig. 72.—A cheap magnifier well adapted for use in analyzing seeds. The magnifier is set over the seeds, leaving the hands free to separate the seeds as one looks through the magnifier from above.

In the following table are given the results of an experiment to determine the rate at which vitality is lost as indicated by the percentage of germination obtained in each of the 6 years of storage.

Seed.	1 yr.	2 yr.	3 yr.	4 yr.	5 yr.	6 yr.
Wheat............................	80	82.3	77.3	37	15	6
Oats.............................	90.2	93	78.2	67	54	29.5
Barley..........................	97	91	78.5	36	19.5	7.5
Peas............................	94	95	88	64	64	6
Flax............................	81	82	75	49	26	24

Purity and the Analysis of Seeds

The impurities of seeds consist of seeds of other species and of dirt, such as soil particles, chaff, hulls, and other plant fragments. In sowing impure seeds one can not estimate the amount of desirable seeds sown unless the percentage of impurities is previously determined so that allowance can be made. Besides one is likely to sow the seeds of undesirable plants, which choke the crop and cause much trouble and expense in eradicating them. A small per cent of weed seeds is often a serious matter. For example, in sowing Grass seeds which contain only 1 per cent of weed seeds there is the possibility of 20 or more weeds to the square yard. Nobbe found enough weed seeds in a certain sample of Timothy seeds, if sown at the ordinary rate, to supply 24 weeds to every square foot of land. Furthermore, in purchasing impure seeds, unless a deduction from the price is made for the impurities, one pays more than he should for the desirable seeds obtained.

More impurities occur among the smaller agricultural seeds, as Grass, Clover, and Alfalfa seeds, than among the grains, although a few very bad weed seeds, such as those of Quack Grass (*Agropyron repens*), Cow Cockle (*Saponaria Vaccaria*), Corn Cockle (*Lychnis Githago*), and English Charlock (*Brassica Sinapistrum*), are common among the small grains.

Seed Analysis. — A bag of seeds may be analyzed for two reasons: (1) to determine the percentage of the desirable seeds contained or to determine the percentage of impurities regardless of their kinds; and (2) to determine the kinds of impurities and the percentage of each present. In either case the determination is based upon the analysis of only a small sample, which is usually prepared by mixing well a handful or more of seeds taken from different parts of the bag or container, usually from the top, middle, and bottom. From the sample from 2 to 5 grams are weighed out, and the impurities and desirable seeds are then separated, usually by means of a lens like the one in *Figure 72*. By

FIG. 73. — Some weed seeds and fruits commonly found among Red Clover seeds. Enlarged and about natural size. From *Farmers' Bulletin 455*, U. S. Dept. of Agriculture.

dividing the weight of the desirable seeds and the weight of the impurities by the number of grams analyzed, the percentage of each is obtained. Thus, if 5 grams are analyzed and the weight of the desirable seeds found is 4.8 grams, then $\frac{4.8}{5} = 96$ per cent, which is the percentage of purity. In determining the kinds of

impurities and their percentages it is not enough to separate the
impurities and desirable seeds, but the kinds of impurities must
be identified, separated, and the weight necessary for finding the
percentage of each must be separately determined.   In this kind

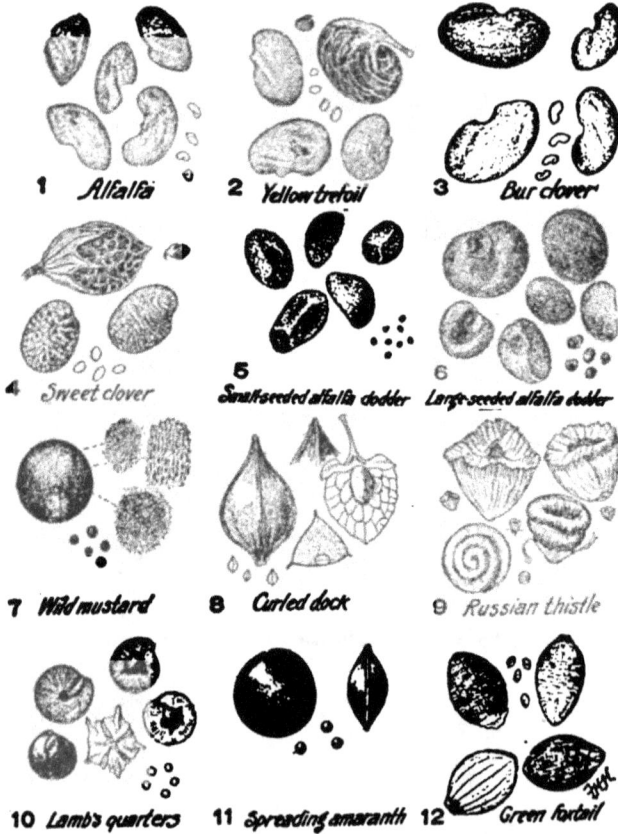

1 Alfalfa   2 Yellow trefoil   3 Bur clover

4 Sweet clover   5 Small-seeded alfalfa dodder   6 Large-seeded alfalfa dodder

7 Wild mustard   8 Curled dock   9 Russian thistle

10 Lamb's quarters   11 Spreading amaranth   12 Green foxtail

Fig. 74. — Some weed seeds commonly found among Alfalfa seeds.   Enlarged and natural size.   Adapted from *Farmers' Bulletin 495*, U. S. Dept.
of Agriculture.

of analysis, the operator, unless he is well acquainted with the
various kinds of seeds, should have at hand for comparison
samples or figures of the seeds of weeds and other plants likely
to occur among the seeds which are being analyzed.   Samples
are better, but figures as shown in *Figures 73* and *74* may serve
quite well.

Nature and Types of Fruits of Flowering Plants

A fruit is difficult to define because not all fruits involve the same structures in their formation. Some fruits are only much enlarged ovaries; but there are others which involve other struc-

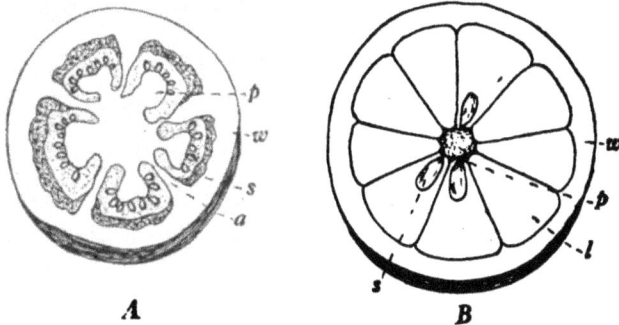

FIG. 75. — A, cross section of a Tomato. B, cross section of an Orange. w, ovary wall; p, placentas; s, seeds; a, partition walls; l, locules.

tures closely related to the ovary. Since fruits involve a number of structures in their formation, it will be best to study some types and then formulate a definition.

Tomato or Berry Type. — The fruit of the Tomato consists of the ovary which has enlarged and become fleshy and juicy. The most edible portion consists of the fleshy enlargements which develop from the inner angle of the locules and almost fill them. These enlargements bear the seeds and hence are the placentas much enlarged. Also the citrus fruits, such as Oranges, Lemons, etc., are of the berry type. However, they have no fleshy placentas. The seeds are attached to the small central core, and the juicy tissues developing from other parts of the ovary and filling the locules constitute the flesh of these fruits. The fleshy and juicy features are characteristics of the berry; and a berry is often defined as a fleshened juicy ovary. (*Fig. 75.*)

FIG. 76. — Lengthwise section through a Plum. s, seed; p, wall of pit; f, fleshy portion of ovary.

Plum or Stone Type. — The Plum, Peach, Cherry, and Apricot, commonly called *drupes*, are fleshy ovaries, but differ from

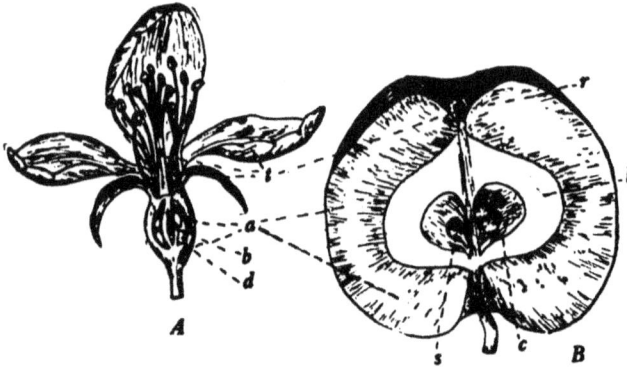

FIG. 77. — Section through flower and fruit of the Apple. *A*, section through the flower. *a*, receptacle; *b*, ovaries; *d*, ovules; *t*, floral organs, calyx, corolla, stamens, styles and stigmas. *B*, section through the fruit. *a*, receptacle; *c*, core; *s*, seeds; *r*, remains of floral parts; *l*, the flesh around the core, bounded on the outside by the conductive vessels, indicated by the lines. The inner portion of this band of flesh is the outer portion of the ovaries, the remainder of it being the inner portion of the receptacle.

the berry type in that the portion of the ovary immediately surrounding the locule hardens into the stone or pit. In *Figure 76*, point out the seed, the pit, and the fleshy portion of the ovary.

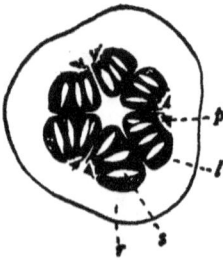

FIG. 78. — Cross section of a Cucumber. *r*, rind consisting of receptacle and ovary wall closely joined; *l*, locules; *p*, placentas; *s*, seeds.

Apple or Pome Type. — The Apple, Pear, and Quince are examples of *pome* fruits, and their structure can best be understood by studying *Figure 77*. The receptacle of the flower is not flat as it is in many flowers, but is hollow or urn-shaped; and the five ovaries are located in the hollow of the receptacle and are grown fast to its sides. The calyx, petals, and stamens are located on the rim of the receptacle and thus above the ovaries. As the fruit develops, the receptacle surrounding the ovaries thickens and forms the greater part of the fruit, while the ovaries form the portion known as the core.

Melon or Pepo Type. — In the Melons, Cucumbers, Pumpkins, and Squashes, which illustrate well the *pepo* type, the ovaries are inclosed in the receptacle, and with the receptacle to

FIG. 79. — Flower and fruit of Strawberry. *A*, section through flower, showing the fleshy receptacle (*r*) and the many pistils (*p*) on its surface. *B*, fruit consisting of enlarged receptacle (*r*), bearing the small hard ovaries (*o*).

which they are closely joined form the rind. (*Fig. 78.*) The placentas are more or less fleshy and in case of the Watermelon, where they form large juicy lobes, they constitute the bulk of the edible portion. In most cases, however, as Muskmelons and Pumpkins illustrate, the placentas break loose from the ovary wall and are removed with the seeds. In what way does the Melon resemble the Apple in structure? How does it differ from the Apple?

Strawberry Type. — In the Strawberry the ovaries develop into hard one-seeded fruits (*akenes*) which appear as small hard bodies over the surface of the much fleshened receptacle. (*Fig. 79.*) In the Strawberry, although the ovaries are included when the fruit is used, the edible portion is the receptacle.

Blackberry Type. — In this type the ovaries develop as small stone fruits, often called *drupelets* (miniature drupes), and with the fleshened receptacle form the fruit. (*Fig. 80.*) Very similar to the Blackberry is the Raspberry, in which the drupelets collectively separate from the receptacle and thus alone form the fruit.

FIG. 80. — Fruit of the Blackberry. *r*, receptacle; *f*, fleshened ovaries.

In developing from a single flower but involving a number of pistils, the fruits of the Strawberry and Blackberry are similar and are classed as *aggregate* fruits.

Pineapple Type. — In the formation of the Pineapple a number of flowers are involved, each of which consists of a small pistil surrounded by large scales and is borne in the axil of a modified leaf. Each ovary with its scales and modified leaf becomes fleshy to form a single fruit. The entire fruit of the Pineapple consists of a number of these single fruits closely packed together on an axis which forms the core of the Pineapple. Since a number of flowers are involved, fruits of this type are known as *multiple* fruits. (*Fig. 81.*)

Nut Type. — In the *nut* type of fruit, the ovary is hard and is generally partly or entirely covered by a husk formed by the perianth or by bracts which grow up from the receptacle. (*Fig. 82.*) Notice the development of the Acorn shown in *Figure 83.*

FIG. 81. — Pineapple. After Koch.

Some Other Familiar Types of Fruits. — In many small fruits the ovaries become dry and often hard as the fruit matures. They are the kind which when small and one-seeded are often called seeds. It has been mentioned that the akenes of the Buckwheat and the cariopsis of the Grasses are fruits with hard ovary walls. In the Clovers, Alfalfa, and Beans the ovary wall becomes dry and hard when mature, forming the structure known as the pod or *legume.* (*Fig. 84.*) Many of the so-called weed seeds are dry ovaries. In many cases, however, other structures are joined with the hardened ovary in the formation of the fruit. In the Dandelion and many other plants of the Composite type, the pappus, consisting of hair-like structures which correspond to the calyx of the ordinary type of flower, remains as a part of the fruit, forming a parachute-like arrangement which enables the

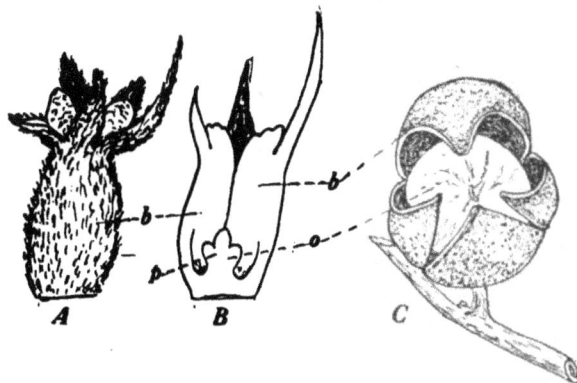

FIG. 82. — Pistillate flower and fruit of a Hickory (*Carya*). *A* and *B*, exterior and interior views of the flower. *C*, the nut. *b*, bracts surrounding the pistil (*p*); *o*, ovary. Flower much enlarged but fruit reduced.

fruit to float in the air. Sometimes, as in the Spanish Needles, the calyx remains on the fruit as spiny appendages. In the case of the Birch, Elm, Ash, and Maple, the fruit known as a *samara* or *key-fruit* has wing-like structures which are outgrowths from the ovary wall.

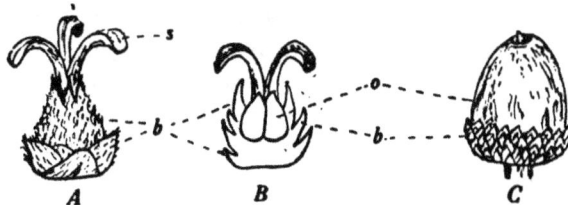

FIG. 83. — Flower and fruit of an Oak (*Quercus*). *A*, pistillate flower, showing the bracts (*b*) which surround the ovary. *B*, section of the flower, showing the ovary (*o*) and the bracts (*b*). *C*, acorn, showing the ovary and cup. *s*, stigmas. Flower much enlarged but fruit nearly natural size.

Definition of a Fruit. — From an examination of the above types of fruits, it follows that a fruit may consist of: (1) simply the ovary either dry or fleshy; (2) ovary or ovaries and receptacle; (3) ovary with perianth or bracts forming a husk; (4) ovary with calyx forming hairs or spines; and (5) a number of single fruits with the modified leaves and floral axis of the flower group. A fruit may be defined as one or more ripened ovaries either with or without closely related parts.

FIG. 84. — The dry coiled fruits (pods) of Alfalfa (*Medicago sativa*). From *Farmers' Bulletin 895*, U.S. Dept. of Agriculture.

Dissemination of Seeds and Fruits

Dissemination has to do with the scattering of seeds from the parent plant. Sometimes the seed is transported naked, but often it is transported enclosed in the fruit or with some larger part of the plant.

The necessity for dissemination is obvious, for if the seeds of a plant were to germinate where formed or on the ground directly beneath, the resultant congestion would prevent the normal development of any of the plants. Green plants must have sunlight and air, and this means that they must have room.

Of course seeds and fruits are not the only means by which plants spread. Many Seed Plants have an additional means in either spreading stems or roots which give rise to new plants as they spread farther and farther from the parent. The Strawberry depends mainly upon its runners, and the Quack Grass much upon its underground stem as a means of spreading. Poplars, some fruit trees, and Canada Thistle are well known to spread by means of sprouts arising from their roots. Most plants which do not have seeds spread by means of spores which in some cases seem to be a more efficient means than seeds are. For example, Wheat Rust, a disease which spreads very rapidly, is spread by spores.

In the dissemination of seeds and fruits, wind, water, and animals are the chief agents. In a few plants there are explosive or spring-like mechanisms which throw the seeds.

Seeds and Fruits Carried by Wind. — The wind is one of the most important agents in the distribution of fruits and seeds. In the Thistle, Dandelion, Wild Lettuce, Fireweed, Ironweed, White Weed, Fleabane, and others, the tufts of downy hairs on the small dry fruits in which the seeds are enclosed enable the fruits with the seeds to be lifted and carried many miles by the wind. In the Milkweeds, the seeds bear long hairs which make them easily carried by the wind. In some plants, as in the Curled and Smooth Dock, Ash, Elm, and Maple, the fruits are winged and easily borne away by a passing breeze. The fruits of some of the

Fig. 85. — Some fruits and seeds disseminated by the wind. *a*, fruits of the Basswood (*Tilia Americana*) and the leaf-like bract which floats in the air and thereby scatters the fruits. *b*, samara or winged fruit of a Maple. *c*, fruit of a Wild Lettuce (*Lactuca Floridana*). *d*, winged fruit of an Elm. *e*, pods of a Milkweed (*Asclepias syriaca*) allowing the seeds to escape to be scattered by the wind. *a*, *c*, and *e* from Hayden.

Grasses are enclosed in chaff bearing long hairs and are easily blown about. The fruits and seeds of Ragweeds, Velvet-leaf, Docks, Pigweeds, Chickweeds, and some plants of the Grass family are blown long distances over the surface of snow, ice, or frozen ground. (*Fig. 85.*)

Some plants break off near the ground after ripening their seeds and are rolled over and over by the wind, dropping their seeds as they go. These are known as the "tumble-weeds" and include the Russian Thistle, Tumbling Mustard, Tumbling Pigweed, Buffalo Bur, Old Witch Grass, and a number of others. (*Fig. 86.*)

Seeds and Fruits Carried by Water. — Plants, such as the Great Ragweed, Smartweeds, Bindweeds, Willows, Poplars, and Walnuts, which grow along streams, have their seeds and fruits floated away during overflows. Sometimes, when the banks of

Fig. 86. — Plants of the tumble weed (*Amaranthus albus*) tumbling over the ground and scattering seeds as they go. After Bergen.

streams cave off, plants with ripened seeds fall into the current bodily and are carried for miles down the stream, finally lodging in fields where their seeds grow. The seeds of plants growing on the upland are washed to the lowlands during rains and seed the bottom fields. Some fruits, as in case of the Coconut, are so resistant to salt water that they can be carried long distances by ocean currents.

Seeds and Fruits Carried by Animals. — Birds eat the fruits of some plants for the outer pulp, and the hard seeds pass undigested. In this way the seeds of the Nightshades, Poison Ivy, Pokeweed, Blackberry, Pepper Grass, and others are distributed. Even the seeds and fruits of Thistles, Dandelion, Ragweeds, and Knotgrass may be eaten in such large quantities that many pass undigested and start new plants wherever they fall. Birds often carry sprigs of plants to places where the seeds may be eaten without molestation and in this way distribute seeds. (*Fig. 87.*) Birds that wade in the edge of ponds, lakes, and streams often carry away on their feet and legs mud containing seeds.

Darwin took 3 tablespoonfuls of mud from beneath the water at the edge of a pond and kept it in his study until the seeds contained developed into plants.   From this small amount of mud, he obtained 537 plants which represented a number of species.

From this it is evident that the mud, carried on the feet and legs of water birds, may be the means of distributing many seeds.

The fruits and seeds of many plants have spines or small hooks by which they become attached to passing animals and are carried far and wide.   Some familiar examples are the burs of Burdock, Cockle Bur, and Sand Bur, and the hooked and spiny fruits of the Buttercups, Wild Carrot, Beggar's Lice, Tick-trefoils, Beggar-ticks, and Spanish Needles.   They catch in the wool, manes, and tails of stock and in the clothing of man, and are carried from one pasture

FIG. 87. — A Chickadee carrying fruit.   From *Bulletin 4*, Iowa Geological Survey.

to another or from one farm to another.   Live stock are important agents in distributing plants on the farm.   The seeds of the Mustards are mucilaginous when wet and, by sticking to the feet of animals or the shoes of man, are carried to new situations. (*Fig. 88.*)

Many plants owe their distribution to man more than to any other agent.   The railways, connecting all of the states and reaching from ocean to ocean where they connect with steamship lines from across the seas, are responsible for the wide distribution of many plants.   For example, the seeds of a number of weeds are shipped across the country with grain and other farm seeds, and also in hay, bedding, packing, in shipments of fruit, and in the coats of live stock.   They fall from the cars as the train travels, and seed the right-of-way where the plants first appear and then later spread to the surrounding fields.   The railways are responsible for the wide distribution of Russian Thistle, Prickly Lettuce, Canada Thistle, and Texas Nettle, which first appear along the railway and later spread to the surrounding farms. Buckhorn, Ox-eye Daisy, and many other weeds are often first found along the railway. Seeds of various kinds are often carried in the packing around nursery stock. Quack Grass Canada Thistle, Ox-eye Daisy, and other weeds are often spread

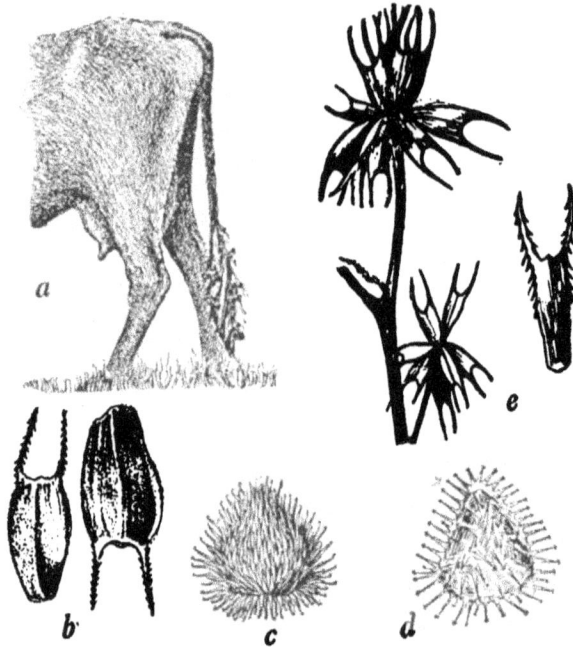

FIG. 88. — Some spiny weed fruits which catch to the coats of animals. *a*, cow with tail loaded with weed fruits. *b*, fruits of Beggar-ticks (*Bidens*). *c*, spiny fruit of Burdock (*Arctium Lappa*). *d*, fruit of Comfrey (*Symphytum*). *e*, fruit of another Beggar-tick. Adapted from Bailey and from Hayden.

in this way. Quack Grass is often carried in straw, and may be introduced on a farm by using straw for covering Grapes and Strawberries. Manure hauled from livery stables is a very important means of introducing plants on the farms where the manure is used. In hauling hay along the highways, seeds of various kinds are dropped and from the highways the plants spread to the fields. Those weeds, such as Quack Grass, White Top, Field Sorrel, and others which are common in meadows, are often spread in this way. When the fields are wet, seeds collect on the wagon wheels and are carried to the highways or to other fields.   Threshing machines are important agents in scattering seeds, for in their traveling through the country seeds of various kinds are jostled from them and seed the fields and highways.

Man scatters many weeds by sowing unclean seed. Clover seed, Alfalfa seed, Grass seed, Wheat, Oats, etc., are often obtained from distant states or even from foreign countries for seeding. Weed seeds are usually present in agricultural seeds, and sometimes they are present in large quantities.

Fig. 89. — The three-valved pod of the Violet throwing its seeds. Much enlarged. After Beal.

In tracing weeds, it has been found that many of the most troublesome ones have come from Europe, Asia, or some other foreign country. Man has carried the seeds and fruits of these weeds across the seas, and most of them have been imported and sown with agricultural seeds.

Fig. 90. — The Squirting Cucumber (*Ecbalium Elaterium*) squirting its seeds from the pod.

Seeds Scattered by Explosive or Spring-like Mechanisms. — In this kind of dissemination the plant itself is the agent which, either by sudden ruptures due to strains or by explosions due to the swelling of certain tissues, is able to throw the seeds often a considerable distance. In the pods of some plants, as in the Vetches, Witch-hazel, Castor Bean, and Field Sorrel, bands of tissue, which ripen under tension, exert such a strain that the pods suddenly rupture with so much violence that the seeds are thrown in every direction. In the Violets the carpels, as they ripen and dry, press harder and harder upon the seeds, which suddenly shoot out as a Watermelon seed may shoot out from between one's pressed fingers. (*Fig. 89.*)   In case of the Impatiens called "Touch-me-not" and the "Squirting Cucumber," tissues within the pod take up water and swell so much that the pod finally explodes and scatters the seeds as shown in *Figure 90.*

CHAPTER VI

GERMINATION OF SEEDS: SEEDLINGS

Nature of Germination and Factors upon which it Depends

Although the resting condition is very essential to the preservation of the life of the seed during transportation and while awaiting favorable conditions for germination, it must be abandoned at some time in order that the embryo may develop into the plant, the production of which is the seed's chief function. By germination of a seed is meant that awakening from the resting condition in which the young plant shows practically no signs of life to a state of active growth. The term germination is used in different ways, being used to designate the beginning growth of such structures as a pollen tube, fertilized egg, and spore, but in each case, however, it refers to the initial growth. Seeds are considered germinated when the radicle and plumule have broken through and project beyond the seed coverings, although germination is not complete until the little plant is able to live independently of the stored food of the seed.

Conditions Necessary for Germination. — The awakening of the seed into active growth depends upon the presence of warmth, moisture, and oxygen. Germination is so dependent upon these three external factors that, if either is lacking though the other two are properly supplied, there will be very little or no germination. Among different seeds, the degree of temperature and the amount of moisture and oxygen required for the best germination vary.

Temperature Requirement. — Seeds vary more in the temperature required for germination than in any other factor. Through experience we have learned that among farm and garden seeds there are different temperature requirements for germination, and that the time of season at which different seeds should be planted must be chosen accordingly. Thus Oats, Wheat, and Red Clover seeds, which have a low temperature requirement, can be planted in the early spring or late fall when the weather and soil are cool, but if Corn or Melons, which have a high temperature requirement, are planted before the weather and ground are warm they will decay and have to be replanted. In considering temperature in relation to germination, three temperatures are usually noted; the *minimum*, the lowest temperature at which germination will occur; the *optimum*, the temperature most favorable for germination; and the *maximum*, or highest temperature permitting germination. As the following table shows, these temperatures are very different for different seeds, sometimes differing as much as 25° or 30° (Fahrenheit).

GERMINATION TEMPERATURES (FAHRENHEIT)

Kind of seeds.	Minimum.	Optimum.	Maximum.
	Deg.	Deg.	Deg.
Oats..........................	32–41	77– 88	88– 99
Wheat, Rye.....................	32–41	77– 88	88–108
Indian Corn	41–51	99–111	111–122
Red Clover....................	32–41	77– 88	99–112
Peas..........................	32–41	77– 88	88– 98
Sunflower.....................	41–51	93–111	111–122
Pumpkin......................	51–61	93–111	111–122
Musk Melon...................	60–65	88– 99	111–122
Cucumber.....................	60–65	88– 89	111–122

Germination, which proceeds most rapidly at the optimum temperature, decreases in rate as the temperature approaches the minimum or maximum as the following table shows in case of Corn, in which the time required for the radicle to break through, though only 2 days at the optimum temperature, was 10 days in a temperature near the minimum. In the majority of cases, the temperature of the soil in which seeds are planted is somewhat below the optimum and, consequently, if the soil tem-

EFFECT OF TEMPERATURE ON RATE OF GERMINATION

Temperature, ° F.	Germinating Period in Hours.	
	Indian Corn.	Red Clover.
42	240	180
55	144	32
75	56	24
87	48	24
102.6	48	24
111.2	80	..

perature is lowered as it often is by heavy rains which fill the soil with water or by days of cool cloudy weather, germination is either very slow or prevented as is well known to every farmer and gardener.

Moisture Requirement. — The amount of moisture required for germination is, in general, that which will completely saturate and soften the seeds. The water absorbed saturates the cell walls and starch grains, and fills the living cells of the embryo and all empty spaces that exist in the seed. Although the amount of water required to saturate different seeds varies, it is always a large per cent, sometimes more than 100 per cent of the dry weight of the seed, as shown in the table below. Reckoning in pounds from the percentages given in the table, 100 lbs. of Corn after being soaked for germination may weigh 144 lbs. and 100 lbs. of White Clover seeds after soaking may weigh 226.7 lbs.

WATER ABSORBED BY GERMINATING SEEDS

Seeds.	Per cent of water absorbed in germination.
Indian Corn	44
Wheat	45.5
Buckwheat	46.9
Rye	57.7
Oats	59.8
White Beans	92.1
Peas	106.8
Red Clover	117.5
Sugar Beet	120.5
White Clover	126.7

Most seeds, though not all, swell as water is absorbed, sometimes more than doubling their dry size. In fact, the per cent of increase in volume is often greater than the per cent of water absorbed, as in case of the Pea which may increase in volume 167 per cent while absorbing only enough water to increase its weight about 100 per cent.

If seeds are confined in a space which they fill when dry, their swelling may exert a force of several hundred pounds and often sufficient to break strong containers. This force is sometimes used in opening skulls in anatomical laboratories, in which case the skulls are filled with dry Peas, which after being moistened swell and force the bones apart.

Oxygen Requirement. — Although seeds are in the optimum temperature and properly supplied with moisture, they will usually not germinate unless oxygen is supplied, as is often demonstrated in the laboratory by the use of some substance to absorb the oxygen in the germinator or by replacing the air in the germinator with hydrogen, nitrogen, or some other substance, so that oxygen is excluded. (*Fig. 91.*) However, since the air is about one-fifth oxygen, seeds receive enough oxygen to germinate well if only air is supplied, although germination is often hastened

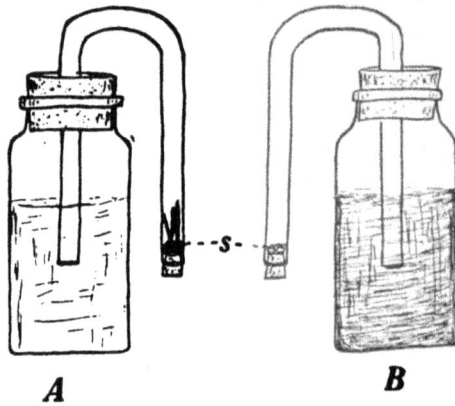

FIG. 91. — The two U-shaped tubes, which contain soaked seeds (*s*) on moist blotting paper at their stoppered ends, are alike except that in *B* the open end of the tube is in pyrogallate of potash, which absorbs the oxygen from the air in the tube, while in *A* the open end of the tube is in pure water, in which case the oxygen still remains in the air of the tube. The seeds germinate well in *A* but not in *B*.

when the amount of oxygen is increased artificially. For example, in an experiment Wheat, requiring 4 to 5 days to germinate in the air, germinated in 3 days in pure oxygen. There are a few seeds, however, which begin to germinate without oxygen, but they soon die unless oxygen is supplied.

For lack of oxygen seeds germinate poorly when planted in the soil so deeply that not enough air is accessible, or when planted in soils with their pores so full of water that the circulation of the air is prevented.

Germinative Processes

Seeds need water, oxygen, and warmth in germination because upon these external factors the internal germinative processes depend. For dissolving and transporting foods water is indispensable; the occurrence of certain chemical processes depends upon oxygen; and in order for both chemical and physical processes to be suitably active, as previously shown (page 90), warmth is required.

Changes in the Stored Food. — The first of the germinative processes has to do with the digestion and translocation of the stored foods. Whether stored outside of the embryo or in the cotyledons, the stored foods, until brought nearer, are beyond the absorptive reach of the cells of the plumule and radicle where they are most needed. But unless foods are in solution, which is the only form in which they can pass through the walls and protoplasm of cells, they can not move from one region of a plant to another. Therefore, since starch, fat, and protein, which are the chief storage foods of seeds, are not readily soluble in water, they must be changed to sugar, fatty acids, peptones, or other soluble forms before being transported. However, this digestive process occurs not only in seeds but also in all plant regions where foods are transported, and also in animals it has its likeness in the digestive process by which foods are made soluble, so that they can pass through the walls of the alimentary canal to the blood, which carries them in solution throughout the body. Both the digestion and transportation of the stored foods are quite noticeable during the germination of some large seeds, as in case of Corn in which the endosperm becomes watery and disappears as germination proceeds, or in case of Beans where the cotyledons in which the food is stored gradually shrink as the young plant develops.

The digestive process in plants as well as in animals is performed by special substances known as *enzymes*, which in case of the seed are secretions of the embryo. Enzymes occur in solution, either dissolved in water or in protoplasm, in all parts of the plant where they either initiate or hasten chemical changes. They are exceedingly important substances because upon them the majority of chemical changes in plants depend. They are specific in their action, that is, as a rule, each enzyme acts on only one kind of a substance, and is concerned with only one or two chemical changes. Consequently, the kinds of enzymes are almost as numerous in the plant as the kinds of substances to be acted upon. Thus for changing starch into sugar there is the enzyme known as *diastase* which is especially active in seeds, but common in other plant organs and in animal saliva. An enzyme secreted by the Yeast Plant and called *zymase* acts on sugar, forming besides alcohol, carbon dioxide which puffs up the dough when Yeast is used in bread-making. This enzyme also occurs in seeds, fruits, and other plant organs. *Lipase* converts fats into soluble fatty acids, and *pepsin* changes insoluble proteins into peptones and other soluble forms. Then there are *oxidases*, enzymes which oxidize substances as the name suggests, and peroxidases which take oxygen away from compounds, and many other enzymes which play an important rôle in the chemical activities of the plant. The exact chemical nature of enzymes has never been determined because of the difficulty in separating them from other protoplasmic substances which enter into and thus complicate the analysis. Nevertheless, there is much evidence that enzymes are protein-like substances. One striking feature of an enzyme is that it does not enter into the chemical action which it causes, and, therefore, a small quantity of an enzyme can keep a chemical action going until a large quantity of a substance is changed.

Although all living cells, whether in the embryo or elsewhere, produce enzymes, sometimes, however, certain cells have the secretion of enzymes as their special function, as in Corn, Wheat, and other seeds of the Grass type, where the epithelial layer of the scutellum has for its special function the secretion of the diastase and other enzymes which are necessary for converting the endosperm into soluble forms.

Transportation of Soluble Foods. — After the foods are made into soluble forms and dissolved in the water present, they pass from one region of the plant to another by the physical processes known as *diffusion* and *osmosis*. Diffusion is probably better known among gases where the spread of odors through a house, the fragrance of flowers through gardens, and smoke through the air are everyday illustrations of it. The spread of indigo, ink, or any substance like salt and sugar through the water in which they are dissolving illustrates it. By diffusion substances, whether dissolved in a gas or a liquid, spread farther and farther from the place where they entered the dissolving medium, and thus toward those regions where they are less concentrated.   In case a number of substances are in solution at the same time, each diffuses independently of the others.   When, for example, sugar, salt, and ink are dissolved in a vessel of water at the same time, each diffuses to all parts of the vessel independently of the others and, consequently, the substances become thoroughly mixed just as the oxygen, nitrogen, carbon dioxide, and other gases of the air by diffusion tend to thoroughly mix.   It is apparent then in case of the seed that foods in a concentrated solution in the endosperm or cotyledons will diffuse to the radicle and plumule, where the food, by being constantly removed from the solution to be built into plant structures, is kept less concentrated.

Osmosis mentioned as another process involved in the transportation of foods is also a diffusion, but differs from the ordinary diffusion just described in that it takes place through a membrane which alters the rate of the diffusion of different substances by allowing some to pass through it more readily than others.   It is by this kind of diffusion that substances pass into and out of living cells, in which case the membrane through which the substances must diffuse is the modified border of the protoplasm. Thus, although foods depend much upon ordinary diffusion for transportation when not passing through membranes, in entering or leaving living cells they must also depend upon osmosis, the nature and principles of which are more thoroughly discussed in connection with the cell (Chapter VII).

The Elaboration of Foods into Plant Structures. — In the early stages of germination the radicle and plumule elongate by the elongation of the cells already present, but soon, however, in certain regions, mainly at or near the tip of the radicle and plumule, there begins cell division followed by elongation, growth, and formation of tissues — the processes upon which the continued development of the young plant depends.   Throughout these processes foods are elaborated: (1) into materials to thicken the cell walls as they become thinner in stretching; (2) into protoplasm which must increase as cells grow and divide; (3) into woody and other elements for strength and conduction; (4) into fatty and waxy substances and cell thickenings for protection; and (5) into the various materials which are peculiar to food-making, reproductive, absorbing, secreting, and other structures which plants form during their development. But the transformation of foods into the various structural elements of the plant involves chemical reactions which take place only when there is energy supplied. This brings us to another process called *respiration* by which the energy required for the chemical changes involved in changing foods into cell walls, protoplasm, and other structures is secured.

Respiration in plants, just as in animals, is an oxidation process in which some food or other elements are burned, as we commonly say, with the result that oxygen is required and energy, carbon dioxide, and water vapor are produced. Respiration occurs only within the cell in connection with which it will be more fully discussed. But since there is no place where respiration is more in evidence than in germination where the cells are extremely active, some of its features should be noted in connection with that process. Furthermore, much about germination can not be understood until something is known about respiration.

Cells, like an electric motor, steam engine, etc., can not do work unless they have energy. Some cells, like the green cells of leaves, are able to utilize the sun's energy for some kinds of work; but when cells are not specially provided with pigments for utilizing the sunlight, they have to depend entirely upon the energy which they produce within themselves. In the sugar and other foods of the seed there is much latent energy which can be released as active energy by oxidizing these substances, which are thereby broken into simpler compounds of which carbon dioxide and water are the simplest and most noticeable ones. It is this oxidizing of substances, so that their stored energy is released, that constitutes respiration, which necessarily must be accompanied by a consumption of oxygen and the production of simpler compounds. It is now clear why seeds do not germinate well when oxygen is excluded as the experiment in *Figure 91* demonstrates. Although most of the energy released is used in carrying on the work of the cell, some, however, escapes as heat, which, like the liberation of carbon dioxide and water vapor, indicates that respiration is going on.

Respiration in seeds is easily demonstrated by germinating seeds in a closed jar, in which the production of heat and carbon dioxide with the accompanying loss of oxygen, and the accumulation of moisture can be demonstrated. By germinating seeds, such as Peas or Beans, in a closed vessel in which a thermometer

is inserted, the temperature of the enclosed air may be raised 10° C.
and sometimes 20° C. by the heat of respiration; and the oxygen of the enclosed air will usually be so nearly used up that the flame of a burning match or splinter is extinguished when inserted ·into the jar. (*Fig. 92.*) To demonstrate the accumulation of carbon dioxide, one may pour lime water into the jar where the seeds are germinating, in which case the calcium hydroxide of the lime water unites with the carbon dioxide of the enclosed air, forming calcium carbonate which is insoluble and when abundant gives the solution a milky appearance. Since the amount of carbon dioxide in ordinary air is not sufficient to give a perceptible precipitate, the milky appearance, therefore, indicates that much carbon dioxide has been added to the enclosed air. Again, the carbon dioxide liberated in germination can be quite accurately measured by drawing the air from over germinat ng seeds through a solution of potassium hydroxide, where the carbon dioxide is caught and its weight calculated from the increased weight of the solution. However, this involves careful weighing as well as seeing to it that the carbon dioxide already present in the air is removed before the air enters the germinator, and that the increased weight of the potassium hydroxide is not partly due to added moisture. This method discloses that many cubic centimeters of carbon dioxide may be liberated by a small quantity of germinating seeds, as shown by the experiment in which 3 Beans with a dry weight

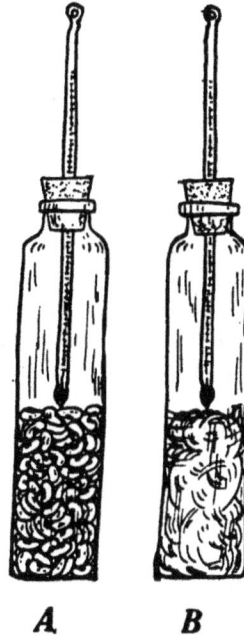

A   B

Fig. 92. — A simple experiment to demonstrate that heat is produced by germinating seeds. The bottle *A* contains germinating seeds, while the bottle *B* contains only moist cotton. The higher temperature, commonly shown by the thermometer in bottle *A*, demonstrates that germination is accompanied by the production of heat. If the bottles are protected against the loss of heat, or if bottles like "Thermos" bottles, which have double walls with air-space between, are used, the results are much better.

of only 1 gram produced $9\frac{1}{2}$ cubic centimeters of carbon dioxide during a germinative period of only 48 hours. That moisture is liberated during germination is obvious, for the air in a closed germinator often becomes so saturated that moisture precipitates on the walls of the germinator.

When green seeds, green hay, or any plant portions in which the cells are quite active are massed together, so that the heat and moisture are retained, they often become very warm and moist due partly to their own respiration and partly to that of the micro-organisms present. The so-called "sweating" of grains in the stack or bin and the heating in the bin when the grain becomes damp due to leaks are phenomena connected with respiration.

Summary. — In germination of seeds the following things take place: (1) the absorption of water which softens the seed coverings and acts as a dissolving and transporting medium of foods; (2) the secretion of enzymes which digest the foods and assist in other processes; (3) the transference of foods by diffusion and osmosis; (4) respiration which supplies energy for the elaboration of foods into plant structures and is accompanied by the absorption of oxygen and the production of carbon dioxide, water vapor, and some heat; and (5) the growth of the radicle and plumule, resulting in the breaking of the seed coverings and the establishment of the young plant in the soil and sunlight.

Testing the Germinative Capacity of Seeds

The loss in crop and labor when poor seed is used may be so serious that no one can afford to plant seeds with a doubtful germinative capacity. It is not enough for seeds to germinate, but they should have vigorous embryos, so that they will germinate quickly and thus rapidly pass through the delicate stage in which the young plant is likely to be destroyed by insects, Fungi, bad weather, and unfavorable soil conditions.

In testing the germinative capacity, as in determining the impurities of a quantity of seeds, decision is based upon the results obtained with a comparatively small number of the seeds as a sample. In case of small seeds, such as Oats, Wheat, Barley, and Clover, Alfalfa, and Grass seeds, tests are ordinarily made with two lots consisting of 200 seeds each and free from impurities. In Corn it is customary to use 6 kernels, 2 from near the tip, 2 from the butt, and 2 from the middle of the ear, with the kernels of each pair selected from rows as far apart as possible.

There are a number of germinators on the market, but, if one is not available, a box of moist soil or sand, or moist rags which are rolled up with the seeds within are good germinators when properly handled. (*Fig. 93.*) A very good germinator is made with two dinner plates and blotting paper as shown in *Figure 94*.

During the test a temperature suitable for the germination of the kind of seeds involved must be maintained. Some prefer to keep the temperature near that of the soil, so as to more nearly

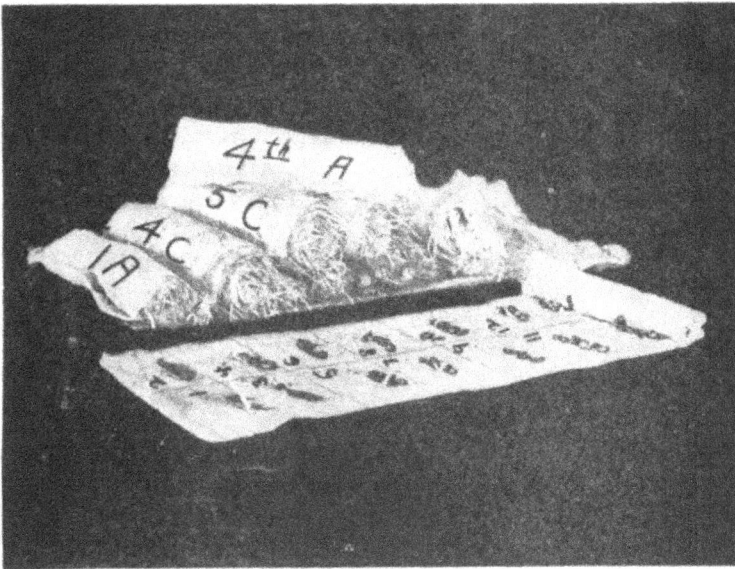

FIG. 93. — Doll rag testers, consisting of moist rags properly labeled and rolled up with the seeds within. After H. D. Hughes.

imitate the soil conditions under which most seeds do not germinate so well as they do in germinators. The germinator should be opened each day to note the germinated seeds and to allow the entrance of fresh air, if ventilation is not otherwise provided. At the end of the germinative period, the results are usually expressed in percentages found by dividing the number of germinated seeds by the number in the lot and multiplying by 100. Thus if 190 of a lot of 200 germinated, $\dfrac{190 \times 100}{200} = 95$ per cent. The percentage of germination will vary for different lots and the greater the number of lots tested, the more the results will be checked and, accordingly, the safer will be the conclusions.

In estimating the germinative capacity of seeds, the time allowed for germination must be considered; for seeds having weak embryos and, therefore, unfit for planting may give a high percentage of germination if allowed enough time. It is, there-fore, necessary to fix a time limit, and in doing so the ger-minative speed characteristic of the type of seeds involved and the temperature of the germinator must be consid-ered; for some seeds naturally germinate more slowly than others, and the effects of low and high temperatures on ger-mination are already known to the student (page 90). Furthermore, kinds of seeds differ so much in germinative capacity that a percentage of germination considered good for one kind of seeds would be con-sidered poor for another. Thus 70 per cent germination is good for Parsnip seeds but very poor for Wheat or Corn. In the following table[1] the number of days in which the seeds should germinate enough to show their germinative capacity, and the percentages of germination considered good for first-class fresh seeds, one year with another, are given.

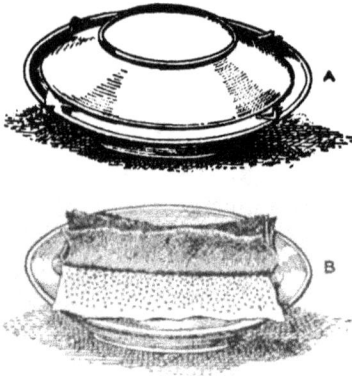

FIG. 94. — Simple germinator. A, closed. B, open. After F. H. Hillman.

Seed.	Germination period, days.	Good germination, per cent.
Red Clover	6	90
Alsike Clover	6	90
White Clover	6	90
Alfalfa	6	90
Timothy	6	96
Bluegrass (Kentucky)	28	80
Millet	5	95
Wheat	3	95
Oats	3	93
Barley	3	95
Flax	3	95
Corn	5	92

[1] Testing Farm Seeds in the Home and in the Rural Schools. *Farmers' Bulletin 428*, U. S. Dept. of Agriculture.

Seedlings

After the radicle and plumule have escaped from the seed coverings, the young plant passes into the seedling stage, which lasts until the young plant becomes entirely self-supporting, that is,

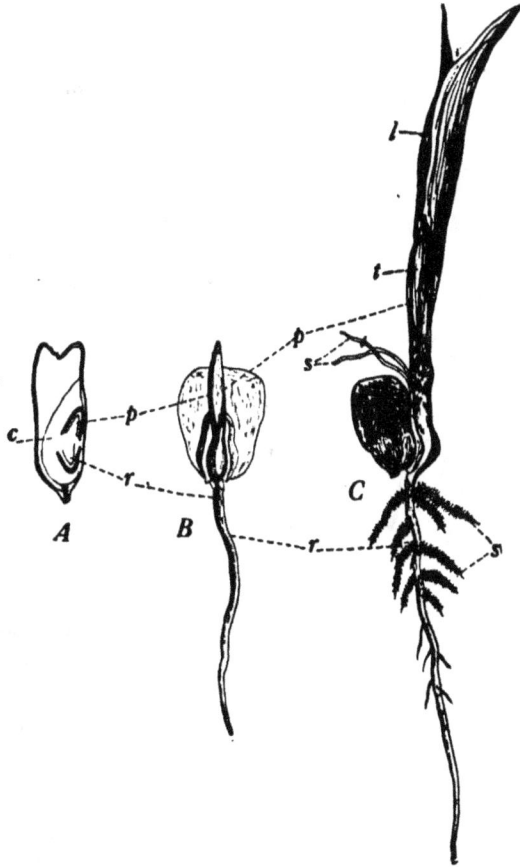

FIG. 95. — Early stages in the development of the Corn seedling. *A*, section through kernel, showing cotyledon (*c*), radicle (*r*), and plumule (*p*). *B*, after germination with radicle or primary root (*r*) and plumule (*p*) much elongated. *C*, radicle (*r*) and plumule (*p*) much further developed; *s*, secondary roots; *l*, leaves; *t*, coleoptile.

until it no longer receives any of its food supply from the seed. From the seedling stage the plant passes into the adult stage, except in trees where a sapling stage occurs. However, the division of a plant's life-cycle into successive stages is somewhat artificial, for the stages so overlap that they can not be separated. In this presentation we are chiefly concerned with the seedling stage — the stage in which plants present differences that sometimes must be reckoned with in choosing proper methods of planting and cultivating, and that often explain the peculiar features of the plant in the adult stage. Among our cultivated plants there are four rather distinct types of seedlings as those of the Grasses, Onion, Beans, and Peas illustrate.

Seedlings of the Grass Type. — The seedlings of all Grasses are so similar in type that their essential features may be learned by studying the seedling stage of Corn. From *Figure 95*, showing the development of the Corn seedling, it is seen that the radicle develops directly downward, forming the first root called *primary root* from which *secondary roots* arise as branches. However, not all secondary roots arise at this time from the radicle, for some often grow out from the stem just above or below the cotyledon. The plumule, although developing more slowly at first than the radicle, soon breaks through its sheath-like covering (*coleoptile*) and rapidly elevates its leaves to the light. As the plumule is

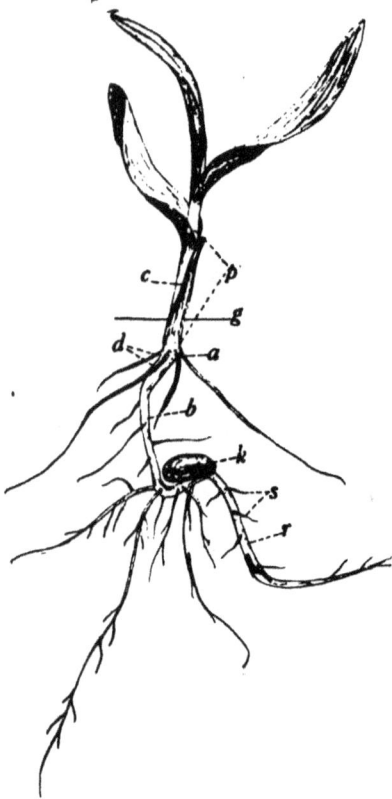

FIG. 96. — A later stage of the Corn seedling. *g*, ground line; *p*, plumule; *a*, first node with permanent root system; *b*, portion of stem between the first node and kernel; *k*, kernel; *r*, radicle or primary root; *s*, secondary roots of the primary root system; *d*, permanent root system; *c*, coleoptile. About half natural size.

unfolding its first leaves to the light, a zone, called a *node*, is formed at its base about 2 inches under the surface of the soil, and from this node and others soon forming above it, there arise roots of a much larger and stronger type than those formed from the radicle and from the stem in the region of the cotyledon. These secondary roots, which are outgrowths of the plumule since they arise from its nodes, constitute the *permanent root system*, which as the name suggests remains active as an anchoring and

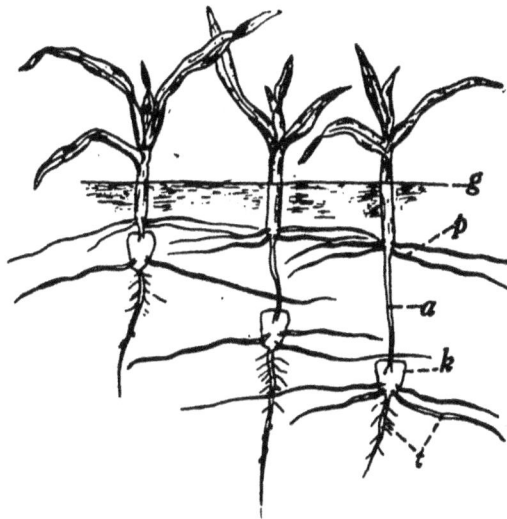

FIG. 97. — Diagram showing the effect of planting Corn at different depths. *g*, ground line; *p*, permanent root system, which always develops at about the same distance under the surface; *a*, temporary region of the stem, which is much longer in deep planting; *k*, kernel; *t*, temporary root system. Modified from "Elementary Principles of Agriculture" by Ferguson and Lewis.

absorptive system as long as the plant lives.   After the permanent roots are established (about 10 days after planting) the first roots, which are known as the *temporary roots* since they serve the plant only till the permanent roots are established, develop no further and remain as vestigial structures until they finally disappear.

Also included among the temporary structures is the portion of stem between the first node and kernel.   (*Fig. 96.*)   During the early stage of germination, this stem portion performs two important functions: (1) by its elongation the plumule is assisted in reaching above the soil; and (2) through it the endosperm and substances absorbed by the temporary roots reach the plu-

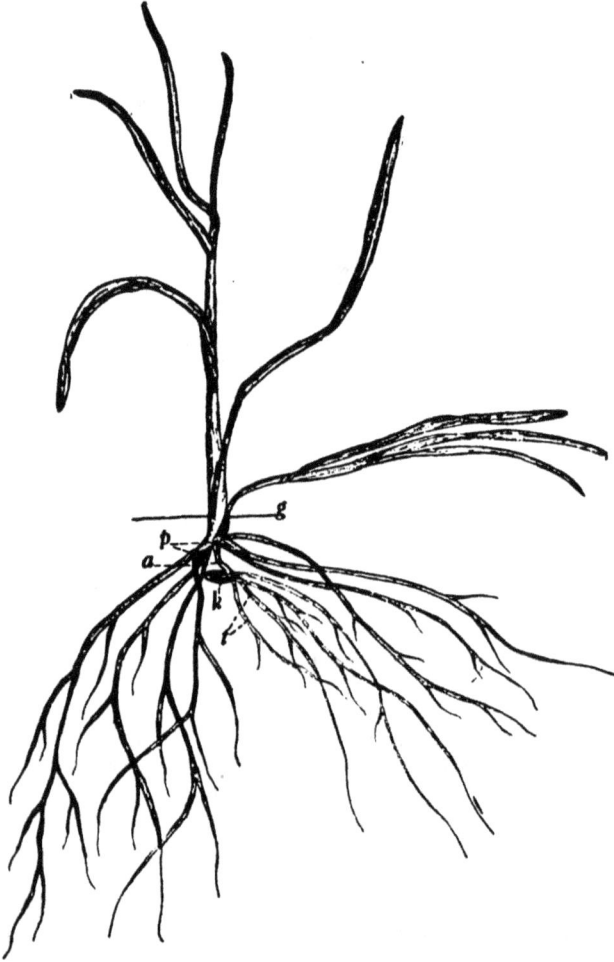

Fig. 98. — Seedling of Wheat after the permanent root system is established. *g*, ground line; *p*, permanent root system; *a*, temporary stem portion; *k*, grain; *t*, temporary root system. About half natural size.

mule. But after the permanent roots are well established, there is no longer any need for this stem region, which now being without a function makes no further development. Nevertheless in connection with it, there is a principle which is reckoned with in growing certain plants of the Grass type. According to the depth of planting this temporary stem region is long or short. (*Fig. 97.*) This is due to the fact that the first node and, consequently, the first of the permanent roots are always established about the same distance under the surface of the soil, regardless of the depth at which the seed was planted. Therefore,

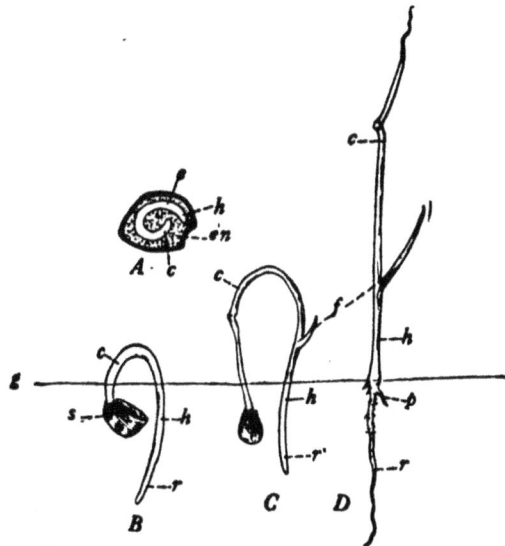

FIG. 99. — Stages in the development of the Onion seedling. *A*, section through an Onion seed showing endosperm (*en*) and embryo (*e*) with the hypocotyl (*h*) and cotyledon (*c*) indicated. *B*, seed germinating; *g*, ground line; *s*, seed; *c*, cotyledon; *h*, hypocotyl; *r*, radicle. *C*, seedling more developed; *c*, cotyledon which is being pulled out of the seed; *h*, hypocotyl; *r*, radicle; *f*, first leaf. *D*, a later stage of the seedling with cotyledon free from the seed and permanent root system (*p*) developing.

a deep permanent root system, which is often desirable in order that the plant may withstand drought, is not secured by deep planting — a fact which has been well demonstrated in case of Corn and the small grains. Moreover, if the seed is planted too deeply, its food and energy may be exhausted before the plumule reaches the light, in which case the seedling is unable to continue its development.

However, after the permanent roots are established they may

be put deeper in the soil by adding dirt around the plant. In semi-arid regions where a deep permanent root system is desired, the ground is often listed, that is, plowed into deep furrows, and the Corn planted in the bottom of the furrows. Then as the furrows are gradually filled in cultivation, the permanent roots are buried deeper in the soil, where there is a chance for moisture during drought. In this same connection, one can see some advantage in drilling small grains in that the roots of the plants will be buried deeper as the dirt from the ridges is carried into the drill furrows during rains and thaws.

In the small grains, such as Wheat, Oats, Barley, etc., although the temporary system is just as prominent as in Corn, there is, however, a difference of minor importance to be noted in the number of primary roots, which is one in Corn but two or more in the small grains. (*Fig. 98.*)

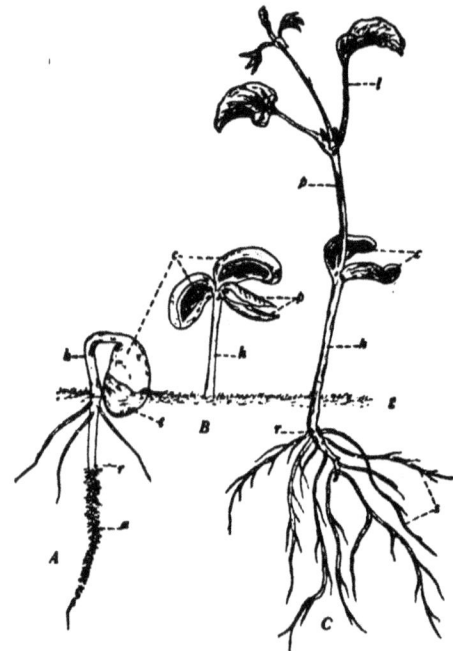

FIG. 100. — Stages in the development of a Common Bean seedling. *A*, the cotyledons (*c*) being pulled out of the ground by the hypocotyl (*h*). *t*, testa; *r*, radicle; *a*, root hairs; *g*, ground line. *B*, the hypocotyl has straightened, and the cotyledons have shed the testa and spread apart, thus giving freedom to the plumule (*p*). *C*, stage with plumule developing stem and leaves (*l*), root system much enlarged by secondary roots (*s*), and cotyledons (*c*) shrinking through loss of stored food.

The presence of the temporary system, although occurring in other plants, is a notable feature of the Grass seedlings. Another feature to be noted is that the cotyledon remains where the seed was placed in planting, that is, it is not pushed up out of the soil by an elongating hypocotyl.

Onion Seedling. — The seedling of the Onion represents another type of monocotyledonous seedlings. In this type the hypocotyl elongates and pushes the cotyledon above ground. (*Fig. 99.*) As in the Grass seedlings, the primary root system is temporary — a feature quite common in Monocotyledons, although in some it lives much longer than in others.

Seedlings of the Common Bean Type. — The seedling of the Common Bean is representative of those dicotyledonous seedlings in which the cotyledons through the elongation of the hypocotyl are carried above ground, sometimes several inches or even a foot in some Beans. Squashes, Cucumbers, Pumpkins, Melons, Radishes, Turnips, Castor Bean, Maples, Ashes, Clover, Alfalfa, etc., besides many of the Beans have this type of seedling. In seedlings of this type the first root system is usually the permanent one and soon firmly anchors the hypocotyl which then by an arching movement pulls the cotyledons out of the ground in such a way that they offer the least resistance in passing through the soil and afford the most protection for the delicate plumule. (*Fig. 100.*) In some cases, as in the Melons and Pumpkins, the hypocotyl also assists in casting

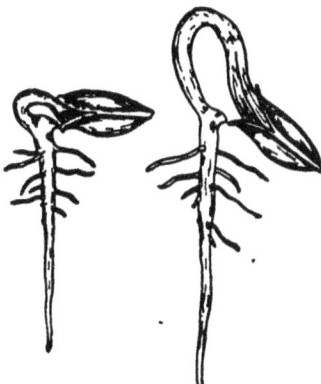

Fig. 101. — Squash seed germinating, showing the peg by which the seed coat is held while the cotyledons are pulled out of the seed coat by the arch of the hypocotyl. Somewhat reduced.

off the seed coat, in which case the arch of the hypocotyl pulls the cotyledons out of the seed coat while the latter structure is held in place by a peg-like structure of the hypocotyl. (*Fig. 101.*) In most cases, however, the seed coat is torn and gradually pushed off by the growth of the seedling. Since the first root system is usually the permanent one, its depth is closely related to the depth of planting.

The plumule remains small and enclosed between the cotyledons until pulled out of the soil. Then by a straightening of the hypocotyl arch and the spreading of the cotyledons, it is fully exposed to the light, where it develops all of the plant above the cotyledons.   Thus most of the stem and all of the leaves, flowers, and fruit of the adult stage are produced by the plumule.

The cotyledons, which are commonly fleshy in these seedlings, enlarge after reaching the light and their color changes to green, which with the presence of stomata indicates that they function to some extent like ordinary leaves in the manufacture of foods.   However, it is only a short time till most of them, especially the fleshy ones, begin to show shrinkage which continues as the food is used for growth, until much shriveled and dried they fall from the plant.   In some cases, as in the Buckwheat and Castor Bean where the seeds are albuminous, the thin cotyledons are more leaf-like and function like ordinary leaves for a considerable time, although in arrangement, shape, or size they are never just like ordinary leaves and never so long-lived. (*Fig. 102.*)   Where the cotyledons are large, much force is required to pull them through the soil, and, consequently, when the ground is hard or covered with a crust, seedlings of this type often fail to develop.

Fig. 102. — Seedling of Castor Bean, in which the cotyledons persist and function like leaves for some time.

As to how the development of both radicle and plumule proceeds until the adult stage is reached, that depends much upon the kind of plant.   In most cases the radicle forms a central root which, although prominent at first, may be much obscured in the adult stage by large secondary roots developing from the base of the stem.   In some plants, as in Red Clover and Alfalfa, the radicle forms a prominent tap-root which enables the plant to penetrate deeply into the soil in its adult stage.

In the Morning Glory, where the stem called the vine may be many feet in length, there is extreme elongation of the plumule. On the other hand, as in some Clovers and·Alfalfa, the plumule and hypocotyl form a short thick stem, called the *crown*, which is barely

FIG. 103. — Development of a Red Clover seedling.   *A*, cotyledons being pulled out of the ground by the hypocotyl (*h*); *r*, radicle; *a*, root hairs; *t*, testa; *c*, cotyledons; *g*, ground line.   *B*, a more advanced stage, showing some development of the plumule (*p*); *b*, first real leaf; *d*, second real leaf.   *C*, a later stage, showing that the plumule has formed more leaves (*e*) but has elongated very little.

above the surface of the ground, and from which the branches arise that bear the leaves, flowers, and fruit.   (*Fig. 103.*)

Seedlings of the Pea Type. — The seedlings of the Pea and Scarlet Runner Bean represent those dicotyledonous seedlings in which the hypocotyl remains short.   Thus the cotyledons remain underground and the plumule is pushed to the surface by the elongation of the stem of the epicotyl just as occurs in the Grass seedlings.   But in these seedlings, in contrast to those of the

Grass type, both the stem of the epicotyl and the primary root system are usually permanent. In many seedlings of this type, the cotyledons are probably so much distorted in connection with food storage, that they could not function as leaves if raised to the light. Again, it is claimed that these seedlings can come up through harder ground by not having to raise their cotyledons. (*Fig. 104.*)

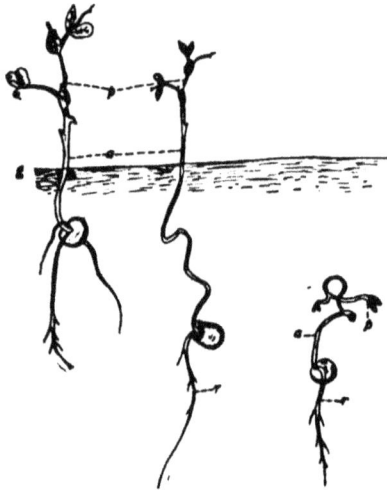

Fig. 104. — Seedlings of the Pea, showing how the seedling develops and the effect of different depths of planting. *p*, plumule; *a*, stem portion of epicotyl; *g*, ground line; *r*, radicle. The seedling at the right is so deep in the soil that it is unable to push the plumule out of the ground.

Size of Seedlings. — There is no feature in which seedlings vary more than in size. This might be illustrated by placing the seedling of Timothy or Clover by the side of a Coconut seedling. In general, the size of the seedling corresponds to the size of the seed. The size of seedlings is reckoned with in our methods of planting different seeds. Thus seeds, like Corn and Beans, are planted several inches deep in the soil, while seeds, like those of Lettuce, Clover, and Timothy, are sown on the surface, and covered only lightly if at all. In small seedlings there is not enough food to enable the plant to reach through thick layers of soil. Tests have shown that not many Clover seedlings get through the soil when the seeds are planted even 2 inches in depth.

Summary of Seedlings. — Seedlings of Flowering Plants are either monocotyledonous or dicotyledonous on the basis of the number of cotyledons. Among the Monocotyledons the temporary root system is a prominent feature, and the cotyledon may remain in the ground as in the Grasses or be raised to the light as in the Onion. In Dicotyledons the first root system is usually the permanent one and may consist mainly of a tap-root or of many roots nearly equal in size. In many Dicotyledons the cotyledons are raised to the light where they function to some extent like ordinary leaves. The fleshy ones, however, lose their stored food in a short time and fall from the plant. In some cases, as the seedlings of Buckwheat, Morning Glory, and Cotton illustrate, the cotyledons become more leaf-like and persist longer, although they are always easily distinguished from true leaves. In some Dicotyledons the cotyledons remain in the soil and the plumule is raised to the light by the elongation of the stem of the epicotyl.

CHAPTER VII

CELLS AND TISSUES

Structure and Function of Cells

Position of the Cell in Plant Life. — Before proceeding to the study of the adult stage of the plant more must be known about the cell. If with a sharp razor a very thin section from any part of a plant is made and observed with a microscope, it will appear to be divided into many small divisions. A section through the growing portion of a root looks like *Figure 105*. These little

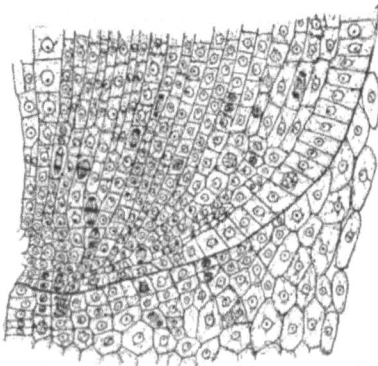

divisions with what they contain are the cells. Cells vary much in shape and are so small that usually four or five hundred of them could be laid side by side on a line not more than an inch in length. They are rarely more than $\frac{1}{100}$ of an inch, and sometimes less than $\frac{1}{1000}$ of an inch in diameter. Although cells are so exceedingly small, nevertheless, it is within them that all life processes take place. For this reason cells are often

FIG. 105. — A small portion of a lengthwise section through the growing region of a root showing the cells. Very much enlarged.

defined as the units of all plant and animal life. Plants need phosphate, nitrates, etc., because the cells must have them. All the problems of the plant relating to the soil, light, temperature, etc., are problems of the cell. The plant is made up of a countless number of cells and the activities of the plant are simply the sum of the activities of the many cells of which the plant is composed.

Discovery of the Cell and Its Structures. — That plants and animals are composed of cells was not revealed until the invention of the microscope, which, although very rude in its con-

112

struction and efficiency as compared with microscopes of today, was beginning to be employed by Robert Hooke (1635–1703) and others in the seventeenth century in the study of plants. Robert Hooke, one of the earliest to study plants with the microscope, examined thin sections of cork, and found the cork to be composed of numerous small compartments which he called cells on account of their rough resemblance to the cells of a honeycomb. Of course in dead tissue like cork the cell contents are absent, and Robert Hooke saw only the cell walls enclosing the spaces from which the active substance of the cells had departed. However, through investigations which followed those of these earliest investigators with the microscope, it gradually came to be recognized that the important part of the cell is the substance which fills the compartments. By extending the study to many kinds of tissues of both plants and animals, it was finally recognized that the substance filling the cell is the only living substance in plants and animals and the substance which builds the cell wall and the entire organism. Various names were at first applied to this substance before the term *protoplasm* suggested by Hugo Von Mohl was adopted by both botanists and zoologists. As the word protoplasm, which is a combination of *protos* (first) and *plasma* (thing formed), signifies, this substance was considered the first organic substance formed from the inorganic materials taken into the plant. The idea that the protoplasm is the essential substance and that the cell is the unit of plant and animal structure was quite thoroughly elaborated by Schleiden (1838) and Schwann (1839) and became generally accepted.

Protoplasm. — The protoplasm, as already noted, is the living substance of plants and animals. The protoplasm of an individual cell is often called a *protoplast*. Protoplasm is a fluid substance which varies much in its consistency, sometimes being a thin viscous fluid like the white of an egg, and sometimes being more dense and compactly organized. Chemical analyses show that protoplasm has the composition of protein, although such analyses necessarily kill the protoplasm and consequently do not give us a true knowledge of the protoplasm as it is while living. Although the protoplasm of higher plants usually exhibits no motion except when dividing, there are cases, however, as in the hairs of the Pumpkin and Wandering Jew, where the protoplasm, when under the microscope, can be seen streaming around the cell wall or across the cell from side to side or end to end.

The protoplasm consists of a number of structures which differ in organization, and each of which has one or more special functions. (*Fig. 106.*)   One of the most conspicuous of these structures is the *nucleus*, which is a comparatively compact protoplasmic body, usually spherical in shape.   Although usually centrally located in actively growing cells, the nucleus commonly has a lateral position in old cells.   The nucleus is enclosed by a membrane, called the *nuclear membrane*, and is filled with a liquid known as *nuclear sap*, which consists of water and dissolved substances. However, nuclear sap is usually colorless and, therefore, not visible.   Within the nucleus also occur one or more small globular bodies known as *nucleoli* (singular *nucleolus*) and much chunky or granular material known as *chromatin*, which is regarded as the most important part of the nucleus and is so named because it stains so readily when stains are applied to the cell.   Around the nucleus and filling up the general cavity within the cell wall is that portion of the protoplasm, known as *cytoplasm*, which is a loose spongy structure full of many cavities called *vacuoles*. The vacuoles are filled with a liquid called *cell sap*, which like the nuclear sap consists of water containing dissolved sugars, salts, and other substances.   The border of the cytoplasm is in contact with the cell wall and is modified into a membrane known as the *cell membrane*, which, since it is closely applied to the cell wall, can not ordinarily be seen until the cell is bathed in salt water or some other solution strong enough to shrink the protoplasm, so that the cell membrane is drawn away from the wall where it can be seen.   (*Fig. 107.*)

Within the cytoplasm commonly occur a number of small bodies

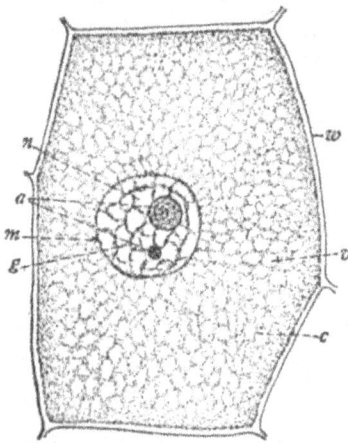

FIG. 106. — A growing cell. *w*, cell wall; *c*, cytoplasm; *v*, vacuoles filled with cell sap; *n*, nucleus; *a*, nucleoli; *m*, nuclear membrane; *g*, chromatin granules. Enlarged about five hundred times.

known as *plastids*, which are masses of cytoplasm but denser than ordinary cytoplasm. (*Fig. 108.*) They often develop pigments as in case of leaves, stems, and other green organs where they develop *chlorophyll*, the pigment upon which the green color of

these organs depends. Plastids containing chlorophyll are called *chloroplasts* and are very important structures because they have so much to do with making plant food. Plastids which occur in the petals of some flowers have yellow or red pigments. Plastids which are colorless, having no pigments at all, are called *leucoplasts*. Starch grains and other small bodies (*chondriosomes*) not

FIG. 107. — Cells with protoplasm (*p*) shrunken to show the cell membrane, which is represented by the dotted line surrounding the protoplasm.

shown in our figure are also commonly present in the cytoplasm.

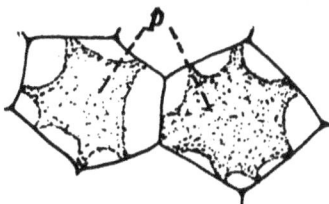

Cell Wall. — The cell wall is formed by the protoplasm and may be variously modified by it. In actively growing cells the wall is thin and composed of *cellulose* — a substance which allows

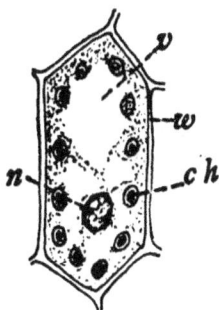

the wall to stretch as the protoplasm expands in growth. As the cell develops, the protoplasm in many cases thickens the cell wall by depositing new layers of material, which may be of cellulose or of some other substance better adapted to the function which the cell is to perform. In nearly all plants but in trees more especially some cells deposit *lignin* in their walls, thus becoming the wood cells which give rigidity to the plant and which we use in the form of lumber. In the bark of trees, Potato skins, and other structures for protection, fat-like substances are deposited in the walls of the cells which then are known as

FIG. 108.—Cell from a leaf. *w*, cell wall; *n*, nucleus; *v*, a large vacuole in the cytoplasm; *ch*, chloroplasts.

cork. Sometimes, as in the so-called *bast fibers*, which are the strengthening fibers especially prominent in Flax and Hemp, the walls are extremely thickened with cellulose. The same is true in Date. seeds and Ivory Nuts where the walls are extremely thickened with cellulose to be used as a food during germination.

There are many ways in which cell walls are modified as will be seen in the study of tissues.

Processes Involved in Cell Activity. — The chief of cell activities is *growth* which will be discussed in connection with the different plant organs. But growth, besides being much under the influence of external conditions, such as temperature and light, depends upon *metabolism* — the process by which materials are changed into forms which have to do with growth. In connection with growth, metabolism, and other physiological processes of the cell, osmosis and respiration are involved, both of which were shown to be important processes in seed germination. In germination and other physiological processes they are important because of their connection with the other processes of cells. Osmosis is a physical process which occurs wherever two liquids differing in concentration are separated by a membrane which they wet, and hence is not a cell activity except in so far as the protoplasm controls it when occurring in connection with the cell. Respiration, on the other hand, is a physiological process and only occurs in connection with protoplasm.

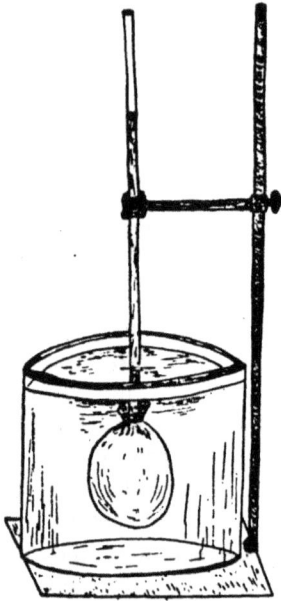

FIG. 109.— Experiment demonstrating osmosis. The pig's bladder was filled with a sugar solution and then the tube was attached. The water from the jar was drawn into the bladder and the solution in the bladder forced up the tube.

Osmosis. — Osmosis may be defined as that kind of diffusion by which liquids pass through membranes and its principles can be best understood by the study of an illustration as shown in *Figure 109*. Thus if a pig's bladder, filled with a sugar solution and having a long glass tube fastened in its neck, is submerged in a jar of water, water will pass in and force the solution up the glass tube. If, on the other hand, a sugar or salt solution stronger than the one in the bladder be placed in the jar, the water slowly passes out of the bladder. Thus the water passes from the weaker solution through the membrane to the stronger. Sometimes some of the dissolved substances may pass through the membrane, but often the membrane permits only the water to pass, in which case it is known as a *semi-permeable* membrane. In case of the pig's bladder not much sugar is allowed to pass through its wall, which is, therefore, semi-permeable in reference to this particular solution. When a membrane will allow a dissolved substance to pass, it is said to be permeable to that substance. Most membranes are permeable to some substances and impermeable to others.

The causes of the movement of the water or other solvents from the less dense to the denser solution are not thoroughly understood. Some think that it is due to the affinity of the dissolved substances for the solvent, which is pulled to the substances with a force increasing with the amount of the substances in solution. Others think that it is due to the checking of the diffusive power of the dissolved substances by the membrane, which permits the two liquids to approach an equilibrium only through the passing of more of the solvent to the denser solution.

In comparing osmosis in the cell with the illustration, the cell membrane corresponds to the wall of the pig's bladder, the cell sap to the solution within the bladder, and the solutions around the cell correspond to the water or solutions in the jar. If the cell sap in denser than the solution on the outside of the cell membrane, then water with those dissolved substances to which the membrane is permeable will pass in; but, on the other hand, if the cell sap is less dense than the solution without, water and probably some dissolved substances will pass out. Thus the passing of liquids through the cell membrane from a less dense to a denser liquid is also the chief feature of osmosis in cells. It should also be noted in connection with osmosis in cells: (1) that the more the two solutions separated by the cell membrane differ in concentration, the more rapid is the process of osmosis; and (2) that the solvent, which is water in case of cells, passes through the membrane independently of its dissolved substances, which are either carried along or left behind according to whether or not the membrane is permeable to them.

However, it is only in principle and not in practice that osmosis as demonstrated with the pig's bladder is identical with that in the cell. In the first place, instead of a solution containing only one dissolved substance, both the cell sap and the solution around the cell usually carry in solution a number of substances, each of which in its osmotic influence is independent of the others, although the osmotic influences of all are combined in determining the osmotic force of the solution. In the second place, the cell membrane is a living membrane and, therefore, able to alter its permeability, so that it may be permeable to certain substances at one time but not at another. Another peculiar feature of protoplasm is that substances are often allowed to pass in more readily than out. Thus root hairs, which take in many substances from the soil, do not allow the sugars and many other substances in their cell sap to pass out. If the cells of a red Beet are laid in a strong salt or sugar solution, the water will pass out but the coloring matter will be retained. Furthermore, when some cells are placed in very dilute solutions of dyes as methylene blue, the dye accumulates in the cell sap, which, therefore, becomes much more colored than the surrounding solution. In this way various kinds of substances which are allowed to pass in more readily than out may become more concentrated in the cell sap than in the solution without.

It is now seen that by osmosis cells obtain their water supply which they pull from the soil, surrounding cells, conductive tracts, or whatever surroundings they may have that puts them in contact with water. Furthermore, the more concentrated their cell sap, the more forcibly and rapidly they can draw water from their surroundings. Osmosis, although chiefly concerned with supplying cells with water, assists some in supplying cells with dissolved minerals, sugars, and other substances, which the cell membrane permits to be carried in with the water. But in connection with osmosis substances may pass into and out of cells by the same principles which are active in ordinary diffusion. Thus if substances are less concentrated in the cell sap than without and the membrane is permeable to them, they will diffuse to the cell sap, more or less independently of the movement of water, although if the water is moving in the same direction the substances will move more rapidly. Likewise substances diffuse out of cells when more concentrated within than without, provided the cell membrane is permeable to them.

Pressure Within the Cell. — In the case of the pig's bladder, it is seen that the flow of water into the interior increases the amount of solution within until some of the solution is forced up the tube. The solution rises in the tube because the increase in the amount of solution within the bladder requires more space, and is, therefore, accompanied by an increase in pressure against the wall of the bladder. This pressure, which in this case depends upon the concentration of the sugar solution in the bladder, might become so great as to burst the bladder, if no tube for an outlet were provided. This pressure, known as *osmotic pressure*, has been found to follow quite well the laws governing gas pressure. Consequently, if the number of molecules of the dissolved substance contained in a certain volume of the solution is known, the osmotic pressure can be calculated. Thus 342 grams of Cane sugar in 1 liter of solution (called a gram-molecular solution) will exert a pressure of about 22.3 atmospheres or 336 lbs. and in whatever proportion the number of grams is increased or decreased, the pressure is altered in a similar proportion. Osmotic pressure in cells, where it is called *turgor* pressure, is usually not less than 50 lbs. and often more than 100 lbs. The rigidity of organs such as leaves, soft stems, and roots is largely due to turgor pressure, as can be easily shown by immersing strips of a fresh Beet or Radish in a strong solution where they lose water and become flaccid. The wilting in leaves when exposed to excessive evaporation is due to the loss of turgor pressure, which occurs whenever cells lose water more rapidly than they absorb it. The preservative value of such substances as salts and sugars when applied to meats and fruits depends largely upon the withdrawal of water from the micro-organism, so that they can not become active. Wilted cells, if not dead, will also draw in water and again become turgid when put in contact with moisture. In this way flowers are revived by placing their stems in water, and Cucumbers, Lettuce, and Celery are made crisp by putting them in cold water. Sometimes, as the pollen of some plants illustrates when immersed in water, the pressure becomes so great that the cells burst. Even fruits, such as Plums, sometimes burst on the trees from this cause when the weather is warm and moist.

The Character of the Cell Membrane After Death. — With the death of the cell, the cell membrane ceases to be an osmotic membrane and thus becomes permeable to all substances in solution. After the cell membrane is dead substances pass through it, either into or out of the cell, almost as easily as through a piece of cloth. Consequently, osmotic pressure is lost when cells die and the substances ordinarily retained are allowed to diffuse out. This is easily demonstrated by soaking plant tissues in water before and after death. Thus, if from a fresh red Beet a strip is cut, washed thoroughly so as to remove the contents of the injured cells, and then soaked in water at a temperature not destructive to the life of the cell, it will be found that the pigment, sugar, and other substances of the cell are retained; but if the strips are put in water hot enough to kill the cells, then the pigment, sugar, and other cell substances diffuse out into the water. That pools in which dead leaves fall soon become colored is a common observation. The fact has significance for the farmer who has learned by experience that, when hay that is down is caught in a rain, more of the elements are washed from the cured hay than from that more recently mowed and hence still partly green.

Nature of Plant Food. — Besides oxygen, which is chiefly used in respiration, various substances, such as water, sugar, acids, salts, and carbon dioxide, enter the protoplasm where most of them have some use related to the growth of the plant. But as to whether or not all should be considered as plant foods, not all students of plants agree; for, although all of these substances have to undergo transformations in becoming cell structures, some are more nearly ready for use than others. This may be illustrated by comparing sugar with carbon dioxide and water. In the leaves or wherever chlorophyll is present, carbon dioxide and water have their elements dissociated and combined in such a way as to form sugar which can be used directly for respiration or by minor chemical changes be transformed into cell walls. Thus sugar, since it is more nearly ready for use, may be called a food and the carbon dioxide and water may be called elements from which food is made. Likewise protein, which is closely related to protoplasm, may be regarded as a food, while the mineral salts, such as nitrates, phosphates, sulfates, etc., which are necessary in the formation of proteins, may be egarded as the elements from which food is made. Some investigators restrict the term plant food to the more complex substances, such as sugars, starch, proteins, fats, and amino acids, while others include some of the simpler elements, especially the mineral salts. In this presentation water, carbon dioxide, and the mineral salts are regarded as elements used in the formation of foods.

Respiration

The general features of respiration were discussed in connection with seed germination where respiration is not only prominent but also must be reckoned with in understanding the germinative process. There it was stated that respiration takes place only within the cell and that it is comparable to ordinary combustion in that it is an oxidation process resulting in the breaking down of substances into simpler elements with the release of potential energy.

It is a well known fact that whenever carbon and oxygen are united energy is released. This is the principle employed in heating plants, steam engines, etc. where energy in the form of heat is obtained through the union of oxygen with the carbon in the coal, wood, or some other combustible substance. If sugars, starches or other substances containing carbon were used for fuel, the same results would be obtained. In the cell, however, since most of the energy released is used in protoplasmic movements, and in chemical changes involved in enlarging cell walls, making more protoplasm, etc., not much is exhibited as heat, although enough that all living plant parts are generally a little warmer than their surroundings, sometimes 2 or 3 degrees in case of large flowers and often much more in germinating seeds. Again, although the rate of respiration increases with the temperature up to a certain point, respiration proceeds in a lower temperature than does ordinary combustion. In fact, a temperature high enough to start the combustion of most substances is entirely too high for respiration, which in most plants ceases before 60° C. is reached. Also in respiration the process of oxidation is initiated and kept going by enzymes or directly by the protoplasm, while there are no such agents involved in combustion. Thus, although similar in results, in operation respiration is very different from combustion.

In combustion there is a constant ratio between the oxygen used and the carbon dioxide produced. Thus in the combustion of Grape sugar, as illustrated by the formula $C_6H_{12}O_6 + 6\,O_2 = 6\,CO_2 + 6\,H_2O$, the ratio $\dfrac{6\,CO_2}{6\,O_2}$ is 1. In respiration, however, although the ratio is often unity, it varies much, sometimes being greater and sometimes much less than unity. In germinating seeds, tubers, and bulbs containing starch and sugars, and in many other plant structures, the volume of oxygen consumed during active respiration is equal to that of the carbon dioxide given off; but in the germination of seeds containing fats and fatty oils, the volume of oxygen consumed is greater than that of the carbon dioxide given off, in which case some of the oxygen is apparently used in changing the fats and fatty oils to other forms of food having a larger proportion of oxygen.

In higher plants the substances oxidized are organic compounds including the sugars, fats, proteins, organic acids, and probably the protoplasm itself. Some lower forms of organisms oxidize inorganic compounds. Some Bacteria obtain energy by oxidizing the ammonia of ammonia salts to nitrites, while others obtain energy by oxidizing the nitrites to nitrates. Various other substances, such as hydrogen sulphide and iron, are oxidized by certain Bacteria to secure energy.

There are some forms of respiration which can continue when oxygen is excluded and the one of them best known is *fermentation*, which is prominent in the Yeast Plant and other fermenting organisms. When proceeding in the absence of oxygen, such forms of respiration are known as *anaërobic respiration*, that is, respiration in the absence of air. In fact, some micro-organisms can not carry on their processes well except in the absence of air. One kind of anaërobic respiration, which is very similar to if not identical with fermentation, can be detected in seeds, fruits. and all living plant parts when oxygen is excluded, so that the process is not obscured by ordinary respiration. This kind of respiration is considered by some to be the initial stage of ordinary respiration, thus being closely related to it.

The peculiar feature about fermentation in the absence of air is that oxidation of carbon continues with the release of energy and the production of carbon dioxide, although no oxygen is obtainable from without. Furthermore, fermentation, whether in the presence or absence of air, differs from combustion and ordinary respiration in the completeness with which the substances involved are broken down. This may be illustrated in the case of the fermentation of sugar by Yeast, in which case, as shown by the equation $C_6H_{12}O_6 = 2 CO_2 + 2 C_2H_6O$, the molecule of sugar is broken into 2 molecules of carbon dioxide and 2 of alcohol, while in case of combustion and often in respiration the molecule of sugar is broken into carbon dioxide and water, as shown in the equation $C_6H_{12}O_6 + 6\ O_2 = 6\ CO_2 + 6\ H_2O$. In respiration the breaking of the sugar into carbon dioxide and alcohol is probably the first step which is then followed by the breaking of the alcohol into carbon dioxide and water. From the equation in case of the fermentation of sugar it is seen that the energy is obtained by uniting the oxygen and carbon, both of which are present in the molecule of sugar. Thus by the use of the oxygen within the compound broken down, some oxidation can occur when there is no oxygen available from without.

Instead of alcohol other substances may be produced by fermentation according to the nature of the fermenting organism and the kind of compound fermented. Thus in the fermentation of cider by certain kinds of Bacteria alcohol is first produced and later acetic acid. In the souring of milk the Bacteria break the milk sugar into lactic acid. Although sugars are the substances involved most in fermentation, other compounds are known to be involved. Even decay, caused principally by Molds and Bacteria, is regarded as a kind of fermentation, in which case many kinds of substances are involved.

The injury caused by Fungi and Bacteria is often due largely to the by-products of their respiration and growth. Partly in this way Fungi damage or destroy plants upon which they live. Many of the Bacteria associated with diseases produce poisons known as toxins which cause injury or death in animals and sometimes in plants. To combat some of these toxins antitoxins are used.

Thus respiration whether aërobic or anaërobic is that oxidation process by which cells secure energy to carry on their work. Any condition, such as a low or high temperature, absence of food, or lack of oxygen, which hinders respiration, holds cell activity in check and thus impedes plant growth. Furthermore, due to the liberation of heat and moisture which may become destructive when allowed to accumulate, respiration must be reckoned with in the storing of plant products.

Cell Multiplication

As previously stated (page 112), cells are exceedingly small structures and a small size seems preferable in both plants and animals where numerous small cells rather than a few large ones

is the rule.   Consequently, as a cell grows, a size is soon attained
at which division must occur.   By division the cell becomes two
cells of half the parent size, and each of the new cells has all of the
structures of the parent cell and the ability to repeat the processes of growth and division.

It is by the growth, division, and differentiation of cells that
both plants and animals become adult individuals.   In the fertilized egg, the first stage of an individual's existence, cell division
begins usually in a few hours after fertilization and continues
throughout the life of the plant, although interrupted at various
times.   Although the cell divisions are countless in number in the
higher plants, they all proceed in the same way throughout the
plant, except in the anther and ovary where a peculiar type of
division to be discussed later occurs.

In some simple plants, as Bacteria and the Yeast Plant where
cell division is of a simple type, the processes of division may occupy only a few minutes, but in the higher plants where cell division is more complex, the processes of division often require two
or more hours, and so far as we know the processes are continuous
throughout the entire period.   Most of this time is occupied by
the division of the chromatin about which cell division centers.

Although cell division consists of a continuous series of events,
a few stages in the process, as shown in *Figure 110*, will suffice to
give an understanding of cell division as it occurs in the higher
plants.   Thus starting with the chromatin in a granular condition and scattered through the nucleus, the first step in division
is the organization of this chromatin into a thread which then is
segmented into segments known as *chromosomes*.   The number
of chromosomes into which the thread segments is definite for
each plant or animal, although varying much in different species,
ranging from two in some worms to more than one hundred in
some Ferns.   However, in many of our common plants and animals the number ranges from sixteen to forty-eight.   In man
there are forty-six or forty-eight, in Tomatoes twenty-four, and
in Wheat sixteen.   The chromosomes, which have no definite
arrangement when first formed, soon arrange themselves in a
plane across the cell.   As they assume this arrangement, the
nuclear membrane disappears, thus allowing the chromosomes to
come in contact with the fibers, known as *spindle fibers*, which
seem to be special provisions of the cytoplasm for bringing about

the distribution of the chromosomes. At this stage it becomes apparent that each chromosome consists of two pieces or halves each apparently having split longitudinally. The halves of each chromosome now separate, pass to opposite ends of the cell where the new nuclei are formed. Thus each new nucleus gets as many halves, which soon grow to full size chromosomes, as there were chromosomes in the parent cell. As the new nuclei are forming

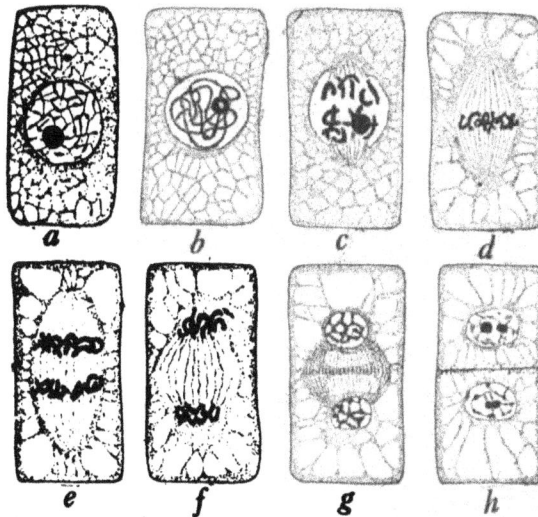

Fig. 110. — Cell division. a, cell in resting stage. b, chromatin formed into a thread. c, the thread of chromatin broken into segments called chromosomes. d, chromosomes arranged across the cell for division. Notice the threads called spindle fibers running through the cell and that the nuclear membrane has disappeared. e, chromosomes have split and the halves are passing to opposite ends of the cell. f, chromosomes have reached the points where they are to form new nuclei. g and h, new nuclei and cross wall between them forming. After Stevens.

a cross wall is formed, which divides the cytoplasm, and cell division is now complete. Instead of one cell there are now two, each of which after growing to full size will divide in the same manner as the parent cell.

Except in certain regions where cell multiplication is the special function, most cells of the plant sooner or later lose their ability to grow and divide as a result of their modifications which adapt them to their special functions. Thus after cells are

thoroughly modified for protection, absorption, strength, conduction, food-making, etc., in most cases growth and division ceases.
This brings us to the *tissues* which are groups of cells so modified
as to be adapted to special functions and upon which the various
activities of the plant depend.

General View of Tissues

The most important tissues of Seed Plants are those which have
to do with growth, protection, support, conduction, secretions,
absorption, food manufacture, food storage, and reproduction.

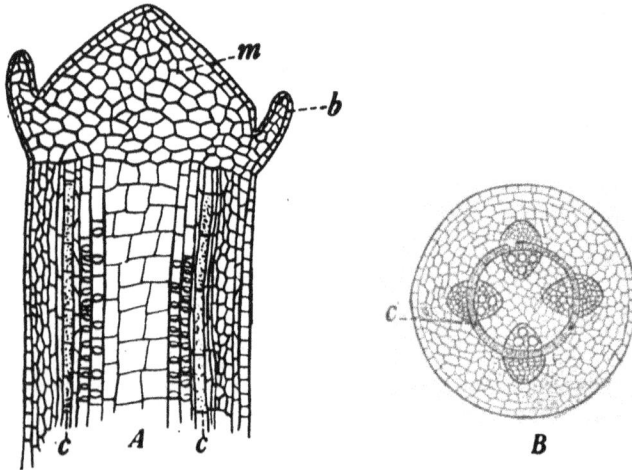

FIG. 111. — *A*, lengthwise section through a tip of a stem, showing the
apical meristem (*m*) from which branches (*b*) are arising and from which cambium (*c*) and other tissues are being formed below. *B*, cross section of a
stem, showing the cambium and its position in reference to other tissues.

Tissues Connected with Growth. — Since the cells of most tissues are no longer capable of growth and division after completing
their modifications, there must be provided at certain places in
the plant groups or bands of cells which retain their ability to
grow and divide throughout the life of the plant, for otherwise
the growth of the plant would soon cease. Such cells, forming
the *meristematic tissues* or *meristems* (from the Greek word meaning "to divide"), are present at the stem and root tips and in the
cambium, where their chief function is the multiplication of cells,

so that the different tissues may be enlarged as the growth of the plant demands. By means of a meristem at their tips, roots and stems elongate, and by means of the cambium they increase in circumference. However, the meristems at the growing apices are the first sources of all other tissues, even of the cambium, and for this reason are known as the *primary meristems.* (*Fig. 111.*)

Meristematic cells are characterized by having thin cellulose walls, large nuclei, and dense cytoplasm — features which enable the cell to grow and divide rapidly. Closely related to the meristematic cells are the *parenchyma cells,* which also in most cases have thin cellulose walls but are less active in dividing. Parenchyma cells occur scattered throughout the various plant tissues and constitute the food-making tissues of leaves and stems, and most of the pith of plants.

Protective Tissues. — For protection against destructive agencies plants have their outer cells modified into protective tissues,

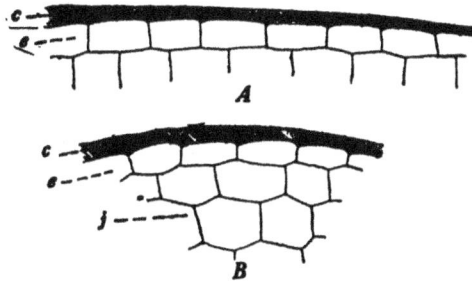

Fig. 112. — *A*, epidermis of a leaf showing epidermal cells (*e*) with their outer cutinized walls (*c*). *B*, the flesh (*j*) and rind of a Jonathan Apple showing the thick, cutinized, outer walls (*c*) of the epidermal cells (*e*). Much enlarged.

such as *epidermis, corky rind,* and *bark,* which lessen evaporation and prevent the entrance of destructive organisms. The most common protective tissue is the epidermis which consists of one or more layers of cells forming a jacket about the plant. The outer walls of the exterior layer of epidermal cells are usually thickened and contain a waxy substance called *cutin* which makes them waterproof. (*Fig. 112.*) Most plant organs are at first protected by an epidermis, but in the older portions of stems and roots the epidermis is often replaced by cork tissue, which is usually

much thicker and more protective than an epidermis. (*Fig. 113.*)
The cork covering may be more or less flexible, as the rind of an

FIG. 113. — A small portion
of a section through an Irish
Potato. *r*, rind composed of a
number of layers of cork cells.
s, tissue filled with food. Highly
magnified.

Irish Potato or Sweet Potato, or
harder and more brittle, as in the
bark of trees, where it reaches its
extreme thickness. Cork tissue consists of dead cells in the walls of
which there is deposited a waxy
substance much like cutin but called
suberin to which much of the protective character of cork is due.
Cork coverings afford more protection than an epidermis, but on account of their opaqueness, they are
not suitable except where it is not
necessary for light to penetrate to
the inner tissues.

The protection afforded by an
epidermis and cork is often brought
to our notice in case of fruits, tubers,
and fleshy roots. Thus Apples,
Oranges, and most fruits which may be kept a long time, if
uninjured, soon decay when their rinds
are broken. The efficiency of a corky
rind to protect against the loss of water
is shown by the experiment in which a
peeled Irish Potato lost sixty times as
much water in 48 hours as an unpeeled
one of equal weight.

Furthermore, cork tissue has an additional function in the healing of
wounds where, by the development of
a callus-like mass of cork, the opening of the wound is closed and the
break in the protective covering of
the plant thereby repaired. It is important to recognize this fact in pruning where the promptness as well as the
thoroughness of the healing depends much upon how the wound
is made.

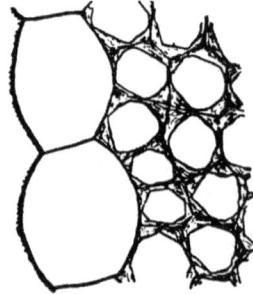

FIG. 114. — Some collen-
chyma cells from the stem
of a Dock (Rumex) showing
the cells thickened mainly
at the angles. After Chamberlain.

Strengthening Tissues. — In order to endure the strains to which they are exposed, both stems and roots must have strengthening tissues so as to be tough and rigid. Strengthening cells, although of different types, have much thickened walls and in most cases are much elongated.

In one kind of strengthening tissue, known as *collenchyma*, which often occurs in the younger regions of stems, the cell walls are thickened chiefly at the angles, thus leaving thin portions in the side walls through which the protoplasm receives enough materials to maintain life in spite of the modifications. (*Fig. 114.*)

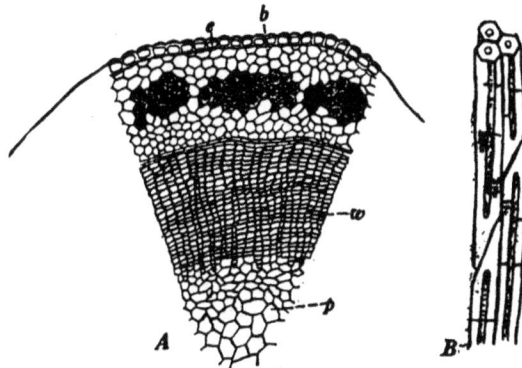

FIG. 115. — Bast fibers of Flax. *A*, a portion of a cross section of a Flax stem, showing the bast fibers. *e*, epidermis; *b*, bast fibers; *w*, woody part of the stem; *p*, pith. *B*, longitudinal view of a number of bast fibers. Much enlarged.

A kind of strengthening tissue, in which the cell walls are quite evenly thickened with cellulose, occurs in the older regions of stems between the epidermis and woody cylinder, and consists of *bast fibers*, the fibers upon which the value of Flax, Hemp, etc. as fiber plants depends. *Fig. 115.*) Bast fibers are much elongated cells and so spliced that they form thread-like fibers which are easily combined into larger fibers for making linen cloth, twine, ropes, and other textiles. Bast fibers may occur also in leaves and roots where they are usually not so prominent, however, as in stems.

In the woody portions of plants, especially in all trees except the evergreens, there occur along with the conductive tissues *wood fibers*, in which the walls of the much elongated cells are not only much thickened but also made woody — a feature in which they differ from collenchyma and bast fibers, where the thickenings are mainly of cellulose. (*Fig. 116.*) Where the wood fibers are abundant, as in Oaks, the wood is compact. Likewise, due to a greater number of wood fibers, fall wood is more compact than spring wood.

FIG. 116. — A wood fiber, consisting of a much elongated cell with thick woody walls.

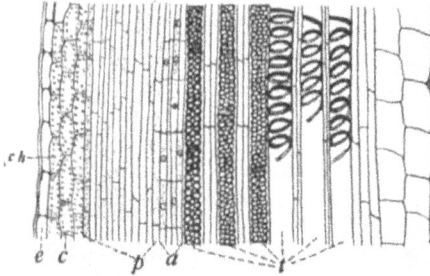

FIG. 117. — Very much enlarged lengthwise section through an Alfalfa stem, showing the conductive and food-making tissues of the stem. *t*, tracheae (commonly called xylem), which constitute the water-conducting tissue; *p*, the conductive tissue (commonly called phloem), which conducts the food made by the leaves; *c*, the food-making and storage tissue (cortex) just under the epidermis (*e*). The cells of the cortex contain chloroplasts (*ch*). *a*, cambium.

Conductive Tissues. — The conductive tissues of plants are of two kinds, *xylem* and *phloem*, which occurring together form the *vascular bundles* through which water, mineral salts, and foods are distributed to all parts of the plant. (*Fig. 117.*) The xylem is devoted chiefly to carrying water with what it may have in solution and the phloem to carrying foods. Furthermore, the xylem and phloem differ in that the conductive cells of the former are empty while the conductive cells of the latter retain their protoplasm. In Conifers, such as Pines, Firs, etc., the water-conducting cells have tapering ends and do not form a continuous series. They have peculiar pits in their walls, known as *bordered pits*, through which the liquids pass from cell to cell. They are commonly known as *tracheids*, meaning "trachea-like." Other plants have tracheids, but tracheids with bordered pits are characteristic of Conifers. The tracheids are also important strengthening as well as conductive tissue. (*Fig. 118.*) In Flowering Plants, although tracheids are present, the water-conducting tissue is composed mainly of cells which fit together end to end and thus form a continuous series. The end walls of the cells of the series are resorbed and thus are formed continuous tubes, called ducts, vessels, or *tracheae*, the last name referring to their resemblance to the human trachea. In the phloem, the main conductive tissue is composed of the *sieve tubes*, which are so named because of the perforations in their walls. Unlike tracheae, which have thickened woody areas in their walls, sieve tubes have thin cellulose walls and retain their protoplasm. With the sieve tubes usually occur thin-walled elongated cells, known as *companion cells*, and parenchyma cells, both of which aid in conduction.

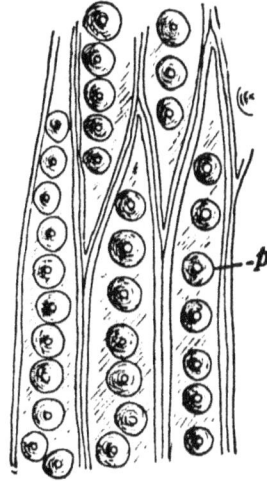

FIG. 118. — Tracheids from wood of Pine, showing the tapering ends and the bordered pits (*p*). After Chamberlain.

Absorbing Tissues. — In the higher plants, where the plant body is differentiated into roots, stem, and leaves, the roots are especially devoted to absorption. In case of soil roots, the root hairs,

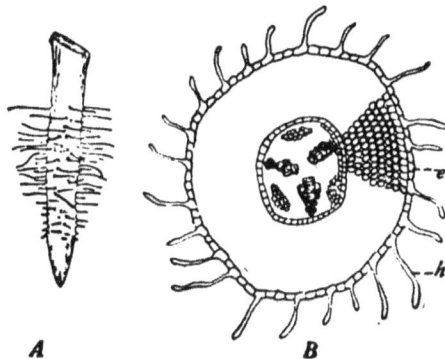

FIG. 119. — *A*, root hairs, the absorptive structures of roots, as they appear in a surface view of the tip of a root. *B*, cross section of a root, showing that the root hairs (*h*) are projections of the epidermal cells (*e*).

which spread into the soil where they take up water by means of osmosis, are the chief absorptive structures. (*Fig. 119.*) There are some plants, however, which live on other plants, in which case the root tissues absorb directly from the tissues with which they are in contact. In some cases the leaves absorb, as in the Sundew (*Drosera*), Venus's Flytrap (*Dionæa muscipula*), and Pitcher Plants (*Sarracenia*), where the eaves are especially constructed for catching and absorbing insects.

Food-making Tissues. — The principal food-making organs are the leaves where the cells are provided with chloroplasts and so arranged that they can obtain the raw materials from which foods

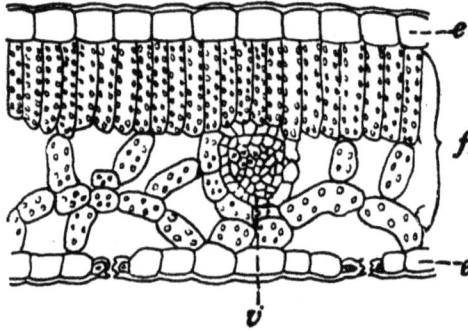

Fig. 120. — Cross section of the leaf. *f*, food-making tissue; *e*, epidermis; *v*, cross section of a vein.

are made. (*Fig. 120.*) However, food-manufacture is not limited to leaves, for all green stems have just under their epidermis a band of green cells, known as the *cortex*, in which food is manufactured as long as light and air are not excluded. (*Fig. 117.*)

Storage Tissues. — Any living cell usually contains some stored food, but there are cells which have food storage as their chief function. This is true in the endosperm and fleshy cotyledons of seeds, and in Irish Potatoes, Sweet Potatoes, and in other tubers and roots where the cells enlarge and become packed with food. In the pith some water is usually stored and often much food, as is well known in the case of Sugar Cane and Sorghum in which the pith contains much sugar. Throughout the wood of trees there are thin-walled living cells, forming the *medullary rays*, which function as a storage tissue. In Maple trees the sugar occurring in the spring sap comes from the starch which was stored chiefly in the medullary rays during the previous season. For water storage some plants have special tissues, while others like the Cacti store it throughout the plant body.

Secretory Tissues. — Secretory tissues, although not so essential and no so common among plants as the other tissues discussed, perform an important function in some cases. Most showy flowers have secreting tissues, known as *necta glands*, located at the base of the corolla or calyx. (*Fig. 121.*) These glands secrete the *nectar*, which, by attracting insects, aids in securing cross-pollination. Furthermore, honey is made from nectar, and the value of a plant as a bee-plant depends upon the amount and quality of nectar secreted by its nectar glands. On the leaves, stems, or fruits of many plants, such as Mints, Oranges, Lemons, etc., there are glands whose secretions give the plan a peculiar fragrance. In he stems and leaves of Conifers occur long tubes or ducts, known as *resin ducts*, which are lined with secretory cells that secrete resin from which pine tar, rosin, turpentine, and other valuable products are made. Much like the resin ducts are the *milk* or *lactiferous vessels* of the Milkweeds (*Asclepiadaceae*), Spurges (*Euphorbiaceae*), Dogbanes *Apocynaceae*), and other plant families where milk-like secretions occur. There are numerous secretions many of which, however, are secreted by cells in which secreting is not the special function.

Fig. 121. — A Buckwheat flower with sepals removed from one side to show the nectar glands (*n*). After H. Müller.

Reproductive Tissues. — Reproductive structures are of two kinds, sexual and asexual. Any portion of a plant, as a bud, tuber, stem, or root which may function in producing new plants, is regarded as an asexual reproductive structure. Some plants, as Irish Potatoes, Sweet Potatoes, and Strawberries illustrate, are quite generally propagated asexually.

In the higher plants the sexual reproductive tissues are those of the flower, and more especially those of the stamens and pistils with which the student is familiar. Although the eggs and sperms are the chief reproductive cells, all the tissues of the stamens and pistils are related to fertilization, which is the chief feature in sexual reproduction.

In plants like Ferns, Mosses, and Algae, where there are no flowers, the sex cells are commonly borne in special organs, called sex organs, which are so constructed as to favor fertilization.

Summary of the Cell and Tissues. — The cell is the unit of plant and animal life. It contains the living substance, known as protoplasm, which is usually enclosed in a cell wall. The protoplasm is composed of a nucleus and cytoplasm. Cells receive water, food, and mineral elements through osmosis and ordinary diffusion, and obtain energy through respiration. Cells multiply by division. Cell multiplication is accompanied by cell modifications which result in the differentiation of the cells into tissues. Some tissues consist of only the modified cell walls, the protoplasm having died and disappeared after the modifications of the walls are complete. The higher plants have many tissues, each of which has one or more functions. The meristematic tissues enable the plant to continue growing; epidermal and cork tissues protect the plant from drying and from attacks of destructive organisms; collenchyma tissue, bast fibers, and wood fibers enable the plant to support itself in a favorable position in spite of the force of gravity and winds; vascular bundles, like the circulatory system of animals, supply the other tissues with materials; the absorbing tissues take from the soil, or other substrata, the water and dissolved substances which the plant must have; the storage tissues hold the water or food in reserve for future use. The stored water is used during dry seasons, and the stored food is used for the growth of new plants, as in case of seeds, tubers, etc., or for the new growth of leaves and flowers at the end of a dormant period, as in case of trees. The food-making tissues furnish the food which all parts of the plant must have. Secretory tissues assist in cross-pollination by providing secretions which attract insects, furnish nectar from which honey is made, and give us many other products, such as resin, turpentine, etc.

CHAPTER VIII

ROOTS

General Features of Roots

The higher plants consist of roots and shoots. The roots are generally underground structures, while the shoot is the aërial portion consisting of the stem with its leaves, buds, flowers, and fruit. Plants like the Algae, which live in the water where all parts of the plant can absorb directly from the surroundings, do not need roots, although they often have structures known as *holdfasts* which anchor them; but holdfasts are too simple in structure to be called roots. Even in the Mosses, which are mainly land plants, instead of roots there are hair-like structures, called *rhizoids*, which anchor the plant to the substratum. True roots are complex structures and are characteristic of Ferns and Seed Plants.

Although we think of roots as underground structures, there are, however, a few plants having roots adapted to living in other situations, as in the water, air, or the tissues of other plants. But with few exceptions our cultivated plants depend upon soil roots, which, therefore, deserve most attention.

Being underground structures, soil roots normally arise from the stem's base, from which they radiate by elongating and growing new branches, which in turn branch and rebranch until the soil about the plant is quite thoroughly invaded by its root system. Usually a plant's root system, tapering into numerous branches almost hair-like in size, is more branched and spreads farther horizontally than its stem system. The profuseness with which roots branch is well shown by the estimated root length of some plants. Thus the length of all the roots of a single Wheat or Oat plant, laid end to end, is estimated at 1600 feet, or more than a quarter of a mile. For a vigorous Corn plant the estimated root length is more than a mile. Certainly in some trees the root length would much exceed that of Corn.

The size of a plant's root system, in general, varies with that of the shoot, for the larger the shoot, the larger the root system necessary to supply the adequate amount of water and mineral matter, and to furnish sufficient anchorage. As to the size of the roots of a plant, that depends upon the size of the shoot, the number of roots, and the distances of roots from the stem. The relation of the size of roots to that of the shoot is well shown in case of trees, where the roots directly connected with the stem and known as *main roots* increase in diameter from a few millimeters often to a foot or more as the shoot passes from the seedling to the mature stage. Where there is only one main root, as in Alfalfa and the Dandelion, its size is directly in proportion to the size of the shoot, usually being as large or even larger in diameter than the short stem of the crown. On the other hand, when the roots leading from the stem are numerous, as in the Grasses and numerous other plants, all are relatively small. As to the size of a branch root, that depends much upon its distance from the stem or main root, for all roots branch and rebranch until the branches are fibrous-like, usually being a millimeter or less in diameter at their tips. It is in connection with these fiber-like branches, which are the absorptive regions, that roots show most uniformity; for the roots of all plants taper down to these fiber-like branches, which are practically uniform in size for all plants. This uniformity in size is probably due to the fact that only roots with a very small diameter are efficient absorbers.

The texture of roots is always soft at the tips where the cells active in division, elongation, and absorption have thin cellulose walls, which readily yield to pressure or strains. But not far back of the absorptive region there are formed strengthening fibers, which afford a toughness that enables the root to endure the strains in connection with its anchorage function. Furthermore, roots, in their older regions, are covered with cork which adds firmness to the texture. In shrubs and trees the roots, in their older regions, become as woody and just as hard as the stems.

As to duration, roots may be short-lived, serving the plant only in the seedling stage, as in case of temporary roots, or they may last as long as the plant, as in case of permanent roots. The life of permanent roots is one, two, or many years according to whether or not the plant is annual, biennial, or perennial.

Interdependence of Shoot and Root. — Upon the roots the shoot depends for water, mineral matter, and anchorage, while upon the shoot the root system depends for food.   Neither could survive without the other.   Moreover, if either is hindered in its development, the other likewise will be stunted.   For this reason when pots in case of potted plants prevent the further development of the root system, the growth of the shoot is checked and the plant has to be repotted.   Again, the cutting away of the roots of a shade tree in excavating for a sewer or sidewalk often kills the tree due to diminished water supply.   A number of instances can be cited to show the dependence of the roots upon the shoot.   For example, it is well known that the roots of Asparagus will not make a good growth unless the shoots are allowed to grow during a part of the summer, in order that food may be provided for the growth of the roots.   Furthermore, it is a common practice in eradicating such weeds as Canada Thistle and Quack Grass, to starve the underground structures by keeping down the shoots.   To enable plants to establish a good root system, in order that there may be a well developed shoot, is one of the chief aims in cultivation.

The most necessary material absorbed by plants is water, which is supplied almost entirely by the roots in higher plants, and serves at least a half dozen different purposes.   *First*, water is necessary, and in large quantities too, to prevent the shoot from becoming dried out through loss of water to the surrounding air. Leaves and also stems, unless the latter are well covered with bark, are constantly having water evaporated from them and, unless this loss is compensated, the shoot will soon die.   *Second*, water enables the cells to maintain their turgidity, which maintains the leaves and other soft tissues of the shoot in a rigid position, and thus in a position suitable for work.   *Third*, water is an essential constituent of sugar, starch, and other foods made by the shoot.   *Fourth*, water as the plant's solvent is the medium through which substances in solution are distributed through the plant. Thus through water as a medium, the mineral elements of the soil and the foods made in the leaves are carried to all parts of the plant.   *Fifth*, it is in the form of a solution in water that substances in the plant react chemically with each other.   *Sixth*, water is an important constituent of protoplasm, cell walls, and other plant structures, usually being more than 90 per cent of their fresh weight.   Thus it is no wonder that plants must have water or they soon perish.

In *anchoring* the shoot most soil roots perform an important function, except in those plants with stems prostrate on the ground or climbing supports. In plants with upright stems, as in trees, the strains due to winds and gravity when the plant is bearing foliage and fruit is often enormous. However, the root system is usually able to hold the plant in place, although the strains may break off branches or even the main stem. It is by spreading laterally and profusely branching, that roots become so firmly attached to large masses of soil that they can endure enormous strains.

In addition to anchoring the plant and furnishing it water and mineral matter, in many plants the roots function as storage organs, in which some of the food made by the shoot each year is stored for use in the development of new shoots each succeeding year. This function is especially obvious in many plants which die down in the fall and grow up again in the spring.

Thus the root depends upon the shoot for food while the shoot depends upon the root: (1) for water and mineral matter; (2) for anchorage; and (3) often as a storage organ.

Types of Root Systems. — There are various irregularities among root systems, due to the alterations which a root system must make in adjusting itself to obstructions and the uneven distribution of water and mineral matter in the soil. For this reason root systems are less symmetrical than shoots. However, despite these irregularities there are some inherent differ-

Fig. 122. — The fibrous roots of Corn.

ences that are so regular as to be typical of certain plants.

In the Corn, Wheat, Oats, and Grasses in general, there is the type of root system, known as the *fibrous root system*, in which there are no dominant main roots, but all roots are small and with their numerous fine branches form a system resembling a fine brush when the dirt is washed away. (*Fig. 122.*) This type of root system is common among weeds, trees, and many cultivated plants. In addition to the underground roots, some of the Grasses, as Corn illustrates, develop *prop* or *brace roots*, which grow out from nodes above the ground into which they finally reach to afford additional anchorage. However, brace roots are not necessarily an accompaniment of fibrous root systems, for they may occur in connection with other kinds of root systems.

The *tap-root system*, in which there is one large main root from which small lateral branches arise, is typical of the Alfalfa, Red Clover, Beets, Dandelion, and numerous other plants. Tap-roots usually grow directly downward, penetrating into the deeper layers of the soil where more moisture is available. (*Fig. 123.*) For this reason, the tap-root system is best adapted for dry regions and is, therefore, characteristic of drought resistant plants. Although the tap-root is more common among herbaceous plants, it occurs, nevertheless, among trees, where it often interferes with transplanting, as in case of Hickories, Oaks, and Maples. (*Fig. 124.*)

FIG. 123. — Alfalfa, a plant with a prominent tap-root.

FIG. 124. — Young Shellbark Hickory, showing the tap-root. After *Farmers' Bulletin 173*, U. S. Dept. of Agriculture.

Tap-roots are also convenient storage organs in which food is stored for the growth of the new shoot the next year. This fact is well illustrated in Alfalfa, Clover, and the Dandelion, where the shoots die down in the fall to be followed by new ones in the spring. Thus the tap-root system is well adapted to the perennial habit. In some plants, as Radishes, Beets, Carrots, Turnips, etc., where the storage function is quite prominent, the tap-root is tender and of much importance as a vegetable. (*Fig. 125.*) From some fleshy roots valuable products are extracted, notably the Sugar Beet from which most of our sugar is obtained.

Fig. 125. — Sugar Beet, a plant with a fleshy tap-root.

Plants having prominent tap-roots with short lateral roots can be grown close together without injury. Due to this fact and to the size of the shoot, such plants as Clover, Alfalfa, Beets, and others with the tap-root system grow well when crowded.

The *fascicled root-system*, consisting of a cluster of roots all of which are much enlarged in connection with the storage of food, is characteristic of a few plants of which the Sweet Potato and Dahlia are two that are well known. (*Fig. 126.*)

Adventitious roots, so named because of their occurrence in unaccustomed places, may be mentioned here, although the classification pertains to the place of occurrence and not to any peculiar feature of the root itself; for any root, whether fleshy or fibrous, developing from leaves or from stem regions where roots are not normally present is called adventitious. All roots may be regarded as adventitious except those, known as the primary ones, which develop directly from the radicle of the embryo.

Fig. 126. — A portion of a Sweet Potato plant, showing the fascicled roots.

The ability of many shoots to develop roots from various regions of the stem is of much service in plant propagation.   When canes of some varieties of Raspberries bend over and touch the ground, they become rooted at their tips.   If the canes are cut, the rooted tip then becomes a new plant.   This is a common method of propagating Raspberries.   If the branches of the Grape Vine, or, if many of our shrubs are bent to the ground and a portion covered with soil, roots will develop on the buried portion, which thereby becomes a means of obtaining new plants.   Geraniums, Coleus, Roses, and many other plants are propagated by cutting off branches and setting them in moist sand where they develop adventitious roots and become new plants.

Depth and Spread of Root Systems.[1] — Roots must go deep enough and spread far enough laterally to meet the demands of the plant for absorption and anchorage, both of which in general must conform to the size of the shoot.   On this account, trees need a deeper and wider root system than a Corn plant.   But aside from these differences which relate to the size of the shoot, root systems of different plants differ in the depth and spread according to: (1) the conditions of the soil in relation to moisture, mineral matter, and air; (2) the type of root system; and (3) the difference in the disposition of the roots of different plants, although similar in type.

Roots, like all other plant portions containing living cells, must have oxygen for respiration.   For this reason the region of the soil just under the surface where air is accessible is more favorable for root activity than the deeper soil regions.   Besides, more of the necessary mineral matter is available in the surface layers of the soil.   Consequently, root systems increase by extending proportionately much more laterally than downward, except in cases where there is extensive development of a taproot, as in such plants as Alfalfa and the Mesquite.

Studies made of the roots of Corn show that under ordinary conditions the roots extend laterally, most of them being only from 3 to 6 inches under the surface, until they reach a distance of about 1½ feet from the plant, and then they extend downward as well as laterally, often having a depth of 3 or 4 feet when the

[1] The Roots of Plants. *Bulletin 127*, Kansas Agr. Exp. Sta. Root Systems of Field Crops. *Bulletin 64*, N. Dakota Agr. Exp. Sta. Corn, its Habit of Root Growth, Methods of Planting and Cultivating, Notes on Ears and Stools or Suckers. *Bulletin 5*, Minnesota Agr. Exp. Sta.

plant is mature. In the Irish Potato the roots may reach a depth of 3 feet after extending laterally 2 or 3 feet, but for most of their length they are within a few inches of the surface. It may now be seen that deep cultivation may injure Corn, Potatoes, and other plants with a similar root habit by tearing away the roots. In Wheat, Oats, and Barley, the root systems do not extend so far laterally as in Corn but deeper into the soil, reaching a depth of 4 to 5 feet. Flax and Kafir Corn have fibrous root systems which feed mainly from the surface soil. Plants with shallow roots are called surface feeders, and are considered " hard on the land," because they exhaust the moisture and mineral matter in the surface soil.

In trees, although the lateral roots may reach a length of nearly 100 feet, they still remain near the surface. In the Soft Maple, lateral roots 80 feet in length have been found to range in depth from 8 inches to 2 feet. In old Apple trees the lateral roots, which may be 60 feet or more in length, usually have a depth ranging from 2 to 5 feet. Since trees by the surface habit of their roots take the moisture and mineral matter from near the surface, it is clear why crops do not grow well around them even when not affected by their shade.

Some fruit trees, such as the Cherry and Pear, send their roots several feet into the soil and, therefore, require a deeper soil than some other kinds of fruit trees. The Quince, commonly used as a stock on which to graft Pears, has a shallow root system, and so has the "Paradise" Apple on which Apples are often grafted. The fact that Pears grafted on Quinces or Common Apples grafted on the "Paradise" Apple bear younger than they do when grown on their own roots, shows that the shoot and root system are very closely related in their activities. The deep root systems occur generally in connection with tap-roots, which sometimes reach extraordinary depths. Also the lateral roots in a tap-root system are usually well under the surface. For example, in Sugar Beets the lateral roots are 6 inches or more under the surface, and, therefore, not usually disturbed by deep cultivation. On account of having a deep root system, Beets require a deep and well loosened soil.

As to the depth reached by tap-roots, 5 or 6 feet is common in Alfalfa, and a depth of 31 feet has been recorded. The tap-root of the Mesquite, which is a native of desert regions, has been known to reach a depth of 60 feet.   Plants with the Alfalfa type of root system are not only drought resistant, but also loosen the subsoil, which is thereby put in better condition for those plants with roots less able to penetrate a hard subsoil.

Root Structure

As the student already knows, plant organs consist of tissues, each of which on account of the peculiar structure of its cells is especially adapted to do a certain kind of work. In roots there are tissues to perform the following functions: (1) protection; (2) growth; (3) absorption; (4) conduction; and (5) strengthening. Root tips show on their surface rather distinct regions, which differ in color, texture, or some other feature that can be seen without a microscope. Often, but not always, the small protective cap, which is the actual end of the root, can be identified by its brownish color. The smooth whitish zone, which is usually a conspicuous region of the tip, is where cell multiplication and growth are most prominent. Just back of this is the absorptive zone, bearing numerous root hairs which are more conspicuous when grown in moist air or moss where there are no soil particles to influence their shape. (*Fig. 127.*) Back of the absorptive region, where protective and strengthening tissues are becoming prominent, the root is firmer in texture and darker in color; and

Fıɢ. 127. — Tip region of a root of Red Clover, showing root hairs.

these features become more prominent with age, as is well demonstrated in shrubs and trees where the older parts of roots are woody and covered with thick bark.

Cellular Anatomy of the Root Tip. — If with the aid of a microscope a lengthwise section through a root tip is studied, more may be learned about the character of the different tissues. (*Fig. 128.*) The *root cap* now appears as a well defined structure, consisting of many cells loosely joined into a covering, which is thickest directly over the end of the root. Next to the root cap is the zone of cells active in division and constituting meristematic tissue. Back of this is the growth zone, in which the chief activity is cell enlargement to which the elongation of the root is due.   Other

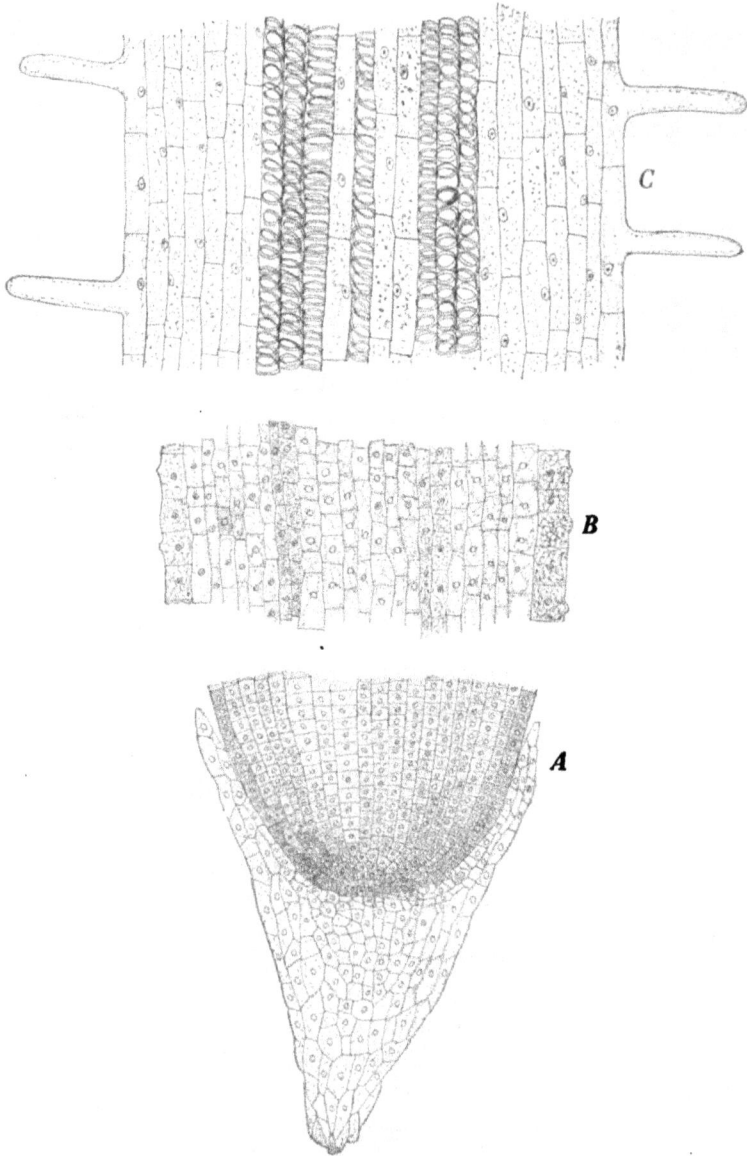

FIG. 128. — Longitudinal sections through root of Onion at the following regions. *A*, through the tip showing the root cap and meristematic zone. *B*, through the zone of elongation. *C*, through absorptive region or hair zone. Highly magnified.

regions of the root increase in diameter, but almost all elongation takes place in the growth zone, as shown in *Figure 129*. The meristematic zone is thus so situated that the new cells formed by it may be added both to the root cap, the thickness of which is thereby maintained in spite of its being rapidly worn away on its outer surface, and to the growth zone, the older portions of which are constantly taking on the features of the absorptive zone just behind. The growth zone merges imperceptibly into the absorptive zone where the following tissues become quite well defined: (1) a surface layer of cells constituting the *epidermis* which has most to do with absorption, the special absorptive agents being the *root hairs*, which, as the section shows, are merely projections of the epidermal cells; (2) a broad band of cells just beneath the epidermis and constituting the *cortex*; and (3) a group of conductive tissues forming a central cylinder, known as the *vascular cylinder*.

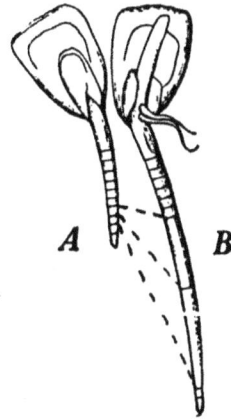

FIG. 129. — The radicle of a Corn seedling marked to show the regions of elongation. *A*, radicle just after being divided into spaces of about $\frac{1}{20}$ of an inch in width. *B*, radicle several hours after marking, showing the region where elongation is taking place. Modified from Andrews.

It is to be noted that the epidermis of roots, unlike that of leaves and stems, has no cutinized walls and contains no stomata or other openings for the entrance of air, although so many active cells require much oxygen for respiration. However, openings are not necessary, for the uncutinized walls offer practically no resistance to the passage of water, which usually carries in solution oxygen enough to support quite active respiration.

Through the development of the root hairs the absorptive surface of the root system is much increased, and may be thereby increased from five to six times in Corn, about twelve times in Barley and as much as eighteen times in some other plants. All root hairs are able to absorb regardless of their size, which ranges from a slight bulge near the growth zone of the root to often more than an inch farther back. They live only a few days, but, as they die off behind, new ones form ahead, and in this

way the absorptive zone moves along just behind the advancing
tip.   The root hairs grow out more or less at right angles to the
surface of the root, and are able on account of their flexible
slimy walls to push through small openings and around the soil
particles against which they flatten and to which they become
glued fast, thereby coming in close contact with the water films
around the soil particles.   Why the region of elongation is near
the tip is now clear, for, if behind the absorptive zone, the hair
region would be pushed ahead and the root hairs thereby torn
away.

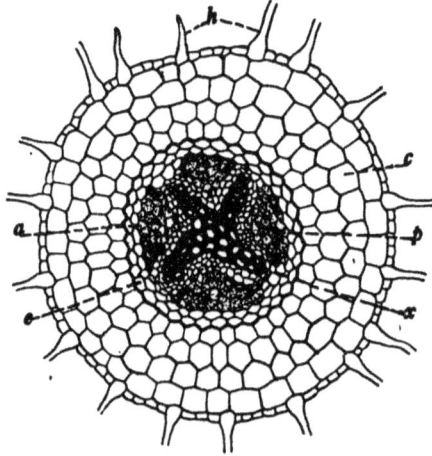

FIG. 130. — Cross section of a root through the absorbing region. x,
xylem; p, phloem; a, pericycle; e, endodermis; c, cortex; h, root hairs.
Highly magnified.

The cortex, consisting of many layers of parenchyma cells,
transports the substances absorbed by the root hairs to the conductive tissues, and in fleshy roots also serves as a storage region.
    The vascular cylinder contains the conductive tissues, notably
the *xylem* and *phloem*.   The xylem and phloem and their positions in reference to each other are best seen in a cross section of
a root, as shown in *Figure 130*.   The xylem occupies the center and has strands radiating from the center like the spokes of
a wheel.   Between the spokes of the xylem and near their outer
ends are the phloem strands.   Inasmuch as the absorbed substances are carried to the shoot by the xylem, this alternate ar-

rangement of xylem and phloem shows adaptation, in that, it permits the absorbed substances to reach the xylem without passing through the phloem.   The vascular cylinder is bordered by a chain of cells, known as the *pericycle*.   The pericycle joins the *endodermis* or *starch sheath* which is the chain of cells forming the innermost layer of the cortex.   Aside from the fact that branches or lateral roots develop from the pericycle, the functions of the endodermis and pericycle in roots are not well understood.

Anatomy of the Older Portions of the Root. — Not far back of the hair zone, as indicated by the brownish color and the sloughing off of the epidermis with its dead root hairs, there appear some anatomical changes, such as the formation of a corky covering, enlargement of conductive and strengthening tissues, and the development of branches.   As this region of the root becomes older, these anatomical changes become more prominent.

Since the epidermis behind the hair zone dies and falls away, absorption is limited to the tip region of the root.   Accompanying the death of the epidermis, a protective tissue is developed by the layers of cells beneath.   Usually the cells just beneath become cutinized and take the place of the epidermis as a covering.   In Grass roots the layers of cells just beneath the epidermis thicken their walls, thereby forming over the root a hard woody rind similar to that of Grass stems. Commonly in roots there is also formed in the region of the pericycle a meristematic band of cells, known as the *cork cambium*, which by dividing parallel to the surface of the root adds layers of cork on its outer side and cortex cells on its inner side, thus forming a protective covering and a secondary cortex which it also en-

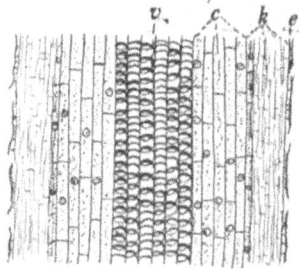

FIG. 131. — Diagram of a lengthwise section through the region of the root back of the hair zone, showing the changes in the epidermis and cortex. *e,* epidermis dead and sloughing off; *k,* cork cambium on the inner side with cork and dead cortex between it and the epidermis; *c,* secondary cortex; *v,* vascular cylinder.   Highly magnified.

larges as the root grows older.   Since cork is impervious to water and the foods contained, by the formation of cork in the region of the pericycle, the first or primary cortex has its conductive connections with the vascular bundles cut off and its death must follow. (*Fig. 131.*) The dead epidermis and cortex form the outer portion of the bark, which thickens as cork is added by the cork cambium, and in roots living a number of years, like those of shrubs and trees, may become quite thick, and broken and furrowed, as in the large roots of trees. As a provision for strength, fiber-like strands of strengthening tissue are commonly formed in the secondary cortex.

In order that the vascular cylinder may have adequate conductive capacity in the older portions of the root, it, too, must enlarge, for as the absorptive surface of the root increases ahead by the multiplication of branches, not only is there an increase in the amount of absorbed substances which the xylem must carry to the shoot, but also an increase in the amount of food which the phloem must carry to feed the greater number of branches of the root. In the formation of xylem in roots, the portions first formed are the radiating strands or spokes which enlarge by developing toward the center where they usually come together, thus forming the solid central core of xylem as shown in *Figure 132.* However, in some plants, as in Corn and many other Monocotyledons, the xylem strands never come together, and consequently a central pith is left, around which the strands of xylem are arranged. In all roots the xylem strands are at first enlarged by this centripetal development. In some short-lived roots of Dicotyledons and in the roots of most Monocotyledons, the enlargement of the xylem is due to this centripetal development and the development of new vascular bundles between the old ones as the root becomes older. In Dicotyledons and also in the Gymnosperms, the group to which Pines, Firs, Spruces, etc., belong, the vascular cylinders of most roots are increased also as shown in *Figure 132.* It is seen in *A* of *Figure 132* that the phloem and xylem are not in contact. Lying between them are cells which have not been modified into definite tissues. Some of these cells become meristematic and so arranged as to form a continuous band of cambium, known as the *cambium ring*, which by curving outward passes on the outside of the xylem, and by curving inward passes on the inside of the phloem, thus separating the xylem and phloem regions of the vascular cylinder as shown at *B*. The cambium cells, in the main, divide parallel to the surface of the root, and divide in such a way that the layers of new cells on the inside of the cambium are about

equal in number to those on the outside.   The new cells next to
the xylem become modified into xylem, at first filling in between
the strands of the primary xylem, and the cells formed next to
the phloem are changed into phloem.   In this way the vascular

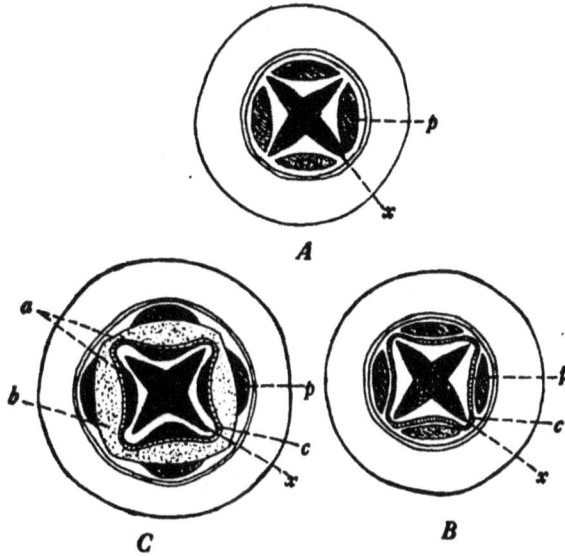

FIG. 132. — Diagrams showing how the xylem and phloem of roots are
increased. A, cross section of a root showing xylem (x) and phloem (p)
before the cambium is formed. B, cross section of root showing xylem (x)
and phloem (p) after the cambium ring (c) is formed. C, cross section showing the xylem (x) and phloem (p) shown in A and B and the new xylem (a)
and new phloem (b) which have been formed by the cambium (c). Adapted
from J. M. Coulter.

cylinder is increased in diameter as shown at C.   In roots which
live many years, like those of trees, the layers of xylem formed
each year form annual rings like those occurring in woody stems;
and the outer layers of the phloem, with the cortex and other
tissues outside of the phloem, constitute a bark like that of
woody stems.   In fact, it is only by the presence of their early
root anatomy that sections of such roots can be told from sections of stems.   In some fleshy roots, as Beets illustrate, a number of cambium rings form outside of the first one, and the
growth resulting from each appears as a ring when a cross-section
of the root is made.

Another anatomical feature connected with the older portions of roots is the development of branches, which begin to develop some distance back of the hair zone and in the way shown in *Figure 133*. In Seed Plants the branch roots, which are called *secondary*, *tertiary*, and so on according to their distance from the main root, develop from the pericycle and usually in the region closest to the xylem. In forming a new branch, a few cells of the pericycle in the region where the branch is to appear begin to divide parallel to the surface of the root. The new cells at first appear as a slight elevation on the pericycle, but by rapid growth this elevation of cells soon pushes through the cortex and other overlying tissues, and becomes a branch with vascular cylinder and other tissues continuous with those of the root of which it is a branch. Of course the farther from the root tip, the older and more fully developed are the branches.

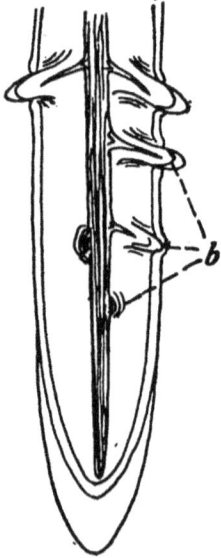

FIG. 133. — Lengthwise section through a root, showing how branches arise. The branches (*b*) originate in the region of the vascular cylinder and push through the cortex, finally reaching the exterior.

One important feature in connection with the branching habit is that, when the end of a root is cut away, the remaining portion is stimulated to develop branches. It is due to the ability of roots to branch, that trees and other plants with their roots heavily pruned in transplanting are usually able to provide a new root system and become established in their new location.

Factors Influencing the Direction of Growth in Roots

Roots and stems respond very differently in respect to gravity. Primary roots grow toward the center of gravity, while most stems grow in the opposite direction. This earth influence is known as *geotropism*. *Geo* comes from a word meaning earth and *tropism* means turning. So the word, geotropism, means earth-turning, and refers to the turning of the root and stem in response to the influence of gravity.   Primary roots are positively geotropic (growing toward the earth's center), while most stems are negatively geotropic (growing directly away from the earth). Lateral roots, as well as most branches of stems, grow more or less

FIG. 134. — The radicle or primary root of the Sunflower growing downward in response to gravity.   After Osterhout.

horizontally and, when strictly horizontal, are neither positively nor negatively geotropic.   What is shown in *Figure 134?*

Roots, especially primary roots, are sensitive to moisture and grow towards it when more moisture is needed.   The tropism induced by water is called *hydrotropism*.   Most roots are to a greater or less extent positively hydrotropic.   Notice what is shown in *Figure 135*.   In response to the water influence, the roots of most cultivated plants grow deeper in the soil during

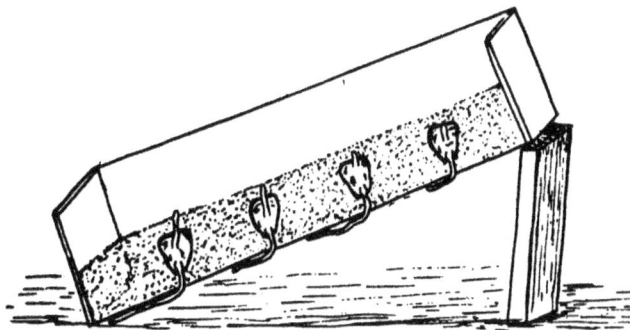

FIG. 135. — An experiment to show the effect of moisture upon the direction of the growth of roots.   The box containing moist sawdust in which the Corn is planted has a bottom of wire netting.   After the roots grew through the meshes, thus coming in contact with dry air, they changed their direction and grew along the bottom of the box, thus keeping in contact with moisture. Adapted from Osterhout.

a dry season than during a wet season.   When there is abundance of moisture in the soil, Corn roots may grow within 2 inches or less of the surface, but are 3 inches or more under the surface when there is a lack of moisture, and usually penetrate the soil to a greater depth. The roots of Willows and Poplars will extend long distances in response to moisture. When these trees grow near a well, their roots often grow down the sides of the well until the water is reached. In seeking water and air the roots of trees and weeds grow into drain tiles and sewers, often clogging them.

Stems, in general, grow toward the light, while most roots shun the light. Roots are said to be *negatively heliotropic*, while stems are *positively heliotropic*. *A ërotropism*, growth toward those regions of the soil where air is more plentiful, *Chemotropism*, growth toward certain substances, and *Traumatropism*, growth away from injurious bodies, are other movements of roots.

The Soil as the Home of Roots

In the most general meaning of the term, the soil is that uppermost layer of the earth's crust in which, by means of their root systems, plants are able to obtain the substances necessary for growth. However, in agriculture. the term soil is often applied to the layer which is tilled, and the term subsoil to that which lies beneath. Although the term soil is used in different ways, we usually think of the soil as extending down to where the dark color changes to a light, due to the absence of humus. The depth of the soil varies greatly in different localities, ranging from a few inches to several feet.

As to *origin*, the soil is fundamentally pulverized rock of which there are a number of kinds, such as granite, limestone, sandstone, shales, etc., each of which gives some special property to the soil. Various agencies, such as wind, water, ice, chemicals, temperature variations, and plants are active in breaking all rocks into a pulverized form. They may be very finely pulverized into clay, as the silicates are, or left in the form of fine sand, coarse sand, or gravel.

The *rock constituents* of any bit of soil, even of the finest clays, are exceedingly various in size and shape as a microscopical examination shows. The irregularity in size and shape makes it impossible for the particles to pack closely, and thus insures the open spaces which are estimated to be from 25 to 50 per cent of the volume of cultivated soils. (*Fig. 136.*) The spaces are exceedingly important, for they permit the circulation of water and air which the roots and micro-organisms of the soil must have. Although not tightly packed, the particles adhere to each other when moist, and this feature and the weight of the soil enable roots to obtain a firm anchorage.

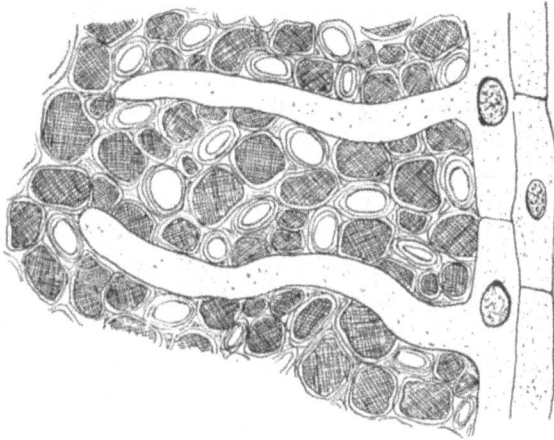

FIG. 136. — Diagram of two root hairs and the soil around them. The soil particles are shaded and the light area around each soil particle represents a film of water. The large light areas among the soil particles are air spaces. Modified from J. G. Coulter.

Water, Air, and Humus of the Soil. — To the plant the water of the soil has two important functions. *First,* it is the reservoir upon which the plant depends for water. *Second,* water is the solvent in which the soil substances become dissolved before entering the plant.

The amount of soil water varies for different kinds of soils, and for the same soil at different times. Thus garden soil rich in humus or a very heavy clay soil will hold two or three times as much water as a sandy soil. Just after a heavy rain soils are saturated with water, that is, all of the spaces are filled. But much of this water, known as *free water,* gradually sinks away toward the center of the earth in response to its own weight, leaving the pores partially empty. The water then remaining in the pores consists chiefly of *capillary water,* which is held in the pores by the force of capillarity. In addition to the capillary water, which does not respond to the influence of gravity, there is also the *hygroscopic water,* which remains, after the capillary water is removed, as a thin film around each particle and so firmly held that it can not be driven off except by the application of heat. The driest of "air dry" soils still contain considerable hygroscopic water, as shown by their loss in weight when they are further dried in an oven.

Plants depend mainly upon capillary water, although in some cases, especially in soils with high hygroscopic power, some hygroscopic water may be available to the plant. When soils are saturated, as after heavy rains or in bogs and swamps, there is more water present than the plant needs, and, besides, the air which roots must have is driven from the soil pores. Experiments have shown that, in general, a soil is best adapted to plant growth when the water present is not more than 60 per cent of the amount required for saturation, or, in other words, when about two-fifths of the pores are open for the circulation of air.

The forces which resist the pulling away of hygroscopic and capillary water from the soil particles tend to keep the water equally distributed. Thus as water is lost from the pores in the surface soil, either by evaporation or root absorption, it is replaced by water moving up from below through the force of capillarity. Consequently, as a root absorbs, the movement of water toward it from all around enables it to obtain water from regions several feet away. In fact, capillarity has been known to raise water to a height of 10 feet in one kind of soil. Again, in hygroscopic water the thin films, which are like stretched rubber around the soil particles, are connected where the soil particles touch, and to compensate the greater water loss one film may have over others, there is such a movement of water between the films that all for a considerable distance around share in the loss. Thus, due to the forces of capillarity and the surface tension of hygroscopic films, soil water tends to move to the point where it is being absorbed. It is now clear why the soil becomes so evenly dry around a plant.

Air in the soil is necessary for the respiration of roots and micro-organisms. It is also of use in oxidizing poisonous substances which result from the decay of organic matter in the soil, so that their poisonous effects on roots are destroyed.

Humus consists of organic matter in a state of decomposition. When only partially decayed as in some bogs where it accumulates in large quantities, it forms *peat*. It gives to soils the dark color which is characteristic of good soils, such as *loams* where it occurs well mixed with sand and clay. It adds to the soil various organic substances, some useful and some harmful, enables the soil to retain more moisture, makes the soil light, and makes the soil a suitable place for micro-organisms to live.

Soil Micro-organisms. — The soil is the home of innumerable organisms, some plants and some animals, all of which are related to soil fertility. They are of three kinds, *Fungi, Bacteria*, and *Protozoa*. These organisms, influencing the soil fertility and having their activities in turn influenced by the soil conditions, add to the complexity of soils, which are still far from being understood.

Many *Molds* occur in the soil, where their thread-like filaments, like those of Bread Mold, aid in breaking up the organic matter into soluble compounds. Besides Molds, there are other kinds of Fungi which act on the soil constituents, as in case of Toadstools which invade the soil with their root-like filaments. Furthermore, some Fungi are so intimately connected with the roots of some plants as to replace the root hairs. In this case the Fungus weaves around the root a close covering of filaments, thus forming with the root the structure, known as the *mycorrhiza*, in which the filaments of the Fungus absorb water and soluble substances, which afterward are

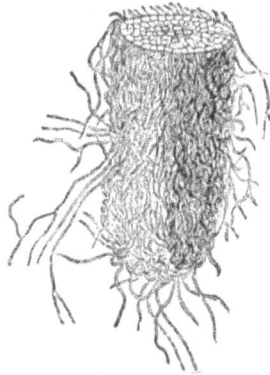

FIG. 137.—A Mycorrhiza on a rootlet of the Beech. The felt-like mass of mycelial threads closely enwraps the root tip, extending back to beyond the hair zone and spreading into the soil like root hairs. After Frank.

transmitted to the root. (*Fig. 137.*) Pines, Beeches, Oaks, Blueberries, and Orchids are some of the more familiar plants in which the mycorhizas occur. Plants, like Blueberries, are so dependent upon Mycorhizas that they can not be grown unless the proper Fungus is present in the soil.

The *Bacteria*, the smallest of all living organisms and well known in connection with diseases of animals and plants, are exceedingly abundant in soils, often many millions being present per cubic centimeter of soil. Like the Fungi, the Bacteria of the soil are dependent in their development upon the presence of some organic food material, such as decaying plant or animal matter. They are of various kinds and perform various functions, the most important of which has to do with making nitrogen available for root absorption. The importance of the Bacteria concerned with providing available nitrogen in the soil is due to the fact that nitrogen is an indispensable constituent of protoplasm, and, although composing four-fifths of the air, it is only available when it occurs in the form of a soluble salt in the soil where it is taken in through the roots. To maintain in the soil an adequate supply of available nitrogen, which is constantly being lost by the removal of the crop and through drainage, is an important problem in maintaining soil fertility. The Bacteria provide available nitrogen in two ways. *First*, some kinds act on the ammonia which is usually abundant where there is humus, forming nitrates, which are soluble, and in which form the nitrogen is available to our higher plants. *Second*, certain kinds of Bacteria use the free nitrogen of the air in forming the nitrogenous compounds of their bodies, which after death release these compounds to the soil, and in this way the soil has its nitrogen increased. Thus while some Bacteria change the nitrogenous substances already present in the soil into forms which can be used as a source of nitrogen by the higher plants, these forms, by adding nitrogenous compounds through the rapid multiplication and early death of their bodies, actually increase the nitrogen content of the soil, and for this reason are of most importance in maintaining the soil fertility. Although many of these Bacteria which fix the free nitrogen of the air live free in the soil, there are some, however, which live in the roots of some of the higher plants, especially in those of Clover, Alfalfa, Beans, and other Legumes. In this case they live in the nodules formed on the roots, and the relation between the Bacteria and the higher plant is said to be one of *symbiosis*, a name applied to such an intimate association of organisms. In this case both organisms are benefitted; for the Bacteria obtain some food from the higher plant and the latter obtains nitrogenous compounds from the dead bodies of the Bacteria. (*Fig. 138.*)

However, not all kinds of soil Bacteria are so indispensable, for there are some which have harmful effects, in that they tend to lessen the nitrogen content of the soil by so thoroughly decomposing the nitrogenous compounds that the nitrogen escapes from the soil as free nitrogen or as ammonia gas. Among so many kinds of soil Bacteria, breaking up compounds in different ways to secure energy and food, not all results of their activities in the soil can be expected to be desirable ones.

The *Protozoa*, which are small one-celled animals of which the Amœba is one type, are abundant in rich soils, where they are thought to exert a harmful influence on the soil fertility by feeding on the Bacteria. The evidence for this accusation is that soils are more fertile after being subjected to temperatures or poisons which kill the Protozoa but leave the Bacteria unharmed.

Soil Solution. — The soil water and the various mineral matters and organic substances dissolved in it constitute the soil solution. The dissolved organic substances are of use to the soil micro-organisms, but it is mainly water and mineral matters that higher plants need to obtain from the soil solution. The most important of the mineral elements for crops are *nitrogen, phosphorus, potassium, sulphur, calcium, iron,* and

Fig. 138. — Nodules on the roots of a Pea. Modified from Palladin.

magnesium. These occur in compounds known as mineral salts, which, although very essential to plant growth, are present in very small quantities, usually constituting less than one per cent of the best of soil solutions. Of these, nitrogen, phosphorus, and potassium are in most demand by crops, and the ones most likely to be lacking. Consequently, in maintaining soil fertility, the chief problem is to conserve and restore these elements. The value of artificial fertilizers and manures depends chiefly upon the amount of these elements contained. In most soils, iron, sulphur, and magnesium are present in sufficient quantities. Calcium must always be present to neutralize the acids, for both roots and soil Bacteria are very sensitive to acids. Calcium is added to the soil in the form of lime or limestone. On the other hand, when soils contain too much of an alkali, such as sodium carbonate, plants will not do well until the condition is changed by the addition of gypsum or some other substance capable of breaking up the alkali.

Each of the mineral salts which plants require, apparently, is so specially related to the nutrition of the plant, that not one of them can be omitted, although all others are present in suitable quantities. This fact is demonstrated by growing plants with their roots in distilled water to which the different mineral salts can be added in such proportions as the experiment demands. When the salts are added in such proportions that the solution imitates a soil solution, such as ordinary spring or well water, many herbaceous plants are able to grow in it till they have flowered and produced seed. In fact, aside from the lack of anchorage and having to supply their roots with oxygen from the shoot, plants may do almost as well as when rooted in the soil. For some plants the water culture gives good results, when the salts are in such a proportion that 2 liters of the solution contain 1 gram of potassium nitrate, ½ gram of iron phosphate, ¼ gram of calcium sulfate, and ¼ gram of magnesium sulfate. The results of omitting some of these salts are shown in *Figure 139.*

FIG. 139.—Water cultures of Buckwheat, showing effect of the lack of the different mineral elements: 1, with all the elements; 2, without potassium; 3, with soda instead of potash; 4, without calcium; 5, without nitrates or ammonia salts.

Root Absorption. — For the process of osmosis upon which the entrance of water into the root depends, the epidermal cells of the root tip are especially fitted. By means of the root hairs they have a large surface in contact with the soil solution. Having thin cellulose walls against which their protoplasm is spread out into a thin lining, root hairs afford an easy entrance of water into their large vacuoles. (*Fig. 140.*) As the student already knows from his acquaintance with osmosis, the entrance of water into the epidermal cell depends upon the concentration

FIG. 140. — Root hair showing the thin layer of protoplasm and large vacuole. After Frank.

of the substances in solution in the cell sap. Water is drawn
into the root hairs only when the density of the cell sap is
sufficient to exert an osmotic force that overcomes the osmotic
force of the solution without and the forces by which the soil
holds on to the water. On the other hand, when the forces
without are stronger than the osmotic force of the cell sap,
then water will be drawn out of the root. This latter condition,
which is likely to be disastrous to the plant, occurs when there
is an excessive amount of mineral salts in the soil solution, or
when the soil becomes so dry that the forces with which the
soil holds on to the water become so great as to overcome the
osmotic force of the cell sap. By watering plants with nutrient
solutions which are too strong, the soil solution may become so
concentrated as to injure the plants.

The entrance of the dissolved mineral salts into the root hairs
depends chiefly upon two things: *First*, the cell membrane must
be permeable to them. *Second*, the membrane being permeable
to them, they pass into the root hairs by the laws of diffusion. Thus, if a salt is more concentrated without than within
the root hairs, it passes into them until it is as plentiful within
as without. Also substances may diffuse out of the root hairs
when more concentrated within than without. Although the
movement of the salts may be influenced in rate by the movement of the water, experiments show that the amount of mineral salts which enter the plant is quite independent of the
amount of water absorbed. However, in being alive, the cell
membrane presents some features not found in connection with
dead membranes. One peculiar feature is that it can alter
its permeability from time to time, and another is that, although it allows many substances to pass in, it allows very
few to pass out. In being permeable to some substances and
not to others, roots are thereby able to exercise *selective absorption*, which in general favors the entrance of the more useful
substances, although roots by no means keep out all harmful
substances.

From the epidermal cells, the water and mineral salts pass
through the cortex to the xylem vessels through which they reach
the shoot. (*Fig. 141.*)

Factors that Hinder Absorption. — The forces concerned in
capillarity and surface films increase as the water of the soil de-

creases.   They retard absorption and may become so great as to
actually prevent it.   The wilting of plants when the soil becomes
dry is not due to the fact that there is no water in the soil, but to
the fact that the roots can not pull the water, known as the *unavailable water*, away from the soil particles.   It has been found

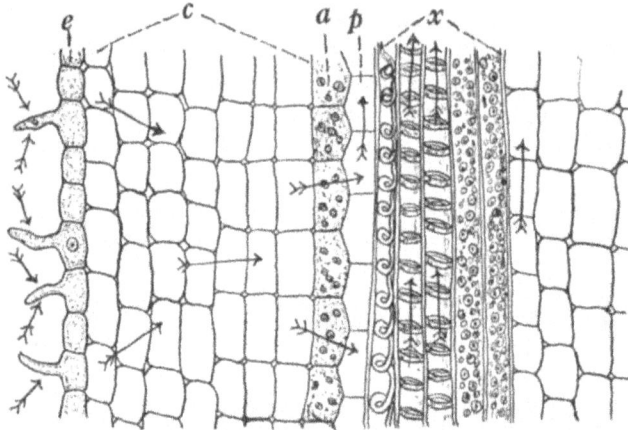

FIG. 141.—Lengthwise section through a root, showing the way the water
and mineral substances of the soil reach the vascular bundles. *e*, epidermis
with root hairs; *c*, cortex; *a*, endodermis; *p*, pericycle; *x*, xylem of vascular
bundle.   The arrows indicate the way the water and dissolved substances
pass to the vascular bundles.   After MacDougal.

that most plants wilt when the soil moisture is reduced to 4.6 per
cent in medium fertile garden soil, 7.8 per cent in sandy loam, and
49.7 per cent in peaty soil.   From these figures it is seen that the
amount of unavailable water depends much upon the kind of soil.
As shown in the table below, it also depends much upon the kind
of plant, for plants differ widely in their ability to pull water
away from the soil particles.

UNAVAILABLE WATER FOR DIFFERENT PLANTS IN LOAM SOIL

Plant.	Unavailable water.
	Per cent.
Cabbage	5.8
Corn	5.9
Oats	6.2
Asparagus	7.0
Lettuce	8.5
Cucumber	10.8
Pondweed (a water plant)	24.8

On the other hand, when the soil water is so plentiful that air is excluded from the soil, root growth is retarded and absorption thereby hindered. For this reason wet lands have to be drained.

In retarding growth as well as slowing down osmosis, a low temperature of the soil retards absorption. This fact is related to winter killing, which is sometimes due to the fact that the roots can not absorb water from the cold or frozen soil about them as rapidly as it is lost from the shoot.

There are other factors, such as the presence of alkalies and certain acids in the soil which hinder absorption by their injurious effects on roots.

Root Pressure. — The absorptive action of roots sometimes manifests itself in forcing water through the stem, acting much like the pump which forces the water through the city's water mains. This pressure exerted by roots is known as *root* or *sap pressure*, and is one cause of the so-called *bleeding* of plants when they are injured. In most plants of the temperate regions, root pressure is only evident in the spring when the plants are not losing much water by evaporation and are gorged with sap. When Grapes are pruned in the spring, they usually bleed profusely. A vigorous European Grape will sometimes bleed a liter per day. A Maple tree may exude from 5–8 liters in a day.

Measurements show that sap pressure is often several pounds to the square inch. In the following table the pressure is recorded in millimeters of mercury (760 millimeters of mercury = 1 atmosphere or about 15 lbs. of pressure to the square inch).

Red Currant   358
Sugar Maple   1033
Black Birch   2040
European Grape   860

Substances Given off by Roots. — Roots give off carbon dioxide. The milky appearance of lime water in which roots are grown is evidence of this fact (page 97). In the soil the carbon dioxide unites with the water, forming carbonic acid, which has an important dissolving action upon the soil minerals. This fact is demonstrated by the etching effect roots have when grown in contact with the surface of polished marble.

There is much evidence that roots also give off oxidizing enzymes whereby the poisonous substances of the soil are oxidized to harmless forms.

It has been demonstrated in case of some plants that roots excrete poisonous substances which tend to impede further root activity. These deleterious substances, with those formed through the decomposition of roots and other organic matter, may be responsible for much of the soil sterility that is so commonly attributed to the lack of the necessary mineral salts. In fact, some think that the value of fertilizers depends mainly upon their neutralizing effect of these deleterious substances. The improvement of the soil, when fields are allowed to lie fallow, is, at least, partly due to the disappearance of these deleterious substances through oxidation. It seems that in many cases the deleterious substances are more poisonous to the roots of plants of the same kind, and this may help explain the value of crop rotation.

Water, Air, and Parasitic Roots

Water Roots. — When branches of some herbaceous plants are cut off and set in water, roots develop from the submerged portion. Branches of the Geranium and Wandering Jew root readily in water and will grow for a long time in ordinary river or well water. The twigs of Willows will develop water roots when set in water. Willows, growing on the edge of ponds and streams, develop roots which penetrate the soil and also roots which dangle in the water. There are a number of small Seed Plants, like the Duckweeds, which float on the surface of the water and have no roots other than water roots. (*Fig. 142.*)

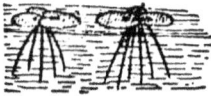

Fig. 142. — Lemna, a floating water plant, which has only water roots. Slightly magnified. After Stevens.

Air Roots. — Some plants depending upon soil roots also develop air roots. The brace roots of Corn are at first air roots and later enter the soil. Some climbing plants, like the Poison Ivy, develop air roots which attach the plant to the support. Many Orchids and some plants of the Pineapple family grow supported on other plants and have only air roots. The *Tillandsia*, called Spanish Moss, although not a Moss at all, is very common in southern regions, growing on the branches of trees with its roots dangling in the air.

Air roots differ in structure from soil roots. Air roots, unless they are growing in wet shady places, are not in a good position for absorption. Air roots of climbers, as in the Poison Ivy, do no absorbing, and serve only to attach the plant to the support. Those air roots that absorb usually have no root hairs, and the absorbing is done by a sponge-like mantle of cells, called *velamen*, covering the root. In some cases, as in many tropical climbers, the air roots reach to the ground or to cup-shaped leaves where water is obtained. The air roots of the Orchids which live on damp tree trunks or rocks of tropical countries take up moisture when there is rain or dew. Such plants, called *epiphytes*, flourish without the assistance of soil roots.

Parasitic Roots. — There are a large number of plants, called *parasites*, that depend upon other plants for food. The Dodder is dependent upon other plants for its food and obtains it by sending roots into the plant upon which it is growing. Dodder has no food-making pigment and the young seedling soon perishes unless it can obtain food from some other plant. The thread-like seedlings are sensitive to touch and coil about weeds, Clover, Alfalfa, or other plants which they may chance to hit in their growth.

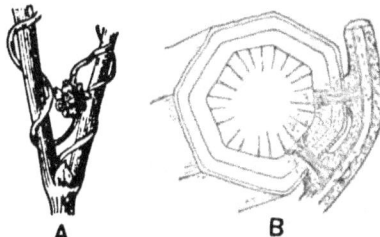

FIG. 143. — *A*, Dodder (*Cuscuta Europæa*) living on a Hop Vine; *B*, diagrammatic drawing of a cross section of the Hop Vine showing the roots of the Dodder having penetrated the tissues of the Hop Vine. After Kerner.

If the plant has suitable food, then the Dodder grows roots into its tissues and absorbs food from it. Clover, Flax, and Alfalfa are attacked in this way and much injured by Dodder. Dodder is considered a destructive weed, and seed containing only a little Dodder seed is undesirable for seeding. (*Fig. 143.*)

The Mistletoe lives upon trees, the roots penetrating the branches and withdrawing the necessary foods. Many plants, such as the Beech Drop, Broom Rape, etc., live on the roots of other plants.

Propagation by Roots

The production of new plants from seeds, stems, leaves, or roots is called plant propagation. Since roots readily produce adventitious buds which can develop into new plants, they are much used in the propagation of some kinds of plants. For example, Sweet Potatoes, which rarely produce seed, are propagated by means of the shoots which develop from the fleshy roots. The roots are planted early in the spring in specially prepared beds, usually hot beds, where they develop buds which grow into stems bearing leaves and roots, as shown in *Figure 144*. These young plants (slips) are broken loose from the potato and planted in the field after all danger of frost is passed. The abundance of stored food enables each potato to produce many slips.

Fɪɢ. 144. — Sprouting of the Sweet Potato. *A*, potato with sprouts in different stages of development. *B*, sprout, or slip, broken loose from the potato and ready to be set out.

From the roots of the Red Raspberry [1] and some Blackberries, new stems called suckers grow up. These suckers with a small portion of the parent root are used in starting new plantations. The larger roots of the Raspberry and Blackberry are often dug up in the fall, cut into pieces, and stored until spring when they are planted in the field. From these root segments new plants are produced. Roses are often propagated by root cuttings. When plants can be propagated either by root cuttings or by seed, it is generally better to use cuttings, because plants obtained from cuttings usually grow faster and are more likely to be like the parent plant than they are when grown from seed.

[1] Raspberries. Farmers' *Bulletin 213*, U. S. Dept. Agr. Culture of Small Fruits. *Bulletin 105*, Oregon Agr. Exp. Sta. Dewberry growing. *Bulletin 136*, Colorado Agr. Exp. Sta.

Some trees, like the Black Locust and Silver-leaved Poplar, are troublesome because of the readiness with which sprouts spring up from the roots. Some of the weeds, such as Canada Thistle and Field Sorrel, spread by developing new plants from buds on their spreading roots. When the Dandelion is cut off several inches under the ground, it often grows up again from the portion of the root left in the ground.

CHAPTER IX

STEMS

Characteristic Features and Types of Stems

The stem, usually consisting of trunk and branches, is the fundamental part of the shoot. Upon the stem the other structures of the shoot, such as leaves, flowers, and fruit, depend for their support in the air and sunlight — the position most favorable for leaf-activity, pollination, and scattering of seed and fruit.

Roots, stems, and leaves are intimately related in their activities, and the efficiency of one affects the efficiency of the others. The productivity of most of the cultivated plants depends not only upon a good root system, but also upon a good stem system. In some plants, such as Beets, Turnips, Radishes, Lettuce, and a few others which have very short stems during much of their life, not so much importance is attached to the stem, but even these plants, in order to complete their life cycle, must eventually develop stems upon which to bear flowers and seeds. Among such plants as the trees and grains, the stem is very important. The value of a tree for shade, lumber, or fruit depends largely upon the character of the stem. Likewise, a Corn or Wheat plant with a well developed stem is able to produce larger ears or a better head than a plant with a stem poorly developed.

In comparing stems with roots the following things may be stated. *First*, stems bear leaves and flowers, while roots do not. *Second*, stems are divided into nodes and internodes but roots are not. *Third*, stems branch at the nodes, while in roots branches arise anywhere. *Fourth*, in stems pith is nearly always present, while in roots it is usually absent.

The *nodes* are the narrow zones, often more or less swollen, at which the leaves and buds as well as the branches arise. The *internodes* are the zones between the nodes. The division of the stem into nodes and internodes is quite noticeable in the stems of Corn and other Grasses, where the nodes divide the stem into distinct segments. By the elongation of the internodes, the

166

leaves are separated and better exposed to the light. If the internodes are short, as in the stem of the Dandelion, the leaves are much crowded. Also in such plants as Beets, Radishes, Turnips, and Lettuce the stem at first has short internodes and the leaves are much crowded.

On the ends of branches as well as in the axils of leaves, occur the *buds* which have much to do with the growth of stems. The stem elongates by the development of new nodes and internodes from the terminal buds, while branches develop from the buds occurring in the axils of the leaves.

Branching of Stems. — Since branches develop from the buds located in the axils of the leaves, the arrangement of branches tends to follow the leaf arrangement. Plants having two leaves at a node and on opposite sides of the stem, as in the Maple, tend to have branches with the opposite arrangement. Likewise, plants with leaves occurring one at a node and on alternate sides of the stem tend to have the alternate arrangement of branches, as Elms illustrate.

The amount of branching varies much among plants. Among herbaceous plants the stems of many of the Grasses branch very little and are called *simple stems*, while in some plants, as Clover and Alfalfa

FIG. 145. — Pines, showing the excurrent type of stem. After Fink.

illustrate, there is very much branching. Branching reaches its maximum among the trees, where often there is branching and rebranching until the youngest branches are so numerous and small, as in the Elms and Birches, that the tree may be somewhat brush-like in appearance.

Branching is directly related to leaf display, for it not only enables the plant to bear more leaves, but makes a better exposure to sunlight possible. Branching is also related to flower and fruit production, for a well branched tree can produce more flowers and fruit than one that is less branched, provided the food supply is sufficient. In plants used for forage, such as Clover and Alfalfa, the amount of hay produced by a plant depends largely upon the extent of branching.

In some plants, as in the Pine shown in *Figure 145*, the stem system consists of a main axis and many lateral branches, forming what is known as the *excurrent* type of stem. In others, as in the Elm shown in *Figure 146*, the main stem is divided into two or more branches, which are soon lost in numerous branches, forming the *deliquescent* type of stem. Among fruit trees and forest trees, there is so much difference in habits of branching that many kinds of trees can be identified by their branching habit.

Work Done by Stems. — There are four important functions of stems. They support the aërial structures, conduct materials, make food, and serve as regions of storage.

Fig. 146. — Elm tree, showing deliquescent type of stem.

The *supporting* function consists in carrying the weight of the leaves, flowers, and fruit, and in elevating them to a position most favorable for performing their functions. There is strong competition among plants for light, and it is through the elongation of the stem that plants lift their leaves higher in the air and often escape the shade of neighboring plants. Some plants, such as the Grape, Poison Ivy, Morning Glory, Beans, and Peas, which have weak stems, secure better light by climbing a support, such as a wall, fence, or the stems of other plants.

As a *Conductive* structure the stem occupies an important position, for through it the leaves and roots exchange materials. Consequently, the vascular bundles, forming a continuous conductive system from roots to leaves, are prominent structures in stems. Through the conductive system the leaves receive water and mineral salts from the soil and the roots receive the food made in the leaves. For this reason any injury to the stem, such as girdling, which severs the conductive system is likely to seriously injure the plant. In fact, girdling is a common method employed in killing trees.

In the *manufacture* of plant foods stems may assume considerable importance, although seldom so much as leaves, which have food-making as their primary function. Being well exposed to light and well provided with chlorophyll, leaves are especially adapted to carry on *photosynthesis* — the process by which food is manufactured. However, any portion of a plant containing chlorophyll to which sunlight and air are accessible can make food, and the stems of practically all plants that make their own food have some portions that are green and, therefore, able in some degree to carry on photosynthesis. For example, the young twigs of trees are almost as green as the leaves and no doubt make considerable food. As the twigs grow older, the green layer is covered by bark, which excludes the light that is necessary for photosynthesis. In the Box-elder, Sassafras, and some other trees, not only the young twigs but portions of the older branches are green, and probably able to make food. In most of our short-lived plants, such as Corn, Sorghum, Kafir Corn, Tomatoes, Melons, Clover, Alfalfa, Beans, etc., the entire stem is green and able to carry on photosynthesis. In some plants, such as the Cacti, which have no leaves, all of the food must be made by the stem. In the garden Asparagus the leaves are scale-like and food is made chiefly by the stem and its many, small, lateral branches. Some plants which have scale-like leaves, have green lateral branches so expanded as to resemble leaves, as the Smilax (*Myrsiphyllum*), common in greenhouses, illustrates. Such branches are called *Cladophylls*. (*Fig. 147.*)

As to the *storage* function of stems, there is much difference among plants, but in nearly all stems there is some accumulation of substances, such as water, sugars, and starch. During the wet season the stems of some Cacti take up large amounts of water, which supply the plant during the dry season. In the stems of Sorghum and Sugar Cane, so much sugar is accumulated and retained that these plants are grown for the sugar which they afford. In the stems of trees much food is stored in the form of starch, and when transferred to growing regions during early spring, it is changed to sugar, in which form it occurs in solution in the sap of the tree. The so-called maple sap obtained from the Sugar Maple is a good illustration of sap which contains much stored food in the form of sugar. In early spring before the leaves appear, the trees are so gorged with sap that it can be drawn off by boring into the wood and inserting spiles. This sugar comes from reserve food accumulated when the leaves are active, and serves as a supply for the growth of new foliage at the beginning of the growing season.

FIG. 147. — A branch of Myrsiphyllum, showing the cladophylls (a), and the scale-like leaves (b).

Some stems, notably those of the Irish Potato, contain large amounts of starch on account of which they are valuable for food. Another tuber-like stem similar to that of the Irish Potato is produced by the Jerusalem Artichoke — a plant of the Sunflower type and often grown on account of the food value of its underground tubers.

Many of the early spring plants, such as Spring Beauty, Dutchman's Breeches, Wind Flower, some Violets, and many other plants having a supply of food at hand can spring up quickly, flower, and accumulate another supply of food before the sunlight is excluded by the forest foliage. Such plants, being seen only in April or early May, have what is called the *vernal habit*, i.e, they live their life cycle in the spring of the year. The food reserve of stems has much to do with the vernal habit.

Classes of Stems. — There are many ways in which stems may be classified. Stems are classified as *monocotyledonous* or *dicoty-*

ledonous, according to whether or not they belong to Monocotyledons or Dicotyledons. However, it is more in structure than
in external characters that these two types of stems present
important differences.

As to hardness stems are often classified as either *herbaceous* or
woody. Stems that are typically herbaceous, like those of Clover,
Alfalfa, Tomatoes, and others which develop very little woody
tissue, are soft and short-lived, usually living but one year. It is
among trees, where the amount of woody tissue reaches its maximum, that the best examples of woody stems occur. However,
between herbaceous and woody stems there is no distinct line of
division, for most herbaceous stems are woody in their older
regions and all woody stems are herbaceous in their younger
regions. The terms, herbaceous and woody, refer, therefore, to
the amount of woody tissue present, and not to the presence or
absence of it.

As to length of life stems may be classified into *annuals, biennials*, and *perennials*. Annual stems live but one growing season.
The stems of most herbaceous plants are annuals, dying down to
the ground either before or after frost comes, as in case of most
vegetables, weeds, and Grasses. But annual stems and annual
plants must not be confused, for many plants, like Alfalfa, Quack
Grass, and Canada Thistle, which live many years, thus being
perennial in habit, have annual stems which grow up in the spring
and die down in the fall. When the plant is annual, roots, stem,
and all other parts die at the end of the growing season, and
the plant must be started anew from seed.

In plants, such as Turnips, Carrots, and Beets, which require
two years to complete their life cycle, and are, therefore, known
as biennials, the stem remains short during the first growing season,
forming a mere crown at the top of the root. During the second
growing season, stems develop which bear flowers and seeds,
and then the entire plant dies. In some biennials, as Cabbage
and Rape illustrate, the stem is prominent during the first season,
although it elongates much more during the second season in
preparation for bearing flowers and seeds, as shown in *Figure 148*.
In Red Clover, Sweet Clover, and many weeds with the biennial
habit, the portion of the stem known as the crown is biennial,
while the branches arising from the crown are annuals.

Perennial stems, so described because they live year after

year, are typical of shrubs and trees, although they occur among herbaceous plants, notably in the Ferns, Sedges, and Grasses where the underground stem, which is well protected by a covering of earth, is able to persist for many years.

As to position stems are classified into *aërial, submerged,* and *underground*. Submerged stems are of least importance, being characteristic of plants which grow in lakes or sluggish streams, where the plant is often supported by the buoyant power of the water rather than by its stem system. Aërial stems are of most importance to us, although there are some valuable underground stems.

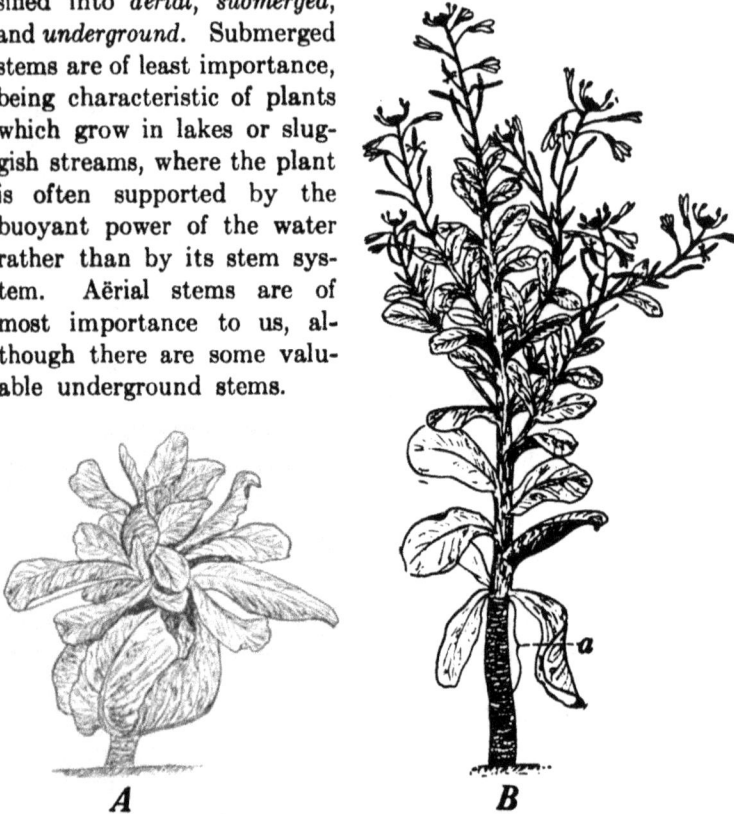

Fig. 148. — Two stages in the development of a Cabbage plant. *A*, plant at the beginning of the second season's growth with flowering stem pushing out of the head. *B*, Cabbage plant in flower near the end of the second growing season. *a*, scars left by the falling of the leaves of the head.

Aërial Stems. — Most of our cultivated plants as well as most weeds have aërial stems. Since aërial stems keep above ground, they are best adapted to expose leaves to the air and sunlight. Aërial stems may be *erect, prostrate,* or *climbing*.

The *erect stem* is the common type of aërial stem, and is best adapted for leaf display. Having the erect position, it can branch and display leaves on all sides, and by elongation can lift its leaves above the shade of other plants.

Erect stems show a striking contrast to primary roots in the way they respond to gravity and light. While the main axis of primary roots is positively geotropic and negatively heliotropic, the trunk of erect stems behaves in the opposite way, thus growing away from the center of the earth and toward the light. But, like lateral roots, the branches of the shoot tend to take a horizontal or *plagiotropic* position, in which they appear indifferent to both light and gravity. However, this indifference to gravity and light on the part of the branches of the shoot seems to depend upon influences exerted by other parts of the stem; for, if the upper part of the shoot is removed, then the horizontal branches remaining show a strong tendency to become erect.

Erect stems, being wholly self-supporting and much exposed to winds, surpass other stems in amount of strengthening tissue developed. From this type of stems where woody tissue reaches its maximum development, as in trees, we obtain timber. However, erect stems are not always sufficiently strong to endure the strains to which they are exposed, as is well known in case of grains where the so-called "lodging" often occurs.

In size erect stems surpass all others. The most remarkable erect stems are those of the giant Sequoias, one of which is shown in *Figure 149*. These giant trees, which are natives of the western mountains, may attain a height of 400 feet, a circumference of more than 100 feet, and live to be more than 4000 years old.

The *prostrate stems* of Pumpkins, Melons, Squashes, Cucumbers, Strawberries, and Sweet Potatoes are well known to the student. They are not strong enough to maintain an erect position, and lie stretched upon the ground. Prostrate stems are common among such weeds as the Five-fingers and Spurges. Some plants, as Crab Grass and Buffalo Grass illustrate, have both erect and prostrate stems. In this case the erect stems arise as branches from the prostrate ones.

The prostrate position is not a good one for leaf display; for leaves can be displayed only on the upper side and not all around as in erect stems. Prostrate stems are also not able to escape the shade of surrounding plants and, therefore, thrive best where erect plants are few, as on sandy beaches or river banks.

However, prostrate stems have some distinct advantages over erect ones. Since they do not have to support much weight, they

FIG. 149. — One of the giant trees of the West, called "Grizzly Giant." From Forestry Bulletin.

can grow very long and slender without developing much strengthening tissue. Furthermore, they are not so much exposed to loss of water by evaporation as erect stems are. The prostrate position is also more favorable for vegetative propagation, for as the stems grow over the ground, the nodes may produce roots from their lower and stems from their upper surface, and thus new plants are started which become independent by the death of the parent stem. This method of propagation is common in the Strawberry where the prostrate stems, known as *runners*, produce roots at their tips and start new plants which soon become independent by the death of the runner. (*Fig. 150.*) Some of the Grasses and weeds are able to spread very rapidly by this method of propagation.

This disposition of nodes to grow roots and start new plants is an important feature in the propagation of plants. Not only the

Fig. 150. — Prostrate stem (runner) of the Strawberry producing new plants at the nodes.

nodes of prostrate stems will do this, but the nodes of most stems are able to produce roots as well as branches and leaves, if placed in proper conditions. Much use is made of this feature in propagating many of our useful plants as we shall see later.

Climbing Stems. — Some familiar examples of climbing stems are those of the Pea, Grape, Hop, Woodbine, Poison Ivy, and Morning Glory. Climbing stems, like prostrate stems, grow long and slender, and are not strong enough to support themselves in an erect position. They raise themselves into the light by climbing a support, such as a fence, wall, or some erect plant. Some kinds of Beans having climbing stems are often planted with the Corn, so that they may have the Corn stems for support, or when planted alone, each plant is provided with a stake for a support. Sweet Peas, Hops, and most Grapes are other familiar plants requiring supports. The Woodbine and some wild Grapes are quite notable climbers, often climbing to the tops of tall trees.

(*Fig. 151.*) Many of the most notable climbers are in the tropical regions.

Climbing stems have no more space for the display of leaves than prostrate stems have, because one-half of the space for leaf display is cut off by the support; but the climbing position is much better than the prostrate position for escaping the shade of other plants.

One interesting feature of climbing plants is their different ways of climbing a support. The Bean, Morning Glory, and Hop climb by twining around the support. They are called *twiners*. These plants can not climb a wall, for they must have a support which they can wrap about. (*Fig. 152.*) The Sweet Pea and Grape Vine illustrate climbing by means of tendrils which hook about the support. Tendrils are usually modified leaves or stems, although sometimes of doubtful origin. (*Fig. 153.*) In some tendril climbers, as in the Japan Ivy, the tendrils have swollen ends which flatten against a wall or other supports, where they se-

FIG. 151. — A Grape Vine climbing over a dead Elm tree.

crete a mucilaginous substance by which they are able to hold on tenaciously. In case of the English Ivy, the plant is held to the wall by roots which are as efficient as tendrils. The Virginia Creeper climbs by means of both roots and tendrils. In being able to climb vertical walls of stone or brick, the Ivies are well adapted for wall vines for which they are much used. (*Fig. 154.*)

Underground Stems. — The Potato, Onion, and Artichoke are familiar examples of underground stems. Many of the plants grown in the greenhouse and on the lawn for decoration, such as the Lilies, Hyacinth, Tulip, Crocus, etc., have underground stems. This type of stem is common among plants with the vernal habit. Many of our useful Grasses, as Red Top, Kentucky and Canada Blue Grass, Orchard Grass, and others have perennial subterranean stems from which aërial stems are sent up each year. Grasses of this type live many years and are the Grasses which produce our permanent pastures. Grasses of this type are also chosen for lawns, because their spreading underground stems produce a compact sod and send up a thick aërial growth. Quack Grass, Johnson Grass, some Morning Glories, Poison Ivy, and many other weeds have underground stems, and it is due to this feature that such weeds are hard to eradicate. Cutting off the aërial stems of these weeds does not kill the plant; for the underground portion still lives and is able to send up more aërial stems.

Fig. 152. — Morning Glory twining around a Corn stalk.

Underground stems are least adapted for displaying leaves and bearing flowers, and they must either produce leaves and flower stalks long enough to reach above ground or grow branches which become aërial stems upon which the leaves, flowers, and fruit are borne.   In most cases aërial stems are produced, and the leaves of the underground stem are mere scales.

Although the underground stems are the least adapted for leaf display, they have some advantages that aërial stems do not have.

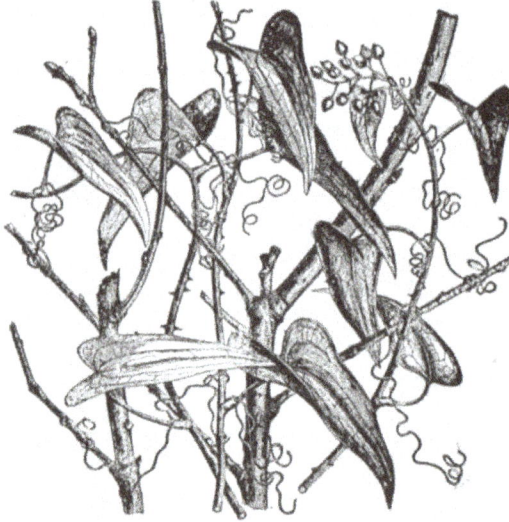

FIG. 153.   Smilax climbing over bushes by means of tendrils.
After Kerner.

They are much less exposed to drying and freezing, and escape being pastured off by stock.   They are safe places for the storage of food, and most underground stems do have much reserve food, which is used in the growth of new aërial shoots at the opening of each growing season.   Herbaceous plants are able to persist for many years, if they have an underground stem from which new shoots may arise each year.   In other words, an underground stem is one of the features that makes it possible for herbaceous plants to be perennials.   The underground position is an advantageous one for vegetative propagation, because not only are the nodes favorably located for establishing roots, but the supply of reserve food and protection from drying and freezing makes it possible for even small segments of underground stems to live and develop separate plants.   When an underground stem like that of Quack Grass is hoed to pieces, each segment, if it has a node, will develop a new plant. Weeds of this type are multiplied rather than destroyed by plowing and discing.

Underground stems may be much elongated or they may be short and thick. In their subterranean habit, they resemble roots, and one may easily mistake some types of them for roots, unless the stem characters are well in mind. However, the presence of nodes, internodes, and leaves, although the latter are usually scale-like, serve to identify the underground structure bearing them as a stem. For example, the so-called eyes of the Irish Potato are buds and are located in the axils of small scales which mark the nodes of the tuber. (*Fig. 155.*) On some the scale-like

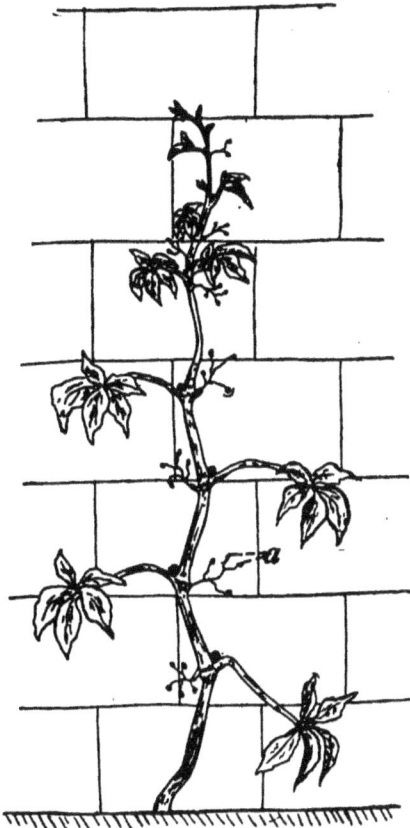

FIG. 154. — A Woodbine (*Ampelopsis climbing a stone wall. a*, tendrils.

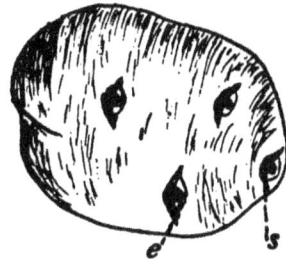

FIG. 155. — Irish Potato. *e*, eyes; *s*, scale leaves.

leaves are large and fleshy, while on others they are very inconspicuous. Underground stems differ so much that they have been classified into *rhizomes* or *rootstocks, tubers, bulbs,* and *corms.*

Rhizomes are very much elongated underground stems. They are so named because of their resemblance to roots (the word rhizome meaning root-like). They are commonly called rootstocks. The rhizome is one of the most common forms of underground stems, being the kind of underground stem most common among Grasses and weeds. Many wild plants, such as the Ferns, May Apple or Mandrake, Solomon's Seal, Iris, Water Lily, and others, have rhizomes. (*Fig. 156*.)

. Fig. 156. — Rhizome of the Mandrake (*Podophyllum*), showing aërial
shoot and two scars (*a*) left by previous shoots.

One striking feature is the difference in the way that rhizomes and their aërial shoots respond to gravity and light. While their aërial shoots grow toward the light and away from the earth, the rhizome elongates horizontally under the surface of the ground, neither seeking the light nor growing away from the earth.

Rhizomes grow best at certain depths in the soil, and, if the depth is changed by adding or removing soil from over them, they will grow up or down until the required depth is reached. By a covering of manure or straw, the rhizomes of Quack Grass and some other weeds may be induced to grow to the surface or even out of the ground. Such weeds are sometimes eradicated by removing the covering and exposing the rhizomes to drying and freezing after they have been induced to grow to the surface.

Rhizomes elongate and push forward through the soil by growth at one end. It is near this growing end that the aërial portions are produced from season to season. As the rhizomes push forward, the older portions behind die away, and if the rhizome is branched, as many of them are, the branches become separated and form independent rhizomes. The creeping and branching habits of rhizomes are important features for vegetative propagation. Rhizomes are able to creep through a soil which is already well occupied by other plants, and consequently, plants having rhizomes are able to spread where there is no chance for seed to develop.

Fig. 157. — Cross section of an Onion above and lengthwise section below. c, main bud; b, small buds; s, stem; r, roots; f, fleshy scales. After Andrews.

The *tuber* occurs among plants where certain regions of the undergound stem or its branches become much enlarged in connection with food storage. The most familiar tuber is the Irish Potato. The nodes are marked by the scale-like leaves in the axils of which occur the small buds or eyes. The presence of nodes identifies the Potato tuber as a stem structure. It is the stem portion of tubers that is prominent, the leaves and buds being small. Another tuber with nodes more prominent than in the Irish Potato and also of some value for food is the Jerusalem Artichoke.

In *bulbs* the leaves or leaf bases are more prominent than the stem, which is short, erect, and enclosed by the leaf structures. Most of the food is stored in the leaf structures rather than in the stem. Some common bulbs are those of the Onion, Lily, Hya-

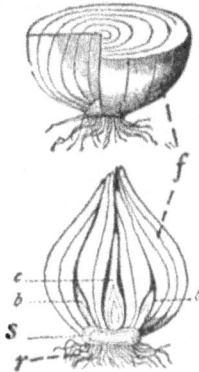

cinth, and Tulip.   The edible portion of the Onion bulb consists mainly of the fleshy scale-like leaves, in which the food has been stored.   (*Fig. 157.*)

Not all bulbs, however, are produced underground, for small Onion bulbs, called *bulb-lets*, often replace flower buds in the common Onion. These small bulbs are sometimes known as "Onion sets." Some Lilies also produce small bulbs in the leaf axils. Such bulbs, although they resemble underground bulbs in structure, are not formed in connection with underground stems.

Corms are very short, solid, vertical, underground stems, usually bearing roots on their lower and leaves and buds on their upper surface. However, buds may arise anywhere and roots are sometimes present at the upper end of the corm, as in the Jack-in-the-pulpit. Corms are usually marked by scar-like rings left by the decay of former leaves. From the buds of the old corm new corms develop.   (*Fig. 158.*)   The most familiar corms are those of the Indian Turnip, Crocus, Timothy, Cyclamen, and Gladiolus.

FIG. 158. — A corm of Gladiolus, showing young corms developing at the base of the old one.

General Structure of Stems

Stems have a cylindrical shape, which is associated with the circular arrangement of their strengthening tissue. By being arranged in a circle and near the periphery of the stem, the

strengthening tissues assume a tube-like arrangement, which is well
known to engineers as the arrangement in which the most strength
with a given amount of material can be secured.   The truth of
this principle is demonstrated in the construction of bicycle
frames, where much strength with little weight is secured by using
large tubes instead of solid rods.   Again, having the cylindrical
form, stems can be equally resistant to strains from all directions.

Stems taper and also decrease in age from the base of the trunk
to the end of the twigs where
the stem tissues are in process
of formation from the apical
meristems.   The apical meristems are also known as primary meristems because they
form other meristems, notably
the cambiums.   It is on the
new elongation at the tips of
the stem, that the leaves appear
anew each year.   The nodes,
the regions where leaves and
buds occur, are separated by
the elongation of the internodes, and in this way the
leaves, which are younger and
more crowded the nearer the
tip, are separated and exposed
to the light.   In most annual
stems the nodes are all formed
very early, and elongation
thereafter consists chiefly in

FIG. 159. — Lengthwise section
through the stem of a Corn seedling,
showing the apical meristems (*m*), the
nodes (*n*), and the short internodes (*i*).

the lengthening of the internodes, which thereby separate the
leaves so that they can unfold and expand to their mature size.
Thus, as shown in *Figure 159*, the nodes and internodes of a Corn
stem are all present in a Corn seedling two or three weeks old.

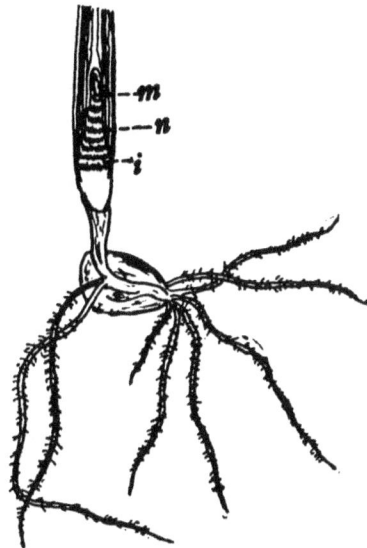

In most herbaceous stems, where there is no need of corky bark
and almost the entire stem is leaf bearing, the stem is active
throughout in the manufacture of food.   But in perennials, such as
shrubs and trees, photosynthesis is limited to the young branches
where the leaves are borne and the light is not excluded from the
green cortex of the branches by a corky covering.   In passing

from the leaf bearing portion of a branch to the regions behind where food manufacture is being abandoned, the following structural features are plainly seen.

First, there are the leaf scars, left where the leaves fell away, and interesting because of the way they are formed. (*Fig. 160.*) As the time approaches for leaves to fall, a cork-like layer, known as the *absciss layer*, forms across the base of the leaf, severing the direct connections of the leaf with the twig and remaining as a covering over the scar after the leaf falls. The absciss layer closes the openings which would otherwise be left by the falling of the leaf, and thereby prevents the entrance of destructive organisms into the twig. It is in connection with leaves which still remain on the tree after the absciss layer is formed that the various autumn colors occur due to changes in the dying leaf tissues.

Second, there are the lens-shaped dots, known as *lenticels*, which, although common on the branches of all woody plants, are especially conspicuous on the branches of the Cherry and Birch. (*Fig. 161.*) The formation of lenticels accompanies the formation of bark. In the young twig, where the protective covering is an epidermis, air is supplied to the tissues beneath through the slit-like openings of the stomata; but, as the twig becomes older and bark is formed, the stomata are replaced by lenticels. Lenticels are stomata distorted and transformed in structure by the development of bark. Just beneath each stoma, instead of cork, there is formed a loose mass of cells, and this loose mass of cells is pushed up into the opening of the stoma, as shown in *Figure 162*, rupturing the stoma and surrounding cells and thus

Fig. 160. Twig of the White Walnut, showing leaf scars (*a*).

Fig. 161.—Twig of Birch, showing lenticels.

forming a lenticel.   Through this loose mass of cells air easily circulates and reaches the tissues beneath.   As the twig increases in diameter and the bark is stretched, the lenticels are enlarged and, when they remain visible on the older bark, form the characteristic bands as on the older bark of Cherries and Birches.

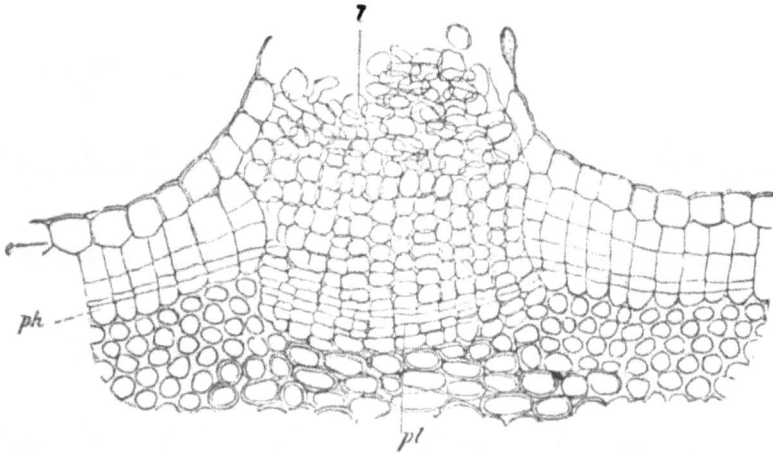

FIG. 162. — Section through a lenticel of the Elder (*Sambucus nigra*). *e*, epidermis; *ph*, cork cambium or phellogen; *l*, loosely joined or packing cells of the lenticel; *pl*, cambium of the lenticel.   Much magnified.   After Strasburger.

Third, as the twig becomes older, the bark increases in thickness, cutting off the light from the green tissue beneath, which, consequently, loses its green color and no longer functions in the manufacture of food.

On each leaf scar there are dots, which are the severed ends of the vascular bundles, known as leaf *traces*, that branched off from the vascular cylinder of the stem to enter the leaf, where by profusely branching they form the veins and numerous veinlets of the leaf.   In turning aside to enter the leaf, the leaf traces leave a gap in the vascular cylinder of the stem, and around this gap the vascular bundles of the bud in the axil of the leaf connect with the vascular cylinder of the stem.   (*Fig. 163.*)   Thus through the branching and rejoining of bundles at the nodes, a plant's vascular system becomes quite complex, looking like *Figure 164.*

Stem tips are not covered by caps, as root tips are.   The actual tips of stems are the meristematic tissues.   During the dormant period, primary meristems are usually protected by bud scales, while, during their active period, they receive considerable protection from the young leaves, which, although developing laterally and behind the tips, project forward and are usually so crowded and folded together that they hide the stem tips.

Behind the stem tips the cells formed from the primary meristems begin to elongate and modify into tissues and continue to do so until transformed into the mature tissues of the older parts of the stem. Stem tissues differ: (1) in some im-

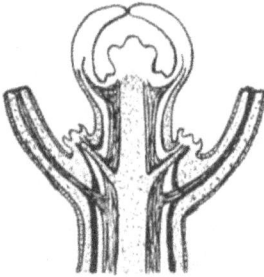

FIG. 163. — Lengthwise section through the apical region of a stem with two leaf stalks and the buds in their axils included, showing the connections of the vascular bundles of leaves and of axillary buds or branches with the vascular cylinder of the stem. The vascular cylinder is represented by shaded strands on each side of the pith, the light area in the center of' the stem. Redrawn from Sargent.

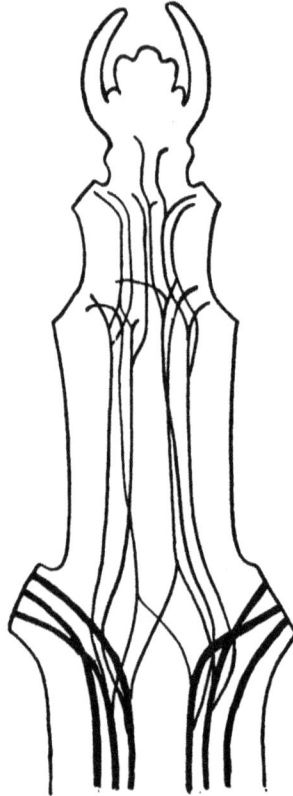

FIG. 164. — Diagram of the vascular cylinder of the young stem of *Clematis viticella*, showing by means of dark lines the branching of the vascular bundles at the nodes to supply the leaves and branches with bundles. Modified from Nägeli.

portant ways according to whether the stem is monocotyledonous or dicotyledonous; and (2) in minor ways according to whether the stem is herbaceous or woody. Thus in trees the tissues of the herbaceous tips differ some from those in the older regions where corky bark and other woody features are developed.

Structure of Monocotyledonous Stems

The most useful of the Monocotyledons are the Grasses of which the Bamboos are the largest representatives. The Lilies, Asparagus, and Palms are some other Monocotyledons that are familiar. Nearly all Monocotyledons are herbaceous, although there are a few, notably the Palms and Bamboos, that are woody.

The characteristic arrangement of the tissues of monocotyledonous stems, as they appear to the naked eye, can be seen in the

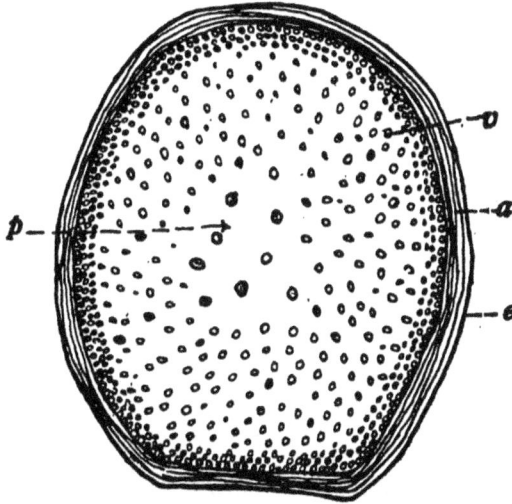

FIG. 165. — Cross section of a Corn stem. *a*, rind; *v*, vascular bundles; *p*, pith; *e*, epidermis.

cross section of a Corn stem, as shown in *Figure 165*. In this section three features are prominent. *First*, there is the rind-like portion, forming the outer region of the stem and affording protection and strength. The cells of this outer region contain chlorophyll and also function to some extent like leaves in the manufacture of food. *Second*, there is the pith, left white in our drawing and filling the entire cavity within the rind. *Third*, there are the vascular bundles (shown by dots) which, although scattered throughout the pith, are more numerous near the rind, thus tending to form a hollow column, which, as previously pointed out, is the best arrangement for strength. In monocotyledonous stems the tissues are run together and consequently are not so grouped as to form distinct regions, such as pith, vascular cylinder, and cortex, which are more or less distinct regions in Dicotyledons.

When cross sections of the Corn stem are studied with the microscope, such anatomical features as shown in *Figure 166* may be seen. The cells of the rind are rectangular in shape, consist of a number of rows, and their walls are thickened and made woody for strength. The woody feature of the rind is characteristic of Grasses and Sedges, being much less prominent in other monocotyledonous stems, as, for example, in Lilies and Asparagus. The outer row of cells of the rind constitute the epidermis, although in the Grasses the epidermal cells differ very little from other rind cells, except that they have silica and cutin deposited in their outer walls. The vascular bundles, containing numerous cells, show three or four large openings which are the large vessels of the xylem. Besides the large size of the pith cells as shown in the drawing, other features not shown, such as their storage function and their being so loosely joined as to form a spongy filling for the stem, should be mentioned.

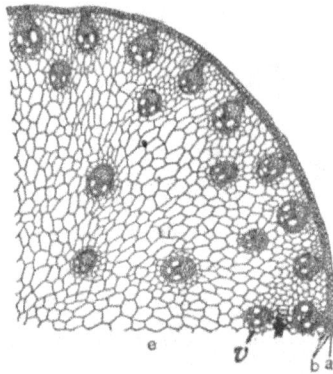

FIG. 166. — A portion of a cross section of a Corn stem much enlarged. *a*, epidermis; *b*, the band of strengthening cells under the epidermis and often called cortex; *v*, vascular bundles; *e*, pith. After Stevens.

To study the complex structure of a vascular bundle, we must turn to a more highly magnified cross section of the bundle as shown in *Figure 167*. The vascular bundle consists of strengthening and conductive tissues, the latter of which is composed of the *xylem* and *phloem*, — the chief structures of all vascular bundles. In respect to the character of the vessels composing them, xylem and phloem show much uniformity throughout Flowering Plants.

In the *xylem* the conductive tissues consist mainly of large vessels, known as *spiral, annular,* or *pitted* vessels according to the character of the thickenings in their walls, as partly shown in *Figure 168* and more fully shown in *Figure 169*. The woody thickenings, which strengthen the cellulose walls of the vessels so that they do not collapse under the pressure of surrounding tissues, may form rings as in annular vessels, spirals as in spiral vessels, or be more generally distributed over the wall, leaving only small unthickened areas which constitute the pits characteristic

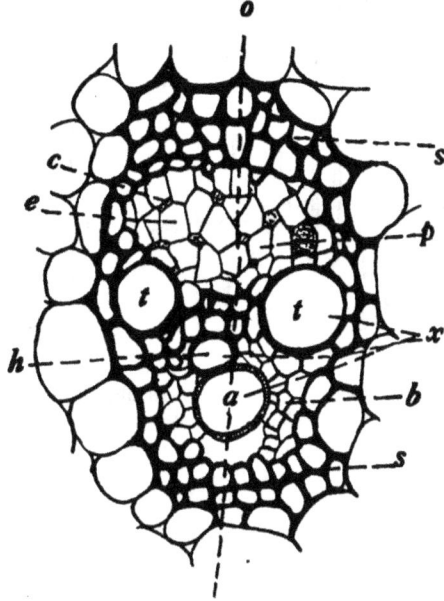

FIG. 167. — Cross section of a vascular bundle of Corn highly magnified. *s*, strengthening tissue; *p*, phloem consisting of sieve vessels (*e*) and companion cells (*c*); *x*, xylem consisting of annular vessel (*a*), spiral vessel (*h*) and pitted vessels (*t*); *b*, parenchyma cells.

of pitted vessels. The xylem vessels are free from protoplasm and are composed of cells joined in series with end walls resorbed. They are known as tracheae, and are quite tube-like in structure and function. Through them the water and mineral salts from the roots are carried, some reaching the leaves and buds while much leaks out through the cellulose portions of the walls to supply the tissues of the stem. Around the vessels are the thin-walled parenchyma cells which may function some in conduction.

In the phloem there are sieve vessels and companion cells. The sieve vessels are composed of cells joined in series and so named because of the perforated areas occurring in their end and side

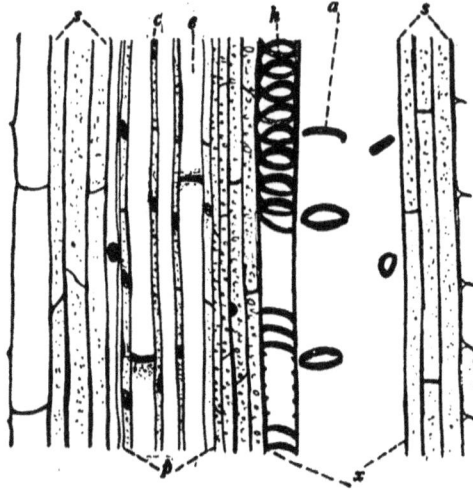

Fig. 168. — Lengthwise section through a vascular bundle of Corn, the knife splitting the bundle as shown by the line (o) in *Figure 167*, thus missing the pitted vessels. *x*, xylem showing spiral vessel (*h*) and annular vessels (*a*) which have been so torn by the growth of the stem that only the rings are left; *p*, phloem consisting of sieve vessels (*e*) and companion cells (*c*); *s*, strengthening tissue. Highly magnified.

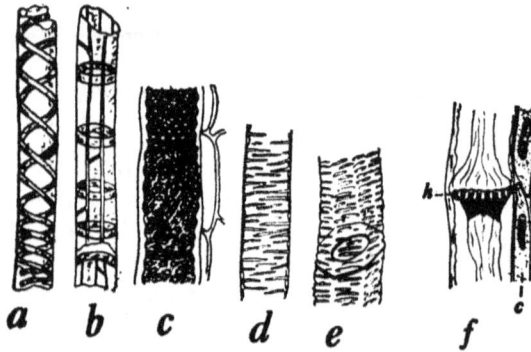

Fig. 169. — Vascular elements common among Ferns and Seed Plants. *a*, spiral vessel; *b*, annular vessel; *c*, pitted vessel; *d*, reticulated vessel; *e*, scalariform vessel; *f*, elements of the phloem showing sieve vessel with sieve plate (*h*), and companion cell (*c*). Highly magnified. *a* and *b*, after Bonnier and Leclerc Du Sablon; *c*, after De Bary; *d*, modified from Barnes; *e*, modified from Cowles; and *f*, from Strasburger.

walls.   The sieve vessels, assisted by the companion cells, which
are also thin-walled, elongated, living cells, conduct the foods
manufactured in the leaves, such as proteins and the carbohydrates of which sugar is the chief one.   The strengthening cells,
which are more numerous at the outer margin of the xylem and
phloem, form a sheath around the vascular bundle.   One peculiar
feature of the vascular bundles of Monocotyledons is that there
is no provision whereby the bundle can increase its tissues, and
for this reason it is known as a *closed* vascular bundle.   In monocotyledonous stems, where there is no special provision for growth

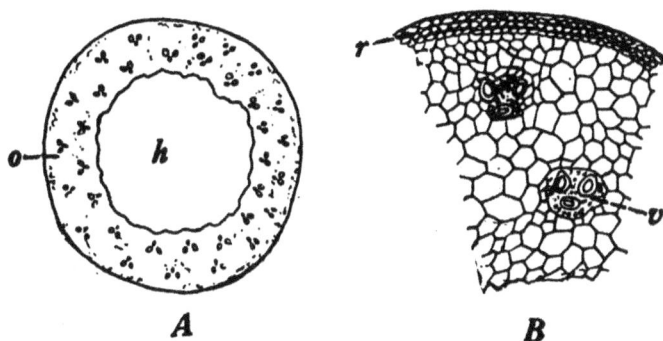

Fig. 170. — Cross sections of a Barley stem.   *A*, section across the entire stem showing the hollow (*h*) and the outer region (*o*) in which the vascular
bundles occur.   *B*, a section of the outer region much enlarged.   *r*, rind composed of strengthening cells; *v*, vascular bundles.

in diameter, growth is mainly in length, and often results in the
development of extremely slender trunks, like those of Palms and
Bamboos.

In many Grasses the stems are hollow throughout the internodes, as shown in *Figure 170*, in which case the vascular
bundles are limited to a zone just within the rind.   In most
Monocotyledons not belonging to the Grass or Sedge family,
the outer region of the stem is less firm in texture and in a few
Monocotyledons, as in the Yuccas and Dragon Tree, some of
the cells in the outer region of the stem divide like a cambium,
adding cells which form new vascular bundles and other tissues.
In this way the Dragon Tree may continue to grow in diameter
for thousands of years and attain a diameter of many feet.

Closed vascular bundles and their scattered arrangement are the chief distinguishing features of the anatomy of monocotyledonous stems.

Structure of Herbaceous Dicotyledonous Stems

Herbaceous Dicotyledons constitute an important group, for they include many forage plants, notably the Clovers and Alfalfa, some important fiber plants as Flax and Hemp, most vegetables, and many greenhouse plants. In the tropical countries there are a few Gymnosperms that are herbaceous, but in general features their anatomy is quite similar to that of herbaceous Dicotyledons.

All stems of the herbaceous dicotyledonous type, whether they are stems strictly herbaceous throughout or only the young branches of woody stems, have pith, vascular cylinder, and cortex which occupy well separated regions when well developed. Cross sections appear to the naked eye about as shown in *Figure 171*. The epidermis, cortex, and phloem form the soft outer zone, while the xylem forms the woody cylinder just within the soft zone, and encloses the pith, which occupies the center of the stem. In order to trace the development and study the anatomy of the different tissues, we must turn to highly magnified sections as shown in *Figure 172*.

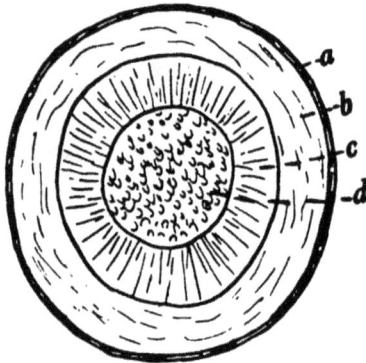

Fig. 171. — Diagram of a cross section of a well developed herbaceous stem, showing the epidermis (a); band of tissue (b) composed of cortex and phloem; xylem cylinder (c); and pith (d).

The *Cortex*, which is the larger part of the outer zone of tissues, is covered by the epidermis, and includes the *starch sheath* as its innermost layer. Just under the epidermis some of the cells of the cortex are transformed into collenchyma cells, which are particularly abundant in the angles of the stem shown in the Figure but more generally distributed around the stem in many other plants. The collenchyma cells, often noticeable in sections on account of their whitish glistening appearance, have much thick-

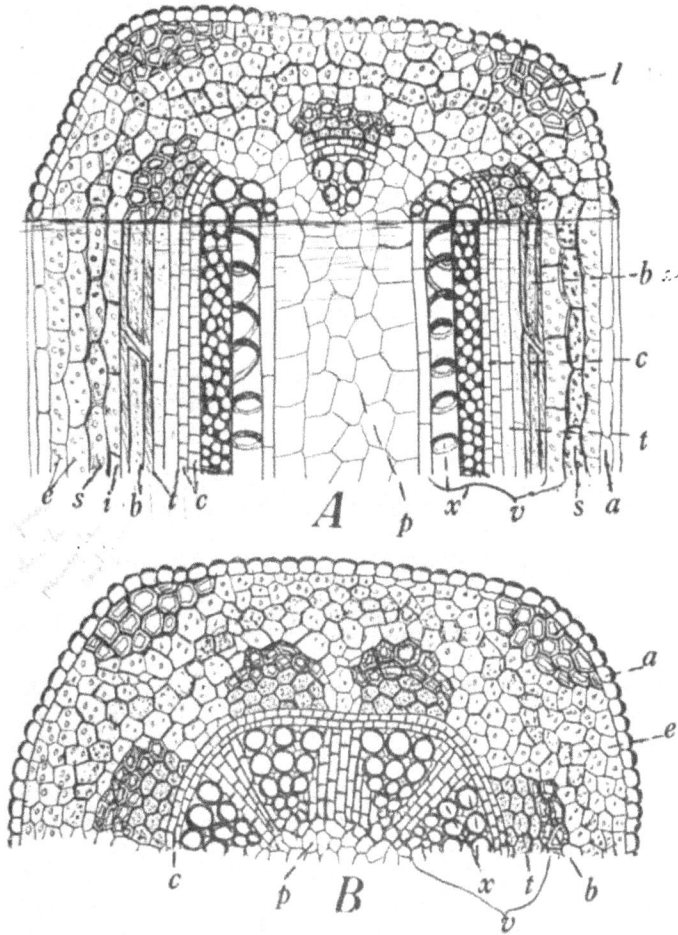

FIG. 172. — Diagrams of highly magnified sections of an Alfalfa stem. *A*, both cross sectional and lengthwise views of the tissues near the tip of the stem. *a*, epidermis; *l*, collenchyma; *e*, chlorenchyma of the cortex; *s*, starch sheath; *i*, pericycle; *b*, bast fibers; *t*, conductive portion of the phloem containing the sieve tubes and companion cells; *c*, cambium; *x*, xylem; and *p*, pith; *v*, vascular bundle. *B*, section farther from the tip, showing cambium ring and the closing together of the bundles. Lettering as above.

ened but elastic walls. Being formed early, they are of much importance in affording strength to the young regions of the stem where bast fibers and woody tissues are not yet well formed. Most of the cortex is made up of thin-walled parenchyma cells, known as *chlorenchyma*, since they contain chloroplasts and function like the cells of leaves in the manufacture of food, being supplied with air through the stomata of the epidermis. The starch sheath, comparable to the endodermis in roots, is not distinct from the other cells of the cortex in most stems. Its function is

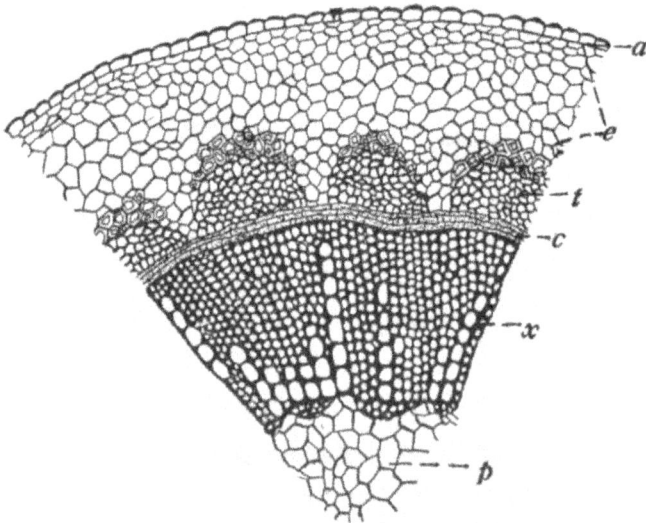

FIG. 173. — A portion of a cross section from near the base of an Alfalfa stem. *x*, xylem, which has formed a compact cylinder; *p*, pith; *c*, cambium; *t*, phloem; *e*, cortex; *a*, epidermis. Highly magnified.

in dispute. Some think that its function is to conduct carbohydrates, while others think that it is the tissue which perceives geotropic stimuli, and is thus responsible for the direction that stems take in response to gravity.

The vascular cylinder, consisting of vascular bundles so joined as to form a compact cylinder in the older regions of the stem, as shown in *Figure 173*, at first consists of separate vascular bundles having a circular arrangement about the stem and widely separated by bands of pith. At the outer border of each mass of phloem are *bast fibers*, often called *sclerenchyma* fibers, — an im-

portant strengthening tissue common to all dicotyledonous stems. Centerward and matching each mass of phloem, is a mass of xylem, wedge-shaped in outline with point towards the center of the stem.   This opposite arrangement of phloem and xylem contrasts with the arrangement in roots, where phloem and xylem alternate. Between the phloem and xylem is the cambium, the meristematic tissue whereby the vascular tissues can be increased indefinitely. Vascular bundles provided with cambium are called *open* bundles, and are characteristic of Dicotyledons and Gymnosperms, whether herbaceous or woody.   During further development, the cambiums of the different vascular bundles extend through

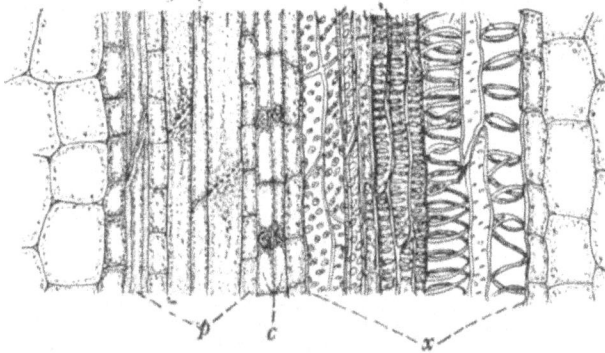

FIG. 174. — Lengthwise section through a vascular bundle of a herbaceous dicotyledonous stem. *x*, xylem showing pitted, annular, spiral and scalariform vessels; *p*, phloem showing sieve vessels and companion cells; *c*, cambium. Highly magnified. Modified from Hanson.

the intervening pith and connect to form the continuous cambium ring.   Then due to the activity of the cambium ring in the formation of other vascular bundles between those first formed and in the enlargement of all, the intervening pith, excepting narrow strands of it called pith rays, is crowded out, and finally a compact vascular cylinder as shown in *Figure 173* is formed. In many herbaceous Dicotyledons, such as the Giant Ragweed and others that grow rapidly, the cambium is so active in adding new xylem on its inner side and new phloem on its outer side that both phloem and xylem constitute zones of considerable thickness at the end of one summer's growth.   The zone of xylem is often so prominent that the basal portions of such stems are considered woody.

The vascular bundles of all Dicotyledons are very similar to those of Monocotyledons in structure and function of conductive vessels, but differ essentially in having cambium. (*Fig. 174.*) The conductive tissue of the xylem consists chiefly of annular, spiral, pitted, and scalariform vessels — the latter being so named because the thickened areas, separated by slit-like thin areas, are so arranged, one above another, as to resemble the rounds of a ladder. As in Monocotyledons, the xylem vessels, probably assisted by the neighboring parenchyma cells, are the passage ways through which the water and dissolved substances absorbed by the roots are distributed throughout the shoot. In addition to sieve tubes and companion

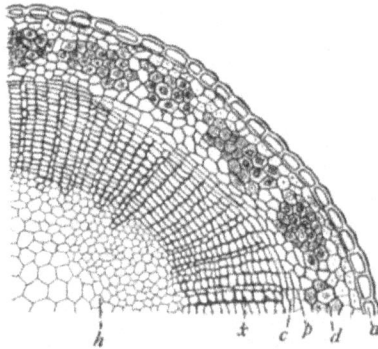

FIG. 175. — Cross section of a Flax stem. *a*, epidermis; *d*, bast fibers; *c*, cambium; *p*, phloem; *x*, xylem, *h*, pith. Enlarged.

cells, the phloem of Dicotyledons generally contains many thin-walled parenchyma cells, which serve in conducting the carbohydrates and also as storage places for proteins. The sieve tubes and companion cells conduct the proteins and a part of the carbohydrates. The bast fibers, which commonly occur in connection with the phloem of all Dicotyledons, are tough flexible strands adapted to afford strength. In fiber plants, such as Flax and Hemp, the bast fibers are well developed and their importance in the manufacture of fabrics, as the manufacture of linen from Flax, is well known. (*Fig. 175.*)

In contrast to the stems of Monocotyledons, the stems of Dicotyledons and Gymnosperms have as their distinctive features the circular arrangement of vascular bundles and the presence of cambium. The stems of Dicotyledons and Gymnosperms, since they increase in diameter by the addition of new layers of xylem or wood on the outside of that previously formed, are called *exogenous* stems. The stems of Monocotyledons are called *endogenous* — a term adopted when botanists had the erroneous notion that monocotyledonous stems grow by the addition of new tissues on the inside of the older ones.

Structure of Woody Stems

Woody stems, characteristic of the shrubs and trees of Dicotyledons and Gymnosperms, are fundamentally the same in structure as herbaceous dicotyledonous stems, for the

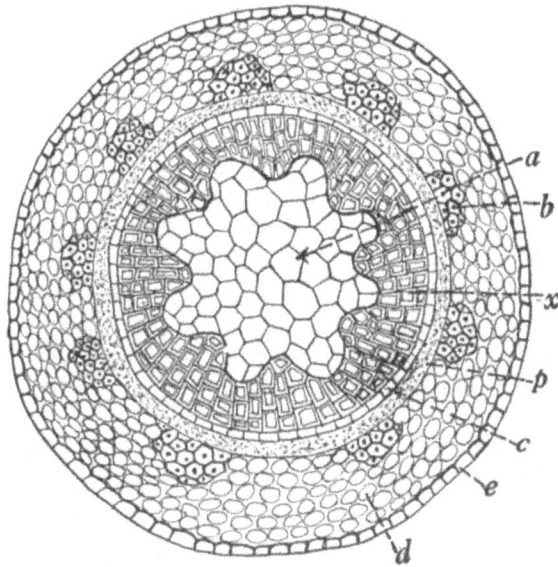

FIG. 176. — Diagrammatic drawing of a cross section of a young Apple twig. *e*, epidermis; *d*, cortex; *b*, bast fibers; *p*, phloem; *c*, cambium; *x*, xylem; *a*, pith.

circular arrangement of vascular bundles and presence of cambium are likewise their distinctive structural features. They, too, are exogenous. Their herbaceous tips, being similar in structure to the herbaceous dicotyledonous stems just described, need no special attention. (*Fig. 176.*) Aside from the lenticels already mentioned, the features most peculiar to woody stems are the *annual rings* of the woody cylinder and the *corky bark* which replaces the epidermis and some or all of the cortex. Also the *medullary rays* are commonly better developed in woody stems than in herbaceous stems. These features are directly associated with the perennial habit and the capacity to add new layers of xylem and phloem each year and thus increase

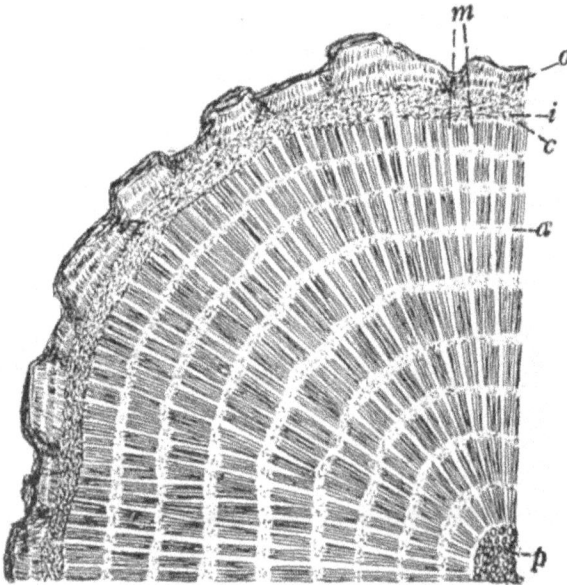

Fig. 177. — Cross section of an Oak branch from a region nine years old. *o*, outer corky bark; *i*, inner bark; *c*, cambium; *a*, annual rings; *m*, medullary rays; *p*, pith.

in diameter. In well developed woody stems, as shown in *Figure 177*, there are three regions, bark, woody cylinder, and pith, although the latter is often so small in amount as to appear absent. The bark, consisting of outer and inner bark, the latter of which contains the active phloem, extends centerward to the cambium, which, although distinctly separating the bark and wood, is so inconspicuous, except under the microscope, that bark and wood appear directly joined. The annual rings are the circles in the wood, and the medullary rays show as radiating lines traversing the bark and wood, reaching part way or all the way to the pith.

The *bark*, characteristic of woody plants, is originated by the cork cambium which forms as an inner layer of the epidermis or in the cortex beneath. (*Fig. 178.*) As the branch increases in diameter, the epidermis seldom grows in proportion, but usu-

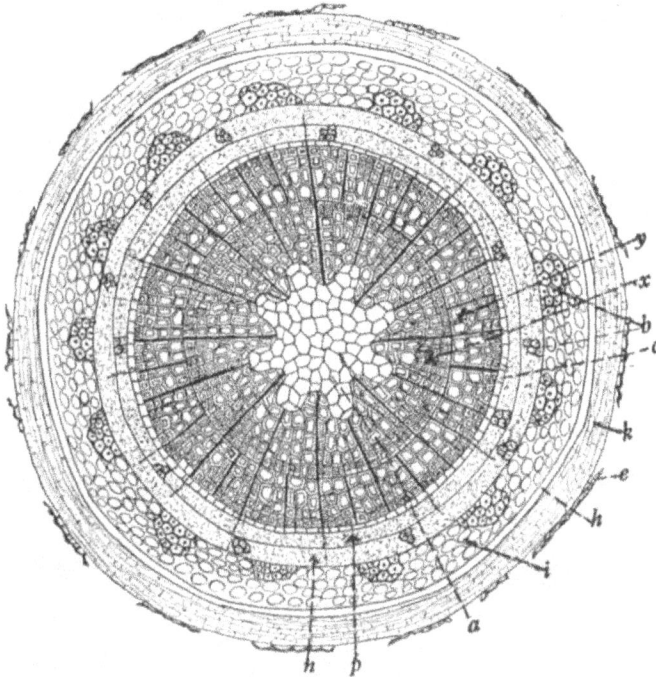

FIG. 178. — Diagrammatic drawing of a cross section of an apple twig after completing two seasons growth. *e*, epidermis sloughing off; *k*, cork; *h*, cork cambium; *i*, inner cortex; *n*, the phloem formed the first season; *p*, phloem formed the second season; *c*, cambium; *x*, xylem formed the first season; *y*, xylem formed the second season.

ally dies and sloughs off, and its protective function is assumed by the cork formed beneath and gradually thickened as the stem grows older. In some cases the cork cambium produces cortex cells on its inner side as well as cork on its outer side, in which case the cortex is increased in thickness. Since cork is impervious to water, the tissues on its outside, having their water supply cut off, soon die and with the epidermis and cork form the dead outer bark. In a few trees like the Beech and Fir the original cork cambium may renew its activity year after year, but usually the cork cambium is replaced each year by a new one formed just beneath. The inner bark consists of the inner cortex and the elements of the phloem made up of sieve tubes, companion cells, parenchyma cells, and bast fibers. After years of growth the outer layers of phloem die and thus on trunks of trees of much age, the inner living bark contains only the inner layers

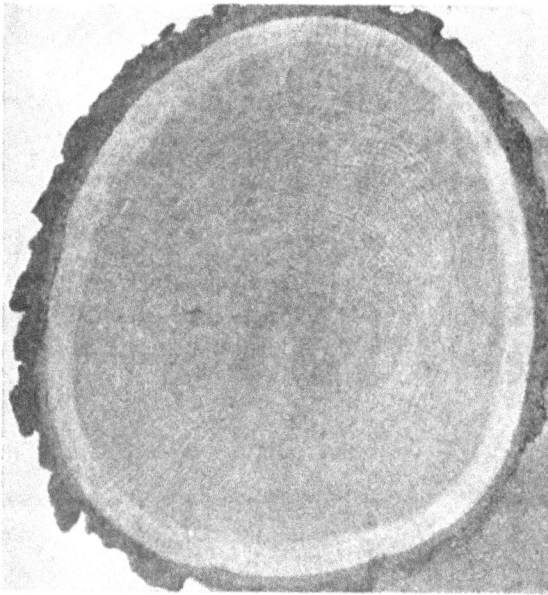

FIG. 179. — Cross section through the stem of a Black Oak, showing heartwood and sapwood. From Pinchot, U. S. Dept. of Agr.

of phloem, the older layers of phloem having become a part of the outer bark. Due to the addition of cork and the increase of the phloem and woody cylinder in thickness, the bark, which is unable to increase in circumference except in a few cases, as in Beeches, is usually broken and slowly exfoliated. It is usually broken into furrows, which are thought to serve the same purpose as lenticels in letting air into the stem tissues beneath.

The *woody cylinder*, consisting of the xylems of numerous vascular bundles closely joined, functions chiefly in the conduction of the water and mineral salts supplied by the roots. However, much stored food in trees is transferred to the growing regions through the xylem. This is especially true in the early spring as well known in the case of Maples where the xylem carries a large amount of sugar in the spring sap. In Gymnosperms the xylem consists chiefly of tracheids through which the water ascends by passing from one cell to another through the thin places of the bordered pits which are provided in their cell walls. In woody

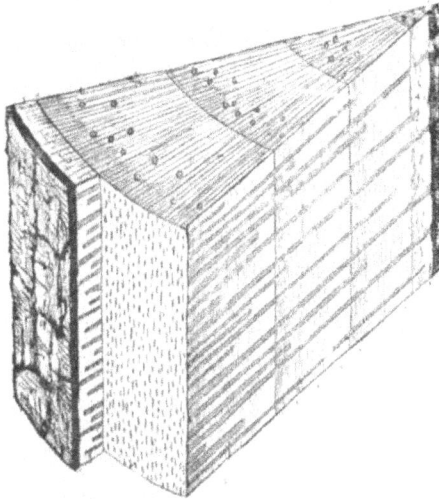

Fig. 180. — Piece of a stem of Scotch Fir four years old, showing the medullary rays as they appear in cross, radial, longitudinal, and tangential longitudinal sections of the stem. Enlarged six times. After Strasburger.

Dicotyledons the xylem consists of tracheae of the annular, spiral, pitted, and scalariform type, among which are intermingled wood fibers, wood parenchyma, and some tracheids.

The xylem tissues formed in the spring, when there is need for rapid transportation of water and dissolved substances to the expanding tips, consist of large cells with large cavities and thus give to the spring wood that open, porous character which contrasts so much with the compact character of the fall wood that the annual rings result. Annual rings, as their name indicates, are formed usually only one each year and consequently their number indicates quite well the age of the tree. Since the cam-

bium adds new phloem on its outside at the same time that it adds
new xylem within, annual rings occur in the bark as well as in
the wood; but in the bark where the tissues are soft and therefore crushed, the annual rings are either indistinct or obliterated.

In some woody stems having many annual rings, only the outer
annual rings which constitute the sap wood, recognizable by its

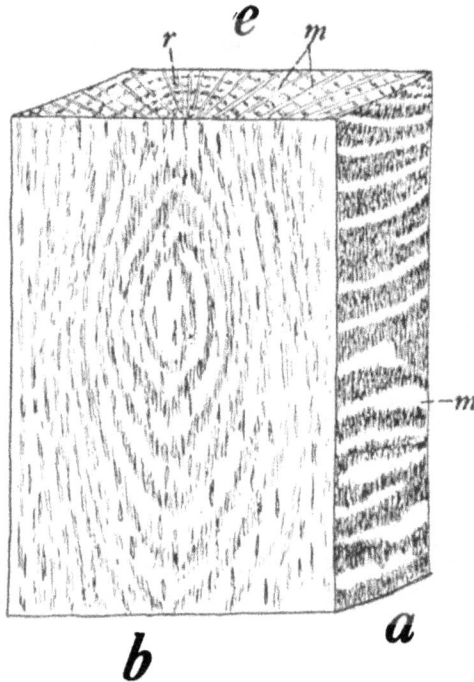

FIG. 181. — A piece of an oak board. *e*, end of the board showing medullary rays (*m*) and annual rings (*r*); *a*, edge of the board showing the medullary rays (*m*); *b*, broad surface of the board showing the annual rings consisting of light and dark bands.

light color, are active in conducting. (*Fig. 179.*) Sap wood is
often called the living wood because, although much of it is dead,
the cells of the medullary rays and wood parenchyma are alive,
while the *heart wood* is practically all dead. Heart wood is usually recognized by its dark color due to deposits of various substances, principally in the cell walls.

The medullary rays are also formed by the cambium and are
of two kinds: (1) those extending from pith into bark and known

as *primary rays*; and (2) those reaching only part way through the wood and known as *secondary* rays. (*Fig. 180.*) The medullary rays are composed of thin-walled living cells, which function in food storage and in the transportation of materials laterally through wood and bark. They are narrow plates of cells, one or only a few cells in thickness, and extend up and down through the stem only very short distances as may be ascertained in *Figure 180.*

Both annual rings and medullary rays have an economic importance in connection with lumber, where they form the beautiful figures on the surface of cabinet woods. When lumber is *quarter sawed*, that is, sawed so that the broad surface of the board is parallel with the medullary rays, then its beauty is due to the medullary rays which form the smooth-looking blotches as shown on the edge of the board in *Figure 181.* When *plain sawed*, that is, sawed at right angles to the medullary rays, the beauty of the board is due to the figures formed by the annual rings as shown on the broad surface of the board in *Figure 181.*

In *summarizing,* corky bark, annual rings, and prominent medullary rays may be stated as the distinguishing features of woody stems. Like herbaceous dicotyledonous stems, they are characterized by the circular arrangement of vascular bundles and presence of cambium — features which distinguish them from monocotyledonous stems where the vascular bundles have the scattered arrangement and cambium is absent.

CHAPTER X

BUDS; GROWTH OF STEMS; PRUNING; PROPAGATION BY STEMS

Buds

Nature of Buds. — Buds contain a partially developed portion of a stem with leaves and also flowers, when present, in an embryonic state. A close study of buds, like those of fruit trees, shows that the stem portion contained is very short and that the leaves and flowers, although they may be seen with a microscope of low power or often with the naked eye, are very rudimentary. Buds are often defined as undeveloped shoots. The most important thing about a bud is that it contains the meristematic tissues upon which growth in length (primary growth) and the formation of new leaves and flowers depend. For this reason, when the bud on the end of a branch is removed, the branch can grow no more in length at that point. (*Fig. 182.*)

FIG. 182. — Lengthwise section through a Hickory bud. *a*, furry inner scales; *b*, outer scales; *l*, folded leaf; *m*, apical meristem; *r*, region to which the scales are attached. Modified from Andrews.

Buds are common to all plants, but they are most noticeable in perennials, such as trees which have dormant periods occurring during the winter season in temperate regions or during dry seasons in warm countries. The buds of these plants are known as *resting buds* and are usually covered with scales which protect the inner portions from drying and other destructive agencies. The scales overlap, forming a covering of more than one layer, and are often made more protective by becoming hairy or waxy. Bud scales are closely related to leaves and, in most cases, are simply modified leaves. Sometimes, however, they are modified stipules which are leaf appendages.

204

In plants, like annuals and those that live in the tropics, the buds usually have no protective scales and are called *naked* buds. *Scaly buds* are characteristic of plants which must pass through seasons that are unfavorable for growth, and may be considered a device for maintaining partially developed stem portions in a protected state, and in readiness to assume rapid growth at the opening of the growing season.

FIG. 183. — Flower bud of the Pear, in which the flowers are pushing the scales apart and coming out of the bud. After Bailey.

Opening of Buds. — The bud scales are forced open by the growth of the young shoot within. The resumption of growth by the parts enclosed is first shown by the swelling of the bud. When the young shoot resumes growth at the beginning of the growing season, it grows with remarkable rapidity and in a few days pushes out of its scaly covering. (*Fig. 183.*) After the shoot has escaped, the scales usually fall off, leaving a scar about the branch at their place of attachment. The bud has now disappeared and in its place there is a new growth bearing leaves or flowers, or sometimes both.

FIG. 184. — Plum branch showing regions of different ages as indicated by the scars resulting from the falling away of the bud scales. Described in text.

The scars left by the scales remain until the bark is sufficiently developed to obscure them, and serve to indicate the age of the different regions of a branch. In *Figure 184*, the portion beyond the scar (*a*) is the last season's growth. The portion between (*a*) and (*b*) is two years old, and the portion between (*b*) and (*c*) is three years of age. Thus the age of a given region of a branch is indicated by the scars on the branch as well as by the annual rings in its woody cylinder.

Position of Buds. — Buds are either *terminal*, located at the tip of the stem: or *lateral*, occupying positions on the side of the stem. (*Fig. 185.*) The plumule is the first terminal bud of the seedling. The terminal bud is usually larger and stronger than the lateral ones, and its shoot usually makes more growth than the shoots of lateral buds.

Lateral buds usually occur in the leaf axils and when so located are called *axillary* buds. In many plants extra buds called *accessory* buds occur, which may stand just above the axillary bud, as in the Butternut, or on either side of it, as in the Box-elder. (*Fig. 186.*)

Buds, called *adventitious buds*, often spring from stems, from roots, or even from leaves without any definite order. In propagation by cuttings or layers, adventitious buds often have an important part in the formation of roots, and sometimes in the formation of stems. Thus in the propagation of Sweet Potatoes, adventitious buds are depended upon to develop the new plants. In *Figure 187* is shown the sprouts springing from the adventitious buds on the stump of the Basket Willow. In this case the sprouts are harvested after they become large enough to be woven into baskets, and a new lot of sprouts is then produced from other adventitious buds. In this way one can secure many crops of stems from one stump.

FIG. 185. — Branch of the Hickory, showing large terminal bud (*t*) and smaller lateral buds (*l*).

FIG. 186. — Accessory buds of the Butternut and Box-elder. *A*, twig of Butternut; *t*, terminal bud; *a*, accessory buds; *x*, axillary bud; *l*, leaf scar. *B*, accessory buds (*a*) and axillary bud (*x*) of the Box-elder. After Bergen.

On the other hand, adventitious buds are often a source of trouble, as in the clearing of ground where the sprouts developing from the adventitious buds on the stumps and roots tend to reoccupy the ground from which the trees and shrubs have been removed. However, in case of some valuable trees like the Chestnut, the sprouting habit is utilized in the production of a new crop of trees. (*Fig. 188.*) In some forage plants, as Alfalfa illustrates, a number of crops of hay can be obtained each year because of the continuous development of adventitious buds on the crown or basal portion of the stem. (*Fig. 189.*)

What Buds Contain. — Some buds contain only flowers, some only leaves, while some contain both flowers and leaves. Buds are called *flower buds, leaf buds,* or *mixed buds* according to what they contain. In such fruit trees as the Apricot and Peach, the buds contain only flowers or only leaves, while in the Apple and Pear the buds contain both flowers and leaves, or leaves only. (*Figs. 190* and *191.*)

Flower buds, or fruit buds as they are often called, are usually broader and more rounded than leaf buds and can often be identified by their position on the branch. For example, in the Peach and often in the Apricot the fruit buds are lateral buds on the current season's growth, while in the Apple and Pear they are usually the terminal buds of the stunted lateral branches

FIG. 187. — Basket Willow from which many crops of branches are obtained through the development of adventitious buds.

called fruit spurs which are located on those portions of the larger branches two or more years of age. In Cherries and Plums the fruit buds occur in clusters on the sides of the spurs. In grapes the flowers occur on the sides of the current spring shoots. The shape and place of appearance of fruit buds varies much in the different classes of fruits, and it is important that one should know their location and time of formation, for such information is valuable in deciding how and when to cultivate and prune.

Fig. 188. — Chestnut sprouts growing from stumps.
After Gifford Pinchot.

Formation of Buds. — The buds of plants which have a rest period are formed during one season, lie dormant during the rest period, and open at the beginning of the next growing season. Thus the buds of our fruit trees, which produced flowers and leafy shoots this year, were formed last year. As the new shoots develop each year, new buds are formed in the axils of the leaves and at the apex of branches, and in these buds are the flowers and leaves which appear the following year.

A study [1] of the development of the buds of our fruit trees has shown that the parts of a bud are formed during the summer and fall and are often so well developed before frost comes that the flowers and leaves may be identified if sections of the buds are

FIG. 189. — Alfalfa plant, showing development of branches on the crown. *h*, a main branch of the crown; *s*, stumps of branches which have been mowed off; *n*, new branches.

studied with the microscope. Thus the character or content of the buds of our fruit trees is determined several months before the buds open. The appearance of a heavy bloom in the orchard means that the conditions prevailing during the previous summer and fall favored the formation of flower buds. It is common observation that fruit trees bloom more profusely some seasons than others. Evidently there are certain conditions which favor the formation of flower buds and by controlling these conditions one can control to a certain extent the fruitfulness of a tree.

[1] Fruit-bud Formation and Development. *Annual Report*, pp. 159-205, Virginia Agr. Exp. Sta., 1909-1910.

The formation of flower buds is known to be closely related to the food supply.[1] Flower buds are formed in greatest abundance when there is more reserve food than is needed for growth. When a plant is growing rapidly and using all the food as fast as the

FIG. 190. — Fruit buds of the Apricot, in which case a fruit bud contains a single flower and no leaves. After Bailey.

leaves make it, few flower buds are formed. Furthermore, if a tree has exhausted its food supply in producing a heavy crop of fruit, not many flower buds are formed, and as a result the tree will bear very little fruit the following year. Any condition that leads to an accumulation of reserve food, such as checking growth by the removal of terminal buds or by cutting down the water supply from the roots, favors the formation of flower buds.

FIG. 191. — Twig of the Crab Apple at time of blooming. The terminal shoot (a) has developed from a leaf bud, no flowers being produced, while the lateral shoots (b) have come from mixed buds, both leaves and flowers having been produced.

[1] Studies in Fruit Bud Formation. *Technical Bulletin 9*, New Hampshire College Agr. Exp. Sta., 1915.

Some Effects of Pruning, Root Pruning, Ringing and Stripping on the Formation of Fruit Buds on Dwarf Apple Trees. *Technical Bulletin 5*, Virginia Agr. Exp. Sta., 1915.

Occasionally *ringing* is employed to induce the formation of fruit buds, in which case a narrow ring of bark is removed from the trunk or branches in order to sever the phloem, and thus, by cutting off the escape of the foods to the roots, bring about their accumulation in the branches. Favorable conditions for food formation in the leaves, such as light and free circulation of air and the addition of soil fertilizers, also have an effect upon the formation of fruit buds.

Active and Dormant Buds. — Many more buds are produced than can develop into branches, for, if all buds were to develop, branches would be so numerous and crowded that none of them could do well. The food supply and proper light relations permit the expansion of only a few buds. Consequently, many buds lie dormant one or more seasons or throughout the life of the plant. Usually the more terminally located a bud is, the more likely it is to be active. Thus the terminal buds of the main branches are less likely to be dormant than the terminal buds of the branches less prominent, and of the lateral buds often a large per cent remain dormant. An examination of the branches of most trees shows many leaf scars with dormant buds which most likely will remain dormant and finally become obscured by the thickening of the bark, just as many others have.

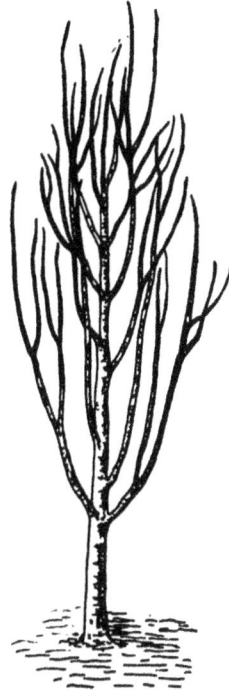

FIG. 192. — Sweet Cherry, a type of tree in which terminal growth is prominent, resulting in the development of a central shaft called a leader. After L. H. Bailey.

The dormancy of buds seems to be due to checks imposed upon them from without and not to conditions within the bud, for most dormant buds can be induced to become active by the removal of the active buds. Thus when the terminal buds of branches are removed, some of the dormant lateral buds become active. Use is made of this principle in inducing shade trees and fruit trees to acquire certain desirable shapes.

In most cases the terminal bud of the main branch is largest
and its shoot makes the most growth during a growing season,
sometimes producing a growth of several feet in a season, while
growth from buds not so terminally located is usually much
less.

The shape of a tree depends much upon the relative development of main and lateral branches.   When terminal growth is
very strong, lateral growth is weak and the tree develops a cen-

FIG. 193. — Sour Cherry, a tree which has strong lateral growth and
consequently no leaders.   After L. H. Bailey.

tral stem, called *leader*, with lateral branches more or less sup-
pressed.   This kind of growth is common among Poplars, Pines,
and even some fruit trees have it, as the Sweet Cherry in *Figure
192* illustrates.   Trees with this habit of growth tend to grow tall
and slender.   To induce such trees to grow low and bushy the
terminal buds must be removed, so that lateral branches will develop.   When terminal growth is weak, lateral growth is stronger,
and the tree is commonly much branched and leaders are absent,
as the Sour Cherry in *Figure 193* illustrates.   This habit of
growth is characteristic of Maples and many other trees.   There

are, however, some plants, like the Lilac shown in *Figure 194*, in which the terminal bud is replaced by two lateral ones, but such is not the rule among plants.

Growth of Stems

Phases of Growth. — In growth three things occur: (1) the addition of new cells by the meristematic tissues; (2) the elongation of cells; and (3) their modification into tissues. The first phase must precede the other two, but elongation and modification accompany each other, for cells begin to modify into tissues before completing their elongation. In short-lived plants, such as annuals, the first phase is most prominent in the seedling stage, during which most of the cells upon which growth in length depends are formed from the apical meristems. In Corn most of the cells are formed during the first three or four weeks of growth. During the remainder of the growth period the cells elongate and modify into the tissues of the mature stem. In perennials the three phases are repeated each year as is well illustrated by the yearly growth of trees. But even in

Fig. 194. — Branch of the Lilac, showing the terminal buds replaced by two lateral ones.

trees most of the cells which have to do with the growth in length are formed in the buds during the previous year; and to their remarkably rapid elongation is due the conspicuous phase of spring growth in which the shoot elongates and leaves and flowers expand into almost full size in a few days.

Regions of Growth. — The principal regions of growth are at the apices of stems, where growth in length occurs by the addition of new nodes and internodes, and at the cambium layer, where growth in diameter takes place. In such stems as those of the Grasses, the basal portion of each internode functions for some time as a meristem and thereby aids in the growth in length of the internode. It is due to this feature that Corn stems, before they reach maturity, are easily broken off just above the node.   Furthermore, in having this meristematic zone, stems of the Grasses, when blown down, are able to become partially erect by bending in the region of the node due to a more rapid growth of this region on its lower side.

Since the stem segments are added in succession at the apex, a stem soon comes to have segments in various stages of development, for while those at the apex are just beginning to elongate, those at the stem's base may have completed their elongation and formation of tissues. This feature is illustrated in *Figure 195*, although none of the segments are yet mature.

Primary and Secondary Growth. — In both stems and roots, apical growth, since from it the tissues of the stem and root first originate, is called *primary growth*, while growth from the cambium is known as *secondary growth* because it is chiefly concerned with adding more tissues of the same kind to those already formed from the apical meristems.   Tissues are also called *primary* or *secondary* according to whether they originated from the primary meristems or from the cambium.

Character and Rate of Growth in Stems. — Since elongation or enlargement is the most conspicuous phase of growth, it is employed in determining the character and rate of growth.   Although the most conspicuous, neverthe-

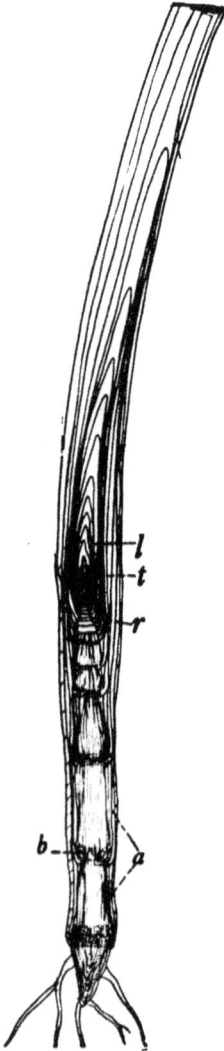

Fig. 195. — Lengthwise section through the stem of a Corn plant, the plant being about two feet high. *l*, leaves; *t*, tassel, *r*, region of stem where internodes have not elongated, *a*, internodes which have undergone the most elongation; *b*, meristematic region at the base of the internodes.

less it is so slow, except in a few cases, that it is imperceptible to the unaided eye; and, therefore, to directly observe it, the growing organ must be watched under the microscope. However, in measuring growth in large organs, such as stems, leaves, and roots, other methods that are more convenient are usually employed. Thus by marking a stem into segments as shown

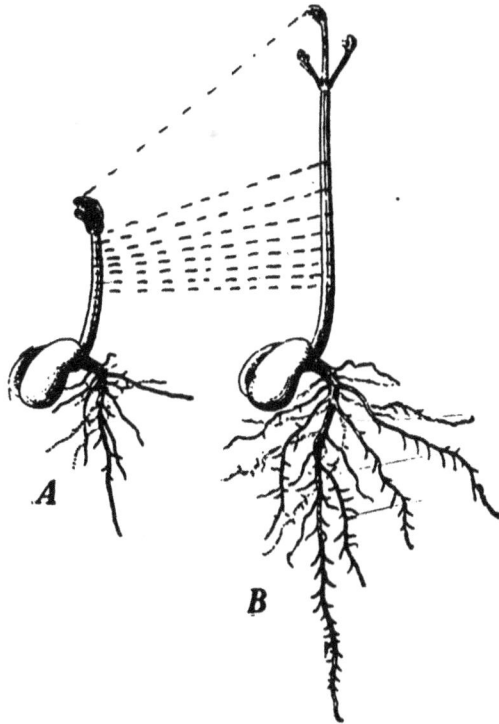

FIG. 196. — Stem of a seedling marked to show the regions of most elongation. *A*, stem just after marking. *B*, stem after a few hours growth.

in *Figure 196* and observing the spread of the marks apart, one can easily determine what part of the stem is most active in elongation. Special kinds of apparatus run by clockwork, one of which is known as the *auxograph* (meaning "growth writer") and another as *auxanometer* (meaning "growth measurer"), have been so devised that the rate and fluctuations in growth are recorded by a pen which indicates the character of the growth throughout a considerable period by curvatures in the

line which it makes on the paper carried around on a revolving
drum. (*Fig. 197.*) Such an apparatus has the advantage in that
one can see just how growth proceeds at any period during day or
night, if the apparatus is so manipulated that the hour at which
any part of the line is made can be determined. Measurements
by such an apparatus show that the rate of growth of an organ
is not uniform, but, beginning slowly, it gradually rises to a point
where growth is most rapid and then gradually falls away, finally

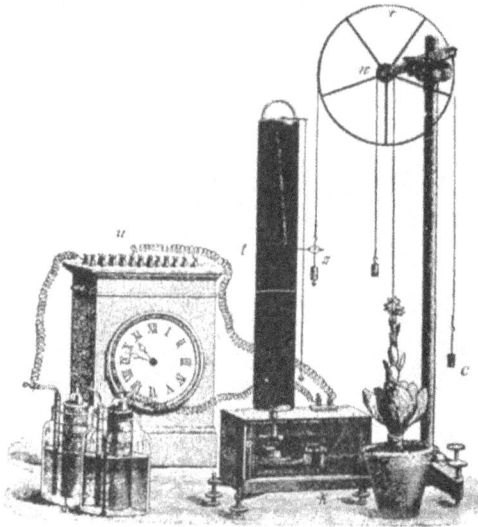

FIG. 197. — Auxanometer in operation. As the plant elongates, the small
pulley (*w*) revolves, revolving with it the large pulley (*r*) which magnifies
the motion and transmits it to the marker (*z*) that marks on the drum (*t*).
The drum is revolved by the apparatus (*k*) at its base and this apparatus
is connected with the clock (*u*). After Pfeffer.

ceasing as the organ approaches maturity. This mode of enlarging, which is commonly known as the *grand period*, is characteristic not only of stems, but also of fruits, flowers, leaves, and roots.
The fundamental cause of the grand period in any organ is due to
the fact that cells themselves enlarge in this way. Unlike leaves,
flowers, and fruit where the expansion is quite even throughout,
stems expand by each internode going through its grand period
independently of the other internodes. Thus between the upper
internodes in which the grand period is just beginning and those

toward the stem's base where the grand period is over, there are internodes in various stages of the grand period. Due to the overlapping of the grand periods of the different internodes, the elongation of the stem as a whole is quite uniform. In roots the grand period is passed through very quickly and is evident only near the tip.

The *rate* of growth also depends much upon the kind of plant and upon moisture, temperature, and light. While some plants, like Corn and Giant Ragweeds, grow to a height of six feet or more in three or four months, the seedlings of some Pines and Oaks grow only a few inches during an entire season. Some vines like the Hop plant may grow a stem more than twenty-five feet in length in one growing season. Most weeds grow more rapidly than cultivated plants and, if let alone, soon exceed them and cut off the light. Measurements have shown that some kinds of Beans and Peas can elongate about two inches and Wheat about four inches in forty-eight hours. In perennials, such as trees, growth is very rapid in the spring, after which it slows down during the remainder of the season.

The *moisture* of the soil and air is an important factor in growth. It is common knowledge that plants are checked in growth when the ground becomes dry. The moisture of the air, although not of use to the plant in the same way that the soil moisture is, checks the evaporation from the plant and thereby influences growth. When the atmosphere is full of water, as on "muggy" days, there is not much evaporation and the cells easily retain the high turgor pressure upon which rapid growth depends. It is partly due to the greater humidity at night that many plants grow faster then than in the day time. That the cells of plants are often more turgid at night than in the day time is shown by the fact that soft stems, like those of Corn and Sorghum, are more flexible and not so easily broken off in the latter part of the day as they are at night or in the morning. For this reason, the afternoon, when the cells are least turgid, is the best time to lay-by Corn. The function of water in enabling cells to stretch is an important one, for enlargement consists in stretching the protoplasm and cell walls without much increase at first in dry weight. Thus the dry weight of an internode of a stem is about the same at the end as at the beginning of the grand period, although the size may increase many times. In fact seedlings, before they

become active in the manufacture of food, often have a dry
weight less than that of the seed.

Temperature is the most important factor in growth and, just
as in the germination of seeds, the minimum, maximum, and

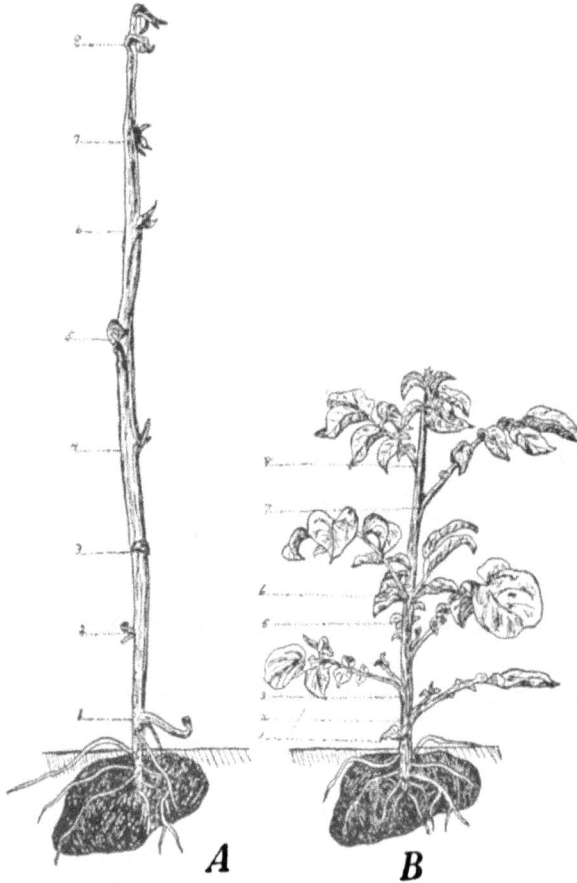

FIG. 198. — Two Potato plants, one of which was grown in the dark and
the other in the light. *A*, plant grown in the dark. *B*, plant grown in the
light. After Pfeffer.

optimum temperature for growth vary with the kind of plant
as shown in the table on next page. For example, the optimum
temperature is between 90° and 95° for Corn, between 80° and
85° for Barley, and about 70° for White Mustard, one of the
weeds. Thus when the days and nights are so cool that such

plants as Corn, Beans, and Pumpkins grow slowly, White Mustard and other plants with a low optimum grow rapidly.   In general, arctic plants have a lower optimum than tropical plants, and consequently plants transferred from one region to the other

FIG. 199. — Pines grown much crowded and consequently producing slender trunks.   From *Bulletin 24*, North Carolina Geological and Economic Survey.

usually do not thrive until they become acclimated, that is, until the plant's protoplasm becomes adjusted to the temperature of the region.

GROWTH TEMPERATURES IN FAHRENHEIT

Plant.	Minimum.	Optimum.	Maximum.
	Deg.	Deg.	Deg.
Barley............................	41	83–84	99–100
White Mustard....................	32	69–70	82–83
Scarlet Runner Bean.............	49–50	92–93	115–116
Corn............................	49–50	92–93	115–116
Pumpkin.........................	56–57	92–93	115–116

Indirectly *light* is very essential for growth because of its importance in the manufacture of plant foods. But directly light has little effect, unless it is intense, and then it checks growth. That most plants grow faster at night than in day time is well known; and, although much of the increase in the rate of growth at night is due to the greater humidity of the air, some is due to the absence of the inhibitive effect that the sun's rays have on

FIG. 200. — Pines growing in the open where their trunks are short and much branched. From *Bulletin 24*, North Carolina Geological and Economic Survey.

growth. In Bacteria, where the protoplasm is not protected by pigments, the sun's rays so inhibit growth that they have an important germicidal effect.

On the other hand, if plants do not have sufficient light, they are affected in various ways. For example, when plants are grown in the dark, as the Potatoes in *Figure 198* illustrate, the stems are excessively elongated, the leaves are abnormal, and the plant lacks chlorophyll, on which account the plant is said to be *etiolated*. Even plants grown in the shade, having the light only partially cut off, are usually taller and more slender than plants grown in the light. Thus many forest trees which have short, thick, and much branched trunks, when growing in pastures, grow tall slender stems with branches only at their tops when grown in forests where they are much shaded. It is for this reason that most forest trees grow trunks more valuable for lumber when grown in thick stands. (*Figs. 199* and *200*.) This principle is observed in growing Sorghum and Corn chiefly for fodder, in which case the plants are grown in thick stands, so that their stems will be finer and, therefore, better for feed. Such a response to shade is often an advantage to plants, for it is through the elongation of their stems that plants compete for light by endeavoring to raise their leaves above the shade of neighboring plants.

Also the development of stem tissues is more or less influenced by light. Stems grown in diminished light do not have their mechanical tissues so well developed. For example, when grain plants receive insufficient light on account of being much crowded, they have commonly weak stems and are likely to lodge. The bast fibers of flax are finer when the plants are thick on the ground, and when flax is grown for fibers it is commonly grown in thick stands.

Pruning

Pruning consists in cutting away portions of the plant and is done for reasons too numerous for more than a few to be mentioned here.

First, trees that tend to grow tall and slender may be induced to acquire a low thick top by subjecting them to the process called "heading-in," which consists in pruning the main branches so that growth in height is checked and a good development of lateral branches is induced. This method is often used in controlling the shape of shade and fruit trees. It is by this means that hedges are made to grow low and dense and thus capable of turning stock when used for fences.

Second, often, as in case of fruit trees, pruning has for its purpose the checking of growth which has been so thoroughly exhausting the food supply as to result in a shortage of fruit buds. In this case growth is checked by removing the terminal buds from the leaders and the food supply thereby conserved.

Third, plants are sometimes pruned to delay maturity. For example, in growing Sweet Peas the young pods are pinched off so as to conserve the food material and thereby prolong the flowering period of the plant. In contrast to this practice, often in case of nursery trees, the leaves are stripped off so as to cut off the food supply and thereby hasten maturity in order that the trees may be in a better condition to stand the winter.

Fourth, fruit trees are often pruned to induce the development of an open head so as to secure better lighting for the interior branches. Such pruning is necessary in trees with heads so compact that the interior branches are not able to function properly in the manufacture of food or in bearing fruit because of the lack of light.

Fifth, when fruit trees are set out, it is necessary to prune the top to safeguard the trees against injuries from excessive evapo-

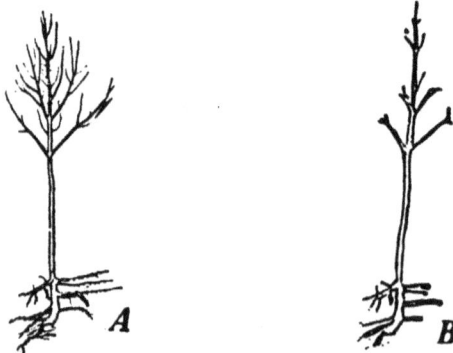

Fig. 201. — *A*, tree just received from nursery. *B*, same tree with top and roots pruned in preparation for setting in the ground. From Alfred Gaskill.

ration. Since the trees have their absorbing power much reduced through the loss of many roots broken and cut away in transplanting, the development of a large leaf surface must be prevented or the intake at the roots and outgo at the leaves will not be properly balanced. (*Fig. 201.*)

Sixth, the appearance of a tree as well as its protection against further injury requires the removal of dead and diseased branches. One can do much toward preventing some plant diseases, such as Fire Blight and Black Knot, from spreading to healthy trees by removing and burning the diseased branches of affected trees.

Seventh, by a severe pruning of the top, trees which are beginning to fail from general debility are often rejuvenated. This kind of pruning, which is characterized as severe because so much of the top is removed, is known as "pruning for wood." By the removal

Fig 202. — An Apple tree which has been severely pruned, its main branches having been cut back. After G. H. Powell.

of much of the top the balance between the top and roots is upset, and as a result a much larger supply of water and mineral salts is received by the remaining branches, which consequently become invigorated and much more active in growth. (*Fig. 202.*)

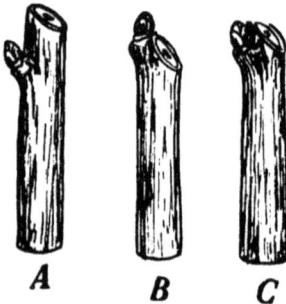

FIG. 203. — Twigs pruned, showing the cuts at different distances from the bud. *A*, the cut is too far from the bud. *B*, the cut is so near the bud that the bud is probably injured. *C*, the cut is at the proper distance from the bud. Why are the cuts made obliquely?

Wounds and their Healing. — The removal of a branch exposes the stem tissues, and makes an opening where destructive organisms, which may injure or even destroy the plant, can enter. Unless wounds are quickly healed over, the plant will suffer.

Since tissues that are much specialized, such as wood and corky bark, have lost their ability to grow, the meristematic tissues or cambiums must be depended upon to heal the wound. If the conditions are favorable for growth, the cambiums and the cells newly formed from them develop a mass of tissue known as the *callus*, which spreads over the wound and forms a cap-like covering. The development of the callus depends very much upon the nature of the wound and where it is made. The cut should be made with a sharp tool, and so made that the stem will not be split. When a small branch is cut off, the cut should be made just above a bud, as shown in *Figure 203*, so that the leaves developed from this bud will supply food for the formation of the callus. If the wound is too far above a bud, or if the cut is so close that the bud is destroyed, then there will be a dead stump which will not heal. Side branches should be pruned close to the main branch, so that the cambium of the main branch can heal the wound. In *Figure 204* is shown an example of improper

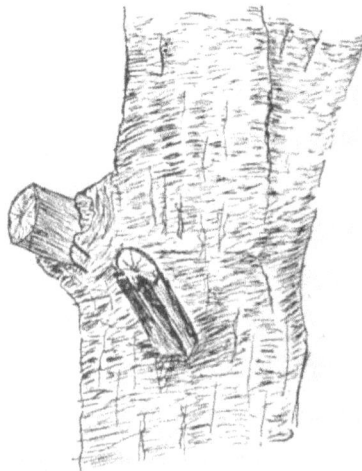

FIG. 204. — An example of bad pruning, showing the dead stubs of branches which may lead to the destruction of the tree. After Bailey.

pruning, in which case there is a stump which will not heal and its decay may result in the destruction of the tree. In *Figure 205* is shown a cut made in the proper way. In this case a callus is forming and enclosing the wound.

The Propagation[1] of Plants by Means of Stems

Some plants, of which the Irish Potato is a familiar example, are propagated almost entirely by planting portions of their stems, which are capable of developing roots and shoots from their nodes. (*Fig. 206.*) A notable example in Southern countries is

FIG. 205. — An example of a wound so made that a callus is closing over it. After Bailey.

the Sugar Cane, which is propagated by planting sections of stalks from which new plants develop. In the propagation of fruit trees, Grapes, Cranberries, Roses, Geraniums, Carnations, and many other plants, stems are used, although not always in the same way.

Propagation by stems is often preferable to propagation by seeds, because by the former method the new plants are more likely to be of the parent type. This fact is demonstrated in propagating Apple trees, which seldom come true from seeds, but do when propagated by grafting. Another advantage of propagation by stems is that new plants can be obtained in less time than by seeds. By means of cuttings new Geraniums or Carnations of considerable size are obtained in a few weeks. Propagation by stems may be by *cuttings, layering, grafting,* or *budding.*

Cuttings. — In the study of prostrate and underground stems, it was noted that nodes of stems can develop roots as well as shoots. This makes it possible for a portion of a stem to become an independent plant under proper conditions. Consequently, many plants are reproduced by setting detached portions of their

[1] The propagation of plants. *Farmers' Bulletin 157*, U. S. Dept. of Agriculture.

stems in soil, sand, or water where they develop roots and become as self-supporting as the parent plant. Such detached portions are known as *cuttings* and consist of a small portion of a stem, as *Figure 207* illustrates, or only of a leaf, as in the propagation of

FIG. 206. — The Irish Potato, showing new plants developing from the eyes.

FIG. 207. — Geranium cutting, showing the roots developing at the cut end.

Begonias and a few other plants having fleshy leaves as shown in *Figure 208*. Among cultivated herbaceous plants which are propagated by cuttings, the Irish Potato, Geranium, Carnation, and Coleus are familiar examples. In Southern countries the use of cuttings is well illustrated in the propagation of Sugar Cane, as shown in *Figures 209* and *210*. Other plants of the Grass family, as Johnson Grass and Bermuda Grass, are sometimes propagated by cutting the underground stems into short pieces, which are used in setting fields to grass. Unintentionally, but often to his sorrow, the farmer helps bad weeds, such as Quack Grass and Marsh Smartweed (*Polygonum Muhlenbergii*), to spread by scattering portions of their underground stems while putting in and cultivating crops.

Cuttings, known as *hard-wood cuttings*, are commonly employed in propagating such woody plants as the Grape, Currant, Gooseberry, Willows, Poplars, and many ornamental shrubs. They may be made in different ways as shown in *Figure 211*, but in each case they must have at least one bud.

Layering. — A layer is a branch which is put in contact with the soil and induced to develop roots and branches while still in contact with the parent plant. After a layer has developed roots and branches, it is separated from the parent and becomes an independent

Fig. 208. — The Life Plant (*Bryophyllum calycinum*) developing young plants on the margins of the leaves. About one-half natural size.

plant. There are different methods of layering, but usually the branches are bent to the ground and covered with dirt. In layering Grapes, a vine is stretched along in a shallow trench and buried throughout its entire length as shown in *Figure 212*. Raspberries and many shrubs are propagated by layering.

Grafting. — Grafting is the common method used in propagating fruit trees, and consists in so joining parts of different plants that they unite their tissues and live together as one plant. In grafting there are two members involved, the *stock* and *cion* or *scion*. The stock, which may be a root, stump, or almost the entire shoot, is the member which remains in contact with the soil, while the cion is the portion of a shoot, usually a twig or branch, which is to be made to grow on the stock. Since only growing tissues, such as the cambiums, are able to unite and heal wounds, it is necessary in grafting to have the cambiums of the stock and cion so adjusted that they can become grown together and thus form a perfect union. (*Fig. 213.*) However, only plants closely related can be successfully grafted, for in the protoplasms of un-related plants there are factors, probably differences in chemical nature, which prevent the union of the cambiums.

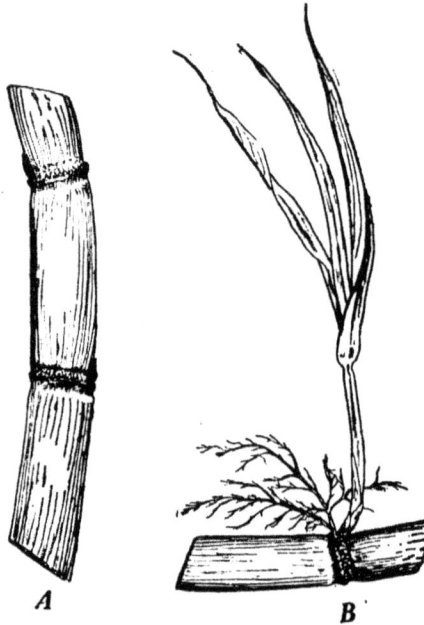

Fig. 209. — Cuttings of Sugar Cane. *A*, cutting, showing two nodes and a bud at each node. *B*, cutting, showing a new plant which has developed from a bud at the node. Adapted from N. A. Cobb.

When grafting is successful, the cion becomes as closely related to the activities of the stock as ordinary branches are. Through the stock the cion receives water and mineral elements from the soil, while the stock receives some of the foods made by the leaves of the cion. However, with all of this close connection, the nature of both stock and cion remains in most cases practically unchanged and each, therefore, continues to produce fruit unchanged in type. This feature is important for two reasons. *First*, it enables one to combine the desirable features of two plants into one individual where the desirable features, although remaining unchanged in nature, may assist each other in functioning. Some fruit trees bear delicious fruit, but on account of poor root systems or other causes they are not hardy. On the other hand, some trees are hardy but produce poor fruits. Now by grafting cions from the trees bearing delicious fruits on the hardy trees as stocks, one may obtain individuals that are hardy and at the same time bear

Fig. 210. — Cuttings of Sugar Cane being properly placed in the trenches, after which they are covered by dragging dirt into the trenches. After N. A. Cobb.

delicious fruits. *Second*, it enables one to preserve *bud sports*, which are individual branches that show qualities strikingly different from other branches of the same plant. Since bud sports rarely take root from cuttings or come true from seed, grafting is usually the only way of preserving them; and so important are bud sports that most of the best varieties of such fruits as Apples, Pears, and Oranges have originated as sports, which, after being grafted on stocks, became trees which by further grafting have been multiplied.

Often minor influences of the stock on the cion, such as dwarfing, hastening the fruiting period, or altering the time of blossoming, are desirable, and are obtained by grafting the cion on suitable stocks. For example, Pears are dwarfed and fruit at an earlier age when grafted on the Quince. Apples are influenced in the same way when grafted on the so-called " Paradise " stock, a name given to certain surface-rooting dwarf varieties of Apples. By grafting Pears on Pear stocks raised from seed or by grafting Apples on stocks raised from the seed of the Crab Apple, larger and longer-lived trees, which do not fruit so soon, are secured. It is claimed that in some cases the quality of the fruit is changed, having more sugar or more acid according to the nature of the stock. One of the most interesting and for a long time a very puzzling result of grafting is the *chimera*, which arises when a bud develops from the wound callus in such a way that the tissues of both cion and stock grow out together to form the branch. The tissues of the members may grow out side by side, in which case each member forms a side of the branch, or the tissues of the members may be so related to each other that one member forms the core and the other the covering of the branch. In either case both members may be represented in the leaves, flowers, and fruit of the branch and be the cause of very peculiar combinations of characters. For example, in Apples one side of the fruit may be of one variety and the other side of another variety. In grafting together Tomatoes and the Black Nightshade, the latter of which has small black fruits, chimeras in which one member formed the core and the other the covering of the branch have been obtained. As a result very queer fruits have been produced. Some resembled tomatoes in size but had the black skin of the Nightshade berry, while others were similar in size to the small berry of the Nightshade but had the yellow or red skin of the Tomato. Also in the character of the leaves and flowers, these chimeras presented queer combinations. By a study of chimeras produced experimentally, as those of the

Fig. 211.—Hardwood cuttings. *a*, simple cutting; *b*, heal cutting; *c*, mallet cutting; *d*, single-eye cutting. After L. C. Corbett.

Tomato and Nightshade just described, an explanation has been obtained for some so-called graft-hybrids, one of note being the *Cytisus Adami* which was produced many years ago by grafting together two shrubs, one having purple and the other yellow flowers.

FIG. 212. — Layering of the grape vine. The vine has been bent to the ground and covered, and from it roots and shoots are developing.

As a result of this graft and further grafting, shrubs having some branches bearing purple flowers and others bearing yellow flowers were obtained. Even a flower might be part purple and part yellow. For a long time some thought these strange plants were true hybrids, but now we are quite sure that they are only chimeras.

Budding. — Budding is similar to grafting, the principal difference being in the character of the cion. In budding, instead of twigs or branches, only a small strip of bark bearing a bud is used. This strip of bark, which is cut so that it has cambium on its inner face, is inserted into the young bark of the stock in such a way that the cambiums can unite. A study of *Figure 214* will show how the bud is inserted. After a T-shaped cut is made in the young bark of the stock, the bark on the edges of the cut is lifted and the cion is slipped in, the lifted bark on each side holding it in place. After the cion is in place, it is fastened more firmly by wrapping strings around the stem just above and below the inserted bud. Peaches are quite commonly propagated by budding and sometimes Apples, Pears, and other fruit trees are propagated in this way.

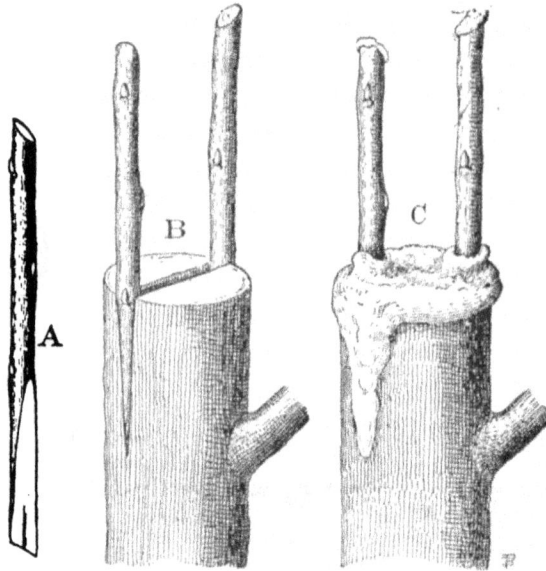

FIG. 213. — Cleft Grafting. *A*, cion; *B*, cions inserted in cleft of stock; *C*, the wound covered with wax. After G. C. Brackett.

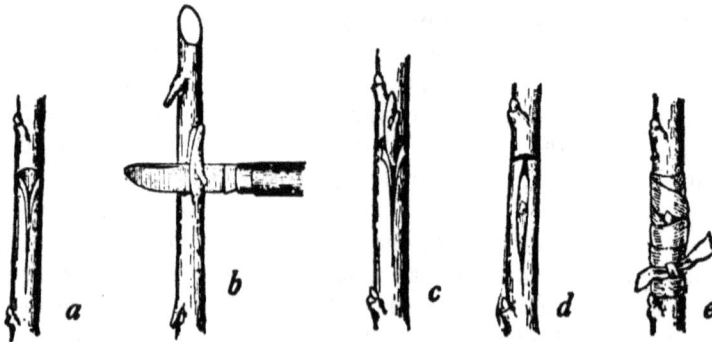

FIG. 214. — Budding. *a*, opening of bark for insertion of bud; *b*, removing the bud; *c*, inserting the bud; *d*, bud inserted; *e*, bud properly wrapped. After G. C. Brackett.

CHAPTER XI

LEAVES

Characteristic Feature of Leaves

Ordinary green leaves, known as foliage leaves, may be defined as the food-making organs of the plant. The green cortex of stems makes some food, but usually the greater part of it is made in the leaves. Leaves are constructed especially for utilizing the carbon dioxide of the air and the water brought up from the roots in the manufacture of sugar. Although starch may sometimes be the first food product formed by the leaves from carbon dioxide and water, the evidence indicates that ordinarily the first product is sugar from which starch is formed later. Sugar then may be regarded as the fundamental plant food, since from it or from the proteins of which it is the chief element, plants build by chemical transformations all of their structures and organic materials of whatever kind. Leaves transform sugar, when it is abundant, into starch which serves as a storage form of sugar. Although proteins can be made in any living part of the plant, it has been demonstrated that leaves are very active in the formation of this food. Although proteins may be regarded as a secondary food since they depend upon sugar as their chief foundational element, they are exceedingly important because from them the protoplasm, the living substance of the cell, is formed. Proteins, although of various kinds, are formed by combining chemically the mineral elements of the soil, such as nitrogen, sulphur, and phosphorus, with the elements of sugar. Since leaves manufacture sugar and are well supplied with the mineral elements, they are well equipped for the manufacture of proteins.

The efficiency of green tissue in making sugar depends upon exposure to light and air, and the foliage leaf may be considered a device for securing good exposure of green tissue. The elevating of leaves into light and air by the stem, and their arrangement, position, form, and structure are related to the problem of securing suitable exposure, and thus to food manufacture.

233

The variations in form and structure of leaves is so great that they are often used in classifying plants, and for this purpose many technical terms have been devised to describe these variations. Since most of these variations concern only those who are interested especially in the classification of plants, only the most common ones will be considered in this presentation.

Primary and Secondary Leaves. — Leaves may be divided into *primary* and *secondary*. The cotyledons are examples of primary leaves. The cotyledons are parts of the embryo and hence precede the stem in development, while the leaves developing later and called secondary leaves arise from the stem. The secondary leaves are usually numerous, while the primary leaves are few in number. Primary leaves are usually short lived and often fall away as soon as their stored food is exhausted. Generally they disappear while the plant is still quite small. Consequently the leaves of plants that attract attention are the secondary ones, and when the term leaves is used, secondary leaves are usually meant.

Development. — Leaves develop upon the sides of the growing points of stems and first appear as mere swellings, the smallest swellings being near the apex. It follows then that the oldest leaves are at the base of the stem or twig. Thus in a Corn stalk, for example, the leaves decrease in age from the lowest leaf on the stalk to the highest. Swellings similar to those that become leaves appear later just above the leaf swellings, and these become the buds which appear in the axils of the developed leaves. In woody plants which prepare for a rest period, the leaves are partly developed during the previous season, and rest in the bud in a miniature form until the following spring when they burst from the bud scales and in a few days complete their development.

Fig. 215. — Leaf of the Apple. *b*, blade; *p*, petiole; *s*, stipules; *r*, leaf base.

Parts of a Leaf. — In a typical foliage leaf, such as that of the Apple shown in *Figure 215*, there are three parts: the expanded portion or *blade;* the leaf stalk, called *petiole*, which supports the blade and makes connection with the twig; and a pair of small leaf-like appendages at the base of the petiole, known as *stipules*. The portion of the leaf at the point of contact with the twig or stem is called the *leaf base*. The leaf base is generally enlarged so as to form a sort of cushion by which the leaf is attached to the stem.

The leaves of most plants are not typical, but have one or more parts lacking. The stipules are very frequently absent. The leaves of the Thistle, Wild Let-tuce, Mullein, and many other plants have no petioles, the blade being directly attached to the stem. Such leaves are said to be *sessile* (mean-ing sitting). (*Fig. 216.*) In Corn, Wheat, Oats, and Grasses in general the leaves have no petioles and the leaf base is much expanded and enwraps the stalk completely for a considerable distance above the node. A leaf base enwrapping or sheathing the stem as just described for the

FIG. 216. — Sessile leaf of a Thistle.

Grass type of leaf is called a *leaf sheath*. At the juncture of the blade with the sheath in the Grass type of leaf occurs an outgrowth which fits closely to the stem and is known as the *ligule* or *rain guard*. In the Corn and some other plants of the Grass type small projections, known as *auricles*, occur at the base of the blade. (*Fig. 217.*) Leaves designated as *perfoliate* have their blades so joined around the stem that the stem appears to pass through the leaf as shown in *Figure 218*.

Leaf Blade. — In general, the leaf blade is expanded into a broad thin structure; but all gradations exist between such forms and those that are thick and fleshy or even cylindrical.

The border of the blade, called *margin*, may be smooth or quite irregular, and the character of the leaf margin is one of the features used in classifying plants. When the margin is smooth, as that of the Corn leaf, it is said to be *entire*. Irregular margins differ much in the form and depth of the indentations, as illus-trated in *Figure 219*. The margin may be cut up by many small notches, as the margin of the Apple leaf shown in *Figure 215*, or

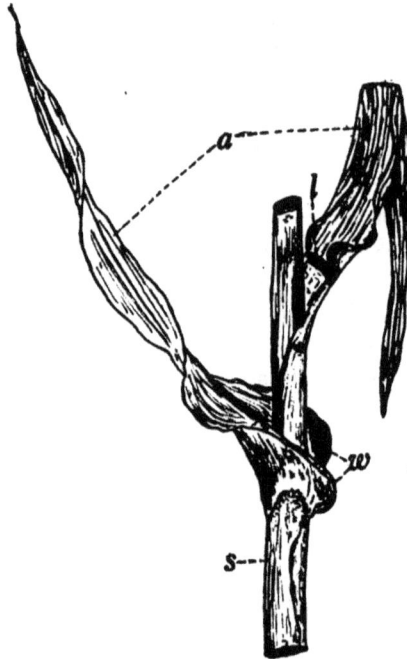

Fig. 217. — A portion of a Corn plant showing two leaves. *a*, leaf blade; *s*, leaf base called leaf sheath; *w*, auricles; *l*, ligule or rain guard.

Fig. 218. — Cup Plant (*Silphium perfoliatum*), a plant with perfoliate leaves.

the notches may be very deep and divide the blade into lobes, as the leaves of the Gooseberry, Cotton, Dandelion, some Oaks, Maples, and many other plants illustrate. In some cases the blade is so divided that it is made up of independent portions united to a common stalk, each independent portion being called a *leaflet*. Many familiar plants, such as Clover, Alfalfa, Vetches,

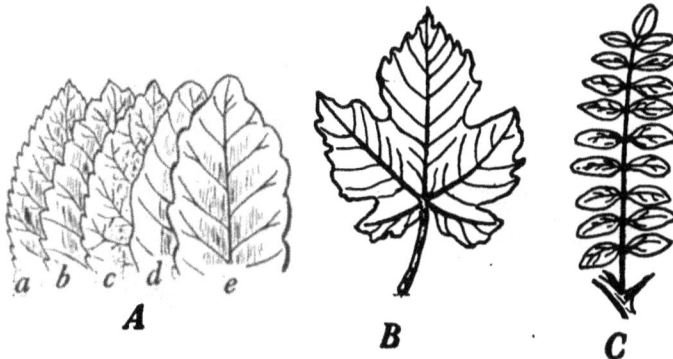

Fig. 219. — *A*, Margins of leaves. *a*, serrate; *b*, dentate; *c*, crenate; *d*, undulate; *e*, sinuate. *B*, lobed leaf of Grape. *C*, pinnately compound leaf of Black Locust. *A*, after Gray.

the Walnut, Ash, Locust, and Sumach, have leaves divided into leaflets. The number of leaflets into which the leaves of different plants are divided varies widely. In the leaves of Clover and Alfalfa three leaflets are common, while leaves of the Black Walnut often have twenty or more leaflets. (*Fig. 220.*) Leaves divided into leaflets are said to be *compound*, while those less divided are called *simple*.

Leaflets resemble simple leaves and in case of some compound leaves it is possible for one to mistake the axis to which the leaflets are attached for a branch of the stem and the leaflets for leaves. However, since buds occur only in the axils of leaves, one can tell whether the leaf-like structure is a leaf or a leaflet by the presence or absence of a bud in its axil.

Exposure to Light. — Unless the leaf is properly exposed to light, it can not be an efficient food-maker. It is not always a problem of securing enough light, but often one of escaping light that is too intense; for too intense light often injures leaves and consequently checks them in their work. The adjustment to light, therefore, is a delicate one, and many leaves do not have the proper amount of light.

The more or less horizontal position which the leaves of many plants assume enables them to receive the direct and most intense rays on their upper surface. Leaves in this position receive more light rays than those having the oblique or vertical position.

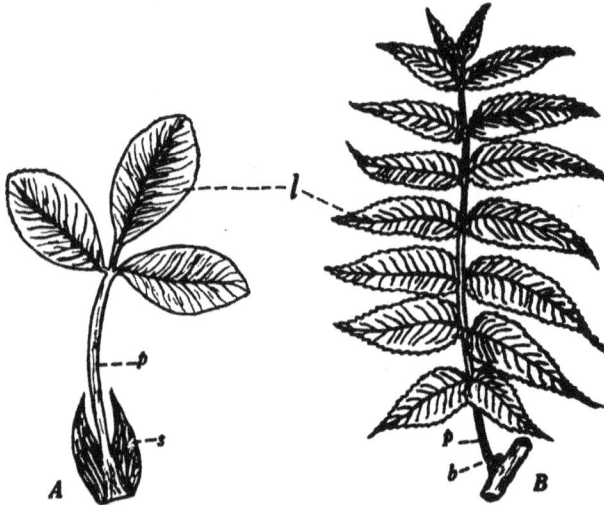

FIG. 220. — Leaves divided into leaflets. *A*, leaf of Alfalfa with three leaflets. *B*, Walnut leaf having many leaflets. *l*, leaflets; *p*, petiole; *s*, stipules; *b*, bud.

The separation of leaves through the elongation of the internodes is another means of securing better exposure. For example, during the early growth of the Corn plant, the leaves are closely packed around the growing point of the stem and only the outer ends of the blades are well exposed. But through the elongation of the internodes, all of the leaves are finally separated, so that at the time the tassel and ears appear all portions of the leaves receive light.

The way leaves are arranged on the stem is also an important feature in securing proper exposure. There are three common arrangements, *alternate*, *opposite*, and *whorled*. In the alternate arrangement, there is but one leaf at a node and they appear to alternate, first on one side of the stem, then on a different side.

The leaves of Corn and other Grasses are good examples of the alternate arrangement. In Corn, for example, the second leaf appears at the next node above and on the opposite side of the stem from the first leaf, and the third leaf appears at the third node and almost directly over the first leaf. Usually on account of a slight twisting of the stem, the leaf blades do not occur

FIG. 221. — Tobacco, a plant with the alternate arrangement of leaves. After Hayes.

directly over each other, but extend in slightly different directions, so that the lower leaves are not directly in the shade of the upper ones. In fruit trees and many other plants having the alternate arrangement, the second leaf is not quite on the opposite side from the first and neither is the third leaf usually over the first. (*Fig. 221.*) The leaves are so arranged that no large open spaces appear in looking in from the end of the twig as shown in

FIG. 222. — End view of an Apple twig, showing the leaves alternately arranged and so located in reference to each other that all receive light.

FIG. 223. — A Wild Sunflower with opposite arrangement of leaves. After Bailey.

FIG. 224.—Sweethearts (*Galium Aparine*), one of the weeds having leaves in whorls. After Beal. Mich. Agr. Exp. Sta.

Figure 222. Many trees as well as many herbaceous plants, such as Cotton, Clover, Alfalfa, Tomatoes, Potatoes, Buckwheat, and Flax, have the alternate arrangement of leaves. In the opposite arrangement two leaves appear at each node on opposite sides of the stem, and neighboring pairs are set more or less at right angles to each other, so that as one looks down from above each pair of leaves alternates in position with the pair above and with the pair below it as shown in *Figure 223.* The opposite arrangement is also common among both woody and herbaceous plants. In the whorled arrangement more than two leaves occur at a node, as illustrated in *Figure 224.* In this arrangement the leaves are also so placed as to shade each other as little as possible.

FIG. 225. — Dandelion viewed from above. The leaves form a rosette and the lower leaves are much longer than the upper ones. After Stevens.

In plants, like the Dandelion and Plantain, which have very short stems bearing many leaves, the leaves form a mat, called a *rosette,* on the surface of the ground. It is readily seen that leaves so closely crowded as they are in the rosette must shade each other considerably, but they have the advantage of being exposed less than those on elongated stems to the loss of water by transpiration. In the rosette much shading is eliminated by a difference in length of petioles, for the outer and under leaves of the rosette have longer petioles which push their blades beyond those of the upper leaves, and in this way they escape the shade of the leaves above. This feature is noticeable in the rosette of the Dandelion shown in *Figure 225.* Another arrangement of leaves which is favorable to light exposure is called a *leaf mosaic,* being so named

FIG. 226. — Nasturtiums showing mosaic arrangement of leaves.

from the fact that the edges of the leaves, as viewed from above,
fit together like the little tiles of a real mosaic. The fitting
together in this way is the best arrangement for the individual
leaves in a large mass to receive light. (*Fig. 226.*) A general
mosaic arrangement of leaves may be observed in connection with
almost every broad leaved plant, but is most noticeable in the
Ivies where their mosaic of leaves often completely cover the
surface of a wall. In case of stems exposed to direct light on
only one side, as the horizontal branches of trees, and stems
prostrate on the ground or in contact with a support, such as
Cucumbers, Melons, and climbing vines, the petioles of those

Fig. 227. — Maple twig, showing mosaic arrangement of leaves.

leaves on the under side of the stem usually curve so as to bring
the blades to the light. For example, in looking up into a tree
in full foliage, one will notice that the horizontal branches are
comparatively bare underneath, the leaf blades being displayed
on the upper side as a mosaic. (*Fig. 227.*)

When plants receive light from only one side, as plants grown
in a room near a window, the entire plant usually bends toward
the light, thus bringing the leaf blades into a better position for
exposure. (*Fig. 228.*)

General Structure of Leaves

Although diverse in form and arrangement, foliage leaves
show much uniformity in structure, being so constructed as to be
adapted to the function of food-making. In general, they have

FIG. 228. — Geranium growing near a window, toward which it is bending and thereby bringing the leaves in a better position in reference to light.

three kinds of tissues. *First*, there are the conductive tissues which bring the water and mineral salts to the leaf and carry away the manufactured foods. *Second*, there is the protective tissue consisting of epidermis which protects the delicate tissues within the leaf against drying, intense light, the entrance of destructive organisms, and to some extent gives rigidity to the leaf. In some cases there are special strengthening tissues developed within the leaf, either in connection with the conductive tissues or separately. *Third*, most important of all is the food-making tissue, known as the *mesophyll*, because it fills the interior of the leaf. The green mesophyll is usually called *chlorenchyma* because of its green color.

The Conductive Tissues. — The conductive tissues of leaves consist of vascular tissues similar to those of the vascular bundles

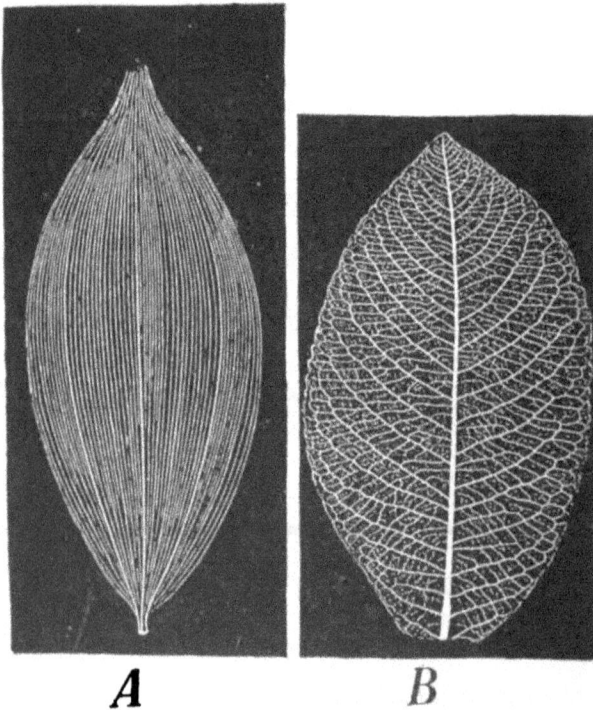

Fig. 229. — *A*, leaf of Solomon's Seal, showing parallel veining; *B*, leaf of Willow, showing net veining. After Ettinghausen.

of stems and roots. They constitute the veins. The veins are simply branches of the vascular bundles of the leaf trace, and the leaf trace is a branch of the vascular cylinder of the stem. Thus through the direct connection of the vascular tissues of the leaves with those of the stem, which in turn are in direct connection with the vascular tissues of the roots, all parts of the plant are brought into close communication for the exchange of materials.

The veins run through the mesophyll of the leaf and form a frame-work, which with its numerous fine branches, known as *veinlets*, resembles a fine-meshed net when a leaf is held up to the light. The finest veinlets can be seen only with the aid of the microscope. It is by this profuse branching of the veins and veinlets that all parts of the mesophyll are brought into direct contact or close relation with the conductive tissues. Although the larger veins are often thicker than the leaf and form prominent ridges on its under side, they taper down to the veinlets which are well buried within the mesophyll.

The character of the veining, known as *venation*, differs considerably in different leaves and there are two types of venation of some prominence. (*Fig. 229.*) One is the *parallel-veined* type, in which there are a number of parallel principal veins with obscure cross veins. This type is familiar in Corn leaves and is characteristic of monocotyledonous plants in general. The other is the *net-veined* type, in which there is one or only a few principal veins and their branches so fork and join each other that a quite noticeable network of veins and veinlets is formed as Maple or Oak leaves will illustrate. This type is characteristic of Dicotyledons. Many leaves have one large primary vein called *midrib*. Some leaves have a number of primary veins, which are then called nerves, and a leaf is described as three-nerved, five-nerved, or whatever the number may be.

Epidermis. — The epidermis forms a continuous covering over the leaf except where it is broken by the openings of the stomata. The stomata, although microscopical in size, afford the openings necessary for the exchange of gases between the interior of the leaf and the outside air. The epidermis is usually one layer of cells in thickness, but in some leaves, especially those of dry regions, it is often thicker. Except in the cells of the stomata, the epidermis usually contains no pigments, although it may appear to have since the green color of the mesophyll beneath readily shows through it. Sometimes the epidermis contains a red pigment, called anthocyan, which causes a part or all of the leaf to be red. Red pigment is often noticeable in the leaves of Sorghum and is common in some greenhouse plants of which the Wandering Jew is a familiar example. The epidermis when smooth has the appearance of having been greased, due to the deposits of cutin in its outer cell walls. Cutin usually forms a thin film called *cuticle* on the outer surface of the epidermis. Being a waxy substance and impervious to water, it makes the epidermis more protective against the loss of water. Sometimes, as in Cabbage, a waxy substance that can be easily rubbed off is deposited on the outside of the epidermis. Frequently, as the common Mullein and some Thistles illustrate, the epidermis develops hairs, which are sometimes so long and dense as to give the leaf a white woolly appearance. Some leaves, as those of the Mints illustrate, have glands that secrete fluids to which the odor of the plant is due. Some plants are cultivated on account of the commercial value of their glandular secretions. In many cases the epidermal secretions of leaves, if not unpleasant to the sense of smell, are to the taste, and therefore may protect plants against being eaten by stock. In fact all of the epidermal modifications are supposed to be related to the protection of the plant in one way or another.

Mesophyll. — The mesophyll, as the term suggests, occupies the middle region of the leaf and its distinctive feature is its green color upon which the power to manufacture food depends. It is soft spongy tissue and is composed of a number of layers of cells which surround the smaller conductive tracts and fill the spaces between.

FIG. 230. — A much enlarged surface view of the lower epidermis of a Bean leaf. *a,* epidermal cells; *s,* stomata; *g,* guard cells; *t,* slit-like opening between the guard cells through which gases pass.

It is so delicate in structure and so closely joined to the epidermis that in most leaves it is difficult to remove the epidermis without tearing away some of the mesophyll.

Cellular Structure of Leaves

To learn the finer structural features of leaves, a microscope must be employed, so that the cells of the different leaf tissues may be studied.

A surface view of a small portion of epidermis stripped off and highly magnified is shown in *Figure 230*. The epidermal cells in this view are irregular in shape, but so closely fitted together that no openings occur except through the stomata. A stoma (singular of stomata) is a definite structure, consisting of two curved cells, known as *guard cells*, which are so fitted together as to enclose a slit-like opening. The guard cells are so named because they regulate the size of the opening. Some plants, such as the Grasses of which Corn is a familiar example, have a peculiar type of guard cells as *Figure 231* shows. In this case the guard cells are enlarged at the ends, and resemble dumbbells in shape. However, this difference in shape seems to have nothing to do with their behavior, for they open and close their slit-like opening just as the ordinary type of guard cells is able to do.

By changes taking place within the guard cells, the stomata are opened and closed, but the causes of such changes are not definitely known. The guard cells have chloroplasts, and there is considerable evidence that the chloroplasts have something to do with bringing about these changes. Since chloroplasts make sugar and have the power to transform sugar into starch

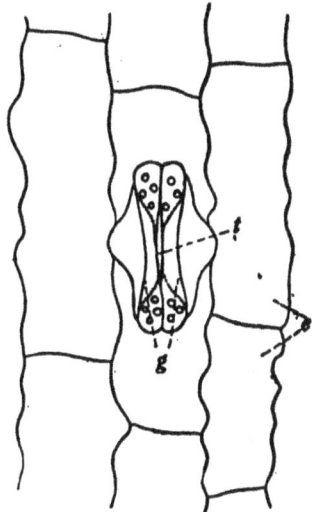

FIG. 231. — A much enlarged surface view of the epidermis of Corn, showing one stoma. *g*, guard cells; *t*, slit-like opening; *e*, epidermal cells. The chloroplasts are in the ends of the guard cells.

or starch into sugar, it is evident that they can alter the concentration of the sugar in the cell sap and in this way alter the turgor pressure of the guard cells. For example, if the chloroplasts of the guard cells manufacture much sugar which is allowed to concentrate in the cell sap, then by the principle of osmosis the guard cells draw in water forcibly and develop a high internal pressure which tends to expand them and alter their shape. On the other hand, if the chloroplasts remove the sugar from the cell sap by changing it into starch, which is insoluble, the result may be that the guard cells then tend to shrink through lack or loss of water, since their power to draw in and retain water decreases with the loss of dissolved substances from their cell sap. Regardless of what the chloroplasts have to do with it, it is obvious that when the guard cells are swollen with water they bow out, that is, curve away from each other and make the slit larger. On the other hand, when the guard cells are shrunken through the loss of water, they straighten and make the slit smaller. Hence the stomata tend to open when the water supply is abundant and close when water is scarce.

The importance to the plant of closing the stomata when water is scarce is apparent, for much water can be lost through open stomata. It would seem, therefore, that the guard cells regulate the loss of water from the plant and this they do to some extent. However, it has been found that stomata open in light and close in dark, and this tendency of light to open, conflicts with the tendency of water shortage to close them; for it is during bright hot daytime when the light stimulus to open is probably strongest, that there is the greatest shortage of water. That the guard cells open and close just when they should in order to control water loss is much doubted. The most important feature of stomata is that they permit exchange of gases.

Leaves having the horizontal position have their stomata much more abundant on the under surface; often they are not found at all on the upper surface. On leaves that stand more or less erect, as those of the Grass family and Carnations, the stomata are about equally distributed on both sides, and on leaves which lie on the surface of the water, like those of the Water Lily, they occur only on the upper side. The location of the stomata on the under surface of horizontal leaves is an advantage to the plant, since here the stomata are less likely to become choked with water during rains, and also less water is lost through them by evaporation.

The number of stomata varies much with different plants, but about sixty thousand to the square inch is a fair average. On the leaves of some plants there may be as many as four hundred thousand to the square inch. In the table on the next page are given the number of stomata found on a square millimeter of leaf surface of some common plants.

NUMBER AND DISTRIBUTION OF STOMATA PER SQUARE MILLIMETER OF LEAF SURFACE

Plant	Lower Surface	Upper Surface
Lilac (Syringa vulgaris)	330	0
Alfalfa (Medicago sativa)	160	160
Bean (Phaseolus vulgaris)	281	40
Tomato (Lycopersicum esculentum)	130	12
Cherry	160	0
Pumpkin (Cucurbita pepo)	269	28
Oats (Avena sativa)	{ 27 23	{ 48 25
Corn (Zea Mays)	{ 158 68	{ 94 52

Although stomata are most numerous on leaves, they occur in Flowering Plants wherever there is green tissue to be supplied with gases. They are common on fruits, green twigs of trees, and are present on nearly all parts of the aërial stems of herbaceous plants. On the older twigs and trunks of trees, the stomata are represented by the *lenticels* which are the structures into which stomata are transformed as the stem becomes enclosed in bark. The stomata are distorted and transformed into lenticels partly by the stretching of the bark and partly by the tissue which grows up from beneath and crowds into the stomatal openings.

In order to get a view of the epidermis in cross section and to study the chlorenchyma and veins of a leaf, a thin section must be made and highly magnified as shown in *Figure 232*. In this view an ordinary epidermal cell is rectangular, has a large central cavity separated from the cell walls by only a thin layer of protoplasm, and has the outer wall more thickened than those within. The continuity of the epidermis is interrupted by the stomata, each of which opens into an *air chamber* in the mesophyll just beneath.

The chlorenchyma is composed of thin-walled cells, having thin layers of protoplasm in which the characteristic green bodies (*chloroplasts*) are located. In most horizontal leaves, the cells of the chlorenchyma are differentiated into two distinct groups, the *palisade* and the *spongy* tissue. The palisade tissue is next to the upper epidermis and consists of one or more rows of compact elongated cells in which chloroplasts are especially abundant.

In leaves having an oblique or vertical position, palisade tissue may be present also on the lower side. The spongy tissue, having fewer chloroplasts and so characterized on account of its loose structure, occupies the region between the palisade tissue and lower epidermis or the region between the palisade tissues when there is a lower palisade tissue present. It consists of cells irregu-

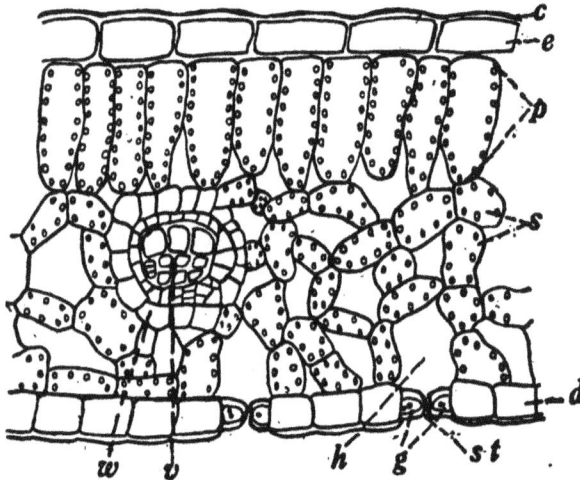

FIG. 232. — Cross section of a Tomato leaf. *e*, upper epidermis; *c*, cuticle; *p*, palisade cells; *s*, spongy cells; *d*, lower epidermis; *st*, stoma; *g*, guard cells of the stoma; *h*, stomatal chamber; *v*, vein; *w*, parenchyma sheath of the vein. The small bodies shown in the palisade and spongy cells are the chloroplasts.

lar in shape and so loosely joined as to provide a system of air spaces which extend in all directions reaching from the stomata into the palisade tissues. In function, which is the manufacture of food, the palisade and spongy mesophylls are identical.

Structurally chlorenchyma cells are well adapted to their function. Their thin cellulose walls permit water and substances in solution to pass in or out readily. They have protoplasm, which, as in all living cells, is the substance endowed with life and, therefore, able to regulate its activities. The cytoplasm (the name applied to all of the protoplasm except the nucleus) only partially fills the cell cavity, forming only a peripheral layer. In this peripheral layer the nucleus and also the chloroplasts are located. Such an arrangement of the protoplasm places the chloroplasts around the cell wall where they are well exposed to light, and provides a large central vacuole which accommodates a large quantity of cell sap consisting of water in which sugar, carbon dioxide, oxygen, mineral salts, and other substances related to the activities of the cell are dissolved. (*Fig. 233.*) Through the layer of protoplasm, the outer border of which behaves as an osmotic membrane, the cell sap osmotically pulls in water from the veins or surrounding cells, and in this way develops a pressure which distends and gives rigidity to the cell. Its cells being rigid, the leaf is rigid and expanded to the light. That this pressure or turgor within the cells gives rigidity to the leaf is shown by the fact that leaves wilt when water is so scarce that the cells can not maintain their internal pressure.

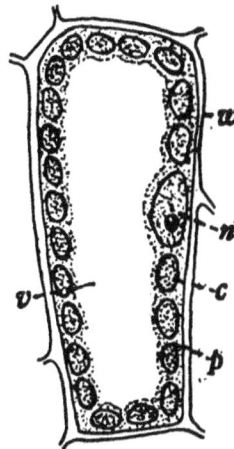

The chloroplasts, usually oval in shape in Flowering Plants, consist of two substances. *First*, the chloroplast has a body which consists of cytoplasm denser than ordinary cytoplasm and known as a plastid. Plastids multiply by constricting into two equal parts, and are as colorless as cytoplasm unless they develop pigments. *Second*, there is the chlorophyll which is the green pigment that saturates the plastid, which is then known as a chloroplastid or by the shorter term *chloroplast*. In the higher plants the

Fig. 233. — Chlorenchyma cell of a leaf, showing wall (*w*) and layer of protoplasm (*p*) containing the nucleus (*n*) and chloroplasts (*c*). *v* is the large central vacuole.

chlorophyll is developed by the plastids and does not occur except in connection with these bodies. Plastids are common in all parts of the plant. In regions where they develop no pigments, the formation of starch from the sugar present is their chief function. They are even abundant in underground organs, such as fleshy stems and roots, which store starch.

The presence of chlorophyll depends mainly upon exposure to light. That chlorophyll disappears in the absence of light is well demonstrated by the fact that leaves lose their green color when light is excluded for a time. Thus Grass under a board or covered with dirt becomes yellow. On the other hand, when leaves lacking chlorophyll, as those of plants allowed to develop in the dark, are brought to the light, chlorophyll develops. Even some underground structures, as Potato tubers, will develop chlorophyll when exposed to the sun. Hence the development of chlorophyll as well as its functioning depends upon the presence of light. Although the body of the chloroplast can make starch regardless of the presence of pigment or light, its power to make sugar depends upon the presence of chlorophyll and light.

The veins in cross section show as colorless often glistening areas in the mesophyll. In the central region of a vein are the two conductive tissues, the xylem and phloem. The xylem, consisting of large, empty, tube-like vessels with spiral, annular, and other kinds of thickenings in their walls, occupies the upper region of the vein. The xylem carries the water and mineral elements to the leaf tissues. In the lower region of the vein is the phloem made up of small thin-walled cells. The phloem carries away the proteins and some of the sugar made by the leaves. The *bundle sheath*, consisting of a chain of cells having large cavities and well adapted to conduction, forms a sheath-like covering around the vein. Through the bundle sheath much of the sugar is carried away from the leaf.

The Manufacture of Food by Leaves

Sugar, starch, and proteins are formed in leaves, but it is the manufacture of sugar that is the special function of leaves. There are various kinds of sugar, but there is considerable evidence that grape sugar, having the formula $C_6H_{12}O_6$, is the chief one formed in leaves. From this sugar as a basis other kinds of sugar, of which cane sugar ($C_{12}H_{22}O_{11}$) is a common one, can be formed by minor chemical changes. The formation of grape sugar is a synthetic process and, since light is necessary, the process is called *photosynthesis*.

Of all plant processes, photosynthesis is the most important, for upon sugar as an indispensable constituent the formation of other kinds of food either directly or indirectly depends. Thus without the formation of sugar, such foods as starch, fats, and proteins could not be formed, and consequently neither plants nor animals could exist. In considering photosynthesis there are two main topics: *first*, the nature of the process in reference to the materials used, the work of the chloroplasts, and the function of light;

and *second*, the various factors which modify the rate of photosynthesis.

As the student already knows, carbon dioxide and water furnish the elements from which sugar is synthesized. The carbon dioxide is obtained from the air through the stomata, while the water is brought up from the roots through the vascular system, which through its numerous fine divisions in the mesophyll supplies either directly or indirectly all of the chlorenchyma cells. The carbon dioxide is dissolved in the water with which it passes into the cells and comes in contact with the chloroplasts where the photosynthetic process takes place. The details of the process involved in forming sugar from carbon dioxide and water are not well known; but, leaving out the intermediate steps, the equation $6CO_2 + 6H_2O = C_6H_{12}O_6 + 6O_2$ represents the nature of the process. From the equation it is seen that there are as many molecules of oxygen liberated as molecules of carbon dioxide used. Whether all or only a part of the $6O_2$ liberated for each molecule of sugar formed comes from the carbon dioxide is not known. It is possible that only the carbon of the carbon dioxide is used, in which case all of the oxygen liberated comes from the carbon dioxide, or it may be that both water and carbon dioxide have their constituents dissociated and some oxygen from each is included in the $6O_2$.

Since photosynthesis removes carbon dioxide from the air to which it returns an equal amount of oxygen, it is obvious that it purifies the air and makes it more wholesome for animal life; for animals in their respiration use oxygen and liberate carbon dioxide, which, if allowed to accumulate, becomes injurious to animals. Not only ordinary respiration of both plants and animals but also fermentation, ordinary combustion, and all other processes which use oxygen and liberate carbon dioxide have their effects on the air counteracted by photosynthesis. On the other hand, the oxidation processes maintain the supply of carbon dioxide for photosynthesis. Thus photosynthesis and the oxidation processes tend to support each other.

Photosynthesis takes place in the chloroplast, but the exact function of either the body or the chlorophyll of the chloroplast is not known. It is generally believed that the chief function of the chlorophyll is to provide energy for the process; and this it does by transforming the sun's rays into available forms of energy.   The need of energy for photosynthesis is easy to understand.   The combining of the elements of carbon dioxide and water into sugar is preceded by a process of dissociation in which carbon dioxide and probably water are in part at least separated into their elements.   But carbon dioxide and water are very stable compounds, and to separate them into their atoms requires much energy.   To force the atoms of CO_2 to separate requires an energy expressed by a temperature of 1300° C.   It is obvious that sunlight will not decompose carbon dioxide and water; for, if so, these elements would be decomposed in the air.   Therefore, the chlorophyll must change the sun's rays into a form of energy which is available for bringing about these dissociations.   However, this energy consumed in bringing about these dissociations is not lost, but is stored in the sugar as latent energy to be released when the sugar or the compounds formed from sugar are broken into simpler compounds or into carbon dioxide and water.   Thus another relation of photosynthesis to respiration and other oxidation processes now appears.   Photosynthesis stores the sun's energy in chemical compounds which, when broken into simpler compounds by respiration, become a source of energy for all other plant or animal activities.   It is also the sun's energy that is released when coal, wood, oil, and other plant or animal products are burned.   Thus the chloroplasts, enabled by their chlorophyll to utilize the sun's energy, stand out as the plant structures upon which our supply of both food and energy depends.

The utilization of only certain rays of the sun accounts for the color of leaves.   When chlorophyll is boiled out of leaves with alcohol and the solution is viewed with a spectroscope, it is seen that the red and blue rays are absorbed while most of the green rays are allowed to pass through.   This experiment demonstrates that chlorophyll uses the red and blue rays for energy and allows the green rays to escape.   Thus leaves are green because from them only green rays come to our eyes.

By imagining a chloroplast as a factory, the process of photosynthesis may be summarized in the following way: the chlorophyll is the machinery by which sunlight, the source of power, is applied to the work; carbon dioxide and water are the raw materials; sugar is the product synthesized; and oxygen is a by-product.   The veins are the lines of transportation which bring up the water from the roots and carry away the manufactured products to all parts of the plant.

The formation of starch, although common in leaves, does not depend upon the presence of light except in so far as light is necessary in providing sugar; for starch is formed abundantly in many roots, tubers, and other structures where light is excluded. Starch, as its formula $(C_6H_{10}O_5)n$ shows, is very similar to sugar of which it is considered a storage form. Consequently its abundance in leaves where sugar is being formed is to be expected. Sugar is changed to starch not only to make room for more sugar, but also to prevent injuries that may result from its accumulation. According to the laws of osmosis, as the sugar content of the cell sap of the chlorenchyma cells increases, their internal pressure increases. Consequently when the chloroplasts are very active, the changing of the sugar into starch, which is insoluble in the cell sap, is necessary to prevent the internal pressure of the chlorenchyma cells from becoming so high that there is danger of bursting.

The transformation of sugar into starch not only prevents the accumulation of the sugar from interfering with the process of photosynthesis, but also enables the plant to have in storage food which can be drawn upon when conditions are unfavorable for photosynthesis. Thus at night when photosynthesis is inactive, the starch in the leaves is changed to sugar and carried to those regions where it is needed for growth, and in this way the plant is able to maintain its growth at night as well as in the daytime.

However, starch is not stored in all parts of the plant so temporarily as in foliage leaves. In some organs, such as seeds, fleshy roots, tubers, and stems of trees, starch is stored to remain as a food supply for next season's growth. Since the starch stored in all parts of the plant is transformed sugar which is made mostly in the leaves, the dependence of such structures as seeds, roots, and tubers upon leaves is obvious; for it is only as the leaves supply the sugar that these storage structures can form starch.

The amount of starch formed in foliage leaves is closely related to the rate of photosynthesis. In general, the more active the process of photosynthesis, the greater the amount of starch formed. For this reason the amount of starch present in leaves can be used in determining the rate of photosynthesis.

Starch occurs in the form of *starch grains*, which are light in color and have a characteristic shape and structure as shown in *Figure 234*. When starch grains are treated with iodine, they turn dark blue, and this color test can be applied directly to the leaf to indicate the amount of starch present and, therefore, the rate of photosynthesis. In applying the test, the leaf is first treated with hot alcohol to remove the chlorophyll. The leaf,

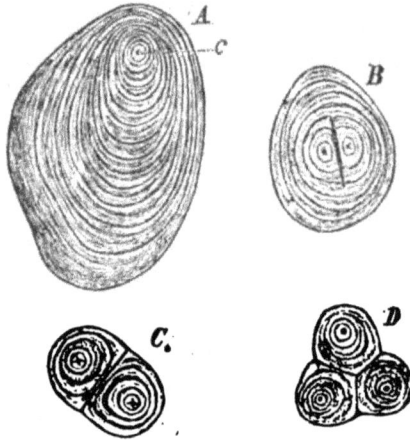

FIG. 234. — Starch grains from a Potato tuber. *A*, simple grain; *B*, half-compound grain; *C* and *D* compound grains. *c*, hilum. Enlarged 540 times. After Strasburger.

now almost white, is immersed in the iodine solution which turns it blue, if starch is present, with the depth of blue roughly indicating the amount of starch present. If no starch is present, then the leaf takes only the brownish color of the iodine solution. This test is of considerable service in experiments on photosynthesis as its application in *Figure 235* shows.

Proteins are made in leaves, but in what part of the leaf they are made is not known. The main evidence that they are formed in leaves is that large quantities of them are being continuously carried away through the veins to the stem. That light is essential in the formation of proteins is doubtful, for there is considerable evidence that the energy employed in their synthesis comes from chemical action and not directly from sunlight. Although proteins are of many kinds, all are formed by combining the elements of sugar, which is the foundational substance, with nitrogen, sulphur, and phosphorus derived from the mineral salts of the soil.   Even if the construction of proteins in leaves does not depend upon light, it is obvious that leaves are well equipped for such work, since they manufacture sugar and the water brought up from the soil supplies them with an abundance of mineral salts.

Factors Influencing Photosynthesis. — The factors influencing photosynthesis are light, temperature, moisture, and amount of chlorophyll.

That light is absolutely essential for photosynthesis is easily demonstrated by applying the iodine tests to two sets of leaves after one set has been kept in the dark and the other in the light for a few days. Even by shading only a portion of a leaf the necessity of light for photosynthesis can be demonstrated as shown in *Figure 235*. For photosynthesis sunlight is best, although some photosynthesis will take place in artificial light that has a suitable intensity. It has been demonstrated in

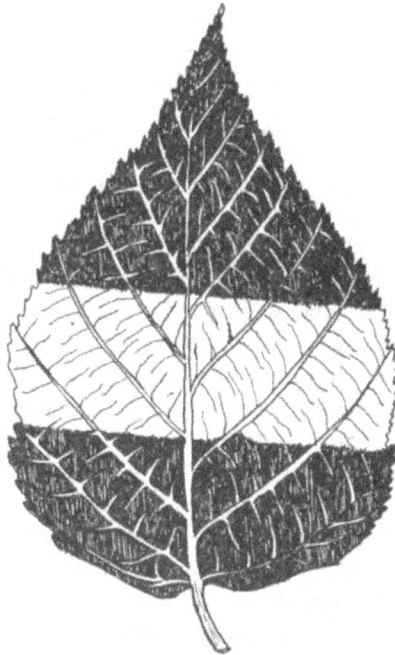

Fig. 235. — A leaf showing the relation of photosynthesis to light, as indicated by the amount of starch formed. After covering the area represented by the light band, the leaf was left exposed to the sunlight for a few hours, then removed from the plant and the iodine test applied. The area protected has no starch while the areas exposed are quite dark, due to the presence of much starch. Adapted from Palladin.

greenhouses that some plants, at least, carry on photosynthesis at night if the proper kind of electric light is provided. For many plants the direct rays of the sun are too intense, in which case photosynthesis is most active in strong diffuse light. It is partly for this reason that Pineapples, Tobacco, Potatoes, Cotton,

Lettuce, and some other plants grow better in some localities under the shade afforded by slats or light cotton cloth. In green-houses during the summer months it is usually necessary to protect the plants against the intense rays of the sun either by painting the glass or by some other means. Of course in shading plants not only more favorable light for photosynthesis is often provided, but the plants are also benefitted by being protected from intense heat, excessive evaporation, and from hail and winds. In many plants, as those of the Grass family, which seem to thrive well under the direct rays of the sun, the surfaces of the leaves slant so as to shun the intensity of the direct rays.

On the other hand, it is very common for leaves to be so situated that they do not receive enough light. This is commonly true of the lower leaves of the small grains, Clover, Alfalfa, and other plants grown in thick stands. Often the leaves on the interior branches of trees do not receive sufficient light. It is for this reason that fruit trees with open heads have better light relations for their interior branches than is afforded by trees with a compact head.

Plants growing in the house are usually insufficiently lighted, especially if they are not very near a window. The problem of overcoming so far as possible the insufficient lighting in green-houses during the winter months is of chief concern in greenhouse construction, determining largely the quality, thickness, and shape of the glass, and the nature of the frame.

What should be considered active photosynthesis, as deter-mined by the amount of starch produced per unit of time, varies widely with different plants. However, investigations show that a number of plants can produce 1 gram of starch per square meter of leaf surface per hour under conditions favorable to active photosynthesis. At this rate a leaf area of a square meter can produce 10 grams of starch in a day of 10 hours. To do this, all of the carbon dioxide would be taken from 250 cubic meters of air. Carrying the calculation further in regard to the use of carbon dioxide, it has been estimated that a yield of 300 bushels of potatoes on an acre involves, including tops and all, about 5400 pounds of dry substance, and to form this, all of the carbon dioxide over this acre to a height of $1\frac{1}{3}$ miles would be used, provided no carbon dioxide were added to the air in the mean-time. This estimate emphasizes the importance of respiration, combustion, and all oxidation processes in maintaining the supply of carbon dioxide for photosynthesis. Roughly estimated, 150 square meters of leaf area will use up in one summer all of the carbon dioxide which an average man produces through respiration in one year.

When one considers that the amount of carbon dioxide in the air is only about 0.03 per cent, that is, about 3 parts in 10,000 parts of air, it is surprising that plants can make sugar as rapidly as they do. Sometimes, as around cities with many factories, the per cent of carbon dioxide may be a little higher but it is always exceedingly low. Of course carbon dioxide is present in solution in the soil water; but it is easily demonstrated that this carbon dioxide is of practically no help to plants in photosynthesis. To compensate for the limited amount of carbon dioxide, it is obvious that leaves need broad surfaces and a thorough distribution of chlorophyll, so that their absorbing surface may be large. However, with all of these adjustments of the plant, it has been demonstrated that the normal supply of carbon dioxide is often insufficient for the maximum amount of photosynthesis; for some plants, when surrounded by air in which the amount of carbon dioxide is increased up to 1 per cent, show a corresponding rise in photosynthetic activity.

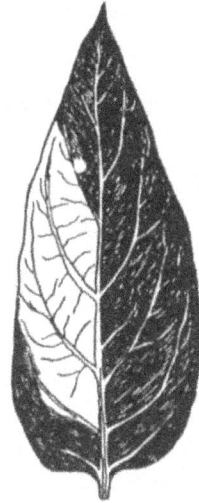

Fig. 236. — Leaf, showing the effect on photosynthesis of closing the stomata. The stomata on the under surface of the white area were closed by covering the epidermis with vaseline, thus filling the stomata and excluding carbon dioxide. After Palladin.

Since stomata are the openings through which carbon dioxide enters the leaf, their number per area of leaf surface and the extent to which they are open affect the amount of this gas that reaches the mesophyll. That photosynthesis is inhibited when stomata are closed is demonstrated by the experiment shown in *Figure 236*. The experiment shows the necessity of keeping the stomata free from dust and other bodies, such as spores of plants and secretions of insects, that clog the stomatal openings. It is for this reason that we are advised to cover house plants with a thin cloth while sweeping. Also for this reason it is well to spray with clean water or even wash the leaves of plants with clean rags, so as to open any stomata that may be clogged. Plants are often much injured by the clogging of their stomata, as in case of hedges along roadsides or plants around cement factories.

As for other plant processes, there is an optimum temperature at which photosynthesis is most active, and above or below this temperature photosynthesis diminishes. The optimum temperature, although varying considerably for different plants, is not far from 80° (Fahrenheit) for most plants in our region. Temperatures unfavorable for photosynthesis not only affect the yield of crops but also may lengthen the time required for maturity, as in case of Corn when the summer is cool.

Since water is one of the materials for making sugar, it must be present in sufficient quantities to supply this demand. Furthermore, the lack of water tends to cause the stomata to close and may thereby diminish the amount of carbon dioxide entering the leaf. In some cases, as in Corn, the lack of water causes the leaves to roll, in which case there is not a good exposure to light.

For the most active photosynthesis an abundance of chloroplasts well supplied with chlorophyll is also necessary. As farmers know, Corn pale in color does not grow so rapidly as Corn that is dark green.

Transpiration from Plants

Transpiration is the loss of water in the form of vapor from living plants. Transpiration, although similar in many ways to ordinary evaporation, differs from the latter process in that it is modified by the structures and vital activities of the plant. By transpiration plants are almost constantly losing water to the air. It is for this reason that shoots quickly wilt when their connections with roots are severed, so that they receive no water from the soil to compensate for the loss of water to the air. The rapidity with which green grass or weeds wilt when mowed on a hot day is a matter of common observation. Transpiration is not limited to leaves; but all parts of plants above ground are exposed to transpiration. Fruits and seeds, although usually jacketed in a rather heavy covering, lose water during storage. Even during winter, the buds, twigs, and branches of trees are continuously losing water to the air. However, the leaves, on account of many openings and the exposure of much surface, are the regions where water is lost most rapidly. Transpiration is the chief enemy of plants and is an important factor in determining the form, structure, and distribution of plants.

The loss of water is not so much under the plant's control as photosynthesis and respiration are. Unless the air about the plant is already saturated with moisture — and it seldom is — it will take up water wherever water is available, and the moist tissues of plants are available sources of moisture. The air circulating through the inter-cellular spaces of the leaf receives moisture from the tissues, and consequently its moisture content becomes greater than that of the air outside of the leaf. But according to the law of diffusion, the water-vapor diffuses from the air within through the stomata to the drier air without, and this diffusion continues as long as the air within the leaf receives sufficient moisture from the tissues to maintain a moisture content greater than that of the air without. The more the moisture content of the air within and without differs, the more rapidly the plant loses water.

Transpiration can be easily demonstrated by enclosing a potted plant in a bell jar, taking the precaution to cover all evaporating surfaces, except the plant, with rubber cloth or wax. It can be demonstrated also by enclosing a branch of a plant in a flask. In a short time moisture collects on the glass, at first as a mist which may later form into drops and run down the sides of the jar or flask. (*Fig. 237.*) This indicates that the plant loses water to the air, which consequently becomes so nearly saturated that moisture is condensed on the glass. If a plant with pot protected from evaporation is exposed to transpiration and weighed at intervals, the loss in weight due to the loss of water through transpiration is quite marked.

The amount of water transpired, although varying much with conditions and in different plants, is always a large proportion of the amount absorbed. Despite the fact that much water is used by the plant in making sugar and other compounds and in maintaining the turgor of cells, much the larger proportion of the water taken in by the roots passes through the plant and out into the air. The amount of water transpired under various conditions ranges from almost zero up to 300 grams or more per square meter of leaf area per hour. For this unit of leaf area per hour, transpiration in greenhouses often drops to 10 grams or less at night and rises to 50 and often to 100 or more grams during the day. For plants outside where there is more exposure to transpiration the variation is much greater.

As compared with the dry weight produced, the amount of water transpired by the plant is surprising. It has been esti-

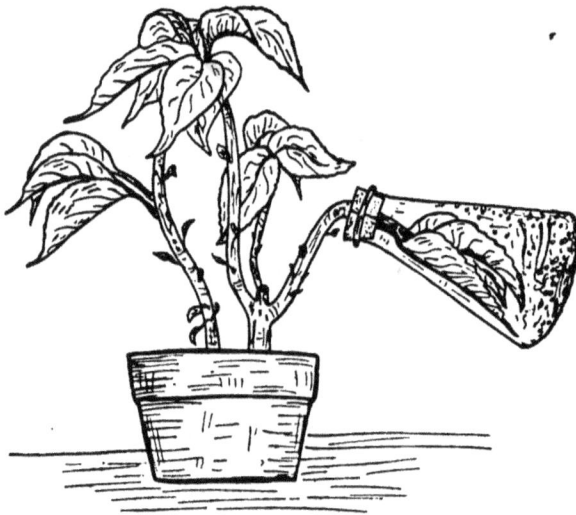

FIG. 237. — Branch of a plant enclosed in a flask in which the air has become so moist through transpiration from the enclosed leaves that moisture has condensed on the flask.

mated that in the Central United States about 425 pounds of water are transpired for each pound of dry matter produced by the plant. It is stated that for the production of one pound of dry matter, Corn requires 272, Potatoes 423, Red Clover 453, and Oats 557 pounds of water. Calculated on the same basis, the production of one acre of Oats of average yield requires 945 tons of water. According to estimates, an Apple tree having thirty years of growth may lose on an average of 250 pounds of water per day, or possibly 18 tons of water during a growing season. An orchard of 40 such trees would transpire about 700 tons in a season. It has been estimated that even an acre of Grass may transpire from 500 to 700 tons of water during a season. Now, if an orchard is in sod, then there is the loss of water from both trees and Grass. These estimates show the importance of maintaining for plants a suitable supply of moisture in the soil.

Conditions Affecting Transpiration. — The humidity of the air, temperature, light, and velocity of wind influence transpiration.

The *Humidity* of the air is an important factor in transpiration. Other conditions remaining constant, transpiration, in general, increases with the dryness of the air. For this reason hay cures quickly when the atmosphere is dry. It is also during hot days when the air is dry that plants are most likely to wilt.

Since *heat* hastens evaporation, transpiration usually rises with the temperature of the surrounding air. Also light, such as the bright sunshine that is common on hot days, is an important factor in raising the temperature of leaves, which thereby have their transpiration increased. In bright sunlight, a large per cent of the light absorbed by leaves is changed to heat, which may raise the temperature of the leaf to 10° or 15° C. higher than the temperature of the surrounding air; and this surplus of heat induces a more rapid vaporization of the water within the leaf.

The velocity of the wind is an important factor in transpiration; for it is well known that the movement of the air has an important effect on the rate of evaporation. Thus wind moving 30 miles an hour evaporates water about 6 times as rapidly as calm air. It is for this reason that muddy roads dry more rapidly on windy days. When the air is calm, the air about the plant becomes more nearly saturated and consequently ceases to take water from the plant so rapidly; but when the air is dry and rapidly moving, the plant is constantly enveloped in dry air which permits very little diminution in the rate of transpiration. When winds are both hot and dry, they are very destructive to plants. The dry hot winds of some of the Western states sometimes rob plants of water so rapidly that crops are killed in a few hours.

Advantages of Transpiration. — Transpiration is an advantage to the plant in two ways. *First*, it is an important factor in maintaining the flow of water and dissolved substances from the roots to the leaves and other portions of the shoot. *Second*, by lowering the temperature of plants, it often prevents injury from excessive heat.

As the student well knows, the movement of water and dissolved substances into and out of living cells is in accordance with the laws that govern the passage of liquids through membranes. But in passing from roots to leaves and other parts of the shoot, the water with the substances in solution passes through the tube-like xylem vessels, which are composed of the cell walls of dead cells, and in such cells, with cell membrane and all parts of the protoplasm absent, the structural features upon which osmosis depends are not present. Of course throughout the stem and roots the osmotic activity of living cells around the xylem may have something to do with the movement of liquids through the vessels, but this force combined with capillarity and root pressure seems entirely inadequate to carry water from the roots to the tops of tall trees. That transpiration has much to do with the movement of water through the xylem vessels has been quite well demonstrated by a number of experiments.

A column of water, due to the coherence of the water molecules, holds together much like a thread or rope. The coherence of water molecules is shown by the way water drops maintain themselves when hanging on the end of a pipette or on the eave of a building where, by accumulating and freezing while still clinging, they form icicles. It has been demonstrated that even very small columns of water, like those reaching from roots to the leaves through the xylem vessels, are able to endure heavy strains without breaking. Regarding the columns of water through the vessels as small but tough threads with one end in contact with the soil water at the roots and the other end in contact with the cell sap in the mesophyll cells of the leaf, it is evident that whenever water becomes scarce in the mesophyll cells through transpiration, then by osmosis these columns of water will be pulled in until the cells of the mesophyll are so filled with water and their cell sap so diluted that they no longer have the osmotic force to overcome the resistance of the water columns. But since transpiration is practically continuous, although varying much in rate at different times, the water columns are drawn into the cells of the mesophyll almost continuously, and hence the apparently continuous flow of water and dissolved substances through the xylem of plants. Thus, transpiration, by removing the water from the cells of the leaf and thereby causing the dissolved substances in the sap of these cells to become more concentrated, brings about the osmotic force by which the cells of the leaf draw in the water columns. The energy contributed by transpiration is really the heat-energy involved in changing water into vapor, in which form the water escapes from the plant. Such seems to be the relation of transpiration to the ascent of sap, but what other factors are involved and to what extent we have no definite knowledge, and, therefore, we may attribute too much to transpiration.

It was once generally believed that the flow of water through the plant is necessary to transport the mineral elements of the soil to the different regions of the shoot, and that the amount of the mineral elements reaching the leaves and other parts of the shoot is directly related to the amount of water flowing through the plant and, therefore, to transpiration. But some experiments indicate that in some cases,. at least, the process of diffusion by which the mineral elements and other substances in solution pass to those regions where they are less concentrated, regardless of the movement of the water in which they are dissolved, can supply the mineral elements to different parts of the shoot as rapidly as needed. In fact, in case of Tobacco plants, analyses have shown that plants grown in the shade may have a higher mineral content than plants grown exposed to excessive transpiration. In other words, the plants through which the least water flows may take the most mineral from the soil. However, since the water carries the dissolved substances along in its current, the movement of water through the plant tends to aid diffusion in the distribution of the elements in solution.

Since transpiration, like evaporation, is a cooling process, it often prevents leaves from becoming overheated. Sometimes bright sunshine, following a summer shower which has filled the air with moisture, results in the leaf injury known as *scalding*. Under these conditions, transpiration is checked and the temperature of the leaf becomes too high. As a large part of the sunlight is changed into heat by the leaf, the heat accumulates very rapidly in bright sunshine. It has been found in the case of some leaves that the excess of heat, if transpiration be stopped, may raise the internal temperature of the leaf to the death point in a few minutes. Transpiration, therefore, rids the leaf of the dangerous excess of heat.

Dangers Resulting from Transpiration. — So long as water from the roots can be supplied as rapidly as water is lost by transpiration, the plant is not in danger.   But it is not uncommon to see Corn with leaves rolled and Potatoes, Cotton, Clover, and other plants wilted during dry hot days.   These plants are losing water faster than it can be replaced from the roots.   These plants are in danger because their living cells are becoming dry, and too much drying results in death.   More plants die on account of transpiration than anything else.

The important thing for the plant is the maintenance of a proper balance between supply and loss of water.   The plant can endure rapid transpiration, if a copious supply of water is coming up from the roots; but, if the ground is dry about the roots, the root system small, or water hard to obtain from the soil, as is the

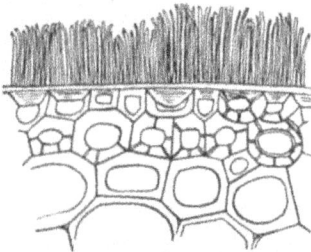

FIG. 238. — A portion of a cross section through a node of Sugar Cane, showing rods of wax secreted by the epidermis.   Enlarged many times.   After De Bary.

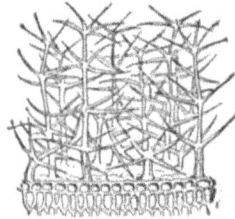

FIG. 239. — A portion of a section through a Mullein leaf, showing the epidermis with its branched hairs.   After Andrews.

case in soils that are cold or frozen, then even a small amount of transpiration may be injurious.

Protection against Injuries Resulting from Transpiration. — Plants may be protected against the injurious effects of transpiration by having their transpiring surface modified, or by having the soil moisture increased or conserved.

There are various ways in which plants modify their transpiring surface.   Some plants, such as the Carnation, Pine, and many plants of the desert, have the epidermis of their leaves covered with a heavy layer of cutin.   Sometimes, as in Cabbage, Sugar Cane, and Wheat, the epidermis is covered with a waxy bloom. (*Fig. 238.*)   Many plants are protected by a covering of hairs. (*Fig. 239.*)   Some plants, such as the Cacti of the desert, have reduced their leaves to mere spines which offer only little transpiring surface.   (*Fig. 240.*)   By reducing the number of stomata, as in many Grasses, or by sinking the stomata in special epidermal cavities, as in the Carnation, transpiration is reduced.

FIG. 240. — A globular cactus, an example of a plant having leaves replaced by spines. After J. M. Coulter.

Sometimes, as in the Corn, the rolling of the leaves decreases the surface exposed and lessens transpiration.   (*Fig. 241.*)   The

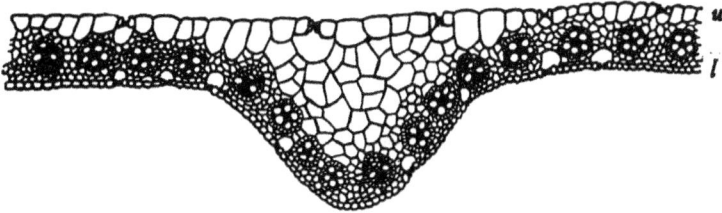

FIG. 241. — Cross section of a Corn leaf. *l*, lower epidermis; *u*, upper epidermis. Notice that the cells are larger on the upper side than on the lower side of the leaf. The cells of the upper epidermis, being larger, shrink more than those of the lower epidermis, and thus cause the rolling of the leaf in dry weather. Much enlarged.

leaves may have an edgewise position and thereby avoid the direct rays of the midday sun, as Wild Lettuce illustrates.

The shedding of leaves from the plant is an important means of protection.   Many of our trees shed some of their leaves during a summer drought and thereby decrease their transpiring surface. Of course this is not a protection to the leaves but to the plant. Most trees of the temperate region shed all their leaves in autumn. Such trees are known as *deciduous*. This shedding of leaves in autumn protects the plant against transpiration during winter. Even with leaves absent, trees are sometimes killed by transpiration from buds and twigs. The killing by transpiration in winter is not due to a great water loss, but to the inability of the roots to furnish water to compensate for the loss. Since the roots of most trees are not far below the surface, a deep freeze may freeze the water about them. Even when the soil is cold, roots take up water slowly, and when the water is frozen into ice, they can not absorb it at all. With only a little water furnished by the roots, a small amount of transpiration may be sufficient to cause the death of the cells in the buds and twigs.

In transplanting trees, it is usually necessary to prune the top, because the root system has been partly broken and cut away, and consequently is not able to furnish enough water to compensate for the amount transpired from a shoot of normal size. Pruning the top results in fewer leaves and hence less transpiring surface. Even after trees have been transplanted and well established, a reduction of the transpiring surface by pruning the top is often helpful, but usually the pruning of such trees has other purposes as pointed out in the study of buds. However, since the leaves are food-making organs, only a limited number of them can be removed or the plant will suffer from starvation.

Supplying moisture to the soil protects against injuries resulting from transpiration. Plants in the greenhouse must have the soil about their roots kept moist by watering. In the dry western regions water is supplied to the soil by methods of irrigation.

Much can be done in protecting against transpiration by conserving the moisture of the soil. If an orchard is in sod, many tons of water will be lost from the soil through the transpiration of the grass. By plowing and keeping the ground free from grass and weeds, the water of the soil is conserved for the fruit trees. In regions where dry farming is practiced, the ground is fallowed during one year and then seeded the second year. Fallowing consists in keeping the ground plowed and well harrowed, so that the surface will be covered with a mulch and be free from vegetation. This treatment allows the water from snows and rains to soak into the soil readily and also prevents much loss of water through evaporation. This stored-up water is then used by the crop during the second year.

Many plants which live in dry regions have regions of water storage. For example, the Cacti store much water in their stems and this storage enables them to withstand very dry periods. Some plants, like the Begonia, have special cells in their leaves for the storage of water. (*Fig. 242.*) In many plants, as in Corn, much water is stored in the pith.

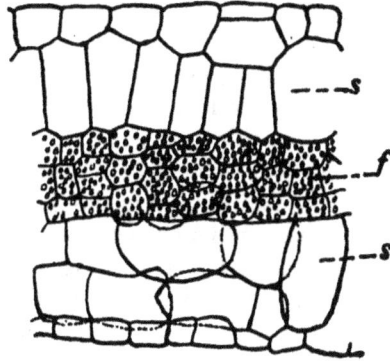

FIG. 242. — A small portion of a cross section of a Begonia leaf, showing water storage cells (*s*) and chlorenchyma (*f*).

Thus it is seen that transpiration is helpful when the water lost does not exceed the supply furnished from the roots; also that the rate of transpiration depends much upon temperature, humidity of the air, light, and velocity of the wind; and that the dangers of transpiration may be overcome by modifying the transpiring surface or by maintaining an adequate supply of water in the soil or in storage regions of the plant.

Respiration

Although respiration is a fundamental process in all living cells, leaves afford a good place for observing the outward signs of it. Most of the oxygen used in the respiration of the plant enters at the leaves from which place it is carried to all parts of the plant. Also through the leaves much of the carbon dioxide produced by respiration escapes to the air. Respiration and photosynthesis, although occurring together in leaves, are wholly separate processes as shown by the ways in which they differ. *First*, photosynthesis occurs in chloroplasts and is a synthetic process, in which the elements of carbon dioxide and water are built into compounds with the storage of latent energy, while respiration occurs in all parts of the protoplasms and is a process in which compounds are broken into their constituents, usually through oxidation, with the result that the latent energy is released to be used in various kinds of work. *Second*, photosynthesis uses carbon dioxide and releases oxygen, while respiration uses oxygen and releases carbon dioxide. Hence one liberates the gas which the other uses, and in this way the two processes tend to support each other. When both processes are active at the same time, as during the day, each process tends to obscure the other by using the gases liberated before these gases escape from the leaf. However, when photosynthesis is active, the amount of carbon dioxide used and oxygen liberated is so much greater than the gaseous exchanges of respiration that the latter process is entirely obscured. On this account, botanists once thought that respiration was a process performed only by animals and that the plant breathes in a way just opposite from that of animals. Of course further investigations showed that plants respire just the same as animals do, but in addition green plants carry on photosynthesis which, when active, so much obscures respiration that the latter process had escaped notice. *Third*, photosynthesis depends upon the presence of light, while respiration is independent of light, being active at night as well as in the daytime. At night when there is no photosynthesis to obscure respiration, plants take in oxygen and liberate carbon dioxide just as animals do, and the notion once prevalent that plants purify the air is only true of them when they are engaged in photosynthesis.

Respiration and transpiration, although influencing each other to some extent, are also distinct processes. Since respiration liberates energy, some of which is in the form of heat, respiration may increase transpiration by raising the temperature of the leaf. Furthermore, respiration in breaking down compounds releases water in the form of vapor, in which form it readily escapes to the air. On the other hand, when transpiration reduces the water content of cells so much as to interfere with the activities of the protoplasm, then respiration may be retarded.

Special Forms of Leaves

In contrast to the leaves which we have been studying, there are some leaves which have become so modified as to resemble ordinary leaves very little. Some have become so changed that

FIG. 243. — A portion of a Sweet Pea, showing one leaf (*l*), a portion of which is transformed into a tendril (*t*).

they have lost much or all of their power to make food, and have become apparently useless or have taken on other functions.

A very common modified form of the leaf is the *scale*. The most familiar example of scales is furnished by the buds of shrubs and trees, where they form a protection for the inner vital portions of the bud. These scales are considered leaves which have been prevented from developing by being so closely crowded in the overlapping arrangement. The leaves of underground stems, which do not get to the light, appear as small scale-like bodies without green tissue, and apparently have no function. Sometimes scales are fleshy and are used for food storage, as in Lily bulbs, Onions, etc.

FIG. 244. — A branch of a Barberry, showing the leaves transformed into thorns.

In the Asparagus the leaves are scale-like and the food-making is mostly done by the stem.

Leaves may sometimes develop into tendrils, either the entire leaf or only a part of it becoming tendrils, as in the Sweet Pea. (*Fig. 243.*)

In the Barberry and some other shrubs, the leaves are so modi-

Fig. 245. — Pitcher Plant, showing pitcher-like leaves (*l*).

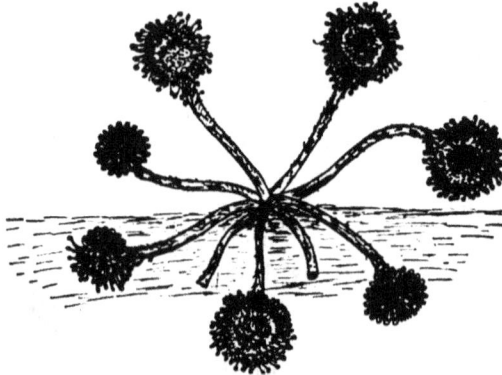

Fig. 246. — Sundew, showing the leaves which catch and digest insects.

fied as to form thorns. (*Fig. 244.*) Sometimes, as in the Common Locust, only a portion of the leaf is devoted to the formation of thorns.

The most interesting special forms of leaves are those adapted to catching insects. Plants with such leaves are often called "carnivorous plants" or "insectivorous plants." The "Pitcher Plants" are so named because the leaves form tubes or urns of various forms, which contain water, and to these pitchers insects are attracted and then drowned. (*Fig. 245.*) The plants known as "Sundews" have their leaves spread on the ground and clothed with secreting hairs. (*Fig. 246.*) These secretions not only entangle insects but digest them. In the "Venus Flytrap," portions of the leaves work like steel traps and hold the insects fast until digested. (*Fig. 247.*)

Uses of the Photosynthetic Food

In plants, as in animals, the chemical processes upon which growth and other vital activities depend are both constructive and destructive. While the simpler elements are being transformed into complex substances, complex substances through

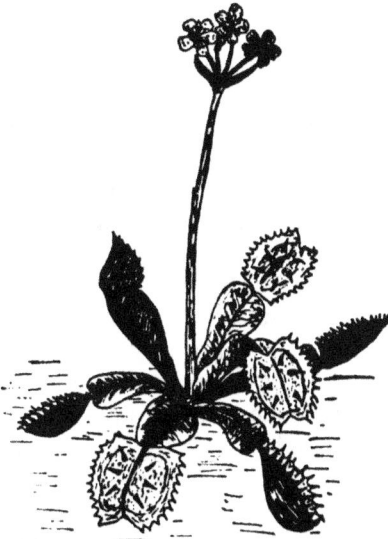

FIG. 247. — Venus Flytrap, showing the leaves which open and close in catching insects

respiration and other destructive processes are being broken into simpler substances. These chemical transformations constitute *metabolism*, and are said to be *anabolic* when constructive and *catabolic* when destructive. Through the plant's metabolic processes numerous substances are formed, of which protoplasm, proteins, sugars, starches, fats, oils, hemicellulose, amino-compounds, cellulose, wood, cutin, suberin, enzymes, acids, tannins, glucosides, and alkaloids are common ones. All of these substances are thought to be of some use to the plant, although the exact function of some of them is not definitely known.

The photosynthetic grape sugar, since there is much evidence that in most cases it is the chief food formed by photosynthesis, may be regarded as a foundational food; for the photosynthetic sugar furnishes either all or an important part of the constituents of which all other plant substances are composed. Even if light is essential to the formation of proteins, which are formed so abundantly in leaves and carried away like the photosynthetic sugar to other parts of the plant for use, sugar is an important constituent of proteins and is therefore a basal substance in their formation. Since animals obtain their food either directly or indirectly from plants, it is evident that the photosynthetic sugar is also the basal food for animals.

The various metabolic changes in the plant have to do with providing living protoplasm, a frame work, reserve foods, secretions, and energy.

Protoplasm. — It is in connection with protoplasm, the living substance of both plants and animals, that the metabolic processes occur. Protoplasm not only transforms substances enclosed within it but by means of enzymes which it secretes it is also able to act on substances with which it is not in contact. Within the protoplasm sugar is synthesized by the chloroplasts, and starch, proteins, fats, and many other plant products are constructed. At the same time substances are being constructed in the protoplasm, substances are also being decomposed, so that within the protoplasm substances resulting from both constructive and destructive processes are always present. So it is not at all strange that many kinds of substances are present in the protoplasm. Some, like starch and some proteins, are insoluble, while many, like the sugars and acids, are dissolved in the nuclear and cell sap. That protoplasm can transform substances with which it is not in contact is well illustrated in seeds, where enzymes secreted by the embryo diffuse out to the endosperm and transform it into soluble forms of food.

One of the important constructive processes of protoplasm is the formation of protoplasm. As the plant grows and more cells are formed, more of the elements of chromatin, nucleoli, cytoplasm, and all other protoplasmic structures must be formed.

As to the chemical composition of protoplasm in its living state, we have no definite knowledge. Chemical analyses of dead protoplasm show that a large number of substances are present, of which proteins are the largest and most essential part. The different kinds of proteins vary in composition, but all are composed chiefly of carbon, hydrogen, oxygen, and nitrogen. In addition to these elements, most proteins contain a small amount of sulphur and some proteins also contain a small amount of phosphorus. By chemically combining in certain proportions the carbon, hydrogen, and oxygen of the sugar with the nitrogen, sulphur, and phosphorus obtained from the soil, proteins are formed, but as to how the proteins are transformed into living protoplasm no one knows.

Framework of the Plant. — Protoplasm, since it is a semifluid, has no definite shape except when enclosed in a framework. It is by means of a framework that higher plants are able to so shape themselves as to be adjusted to the soil, air, and sunlight.

The cell walls constitute the framework. They are so joined as to divide the plant into the compartments in which the protoplasts or individual masses of protoplasm reside. The fact is, however, that each cell is enclosed by walls of its own; but the adjacent walls of neighboring cells are usually so closely joined that the cells appear to be separated by a single wall.

Fig. 248.—Cells with protoplasm shrunken, so that the fine strands of protoplasm extending through the cell walls and connecting neighboring protoplasts may be seen. Highly magnified.

Through very small pores in the cell walls, the protoplasts are commonly connected by small protoplasmic strands, which afford a means of communication between the protoplasts of neighboring cells. (*Fig. 248.*)

The primary substance of which cell walls are formed is *cellulose*, a substance closely related to sugar as its formula $(C_6H_{10}O_5)n$ indicates. In the formula $(C_6H_{10}O_5)n$ each combination $C_6H_{10}O_5$, of which an unknown (n) number are combined in forming cellulose, is a molecule of sugar minus a molecule of water as may be seen from the equation $C_6H_{12}O_6 - H_2O = C_6H_{10}O_5$. Thus the formation of cellulose involves no other elements than

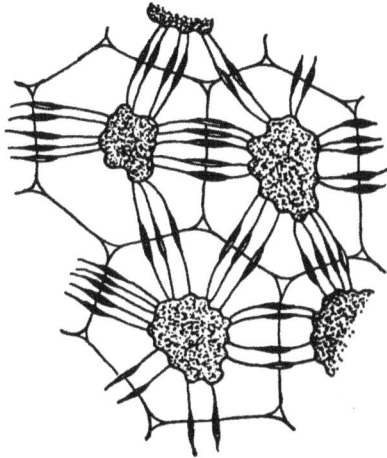

those of grape sugar and only slight changes in their proportion.

Cellulose is a suitable material for cell walls; for its elasticity permits cells to enlarge, and its permeability allows water and solutions of food to reach the protoplasm. In actively growing cells thin cellulose walls are essential, so that the cells can enlarge; but when the cells are to afford strength, as in case of bast fibers, then the cellulose is so deposited as to form thick walls. Commonly when an important function of the cell walls is to afford strength, another substance called *lignin* is formed from the sugar and combined with the cellulose, thus forming the wood characteristic of the trunks of trees and shrubs but also common in herbaceous plants. Also in the shells of some nuts and the coats of many seeds, lignified walls are common. Woody walls, like cellulose walls, are permeable to water and solutions, and for this reason are not adapted for protective coverings, where the prevention of loss of water is an important function. In forming waterproof walls, a portion of the sugar or cellulose is converted into fatty or wax-like substances known as *cutin* and *suberin*. Cutin is common in the outer walls of epidermal cells, while suberin occurs throughout the walls of cork.

Occasionally in the formation of cell walls, some of the sugar is converted into substances which swell and become mucilaginous when wet, as the seed coats of Flax and some Mustards illustrate.

Some other substances which are formed from sugar and associated with cellulose, lignin, cutin, and suberin in cell walls are the *pectic* compounds. The pectic substances (pectin, pectose, and pectic acids), although much like cellulose, are more easily decomposed by certain acids and alkalies. They are often combined with minerals, and one of the mineral compounds, known as *calcium pectate*, is the chief substance of the middle portion (middle lamella) or oldest portion of walls separating cells.

Besides the various substances formed from sugar, cell walls are often infiltrated with mineral matters, notably *silica*, and these minerals often add much strength to the frame work.

Cellulose and its closely allied compounds serve man in many ways. From cellulose paper is made, and long cellulose fibers, as those of Cotton and Flax, are woven into clothing. The wood of plants is the source of lumber. Being oxidizable, cellulose and its compounds serve as fuel, either in the form of wood, peat, or coal. Man converts cellulose into celluloid, artificial silks, artificial rubber, and powerful explosives, such as gun cotton.

Reserve Foods. — The photosynthetic sugar, which is not used immediately as food, is stored in seeds, stems, roots, and temporarily in leaves for use at some future time. The reserve foods into which the excess of photosynthetic sugar is transformed are of various forms, but are chiefly of three general classes — *carbohydrates, fats,* and *proteins.*

The carbohydrates include the *sugars, starches,* and *hemicelluloses,* and are so named because their proportion of hydrogen and oxygen, being the same as in water, suggested that they were compounds of carbon and water.

Sugars are of various kinds, but only a few occur in considerable quantities in the plant. *Grape sugar, fruit sugar,* and *cane sugar,* the most important of the sugars, are commonly present in the sap of plants. Grape sugar, called *glucose* or *dextrose,* and fruit sugar, called *fructose* or *levulose,* are the simplest of the sugars. They have the same formula $C_6H_{12}O_6$, but differ in the arrangement of atoms. Both are found in all parts of plants, but usually one is more abundant than the other. In sweet fruits and the nectar of flowers, fruit sugar is usually more abundant than either glucose or cane sugar, while in Sugar Cane, where both occur along with cane sugar, glucose is more abundant than fructose. Much glucose accumulates in the stems of Corn and other Grasses. Both glucose and fructose are produced not only synthetically, but also through the decomposition of some of the more complex carbohydrates. Thus when Cane sugar is boiled with hydrochloric acid, glucose and fructose in equal amounts are produced.

Cane sugar, called *sucrose* or *saccharose,* is the sugar of most service to man. It is present in the sap of most plants and accumulates in great abundance in Sugar Cane, Sorghum, Beets, and the Sugar Maple. From the stems of Sugar Cane and the roots of Sugar Beets many million tons of cane sugar are extracted each year. A molecule of cane sugar, as represented by the formula $C_{12}H_{22}O_{11}$, contains a molecule of glucose and one of fructose with a molecule of water dropped in making the combination. The formation of cane sugar is represented by the equation $C_6H_{12}O_6 + C_6H_{12}O_6 - H_2O = C_{12}H_{22}O_{11}$.

Another sugar, known as *Maltose* and having the same formula as cane sugar but differing in arrangement of atoms, occurs in germinating seeds, and is especially abundant in germinating Barley. It is formed when starch is broken into its components. Maltose, when broken into its constituents, gives rise to two molecules of glucose.

The *starches* are the most abundant storage forms of food into which the photosynthetic sugar is converted. They occur in all parts of the plant, but are especially abundant in seeds, tubers, and fleshy roots, where they are extensively used by man for food. The food value of Corn, Wheat, Rice, and other Cereals, and of Potatoes depends mainly upon the starch which they contain.

FIG. 249. — *a*, starch grain of Irish Potato; *b*, starch grain of Wheat; *c*, starch grain of Corn.

The starches, unlike the sugars, are insoluble and occur in the form of definitely shaped bodies, known as starch grains, which vary much in shape, size, and markings in different plants. (*Fig. 249.*) The size, shape, and markings of the starch grains are so characteristic of many plants that by a study of the starch grains in a mixture of ground vegetable products, the constituents can often be determined and the adulterants thereby detected.

Starch and cellulose have the same formula $(C_6H_{10}O_5)n$ but they differ in the number of combinations, $C_6H_{10}O_5$, contained in their molecules. Their exact difference in structure is not known, for the number of combinations, $C_6H_{10}O_5$, contained in a molecule of either starch or cellulose has not been determined. They differ in physical properties as well as chemically. The starches are readily converted back into sugar, in which form they are used by the plant. The starches are broken into simpler compounds by a group of enzymes, and the products formed are dextrin, maltose, and glucose according to the extent to which the starch molecules are broken up.

The *hemi-celluloses* are quite prominent in some seeds, and occur in many other places in the plant. They are much like ordinary cellulose, but, being easily converted into sugar, they are available sources of food and on this account are often called *reserve celluloses*. They are usually very hard substances and are deposited as extra layers on the cell walls. The hardness of

Date seeds and Ivory nuts is due to the hemi-celluloses, in which form these seeds store their reserve food. (*Fig. 250.*)

The *fats* are prominent storage forms of food in a number of plants and usually occur in the form of oils, known as fatty oils. They contain the same elements as the carbohydrates, but have much less oxygen in proportion to carbon, and the hydrogen and oxygen are not present in the proportion to form water. The vegetable fats are chiefly compounds of glycerine and fatty acids. Palmitic, oleic, and stearic acids are the fatty acids commonly found in fats, but there are many others, and the character of the fat formed depends much upon the kind of fatty acid entering into the combination. The fatty oils are usually stored in the seeds, but often in the flesh of fruits and other portions of the plant. *Olive oil* which is pressed out of the fruit of the Olive, *Corn oil* from the embryos of Corn, *Cotton-seed oil* from Cotton seed, *Coconut oil* from Coconuts, *Linseed oil* from Flax seed, and *Castor oil* from seeds of the Castor Bean are well known plant oils and have an important place in our industries.

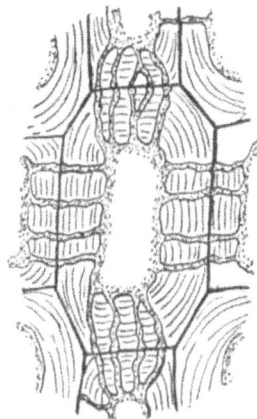

Fig. 250. — Cell walls of Ivory nut, showing the extreme thickening with hemi-cellulose, which is deposited in layers forming striations. The walls are perforated by the canals through which the protoplasmic strands pass. Highly magnified.

The fatty oils are usually present in the storage cells in the form of globules, and like starch are insoluble in the cell sap. Before being consumed by the plant as food, they are converted by means of enzymes into simpler and soluble forms, such as glycerine and fatty acids.

The vegetable fats are not only important animal foods, but are used in many ways by man in the industries. Rape oil and Corn oil are much used for lubricating machinery. Linseed oil is extensively used as a solvent for paint. Palm oil, Cotton-seed oil, and Coconut oil are made into substitutes for butter, besides being used in many other ways. Castor oil, besides being used as a medicine, lubricant, and illuminant, is used in manufacturing dyes. The use of Olive oil in foods is well known. Many of the vegetable oils are used in making the best soaps.

The vegetable *proteins* are of many kinds and they vary greatly in physical and chemical properties. They occur as crystals, granules, or in solution in the vacuoles of the protoplasm, or in intimate association with the protoplasm. They are present to some extent in all plant cells, but are more prominent as storage products in seeds, where they are usually associated with starch and fats. Sometimes, as in the aleurone layer of the cereals, there is little else but proteins. (*Fig. 251.*) The Legumes store considerable quantities of proteins, and for this reason some of them, especially the Beans and Peas, are very desirable for food. (*Fig. 252.*)

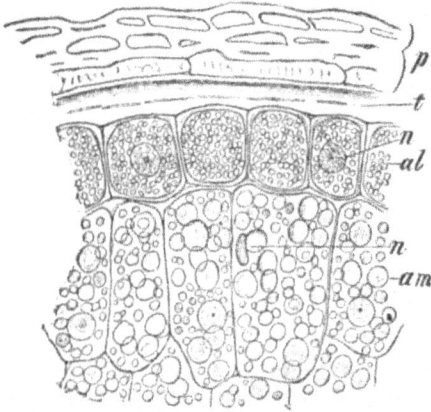

FIG. 251. — Cross section through grain of wheat (*Triticum vulgare*); *p*, pericarp; *t*, testa; *al*, aleurone layer containing numerous protein grains; *n*, nucleus; *am*, starch grains. Enlarged 240 times. After Strasburger.

Proteins differ chiefly from the carbohydrates and fats in that they contain nitrogen. They are known as nitrogenous foods. In addition to nitrogen they usually contain sulphur and sometimes phosphorus; but nitrogen is the chief mineral constituent. The proteins are extremely complex, as the formula $C_{720}H_{1134}N_{218}O_{248}S_5$ for one of them indicates.

The steps in the process by which the photosynthetic sugar and the mineral elements are formed into proteins are not well known; but it seems clear that the elements of the sugar are first

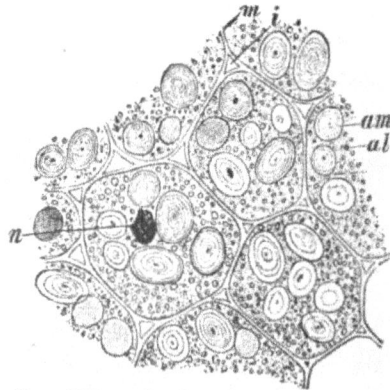

FIG. 252. — Section from a cotyledon of a Pea, showing a few cells; *i*, intercellular space; *am*, starch grains; *al*, aleurone grains; *n*, nucleus. Enlarged 240 times. After Strasburger.

combined with nitrogen to form amino-compounds or amides, which then combine with themselves and other mineral elements to form proteins. The proteins, like the starches and celluloses, are thus supposed to be built up by the combining of simpler compounds. That amino-compounds are involved in the formation of proteins is suggested by the fact that they are nearly always present in plants, and also by the fact that they are produced when proteins are decomposed. Asparagin $C_4H_8O_3N_2$ is one of the most common amino-compounds found in plants, but a number of others, such as *arginin, tyrosin, leucin,* and *tryptophane,* are often found in considerable quantities in the germinating seeds or seedlings of plants.

Plants form many kinds of proteins, but most of them belong to one of the general classes — *albumins, globulins, glutelins, gliadins,* or *nucleo-proteins.* The albumins, the proteins of which the white of an egg is composed, are represented in Peas by *legumelin* and in Wheat and other cereals by *leucosin.* The globulins are common in the Legumes, *legumin* being the chief one. The globulins are probably the most abundant of the reserve proteins in all seeds except cereals. *Glutenin* found in Wheat and *oryzenin* in Rice belong to the glutelins. The gliadins are found in the cereals. Gluten, the substance upon which the tenacity of dough depends, consists chiefly of glutelins and gliadins. The nucleoproteins occur in the nucleus of the cell where they are an important constituent of chromatin. Most proteins are insoluble in the cell sap, and need to be digested by enzymes into soluble and diffusible forms, such as proteoses, peptones, or amino-compounds, before they can be moved through the plant.

Secretions. — A large number of plant substances, differing widely in both composition and function, are often classed as secretions. The important classes of secretions are *volatile oils, glucosides, alkaloids, pigments,* and *enzymes.* Some of the secretions accumulate in glands, which have special cells for secreting and often cavities provided for holding the secretions, as the glands on the leaves of the Mints and in the skin of Oranges illustrate. Some accumulate in long ducts like those in the stems and leaves of the Milkweeds and Pines and are secreted by the cells around these ducts. Many of the secretions, however, are formed in cells, in which secreting is only a minor function, and are usually found in solution in the vacuoles of the protoplasm.

The *volatile oils* differ not only chemically from fatty oils, but also in being volatile. They cause most of the odors of plants. Oil of Peppermint, Sassafras, Cinnamon, Cloves, Cedar, and the oil of the Orange rind are familiar volatile oils. A number of uses to the plant have been assigned to the various volatile oils, such as protection against destructive organisms, attraction of insects in the pollination of flowers, and serving as a storage form of food. Their pleasant odors and tastes add charm to the flowers of many garden plants, and before the chemists learned to make many of them, plants were our chief source of the perfumes and essences of commerce. Their composition suggests their origin from the photosynthetic sugar, since nearly all of them contain only carbon and hydrogen, or only carbon, hydrogen, and oxygen.

Closely related to the volatile oils are a number of substances, such as the Pine resins, india rubber, gutta percha, camphor, and asafetida, which are important commercially, although their use to the plant is not definitely known. From the Pine resins, which are found in the resin ducts of Pines, turpentine, pine tar, rosin, and pitch are obtained. India rubber is the prepared milk-juice obtained from a number of trees of tropical countries. Gutta percha, used in making surgical instruments, in filling teeth, and in a number of other ways, is obtained also from the milk-juice or latex of a number of plants. Camphor is obtained from a number of tropical trees and asafetida from a group of herbaceous plants.

Glucosides are complex substances and are so named because many of them contain glucose as one of their constituents. They may be considered storage forms of food since they yield a sugar when broken down. *Amygdalin*, the bitter substance in the seeds of the Bitter Almond, is one of the best known glucosides. Its formula is $C_{20}H_{27}NO_{11}$, and when decomposed it yields glucose ($C_6H_{12}O_6$), hydrocyanic acid (HCN), and benzaldehyde (C_6H_5CHO). Glucosides vary much in composition and consequently in the products which they yield when decomposed. Thus the glucoside *coniferin* ($C_{16}H_{22}O_8$), found in coniferous trees and Asparagus, yields glucose and *coniferyl alcohol* ($C_{10}H_{12}O_3$) when decomposed.

Glucosides occur in all parts of the plant and are especially abundant in the parenchyma cells of roots, stems, and leaves.

On account of the hydrocyanic acid or other poisonous substances contained, many of the glucosides are poisonous. For example, the *saponins*, which are present in Corn Cockle and Cow Cockle, are poisonous and make the seeds of these plants very objectionable impurities of the small grains. The mustards, a number of which have poisonous seeds, contain *sinigrin*, a poisonous glucoside. In the seeds of some Beans, as the Burma Bean, there is *phaseolunatin*, a poisonous glucoside.

Although it is not known just how glucosides are formed or their exact function to the plant, their structure shows that the photosynthetic sugar furnishes most of the elements. Some of them may be directly synthesized, while others may result from the decomposition of more complex compounds. For the decomposition of each kind of glucoside there seems to be a special enzyme.

The *alkaloids* constitute another group of substances whose origin and function are obscure. Some of the familiar ones are *caffein* and *thein* in Coffee and Tea, *nicotine* in Tobacco, *morphine* from the Poppy, *quinine* from the bark of the Cinchona tree, and *strychnine* from the seeds of Nux vomica. In containing C, H, O, N, they show a close relationship to the amino-compounds. The alkaloids are probably protective substances, since they are often unpleasant to the taste and the most poisonous group of the plant substances. In the preparation of drugs, the alkaloids have a very important place. They are the plant poisons which commonly poison stock in pastures and often people get them by mistake. In Poison Hemlock (*Conium maculatum*) and Water Hemlock (*Cicuta maculata*) there is the poisonous alkaloid, known as *conin*, which is poisonous to stock and man. In the Nightshade family, of which Tomatoes and Irish Potatoes are representatives, there are a number of plants which contain *atropine* and *solanin*, which are poisonous alkaloids. There is a large number of plants, many of which are common, that are poisonous on account of the alkaloids contained. The *ptomaines*, the poisonous substances which Bacteria produce in the decomposition of meats, are alkaloids.

Pigments are the substances upon which the colors in plants depend. Their origin is obscure and in some cases their function is not known. The one most prominent is chlorophyll with the formula often given as $C_{55}H_{72}O_6N_4Mg$. Associated with chlorophyll and probably decomposition products of chlorophyll, are *carotin* ($C_{40}H_{56}$) and *xanthophyll* ($C_{40}H_{56}O_2$), which are usually yellow or orange. Carotin is so named because of its abundance in the root of the Carrot. These pigments are present in fruits, flowers, and autumn leaves, where they produce the yellow and orange colors. *Anthocyan*, a pigment whose formula is not well known, occurs dissolved in the cell sap and is the basis of the reds, purples, and blues in plants, being red when the cell sap is acid and blue when alkaline. Besides having an important place in determining the color of flowers and fruits, it often occurs in leaves and stems.

In addition to the manufacture of food, which is the function of chlorophyll, the pigments, by producing the showy colors of flowers, assist in pollination. They also add to the attractiveness of fruits and thereby assist in the dissemination of seeds. Often the yellow, red, and blue pigments are prominent in leaves and other structures where they seem to have no function.

The *enzymes* are of many kinds and most of the metabolic changes in cells involve the action of enzymes. They are the most general secretions of protoplasm and in all living cells enzymes of some kind are present. So far as chemical analyses have been able to determine, they are similar to proteins in composition. They occur dissolved in the cell sap or in intimate relation with the protoplasm, but often diffuse out of the cell and attack surrounding substances.

Enzymes are specific in their action and hence there are almost as many kinds of enzymes as there are kinds of substances to be acted upon. There is a class of enzymes which acts on proteins, one that acts on carbohydrates, and another that acts on fats. In addition there are enzymes which act on glucosides and other substances of minor importance. The enzymes, called *proteases*, which act on proteins in plants, are of two classes — *ereptases* and *peptases*. Peptases have been found in a number of plants but they are not so generally present as the ereptases are. Ereptases apparently break up proteins more completely than the peptases do. *Bromelin* found in the Pineapple and *papain* in the Papaw (*Carica papaya*) are two well known peptases. Papain is used in making digestive tablets. The proteases break the proteins into soluble forms, such as proteoses, peptones, and amino-compounds, that can be translocated and used as food.

A number of enzymes, such as *diastase, invertase, maltase, zymase,* and *cytase,* are involved in the digestion of the carbohydrates. Diastase, which is especially abundant in germinating seeds, changes starch into sugar. Invertase converts cane sugar into glucose and fructose, and maltase converts maltose into glucose. Zymase, well known as a secretion of the Yeast plant, converts sugar into alcohol and carbon dioxide. Cytase breaks cellulose into simpler compounds.

The *lipases* digest the fats by changing them into fatty acids and glycerine, in which form the fats can be moved in the plant and consumed as food.

For the glucosides there is also a group of enzymes. For amygdalin there is *amygdalase,* and for other glucosides certain other enzymes which decompose them.

Although we know that enzymes have much to do with the metabolic changes in plants, our knowledge of enzymes is comparatively meager. Investigations on the kinds of enzymes and their particular functions are much needed and are receiving much attention by plant chemists.

FIG. 253. — Cells containing crystals of calcium oxalate.

Other secretions so far omitted from our list are the acids and the tannins. *Malic acid, oxalic acid, citric acid, tartaric acid,* and a number of others, known as fruit acids, which function in determining the taste of fruits, are very important to man and assist in seed dissemination when they make the fruit more pleasing to the taste. Some of the organic acids often form compounds with minerals and form crystals. Crystals of calcium oxalate are quite common in plant cells. (*Fig. 253.*) The tannins are bitter astringent substances as any one who has tasted a green Persimmon well knows. They occur throughout plants, but are more abundant in the bark. Tannins harden the gelatine in skins, and before the chemists provided substitutes bark was extensively used in tanning leather. Due to their astringent and antiseptic properties, it is thought that they protect the plant against the action of organisms, such as Fungi and Bacteria.

Stored in all forms of food there is latent energy, which is transformed sunlight, and through respiration the foods are broken
into simpler compounds with the release of energy, which is
utilized in the various kinds of work of the plant.

Summary

Leaves may be classed as primary and secondary. The
primary leaves, represented by the cotyledons, are mainly storage
organs and are usually short-lived. The secondary leaves form
the foliage of plants and are the food-making organs. The form
and arrangement of leaves vary much, but usually result in the
best exposure to light.

The chief tissues of the leaf are the epidermis consisting of protective cells and stomata, the mesophyll containing the working
cells, and the veins, which give strength and supply other tissues
with water and salts and carry away the manufactured products.

The processes taking place in leaves are photosynthesis, transpiration, and respiration. Leaves are especially adapted to
photosynthesis because of their green tissue and exposure to
sunlight. Upon photosynthesis the carbohydrate supply of the
world depends. Respiration is not peculiar to leaves; for it
takes place in all living cells, but can be easily observed in leaves.
Leaves are much exposed to transpiration, which may benefit
the plant or result in injury. The amount of water lost through
transpiration depends upon the character of the transpiring
surface, temperature, humidity of the air, light, and velocity of
wind. A plant may be protected against the dangers of transpiration by having its transpiring surface modified or by being
able to supply water from the soil or storage organs in sufficient
quantities to meet the loss through transpiration.

Leaves may have become modified into special forms, such as
scales, tendrils, thorns, pitchers, or traps.

Through metabolism the photosynthetic sugar is chemically
combined with mineral elements to form proteins and protoplasm, transformed into materials which constitute a framework, changed into storage foods and into various other kinds
of plant products. Through respiration, a phase of metabolism,
plants obtain chemical energy by releasing the latent energy of
sugar or of the compounds of which it is a part.

PART II

PLANTS AS TO KINDS, RELATIONSHIPS, EVOLUTION, AND HEREDITY

CHAPTER XII

INTRODUCTION

Aside from some references to Gymnosperms, and to Yeast, Bacteria, and a few other simple plants, *Part I* is devoted almost entirely to a study of the Morphology and Physiology of the Flowering Plants. The Flowering Plants deserve more attention than other groups, because they are the most highly developed, most attractive, and are the chief source of food, fibers, and many other products related to the welfare of mankind. But in addition to the Flowering Plants, the Plant Kingdom also includes many kinds of plants which do not have flowers. In fact, not much more than half of the 233,000 or more species of known plants are Flowering Plants. About us are many kinds of plants which do not have flowers and some of them are also of much economic importance. The Gymnosperms, the group to which Pines, Spruces, Firs, and some other trees valuable for timber belong, do not have true flowers but have seeds, and are almost as highly developed as the Flowering Plants. The Flowering Plants and Gymnosperms constitute the group called Seed Plants. But there are many kinds of plants, which are often referred to as the simpler plants, that do not even have seeds and some of these are of much economic importance. Well known among the simpler plants are the Ferns, Mosses, Algae, Fungi, and Bacteria. Both the Fungi and the Bacteria are important economic groups. The Fungi cause most of the plant diseases and consequently much destruction and loss among cultivated plants. Many of the Bacteria are indispensable to Agriculture, for they decompose organic compounds, increase the nitrogen of the soil, and do other things that are related to the soil fertility. On the other hand, the Bacteria cause most of the animal diseases and these forms we have to combat.

Some of the simpler forms, like the Bacteria and many Algae, are unicellular plants and hence are extremely simple, while some, as the Ferns illustrate, have complex plant bodies and are comparatively well developed. In addition to the many kinds of plants now living, many other kinds once existed but are now known only by their fossils.

Among the kinds of plants, including both the living and fossil forms, there are almost all degrees of complexity, ranging from the simplest unicellular plants to the most highly developed Flowering Plants. Although varying widely in complexity, the various kinds of plants are evidently related as a study of their structures and habits reveals. Scientists believe that the living forms have come from previously existing forms and hence are related through a common ancestry. They have originated through the process known as evolution, which assumes that the first plants on earth were extremely simple and from these simple forms the more complex forms arose. In response to a changing environment or due to changes arising wholly within, the simple forms gave rise to more complex forms, which in turn gave rise to forms still more complex. Thus through slow changes involving millions of years the highly developed forms were evolved.

Evolution has generally been progressive, giving rise to forms with higher organization, greater perfection of parts, and increased efficiency of function. Sometimes, however, evolution has been retrogressive, and forms have been reduced to simpler forms, through becoming more simply organized and less efficient in function. For example, in this way the Fungi are supposed to have arisen from the Algae. Progressive evolution has not been direct from the simplest to the highest organisms, but has been along many lines which, although usually progressive, have been more or less divergent and this accounts for many kinds of organisms among both plants and animals. Animals and plants can be distinguished in their higher forms on the basis of locomotion, methods of getting food, character of the skeleton, and so on, but in their simpler forms animals and plants are not easily distinguished, and this fact suggests that plants and animals arose as diverging lines from the same preëxisting organism. A diagram of evolution in plants looks like a tree with many branches. The trunk represents the main line and the branches the diverging lines of evolution. The lowest branches with their sub-branches represent the groups of the simplest plants and their relationships. The groups of Seed Plants and their relationships are represented by the topmost branches, and the branches representing other groups are so located as to show the relative complexity and relationships of the various other groups included in the Plant Kingdom.

The origin of a plant from simpler previously existing forms is known as *phylogeny*, while the series of changes which a plant or any living being passes through in attaining a mature condition is called *ontogeny*. Plants are classified in a number of ways, but chiefly upon their phylogenetic relationships. Another basis of considerable importance upon which plants are classified pertains to their place of living and adjustments to environment. Relationships of this kind are *ecological*.

Part II is devoted, although briefly: *first*, to a study of the structure, habits, economic importance, and phylogenetic relationships of the plants below the Flowering Plants; *second*, to a study of some of the important groups of Flowering Plants as to their phylogenetic relationships and economic importance; *third*, to a consideration of plants as to their ecological relationship; and *fourth*, to a special study of evolution, heredity, and the breeding of plants.

Classification of Plants. — On the basis of descent or phylogenetic relationships the Plant Kingdom is divided into four groups called *divisions*. Divisions are divided into *classes*, classes into *orders*, orders into *families*, families into *genera*, and genera into *species*. Species are the units in the phylogenetic classification. Species are aggregates of individuals which are alike in their important characteristics and are therefore regarded as the same in kind. Of course the individuals of a species may vary in a number of minor features. Thus White Oaks vary much in size, shape, and a number of other ways, but in essential features all White Oaks are alike and all belong to the species White Oak. Sometimes some of the individuals of a species show some important differences, and then the species is subdivided, the subdivisions being called varieties, strains, or races. Also for a similar reason it sometimes happens that orders are subdivided into suborders, classes into subclasses, and families into subfamilies.

The scientific names of the phylogenetic groups are Greek or Latin terms and commonly express some characteristic of the group. With some exceptions due to historical causes, the groups are named according to a rather definite plan. The names of the divisions end in -*phyta*, commonly written -*phyte*, from the Greek word *phyton* which means plant. The names of classes commonly end in -*ineae* or -*eae* and are usually derived from some important group included. Thus the Lycopodineae is the class containing the Lycopods, and the Filicineae is the class containing the Ferns.

The names of orders end in -*ales*, and orders are commonly named from some prominent family included. Thus the Rosales are named from the Rosaceae, the Rose family. Names of families usually end in -*aceae* and are commonly derived from some prominent genus, as for example the Liliaceae, which is the Lily family. The names of genera are Latin nouns in the nominative case. Thus *Quercus* is the Oak genus, *Pyrus*, the Apple genus, and *Acer*, the Maple genus. Species have two names, the name of the genus and the name that distinguishes the species. For example, *Quercus alba* is the White Oak, while *Quercus rubra* is the Red Oak. Quercus is the name of the genus, and the terms alba (the Latin term for white) and rubra (the Latin term for red) name the species. In English we simply change the terms about and say White Oak instead of Oak White.

The Divisions of the Plant Kingdom. — The phylogenetic divisions of the Plant Kingdom arranged in phylogenetic order are *Thallophytes, Bryophytes, Pteridophytes,* and *Spermatophytes.*

The Thallophytes are the simplest plants and are regarded as the lowest and most primitive from the standpoint of evolution. The word means *thallus plants*. As previously stated the ending -*phyte* always means plant. Thallus refers to the fact that the plant body has a simple organization. It is not differentiated into roots, stem, and leaves. Bacteria, Toadstools, and Algae are familiar Thallophytes. The plant body of some of them consists of a single cell, which is the simplest plant body possible.

The Bryophytes are so named because they are chiefly *Moss plants*. Besides the Mosses, they also include the Liverworts. The Bryophytes have better organized plant bodies than the Thallophytes and are, therefore, considered higher in the scale of evolution.

The Pteridophytes are so named because they include the *Fern plants*. Most Pteridophytes are Ferns, but this group includes some plants that are not true Ferns.   The Pteridophytes made much advancement in developing tissues and organs.   They have roots, stems, and leaves, and for this reason are regarded as more highly developed than the Bryophytes..

The Spermatophytes are the *Seed Plants*.   With this group we are most familiar, since to this group belong the trees, shrubs, and most of the familiar herbaceous plants.   It is the seed, which is one of their contributions to evolution, that makes many of them so useful.   In this group occurs the greatest display of tissues and organs.

The Spermatophytes consist of two subdivisions, *Gymnosperms* and *Angiosperms:*

The Gymnosperms (Gymnospermae), as the term signifies, do not have their seeds enclosed.   These are the evergreens, such as Pines, Cedars, Spruces, Hemlocks, Firs, etc.

The Angiosperms (Angiospermae), as the term signifies, have their seeds enclosed.   This refers to the enclosing of the seed in an ovary.   Nearly all of the cultivated plants belong in this group.   They contribute the fruits.

A Comparison of Simple Thallophytes with Spermatophytes. — One striking difference between the simplest Thallophytes and the Spermatophytes is in the number of cells of which the plant is composed.   The simplest Thallophytes are unicellular, while the Spermatophytes are extremely multicellular.   A second striking difference between the plants of the two divisions is in the differentiation and specialization of cells which are thereby fitted to perform special functions.   In unicellular Thallophytes one cell performs all of the different kinds of work that the plant has to do, while in Spermatophytes there is a division of labor among the cells;   that is, Spermatophytes have tissues, which are groups of cells especially adapted to do particular kinds of work.

As the cells of multicellular plants become differentiated into tissues and thus specialized in function, they lose the ability to exist independently.   Many unicellular plants can live independently of other cells, but in Spermatophytes, the life of a cell in most cases depends upon the proper adjustment of the cell to the vital processes of other cells of the plant body.   Thus the ability of a cell to perform many functions is lost in becoming adapted to perform one function well.

In organization the cells of Spermatophytes do not differ essentially from those of most Thallophytes. Excepting in the very lowest forms, the cellular structures of Thallophytes are similar to those of the Spermatophytes as a study of the unicellular Thallophyte in *Figure 254* will show. This one-celled plant is composed of protoplasm, which is the living substance, and a wall, which encloses the protoplasm. The protoplasm, as in the cells of higher plants, consists of nucleus and cytoplasm. The nucleus, usually globular in shape, is enclosed by a nuclear membrane and contains one or more nucleoli (small globular bodies) and chromatin (the chunky or granular substance scattered about in the nucleus). In addition to nucleoli and chromatin, the nucleus contains nuclear sap (water containing sugar, salts, and other substances in solution). The cytoplasm, the protoplasm outside of the nucleus, is vacuolate and has its outer border so modified as to form a membrane, which, unless the protoplasm is shrunken, is tightly pressed against the cell wall. Water and solutions enter the protoplasm through this cell membrane by the processes of osmosis and diffusion. All of

F I G. 2 5 4. — A one-celled Thallophyte, *Pleurococcus vulgaris*. *n*, nucleus showing nuclear membrane, chromatin, and a nucleolus. *c*, cytoplasm, in which there is a large lobed chloroplast. × 800. From Strasburger.

these cellular structures have practically the same function here as in the cells of the higher plants. In this particular unicellular plant there is a chloroplast, which, like the chloroplasts in the food-making cells of leaves, is a special protoplasmic body saturated with a green pigment (chlorophyll), which enables it by utilizing the sunlight to carry·on photosynthesis, that is, to form sugar from carbon dioxide and water.

Although consisting of a single cell, this plant performs most of the functions which the most highly organized plants perform, but in a simpler way. In absorbing water and mineral elements directly from its surroundings, it performs the function of roots. In carrying on photosynthesis, it performs the function of leaves. By dividing it gives rise to new individuals and thereby performs the function of reproduction, which is the function of flowers. In such a simple plant there is no function comparable to that of a stem, for there are no distant parts, such as leaves and roots, to be connected and no definite position which the plant must maintain.

It is now clear that in passing from the unicellular condition to the Spermatophyte stage, evolution was along the following lines: *First,* plants became multicellular; *second,* the cells constituting a multicellular plant became somewhat differentiated as to function and structure; *third,* as plants became more multicellular, there was further differentiation which eventually resulted in the establishment of definite structures or organs fitted to efficiently perform special functions.   Such structures in their most highly organized form are the leaves organized for the manufacture of plant food, the roots organized for absorbing and for anchoring the plant, the flowers organized for reproduction, and the stem organized to support leaves, flowers, and fruit in the air and sunshine.

Of course the organs as they occur in Spermatophytes did not arise suddenly, but they, too, underwent a gradual process of evolution, at first arising as simple structures and gradually becoming more complex and better defined.   Through the Thallophytes, Bryophytes, Pteridophytes, and Spermatophytes, including both living and extinct forms, the organs characteristic of the highest type of Spermatophytes gradually arose.

CHAPTER XIII

THALLOPHYTES

Algae (Thallophytes with a Food-making Pigment)

General Characteristics. — The Algae are a familiar group of Thallophytes, for in nearly every lake, pond, and stream, and along the sea coast some forms of them can be found. They commonly appear in fresh water as a green scum or as floating mats of green threads on or near the surface of the water. They often occur in abundance in watering troughs, and sometimes become troublesome by clogging sewers and water mains. Along the sea coast occur the large brown and red forms known as Seaweeds.

Algae are of some economic importance. The Seaweeds are much used as food in some countries, especially in Japan, and from some Seaweeds iodine and potassium are extracted. Along the Pacific Coast of the United States, Seaweeds are an important source of potassium for fertilizers. However, the interest in the study of Algae is not due so much to their economic importance as it is to the fact that a knowledge of them is essential to an understanding of the evolution of the higher plant forms.

Although Algae are water plants, not all Algae live in the water, for there are some forms which live on moist soil or rocks where water is easily obtained, and a few exceptional forms, such as those that live on the bark of trees, have very dry surroundings much of the time. Algae differ from other groups of Thallophytes in having food-making pigments by which they make their carbohydrates. Consequently, they are not saprophytes or parasites, that is, plants which have to depend directly upon other plants for food, but are equipped to live independently. Among them there is a wide range of variation in plant body and methods of reproduction, and four groups of Algae are commonly recognized — *Blue-green, Green, Brown, and Red Algae.*

Blue-green Algae. Cyanophyceae

The Blue-green Algae are the simplest forms of Algae and are the simplest known plants that make their own food. They are so named because of their bluish green color which is due to the presence of chlorophyll and a blue pigment called *Phycocyanin*. Although their size is microscopical, they form aggregations that are often quite conspicuous. There are about 1200 species of Blue-green Algae, and they are widely distributed, occurring nearly everywhere in fresh and salt water and also on wet soil, rocks, and logs. On wet surfaces they form bluish green slimy layers or jelly-like lumps, and in sluggish streams and ponds they form bluish green scums or mats which float on or near the surface of the water. They thrive best where there is organic matter and consequently prefer stagnant to running waters. Some forms are so resistant to heat that they can live in hot springs where the temperature is near the boiling point of water. Some, called *endophytes*, live in the cavities of some of the more highly organized plants, such as the Liverworts and Ferns. Some are associated with Fungi in the formation of Lichens. The Blue-green Algae are of only slight economic importance. When allowed to accumulate, they impart offensive odors to water supplies, but are easily controlled by use of copper salts. It is claimed that livestock are sometimes killed by drinking water that has become foul with Blue-green Algae.

The *plant body* in the Blue-green Algae is a single cell or a colony of cells so joined as to form a filament or plate. When cell division is in only one direction and the cells formed do not separate, then as a result of a number of successive cell divisions a chain or filament of cells is formed. When cell division is in more than one direction and the cells do not separate, then colonies of other shapes are formed. Colonies, although they may resemble multicellular plants, are aggregates of essentially independent cells. One notable feature of the plant body of the Blue-green Algae is the secretion of a gelatinous substance which forms a sheath about the plant. As plants grow and multiply, the gelatinous secretion accumulates and commonly forms a matrix which holds the plants together in slimy layers or jolly-like lumps. The gelatinous sheath holds water and thus protects the plants from drying out. Another notable feature of this group pertains to the organization of the cell. In a few of the most highly developed forms the protoplast is pretty well organized, but in most Blue-green Algae the nucleus and cytoplasm are not clearly differentiated and there are no chloroplasts. The chlorophyll and other pigments are diffused through the cytoplasm and sometimes throughout the entire protoplast.

A simple form of Blue-green Algae is *Gleocapsa* shown in *Figure 255*. This plant, which lives mostly on wet rocks, consists of a single globular cell with a rather prominent gelatinous sheath and is about as simple as a plant can possibly be. By the divi-

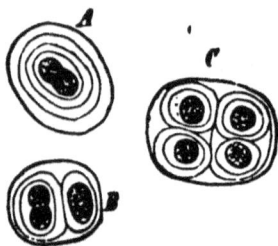

Fig. 255. — *Gleocapsa*, one of the simplest of the Blue-green Algae. *A*, single individual enclosed in a heavy gelatinous sheath and beginning to divide. *B* and *C* show how the plants as they multiply are held together by the gelatinous sheath. × 540. After Strasburger.

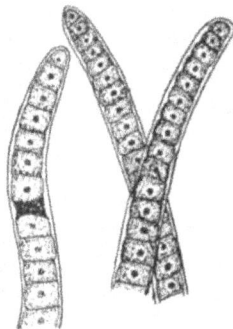

Fig. 256. — Portions of three filaments of *Oscillatoria*. At the left one cell in the filament has died, resulting in segmenting the filament. × 540.

sion of the cell new individuals are formed, which are held together in loose aggregations by the gelatinous secretion from their walls.

One of the common colonial forms is *Oscillatoria*, of which there are about 100 species (*Fig. 256*). They form bluish green felt-like mats in fresh and salt water, and bluish green layers on moist soil. The colony is a filament, consisting of a large number of short cylindrical cells joined end to end and enveloped in a thin gelatinous sheath. Usually the filaments occur together in large numbers, and often there is enough of the gelatinous secretion to hold them together in loose aggregations. A characteristic feature of the plant, as the name suggests, is the swaying and revolving movement of the filament, which sometimes resembles a tiny worm in its creeping and bending to one side and then the other. This movement indicates that the cells of the colony of Oscillatoria work together as a unit and thus the many-celled colony takes on the character of a many-celled plant where the cells are closely associated in the activities of the plant.

Another filamentous form (*Fig. 257*) is *Nostoc*, which is common in fresh water and on moist soil. In this plant the cells are rounded and the filament resembles a chain of beads. Nostoc secretes an extraordinary amount of gelatinous substance and forms jelly-like lumps in which a large number of the plants are held. These jelly-like masses are often more or less rounded, and are of various sizes up to that of a marble or even larger. When growing on soil, they often swell up and glisten after a rain, on which account they have been called "fallen stars."

In Nostoc there is some differentiation of cells. At intervals in the filament ordinary working cells enlarge, lose their contents, and thicken their walls. Being larger in size and almost colorless, they are quite distinct from the other cells of the filament, and thus divide the filament into sec-

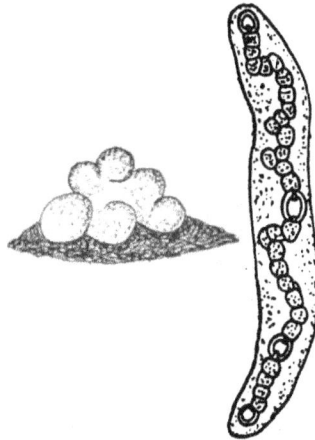

Fig. 257. — *Nostoc.* At the left are jelly-like lumps of Nostoc consisting of numerous colonies. About natural size. At the right is a single colony, showing the gelatinous sheath and the heterocysts, the large cells shown empty, which segment the filament into harmogonia. × 540.

tions called *harmogonia*. These special cells, called *heterocysts*, seem to be concerned with the multiplication of filaments, for it has been observed that the harmogonia break loose at the heterocysts, wriggle out through the jelly-like matrix, and develop new filaments.

Another special kind of cell formed in Nostoc is the *resting cell*, which is formed when periods unfavorable for the growth of the plant appear. In this case certain cells of the filament enlarge, accumulate food, and thicken their walls. These cells are able to endure cold, drought, and other conditions which are destruc-

tive to the ordinary cells of the filament; and, when favorable
conditions for growth return, the protoplast of the resting cell
breaks through the heavy wall and develops a new filament.

In *Rivularia* (*Fig. 258*), another filamentous form, the filament
is apparently differentiated into a basal and apical region. A
heterocyst is the basal cell and the cells decrease in size toward
the apex, so that the filament has a whip-like
appearance.

Besides the features just mentioned in connection with the plant body, there are some
other minor ones which some particular species
of Blue-green Algae have. For example, in
one species the cells of the colony arrange
themselves so as to maintain a regular rec-
tangle. In some forms the colony forms a
branched filament.

Food is manufactured, and water and mineral matters are absorbed by these simple
plants in essentially the same way as in the
more complex plants, but each cell must
manufacture food and absorb water and
mineral matters for itself. Since these plants
live in water or on a moist substratum, they
are able to absorb water and mineral matters
from their immediate surroundings. Having
chlorophyll, they are able to carry on photosynthesis and thereby provide themselves
with carbohydrates. Although the function
of phycocyanin is not known, it is probable
that it assists some in connection with photo-

FIG. 258.—A
single colony of
Rivularia consist-
ing of a large hete-
rocyst and many
vegetative cells
which decrease in
size away from the
heterocyst. × 540.

synthesis. Sometimes there is an additional reddish pigment
developed, which may have something to do with enabling the
plant to utilize the sun's rays in the manufacture of food. The
reddish pigment is so abundant in a few forms that the plants
appear red in mass, as in one group which forms floating colonies
in salt water and has given the name to the Red Sea.

Reproduction in the Blue-green Algae is chiefly by cell division.
They form no sex cells and, therefore, depend entirely upon
vegetative methods of reproduction. By cell division new cells
are formed, which may, according to the species, separate as new

plants, as in Gleocapsa, or remain as a part of a close colony, as in Oscillatoria and other forms where the cells of a colony are closely associated. In filamentous forms the method of multiplying filaments by means of harmogonia may be classed as a method of reproduction. In this case a filament breaks into segments which separate and establish new filaments. The filament may be segmented by heterocysts or by the death of ordinary working cells.

The simplicity of plant body, cellular structures, and methods of reproduction makes the Cyanophyceae the simplest of all groups of independent plants now in existence. The absence of chloroplasts and a well-defined nucleus and cytoplasm clearly distinguishes them from other groups of independent plants. But in the group some advancement is shown. The formation of a colony in which the cells are closely associated looks forward toward the formation of multicellular plants in which the cells are very intimately associated. Also the differentiation of the cells of a colony into ordinary working cells, heterocysts, and resting cells suggests the differentiation of cells in multicellular plants into tissues.

Green Algae (Chlorophyceae)

The Green Algae are the Algae most commonly seen in our lakes, ponds, and streams. They usually have only one pigment, chlorophyll, and their green or yellow-green color is usually quite distinct from that of the Blue-green Algae. Some of the Green Algae are microscopic and some form colonies or multicellular plant bodies that are clearly visible to the naked eye. Although they are small plants, large numbers of them commonly occur together, forming scums or tangles of filaments that are conspicuous. Most of them live in the water but some live on moist earth, rocks, or wood, and a few forms can endure periods of drought. A few forms live in salt water, but nearly all are fresh water plants.

The Green Algae differ from the Blue-green Algae not only in color but also in a number of other ways. Gelatinous substances are secreted in abundance only in the lowest forms of the group, and consequently Green Algae do not commonly form gelatinous masses. They have chloroplasts, and the nucleus is well organized and quite distinct from the cytoplasm. In some, the cells of the colony have their protoplasts joined by protoplasmic strands and have thus become so closely associated that they constitute a multicellular plant. Some reproduce entirely by cell division, but many of them have more specialized methods of reproduction. Many Green Algae form swimming cells called *zoöspores*, each of which is able to produce a new plant directly. Others also form *gametes* or *sex cells* which fuse and form a cell that develops a new plant either directly or indirectly. The simplest gametes occurring in the group are alike as to size, structure, and behavior and are called *isogametes*. When isogametes pair and fuse, a cell called a *zygospore* or *zygote* is formed, and this spore may form zoöspores or develop a new plant directly. The fusion of similar gametes is called *conjugation*. The more advanced Green Algae form morphologically unlike gametes called *heterogametes*, of which the large ones are called *eggs* and the small ones are called *sperms*. The spore formed by the fusion of an egg and a sperm, that is, by the fusion of unlike gametes, is called an *oöspore* and the fusion is called *fertilization*. Often the gametes are produced in special organs called *sex organs*. It is evident that the Green Algae resemble the higher plants much more than do the Blue-green Algae and are, therefore, considered more advanced. It is supposed that from plants like the Green Algae the higher plants have come.

Among the Green Algae there is much diversity in character of plant body and methods of reproduction. About 9000 species are known and these are commonly grouped into five orders — *Volvocales, Protococcales, Confervales, Conjugales,* and *Siphonales.*

Unicellular Motile Green Algae (Volvocales). — These Green Algae are regarded as one-celled plants, although some of them form colonies of considerable size and complexity. They live in the water and chiefly in fresh water. Their vegetative cells have cilia and swim about like the lower animals. It is this motile habit that distinguishes them from other Green Algae. On account of their motility and some animal-like structural features, they are sometimes regarded as animals. They are microscopic plants, but some of them form colonies that are sometimes visible to the naked eye.

Chlamydomonas. — In *Chlamydomonas* (*Fig. 259*), which is regarded as one of the simplest of the Volvocales, the habit of colony formation is lacking and, therefore, each individual swims about independently. This plant is common in fresh water and when seen swimming about under the microscope might be mistaken for a protozoan, a one-celled animal which it resembles.

The *Plant body* consists of a more or less globular protoplast closely invested by a thin membrane through which the two long cilia project at the forward end. There is a large cup-shaped chloroplast, in which there is a protein body called *pyrenoid*. The nucleus is in the cup of the chloroplast; at the base of the cilia are two contractile vacuoles; and not far from these is the *red pigment spot* or *eye spot* which is supposed to be sensitive to light and, therefore, of some use in directing the movements of the individual. In certain species a bright red pigment is often so abundant that, when the plants are numerous, they cause pools to appear red and, when blown over the snow, produce the "red snow" of arctic and alpine regions.

In the number of cells constituting the plant body, Chlamydomonas is

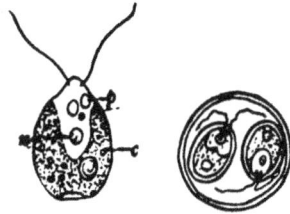

FIG. 259.—*Chlamydomonas,* a simple motile Green Algae. At the left an individual, showing the cilia, the large cup-shaped chloroplast (*c*) containing a pyrenoid, the nucleus (*n*), the two pulsating vacuoles (*p*), and the red pigment spot represented by a black dot near the pulsating vacuoles. At the right an individual which has formed two zoöspores. × 300.

as simple as any of the Blue-green Algae, but in having a chloroplast and well-defined nucleus and cytoplasm, it shows considerable advancement.

Reproduction takes place by means of zoöspores and gametes. In forming zoöspores the plant becomes quiescent and the protoplast divides into two or more ciliated cells which are miniatures of the parent. These daughter cells or zoöspores escape from the mother cell and enlarge to the parent size. Under certain conditions the protoplast may form many small zoöspore-like cells which escape from the mother plant and fuse in pairs to form resting zygospores which later form new plants. Since these small zoöspore-like cells fuse, they are gametes or sex cells and, since they are alike, they are isogametes. The zygospore, a spore formed by the fusion of similar gametes as the prefix (*zygo*) suggests, is commonly a well-protected spore and, therefore, able to resist conditions that are destructive to the zoospores or vegetative cells of the plant. The approach of unfavorable conditions commonly induces the formation of gametes and zygospores. The zygospore remains dormant until favorable conditions return and then produces a new plant. The zygospore is, therefore, a stage in the round of life in which the plant is able to survive unfavorable conditions.

Gametes are supposed to be zoöspores that are too small to function alone. By pairing and fusing, the energies of two gametes are combined in a zygospore which is able to produce a new plant that neither of the gametes could produce alone. Thus the zygospore may also be regarded as a cell in which gametes combine their energies, so that they may be effective in producing new plants. There are two things which indicate that gametes are miniature zoöspores. *First*, gametes and zoöspores grade into each other in size. *Second*, it has been observed that small zoöspores may fuse and, therefore, behave as gametes when poorly nourished, or grow directly into new plants and, therefore, function as zoöspores when well nourished. Thus a zoöspore-like cell may be a zoöspore or gamete according to conditions. Such is the evidence supporting the theory that sexuality arose through the fusion of zoöspores which, on account of size, or conditions of light, temperature, food, etc., were unable to function alone. From this simple isogamous sexuality the more complex heterogamous forms of sexuality have followed. Even in some forms of Chlamydomonas, the gametes pairing often differ some in size and, therefore, suggest heterogamous sexuality.

Pandorina. — The colony, which is one of the notable features of the Volvocales, varies widely in different genera, ranging from 16 cells or less up to 20,000 or more. *Pandorina*, shown in *Figure 260*, is one of the forms producing simple colonies.

The cells or individuals of which the colony of Pandorina is formed are similar in structure to Chlamydomonas. Commonly the spherical colony consists of 16 individuals, held together in a mucilaginous matrix.

Reproduction differs in some ways from that of Chlamydomonas on account of the colony formation. Any individual of the colony may divide into 16 zoöspore-like cells which remain together, escape from the mother colony, and thus become a new colony. The gametes are formed in essentially the same way as the individuals of the new colonies, but they separate and thus swim about independently after leaving the mother colony. When the zygospore germinates, as shown in *Figure 260*, there results a new colony which has only to grow to adult size.

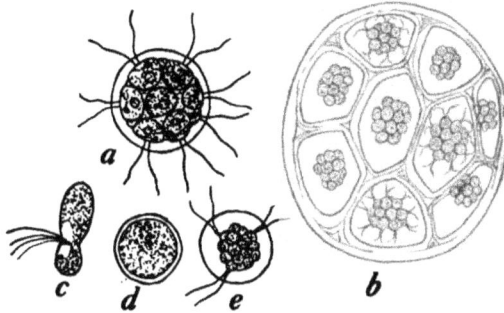

FIG. 260. — *Pandorina morum.* *a*, Motile colony ordinarily consisting of sixteen motile cells (× 475); *b*, colony in which the cells have formed daughter colonies (× 475); *c*, two gametes fusing; *d*, zygospore; *e*, zygospore germinating and forming a new colony. Redrawn with modifications from Oersted.

Among the gametes there is often considerable variation in size and motility, some being smaller and more active than others. The gametes pair and fuse regardless of their size, and, when gametes that are unlike happen to pair, there is a suggestion of heterogamy, although there is no distinct differentiation of gametes as occurs in plants where heterogamy is well established.

Volvox. — The highest expression of colony formation is reached in forms like *Volvox* (*Fig. 261*), where the colony contains thousands of individuals held together in a gelatinous matrix and so arranged as to form a hollow sphere. The colonies of Volvox are often as large as a pin head and hence visible to the naked eye. The two cilia of each individual project from the colony, and by the lashing of the cilia the colony moves through the water by a revolving motion. One can often see them slowly moving about in ditches, ponds, and sometimes in tanks in greenhouses. A microscopical study of the colony shows that the individuals of the colony are connected by protoplasmic strands, and hence so vitally related that the colony of Volvox may be regarded as a multicellular individual rather than a colony.

Reproduction presents some interesting features. At first all cells of the colony are alike, but later considerable differentiation among cells occurs. Some cells of the colony enlarge and pass

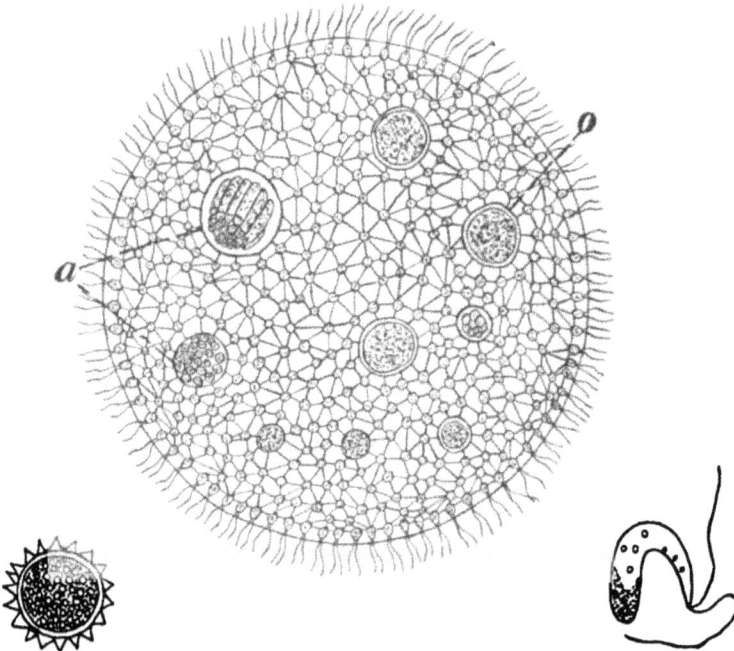

FIG. 261. — *Volvox.* In the colony (*Volvox aureus*) the smaller cells bearing two cilia are the vegetative cells, the enlarged cells (*a*) contain sperms, and the enlarged cells (*o*), varying in size and stages of development, are eggs (× 300). Below and at the right is a sperm, and below and at the left is a oöspore of *Volvox globator*. After West.

into the hollow of the sphere where they form new colonies which escape and grow to adult size. Sexual reproduction in Volvox is heterogamous, for two distinct kinds of gametes are involved. Some of the cells enlarge, lose their cilia, and become filled with food. They are the female gametes or eggs. Other cells of the colony form numerous small motile gametes or sperms which seek the eggs and fuse with them. Fertilization, as this fusing is called since the gametes are differentiated into eggs and sperms, occurs within the hollow of the sphere. The spore formed from the fusion, now known as an oöspore (meaning eggspore), forms a new colony upon germination.

There is much advantage gained by differentiating gametes. The egg, owing to its size and loss of motility, can store much food for the next generation. The smallness of sperms makes it possible for large numbers of them to be produced, and promotes their movements through water.

In summarizing the Volvocales, the following features are the notable ones. The plant body consists of a single motile cell having a chloroplast and well-defined nucleus and cytoplasm. Some swim about independently, but the formation of colonies is a marked feature of the group, and the colonies range from simple to complex ones. By the division of cells new individuals and new colonies are formed. Sexual reproduction advances from isogamy to heterogamy. As in the Blue-green Algae, the formation of colonies is a step toward the formation of multicellular individuals.

Unicellular Non-motile Green Algae (Protococcales). — In contrast to the Volvocales, the absence of cilia, except on reproductive cells, is a notable feature of this group. Some plants of this order are very common on damp soil, walls, and on the bark of trees, where they are often exposed to long periods of drought. Most of the group are aquatic and occur mainly in fresh water. Some enter into the formation of Lichens. Others are endophytic, living in the intercellular

FIG. 262.—*Pleurococcus vulgaris*. Above, a single plant consisting of a single cell with a definite wall, well defined nucleus, and large lobed chloroplast; below, left, plants dividing; and below, right, a group of four separate plants. × 540. After Strasburger.

spaces of other plants, and some give the green color to certain animals, such as the hydra and fresh-water sponge, which eat them. They show considerable variation in their habit of forming colonies and in methods of reproduction.

Pleurococcus. — *Pleurococcus (Fig. 262)*, often called *Protococcus*, is the simplest plant of the group, and may be regarded as one of the simplest of the Green Algae. It forms green coatings, resembling green paint, on flower pots, damp earth or walls, and on the trunks of trees. It is a single, globular, non-motile cell. It has a definite wall, a large lobed chloroplast suggesting several chloroplasts, and its nucleus and cytoplasm are well defined. It reproduces entirely by cell division, thus forming no zoöspores or gametes. They are small plants and a mass of them perceptible to the eye consists of numerous individuals. They divide rapidly when conditions are favorable, and daughter cells recently formed and not yet separated are usually seen when a mass of individuals is observed with the microscope.

FIG. 263. — *Scenedesmus.* Above, a colony of *Scenedesmus quadricanda* consisting of four cells arranged in a row; below, a cell of the old colony forming a new colony. × 600. Drawn from West.

Scenedesmus. — This form, which is common in fresh water, is often classed with the Protococcales. The individuals form simple colonies with the individuals usually arranged in a row as shown in *Figure 263*. There are no zoöspores

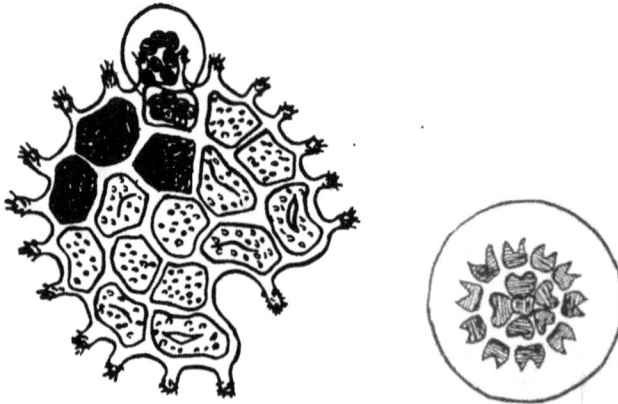

FIG. 264. — *Pediastrum boryanum.* At the left, the plate-like colony of cells, some of which have formed zoöspores and from one of which the zoöspores are escaping; at the right, zoöspores arranging themselves into a new colony. × about 400. From Braun.

or gametes, but reproduction is effected by the division of each cell into daughter cells which escape as a new colony.

Pediastrum. — A more complicated colony occurs in Pediastrum (*Fig. 264*), another form common in ponds and other quiet waters in warm weather. The cells, which are quite numerous in some species, form plate-like colonies in which marginal cells differ in form from those within.

Both zoöspores and gametes are produced in this form. Any cell may form zoöspores, which escape from the mother cell enclosed in a membrane and then arrange themselves into a new colony. Instead of zoöspores the cells may form gametes, which

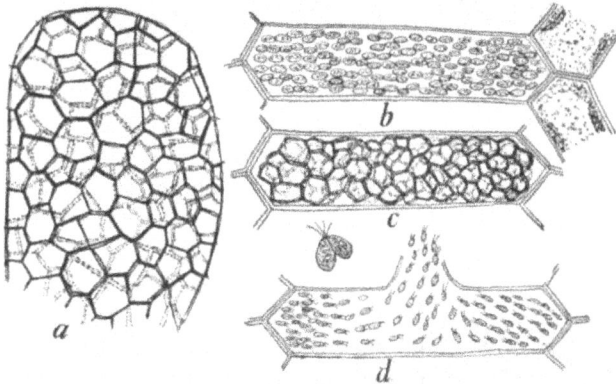

Fig. 265. — Water-net, *Hydrodictyon reticulatum.* *a*, portion of a net (× about 2); *b*, a cell which has formed zoöspores; *c*, the zoöspores formed into a small net within the mother cell; *d*, a cell in which gametes have formed; at the left of the opening through which the gametes are escaping two gametes are shown fusing.

resemble zoöspores but are smaller and more numerous. The gametes, since they are alike, form zygospores, and each zygospore upon germination produces a new colony.

Hydrodictyon. — This is the remarkable Water-net, in which the cylindrical colonies, often a yard or more in length, comprise thousands of cells so joined as to enclose polygonal meshes and thus form a net as *Figure 265* shows. These massive colonies, buoyed up by bubbles of oxygen caught within them, often form extensive floating mats in lakes, ponds, and sluggish streams.

New nets may arise from zoöspores or from zygospores. When a cell reaches a certain size and other conditions are right, its protoplast divides into thousands of zoöspores. These zoöspores do not escape but, after swimming about for a time in the mother cell, they so arrange themselves and grow together at points of contact as to form a miniature net. Through the softening and decay of the wall of the mother cell, the small net is set free and by the mere enlargement of its cells becomes a colony of adult size. The gametes are isogamous and are formed in great numbers by certain cells. As many as 100,000 of them may be produced within a cell. Almost as soon as formed they escape from the mother cell and begin to pair and fuse. The zygospore produces zoöspores which at first pass into a resting stage and later from new nets.

Thus in the Protococcales the individuals may remain separate or form colonies which are exceedingly complex in the higher forms. In the simplest forms, as Pleurococcus illustrates, reproduction is by cell division in which the parent divides to form two new plants, but in the higher forms there is reproduction by zoöspores and isogametes. Since their sexuality does not reach the heterogamous condition, they are not so advanced in this respect as the Volvocales are, but they lack motility and this feature is characteristic of the higher plants, which are adapted to live on land rather than in the water.

FIG. 266. — Sea Lettuce (*Ulva*), a Confervoid Alga having a plate-like plant body. This plate-like plant body is two layers of cells in thickness, bright green, and resembles a leaf in form. Natural size. Redrawn from Bessey.

Confervoid Algae (Confervales). — The Confervales or Confervoid Algae are among the most familiar of the Green Algae. Their plant bodies are usually filaments, commonly consisting of much elongated cylindrical cells closely joined end to end in a single row. The filaments may be several inches in length and in some forms much branched. In a few forms the plant body is plate-like instead of filamentous, as the Sea Lettuce illustrates (*Fig. 266*). The Confervales are common in lakes, ponds, streams, and water troughs, where many of them grow attached and form green hair-like fringes about rocks and other objects. More than 700 species of them are known, and there is considerable variation in plant body and methods of reproduction.

Ulothrix. — *Ulothrix* (*Fig. 267*) is one of the simpler forms of the group, and its filaments, an inch or two in length, form bright green fringes about stones and other objects in lakes, ponds, streams, and troughs. There is some differentiation within the filament, for the basal cell is modified into a holdfast by which the filament is attached to a support. The other cells are alike and each contains one nucleus and a large encircling chloroplast.

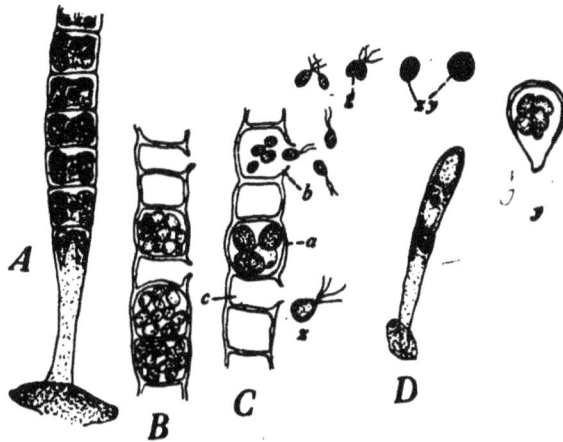

Fɪɢ. 267. — *Ulothrix zonata.* *A*, portion of a filament, showing the holdfast and a number of vegetative cells; *B*, portion of a filament, showing three cells containing gametes; *C*, a portion of a filament, showing gametes escaping at *b*, and zoöspores formed at *a* and escaping at *c*; *D*, a new filament developing from a zoöspore, the character of which is shown at *z*. At *g* gametes are shown fusing to form zygospores. At *zy* a zygospore, just after the fusion of the gametes and when fully mature, is shown. A zygospore which has germinated and produced four zoöspores is shown at *y*. × 200–300. Redrawn with modification from Coulter and from Strasburger.

The plant reproduces asexually by four-ciliate zoöspores, and sexually by two–ciliate isogametes. The zoöspores are formed usually two or more in a cell. They escape together from the mother cell enclosed in a membrane, but soon separate and after swimming about for a short time become attached to some object by the ciliated end and by growth and cell division become new filaments. Some cells produce gametes, which, besides having only two cilia, are much smaller and more numerous than zoöspores. After escaping, the gametes fuse in pairs to form resting zygospores. Upon germination, the zygospore does not produce a new plant directly but, as in Hydrodictyon, produces a number of zoöspores each of which produces a new plant. Thus, instead of one, a number of new plants arise from the zygospore, a feature of advantage in the multiplication of new plants.

Another form, similar in a number of ways to Ulothrix, is Cladophora which has long branched filaments that form long, green, hair-like tufts, which, with one end anchored to a stone or some other object, wave back and forth in moving streams. The cells are multinucleate and contain many chloroplasts. Reproduction is by zoöspores and isogametes, but the zygospore develops a new plant directly.

Oedogonium.—This form (*Fig. 268*), common in lakes and ponds, is similar to Ulothrix in the character of the filament, but shows marked advancement in methods of reproduction. The zoöspores, formed only one in a cell and consequently very large, have numerous cilia forming a crown at the forward end. Sexual reproduction is distinctly heterogamous. The eggs, which are large and packed with food, are borne in much enlarged cells called *oögonia*. Each oögonium bears one egg and is simply a transformed vegetative cell of the filament. Other small cells produce the sperms which resemble the zoöspores except in size. The sperms swim to the oögonia, enter, and fertilize the eggs and thick-walled resting oöspores are then formed. Upon germina-

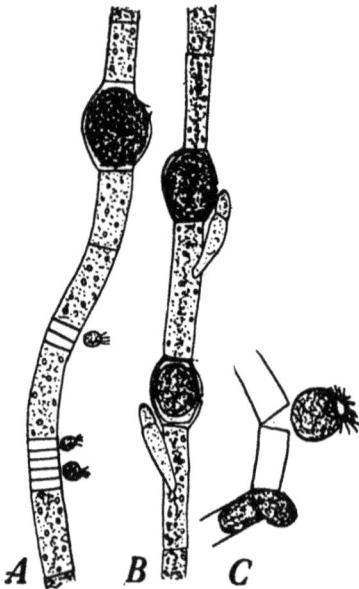

FIG. 268.—*Oedogonium.* *A*, a portion of a filament of *Oedogonium echinospermum*, showing some vegetative cells and oögonium above and some antheridia below from which sperms are escaping; *B*, a portion of a female filament of *OEDOGONIUM HUNTII*, showing oögonia and two dwarf male plants attached near the oögonia; *C*, zoöspores of an Oedogonium escaping from the cells of the filament. × about 300. Drawn from Wolle.

tion the oöspore forms four zoöspores, each of which develops a new filament. In some forms of Oedogonium there are both male and female filaments. In some species the male plants are miniature filaments and attach themselves to the female plants, where they produce sperms in their terminal cells.

Coleochaete. — This form (*Fig. 269*), found growing attached to water plants, has a disk-shaped plant body and also presents some new features in connection with its reproduction. Like Oedogonium it reproduces by zoöspores and sexually by oöspores.

One of the new features is the development of a case around the oöspore by the adjacent cells. This feature suggests a close relationship of this form to the higher Algae, where the formation of a case around the immediate product of the oöspore is a prevalent feature. The second new feature is that the oöspore upon germination develops neither a plant nor zoöspores, but a structure consisting of several cells each of which develops a zoöspore from which a new plant arises. Thus between fertilization and the development of new plants,

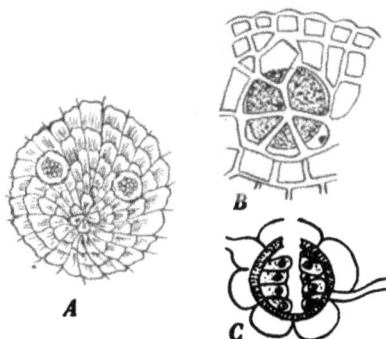

FIG. 269. — *Coleochaete scutata.* A, the plate-like plant body with two oögonia developed ($\times$ 25); B, thick-walled oöspore surrounded by vegetative cells (much enlarged); C, a much enlarged section through the oöspore and its jacket of sterile cells, showing the multicellular body produced by the oöspore, each cell of which produces a zoöspore. Redrawn from Wolle, Atkinson, and Altmanns.

there is introduced a new structural stage and one that is characteristic of higher plants. These new features with others have led to the theory that the higher plants have evolved from Algae of the type of Coleochaete.

In having multicellular plant bodies and more advanced methods of reproduction, the Confervales, as a group, show advancement over the preceding groups. The plant body is a simple filament, branched filament, or a disk-shaped structure. Sexual reproduction, which is isogamous in the lower forms, advances to heterogamy where the two kinds of gametes occur in

special cells and often on different plants.   Also in the higher
forms, the introduction of a case around the oöspore, and a new
structural stage between fertilization and the formation of new
plants, suggests a relationship to the higher plants.   On the other
hand, the simpler forms resemble some of the Protococcales from
which the Confervales have probably been evolved.

Conjugating Algae (Conjugales). — This group is so named
because of the peculiar conjugating habit, in which the contents
of two cells fuse to form zygospores.   Some are unicellular but
many are filamentous.   They include Spirogyra and others that

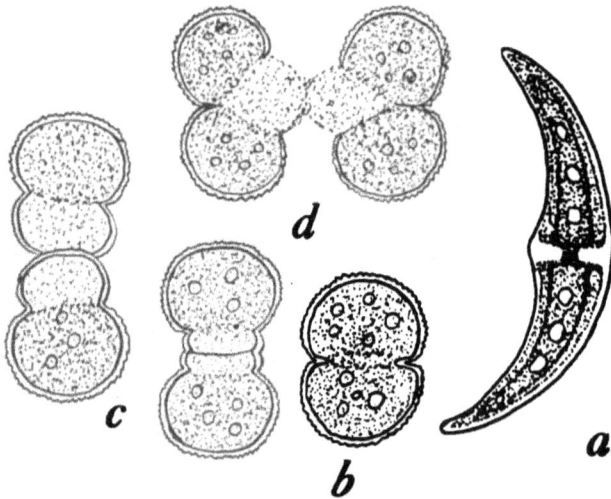

Fig. 270. — *Desmids.* *a* and *b*, two common species of Desmids highly
magnified; at the right of *c*, a Desmid dividing, and at the left of *c*, each
daughter cell resulting from the division developing a new half; at *d*, the protoplasts of two Desmids are escaping and conjugating.   Redrawn from Curtis.

are very common nearly everywhere in fresh water.   They are
free floating, and the filamentous forms often form extensive
floating mats, which are buoyed up by the oxygen entangled
among the filaments.   Some, owing to the shape and arrangement of their chloroplasts, are attractive plants under the microscope.   One peculiar feature of the group is that, although the
plants are aquatic, there are no ciliated cells of any kind.

Desmids. — The simplest of the Conjugales are the *Desmids,*
which are unicellular floating plants that exhibit a variety of
shapes and some are extremely beautiful (*Fig. 270*).   They are

abundant fresh water plants, and in the examination of other forms of fresh water Algae with the microscope one usually finds some Desmids present. The cell is peculiar in being organized into symmetrical halves, which are separated by a constriction that forms an isthmus. The nucleus is in the isthmus, and in each half there is a chloroplast and a number of pyrenoids.

They reproduce in two ways, by cell division and by zygospores. In multiplying by cell division, the cell divides at the isthmus, the halves separate, and the portion of the isthmus remaining to each half develops a new half and thus a new individual is formed. In sexual reproduction the cells pair and the protoplasts, which escape through ruptures at the isthmus, fuse and form a zygospore. Sometimes the cells after pairing become connected by a tube through which the protoplasts reach each other. In either case the entire protoplasts of cells conjugate.

Spirogyra. — *Spirogyra* (*Fig. 271*), very common in ponds, sluggish streams, and watering troughs, is the most familiar filamentous form of the Conjugales and the one most commonly studied in elementary classes. It gets its name from its large and beautiful spiral chloroplasts. Its cells are all alike and it pro-

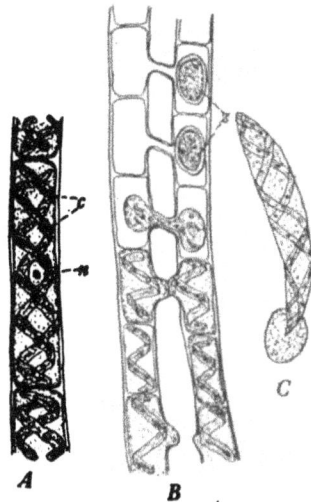

Fig. 271. — A species of *Spirogyra*. *A*, a portion of a filament showing a vegetative cell with its spiral chloroplasts (*c*) and nucleus (*n*) ($\times$ 100); *B*, filaments conjugating and two zygospores (*z*) fully formed; *C*, a zygospore germinating and producing a new filament ($\times$ 150). *A* and *B* from nature, and *C* from Wolle.

duces no zoöspores. Its sexual reproduction, in which the gametes reach each other through tubes, is its important feature. Under certain conditions, filaments pair and line up side by side. In this position, the cells of the filaments grow toward each other in tubular projections which unite and form open passage ways between the cells of the paired filaments. The protoplasts of one filament pass through these tubes and fuse with the protoplasts of the other filament as shown in *Figure 271*. The protoplasts are unlike, for one migrates while the other does not. In behavior the migrating protoplasts may be regarded as sperms and the passive ones as eggs, although they show no differentiation in size or structure. Also, the filament which loses its protoplasts may be regarded as male and the receiving filament as a female individual. The zygospore builds about itself a heavy wall and at the end of a rest period develops directly into a new filament.

It is now seen that the Conjugales stand quite apart from the previous groups in having no zoöspores or swimming gametes,

FIG. 272. — A species of *Vaucheria* (*Vaucheria sessilis*), showing the coenocytic habit of the filament, the oögonia at *o*, the antheridia at *a*, and the sperms escaping from an antheridium and entering an oögonium at *s*.   × 75. Partly drawn from nature and partly diagrammatic.

and in having a peculiar kind of conjugation, in which entire protoplasts fuse and commonly reach each other through tubes. Although the gametes are alike in size and structure, they show some differentiation in the way they behave. The group is considered a highly specialized one.

Tubular Algae (Siphonales). — These Algae, of which there are about 300 species, are so named because the plant body, no matter how long and thread-like, has no cross walls and, therefore, resembles a tube filled with protoplasm. The protoplasm contains many nuclei and many chloroplasts, and may be regarded as a much elongated multinucleate cell or as a filament with cross walls omitted. Such a plant body is called a *coenocyte*. The majority of the Siphonales are marine forms, living in warm seas, but there are a number of species living in fresh water and some on moist shaded soil.

Vaucheria. — *Vaucheria* (*Fig. 272*) is one form of the Siphonales that is common in fresh water and on moist shaded soil. The long filaments, usually much coarser than those of Spirogyra and usually branched, interlace and form felt-like masses, on which account Vaucheria is often called Green Felt. The green or yellowish green felt-like mats of the species growing on moist soil are common in flowerpots and on and under the benches in greenhouses. Other species are common in ponds and sluggish streams.

Vaucheria forms zoöspores and heterogametes. In forming a zoöspore a portion of protoplasm at the end of the filament is cut off from the rest by a cross wall. This severed mass of protoplasm escapes from the filament as a multinucleate and multiciliate zoöspore, large enough to be seen with the naked eye. After swimming about for a time the zoöspore comes to rest and elongates into a new filament.

Sexual reproduction shows advancement in that the gametes are borne in well-defined sex organs, which are

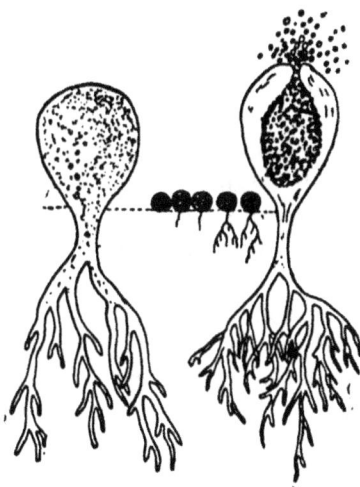

FIG. 273. — *Botrydium granulatum.* At the left, the vegetative plant body, showing the root-like projections below and the balloon-like top above ground; at the right, a plant in which zoöspores have formed and are escaping; between the enlarged plants, plants about natural size. Drawn with modifications from Wolle.

special structures for bearing sex cells. The oögonium, oval in shape, bears one large egg, and the antheridium containing many sperms is near it and is the end cell of a short curved branch. The sperms escape, reach the egg through a special opening in the oögonium, and one of them fertilizes the egg. The heavy-walled oöspore upon germination forms a new filament directly.

There are, however, some Siphonales in which sexual reproduction is of a simpler type. For example, in *Botrydium* (*Fig. 273*), a form with a small balloon-shaped plant body, which is commonly found projecting from moist soil, there are no sex organs and the gametes are alike.

The Siphonales are most peculiar in having a tube-like plant body. In the production of well-defined sex organs they show considerable advancement in sexual reproduction.

Summary of Green Algae. — In having chloroplasts and well-defined nucleus and cytoplasm, the cells of the Green Algae are more advanced than those of the Blue-green Algae. In the simplest forms the plant body is a single cell, either motile or non-motile, and the uniting of cells into colonies is a prominent feature. In the higher forms the plant body is multicellular and in the form of a filament or disk. The multicellular forms have not only established the habit of cells living together to form a complex plant body but have also to some extent differentiated cells. These habits look forward toward the formation of plants consisting of a countless number of cells, which are differentiated into tissues, such as occur in the higher plants. They introduced sex cells which were at first alike, and later differentiated the sex cells, thus introducing eggs and sperms, the sex cells of the higher plants. They also introduced sex organs which are prominent structures in the Mosses and Ferns.

Brown Algae (Phaeophyceae)

These Algae are marine forms, occurring on all sea coasts but more abundantly in the cooler waters. They have two pigments, chlorophyll and a brown pigment called *fucoxanthin*, but the brown pigment obscures the green one and determines the color of the plant. Both pigments probably help in the manufacture of food, although the exact function of fucoxanthin is not known. These Algae grow anchored by holdfasts to the rocks and their bodies are so tough and leathery that they are not injured by the beating of the waves.

Although a few are simple filaments, most of them are much more complex than any of the Green Algae. The plant body of the majority of them not only consists of a greater number of cells, but there is more differentiation among the cells than in the Green Algae. In the largest of them the plant body often attains a length of several hundred feet. As shown in *Figure 274*, the plant body commonly consists of a stalk bearing leaf-like branches and attached to a support by root-like holdfasts. One might think such a plant too complex to be classed as a Thallophyte, for, according to definition, a Thallophyte is a plant not differentiated into roots, stem, and leaves. However, when the structure of these parts that so much resemble roots, stems, and leaves is studied, one finds that they are too simple in structure to be classed as such organs, although they mark a notable advancement over the Green Algae in the differentiation of the plant body. Some have special swollen regions called air bladders, which help

Fig. 274. — One of the Brown Algae, *Macrocystis*, showing the root-like holdfasts, the stem-like axis, and the leaf-like blades. Much reduced. Redrawn with modifications from Harvey.

the plant to float, and in connection with reproduction there is much differentiation shown by some forms.

There are about 1000 species of Brown Algae known and these are divided into two groups, one of which comprises the *Kelps* and closely related forms, and the other, the *Rockweeds* and *Gulfweeds*.

Kelps and Closely Related Forms (Phaeosporales). — This order comprises a number of families of which the *Laminarias* or *Kelps* are the largest forms.

Laminarias. — These are the largest of Algae, and include such conspicuous forms as *Nereocystis*, *Postelsia*, or Sea Palm, and the huge *Macrocystis* (*Fig. 274*), which is sometimes more than 200 feet in length. It is from the massive plant bodies of the

Kelps that much potassium for fertilizers is obtained (*Fig. 275*). Although the Kelps have massive and complex plant bodies, their reproduction, so far as known, is not so complete as that of some Green Algae. Their reproduction is sexual and the small ciliated gametes are borne in special cells which occur in patches

FIG. 275. — Harvesting Kelp on the Pacific Coast. From *Report 100*, U. S. Dept. of Agriculture.

on the surfaces of the leaf-like branches. The zygospore develops a new plant directly.

Ectocarpus. — This form (*Fig. 276*), although belonging to the same order, contrasts strikingly in size with the Kelps, for it is a slender filamentous form not much larger than some of the Green Algae. This form also shows some interesting features in connection with reproduction which is effected through the production of both zoöspores and gametes.

The zoöspores are produced in certain cells which become transformed into *sporangia*. In forming a sporangium, a single cell within the filament or at the end of a branch usually enlarges and its protoplasm divides up into zoöspores. The zoöspores bear their cilia laterally and not terminally as in the Green Algae, but function in the same way by growing directly into new plants.

The gametes are produced in a multicellular structure known as a *gametangium*, and, as in case of a sporangium, the gametangium may be formed from a cell within the filament or from a terminal cell on a short lateral branch.   The small cubical cells composing a gametangium are packed closely together and each

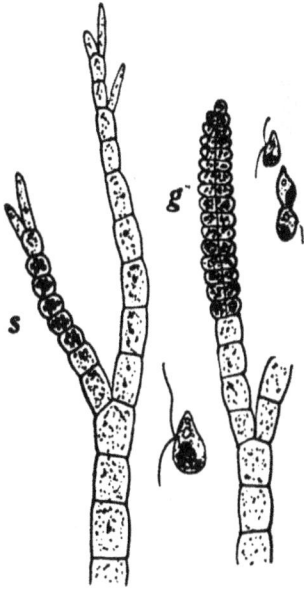

FIG. 276. — Portions of two filaments of *Ectocarpus*, showing reproduction.   At *s* are shown sporangia, and between the filaments, a zoöspore.   At *g* are shown a gametangium and a single sperm and two sperms fusing at the right.   Redrawn with modifications from Curtis.

FIG. 277. — Plant body of *Fucus vesiculosus* (× ½).   In the swollen tips are the conceptacles in which the sex organs occur, and at various places occur bladder - like floats.

produces a biciliate zoöspore-like gamete.   After escaping the gametes fuse in pairs and form zygospores.   In this plant such gradations occur between sporangia and gametangia and between zoöspores and gametes, as to afford considerable support for the theory that gametes are simply zoöspores which are too small to function alone.

Rockweeds and Gulfweeds (Fucales). — In this order the plant body may reach a meter in length, but is usually much

smaller.   Although strictly aquatic, they produce no zoöspores
and their sexual reproduction is much specialized.

Rockweeds. — These are very common Seaweeds and are
especially abundant on rocky shores.   The plant body, sometimes
a foot or more in length, is much branched and has bladder-
like floats and commonly special reproductive structures.   The
Rockweeds are common in fish markets, being used as a packing

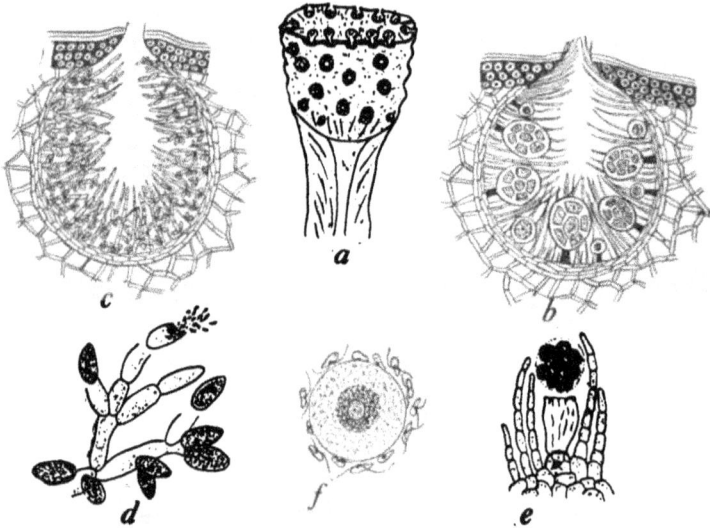

Fig. 278. — Reproduction in *Fucus vesiculosus.*   *a*, section through a
swollen tip, showing sections through some of the conceptacles; *b*, much
enlarged section through an oögonial conceptacle, showing the pore-like opening to the exterior and the oögonia within; *c*, a similar section through a
conceptacle containing antheridia which appear as small bodies on the filaments projecting from the walls of the conceptacle; *d*, antheridia much enlarged and one antheridium shedding its sperms; *e*, oögonium from which
the eggs are escaping; *f*, sperms swarming around an egg.

in the shipment of crabs and other shell fish.   Along the west
coast of South America and also in other countries, Fucus is used
for food by the inhabitants, and it is also used as a fertilizer and
as a source of iodine.

Fucus vesiculosus, one of the commonest of the Rockweeds, will
serve to illustrate the character of the plant body and the peculiar
features of reproduction, the former being shown in *Figure 277*
and the latter in *Figure 278*.   The gametes are differentiated

and are borne in sex organs, which are also quite unlike. The sex organs are borne in hollow conceptacles, which occur in large numbers in the swollen tips of the branches. Each conceptacle opens to the exterior by a pore-like opening. In this species the male and female sex organs do not occur together in the same conceptacles as they do in some species. The oögonium is a large, globular, stalked cell and in this species contains eight eggs, but the number ranges from one to eight in other species of Fucus. The antheridia are borne on the lateral branches of much-branched filaments, which project from the wall of the conceptacle. They are oval cells which produce numerous sperms. A curious feature of Fucus is that the eggs as well as the sperms are discharged from the conceptacle before fertilization. The eggs while passively floating about are surrounded by swarms of sperms, which sometimes, by their vigorous movements, give the eggs a rotary motion. In fertilization one sperm, after penetrating the cytoplasm of the egg, fuses with the egg nucleus and thus an oöspore is formed which develops a new plant.

Fig. 279. — A portion of a plant of *Sargassum vulgare*, showing the floats and the stem- and leaf-like structures. × ½.

Gulfweeds (Sargassum). — The Gulfweeds, well known in connection with the Sargasso Sea, are sometimes a meter in length and are more differentiated than the Rockweeds (*Fig. 279*). In form the stalks and leaf-like branches resemble very much the stems and leaves of the higher plants, although they are very different in structure. The stems are at first anchored by root-like holdfasts and bear many stalked air bladders, which buoy up the plant when attached and float it when torn free. Other short, thick, axillary branches contain the conceptacles. So far as known their reproduction is similar to that of the Rockweeds.

It is now evident that among the Brown Algae there is more differentiation of plant body and more specialization in sexuality than among the Green Algae.   Except in their lowest forms, they show no affinities with the Green Algae and consequently are supposed to have originated independently and probably from such organisms as gave rise to the Green Algae.   Unlike the Green Algae they show no evidence of having led to higher forms.

Red Algae (Rhodophyceae)

These Algae are mainly marine forms, although some forms occur in streams.   Besides the green they have a red pigment called *phycoerythrin* which determines their color.   Some also

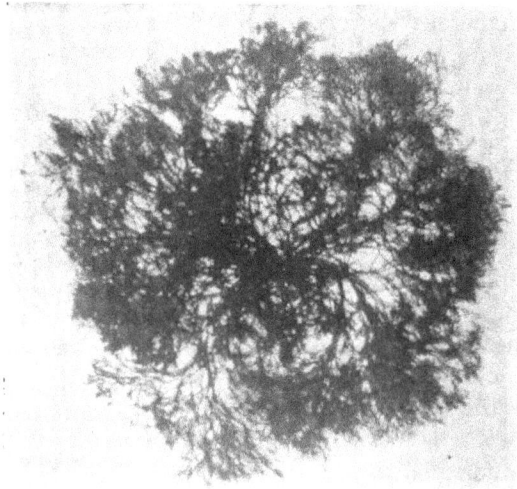

FIG. 280. — A finely branched Red Alga.   Natural size.

have a blue pigment, *phycocyanin*.   They are not so bulky as the Brown Algae, but they exceed them in number of species and are much more diversified in form.   Some are mere filaments no larger than Vaucheria.   They live mostly below low water mark and often at depths of more than 100 feet in clear waters.

The plant body, commonly only a few inches in length, is flat, thin, and flexible and usually much branched.   Some kinds are finely branched, as the Sea Mosses noted also for their beautiful colors of red, violet, and purple (*Fig. 280*).   As in the Brown

Algae, the plant body is commonly differentiated into parts similar in form, although not in structure, to the roots, stems, and leaves of the higher plants. The cells are commonly arranged in such definite lines that the plant body has the appearance of a bundle of closely joined simple filaments. The evident protoplasmic connections between cells and the gelatinization of cell walls are other notable features.

Fig. 281. — Irish Moss, *Chondrus crispus*, much used for food. Natural size.

The life history of some of them is quite complex. They have spores, but their spores and likewise their gametes have no cilia, a curious feature since these plants are wholly aquatic. The female sex organ is multicellular and more complex than the sex organs of the Brown Algae.

Several forms of the Red Algae are of economic importance. Some are used as food, being dried and kept for long periods The gelatinous material obtained from Red Algae forms a delicacy much desired by some people. The form called Irish Moss, shown in *Figure 281*, is collected in large quantities and employed in the manufacture of jelly, which is used directly as food and as the basis for the preparation of other foods. Agar-agar, which is used as a medium in which Bacteria and Fungi are grown, is a gelatinous product obtained from Red Algae.

Nemalion. — This plant is one of the simpler forms of Red Algae. The plant body is a rather soft, cord-like, branching

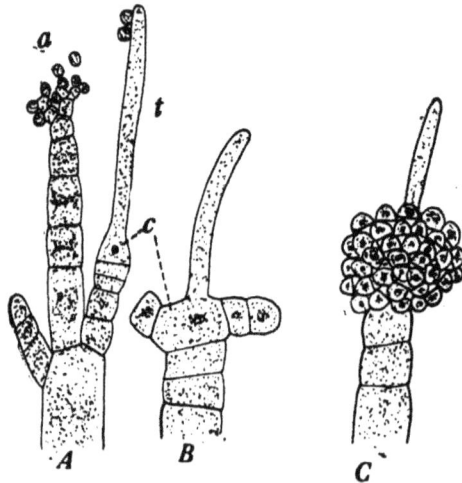

Fig. 282. — Reproduction in *Nemalion*. *A*, a portion of Nemalion, bearing antheridia at *a* and at the right a procarp consisting of carpogonium (*c*) and trichogyne (*t*) to the tip of which two sperms have become attached; *B*, fertilized carpogonium beginning to develop branches on the ends of which the carpospores are borne; *C*, mature cystocarp consisting exteriorly of carpospores. × 100–150. Redrawn with modifications from Bornet.

structure, composed of a large number of filaments, which are held together by a stiff gelatinous substance. There is a central axis of delicate threads and an outer region consisting of short branches pointing outward.

Nemalion produces both spores and gametes (*Fig. 282*). The two kinds of reproduction are intimately related, for the production of spores follows closely as a result of fertilization.

The female sex organ, which is a very peculiar structure in the Red Algae, is called a *procarp*. In Nemalion the procarp is borne on the end of a branch and at first apparently consists of two cells, a basal one called *carpogonium* and a much elongated terminal one called *trichogyne*. The two cells are not separated by a wall and the nucleus soon disappears from the trichogyne and the two cells then appear as a single one with a bulbous base and a hair-like extension. The carpogonium corresponds to the oögonium in other Algae, for it contains a protoplast which functions as an egg.

The antheria, which are borne in clusters at the ends of short branches, are single cells, and the protoplast of each antheridium becomes binucleate and functions as a sperm. After these binucleate protoplasts are discharged from the antheridia, they depend upon water currents to carry them to the female sex organs as they have no cilia. When they come in contact with the trichogyne, the two walls in contact are resorbed, and the two male nuclei of the sperm pass into the trichogyne through the perforation. A number of sperms may discharge their nuclei into the same trichogyne, but only one male nucleus passes on into the carpogonium and fuses with the female nucleus. After fertilization, the carpogonium develops numerous short filaments, each of which bears a spore, called a *carpospore*, at its tip. The carpospores, short filaments, and the carpogonium together constitute the structure known as a *cystocarp*. The carpospores upon germination develop sexual plants, thus completing the life history.

Polysiphonia. — This plant (*Fig. 283*) is a representative of the complex forms of Red Algae. It is a much-branched complex filament and is so named because it has a central row of elongated cells (axial siphon), enclosed by peripheral cells. This plant presents much differentiation and ordinarily a life history involves three types of individuals — male, female, and sexless plants.

The *male plants* bear their antheridia on very short lateral branches which arise from the axial siphon and bear the antheridia somewhat laterally on their tips. The protoplast of an antheridium contains only one nucleus and is not discharged as in Nemalion, but the antheridium breaks off bodily and is floated to the trichogyne.

The female plant produces a procarp more complex than that of Nemalion. The procarp consists of other cells in addition to the carpogonium and trichogyne. The *pericentral cell*, the large cell of the axis from which the carpogonium arises and the vegetative cells, known as auxiliary cells, surrounding the carpogonium take part in forming the cystocarp and are therefore considered a part of the procarp. So in polysiphonia a procarp

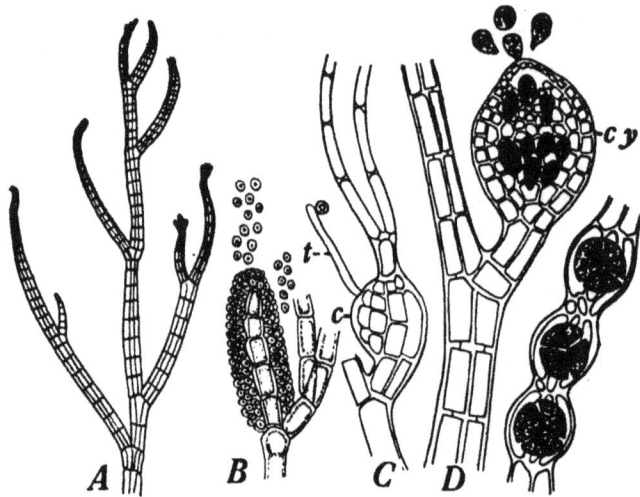

FIG. 283. — *Polysiphonia violacea.* *A*, a part of a plant showing the branching and multicellular character of the filament (× 75); *B*, a branch bearing antheridia, some of which have broken away (× 400); *C*, branch bearing a procarp consisting of carpogonium and adjacent cells at *c* and trichogyne (*t*) to the tip of which a sperm is attached (× 500); *D*, branch bearing a mature cystocarp (*cy*) from which carpospores are shown escaping through an opening in the jacket of the cystocarp (× 75); at the right is a part of a tetrasporic plant bearing three tetrasporangia (× 100).

consists of trichogyne, carpogonium, pericentral cell, and auxiliary cells.

After fertilization, which is essentially the same as in Nemalion, the carpogonium, pericentral cell, and auxiliary cells unite in forming a large chamber from which lobes arise, and on the ends of these lobes the carpospores are produced. In the meantime vegetative cells, growing up from below, form a jacket which encloses the spore-bearing structure, thus completing the formation of the cystocarp (meaning a fruit case), which in this plant is a genuine cystocarp. From this cystocarp the carpospores escape and upon germination produce an asexual or *tetrasporic plant.*

The *tetrasporic plant* in character of plant body is very similar to the sex plants. On it no sex organs occur. It bears spores known as *tetraspores*, so named because the number occurring in a sporangium is four. Why the plant is called a tetrasporic plant is now clear. The sporangia, which have a one-celled stalk, arise laterally from the axial siphon and push their way through the peripheral cells. The tetraspores escape and upon germination give rise to plants that bear sex organs, either antheridia or procarps.

This type of life history in which sexual plants alternate with asexual plants is a feature of considerable significance because it is a feature characteristic of plants above Thallophytes. It is known as "alternation of generations" and its significance will be explained in the groups where it is a well-established feature. The alternation of generations, the cystocarp, and more complex female sex organs are the chief features introduced by the Red Algae.

When Polysiphonia is compared with some of the simplest forms of Algae, as some of the one-celled Blue-green Algae or even Pleurococcus, it is obvious that the Algae made notable advancements. The plant body, a single cell in the simplest forms, becomes a multicellular plant body showing considerable differentiation of parts as to form and function in the higher forms. Reproduction, accomplished entirely by cell division in the simplest Algae, gradually becomes more complex through the groups, involving zoöspores, gametes, the differentiation of gametes, and the development of sex organs.

There is very little reliable data as to how each group of Algae arose. It is not probable that they arose from each other, but probably all have developed independently from some unknown ancestor. Regardless of how they arose, the groups mark in a general way some of the steps in the evolution of the higher plants.

Some Alga-like Thallophytes not Definitely Classified

There are three groups of alga-like plants, the *Flagellates*, *Diatoms*, and *Stoneworts*, which have not been definitely classified.

Flagellates. — These are free-swimming unicellular organisms of fresh water. They have both plant and animal features, on which account they are regarded as intermediate between the plant and animal kingdoms. The protoplast is naked or invested by a membrane which usually contains no cellulose. They are commonly abundant in stagnant water and among Green Algae some are usually present.

Euglena represented in *Figure 284* is one of the most common of the 300 or more species and will serve to show the structure and habits of the group. Euglena is quite commonly seen swimming about under the microscope when Algae are being examined. The slender unicellular body bears a long terminal flagellum, has a chloroplast, eye-spot, and pulsating vacuole. These structures are characteristic of the Algae, such as Volvocales and also of protozoa, the one-celled animals. No sexuality is known, and multiplication is effected by longitudinal fission, a method characteristic of the lower animals. At the approach of unfavorable conditions, as in autumn, .it transforms itself into a thick-walled resting spore which germinates and produces one or more new plants when favorable conditions return. Although it usually makes its own food, sometimes Euglena loses its chlorophyll and lives on organic solutions as a saprophyte, thus demonstrating that the saprophytic may readily originate from the independent habit.

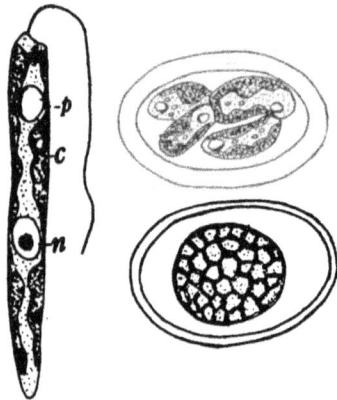

Fig. 284. — A common species of *Euglena* (*Euglena gracilis*). At the left, an adult individual, showing the flagellum, the pulsating vacuole (*p*), the chloroplast (*c*), and the nucleus (*n*) (× 650); at the right and below, Euglena in the spore stage (× 1000); at the right and above, a spore germinating and producing four new individuals (× 1000). Redrawn from Zumstein.

Many of the Flagellates change their forms readily like the Amoeba. Sometimes the individuals form colonies of various shapes and often variously branched.

Such features as the possession of chlorophyll and the formation of thick-walled resting spores suggest a relationship of the Flagellates to plants, while their swimming habits, amoeboid movements, reproduction by longitudinal fission, and such structures as contractile vacuoles and red pigment spots suggest a relationship to the animal kingdom. Consequently, they are regarded as a transition group between plants and animals.

Diatoms. — These one-celled plants are often classed with the Brown Algae on account of their brown pigment, although they differ from the Brown Algae in a number of ways. The Diatoms are a vast assemblage of plants varying widely in form and occurring in vast numbers in fresh water, salt water, and on damp soil. They float or swim commonly on the surface of water and often in such vast numbers as to form a scum. They form a large

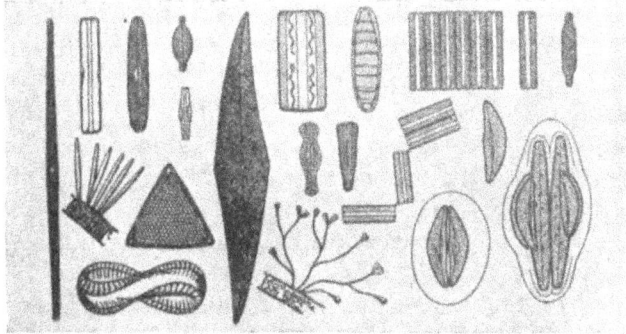

FIG. 285. — Diatoms of various kinds ($\times$ 30–200). In cases where a pair of individuals equal in length are shown, two views of the same Diatom are included. From Kerner.

part of the floating plankton or free-swimming organic world on the surface of the ocean. Many occur as fossils and their silicified walls form a large part of the deposits of siliceous earth in which form they are used in the manufacture of dynamite, scouring powders, etc. Some are free-swimming while others are attached by stalks.

The *plant body* is microscopical and may have most any shape imaginable as may be seen from *Figure 285*. The cell wall, consisting largely of silica, is very rigid and durable and is composed of halves which fit together one over the other much like the two parts of a pill box. The walls of some are delicately but beautifully marked with fine cross lines, which make certain Diatoms suitable objects for testing the definition of microscopes.

Usually there is also a longitudinal line, which is a fissure or series of fine pores through which fine threads of protoplasm project and serve like cilia in locomotion. The halves of the box-like shell of a Diatom are called valves and the appearance of a Diatom depends much upon whether the face of the valve (the valve side), or the side showing the joining of the valves (the girdle side) is seen (*Fig. 286*). The protoplast usually has a large central vacuole with the nucleus suspended in the center by small strands of cytoplasm.

Cell division is the chief method of reproduction. The cell usually divides lengthwise and in such a way that the valves separate with the daughter protoplasts. Each daughter protoplast then develops a new valve on the naked side. In connection with this, a peculiar situation arises. The new valve developed always fits within the old one and consequently there is a gradual reduction in the size of the individuals as division continues, for at each division the daughter protoplast with the smaller valve is necessarily smaller than in the preceding division. However, it has been found that the protoplasts shed their walls when reduction in size has reached a certain degree and in a naked condition grow to full size and then enclose themselves in new valves. This naked protoplast is called an *auxospore* (meaning enlarging spore).

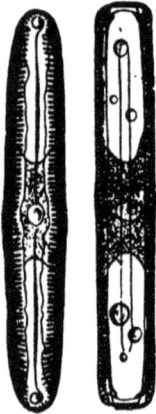

FIG. 286.—A common Diatom, *Navicula viridis*, with valve side shown at the left and the girdle side at the right. In the view of the girdle side one valve is seen to fit over the other. From Strasburger.

It is in connection with these naked protoplasts that the sexual act occurs. Sometimes the protoplasts of contiguous cells conjugate and sometimes the four daughter protoplasts of two contiguous cells escape and conjugate in pairs. The zygospore usually enlarges and then encloses itself in valves.

Thus Diatoms are one-celled and conjugate like some Green Algae, have the color of Brown Algae but have no zoöspores or gametes like the Brown Algae.

Stoneworts. — The Stoneworts constitute the group scientifically known as the *Charales*. Some classify the Stoneworts as

Green Algae because they are green, while others regard them as
so different from any of the Algae as to put them in a separate
class. They grow in fresh and brackish waters and often form
dense masses of vegetation covering large areas. They grow

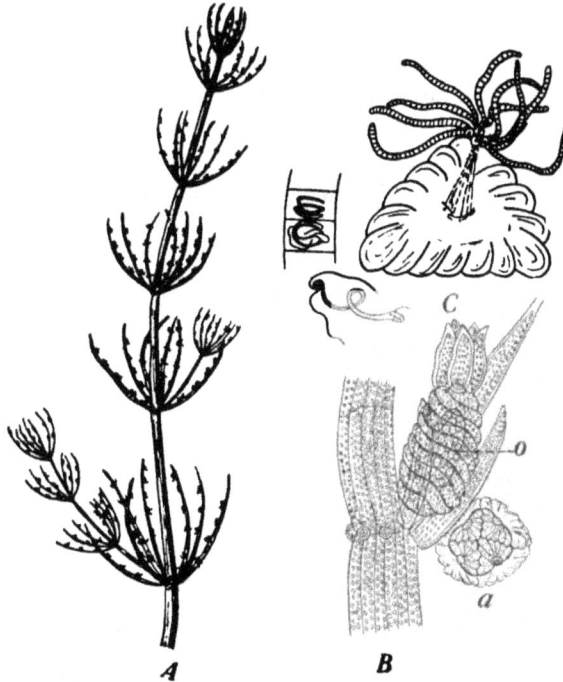

FIG. 287. — *Chara fragilis.* *A*, part of a plant, showing nodes, internodes,
and the two kinds of branches (natural size); *B*, part of a plant, showing a
node bearing sex organs, the oögonium enclosed in its jacket being at *o* and
the antheridium with its shield-shaped wall cells shown at *a* (× 25); *C*, wall
cell of the antheridium, showing the stalk-like projection at the end of which
are borne the filaments in the cells of which the sperms are produced (×
about 50); at the left of *C*, two cells of a filament in which the sperms are
formed, and a single sperm below. Redrawn from Sachs and Thuret.

attached to the bottom and are often so incrusted with calcium
carbonate that they are rough and brittle as the name Stoneworts
suggests.

The plant body has a much branched stem-like axis quite
distinctly differentiated into nodes and internodes (*Fig. 287*).

From the nodes the branches arise in whorls and some branches resemble leaves, while others elongate much more and resemble the main axis.

Their *reproduction* may be illustrated by following that of Chara. There are no asexual spores, but the plant is propagated vegetatively by special tuber-like branches which separate from the nodes and grow into new plants.

Sexual reproduction involves complex structures which are not typical of Algae and which are the most distinguishing features of the Stoneworts. Both antheridia and oögonia (*Fig. 287*) are complex structures. Due to their size and color the sex organs are visible to the unaided eye. Both are developed at the nodes and often close together.

The antheridium is an orange or reddish globular body with a wall composed of eight triangular plate-like cells. From the inner side of each of the wall cells there projects toward the center of the antheridium a much elongated cell which bears a terminal cell. The terminal cell, known as *head cell*, divides into a number of cells and each of these produces a pair of long filaments. Each filament consists of about 200 cells, each of which forms a single sperm. When an antheridium is fully formed, its interior is a tangle of filaments and the sperm output amounts to many thousands. The sperm is a much elongated ciliated structure, resembling the sperms of some of the more complex plants more than those of ordinary Algae.

The oögonium with its jacket is larger and more elongated than the antheridium. The oögonia are often yellow but are not so brightly colored as the antheridia. An oögonium contains one large egg and much stored food in the form of starch and oil. The oögonium is closely invested by cells which grow up from the cells below and, as they elongate, wind spirally around the oögonium, forming a close jacket around it and a crown at its top.

In fertilization the cells of the jacket spread apart at the crown, so that the sperms can enter. After fertilization the jacket hardens, and thus forms a nut-like case for the oöspore. When the oöspore germinates, it does not form a new plant directly but first forms a filament of cells, and the adult plant arises as a branch from this filament. This feature is prominent in the Bryophytes.

It is now evident that the Stoneworts are very different from the ordinary Green Algae, differing from them in structure of plant body, character of sex organs, type of sperms, and life history. They resemble some of the more complex forms of plants more than they resemble the Algae.

CHAPTER XIV

THALLOPHYTES (Continued)

Myxomycetes and Bacteria (Thallophytes lacking food-making pigments)

There are three groups of Thallophytes — the *Myxomycetes*, *Bacteria*, and *Fungi* — which are characterized by the lack of food-making pigments. Having no chlorophyll or other food-making pigments, they are unable to carry on photosynthesis and consequently must depend upon other organisms for their food. Many obtain their food from the decaying bodies of other organisms, while others attack living organisms.

As to how these plants arose, we are not certain. Although some are the simplest of plants, they must have been preceded by green plants, for otherwise there would have been no food for them. They are no doubt degenerate forms of green plants, having lost their food-making pigments as a result of their acquiring the habit of taking food from other organisms. As will be seen later in the study of these groups, the Bacteria have some of the features of the Blue-green Algae, while the Fungi present a number of features found in the Green or the higher groups of Algae. But for the Myxomycetes we have no definite suggestions of any relationships with other groups of plants.

Being dependent plants, these Thallophytes are supposed to have evolved backward, rather than forward. The Fungi, the most complex of the group, present nothing new over the Algae in the way of evolution. To the evolutionists these groups offer very little that is of interest. They concern us chiefly because of their economic importance.

Myxomycetes (Slime Molds)

The *plant body* of the Myxomycetes, commonly called Slime Molds, consists of a large slimy mass of protoplasm not enclosed by cell walls, and hence the term myxomycetes from *myxos* (meaning slime) and *myces* (meaning mold or fungus) (*Fig. 288*). This naked mass of protoplasm is called a *plasmodium*. It is a semi-liquid and is found flowing out of the cracks of rotten logs and stumps, forming white or colored doughy-like masses. They are often found creeping out of the cracks of old plank walks, out of decayed bark, or out of apple pumice around a cider mill. Some of the Myxomycetes are parasites, living in the tissues of higher plants and often causing much injury.

FIG. 288. — Plasmodium of a Myxomycete growing on wood. X about ½.

The plasmodium is multinucleate and is able, by putting out and withdrawing regions of its body, to move about like a gigantic Amoeba. Sometimes the plasmodium breaks up into many smaller portions which are able, by means of cilia or flagella, to move about like the low forms of animals. The Myxomycetes have the characteristics of both plants and animals, and opinions differ as to whether they should be classed as plants or animals.

FIG. 289. — *A*, Myxomycete, *Stemonitis*, in which the plasmodium has been transformed into slender stalked sporangia (*sp*) which bear numerous spores (*s*).

Their *method of obtaining food* consists chiefly in digesting the substances found in other plants. Those forms which live on dead organisms are able to utilize the carbohydrates remaining in decaying organic matter, while those attacking living plants prey upon the tissues of the plant attacked. Those forms living on dead organisms are called *saprophytes*, while those forms living on living organisms are called *parasites*. The living organism attacked is called the *host*.

Reproduction in the Myxomycetes is asexual. The first indication of reproduction in most of the saprophytic forms is the appearance of upward projections on the surface of the plasmodium. Into these projections, which are at first hollow structures, varying in shape according to the species, the remaining protoplasm of the plasmodium passes until they are filled. Often nearly the entire plasmodium is used in forming and filling

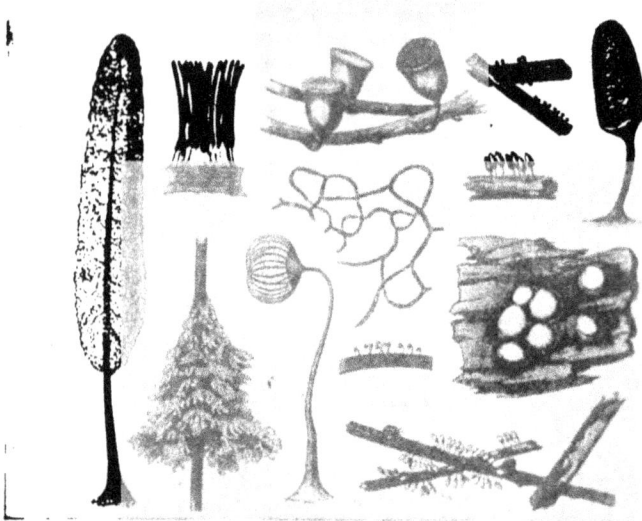

Fig. 290. — Various Myxomycetes, showing various types of sporangia. The large sporangium at the left and the third one from the left, below, have shed the spores, and the capillitium, the lace-like framework of the sporangium, is plainly visible. The larger ones are larger than natural size, the smaller ones are reduced. From Kerner.

the projections. The protoplasm filling the upper part of each projection forms numerous, small, globular spores with heavy

Fig. 291. — Spores of a Myxomycete germinating and producing motile animal-like bodies which usually multiply and later fuse to form a plasmodium. Much enlarged. From Woronin.

walls, and thus the projection becomes a stalked sporangium (*Fig. 289*). In the interior of the sporangium there is often a lace-like framework, called *capillitium*, which assists through its hygroscopic movements in the shedding of the spores (*Fig. 290*).

After the spores are mature, the wall of the sporangium breaks
open and the spores are scattered far and near by wind, animals,
and other agencies. When the spores fall on a suitable object
and conditions are right, the protoplasm breaks out of the heavy
wall and either grows directly into a new plasmodium, or produces cilia, swims about, and multiplies like the simple one-celled
forms of animals (*Fig. 291*), the plasmodium being formed later
by the fusion of these animal-like bodies.

Some Myxomycetes of Economic Importance

Most of the Myxomycetes are saprophytes and consequently
the group is not so important economically as the Bacteria and
Fungi. Of course the saprophytic forms are of some importance

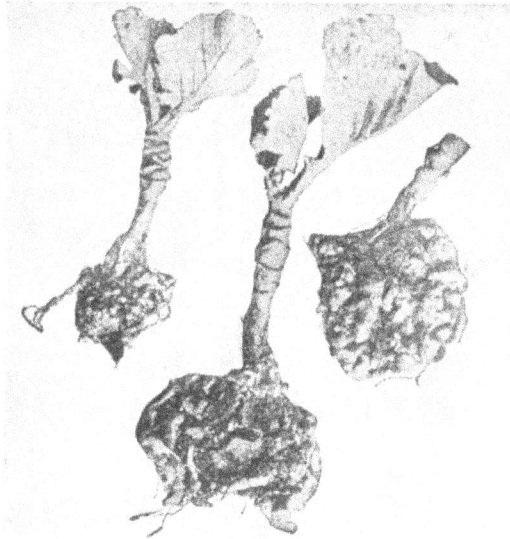

Fig. 292. — Cabbage plants attacked by the Club Root Myxomycete
(*Plasmodiophora Brassicae*) which causes wart-like distortions. From Woronin.

because they disintegrate organic matter and make it soluble, so
that it can soak into the soil and be used by higher plants.
There are, however, a few parasitic forms which attack some of
our useful plants and cause considerable trouble and loss.

Club Root of Cabbage.[1] — This is a disease of Cabbage caused by a parasitic Myxomycete. The Myxomycete gains entrance through the roots and lives upon the cells of the plant. The presence of the parasite causes the wart-like developments on the roots and stem of the Cabbage, and so injures the plant that no head is produced and even death often results (*Figure 292*).

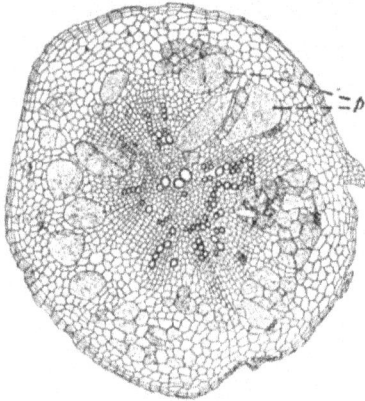

FIG. 293. — Cross section of a root of Cabbage affected with Club Root, showing the plasmodia (*p*) within the tissues. From Woronin.

Within the cells of the Cabbage the plasmodia live and form spores (*Figure 293*). When liberated through the decay of the Cabbage, the spores are carried by water, animals, or wind to other plants. The spores may lie in the ground and infect plants in succeeding years. This disease is not only destructive to Cabbage but often attacks Turnips, Radishes, Rutabagas, and Cauliflower. The important feature in controlling the disease consists in preventing the spores from functioning by burning infected plants, treating the soil with lime or sulphur, and rotation of crops.

Powdery scab of the Irish Potato.[2] — This disease is caused by one or more kinds of Myxomycetes which enter the tubers and roots of the Irish Potato and destroy the tissues (*Fig. 294*). The Amoeba-like plasmodia live in the cells, which, due to the presence

[1] Cabbage Club Root in Virginia. *Bulletin 191*, Virginia Agr. Exp. Sta., 1911.

Studies on Club Root. *Bulletin 175*, Vermont Agr. Exp. Sta., 1913.

Studies on Clubroot of Cruciferous Plants. *Bulletin 387*, Cornell University Agr. Exp. Sta., 1917.

[2] Powdery Scab (Spongospora subterranea) of Potatoes. *Bulletin 82*, U. S. Dept. Agr., 1914.

Powdery Scab of Potatoes. *Bulletin 227*, Maine Agr. Exp. Sta., 1914.

Spongospora subterranea and Phoma tuberosa on the Irish Potato, Vol. 7, No. 5, pp. 213–254, Jour. Agr. Research, U. S. Dept. Agr., 1916.

of the organism, develop abnormally, producing scabby formations which constitute the scabby areas on the tuber or root. The plasmodia are finally transformed into spores which are liberated as powdery masses as the infected tissues die and the spore masses break open. It has been found that the spores can live in the ground for a number of years and may also live adhering to the rind of the Potato. Treating seed Potatoes with weak solutions of formaldehyde or corrosive sublimate to kill the spores adhering to the tubers, and rotating crops, so that the Potatoes are not planted in infected soil are means of controlling the disease.

FIG. 294. — An Irish Potato attacked by a Myxomycete, *Spongospora subterranea.*

Bacteria

Bacteria, of which there are 1400 or more species, are the smallest of plants, and their study requires microscopes of a very high power of magnification. Some spherical forms, visible only through the best microscopes, are less than 0.0005 of a millimeter in diameter, and some Bacteria are known to exist that are ultramicroscopic, that is, too small to be seen with the best microscopes. They are present almost everywhere, occurring in the soil, in water, in the air, and in all organic bodies living or dead. Although so insignificant in size, they are of great importance, because the service of some forms is indispensable to our welfare, while the forms which cause diseases are destructive to both plants and animals. The disease-producing forms are commonly known as germs or microbes. So numerous and important are these simple plants that their study now forms a special subject called *Bacteriology.*

The *plant body* of the Bacteria consists of a single cell. Bacteria are of three general forms: *coccus* forms, which are globular; *bacillus* forms, in which the shape is rod-like; and *spirillum* forms, in which the plant body is a curved rod (*Fig. 295*).

Many of the Bacteria are provided with cilia or terminal flagella, which enable them to move about independently. The cilia are distributed over the body in various ways and are extremely difficult to detect. Some of the motile forms are quite' active and motility is one of the features suggesting that Bacteria are animals. Their cell walls are more or less slimy, and their protoplasm is not definitely organized into nucleus and cytoplasm. These features with their power of resistance suggest a relationship with the Blue-green Algae. They possess no chlorophyll and are almost exclusively parasites or saprophytes. The ability of the protoplasm to endure extreme cold, high temperatures, and drying even surpasses that of the Blue-green Algae. Besides remaining separate or forming filaments, Bacteria commonly have another stage in which numerous individuals are held together in masses or colonies by a matrix of gelatinous substance formed from their walls. This stage is known as the zoögloea stage (*Fig. 296*). These colonies form the characteristic pellicles on nutrient media, as on the water in which hay, Beans, Peas, or other organic substances are decaying, and on bouillon and various solid media (*Fig. 297*). When food is scarce or other conditions unfavorable, some forms shrink their protoplasm and enclose it in an inner heavy wall, thus forming what is called a spore. Enclosed in this heavy wall, they are inactive and extremely resistant to cold, heat, and drying. When transferred by wind or other agents to a suitable medium, they shed the heavy wall and become active again.

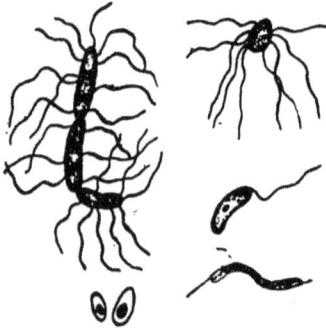

FIG. 295. — Some forms of Bacteria. At the right and above, a coccus form; a bacillus just below; and a spirillum form at the bottom. At the left, above, a chain of bacilli; and, below, bacteria in the spore stage. Very highly magnified.

Their *method of getting food* is essentially the same as in the Myxomycetes. Since they live on or within the food supply, they are in direct contact with the food material, and have only to change it to a soluble form and absorb it through their walls. They secrete enzymes which change insoluble foods to soluble forms and as a result of their activity various substances are produced, the accumulation of which check their activity. Some forms, called *anaërobic*, get along better without air, while others, called *aërobic*, must have air.

Their *reproduction* is accomplished by cell division, which is not so complex and takes place more rapidly than in the cells of

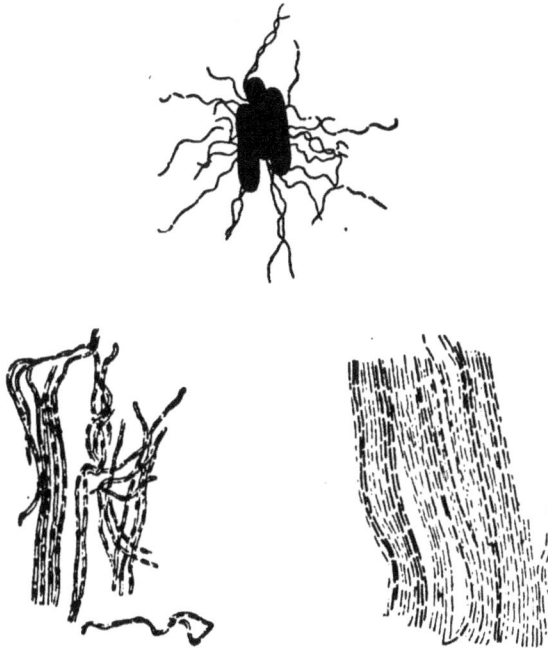

FIG. 296. — *Bacillus subtilis*, a Bacterium of decay. Above, the active form ($\times$ 1500); at the left, below, spore stage ($\times$ 800); at the right, below, the zoögloea stage ($\times$ 500).

the higher plants. Cell division is so rapid that the progeny of one individual often runs into many millions in twenty-four hours. The new individuals may separate immediately after division is complete or cling together in filaments. Sometimes in shrinking the protoplasm and enclosing it in an inner heavy wall in preparation for the resting stage, the protoplasm divides and each separate mass of protoplasm forms a spore. Since each spore is an individual in a dormant protected state, the formation of more than one spore results in the multiplication of individuals.

But a Bacterium commonly forms only one spore, and the formation of spores, therefore, does not generally result in the multiplication of individuals. The spore stage is apparently for protection rather than for multiplication. In the spore stage Bacteria can live where there is no food and when heat and

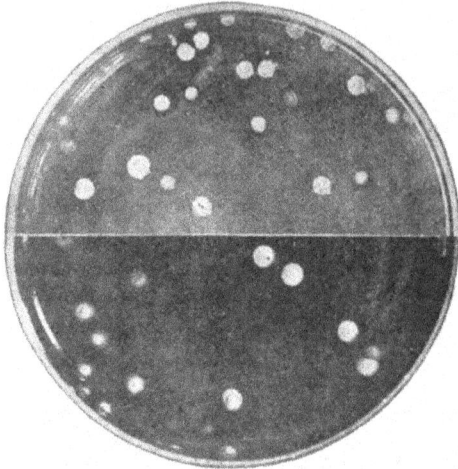

FIG. 297. — A petri dish containing agar upon which are colonies of the Bacterium (*Actinomyces chromogenus*) which attacks Irish Potatoes, causing scabby areas. The white spots are the colonies. From *Bulletin 184*, Vermont Agr. Exp. Sta.

cold are much too extreme for ordinary life. In this condition some Bacteria can endure boiling water for an hour or longer as well as extremely low temperatures. It is the spores of Bacteria that are hard to kill in sterilizing media and other substances. In the spore stage Bacteria can retain their vitality for months or years and, floating about with the dust in the air, reach all kinds of situations.

Some Bacteria of Economic Importance

Bacteria of Decay. — The Bacteria of decay live on dead organisms. By their activity dead organisms, such as straw, weeds, corn stalks, logs, and carcasses of animals, are decomposed into simpler and soluble compounds, in which form they return to the earth and become available nutrients for plants. Their activity helps to rid the earth's surface of débris and to prevent the soil from becoming depleted of plant nutrients. Of course they attack meats, canned fruits, and many other things which we do not wish to have decomposed, but the good they do more than compensates the harm. Methods, such as cold storage, applications of salt and other preservatives, and canning, are employed in checking or preventing the activity of Bacteria in foods. In cold storage the temperature is too low for them to be active. Salt solutions keep them dormant by extracting water from them. In canning those present are killed by heat, and by sealing the cans others are prevented from entering. Alcohol, formaldehyde, carbolic acid, etc., are useful in preventing bacterial action in materials not intended for food.

Bacteria of Fermentation. — These Bacteria attack carbohydrates and break them into simpler substances, such as alcohol, lactic acid, acetic acid, butyric acid, etc. A few forms are shown in *Figure 298*. The product produced depends upon the substance attacked and the kind of Bacteria at work. For example in the fermenting of cider, some Bacteria break the sugar into alcohol and carbon dioxide, while others attack the alcohol, changing it into acetic acid. All the forms working

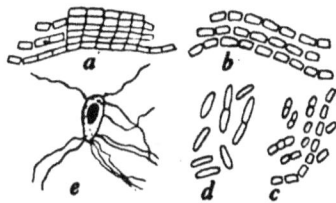

Fig. 298. — Bacteria of fermentation. *a, b,* and *c,* vinegar Bacteria; *d,* Bacteria that ferment milk; *e,* butyric acid Bacteria. × 1000. Redrawn from Fisher.

together change the cider into vinegar. After the vinegar Bacteria become inactive, due to the exhaustion of the food supply or the accumulation of the fermented products, they form the well-known mother of vinegar, which consists of the Bacteria held together in a gelatinous matrix. In milk, certain kinds of Bacteria attack the milk sugar and change it into lactic acid. Another kind produces butyric acid in butter, turning it rancid.

Bacteria of Nitrification and Nitrogen Fixation. — In the soil there are some kinds of Bacteria that change certain nitrogenous compounds of manure and other organic matter into nitrates in which form the nitrogen is available for crops. The advantage to the Bacteria is that they secure energy in this way from these compounds, while the advantage to the soil is that the nitrogen of the compounds decomposed is put in an available form for other plants. The Bacteria use the chemical energy derived from the oxidation of organic compounds in performing the work involved in building up their bodies. There are a few exceptional forms of soil Bacteria which can actually make their own food, and this they do by using this chemical energy, as green plants do sunlight, in the construction of foods from carbon dioxide and water.

FIG. 299. — A young Red Clover plant, showing the root nodules that are associated with the nitrogen fixing Bacteria. From *Farmer's Bulletin 435*, U. S. Dept. of Agriculture.

There are other kinds of soil Bacteria which have the power of actually increasing the nitrogen in the soil. They incorporate the gaseous nitrogen of the air into nitrogen compounds, which they use in building up their own bodies, and when their bodies decay, these nitrogenous compounds are added to the soil, which is thereby enriched. Some kinds of these Bacteria live independently in the soil, while some kinds are associated with higher plants, especially the Legumes, such as Clover, Alfalfa, Beans, etc. (*Fig. 299*). They enter the roots of these plants, and, as a result of the attack, the roots form nodules in which the Bacteria live and carry on their work of fixing nitrogen. It is due to their association with these Bacteria that the Legumes are important in enriching the soil.

Pathogenic bacteria. — These are the disease-producing forms. They prey upon both animals and plants. The disease is the result of their direct attack upon the tissues, or of the poisons, called *toxins*, which they excrete. They produce most of the diseases of human beings, such as erysipelas, tetanus, diphtheria, tuberculosis, typhoid fever, pneumonia, cholera, etc. (*Fig. 300*). Among our domesticated animals, such diseases as hog cholera, splenic fever, glanders, black-leg, etc., are caused by Bacteria. The fighting of these forms, either to exclude, destroy, or neutralize them, is the business of modern medicine and surgery. Besides the dangerous forms which attack animals, there are numerous harmless forms constantly present throughout the alimentary canal.

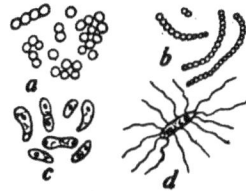

FIG. 300.—Some pathogenic Bacteria. *a*, pus cocci; *b*, erysipelas cocci; *c*, Bacteria causing diphtheria; *d*, typhoid bacilli. × 1500. Redrawn from Fisher.

Among plants the disease-producing Bacteria are almost as busy as among animals. Not only the tender herbaceous plants but even the trees are attacked, and the loss caused every year is large.

FIG. 301. — Potato tuber affected with the Potato Scab caused by a Bacterium, *Actinomyces chromogenus*. From *Bulletin 184*, Vermont Agr. Exp. Sta.

Black-rot of Cabbage. — This disease occurs on Cabbage, Turnips, and other plants of this family. The Bacteria enter through the openings of the leaf and advance through the vascular bundles. They are able to destroy cell walls as well as the living content of the cells. Their presence in the leaf causes a blackening of the veins and a yellowing of the mesophyll. The disease may spread to the stem, where it clogs the vascular bundles and destroys tissues. Plants attacked lose their leaves and are dwarfed or killed.

Potato Scab.[1] — There are a number of organisms which attack the Irish Potato and cause scabby areas and the decay of the tuber. Among this group of organisms producing scab there is one of the higher forms of Bacteria scientifically called *Actinomyces chromogenus* (*Fig. 301*). Among other bacterial diseases of the Irish Potato, Black-leg[2] is of considerable importance, especially in the Southern States.

Pear Blight.[3] — This disease occurs on many fruit trees, but is more serious on Pears and Apples. It is often called Fire Blight or Blossom Blight. The Bacteria enter the young twigs, usually through the flowers, and attack the cambium and cortex. The tips of the twigs with their flowers and leaves soon wilt, and in a few weeks

Fig. 302. — Fire blight on the Pear. The tip of the branch is being killed by the Bacteria. After Whetzel & Stewart.

blacken and die. Sometimes when the attack is quite general, scarcely a flower tip of an infected tree escapes. This not only results in loss of fruit, but the tree is often so disabled that death results. *Figure 302* shows a Pear twig severely

[1] Potato Scab. *Bulletin 184*, Vermont Agr. Exp. Sta., 1914.
[2] Potato Tuber Diseases. *Farmer's Bulletin 544*, U. S. Dept. Agr., 1913.
[3] Fire Blight Disease in Nursery Stock. *Bulletin 329*, Cornell University Agr. Exp. Sta., 1913.

attacked. The Bacteria pass the winter in the infected regions, which are sources of further infection. When growth begins in the spring, a gummy substance carrying the Bacteria exudes from these dead portions, and insects visiting the exudations carry the disease to other trees. How would you combat Pear Blight?

Crown Gall. — This disease is common on fruit trees, and occurs on Roses, Blackberries, Alfalfa, and a number of other plants. The presence of the Bacteria causes an abnormal development of the infected tissues, resulting in the formation of cancer-like swellings. The disease may occur on any portion of the plant but is common on the roots or on the stem near the surface of the ground. In general, nursery stock is more readily affected than older trees. Plants affected are much dwarfed or killed (*Fig. 303*).

Beans, Tomatoes, Potatoes, Sugar Cane, Cotton, and most of our economic plants have some form of bacterial disease, but a further study of the disease-producing forms must be left to courses in Bacteriology and Pathology.

In *summarizing*, the following features should be noted. Bacteria are the smallest of plants, and their plant body consists of a single cell with protoplast poorly organized. The plant body may be globular

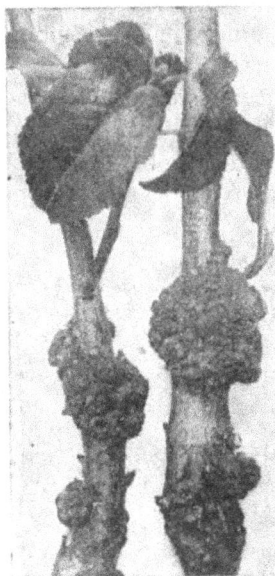

FIG. 303. — Crown Gall on the Cherry tree. The cancer-like swellings are due to the presence of Bacteria. After *Bulletin 235*, California Agr. Exp. Sta.

or rod-shaped, either straight or curved. Some have cilia or flagella and are therefore motile. They are remarkably resistant, especially in the spore stage. With the exception of a few forms, they are saprophytes or parasites. The disease-producing forms are very destructive to both animals and plants. They reproduce by rapid cell division and are spread, partly by wind, partly by water currents, partly by their own locomotion, and partly by the movements of animals with which they are associated. Their structural simplicity, power of resistance, and gelatinization of walls suggest a relationship to the Blue-green Algae.

In connection with Bacteria another group of organisms, known as the *Myxobacteria*, is commonly discussed. As the name suggests, the myxobacteria resemble both the Bacteria and Myxocytes. They differ from the Bacteria in that they form colonies, which in some cases are definite and elaborate in form. Some form colonies resembling a stalk bearing a group of sporangia at its summit. The life histories of the individuals of a colony are essentially the same as those of the Bacteria, differing chiefly in that the resting cells or spores form rod-like cells which escape and assemble to organize the colony.

CHAPTER XV

THALLOPHYTES (Concluded)

Fungi (Thallophytes Lacking Food-making Pigments)

General Discussion. — The Fungi are a very large group of Thallophytes. There are thousands of different kinds of Fungi. Most people know some of the common forms, such as Toadstools, Mushrooms, and Puffballs, and those who live on the farm are probably acquainted with the Rusts and Smuts of our common cereals. Most of the plant diseases are caused by Fungi. Like the Slime Molds and Bacteria, they have no food-making pigment and consequently are either saprophytes or parasites. They attack both animals and plants. Plant Pathology, which is a study of plant diseases, devotes some time to the study of Slime Molds and Bacteria, but is concerned mainly with the Fungi. They attack vegetables, grains, fiber plants, fruits, fruit trees, and forest and shade trees. The destruction which they cause is enormous. Some of the parasitic forms, however, are harmless, and many of the saprophytic forms are beneficial.

It is generally supposed that the Fungi are derived from the Algae, having lost their chlorophyll and independent living. Some of them have plant bodies, zoöspores, sex organs, and sex cells similar to those of the Green Algae, while some have sex organs resembling those of the Red Algae, but have no resemblance in other features. Some have become so modified by their dependent habit of living that they have lost all of their alga-like features. They have made no advancement in evolution, for there is less differentiation of plant body in this group than in the Algae, and methods of reproduction show no improvement, but often are simpler than those of the Algae or have been lost entirely. Those botanists who study plants mainly from the standpoint of evolution devote very little time to the Fungi because they have contributed nothing to evolution. But from the economic standpoint, the Fungi are an exceedingly important

351

group. A knowledge of their plant bodies, methods of reproduction, and how they injure other plants is essential for working out methods of controlling the destructive forms.

The *plant body* of Fungi consists of a mass of colorless branching threads or filaments, and is called a *mycelium* (plural *mycelia*). The individual threads are called *hyphae* (singular *hypha*). The hyphae constituting a mycelium may be loosely interwoven, forming a structure resembling a delicate cobweb, as in the Bread Mold, or they may be woven into a compact body having a definite shape, such as occurs in Toadstools and Mushrooms. The mycelium must be in direct contact with its food supply, which is called the *substratum*.

Sometimes, especially in the case of parasites, special short branches are formed which penetrate the host and absorb food material. These special absorbing branches are called *haustoria*, meaning "absorbers."

Hyphae are modified in various ways for reproduction. Some produce spores, which are sometimes borne in sporangia and sometimes openly on the end or sides of the hyphae. Some are modified into organs for bearing sex cells. These various modifications for reproduction will be learned as the different groups and their types are studied.

Divisions of Fungi. — The Fungi are so much modified by their peculiar life habits that they have either lost or disguised the structures which prove most helpful in the classification of the Algae. The Fungi are divided into four large subdivisions, but the life histories of only three of the subdivisions are well known.

The constant termination of the group names is *mycetes*, a Greek word meaning "Fungi." To this name is added a prefix which is intended to indicate some important character of the group. The three subdivisions in which the life histories are known are named as follows: (1) *Phycomycetes* (Alga-like Fungi) "phyco" coming from "phykos," meaning Seaweed and suggesting the water habits of this group; (2) *Ascomycetes* (Sac Fungi), so named because they bear spores in small sacs called *asci* (singular *ascus*); and (3) *Basidiomycetes*, Fungi which bear spores on small club-shaped hyphae called *basidia* (singular *basidium*). To the Basidiomycetes belong such familiar forms as the Toadstools, Mushrooms, Rusts, and Smuts. The fourth group is known as the *Fungi Imperfecti*. They are those Fungi

which are not known to have a life history of the type characteristic of either of the other subdivisions. Their life histories so
far as they are known are imperfect.

Phycomycetes (Alga-like Fungi)

This group, as their name suggests, resembles the Algae, but it
is a large assemblage of plants which vary widely in both structure and habit. Some of them live
in the water and have zoöspores
and sex organs similar to those of
the Green Algae, while some have
lost their water habits and nearly
all of their algal features. There
are three principal orders — Water
Molds (*Saprolegniales*), Downy
Mildews (*Peronosporales*), and
True Molds (*Mucorales*).

Water Molds (Saprolegniales).—
These are the Fungi showing closest
affinities with the Algae. In fact,
if some of them had chlorophyll,
they could scarcely be told from
some of the Green Algae. They
live in the water where they feed
upon the dead bodies of insects,
fish, and tadpoles. Sometimes they
attack living organisms, as the one
called Saprolegnia illustrates.

Water Mold (Saprolegnia). —
There are several kinds of Water
Molds, but the one called *Saprolegnia*, shown in *Figure 304*, is a
very common one. Although commonly a saprophyte on the floating
bodies of dead organisms, it often
attacks and kills young fish that
are confined in close quarters, on which account it is sometimes very destructive in fish hatcheries. This Fungus, since
it can live on both live and dead organisms, shows that there

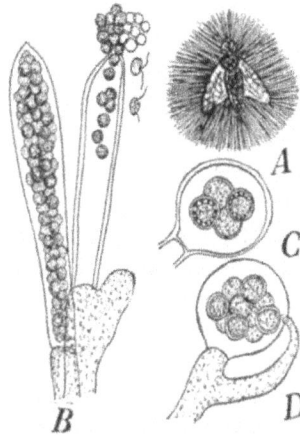

Fig. 304. — A Water Mold
(Saprolegnia). *A*, a fly affected
with Saprolegnia. The fuzzy appearance of the fly is due to numerous hyphae which project from
the body of the fly. *B*, tips of
projecting hyphae which have
formed zoösporangia. From the
zoösporangium at the right the
zoöspores are escaping. *C*, a
tip of a projecting hypha bearing
an oögonium containing a number
of eggs. *D*, an oögonium and antheridium, the latter of which has
pierced the wall of the oögonium
and thereby enabled the sperms
to reach the eggs.

is no sharp line of distinction between parasites and saprophytes. As long as the host is living, the Fungus is a parasite, but upon the death of the host it becomes a saprophyte. Thus a Fungus may be a parasite at one time in its life and a saprophyte at another. Saprolegnia is usually obtained for study by throwing dead insects or pieces of beefsteak into stagnant water from a pond, where the objects usually become infected and soon look like the fly in *Figure 304*.

The mycelium of Saprolegnia is composed of many branched hyphae which extend throughout the tissues of the host. The hyphae are coenocytes. This coenocytic feature suggests a closer kinship to Vaucheria than to the other Green Algae. After the mycelium is well established in the host, numerous hyphae, which cause the fuzzy appearance, protrude from the surface of the host.

The hyphae within the tissues of the host are able to absorb food materials directly. They are also able by means of enzymes to change materials to soluble forms, and in this way the Water Molds bring about the decay of animal bodies in water.

Many of the hyphae protruding from the host become modified for reproduction. Some produce zoöspores, while others produce sex organs. The swollen tips of some of the protruding hyphae are cut off by a cross wall and form sporangia in which are produced numerous zoöspores. These zoöspores escape, swim out, and when in contact with another host produce hyphae that penetrate and infect the new host.

Oögonia and antheridia are also formed at ends of hyphae. The oögonia are spherical and form one and sometimes many eggs. The antheridia are formed on branches near the oögonia. The antheridium comes in contact with the oögonium and pierces its wall with a small tube through which the sperms from the antheridium pass and fertilize the eggs. As a result of fertilization, a heavy-walled oöspore is formed, which after rest grows into a hypha which can penetrate and infect a host.

A peculiar feature in connection with some of the Saprolegnias is the ability of their eggs to develop without fertilization. In most plants, unless the egg is fertilized, it will not develop, but will soon disintegrate and disappear. In some Saprolegnias, the sperms of the antheridium fail to enter the oögonium, or there may be no antheridium developed, and still the egg without fertilization forms an oöspore which can germinate. This peculiar feature, called *parthenogenesis*, meaning reproduction by an egg without fertilization, has been mentioned before (page 50).

The aquatic habit, reproduction by zoöspores, and character of sex organs support the theory that the Water Molds are degenerate forms with the Green Algae as their ancestors. The

Fig. 305.— Leaf of the Grape, showing the downy areas caused by the Downy Mildew, *Plasmopara Viticola*. After W. H. Hein.

coenocytic character of their hyphae suggests a close relationship with the Siphonales.

Downy Mildews (Peronosporales). — These Fungi, which are parasites on the higher plants, cause some serious plant diseases of which the Grape Downy Mildew and Potato Blight are notable ones, and will serve to illustrate the habits of the group. There are about 100 species known and the order is so named because of the downy patches which they produce on the diseased portions of the host.

The Grape Downy Mildew (Plasmopara Viticola). — The Downy Mildew of the Grape, shown in *Figure 305*, is a very common and important one of the many Downy Mildews and often causes much loss in grape-growing districts. Its downy white growth occurs most commonly on the leaves, but the Fungus often attacks the green shoots and fruit (*Fig. 306*). Sometimes it destroys the fruit crop and weakens the vines.

The mycelium consists of coenocytic hyphae, which extend through the tissues of the part attacked. The hyphae grow between cells and send into the cells short branches (haustoria) which absorb the cell contents of the host (*Fig. 307*). The death of the leaf cells resulting from the attack is indicated by the occurrence of yellow or brown areas which may involve much of the leaf. This destruction of leaf tissue diminishes the carbohydrates

FIG. 306. — A bunch of Grapes partially destroyed by the Downy Mildew. From *Farmer's Bulletin 284*, U. S. Dept. of Agriculture.

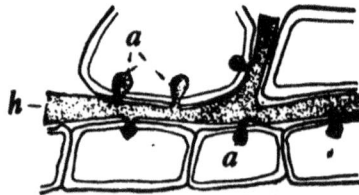

FIG. 307. — The haustoria of the Downy Mildew reaching into the cells of the grape. *h*, hypha; *a*, haustoria. From *Bulletin 214*, Ohio Agr. Exp. Sta.

furnished by the leaves and as a result both fruit and vine may suffer. Often the fruit is directly attacked and destroyed. After the Mildew is well established within the tissues of the hosts, it sends through the stomata numerous branches which constitute the superficial downy patches characteristic of the parasite (*Fig. 308*). On the tips of these protruding hyphae are produced small globular bodies known as *conidiospores* or *conidia*, and the hyphae bearing them are called conidiophores which means "conidia bearing."

The conidia are really small sporangia which break off and are scattered about like spores. When the conidia germinate, instead of producing hyphae they produce zoöspores, which, after swimming about for a few minutes, lose their cilia and begin to produce new hyphae. If favorably located, the new hyphae find entrance to a leaf through its stomata and start the disease anew. The oögonia and antheridia resemble those of Saprolegnia, but are produced on short hyphae within the tissues of the host. The oöspore has a heavy wall and is not liberated until the tissues of the host surrounding it decay. The oöspores are well fitted to endure winter conditions, and as the dead leaves are scattered, the oöspores contained are also scattered, and when freed it is probable that they often start the disease the following year.

Potato Blight[1] (**Phytophthora infestans**). — This Fungus, commonly called the Late Blight of the Potato, is a near relative of the Grape Mildew. It attacks the leaves, stems, and tubers of the Irish Potato and is very rapid and destructive in its work. *Figure 309* shows the leaves of a Potato plant affected with this disease. Like the

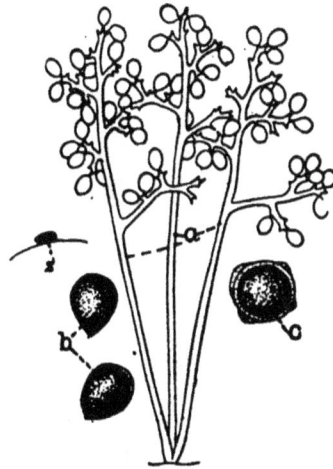

FIG. 308. — Reproduction in the Downy Mildew of the Grape. *a*, conidiophores bearing conidiospores on the ends of their branches; *b*, conidiospores; *c*, oöspore; *z*, zoöspore. Much enlarged. From *Farmer's Bulletin 284*, U. S. Dept. of Agriculture.

Grape Mildew, after the mycelium is well established in the host, conidiophores are produced (*Fig. 310*). The conidia may grow directly into hyphae or produce zoöspores (*Fig. 311*).

[1] Late Blight and Rot of Potatoes. *Circular 19*, Cornell University Agr. Exp. Sta.

Investigations of the Potato Fungus, Phytophthora Infestans. *Bulletin 168*, Vermont Agri. Exp. Sta.

Germination and Infection with the Fungus of the Late Blight of Potato. *Research Bulletin 37*, Wisconsin Agr. Exp. Sta., 1915.

Studies of the Genus Phytophthora. Vol. 8, No. 7, pp. 233-276, Jour Agr. Research, U. S. Dept. Agr., 1917.

The conidia and zoöspores which they produce spread the disease very rapidly in moist weather. Since the zoöspore is a swimmer, it can function more efficiently during moist weather. Moist weather also favors the germination of the conidia. Little is known about the sex organs of the Potato Blight, but in the form which causes the Bean Blight, the sex

Fig. 309. — Leaf of Irish Potato affected with the Late Blight. From *Bulletin 140*, Cornell University.

organs and oöspores occur in the seed coat or cotyledons of the seed, in which case the oöspore is planted with the seed. In the *Phytophthora cactorum*,[1] which is destructive to Ginseng, the sex organs and oöspores have been found in the stem and roots (*Fig. 312*).

There are many Downy Mildews which give us trouble. In fact many of our plants such as Cucumbers, Melons, Beans, Potatoes, Lettuce, Grapes, etc., are attacked and much damaged by Downy Mildews. But the study of the Grape Mildew and Potato Blight has given a general knowledge of their habits. In combatting the Mildews one must reckon with conidiospores, zoöspores, and oöspores.

One is able to check the spread of the disease by spraying the plants with a solution that is poisonous to conidia and zoöspores.

[1] Phytophthora Disease of Ginseng. *Bulletin 363*, Cornell Agr. Exp. Sta., 1915.

A spray that is very commonly used is Bordeaux mixture.[1]   The oöspores live over winter and may perpetuate the disease from year to year.   Portions of diseased plants containing oöspores, when hauled out in manure or scattered about by the wind, may be a means of spreading the disease.

In some forms of the Peronosporales as in *Albugo* or *White Rust*, which forms white blisters on the leaves and stem of the Radish and other plants of the Mustard family, both the sex organs and conidiospores are produced internally. The hyphae form in clusters under the epidermis and form conidiospores in chains which push up the epidermis, forming white blisters which finally rupture and allow the spores to escape.   In this Fungus the conidiospore produces a number of zoöspores.

In this order *Pythium* is sometimes included, species of which attack seedlings in greenhouses, causing the rapid wilting known as damping off, when moisture and warmth are abundant.   Some species of Pythium live in the water like the Saprolegniales in which order Pythium is often put, while other species live in the soil.

Fig. 310. — The lower epidermis of a Potato leaf showing the conidiophores of the Late Blight protruding through the stomata and bearing conidiospores at the tips of their branches. Many times enlarged.

In contrast to the Water Molds, the Downy Mildews are chiefly parasitic, much less aquatic and, having introduced the conidia, they depend less upon water for dissemination.   But like the Water Molds the presence of zoöspores and the character of the reproductive organs suggest a relationship to the Green Algae.

---

[1] The preparation as most commonly made consists of 5 pounds of copper sulphate and 5 pounds of stone lime dissolved in 50 gallons of water.   Potato Spraying Experiments in 1906. *Bulletin 279*, New York Agr. Exp. Sta.   Certain Potato Diseases and their Remedies. *Bulletin 72*, Vermont Agr. Exp. Sta., 1899.

True Molds (Mucorales). — There are a number of Molds
some of which belong to other divisions of the Fungi. The
Molds of this order are characterized by a zygosporic reproduction, on which account they are called *Zygomycetes*. Of the
nearly 200 species known, Bread Mold is the most familiar one.

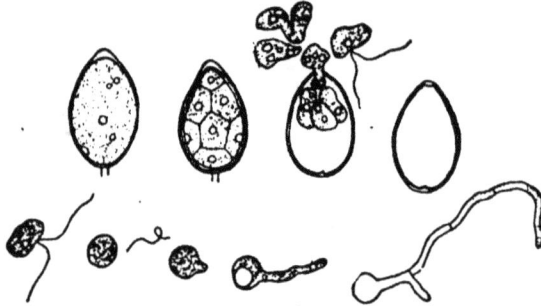

FIG. 311. — Conidia of the Late Blight of the Potato developing zoöspores,
and zoöspores growing hyphae. × about 400. After Ward.

Bread Mold (Rhizopus nigricans). — Bread Mold is very
common about homes, producing a fluffy tangle of hyphae on the
surface of bread, fruit, and other favorable nutrient substances
when left exposed (*Fig. 313*). It is sometimes injurious to
Sweet Potatoes and other vegetables in storage. The fluffy
tangle of hyphae is white while young but becomes dark when old,
owing to the dark color of the mature sporangia.

A strong poison has been found in connection with Rhizopus
nigricans, and it has been suggested that some of the diseases of
stock, such as the "cornstalk disease" and the "horse disease,"
prevalent in some of the Western states, may be due to the toxin
which stock get in moldy fodder or other feed. The toxin
apparently is only effective when introduced into the circulatory
system. This is shown by the fact that rabbits can be fed the
Mold without any injury, but when a little of the sap is expressed
from the mycelium and injected into the blood, the animal dies
almost instantly.

The mycelium consists of numerous coenocytic branching
hyphae. Some of the hyphae penetrate the substratum and
gather food, while others grow above the substratum and produce
the visible fluffy mass. The surface hyphae with more or less

upright growth bear the sporangia, while others running over the surface of the substratum produce at certain places a new set of both penetrating and upright hyphae.   These runner-like hyphae are called *stolons*, and serve to spread the mycelium over the substratum.   The hyphae which penetrate the substratum are able to change the elements of the substratum into soluble forms and absorb them.

The sporangia occur singly on the hyphae and contain numerous aërial spores, which when mature are liberated by the breaking of the sporangial wall. The spores are nearly always present, floating about in the air and resting on objects where they happen to fall.   It is probable that they can live for many years in the dormant state and then germinate when they come in contact with suitable food material.

The Bread Mold has no sex organs, but there is a sexual process which reminds one of the sexual process in Spirogyra. Sometimes, as shown in *Figure 314,* tips of hyphae approach

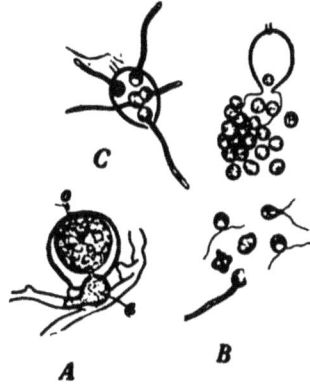

Fig. 312. — Methods of reproduction in the *Phytophthora cactorum*, which attacks Ginseng. *A,* sex organs consisting of oögonium (*o*) and antheridium (*a*). *B,* conidiospore forming zoöspores above, and a group of zoöspores below. *C,* conidiospore producing hyphae directly.   Much enlarged.   From *Bulletin 363,* Cornell University Agr. Exp. Sta.

each other and finally meet.   From each hyphae an end cell is cut off, and these end cells fuse to form heavy walled zygospores. Upon germination the zygospore produces an erect hypha bearing a sporangium of the ordinary type, and the aërial spores developed therein are capable of starting a new series of plants.

Conjugation is only occasionally obtained in Rhizopus nigricans unless the cultures are made in a certain way.   It has been found that in Rhizopus nigricans there are two kinds of plants, which, although looking just alike, behave differently.   They are called strains, one being known as the plus (+) and the other as the minus (−) strain.   When either of these occur alone in a culture then no conjugation takes place, but if both are present then there is abundant conjugation and formation of zygospores. In many laboratories the spores of both strains are kept in stock, and conjugation is obtained whenever desired by using spores of both strains in growing the cultures.

Another Mold of this order is *Pilobolus*, commonly called Squirting Fungus on account of the way it throws its sporangia.

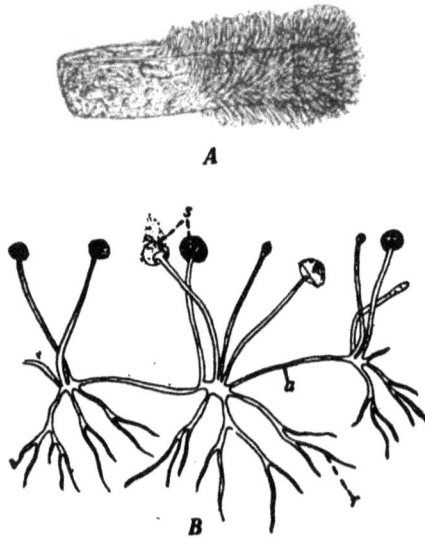

FIG. 313. — Bread Mold, *Rhizopus nigricans*. *A*, piece of bread on which there is a growth of Mold (× ½). *B*, plant body of Bread Mold, showing the hyphae (*r*) which penetrate the bread, the hyphae which grow up and bear the sporangia (*s*), and the hyphae (*a*) (stolons) which grow prostrate on the surface of the substratum and start new plants. (× about 20.)

It is common on stable manure and resembles Bread Mold. The hyphae become turgid and swollen just beneath the sporangia and finally burst, hurling the sporangia with considerable force, whence the name Squirting Fungus.

In the True Molds, where there are no swimming spores, the Phycomycetes become entirely aërial, although the coenocytic plant body and conjugation still suggest a relationship with the Green Algae. The mycelium, a tangle of hyphae with no definite shape in Phycomycetes, shows some differentiation into absorbing, vegetative, and reproductive structures. The chief propagative structures of the group are zoöspores, conidia, and aërial spores.

Oöspores and zygospores tide the plant over unfavorable conditions and produce new plants when favorable conditions return. In combatting the disease-producing Phycomycetes, the control of zoöspores, conidia, and oöspores must be considered.

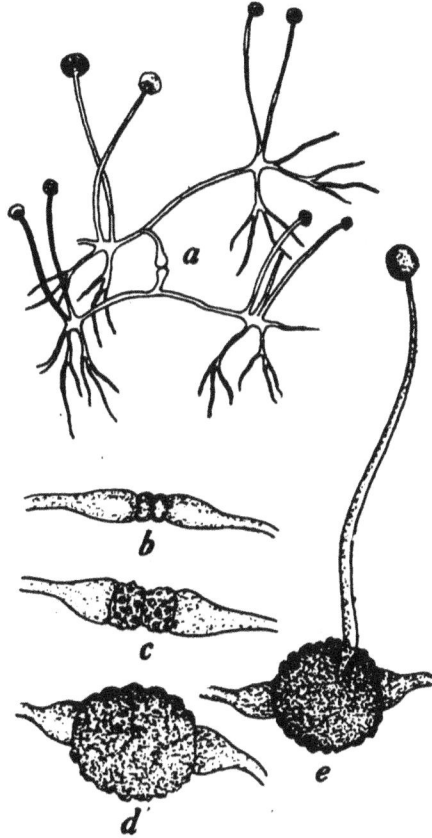

Fig. 314. — Conjugation in Bread Mold. *a, b, c,* and *d* are successive stages in conjugation. At *a* the short hyphae have just come together, while at *d* the zygospore is formed. *e,* zygospore developing a new hypha bearing a sporangium. × about 130.

Ascomycetes (Sac Fungi and Lichens)

General Description. — To the Ascomycetes belong the largest number of Fungi, and most of them are parasites. Many of our most troublesome diseases are caused by these Fungi. Some, like the Yeast Plant, and the Molds which help in making cheese, are useful. Some of the Ascomycetes are used directly as food. The saprophytic forms are useful in hastening the decay of organic matter. But the main reason for their study is the desire to be able to stop the destruction caused by the disease-producing forms.

The Ascomycetes are so named because of the *ascus or sac* which is the characteristic spore-bearing structure of the group. The ascus is an enlarged end of a hypha which becomes a thin walled sac in which spores are produced. Any Fungus producing spores in an ascus is called an Ascomycete. The spores produced in an ascus are called *ascospores*. The Ascomycetes have other spores, but the ascospores are the most general ones.

The Ascomycetes differ from the Phycomycetes in having no zoöspores and in having hyphae divided by cross walls. Many of the Ascomycetes have sex organs and differentiated gametes, but the cell resulting from fusion develops immediately into asci, so there are no resting oöspores to be considered in this group. Taking care of the ascospores takes care of the results of fertilization.

The Ascomycetes vary widely in character of plant body and methods of reproduction. In some the plant body is a structure with a definite form, while in others it is only a scattered mass of hyphae. In some the plant body is very prominent, but extremely inconspicuous in others. Some have well-defined sex organs, while others apparently have abandoned sexual reproduction and have lost their sex organs. Their sex organs resemble those of the Red Algae and this is the feature that suggests their relationship to the Algae. There are about 15 orders and 29,000 species of Ascomycetes. The Morels (*Helvellales*), Cup Fungi (*Pezizales*), Closed Fungi (*Pyrenomycetales*), Naked Ascus Fungi (*Protodi scales*), Mildews (*Peri sporiales*), the Blue and Green Molds (*Plectascales*), and the Yeasts (*Protoascales*) are familiar orders.

The Morels (Helvellales). — Not all of the Fungi of this order are Morels, but the Morels are the most familiar ones. The fleshy plant body with a definite form and often so large as to be quite conspicuous is one of the notable features of the Helvellales. They are mostly saprophytic and the mycelium usually develops underground where it lives on decaying wood, leaves. etc. Here belongs the Edible Morel shown on next page.

The Common Edible Morel (Morchella esculenta). — The common Edible Morel is found in the spring, commonly in May and early June. It is quite generally collected and used for food. It is often called a Mushroom, although it is not the cultivated Mushroom. Morels are usually found in the woods among the leaves and about old logs and stumps. Often they grow in clusters as *Figure 315* shows. The wrinkled top and supporting stalk consist of hyphae so massed together as to form a definitely

FIG. 315. — A cluster of Morels, *Morchella esculenta* ($\times \frac{1}{3}$). Photographed by C. M. King.

shaped plant body. The mycelium absorbs food from decaying organic matter in the earth, and when it is well established in the soil, the portion above ground is produced. The asci with the ascospores are produced in the pits of the wrinkled top which is known as the *ascocarp*. A small portion of a section through a pit, as seen under the microscope, is shown in *Figure 316*. The asci are numerous and each contains eight ascospores. The asci with the intermingling sterile hyphae, called *paraphyses*, constitute a distinct layer, known as the *hymenium*, on the surface of the ascocarp. After the spores are mature, the ascocarp decays and frees the spores which are widely distributed by wind and other agents. When located on favorable organic matter, the spores grow directly into new mycelia.

Although Morels spring up quickly, often apparently over night, much time is required for the development of the subterranean mycelium before the aërial portion is developed. No sexual reproduction has been discovered in the Morels, and the only spore known is the ascospore.

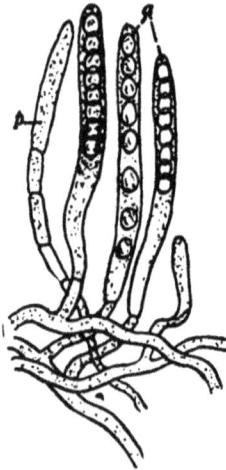

FIG. 316.—Asci (a) of the *Morel,* showing the ascospores (× about 200). The hypha (p) producing no spores is called a paraphysis.

Some other edible Ascomycetes, which command high prices in Europe, are the Truffles, which belong in the order *Tuberales.* The distinctive feature of the Truffles is that the ascocarp occurs wholly underground. The ascocarp, which is tuber-like, is closed except for a small opening and the spores are released by the decay of its walls. Since they are underground, they are very difficult to find, and experts hunt them by the aid of trained pigs or dogs which detect them through the sense of smell. No sexual reproduction has been discovered, but not much is known of their life cycle.

Cup Fungi (Pezizales). — The Cup Fungi include many species most of which are saprophytes. The loose mycelium develops in decaying rich humus, decaying wood, or leaf mold, and when well established it produces above the surface an ascocarp which has the form of a disk, funnel, or cup. Such an ascocarp is called an *apothecium* to distinguish it from other types of ascocarps.

Peziza. — This genus, a species of which is shown in *Figure 317,* is common in the woods and the cup-shaped apothecium is sometimes 2 or 3 inches across and often brightly colored. In one common form the interior of the cup is bright scarlet. The interior of the apothecium is lined with a hymenium consisting of parallel, sterile, hyphal threads or paraphyses among which occur the asci each containing eight spores. By the swelling and rupturing of the asci the ripe spores are expelled and then scattered by the wind. No sexual reproduction has been discovered in Peziza, but in *Pyronema,* a form similar to Peziza, sexual reproduction has been discovered and carefully followed.

Pyronema. — In this form there are sex organs and the apothecium develops as a result of fertilization (*Fig. 318*). The female sex organ resembles that of the simpler Red Algae, such

FIG. 317. — A cluster of Cup Fungi, *Pezizas.* × ½.

as Nemalion. It consists of a globular cell (oögonium) and an elongated tube-like cell (trichogyne or conjugating tube). The

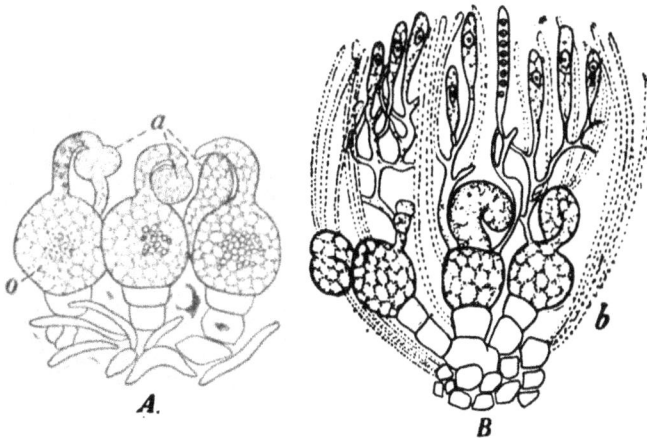

FIG. 318. — Sexual reproduction in *Pyronema confluans.* A, the sex organs at the time of fertilization, showing the antheridia (*a*) in contact and fusing with the trichogynes through which the sperms pass to the oögonia (*o*); B, development of apothecium, showing the oögonia developing ascogenous hyphae which are beginning to form asci at the ends of their branches, and the sterile hyphae (*b*) which grow up among the ascogenous hyphae and form a large part of the wall of the apothecium. Highly magnified. After Harper.

antheridium is a somewhat club-shaped terminal cell which comes in contact with the tip of the trichogyne and fuses with it. Both oögonium and antheridium are multinucleate. The numerous nuclei of the antheridium flow into the trichogyne and pass on into the oögonium where they pair and fuse with the numerous nuclei of the oögonium. From the fertilized oögonium, now known as the _ascogonium_, branches called _ascogenous hyphae_ are developed and on the ultimate branches of these are produced the asci. From beneath the ascogonium sterile hyphae (hyphae producing no asci) grow up among the ascogenous hyphae and constitute the paraphyses of the hymenium. Other sterile hyphae form the wall of the cup-shaped plant body or ascocarp. Usually several oögonia are involved in the formation of a single ascocarp.

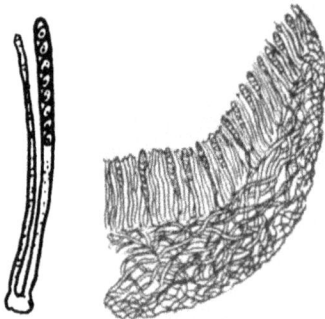

Brown Rot of Stone Fruits (Sclerotinia fructigena). — This Fungus, shown in _Figure 319_, is one of the parasitic forms of the Pezizales. In some years this Fungus is an extremely destructive parasite. It attacks nearly all stone fruits and in some years nearly half of the Plum and Peach crop may be destroyed by this disease. In Georgia the estimated loss in Peaches and Plums caused by this disease in 1900 was between $500,000 and $700,000. To a limited extent it attacks the twigs and flowers and does some damage in this way.

FIG. 319. — _Sclerotinia fructigena._ Above, the apothecia developed on a decayed Plum; at the right, below, section through an apothecium, showing asci and paraphyses; at the left, below, an ascus and paraphysis more highly magnified. After Duggar.

Fruits half size or larger seem to be most susceptible to the attack of the Fungus. The disease first shows as small decayed spots, dark brown in color. The fruit decays rapidly and soon hyphae break through from beneath, forming moldy patches on the surface. The moldy patches contain conidiophores which

produce conidiospores abundantly.   The conidiospores can live
over till the succeeding season and start the disease anew.   The
disease is propagated chiefly by conidiospores.   It was a long
time after the disease was known before ascospores were found
and of course it was not then classed as an Ascomycete but was
put into the class Fungi Imperfecti.   Apparently ascospores are
often not formed at all, and, when they are, they occur in the
diseased fruits after they have dried up and usually fallen from
the tree.   As the fruit decays it dries up into a mummy.   In this
dried-up fruit, regardless of whether it is on the ground or on the
tree, the mycelium becomes changed into compact masses called
sclerotia.   Later, probably the next spring, upon these sclerotia
are developed bell-shaped apothecia in which the ascospores occur
(*Fig. 319*).   Thus in controlling the disease the destruction of
the mummied fruits as well as spraying to kill the conidiospores
that are sticking to the buds and bark are advised.

The Closed or Black Fungi (Pyrenomycetales). — These
Fungi, of which there are about 11,000 species, include both
parasites and saprophytes.   They vary much in form and
manner of growth.   They are chiefly characterized by a superficial, compact, black mycelium looking as if it had been charred
by fire.   The structure in which the asci are produced is a peri-
thecium, a small commonly flask-shaped cavity with a small
pore-like opening.   Many of these Fungi produce destructive
plant diseases, of which the *Black Knot*, *Ergot*, and *Chestnut
Disease* are familiar ones.

Black Knot (Plowrightia morbosa). — This Fungus occurs on
the twigs of Plum and Cherry trees, producing wart-like excrescences as shown at *A* in *Figure 320*.   The mycelium attacks the
cambium, phloem, and cortex, causing at first an abnormal growth
and later the death of these tissues.   As a result of the attack, the
twig is much injured or killed.   The attack is often so general that
the entire tree is killed.   The wart-like excrescences or knots consist of the mycelium and the abnormally developed tissues of the
host.   During the first summer the disease shows as slight swellings, but with the renewed growth of the following spring, the
swellings enlarge rapidly, and during May or June the mycelium
breaks through the bark and forms a dense covering over the surface of the swellings.   From the hyphae forming the covering of
the knot numerous erect hyphae arise which give the knot a

velvety appearance. These erect hyphae are conidiophores and bear conidiospores as shown at *B* in *Figure 320*. The conidiospores are scattered by the wind and upon germination grow directly into hyphae which can penetrate a young shoot and start the disease anew. In late summer after the production of conidiospores is over, the knot becomes black and on its surface occur numerous small papillae which are the flask-shaped perithecia, opening with a pore and lined on the inside with asci as shown at *C* n *Figure 320*. The ascospores are mature and ready to be distributed early the next spring.

It follows then that the disease may be spread during the early spring by ascospores or during late spring and summer by the conidiospores. The destruction of the knots before the shedding of the spores will check the disease. Bordeaux mixture applied at proper times is useful in checking the disease, but most attention should be given to the destruction of the diseased branches.

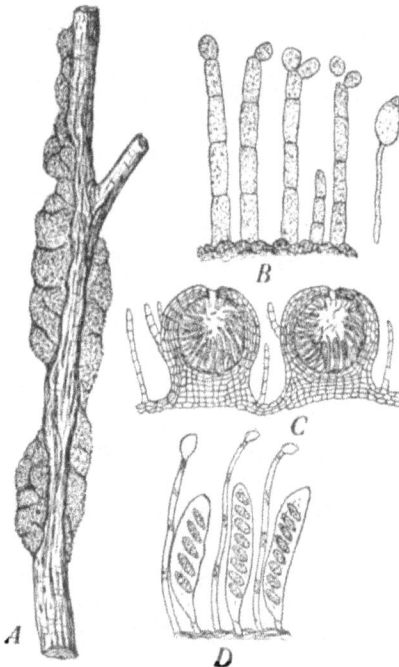

FIG. 320. — Black Knot, *Plowrightia morbosa*. *A*, branch of a Plum, showing the wart-like excrescences caused by the Fungus; *B*, conidiophores producing conidiospores (× 500), and at the right a conidiospore germinating; *C*, two perithecia sectioned lengthwise, showing the asci and paraphyses within (× 50); *D*, asci and paraphyses more highly magnified.

Ergot (Claviceps purpurea and Paspali).[1] — Ergot is a parasite on the young ovaries of the Grasses, being especially common on Rye and occurring sometimes on Wheat, Barley, and a number of

[1] Ergot and Ergotism. *Press Bulletin 23*, Nebraska Agr. Exp. Sta., 1906. Life History and Poisonous Properties of *Claviceps Paspali*. Vol. 7, No. 9, pp. 401–406, Jour. Agr. Research, U. S. Dept. Agr., 1916.

other Grasses. The ascospores affect the ovaries in early summer. In the ovary the mycelium develops, using the food material which the ovary should have. The mycelium produces on the surface of the ovary numerous conidiophores which produce conidia abundantly, and the conidia are disseminated largely by insects which seek the honey dew secreted by the mycelium. After the tissues of the ovary are destroyed, the mycelium becomes transformed into a dark, hard, club-shaped body called *sclerotium* which projects from the spikelet as shown in *Figure 321.* These bodies, which are the so-called Ergot, contain one or more alkaloids which are poisonous to both man and live stock. Stock are sometimes badly poisoned by eating Timothy, Red Top, and other kinds of hay where Ergot is abundant. The sclerotia fall to the ground and pass the winter. The next spring they develop branches which bear rose-colored globular heads, called *stromata*, in which the asci are produced in sunken perithecia.

Fig. 321. — The Ergot Fungus, *Claviceps purpurea.* a, head of Rye, showing projecting sclerotia; b, a sclerotium which has developed stalks bearing globular heads in which the perithecia occur (× 3); c, section through one of the globular heads, showing the perithecia (× 15); d, ascus highly magnified, showing the spindle-shaped ascospores; e, hypha and conidia which develop on the surface of the grain in the early stage of infection. From Tulasne and Strasburger.

The Chestnut Disease (Endothia parasitica). — This disease was introduced from Asia and appeared in New York about 1904. It is very destructive to Chestnut trees, and the estimated loss in New York City and vicinity is more than $5,000,000. For the entire United States, the financial loss up to 1911 was estimated at about $25,000,000. So serious is this disease that legislatures have made special appropriations for fighting it.

The spores are carried by the wind and sometimes by birds and insects. When the spores reach the bark of the Chestnut, they develop hyphae which penetrate and kill the phloem and cambium. The dead bark soon becomes warty with yellowish-brown pustules in which summer spores in great numbers are

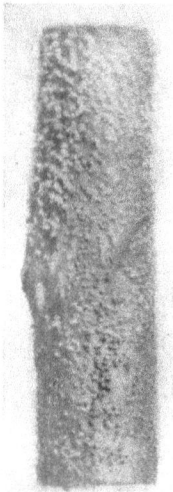

Fig. 322. — Pustules on the bark of a Chestnut caused by the Chestnut Blight Fungus. From *Bulletin 380*, U. S. Dept. Agriculture, 1917.

Fig. 323. — Powdery Mildew on an Apple leaf. The light areas are due to the presence of many superficial hyphae. From *Bulletin 185*, Maine Agr. Exp. Sta.

produced (*Fig. 322*). The summer spores are extruded in threads and spread the disease to other trees. In autumn these same pustules develop deeply buried perithecia in which the ascospores (winter spores) develop. The ascospores germinate the next spring and when carried to other trees start the disease anew. The mycelium in an affected tree renews its activity each year and thus continues to spread, usually downward, until the tree is killed. The deeply buried mycelium is not reached by sprays, and the total destruction of the infected trees is the only available method of checking the disease.

Powdery Mildews (Perisporiales). — This group includes many Fungi, but they are all very similar in their habits. The mycelium commonly occurs on the surface of leaves, but sometimes on the stems and fruits of the higher plants. The myce-

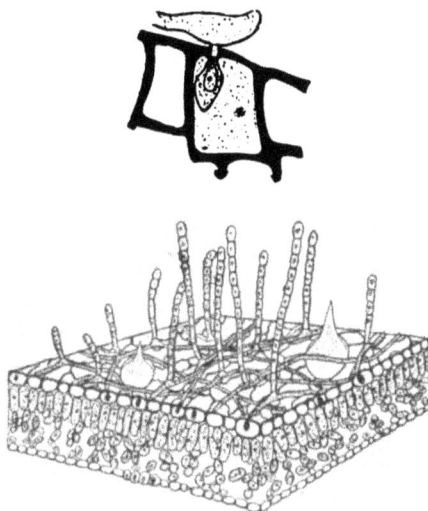

Fig. 324. — Powdery Mildew of the Hop. Below, diagrammatic drawing of a section of a Hop leaf, showing the superficial mycelium which has grown haustoria into the epidermal cells, and produced erect conidiophores bearing chains of conidia ($\times$ about 50). Above, epidermal cell, hypha, and invading haustorium more highly magnified. From *Bulletin 328*, Cornell University Agr. Exp. Sta.

lium forms quite noticeable powdery patches. The asci are produced in closed ascocarps called *cleistothecia*. In *Figure 323* is shown the mildew of the Apple.

The Lilac Mildew (*Microsphaera*) is the one most commonly observed of the Mildews. Often in late summer and autumn, the leaves of the Lilac are so generally covered with the whitish dusty-looking patches, that the entire bush appears covered with street dust. But there are also Mildews that occur on fruit trees, Roses, Gooseberries, Peas, and other cultivated plants, which do considerable damage. From the superficial hyphae haustoria are sent into the host. These haustoria absorb food from the tissues, and often cause considerable injury to the leaves and fruit.

From the superficial hyphæ arise numerous erect conidiophores, which produce chains of conidiospores (*Fig. 324*). The powdery appearance of the Fungus is due to the ascocarps and the numerous conidiospores. The conidiospores are distributed by the wind and, when favorably placed, grow directly into hyphæ, and are the means of producing new growths of the Mildew. Late in the summer and autumn, the superficial hyphæ form

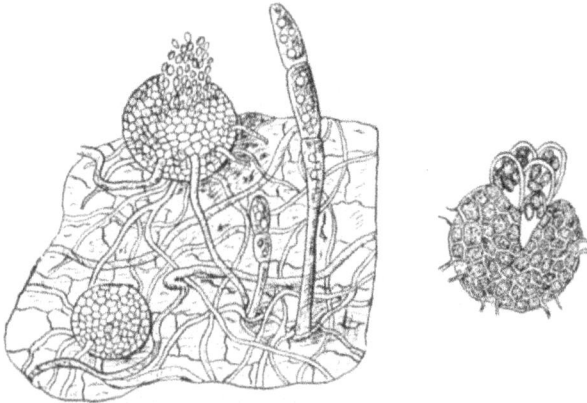

Fig. 325. — At the left, surface of a leaf infected with Powdery Mildew, showing the superficial mycelium, ascocarps, and conidiophores. At the right, a cleistothecium broken open, showing the asci which develop within. From Tulasne and Nature.

globular heavy-walled cleistothecia in which the asci are produced and which, when mature, appear to the naked eye as black dots on the surface of the leaf (*Fig. 325*).

Projecting from the wall of the ascocarp are appendages which may have variously branched tips. Enclosed within the heavy wall of the ascocarp, the ascospores pass the winter. When freed in the spring by the breaking of the ascocarp, the spores may be blown or carried about and germinate upon a new host. The development of the ascocarp is a result of fertilization and the sex organs, like those of Pyronema, suggest those of the Red Algae.

The ascocarp of the Mildews suggests the cystocarp of the

higher Red Algae, such as ·Polysiphonia, for as the ascogenous hyphæ develop from the ascogonium, sterile hyphæ, growing up from below the ascogonium, form a compact hard wall which makes a case for the asci and ascospores, just as the filaments growing up from below the carpogonium produce a case for the carpospores in Polysiphonia.

The Blue and Green Molds (Plectascales). — Superficially these Molds resemble the true Molds discussed under the Mucorales, but their spore masses are generally green or blue, while those of the true Molds are black. There are about 250 known species in this order, but they are saprophytes and only a few of them are of much importance. They bear their ascospores in closed ascocarps or Cleistothecia. *Aspergillus* and *Penicillium* are two familiar genera of the order.

Aspergillus.—These Molds are commonly green on account of their greenish spore masses. One form known as the Herbarium Mold is troublesome in herbariums

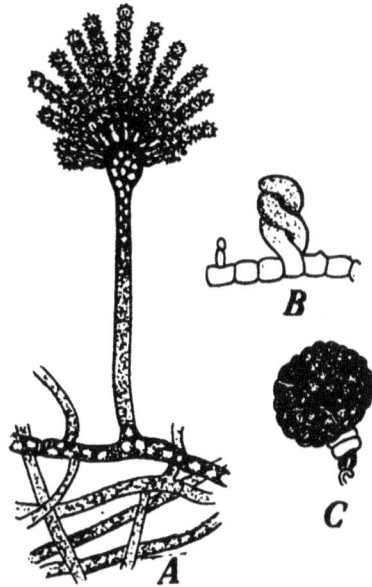

FIG. 326. — A species of *Aspergillus*. *A*, a portion of a mycelium, showing a conidiophore bearing chains of conidia (300); *B*, sex organs coiled about each other and consisting of hyphæ similar in appearance; *C*, the cleistothecium which develops after fertilization and in which the asci develop (× 200).

where it attacks specimens that are not well dried. They often occur along with the true Molds. They will grow on cheese, leather, wall paper, fruit, hay, silage, and on most any damp object from which they can obtain nourishment. Some are poisonous and stock are injured and sometimes killed by eating them in moldy Corn, hay, and silage.

The loose extensive mycelium runs over and through the

substratum, and sends up conidiophores at the ends of which the conidia are borne in radiating chains as shown in *Figure 326.* The spores are scattered mostly by the wind.

The sex organs appear a little later than the conidia and consist of two short hyphal filaments which come together and intertwine spirally. One of these filaments represents the oögonium and the other, the antheridium. After fertilization, ascogenous hyphæ develop from the ascogonium and bear eight-spored asci at their tips. In the meantime other hyphæ grow up from below the ascogonium and a closed case or cleistothecium is formed, within which are the asci intermingled amongst sterile hyphae. The walls of the asci finally dissolve, thus setting the ascospores free within the cleistothecium. Through the decay of the wall of the cleistothecium the spores are finally freed to be scattered by the wind.

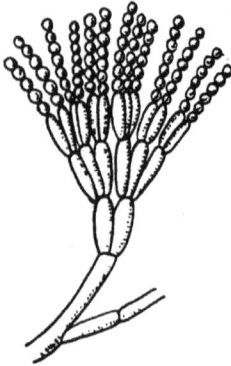

FIG. 327. — A species of Penicillium, showing conidiophores bearing chains of conidia.

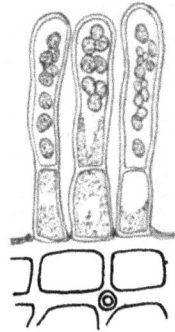

FIG. 328. — A naked-ascus Fungus, *Taphrina pruni* on a plum, showing the asci developed without any covering on the surface of the epidermis (× 400). Redrawn with modifications from Strasburger.

Another Ascomycete which sometimes poisons livestock is the Purple Monascus. It belongs to another order and is a simpler Ascomycete than Aspergillus. It is often present in moldy silage and when fed to livestock may cause death. This mold produces a purple pigment which colors the substratum upon which the mold lives and distinctly colors silage attacked by the Mold.

Penicillium. — A common species of Penicillium is the Blue Mold which develops on shoes or gloves left in damp places, and on lemons, cheese, etc. It often occurs intermingled with Bread Mold on bread. The conidia are borne as shown in *Figure 327.* Its sexual reproduction is similar to that of Aspergillus and the cleistothecia are about as large as a coarse grain of sand.

Certain species[1] give desirable flavors to some kinds of cheese and are quite useful in this connection.

Naked-ascus Fungi (Protodiscales). — This is a small group of parasites which attack seed plants. They produce no ascocarp and the asci are therefore borne exposed (*Fig. 328*). So far as known they have no sexual reproduction. They are regarded as simple Ascomycetes. One common species is the *Exoascus deformans*, which causes the disease known as Peach Curl. The mycelium develops in the tissues of the host and forms on the surface asci which appear as gray powdery films. One species attacks the young ovaries of Plums, causing the malformation known as "Bladder Plums," and one species causes Witches' Brooms on some of our deciduous trees.

Yeasts (Saccharomyces). — The Yeasts are very simple Ascomycetes. In most Yeasts the hyphae are so short and simple that they appear as single globular cells The only reason for calling them Ascomycetes is that under certain conditions the cells form spores and then resemble asci (*Fig. 329*).

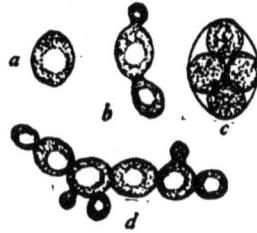

FIG. 329. — Bread Yeast. *Saccharomyces cerevisiae.* a, single plant ($\times$ 600); b, a plant in the process of budding; c, plant which has formed spores; d, plants remaining in contact and forming chains as they are multiplied by budding.

On account of their ability to ferment sugars and produce carbon dioxide and alcohol, they are useful in making bread and in making alcohol, wine, beer, and other liquors which contain alcohol. When placed in dough they grow and work rapidly, and the carbon dioxide produced causes the bread to rise. There are many kinds of Yeasts, and each kind gives a different flavor to the fermented product. For this reason brewers keep pure cultures of certain kinds of Yeasts, which give the liquor the desired characteristics.

Their main method of reproduction is by the rapid division of cells, often called *budding,* in which small cells are apparently pinched off from the parent cell. The cells often remain in contact for some time after being budded off, forming chains of cells.

[1] Cultural Studies of Species of Penicillium. *Bulletin 148*, Bureau of Animal Industry, U. S. Dept. Agriculture, 1911.

Other Ascomycetes. — A study of a few types of the Ascomycetes has given a general notion of their habits but no notion at all of their extensive number. However, with this general acquaintance, other forms can be easily understood. Some other common destructive forms are the Apple and Pear Scab[1] (*Fig. 330*), the Bitter Rot of Apples[2] (*Fig. 331*), Peach Mildew,[3] Black

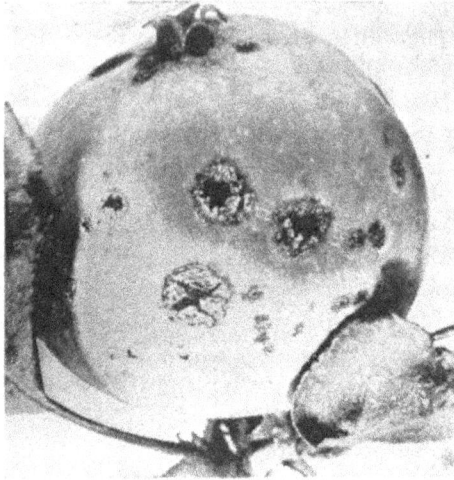

Fig. 330. — Apple attacked by Scab, *Venturia Pomi*. Photographed by Whetzel.

Rot of Grapes,[4] and the Wilt disease of Cotton, Watermelons, and Cowpeas,[5] etc.

Summary of Ascomycetes. — The Ascomycetes have no water habits and their chief resemblance to the Algae is in the character of their sex organs and fruiting bodies. The plant body ranges

[1] A Contribution to Our Knowledge of Apple Scab. *Bulletin 96*, Montana Agr. Col. Exp. Sta., 1914.

[2] Bitter Rot of Apples. *Bulletin 44*, Bur. Pl. Ind., U. S. Dept. of Agriculture, 1903.

[3] Peach Mildew. *Bulletin 107*, Colorado Agr. Exp. Sta., 1906.

[4] The Control of Black-Rot of Grape. *Bulletin 155*, Bur. Pl. Ind., U. S. Dept. Agriculture, 1909.

[5] Wilt Disease of Cotton, Watermelon, and Cowpea. *Bulletin 17*, Division of Vegetable Path., U. S. Dept. Agriculture, 1899.

Also see Spraying Practice for Orchard and Garden. *Bulletin 127*, Iowa Agr. Exp. Sta., 1912.

from a single cell, as in Yeast, to a massive mycelium which in some cases takes no definite shape while in others it forms a definitely shaped fruiting body. In parasitic forms the mycelium sometimes runs through the tissues of the hosts, and sometimes is chiefly superficial, sending only haustoria into the host.

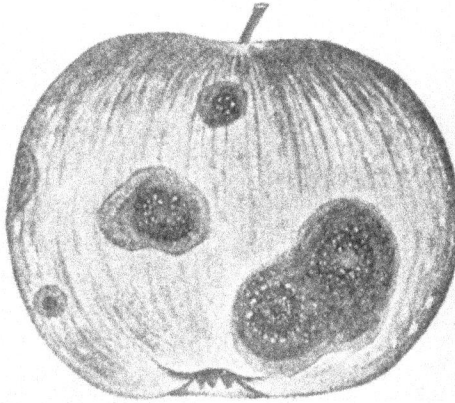

Fig. 331. — Apple attacked by the Bitter Rot Fungus, *Glomerella rufomaculans*. After Alwood.

The spores are of two kinds, conidiospores and ascospores. The conidiospores are borne free on projecting hyphae, and grow directly into hyphae upon germination. The ascospores, the characteristic spores of the group, are borne in asci which are usually produced within a fruiting body or ascocarp, which may be an open structure or a closed one.

In controlling the disease-producing forms one must reckon with conidiospores and ascospores. .

Lichens

Lichens are very common structures which form splotches on stumps, tree trunks, rocks, old boards, etc., and some grow upon the ground. *Figure 332* shows an Apple twig covered with Lichens. They may appear as a crust covering the support; or they may have flat lobed bodies like the one shown in *Figure 333;*

or they may have slender branching bodies like the one shown in *Figure 334*. The slender branches may be erect, prostrate, or hang in festoons from the branches of trees or other supports.

A Lichen, although regarded as a plant, is a structure formed by the association of a Fungus and an Alga. The Fungus involved is in nearly all cases an Ascomycete, and the Alga involved is nearly always a unicellular form of the Green Algae or some form of the Blue-green Algae. The Fungus is a parasite on the Alga, obtaining food from the Alga. The hyphae of the Fungus get food from the Alga by being in close contact, and since the cells of the Alga are rarely penetrated, the Alga apparently is not injured in most cases. A section through a Lichen, as shown in *Figure 335*, shows a meshwork of hyphae and in the meshes the cells of the Alga are held. Usually the hyphae are more closely interwoven in the outer region, thus forming a compact cortical region which encloses the looser region within where the cells of the Alga are usually more abundant. On the under surface filamentous structures are developed which attach the plant body to the substratum. The mycelium of the Fungus thus constitutes the framework of the plant body or thallus.

FIG. 332. — Lichens on an Apple branch. From *Bulletin 185*, Maine Agr. Exp. Sta.

FIG. 333. — A Lichen with a flat lobed body growing on bark. The asci are produced in the small cups. × ½.

The two plants of this association are of mutual help. The sponge structure formed by the Fungus holds water for the Alga, while the Alga makes carbohydrates, some of which can be used by the Fungus. As a result of this mutual help, the Lichen can live on dry barren rocks where other plants cannot exist. Neither

FIG. 334. — A much branched Lichen hanging from the branch of a tree.

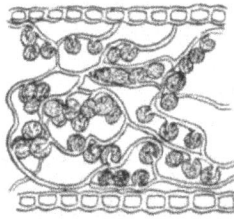

FIG. 335. — A much enlarged section through a Lichen, showing the fungal hyphae and the globular cells of the Alga.

the Alga nor the Fungus could grow in such places alone, for the Alga would lack moisture and the Fungus would lack food. Being so little dependent upon their support for moisture and food, the Lichens are the pioneers on bare and exposed surfaces. They hasten the disintegration of rock and start soil formation. The materials of their dead bodies added to the disintegrate rock form a soil for other plants.

Lichens multiply vegetatively by small scale-like portions, called *soredia*, which separate from the main plant body. Soredia are small masses of hyphae in which some algal cells are entangled and are capable of growing directly into Lichens.

The fungal member of Lichens usually reproduces by ascospores and the algal member by cell division. The asci occur in ascocarps which appear as small cups or disk-like bodies on the surface of the plant body (*Fig. 336*). The sex organs are quite suggestive of the Red Algae. The antheridia occur on branching hyphae and are very small cells which break off and function as sperms. After fertilization, sterile hyphae grow up from below the ascogonium and form the wall of the ascocarp which finally breaks through and appears on the surface of the plant body as a cup or disk.

Besides being the pioneer plants on rocks and other places where they form soil and thus make it possible for higher plants to get a start, they are also of some economic importance in other ways. In northern regions the Lichen known as Reindeer Moss is an important food for animals. Some forms are used as food by man. Although not parasites, they sometimes are harmful to plants upon which they grow. When growing on the twigs of fruit trees, they prevent the bark from functioning properly and also furnish a shelter for various kinds of destructive insects.

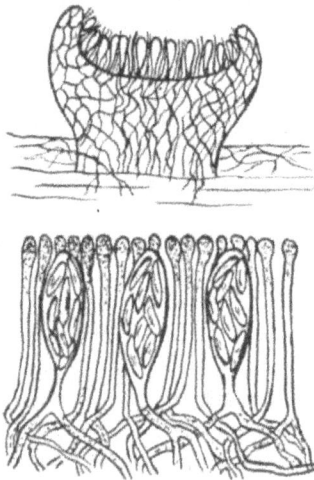

Fig. 336. — Reproduction in Lichens by ascospores. Above, vertical section through a cup (apothecium), showing asci and paraphyses; below, asci and paraphyses shown more enlarged. Redrawn from Schneider.

Basidiomycetes

General Description. — This is the group of Fungi to which Toadstools, Mushrooms, Puffballs, Rusts, and Smuts belong. The group scarcely needs an introduction, because such conspicuous forms, as Toadstools, Mushrooms, and Puffballs are familiar to everybody. In number of forms this group is next to the Ascomycetes. Their characteristic spore-bearing structure is the *basidium*, which is the enlarged end of a hypha with usually four slender branches upon which spores are borne, one spore being borne on the end of each branch. Just as the spores borne in an ascus are called ascospores and are the characteristic spores of the Ascomycetes, so those borne on a basidium are called basidiospores and are the characteristic spores of the Basidiomycetes.

The mycelium of many is saprophytic, living in decaying wood, rotten manure, and other kinds of organic matter. In others, such as the Rusts, Smuts, and other forms, the mycelium is parasitic, living upon the tissues of the grains and other higher plants. Even the saprophytic forms cause some undesirable destruction. They often start in the wounds of fruit trees, shade trees, and forest trees, and the action of their mycelia hastens decay and may lead to the destruction of the tree.

In many forms the mycelium, after it is well established in the region of food supply, produces on the surface of the substratum some kind of a body in which the spores are borne. It will be recalled that this is the habit of the Morel. This body, since it bears the spore, is called a *sporophore* which really means a "spore-bearing body." It is a term commonly applied to a spore-bearing hyphae or to any portion or all of the plant body which has to do with bearing spores. Thus the wrinkled top and stalk bearing it constitutes the sporophore in the Morel. In the Toadstools and Mushrooms, the sporophore is often umbrella-shaped. In some forms which grow on the sides of trees and stumps, the sporophore resembles a small shelf projecting from the support, and in this case the sporophore is often hard. In Puffballs the sporophore is more or less globular. Sporophores are extremely variable in both shape and texture, and are the structures by which those Fungi which have them are classified. The sporophore is the part of the Fungus that attracts attention. It is the portion that is eaten and called a Mushroom. The portion of the mycelium which traverses the substratum is usually hidden, and its presence is not known until the sporophore appears.

Many of the parasitic Basidiomycetes, like the Smuts and Rusts, have no conspicuous sporophores, and the presence of the mycelium is indicated only by the occurrence of unusual structures on the surface of the host plant. In case of Smut the presence of the disease is indicated by the appearance of Smut balls, and in Rusts, by the red or black blisters occurring on the leaves and stem of the host.

Although the basidiospores are the characteristic spores of the group, a number of other kinds of spores occur, which in some cases are more important in reproduction than the basidiospores. Sexual reproduction has been entirely lost by many of the group, and in those where it is retained the fusion is between hyphae, there being no sex organs formed. There are no oöspores or zygospores to be considered in this group.

The Basidiomycetes, of which there are 14,000 or more species, are divided into a number of orders. The most familiar orders are those represented by the Toadstools and Mushrooms (*Hymenomycetes*), Puffballs (*Gasteromycetes*), Smuts (*Ustilaginales*), and Rusts (*Uredinales*).

Toadstools and Mushrooms (Hymenomycetes). — This is the most familiar order to most people, because it includes so many forms like the Toadstools and Mushrooms, which have conspicuous sporophores. In addition to the Toadstools and Mushrooms, the order contains some other rather familiar kinds of Fungi.

FIG. 337. — A poisonous Toadstool, *Amanita bulbosa.* × ½.

The Fungi of this order are chiefly saprophytes, living on decaying wood, leaf mold, rich humus, and manure. Often the organic matter upon which they are living is not visible and they seem to be growing right out of the soil. As the name of the order suggests, they have a hymenium, and the hymenium, which consists of basidia commonly intermingled with sterile hyphae, is borne exposed. Usually the hymenium is on the under side of the sporophore where it is protected from rain.

Those of the order having umbrella-shaped sporophores are popularly called Toadstools and when edible they are popularly called Mushrooms. The term Mushroom, however, is often applied to Morels and all kinds of Fungi that are edible. There are several hundred species of edible Fungi in the United States and more than one hundred of them are of the Toadstool type. Some of the Toadstools are deadly poisonous, as the one shown in *Figure 337*, and many that are not poisonous are tough, fibrous, or ill-tasting and hence not edible. Between edible and non-edible Fungi there are no botanical distinctions or guides. By experience people have learned that some species are edible and some non-edible, and many sad accidents have occurred as a result of not being able to distinguish the poisonous from the edible ones.

The order is divided scientifically into a number of sub-groups according to the method of exposing the hymenium. In the largest and most important group of Hymenomycetes, the hymenium covers the surface of thin radiating plates called gills. These Fungi are known as the Agarics or Gill Fungi. To the Gill Fungi belong most Toadstools and the Field Mushroom (*Agaricus campestris*) which is extensively cultivated for market.

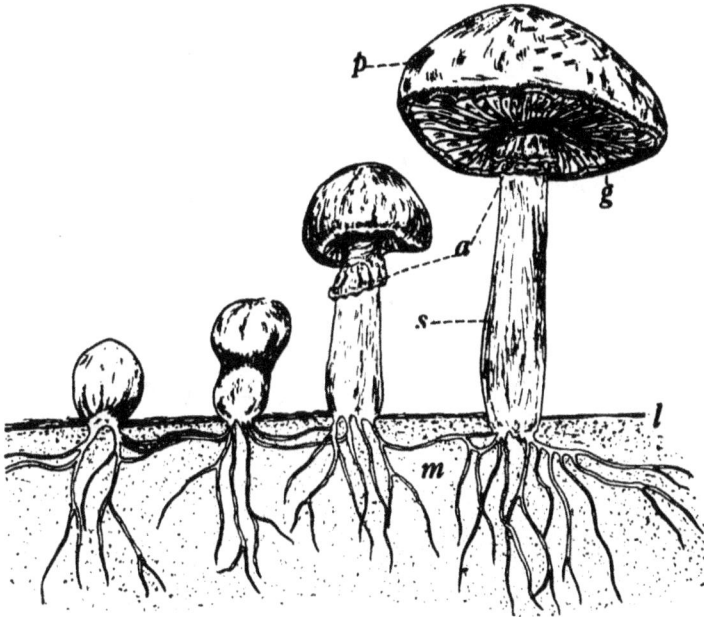

FIG. 338. — Stages in the development of the Mushroom, *Agaricus campestris*. *l*, ground line; *m*, underground portion of mycelium; *s*, stipe; *p*, pileus; *g*, gills; *a*, annulus. × ½.

On account of their structural complexity the Agarics are regarded as highly developed Fungi. They develop as shown in *Figure 338*.

Before developing the sporophore, the mycelium becomes well established in decaying organic matter and this may require considerable time. In the development of a sporophore, there first appears on the surface of the substratum a small spherical body called a button which has a skin-like covering within which the sporophore is forming. This body elongates very rapidly if the weather is warm and moist and sometimes the sporophore attains full size in a few hours. The elongating sporophore finally breaks through the covering of the button, spreads out its umbrella-like top, and the characteristic sporophore appears with remnants of the torn skin-like covering remaining attached.

When mature the sporophore consists of a stalk, called *stipe*, and the expanded umbrella-like top, called *pileus*. On the under

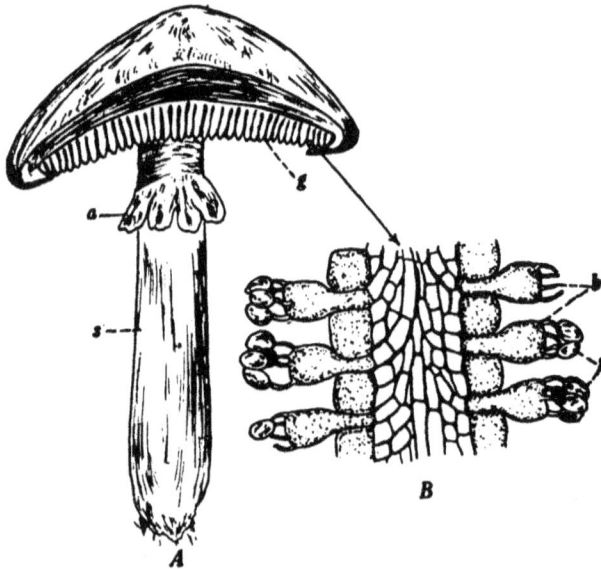

FIG. 339. — Reproductive structures of the Mushroom, *Agaricus campestris*. A, the Mushroom with a portion of its pileus cut away to show the gills. *g*, gills; *s*, stipe; *a*, annulus. B, section through a gill, highly magnified to show the basidia (*b*) and the basidiospores (*r*). Redrawn from Leavitt.

side of the pileus are the thin radiating plates or gills bearing the hymenium in which occur the basidia as shown in *Figure 339*. A fragment of the skin-like covering of the button stage commonly remains attached to the stipe, forming the *annulus* and in some forms, as shown in *Figure 337*, a portion of the covering remains as a cup at the base of the stipe, forming the *volva*. Other fragments of the covering often remain as flecks on the outer surface of the pileus. When the spores are mature, they fall from the basidia and may reach the ground directly beneath or be carried away by the wind. When favorably situated, the spores grow new mycelia, thus completing the round of life. The basidiospore is the only spore formed and no sexuality has been discovered.

Small brick-like masses of organic matter, usually consisting of manure and containing mycelial threads of the Mushroom in a dormant state, are sold on the market, and used in starting Mushroom beds, the mycelial threads contained constituting the so-called Mushroom *spawn*.

FIG. 340. — The Edible Boletus, a polyporus Fungus. × ½.

In another rather common family (*Polyporaceae*) of the Hymenomycetes, the hymenium

FIG. 341. — A *Hydnum*, a Fungus in which the hymenium is borne on tooth-like projections. × ½.

FIG. 342. — A Basidiomycete, *Clavaria*, with a much branched sporophore. × ½.

lines tubes with pore-like openings. These are known as the Pore Fungi, and to this family belong some Toadstools, some of which are edible (*Fig. 340*), and the Bracket Fungi, which form shelf-

like sporophores on the sides of trees and stumps.   In the family
to which the Hydnums belong the hymenium is borne on tooth-
like projections (*Fig. 341*).   In another family the sporophore
is much branched and the hymenium covers the surface of the
branches (*Fig. 342*).   As to the texture of the sporophore, that
varies widely in the different families.   In some families it is
gelatinous and without definite shape.   It is fleshy in the Toadstools and Mushrooms and in some of the Bracket Fungi it becomes as hard and persistent as wood.

FIG. 343. — Some of the roots and the lower portion of the trunk of an
Apple tree which has been killed by the Toadstools.

Destructive Toadstools and Bracket Fungi. — Some Toadstools attack the roots of trees and cause the disease called *Root
Rot*.   This disease occurs on a number of fruit trees, such as the
Apple, Plum, Cherry, and Peach, and on many shrubs and forest
trees.   In *Figure 343* is shown some Toadstools which have
destroyed an Apple tree.   The Toadstools usually cause the death
of the roots, and this results in killing the tree.   The mycelia of
the Toadstools probably enter the roots through wounds.

In *Figure 344* is a Bracket Fungus which causes a disease known as *White Heart Rot*. This disease occurs on fruit trees and many forest trees. The spore enters through a wound and starts the mycelium which penetrates and transforms the heart wood into a white pulpy mass. In *Figure 345* is shown another Bracket Fungus which attacks trees in a similar way and causes the wood to rot and become reddish brown or black. It produces the *Red Heart Rot*. There are many other destructive forms which concern the forester and horticulturist. They start in

FIG. 344. — One of the Bracket Fungi, *Fomes igniarius*, living on the trunk of a living Aspen. It attacks various trees, destroying the wood and causing much damage. From *Bulletin 189*, Bureau of Plant Industry, U. S. Dept. of Agriculture.

wounds where there is some decaying matter, and in pruning it is necessary to guard against the entrance of these Fungi.

Puffballs and Related Forms (Gasteromycetes). — On account of the complexity of their sporophores, the Gasteromycetes are considered the highest of all Fungi. They are saprophytes, growing on decaying wood, leaf mold, rich humus, and manure. They require about the same conditions for growth as do the Toadstools and Mushrooms and are often found growing with them. There are about 700 species, many of which are edible. The sporophore of these Fungi is usually more or less globular in form and the hymenium is enclosed.

The most common and familiar members of the order are the Puffballs, common in the woods and fields, and so named because when pressed upon the spores puff out in cloud-like masses (*Fig. 346*). Some of the Puffballs are a foot or more in diameter when mature and most of them are edible. The sporophore

FIG. 345. — A Polyporus Fungus, *Polyporus sulfureus*, on the Red Oak. It causes the Red Heart Rot of trees. Photo by Dr. W. A. Murrill, N. Y. Botanical Garden.

develops from a subterranean mycelium, and is differentiated into an outer region which constitutes a two-layered skin-like covering (*peridium*) and an interior chambered region (*gleba*) in which the basidia intermingled with sterile hyphae occur. Spores are produced in immense numbers. A Puffball of ordinary size produces many millions of spores. The spores are dark in color due to their heavy walls. They escape from the sporophore through pore-like or slit-like openings in the peridium.

A very interesting Puffball is the Earthstar (*Geaster*) shown in *Figure 347*. In this form the outer layer of the peridium splits into regular segments and these segments are hygroscopic. When the segments are wet they bend back and downward and in this way the outer layer of the peridium spreads out like a star. The inner layer of the peridium opens by an apical pore and allows the spores to escape as in other Puffballs.

The Bird's Nest Fungi (*Fig. 348*), which are close relatives of the Puffballs, show another interesting feature. They are small, usually less than a centimeter in height and width. They develop on twigs and sticks as well as on organic matter that is quite well decayed. One often finds them growing on the benches in greenhouses. The chambers of the gleba become

FIG. 346. — Puffballs, *Lycoperdons.* Three have opened at the top, thus allowing the spores produced in the interior to escape. $\times \frac{1}{2}$.

FIG. 347. — An Earthstar, *Geaster.* About natural size.

enclosed in walls and separate. After the peridium opens, the sporophore is cup-shaped and, with the egg-like chambers of the gleba exposed, resembles a bird's nest full of eggs.

The Stink Horn (*Fig. 349*), noted for its intolerable odor, is another Fungus of this order. Its mycelium feeds on decaying organic matter in the ground.   The sporophore is at first globose, but the gleba soon breaks out of the peridium and is elevated to some distance above ground by an elongating stalk.   The spore masses are slimy and have the odor of carrion.   Certain insects which disseminate the spores are attracted by the odor.

FIG. 348. — A Bird's Nest Fungus, *Nidularia*. About natural size.

Smuts (Ustilaginales). — The Smuts are parasitic Basidiomycetes. In some Smuts, the mycelium, although evident only in local areas, traverses widely through the host, while in others only local areas of the host are attacked.

No sporophores, such as characterize the Toadstools and Puffballs, occur in the Smuts.   There are more than 2000 species of Smuts.   They attack chiefly plants of the Grass family and especially the cereals, the grains of which they commonly displace with powdery black masses of spores.   The financial loss due to Oat Smut alone has been estimated to be $10,000,000 annually in the United States. In addition to the loss due to the destruction of the cereal crops and the lowering of their market price, there is considerable loss due to Smut explosions in thrashing machines.   During the summer of 1914, 300 thrashing machines were blown up or burned in the Pacific Northwest by Smut explosions. Smut dust is highly combustible when dry, and is probably ignited by static electricity in the cylinder of the thrashing machine.   The Smuts are particularly destructive to Oats, Wheat, Rye, and Barley.   Corn Smut is exceedingly common but less destructive.

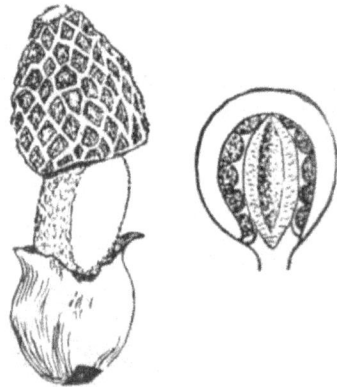

FIG. 349. — Stink Horn Fungus, *Phallus impudicus*.   At the right, vertical section of the Fungus in early stage of development, showing the gleba enclosed by the peridium. At the left, mature stage, showing the gleba elevated much above the peridium.   × ⅓.

The Smut of Oats.[1] — The Smut of the Oats is probably the most common and destructive one of the Smut group. The mycelium of the Oat Smut gets started in the tissues of the Oat plant when the latter is in the seedling stage, and at flowering

Fig. 350. — Loose Smut of Oats. Left, normal head; right, head destroyed by Smut. After *Bulletin 112*, Minnesota Agr. Exp. Sta.

time it masses in the ovaries, which become swollen and finally destroyed and replaced by masses of spores (*Fig. ,350*). A

[1] The following references will be found helpful in understanding the smuts and methods of combatting them.

The Grain Smuts. *Farmers' Bulletin 75*, U. S. Dept. of Agriculture, 1898.

Corn Smut. *Annual Report 12*, Indiana Agr. Exp. Sta., 1900.

The prevention of Stinking Smut of Wheat and Loose Smut of Oats. *Farmers' Bulletin 250*, U. S. Dept. Agriculture, 1906.

The Smuts of Grain plants. *Bulletin 122*, Minnesota Agr. Exp. Sta., 1911.

The Smuts of Wheat, Oats, Barley, and Corn. *Farmers' Bulletin 507*, U. S. Dept. Agriculture, 1912.

Bunt or Stinking Smut of Wheat. *Bulletin 126*, Washington Agr. Exp. Sta., 1915.

study of the formation of these spores shows that they are not basidiospores, for they are not formed on basidia. The hyphae in the smut ball simply divide into cells which separate and become spores. These spores are the so-called *brand spores*, the whole mass of them forming the so-called Smut. The spores are very heavy-walled and appear black in mass. This kind of a heavy-walled spore, which is simply a transformed vegetative cell of the mycelium, is called a *chlamydospore*, a name referring to the heavy protective wall. The spore masses break up when mature and the spores are shed. In handling the grain, especially in thrashing, the spores escape in dust-like fogs. The spores pass the winter on the ground, straw, grain, or wherever they happen to fall. Many of the spores lodge on the Oat grain, falling down between the lemma and palea which enclose the Oat kernel. The following spring the chlamydospores germinate, each producing a small hypha called a *promycelium*, on which the basidiospores are produced. The basidiospores are produced on the end and sides of the promycelium as shown in *Figure 351*. Their number is indefinite and they often multiply by budding after the manner of the Yeasts. They are quite commonly called *conidia* and often *sporidia*, although they are comparable to the basidiospores of the Toadstools and Puffballs. It is on account of the occurrence of the promycelium, which is regarded as a basidium, that the Smuts are classed as Basidiomycetes. Once in contact with a young Oat plant, the basidiospores produce hyphae, known as *infection hyphae*, which penetrate the young plant and start the development of a mycelium.

Fig. 351. — Germination of Chlamydospores. At the left, a spore, and at the right, a spore which has germinated and produced a promycelium bearing basidiospores (c). × about 300.

It has been found that most of the infection in Oat Smut results from the chlamydospores which are lodged on the grain, and that by soaking seed Oats in hot water (132° to 133° F.) for ten to fifteen minutes or in water containing about 1 pint of 40 per cent formalin to 45 gallons of water, the spores can be killed and much loss to the Oat crop prevented.

The Smut of Oats, Stinking Smut of Wheat, and Covered Smut of Barley are very similar in habit and require similar treatment. Sometimes, as in case of the Stinking Smut of Wheat, the infection of the seedling may be due to spores lodged in the soil as well as to spores adhering to the kernel.

Loose Smuts of Wheat and Barley. — The Loose Smuts of Wheat and Barley mature and shed their chlamydospores when the grain is in flower. These spores are borne away by the wind and when falling on the flowers of their respective hosts, grow hyphae into the young kernel. The kernel continues its development, but when mature it has concealed within a tiny Smut plant, which is able, when the kernel is planted, to resume its growth and develop in the grain plant. Much of the damage from these Smuts can be avoided by seed selection. Treatments for these Smuts must aim at killing the tiny Smut plants concealed in the seed grain. Soaking the seed in cold water five hours and then in water 130° F. for ten minutes is recommended.

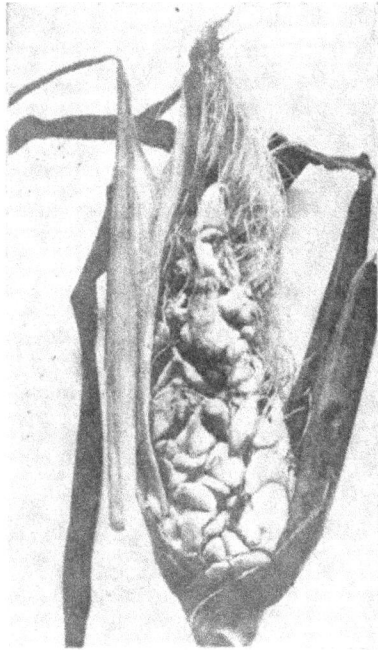

FIG. 352. — Ear of Corn with kernels destroyed and replaced by masses of Smut. From *Farmers' Bulletin 507*, U. S. Dept. of Agriculture.

Corn Smut. — Corn Smut is the most conspicuous of the Smut group. It attacks all tender regions of the Corn plant but does most damage to the flowers which become much enlarged and transformed into Smut balls. Tumor-like developments of the Fungus occur also on the leaves and stem as well as on the ear and tassel. In *Figure 352* is shown an ear in which the kernels are replaced by the tumor-like masses of the Fungus. These Smut bodies have a thin, grayish, hyphal covering, and within the chlamydospores are pro-

duced by the division of hyphae as described in Oat Smut.
When the spores are mature, the skin-like covering breaks, thus
allowing the spores to be scattered. Some spores pass the winter
on the old stalks. Others pass the winter on the ground or wherever they happen to fall. In the spring the chlamydospores germinate and produce the promycelia and basidiospores. The
basidiospores are blown to the Corn and are able to grow hyphae
into the tender regions of the plant and start the disease. Treatment of the seed Corn is, therefore, of little value in combatting
Corn Smut. In what way can Corn Smut be controlled?

Rusts (Uredinales).[1] — Like the Smuts, the Rusts are internal
parasites and only their spore masses are visible externally.
They are so named on account of the red color of their spore
masses. There are about 2000 species of Rusts and they attack
nearly all kinds of plants but more especially members of the
Grass family. Although regarded as degraded parasites, they
are more complex than the Smuts, for they have more kinds of
spores and many of them have alternating stages upon different
hosts. For example, it is well known that Wheat Rust and the
Common Barberry bush (*Berberis vulgaris*) are associated. They
are associated because the Wheat Rust lives one stage of its life
cycle on the Wheat and the other on the Barberry. Each kind
of Rust lives on only certain hosts and the alternating hosts are
plants very different in kind, as those of the Wheat Rust
illustrate.

Rusts, although directly affecting only limited areas of tissue
around the places of attack, commonly attack the host in so
many places that they weaken the host and thereby prevent grain
plants from yielding normally. The financial loss to the farmer
due to Rusts is considerably more than that caused by Smuts.
Some years the loss in the United States due to the Black Rust
exceeds $15,000,000. The Black Rust of which six forms are
distinguished is the most important one of the Rusts.

Black Rust of Grain (Puccinia graminis). — The Black Rust,
sometimes called Red Rust, is a dreaded pest on Wheat, Oats,

[1] Investigations of Rusts. *Bulletin 65*, Bureau of Plant Industry, U. S.
Dept. Agriculture, 1904.

Lessons from the Grain Rust Epidemic of 1904. *Farmers' Bulletin 219*,
U. S. Dept. Agriculture, 1905.

Rust of Cereals. *Bulletin 109*, South Dakota Agr. Exp. Sta., 1908.

Rye, and Barley, and occurs on other Grasses.   The presence of the mycelium in the host is first known through the appearance of reddish spots or lines on the stems and leaves in late spring or early summer.   The reddish spots or lines are regions of spore production.   They are pustules or blister-like structures caused by masses of spore-bearing hyphae which push up the epidermis until it is finally ruptured (*Fig. 353*).   The reddish color of the pustules is due to the reddish color of the spores.   These spores are known as the "summer spores" or *uredospores*. The uredospores, which are produced in great numbers, are scattered by the wind, thus reaching other host

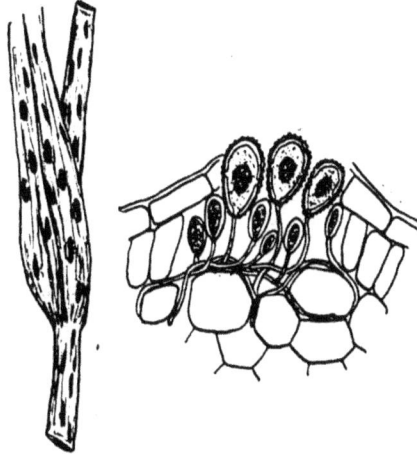

FIG. 353. — Wheat Rust as it appears on Wheat.   Left, portion of a Wheat plant, showing the pustules on the stem and leaf; right, a much enlarged section through a pustule, showing the summer spores ($\times$ 200).

plants into which they grow hyphae and thereby infect. They are chiefly responsible for the rapid spread of the disease during summer.

Later in the summer, when the grain is ripening and the food for the Fungus becomes scarce, the same mycelia produce heavy-walled, two-celled spores, known as *winter spores* or *teleutospores* (*Fig. 354*). These spores are dark in color, giving the pustules a dark appearance — whence the name

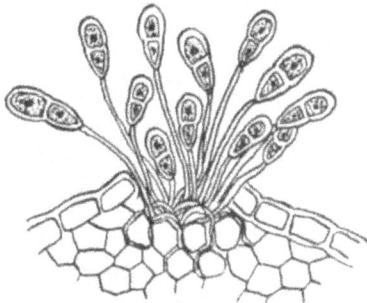

FIG. 354. — A section through a pustule in late summer, showing the winter spores or teleutospores. $\times$ about 200.

Black Rust.   They pass the winter on the straw, ground, or wherever they happen to fall.   The following spring, each cell of the teleutospore produces a promycelium bearing the *basidiospores*, often called *sporidia*, as shown in *Figure 355*. Thus the teleutospore occupies the same position in the life history of Rusts as the brand spore occupies in the life history of Smuts. The basidio spores are scattered by the wind, and in regions where Barberry bushes grow, they come in contact with the leaves of the Barberry where they grow and produce mycelia in the leaf tissues.

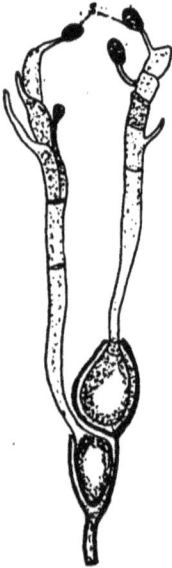

Upon the Barberry, the mycelia produce on the under surface of the leaf small cups called aecidia in which spores are borne in chains as shown in *Figure 356*. These spores are called *aecidiospores* or *cup spores*. The aecidiospores, which are shed in the spring or early summer, are disseminated by the wind and start the disease on the grains or other Grasses, thus completing the life cycle as it is shown in *Figure 357*.

In connection with the development of the aecidiospores there occur on the upper surface of the Barberry leaf very small flask-shaped cups called spermagonia, in which are produced very small spores called *spermatia* or *pycniospores*. The spermatia have no function and the spermagonia and aecidia are supposed to represent the remnants of a sexual apparatus which has become functionless.

Thus four kinds of spores are involved in the complete life cycle of the Black Rust and a fifth kind occurs. The uredospores and teleutospores occur on the grains or other Grasses. The basidiospores are produced by the teleutospores and no host is required, while aecidiospores occur on the Barberry bush.

FIG. 355. — Teleutospore having developed the promycelia bearing basidiospores (s).

If the Black Rust must have all of the stages in order to propagate from year to year, then it seems that there should be little or no Black Rust in regions where there are no Barberry bushes, but such is not the case, for the Black Rust occurs abundantly in fields many miles away from Barberry bushes.

Just how it gets started on the grains in localities where there are no Barberry bushes is not definitely known. It was once

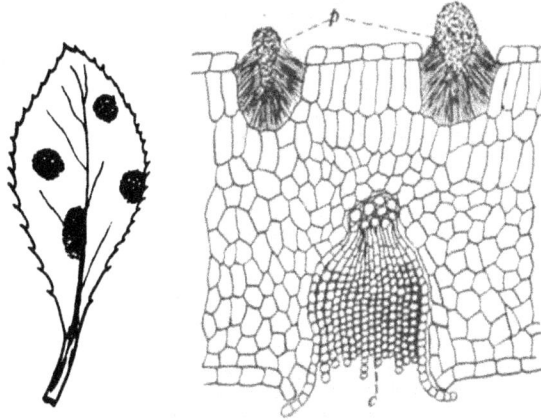

FIG. 356. — Stage of the Wheat Rust on the Barberry bush, *Berberis vulgaris.* Left, leaf of Barberry, showing the affected areas which are reddish, much thickened, and contain many cup-like depressions; right, a very much enlarged section through the affected area of the leaf, showing one of the cups (*c*) with chains of aecidiospores ($\times$ 200). The very small spores at (*p*) are the spermatia or pycniospores.

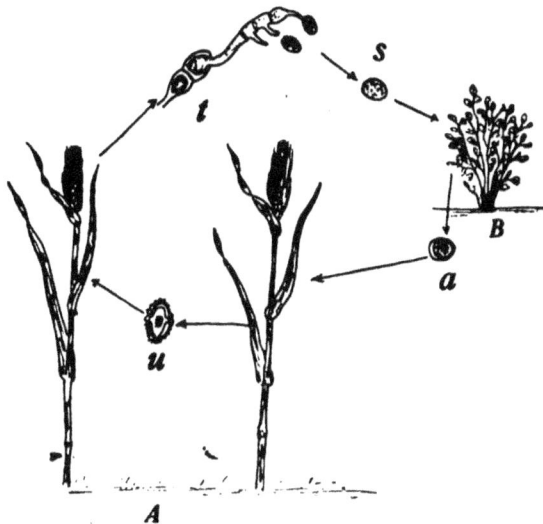

FIG. 357. — Diagram showing the life cycle of the Wheat Rust. *A,* wheat plants; *B,* barberry bush; *u,* uredospore; *t,* teleutospore; *s,* basidiospores; *a,* aecidiospore.

thought that the basidiospores started the disease directly on the Grass host, but experiments have shown that they will not grow on this host. Experiments have also shown that uredospores are ordinarily killed by freezing weather and therefore are rarely able to live over winter where the temperature goes much below freezing. It has been suggested that some hyphae may enter the kernels of the diseased plants and remain dormant until the seed is planted and then infect the seedling, but this theory is not generally accepted. Another suggestion is that the wind carries the uredospores northward from the Southern states where they

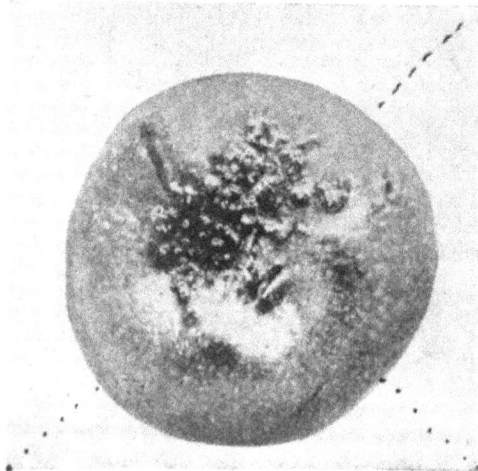

FIG. 358. — Apple affected with Cedar Rust. From *Technical Bulletin 9,* Virginia Agr. Exp. Sta.

are able to live over winter. It is also probable that the aecidiospores may be carried a considerable distance by the wind and thus reach grain fields not in the immediate vicinity of Barberry bushes. Then there is the probability that the disease may start on the wild Grasses growing near the Barberry bushes, and be passed along by the uredospores from one patch of Grass to another until grain fields far away are reached.

No satisfactory preventative for the Black Rust has been discovered. We are not able to control the spores. It is generally believed that the eradication of all of the Common Barberry bushes would do much toward eliminating this Rust. The most hope, however, seems to be in breeding and selecting varieties of grains which can resist the attack of the Rust, and some progress has already been made in this direction.

Cedar Apples and Apple Rust (Gymnosporangium).[1] — There are several Rusts belonging to this group, but the one producing Cedar Apples and the Rust on Apple trees is the most common and the most important of the group. It is common in nearly every region where Red Cedars grow, but does most damage to fruit trees in the Eastern and Southern states. It lives a part of its life cycle on the Cedar, producing gall-like enlargements on the branches, and a part of its life cycle on the Apple tree where it attacks the leaves and fruit, often causing much damage to the fruit (*Fig. 358*). It is the gall-like enlargements on the Cedar tree that are called Cedar apples, although they are not apples at all. In *Figure 359* are shown Cedar apples as they appear in the winter. In the spring gummy branches containing many teleutospores develop on these galls which then look like the one shown in *Figure 360*. The teleutospores produce basidiospores which are blown to the Apple tree where they start the

FIG. 359. — Cedar Apples on the Cedar. This is the way the galls look in winter. From *Bulletin 257*, Wisconsin Agr. Exp. Sta.

---

[1] The Cedar-Apple Fungi and Apple Rust in Iowa. *Bulletin 84*, Iowa Agr. Exp. Sta., 1905.

The Life History of the Cedar Rust Fungus Gymnosporangium juniperivirginianae. *Annual Report 22*, pp. 105–113, Nebraska Agr. Exp. Sta., 1909.

Apple Rust and its Control in Wisconsin. *Bulletin 257*, Wisconsin Agr. Exp. Sta., 1915.

The Cedar Rust Disease of Apples caused by Gymnosporangium juniperivirginianae Schw. *Technical Bulletin 9*, Virginia Agr. Exp. Sta., 1915.

disease on the leaves and fruit. Upon the Apple tree, the aecidia stage is produced, and the aecidiospores are able to attack the Cedar and form new galls, thus completing the life cycle as shown in *Figure 361*.

Pine Tree Blister-rust (Cronartium ribicola). — As its name suggests this Rust attacks Pine trees. It was introduced from Europe about ten years ago and has now become a serious disease in this country. It has its aecidial stage on Pines with five leaves in a fascicle, such as the White Pine and Sugar Pine, and has species of Ribes (Gooseberries and Currants) as the other host. In this Rust the aecidial stage is the most destructive. The mycelium of the aecidial stage kills the cambium and inner bark of Pines, thus causing the death of branches and sometimes of the entire tree. Both uredospores and teleutospores are produced on the infected Currant and Gooseberry bushes, which are apparently very little injured thereby. Pines are infected through the basidiospores. The chief means of checking the spread of the disease is through the destruction of the wild Currant and Gooseberry bushes.

FIG. 360. — A Cedar Apple which has developed the gelatinous branches containing numerous teleutospores. The teleutospores produce sporidia or basidiospores that attack the Apple tree. These gelatinous branches develop in the spring after a rain and while the leaves and shoots of the Apple are young and easily attacked. After *Bulletin 257*, Wisconsin Agr. Exp. Sta.

The damage done to Pine trees is serious and since our Pine forests are valued at many millions of dollars, it is not surprising that our government has put restrictions upon the importation of Pines from Europe and has appropriated large sums of money to be expended in checking this disease.

Asparagus Rust. — Asparagus is often attacked by a Rust (*Puccinia Asparagi*) which is a type of those having but one host. The uredospores, teleutospores, and aecidiospores all occur on the Asparagus.

Some other forms of Rusts of some importance occur on Clover, Alfalfa, Beans, Peas, Beets, Timothy, Corn, Peach trees, etc.

Summary of Basidiomycetes. — Like the Ascomycetes the Basidiomycetes are parasites or saprophytes on land plants and have no motile spores. The Basidiomycetes are supposed to

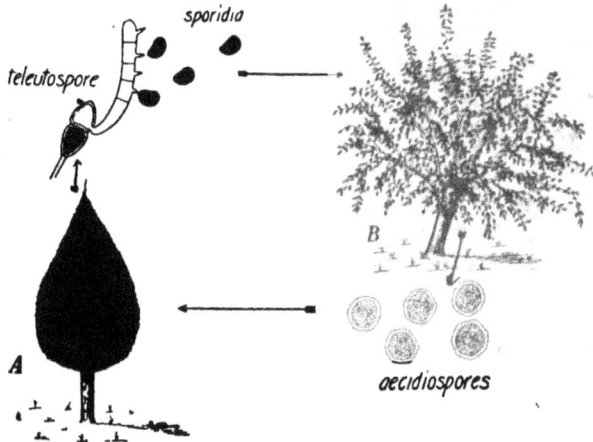

FIG. 361. — Diagram showing life history of the Cedar Rust Fungus. *A*, Cedar tree; *B*, Apple tree. The sporidia from the teleutospores infect the Apple tree and the aecidiospores produced on the Apple foliage during summer reinfect the cedars. From *Technical Bulletin 9*, Virginia Agr. Exp. Sta.

have been evolved from the Ascomycetes, and hence are farthest removed from the Algae, which they resemble very little.

In such Basidiomycetes as the Toadstools and Puffballs, the most highly developed sporophores occur, while in the parasitic Basidiomycetes, as the Smuts and Rusts, the mycelium is scattered through the host and is only visible through the production of spore masses.

Such forms as the Toadstools, Mushrooms, and Puffballs reproduce entirely by basidiospores, while in the reproduction of the Smuts brand and basidiospores are involved, and in the reproduction of Rusts there are four kinds of functional spores — uredo-, teleuto-, basidio-, and aecidiospores, — and the nonfunctional spermatia.

Fungi Imperfecti (Imperfect Fungi)

All Fungi in which the features characteristic of the Phycomycetes, Ascomycetes, or Basidiomycetes have not been discovered in their life histories are classed as imperfect Fungi. It is a heterogenous group, containing numerous Fungi varying widely in characteristics. Investigators think that most of them are the conidial stages of Ascomycetes in which the Ascogenous stage has been abandoned or has not been discovered. Careful investigations have already discovered that a number of Fungi which have been classed as imperfect Fungi have ascogenous stages and are therefore Ascomycetes. As investigations go on no doubt others and probably all of them will be definitely classified in the other groups.

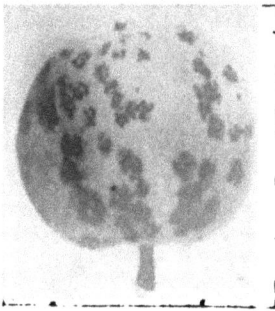

Fig. 362. — Apple affected with Apple Blotch caused by an Imperfect Fungus. From *Bulletin 144*, Bureau of Plant Industry, U. S. Dept. of Agriculture

The spore commonly known in the group is the conidiospore and the character of this spore and the way it is borne are the chief features upon which the group is divided into numerous subdivisions.

Among them are many disease-producing forms, a large number of which produce serious diseases on cultivated plants. The Early Blight of the Potato, Leaf Blight of Cotton, Black Rot of the Sweet Potato, Fruit Spot of Apples, one of the Potato Scabs, Apple Blotch shown in *Figure 362*, and numerous other diseases are produced by these Fungi.

Some special books on Fungi:

HARSHBERGER, JOHN W. A Text-Book of Mycology and Plant Pathology.
STEVENS, F. L. The Fungi which Cause Plant Diseases.
DUGGAR, BENJAMIN M. Fungous Diseases of Plants.
MASSEE, GEORGE. Diseases of Cultivated Plants.
MASSEE, GEORGE AND IVY. Mildews, Rusts, and Smuts.

CHAPTER XVI

BRYOPHYTES (MOSS PLANTS)

Liverworts and Mosses

General Discussion. — In the study of the Myxomycetes, Bacteria, and Fungi, not much attention was given to evolutionary tendencies, for these groups are supposed to be degenerate forms and have contributed nothing of importance in the way of evolution. But in taking up the study of the Bryophytes, we return to the study of evolution which will be emphasized throughout the remaining groups, the aim being to see how Flowering Plants could have originated.

The Bryophytes include two large groups of plants — *Liverworts* (*Hepaticae*) and *Mosses* (*Musci*) — although the term refers to Mosses. The Mosses are more conspicuous and more familiar to most people than the Liverworts, but they are no more important in the study of evolution.

The Bryophytes are of practically no economic importance. They are of very little value for food and rarely harm other plants. They make their own food and therefore do not need to prey upon other plants. The only reason for studying them is that they have contributed to evolution, and a knowledge of them is necessary for an understanding of the higher plants.

The Bryophytes are supposed to have originated from the Algae, and the advancements made by the Algae, such as the establishment of multicellular plant bodies, food-making by photosynthesis, development of gametes and sex organs, and the differentiation of gametes and other cells, are resumed and some of them carried farther by the Bryophytes.

Most Algae live in the water while the Bryophytes in most part live on the land. The Bryophytes are considered the first and most primitive land plants. The Algae are exposed to water while most Bryophytes are exposed to the drying effects of the air. Most Algae soon die when removed from the water and exposed to the air, for they are not protected against loss of water and the air soon dries them out. To live on land a plant must be protected against transpiration, and to become large and erect, a plant must have structures for connecting it to the ground and a stem to support it against the wind. It is believed that the land plants came from Algae, and this means that certain Algae must have acquired the land habit and in so doing ceased to be Algae and became Bryophytes. One can imagine that this transformation came about by some Algae gradually becoming more and more adapted to living on the shore, where they were often stranded, until finally they became so modified as to be fitted to live permanently on land.

Liverworts

The Liverworts are thought to be the group that first acquired the land habit, for, as a group, they are less complex than the Mosses and are also more like the Algae in their moisture requirements. While many of them live on land, there are some forms which still live in water, and it is, therefore, in the Liverworts that the connection between water forms and land forms is most evident. Even most of those Liverworts that live on land are not able to endure dry air and hot sunshine, for, in most part, they must grow in places that are moist or at least shaded. But the Liverworts did much toward establishing the land habit, and it is thought that our strictly land plants originated from such forms as the Liverworts.

The plant body of most Liverworts is a flat body, known as a *thallus*, but in some forms it is differentiated into stem- and leaf-like structures. The thallus form of plant body, although varying much in form according to the species, is usually lobed and often branched. Often the thalli are liver-shaped, and their shape was once thought to signify that these plants possess special virtues in the cure of liver diseases — whence the name Liverworts.

The thallus forms of Liverworts often form mat-like coverings on moist soil or on moist rocks, such as the sides of a cliff. Those Liverworts having better differentiated plant bodies and resembling Moss commonly grow on logs and tree trunks in moist and shady woods. There are about 4000 species of Liverworts and they vary widely in complexity. They are commonly subdivided into three orders — *Marchantiales, Jungermaniales,* and *Anthocerotales.*

The Marchantias. — The Marchantiales include the best known Liverworts, among which are the Marchantias, the most highly specialized Liverworts of this order and the family after which the order is named. The Marchantia common in the north temperate regions is *Marchantia polymorpha.* It grows in moist places, often occurring abundantly in swampy regions, on shaded river banks, and on protected rocky ledges. It often gets started

Fig. 363. — A female and a male plant of *Marchantia polymorphia,* showing the external features of the plant body (about natural size). The two plants, of which *A* is the female and *B* the male plant, differ most noticeably in the character of the gametophores which are the erect stalks with expanded tops (conceptacles) on which the sex organs occur. *r,* rhizoids; *c,* the gemmae cups which are concerned with vegetative multiplication.

in greenhouses where it develops and spreads rapidly on moist soil that is left undisturbed. Being easily obtained, it is one of the Liverworts most commonly studied in botanical laboratories.

The plant body is shown in *Figure 363.* The flat, lobed, green plant body or thallus lies prostrate on the substratum. Often the plants are so much crowded as to overlap, and form aggregations that cover the substratum like a carpet.

Single plants are often several inches in length and breadth, and consist of a number of layers of cells in thickness. On the under surface, cells are differentiated into thread-like structures called *rhizoids*, which attach the plant to the substratum.   In the notches about the margin are cells which function like the meristematic cells of the higher plants, and thus have to do with the addition of new cells whereby the growth of the plant is maintained.   The cells of the upper region of the thallus are differentiated into an epidermis, which affords protection against

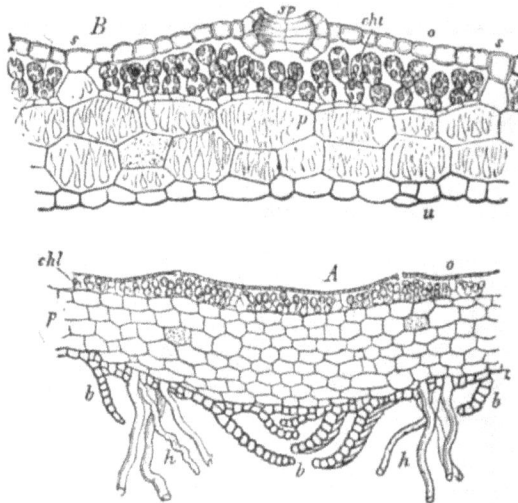

FIG. 364. — Highly magnified cross sections of a thallus of Marchantia. *A*, section through a thick portion of a thallus, showing the following features: the upper epidermis and the chlorenchyma tissue (*chl*) just beneath divided into chambers by partitions (*o*); the layers of cells (*p*) between the chlorenchyma and lower epidermis, giving thickness and rigidity to the thallus; and the lower epidermis with rhizoids (*h*) and scale-like plates of cells (*b*). *B*, section near the margin of the thallus and more highly megnified, showing the following features: upper epidermis (*o*); a chamber of chlorenchyma tissue (*chl*) bounded by the partitions (*s*) and into which the chimney-like air pore (*sp*) opens; the lower epidermis (*u*); and two layers of supporting tissue (*p*). From J. M. Coulter, originally after Goebel.

evaporation, and into tissues which utilize the air and sunlight in manufacturing carbohydrates.   Highly magnified sections through a thallus are shown in *Figure 364*.   In the epidermis are many chimney-shaped pores which permit the air to reach the filaments of food-making cells in the chambers beneath.

On the thalli shown in *Figure 363* are also shown some small cups and some erect stalks with expanded tops.   These structures are further differentiations of the plant body, that are not always present, occurring only during periods of reproduction. The erect umbrella-shaped structures, which are upgrowths of the midrib of the thallus, bear the sex organs and are called *gametophores*, while the cup-shaped structures have to do with a vegetative method of reproduction which will be discussed later.

Since the plant lives spread out on a moist substratum, much of the plant body is in direct contact with moisture and can absorb water and minerals directly. The rhizoids are not roots and are of very little service in supplying water and mineral salts. It is probable that they do nothing more than hold the plant body to the substratum. The filaments of cells in the air chambers on the upper surface are well provided with chloroplasts and carry on active photosynthesis which supplies the plant with carbohydrates. Many of the other cells in the upper region of the plant body have some chloroplasts and no doubt assist some in providing food.

In addition to the sexual method of reproduction, there are two ways of propagating vegetatively or asexually. As the branches of the thalli develop and push ahead, the older regions die away and soon the branches become isolated and form separate plants. This is known as a vegetative or asexual method of reproduction because no spores or sex cells are involved. Another vegetative method occurs in connection with the cups which have been pointed out on the surface of the thalli. In these cups are produced small plates of cells, called *gemmae*, which, when splashed out by rain and suitably located on a substratum, grow directly into new plants. These vegetative methods remind one of the propagation of Strawberries by runners, or of Geraniums by cuttings.

The sex organs are produced upon the umbrella-like tops or receptacles of the gametophores. On the under surface of the much lobed receptacles of the gametophores of the female plants (*A, Fig. 363*) occur the female sex organs called *archegonia*. When a thin section is made through a female receptacle and examined under the microscope, the archegonia are seen projecting from the under surface as shown at *A* in *Figure 365*. Each archegonium consists of many cells so arranged as to form a long hollow neck and an enlarged hollow base called *venter*, in which the large egg is located. It is obvious that an archegonium is much more complex than the oögonium of the algae. In the less lobed receptacles of the gametophores of the male plants (*B*, *Fig. 363*) occur the antheridia, consisting of a stalk and of a jacket of cells which encloses a mass of sperms as shown in *Figure 366*.

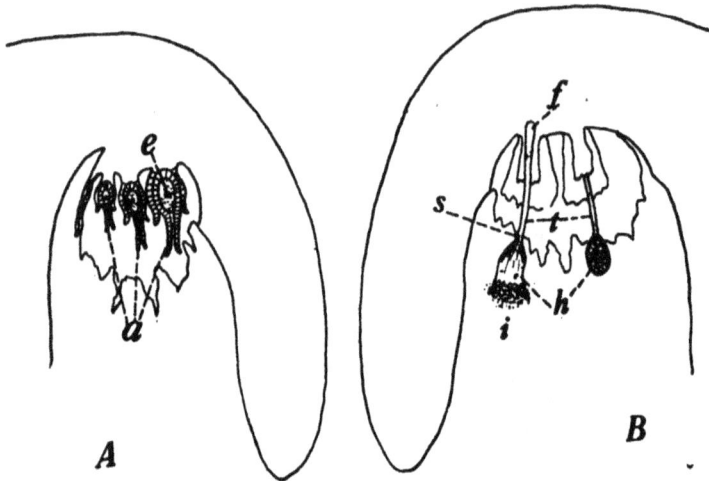

Fig. 365. — Highly magnified vertical sections through the expanded tops or receptacles of female gametophores of Marchantia, showing the sex organs and sporophytes. *A*, section through female gametophore, showing the archegonia (*a*), each of which consists of a neck and an expanded base called venter, in which the egg (*e*) is located. *B*, section through a female gametophore, showing sporophytes (*s*), with their sporangia (*h*), stalks (*t*), foot (*f*), and also showing spores (*i*) escaping from the sporangium of the sporophyte at the left.

Since the sperms are produced on one plant and the eggs on another, the sperms have a considerable distance to be carried to the eggs. .The sperms are splashed about during heavy rains, and, when near an archegonium, they are attracted to the entrance in the neck by an attractive substance which diffuses out of the archegonium. The sperms swim down the canal in the neck of the archegonium and the first one reaching the egg fertilizes it.

The fertilized egg or oöspore remains where it was formed, begins to grow and divide rapidly, and soon produces an oblong, multicellular, brownish body which consists of a stalk that is attached to the receptacle by an absorbing organ called *foot* and bears at the other end a sporangium (*B*, *Fig. 365*). The foot extends into the gametophore and absorbs food which is supplied to the elongating stalk and developing sporangium. In the sporangium are produced numerous spores and also elongated twisted cells called _elaters_, which assist in scattering the spores. When the spores are mature the sporangial wall opens and the spores are scattered. When the spores fall on a moist substratum, they germinate and produce new thallus plants like the ones described.

The Two Generations. — The oblong body produced by the fertilized egg, and consisting of foot, stalk, and sporangium, is regarded as a plant within itself. When fully mature it is so small that one must look closely under the finger-like lobes to find it. It doesn't look much like a plant, since it is so simple and depends upon the gametophore for food and water, but it is this plant that differentiates and becomes the conspicuous

FIG. 366.— Highly magnified vertical section through the expanded top or conceptacle of a male gametophore, showing the antheridia (a) imbedded in the gametophore and consisting of a short stalk and of a jacket enclosing numerous cells which form sperms.

plant body of the higher plants. Since it produces spores, it is called a spore plant or _sporophyte_. When one is reminded that a Corn plant or Apple tree is all sporophyte excepting some microscopical structures within the flowers, then the significance of this small sporophyte of the Liverworts in relation to the origin of the higher plants may be realized.

It is obvious that if this little sporophyte is regarded as a plant, then all of the remainder of Marchantia must be regarded as another plant. This other plant consists of all that has been described as the plant body of Marchantia. It consists of the flat prostrate thallus and the gametophores with the sex organs and gametes. Since it is the function of this plant to bear gametes, it is called _gametophyte_.

It follows then that the complete life cycle of Marchantia involves two plants or generations as illustrated in _Figure 367_. The gametophyte generation develops from a spore and produces gametes, while the sporophyte generation develops from the fertilized egg and produces the spores. It is obvious that this is alternation of generations. Some of the higher Red Algae, as illustrated by Polysiphonia, have an alternation of generations

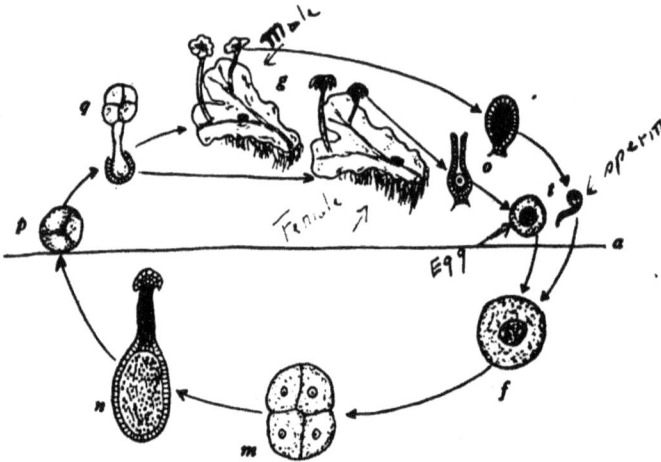

FIG. 367. — A diagram showing the life history of Marchantia. Above the line (a) is the gametophyte generation and below the line is the sporophyte generation. p, spore; q, spore germinating to form gametophyte; g, mature gametophytes; o, sex organs; t, gametes; f, fertilized egg or first cell of the sporophyte; m, fertilized egg dividing; n, mature sporophyte ready to shed spores which are the first cells of new gametophytes.

in their life cycle, but in Bryophytes this feature is so well established that it occurs everywhere in the group and is so evident that it was in the Bryophytes that the alternation of generations was first observed. Alternation of generations is also an established feature of Pteridophytes and Spermatophytes or all plants above the Bryophytes.

One of the interesting features in connection with the transition from the gametophyte generation to the sporophyte generation is a peculiar kind of cell division known as the *reduction division*. It will be recalled that in preparation for cell division the chromatin in the nuclei of cells forms into a definite number of chromosomes, the number depending upon the kind of plant. Now reckoning nuclear content in terms of chromosomes, it is obvious that since fertilization is a fusion of the nuclear contents of a sperm and an egg, the number of chromosomes in the nucleus of the fertilized egg is double that of the sperm or egg. It follows that, unless the number of chromosomes is reduced somewhere in the life cycle of the plant, each generation of plants would have double the number of chromosomes of the preceding generation. This doubling of the chromosome number in each generation

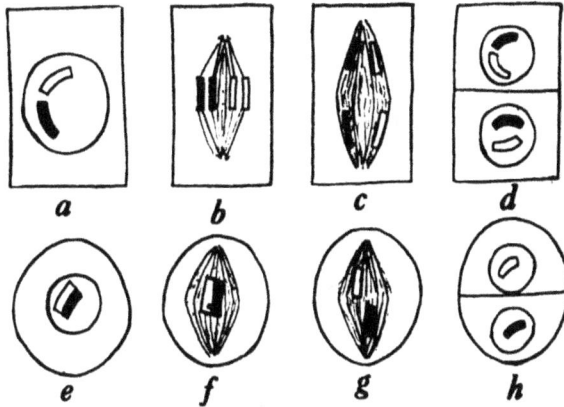

FIG. 368. — Diagrams showing the difference between ordinary cell division and the reduction division. To make the diagrams easy to follow only two chromosomes in each case are represented, but their behavior is typical of all the chromosomes of the nucleus. One chromosome has been blackened and the other left white to indicate that they differ in that one consists of chromatin material of the father parent and the other, of the mother parent of the individual whose cell division is illustrated by the diagrams. The upper diagram illustrates the behavior of chromosomes in ordinary cell division, showing the chromosomes at a soon after organization, their arrangement on the spindle fibers and splitting lengthwise at b, the separation of the longitudinal halves at c, and the formation of the new nuclei at d, with each new nucleus containing a longitudinal half of each of the original chromosomes. In the lower diagram, illustrating the behavior of chromosomes in the reduction division, the chromosomes are paired at e, arranged on the spindle in pairs at f, separated as whole chromosomes at g, and thus each nucleus at h receives one chromosome of the pair and not half of each chromosome as in ordinary cell division.

would soon result in a disastrous piling up of chromosomes. Investigations show that the sporophyte has twice the number of chromosomes of the gametophyte, but that the spores formed by the sporophyte have the gametophytic number. The transition is made in the mother cells, that is, in the cells which form the spores, and by these cells dividing in such a way that the chromosomes are so distributed that each daughter cell gets only half of the number of chromosomes or the gametophytic number. This kind of cell division is called the reduction division and simply undoes the doubling of chromosomes resulting from fertilization. The diagrams in *Figure 368* show how the reduction division differs from ordinary cell division. Cytologically the sporophyte begins with the fertilized egg and ends with mother cells, while the gametophyte begins with the spore and ends with fertilization. More will be said about the significance of the reduction division in connection with heredity where it has an important bearing.

The Riccias. — The genus Riccia, which is often regarded as a subdivision of the Marchantiales, includes the simplest of Liverworts. Some of them are almost entirely aquatic, living sub-

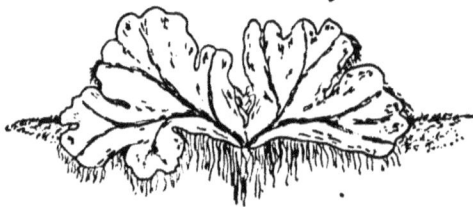

Fig. 369. — One of the Riccias, the simplest of Liverworts. × 4.

merged or floating on the surface of the water, while others live spread out on moist soil. The plant body is a simple thallus, smaller and not so well differentiated as the thallus of Marchantia. (*Fig. 369.*) No gametophores are developed and the sex organs, both kinds of which may develop on the same plant, occur in grooves along the ribs of the thallus. The air pores are not well developed and sometimes rhizoids are absent. The sporophyte, which is also much simpler than the sporophyte of the Marchantias, lacks a foot and stalk, and thus consists of only a sporangium.

When the sporophytes of the Riccias and Marchantias are compared, it is obvious that much more of the fertilized egg has been turned into spores in the Riccias than in the Marchantias. In the Marchantias much of the cell progeny of the fertilized egg, instead of forming spores, is used in forming a foot, stalk, and elaters. Such a diverting of the cells which could form spores into other kinds of work is spoken of as sterilization of sporogenous tissue. One can now see that a sporophyte could become as complex as a Corn plant by becoming more and more multicellular while at the same time most of the cells were used in forming structures, such as roots, stems, and leaves. In this way sporophytes became more and more complex until the highest plant forms were produced.

Porella. — This Liverwort belongs to the Jungermaniales, which order contains the largest number of Liverworts.

The Jungermaniales vary widely in their moisture requirements, some being able to live in dry situations. They are especially abundant in the tropics where they grow on the trunks of trees, on leaves of other plants, and on the ground. Some have thallose gametophytes like the Marchantiales, while others, known as foliose forms, have gametophytes that are differentiated into leaf- and stemlike structures and resemble the Mosses.

Porella is one of the foliose forms of the Jungermaniales and is common on the trunks of trees and fallen logs in the north temperate regions. The character of the gametophyte is shown in *Figure 370*. It has a slender, creeping, branched, stem-like axis bearing two horizontal rows of larger leaves on the dorsal surface and one horizontal row of smaller leaves on the ventral surface. Although much more differentiated as to form, the gametophyte of Porella is much less differentiated as to tissues than the gametophyte of the Marchantias.

The two kinds of sex organs may occur on the same plant or on different plants. The Archegonia occur in groups on the ends of short lateral branches. The antheridia occur in the axils of the leaves of certain branches which can be identified by the closely imbricated leaves.

The sporophyte has a long stalk and the sporangium splits into four valves which spread out and allow the spores to escape. There is more sterilization of sporogenous tissue and a more definite provision for the shedding of spores than in the sporophyte of the Marchantias.

FIG. 370. — A branch of Porella, a foliose Liverwort of the Jungermaniales. × 3.

Thus as compared with the Marchantiales, the Jungermaniales have gametophytes more differentiated in form but less in structure, and have sporophytes characterized by a greater sterilization of sporogenous tissue.

Anthoceros. — Anthoceros is a representative of the Anthocerotales which is a very small group of inconspicuous Liverworts.

Anthoceros and its allied forms are the most interesting of all Liverworts, because their structure suggests the steps by which Pteridophytes, the Fern group, could have originated from the Bryophytes. Anthoceros grows spread out like some of the Riccias and is common on moist soil in north temperate regions (*Fig. 371*). The gametophyte is a simple thallus, much simpler than that of the Marchantias. The sex organs develop in sunken areas on the top surface of the thallus.

FIG. 371. — Anthoceros, showing a gametophyte (*g*) bearing sporophytes (*s*). × about 2.

The remarkable feature is the sporophyte, which differs in a number of ways from the sporophytes of other Liverworts. In the first place the sporophyte is green, which means that it is supplied with chloroplasts and is thereby able to make food for itself, although it has to depend upon the gametophyte for water and mineral salts. This feature suggests the independent sporophyte of the Pteridophytes. The epidermis of the sporophyte even contains stomata for allowing the air to reach the green tissues beneath as in the leaves of higher plants. Evidently, if this sporophyte had roots, it could live independently of the gametophyte. In the second place there is a core or central axis of sterile tissue called *columella* extending lengthwise through the sporophyte, and bands of spore-forming tissue alternate with bands of sterile tissue around this columella. The columella is a characteristic feature of Moss sporophytes, and in this way the Anthocerotales relate the Liverworts to Mosses. If one imagines the bands of sterile tissue which alternate with the bands of spore-forming tissue growing out so as to form leaves, then a leafy sporophyte like those of Pteridophytes would be formed. In the third place there is a meristematic group of cells at the base of the sporophyte by which growth and production of spores are maintained for a period of time.

Mosses

General Description. — In general, Mosses do not need so much moisture as Liverworts do, and are, therefore, more generally distributed. They are common in moist places and some inhabit bogs and streams, but Mosses are also very common in dry places. They live on tree trunks, logs, stumps, rocks, soil, and in bogs and fresh water. In fact one can find Mosses nearly everywhere. They often mass together in clumps and cushion-like masses which hold water much like a sponge. Many Mosses, especially those growing in dry places, can become dried out and then revive when they become moist again. The Mosses as a group have better differentiated gametophytes and sporophytes than the Liverworts.

The Mosses are divided into three groups, *Sphagnales, Andreales,* and *Bryales.* The Sphagnales are the Sphagnums, which live in bogs where the accumulation of their plant bodies forms peat. The Andreales are a very small group of siliceous rock Mosses which will receive no further discussion, although they are interesting because they present a combination of characters which relate them to the Sphagnales, Bryales, and also to Liverworts. The group containing the vast assemblage of our most familiar Mosses is the Bryales. The Bryales, known also as the True Mosses, are the most highly organized of the Mosses.

True Mosses (Bryales). — The most conspicuous part of the Moss plant is the gametophyte, which looks like *Figure 372.* It consists of a leafy stem attached to the substratum by rhizoids. In some Mosses the leafy stem is prostrate, but in many it grows erect. The leaves of the Moss plant, like the leaves of the foliose Liverworts, are quite simple. In most part they are only one cell in thickness. They have no stomata and no palisade or spongy tissues. Although they are called leaves, it is obvious that they are not like the leaves of the higher plants. But their cells contain chloroplasts and they make carbohydrates just as the leaves of the higher plants do. Stomata, palisade, and spongy tissues cannot occur and are not needed until leaves become more than one cell in thickness. The stem is also quite simple in structure, and is not differentiated into the tissues which characterize the stems of higher plants.

The sporophyte is commonly much larger than that of the Liverworts

FIG. 372.—The gametophyte of a Moss, consisting of stem- (s) and leaf-like structures (l), and rhizoids (r) which attach it to the substratum. × about 2.

FIG. 373. — The two generations of Moss. g, gametophyte generation; a, sporophyte generation; s, sporangium of the sporophyte.

and it can be seen usually at a considerable distance projecting from the top of the gametophyte. A plant bearing a sporophyte looks like *Figure 373*.

Most parts of the Moss absorb water and salts directly. Even the leaves are probably able to absorb. The leaves carry on active photosynthesis and supply the carbohydrates. No vascular bundles occur, but in many Mosses there are strands of elongated cells which assist in conducting and distributing the foods. The erect habit and the radiate arrangement of the leaves on the stem enable the plant to make the best use of light.

Knowing that the leafy green plant is the gametophyte, one knows where to look for the sex organs. They are produced on

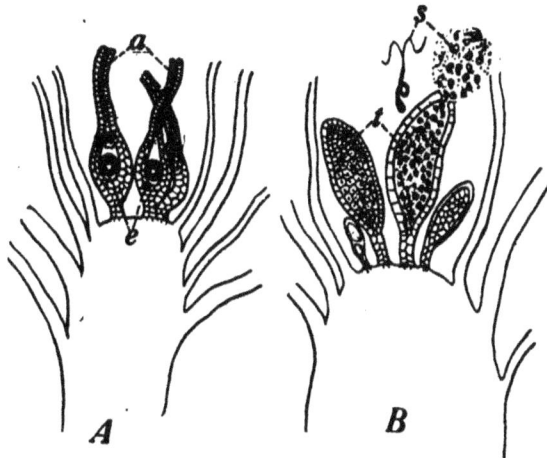

FIG. 374. — The sex organs of Moss. *A*, highly magnified vertical section through the apical region of the stem of a gametophyte, showing archegonia (*a*) with eggs at (*e*). *B*, a similar section through a plant bearing antheridia (*t*). Sperms escaping from an antheridium and one sperm much enlarged are shown at *s*.

the upper end of the stem and are quite well surrounded and hidden by the upper leaves. If one carefully pulls off the terminal leaves from plants that are in the reproductive condition, the sex organs may be found. They stand erect on the stem tip and are so large that they can be seen with a magnifier of very low power. The antheridia can sometimes be seen without any magnifier. The archegonia are flask-shaped and have very long necks, while the antheridia are club-shaped (*Fig. 374*). In many Mosses both sex organs occur on the same plant, but in the one shown in the Figure they occur on separate plants. The male

plants of some Mosses can be identified by a small terminal cup
in which the antheridia are produced.

The antheridia produce numerous swimming sperms, and, when
there is suitable moisture, the sperms reach the archegonia, swim
down the long necks into the venters, and fertilize the eggs.
The fertilized egg begins to grow almost immediately after fertilization, and like the fertilized egg of the Liverworts, it develops
in the place in which it was formed.   By rapid growth and cell
division, it soon forms a spindle-shaped body with one end called
foot pushing into the stem of the gametophyte to absorb food,

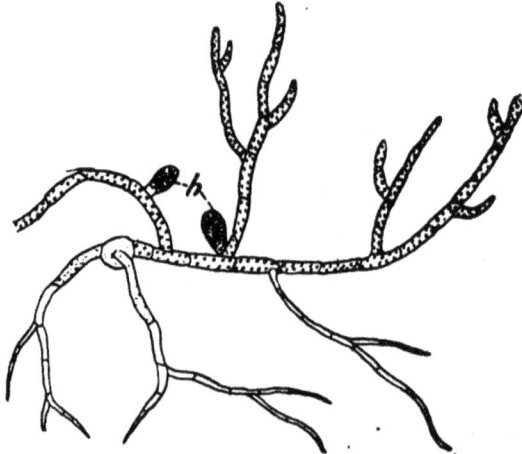

Fig. 375. — A protonema of Moss (× 50). Buds which develop leafy
gametophores are shown at b.

and the other end pushing into the air, forming a stalk called seta
which bears a sporangium at its upper end in which the spores
are produced.   As the sporophyte develops, the venter about the
young sporophyte and also the neck of the archegonium enlarge.
Finally the venter is ruptured and the enlarged archegonium is
carried up by the sporophyte, forming a pointed cap on the top
of the sporangium.   When the spores are shed and fall on a
moist soil, they produce new gametophytes.   However, the
spore does not grow a leafy plant directly, but first produces
an Alga-like filament which branches and creeps over the
substratum (Fig. 375).   From bud-like structures on this filament, the leafy green plants grow, thus completing the life

cycle as shown in *Figure 376*. The Alga-like filament called
protonema is comparable to the thallus of the Marchantias, and
the leafy plants to the gametophores. Although the leafy plants
or gametophores of Moss are not all of the gametophyte, they are
the conspicuous part of it, the protonemas being microscopic in
size. One protonema may produce many buds, and, therefore,
many gametophores.

In Moss the two generations are more noticeable than in the
Liverworts. The gametophytes with their leafy gametophores
present more differentiation than is the rule among Liverworts.

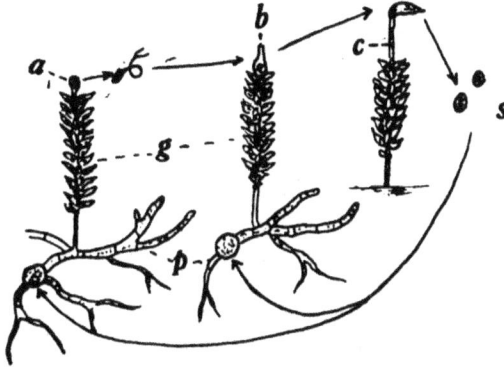

FIG. 376. — Diagram of the life cycle of Moss. *p*, protonemas from
which the gametophores (*g*) have arisen; *a* and *b*, the sex organs with a
sperm shown passing from antheridium to archegonium; *c* sporophyte which
the fertilized egg produces; *s*, spores which grow new protonemas and thus
the life cycle is completed.

The sporophyte, consisting of a large sporangium supported on a
long stalk, or seta, is usually quite conspicuous. It is more multicellular and has carried the sterilization of sporogenous tissue
farther than the sporophytes of most Liverworts have. Not
only is it larger and more multicellular, but it also shows more
differentiation than the sporophytes of Liverworts. The seta
is so differentiated as to have a central strand of elongated
cells for conduction. The sporangium of the Moss-sporophyte
develops at its top a special lid-like structure (operculum) for
opening, and often special tooth-like structures (peristome) are
produced just under the lid and assist in scattering the spores.

In the sporangium there is a columella or axis of sterile tissue, and in the sporangial wall air spaces and filaments of green tissue are provided. In some Mosses the base of the capsule, called *apophysis*, is devoted to food-making rather than to the formation of spores, in which case there is much chlorophyll tissue and many stomata present. This feature is quite important as was pointed out in Anthoceros, because it looks forward to the independence of the sporophyte; for, if the sporophyte can make carbohydrates for itself, it then needs only roots to absorb water and mineral salts, in order to live independently of the gametophyte.

The gametophytes of the Mosses have a remarkable power of propagating vegetatively. Since the sperms depend upon water for transportation and the sex organs are borne above the moist substratum, fertilization rarely occurs in some Mosses, which, therefore, must depend largely upon vegetative propagation. There are a number of ways by which they propagate vegetatively. *First*, by the isolation of branches through the death of the older axes; *second*, the cells of the protonema sometimes separate, become restive, and later from each resting cell a new protonema is developed; *third*, from the leaves and stems of the gametophore new protonemas are often developed; and *fourth*, some Mosses develop gemmae which are commonly borne at the summit of the leafy gametophore.

The Sphagnums (Sphagnales). — The genus Sphagnum includes all of the Mosses of this order. There are about 250 species, and they occur mostly in temperate and arctic regions. They live chiefly in bogs and are commonly called Bog or Peat Mosses. Their slender, branched, leafy gametophores (*Fig. 377*) are pale in color due to the fact that many of the leaf cells as well as many of the outer cells of the stem are empty except for the water and air which they hold, thus containing no chloroplasts. It is due to the ability of these much enlarged empty cells to take up and retain water by capillarity that Sphagnum retains moisture so well when used in germinating boxes or for moist packing around plants. The gametophores are commonly creeping, turning up only at the ends, and they usually form close mats, which gradually thicken by growth above and eventually fill up bogs. Due to the indefinite growth at the tips, gametophores may attain great length and age. In bogs where, due to the lack of drainage, organic acids accumulate and prevent the action of Molds and Bacteria, the dead remains of Sphagnum and accompanying plants do not decay, but are finally transformed into peat, which is a valuable fuel in some countries, especially in Ireland.

Both antheridia and archegonia are stalked and are produced on branches. The sex organs differ from those of the Bryales in their development but are quite similar in appearance when mature.

The sporophyte differs from the sporophyte of the Bryales in having only a very short seta, which is only a neck between the foot and the capsule. In connection with this feature there occurs another characteristic feature known as the *pseudopodium*. The pseudopodium, which replaces the seta in function, is formed by the elongation of the axis of the gametophore just beneath the sporophyte, which is thereby carried up as if it were on an elongating seta. Another peculiar feature of the sporophyte is that the

FIG. 377. — The gametophyte and sphorophyte of Sphagnium. At the left, gametophyte of Sphagnium; at the right, a sporophyte and the pseudopodium; between, a vertical section through the sporophyte, showing the short rounded foot, the short neck-like seta, and the globular sporangium in which the spores are borne in a cavity forming an arch over the columella.

columella does not extend entirely to the top of the sporangium as in Bryales, but the sporogenous tissue arches over the columella. In this respect the sporophyte is like that of Anthoceros.

When the spores germinate, instead of producing a filamentous protonema, they produce a flat thallus that resembles a Liverwort, and from buds on this thallus the leafy gametophores arise. When studied in detail one finds that Sphagnum has a number of features characteristic of Liverworts and a number that are characteristic of the Bryales, while it has some that belong to neither. It is often called a synthetic form, for it combines the characters of Liverworts and True Mosses.

Summary of Bryophytes. — The Bryophytes show progress over the Algae in a number of ways. *First*, the Bryophytes established the land habit, which meant the establishment of a plant body that was adapted to live and function in the air rather than in the water. In establishing the land habit the plant body had to develop tissues to protect against transpiration, sex cells had to be jacketed, and sex organs, now called antheridia and archegonia, consequently became multicellular, and tissues for utilizing the carbon dioxide of the air and sunlight in making food had to be provided. *Second*, although alternation of generations is quite prominent in some of the higher Algae, it is a very distinct feature throughout the Bryophytes. Both gametophyte and sporophyte generations show considerable advancement from the simplest Liverworts, where the gametophyte is a small flat thallus and the sporophyte merely a sporangium, to the highest of the Mosses, where there is a leafy gametophore and a sporophyte with a well developed seta and a sporangium having an operculum, peristome, columella, aërenchyma, and food-making tissues.

It should be noticed, however, that, although the Bryophytes adopted the land habit, they have a swimming sperm which puts a limit on the size of gametophytes, for swimming sperms can travel only short distances and only when water is present. In Mosses and the more complex Liverworts, there is much evidence that a large percentage of the sperms are not able to reach the archegonia. But the spore, since it is protected against drying and can, therefore, be transported by the wind, puts no limit on the size of the sporophyte. This means that the higher plants must consist chiefly of the sporophytic generation.

CHAPTER XVII

PTERIDOPHYTES (FERN PLANTS)

General Discussion. — Ferns are much larger plants than Bryophytes and consequently are much better known by the general public. In the woods Ferns are common and often they can be found in the fields. On account of their large, attractive, feather-like leaves, they are common house plants and are extensively grown in greenhouses. Most Ferns require a moist or shady region, but some are able to grow in dry situations.

In studying the different layers of rock which form the earth's crust, many Pteridophytes are found preserved. In the layer of rock from which coal is obtained, Pteridophyte fossils are very abundant. These fossils show that Pteridophytes were at one time much more abundant than now. Some of these ancient forms were like trees in size and resembled Seed Plants more than any of the present forms do. Although the forms that made most advancement toward Seed Plants have long been extinct, the forms which now exist show us some of the lines along which progress was made.

In beginning the study of Pteridophytes, one should have in mind the features contributed by the Bryophytes, because the Pteridophytes are supposed to have come from forms like the Bryophytes, although we are not able to connect them up with any of the existing forms of Bryophytes. From forms like the Bryophytes, the Pteridophytes inherited the land-habit. They not only inherited those features which enable plants to live, work, and reproduce in the air, but they have improved upon these features, so that in general they are better fitted to live on land than most of the Bryophytes. They have the alternation of generation which the Bryophytes so firmly established and have carried the sterilization of sporogenous tissue so far that the sporophyte is a massive and well differentiated plant body. Probably, instead of speaking of it as sterilization of sporogenous tissue, it would be clearer to say that the fertilized egg now produces an enormous number of cells which go to form vegetative tissues of various kinds, before sporogenous tissue is produced. Thus by delaying the formation of sporogenous tissue, the sporophyte of Pteridophytes has become more and more massive and at the same time with its larger number of cells has formed more kinds of tissues than occur in the sporophytes of Bryophytes. It is the sporophyte, which is the plant that we call the Fern, that is the conspicuous generation in the Pteridophytes. The gametophytes in most cases are quite small and generally simpler than the gametophytes of most Liverworts. In passing from the Bryophytes, where the sporophyte is small, dependent, and relatively simple, to the Pteridophytes, where the sporophyte is so many times larger and differentiated into roots, stems, and leaves so that it lives independently, one is struck with the big jump between the two groups. In the absence of forms to bridge over this gap, the relation between the Bryophytes and Pteridophytes is obscure. The sporophyte with its roots, stem, and leaves is now well advanced toward Seed Plants.

Although the Pteridophytes are known as the Fern group, there are many Pteridophytes, of which Horsetails and Club Mosses are familiar ones, that are not really Ferns. The True Ferns are the most highly specialized and much the largest group of the Pteridophytes, but in order to get a notion of the most important features contributed toward Seed Plants by Pteridophytes, a study of the Ferns should be followed by a study of some other groups of Pteridophytes.

Filicales

The Filicales are composed of the True Ferns and the Water Ferns. The latter are small forms living in the water or mud and are supposed to be an aquatic branch of the True Ferns. Although the Water Ferns present some features of interest to special morphologists, they will receive no attention in this brief discussion. The True Ferns, which are the most abundant and familiar of all Pteridophytes, are even more abundant in the tropics than in the temperate regions. In the tropics the sporophytes of some grow so large as to be called Tree Ferns.

Sporophyte. — Since the gametophyte is very inconspicuous, the sporophyte, or the plant known as the Fern, is the only generation of the Fern which people in general know (*Fig. 378*). There is much range in size of Fern sporophytes, from very small plants like some that are common in our woods, to those as high as a man's head, and to the Tree Ferns of the tropics and greenhouses that may reach a height of forty feet or more.

The *stems* of a few Ferns are erect and may become large like the trunk of a tree, as the Tree Ferns illustrate (*Fig. 379*), but in

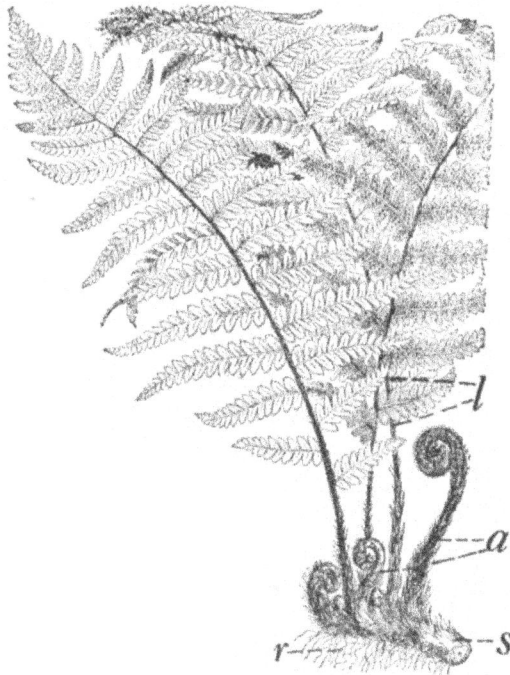

FIG. 378. — A fern sporophyte. *r*, roots; *s*, stem; *a*, young leaves or fronds unfolding; *l*, mature fronds. After Wossidlo.

our common Ferns, the stems remain a few inches under the surface of the ground and, as they elongate and push horizontally through the soil, leaves are produced from the upper and roots from the lower surface. They are called *rootstocks* or *rhizomes*, both terms referring to the root-like feature of growing under the ground.

The stems of Fern sporophytes are woody and have many of

the structures characteristic of the stems of Seed Plants and are, therefore, not merely stems in appearance as the stem-like structures developed by the gametophytes of Mosses and some Liverworts are.   It remained for the sporophyte generation to develop

FIG. 379. — A Tree Fern.   After Bailey.

a real stem.   At the tip of the Fern sporophyte there is a meristematic region which by the rapid growth and division of its cells elongates the stem.   Just behind the advancing tip new roots and leaves are developed and stem tissues are formed.   A cross section of a stem, as shown in *Figure 380*, shows an epidermis, cortex, vascular cylinder, and pith — tissues characteristic of the stems of Seed Plants.

The *roots* too are true roots and are not simple structures like the rhizoids of gametophytes.   They have a root cap, region of growth and elongation, epidermis, root hairs, cortex, and vascular cylinder, thus having the features characteristic of the roots of Seed Plants.

The *leaves*, although true leaves, are generally called *fronds*, a term formerly applied to them because they were considered a combination of leaf and stem.   Fern leaves are usually much branched and are easily identified by the way their veins branch and by the way they develop in the spring.   Their veins branch by forking; that is, a vein divides into two veins of equal size (*dichotomous branching*); and the leaves develop in the spring by unrolling from the base, much like unrolling a bolt of cloth, until their final length is reached (*circinate vernation*). They have epidermis, stomata, and chlorenchyma or food-making tissue, and through their veins run well developed vascular bundles.

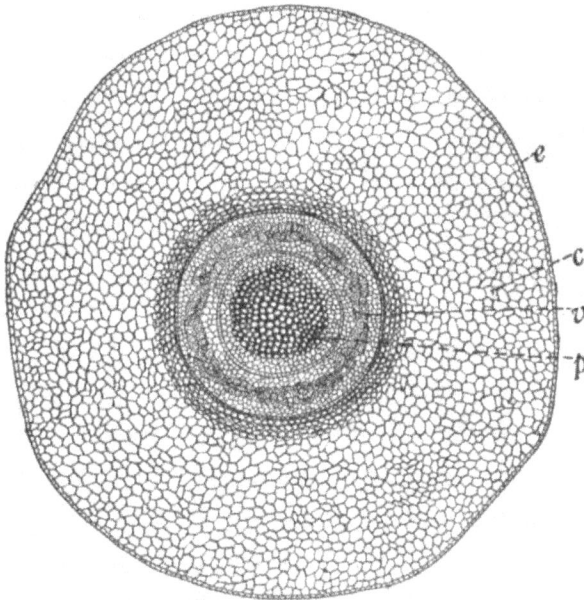

FIG. 380. — A cross section of a Fern stem, showing the epidermis (*e*), the cortex (*c*), the vascular cylinder (*v*), and the pith (*p*).

The *sporangia* occur in the rusty looking spots, called *sori* (singular *sorus*), which are formed at certain times on the under surface of the leaves (*B, Fig. 381*). Each sorus has a membrane-like covering called *indusium*, under which the sporangia are protected. By making a thin cross section of a leaf, so that the section passes through a sorus, the sporangia then appear under the low power of the microscope as shown at *C* in *Figure 381*. A number of sporangia occur in a sorus, but the number varies in different Ferns. The sporangia are usually stalked and flattened, and around the margin there is a row of heavy walled cells forming the *annulus*, which assists in opening the sporangia and scattering the spores (*D, Fig. 381*).

The character of the sporangia and the way they are borne vary much in different Ferns and are much used in the classification of Ferns. In the lowest group of the True Ferns the sporangia are borne in *synangia*, which are apparently composed of united sporangia. In some Ferns the sporangia are borne singly. In some the sori have no true indusium, but the edge of the leaf folds over and protects the sporangia. Then in the shape of the sporangia, presence or absence of an annulus, the location of the annulus, and in the number of spores borne in a sporangium, there are important differences among Ferns. Again there are two ways in which sporangia begin their development. In some Ferns, known as *eusporangiates*, both epidermal and sub-epidermal cells of the leaf are involved in forming the sporangia, while in Ferns, known as *leptosporangiates*, the sporangia are formed entirely from the epidermal cells of the leaf.

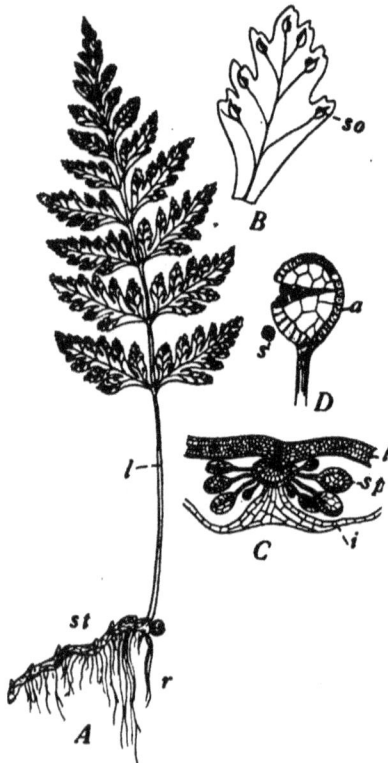

FIG. 381. — A sporophyte and spore-producing structures of a True Fern. *A*, a Fern sporophyte, showing roots (*r*), stem (*st*), and a leaf (*l*) (× about ⅓). *B*, an enlarged view of the under surface of a Fern leaf, bearing sori (*so*). *C*, highly magnified section through a Fern leaf and sorus, with section of leaf shown at *l*, sporangia at *sp*, and indusium at *i*. *D*, a much enlarged view of a sporangium, showing annulus *a* and method of opening to allow the spores (*s*) to escape.

In some of the True Ferns the sporangia are not borne on ordinary leaves, in which case the sporophyte is differentiated into vegetative and spore-bearing regions. Sometimes some of the leaflets are devoted entirely to bearing spores as in the Interrupted Fern (*Osmunda Claytonia*) (*Fig. 382*). In some like the Sensitive Fern (*Onoclea sensibilis*), common along roadsides and in wet meadows, there are two distinctly different kinds of fronds, one of which is entirely devoted to bearing spores and the other entirely to vegetative work (*Fig. 383*). This separation of spore-bearing and vegetative tissues is adhered to more closely in some other Pteridophytes than in the True Ferns, and it is a feature

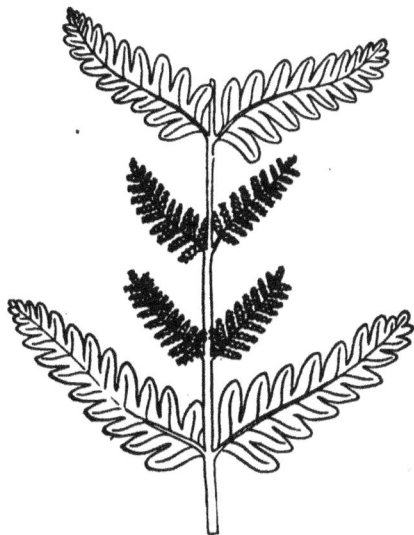

FIG. 382. — A portion of a leaf of the Interrupted Fern (*Osmunda Claytonia*), showing a pair of vegetative leaflets above and below and between them two pairs of spore-bearing leaflets.

FIG. 383. — The Sensitive Fern (*Onoclea sensibilis*), showing a vegetative frond at the left and a spore-bearing frond at the right.

of considerable significance because it is characteristic of Seed Plants.

Gametophyte. — When the spores are shed and fall in moist places, the protoplasm breaks the spore wall and begins the development which results in the production of a gametophyte. In True Ferns a short tube with one or more rhizoids at the spore end is first produced.   The development of this tube, called *germ tube*, is germination.   The germ tube soon reaches its full length, and then it begins to broaden at the outer end and a tiny, green, heart-shaped gametophyte is produced (*Fig. 384*). The gametophyte resembles the thallus of the simplest Liverworts.   When mature it has a cushion-like central axis where the rhizoids and sex organs are developed, and wing-like margins consisting of a single layer of cells.   The game·tophyte is called a *prothallus*, the term referring to the fact that it is thallus-like in form and precedes the sporophyte in reproduction.   In and around Fern beds in greenhouses Fern gametophytes are quite common on the

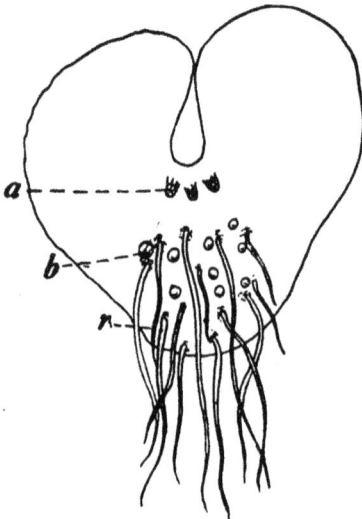

FIG. 384.— Three Fern gametophytes shown about natural size.

FIG. 385. — An enlarged view of the under surface of a Fern gametophyte, showing the archegonia (*a*), the antheridia (*b*), and the rhizoids (*r*).

FIG. 386. — A Fern gametophyte (*g*) bearing a young sporophyte (*s*) with leaf at *l* and root at *r*.

damp walls, damp soil, and on the sides of flower pots.   Occasionally they can be found out of doors about Ferns growing in moist shady places.   They lie flat on the substratum, and the sex organs are borne underneath where there is moisture for the swimming sperms (*Fig. 385*). The chimney-shaped archegonia are near the notch of the prothallus, and the globular antheridia are in the region of the rhizoids. In some Ferns the male and female sex organs are on different gametophytes.

The sperms are active swimmers and reach the egg by swimming down the neck of the archegonium which, like the archegonia of Bryophytes, opens at the top when the egg is ready for fertilization. From the neck of the archegonium, a substance is also discharged, which chemically attracts the sperms.

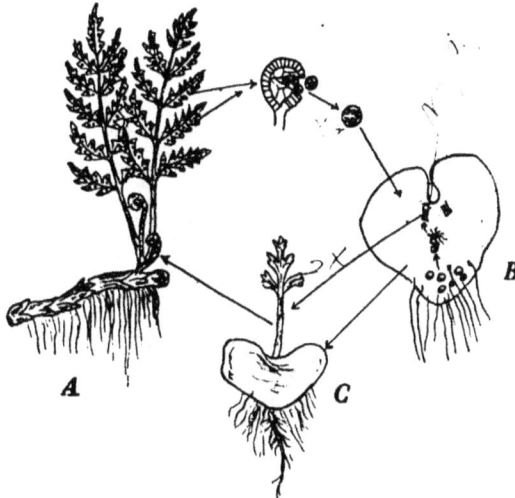

FIG. 387. — A diagram of the life cycle of a Fern. *A*, sporophyte bearing sori in which the sporangia occur. *B*, a gametophyte, a product of a spore and the generation bearing the gametes, the sperms of which are shown passing from the antheridia to the archegonia. *C*, gametophyte bearing a sporophyte, which soon becomes independent and like the one at *A*.

The fertilized egg immediately grows into a sporophyte, which lives on the gametophyte only until it has roots and leaves sufficiently developed to support itself (*Fig. 386*). After the sporophyte reaches maturity, sori are developed and the life cycle is completed (*Fig. 387*). Among a group of gametophytes one usually finds sporophytes in various stages of development and greenhouse attendants sometimes collect and pot the young sporophytes growing in unfavorable places, so that they mature and thereby increase their stock of Ferns. Usually, however,

Ferns are propagated vegetatively in greenhouses, and out of doors, where conditions are usually unfavorable for the development of their delicate gametophytes, many Ferns propagate almost en-

Fig. 388. — A Moonwort (*Botrychium Virginianum*). × about ½.

tirely vegetatively. Some propagate by runners, many by the branching and segmenting of the rhizome, some by buds which fall from the leaves to the ground where they develop new plants, and some by the leaves bending over and taking root at their tips.

Some Plants Resembling True Ferns. — Some plants which resemble the True Ferns, although they belong to another group, are the *Botrychiums* or *Moonworts* that are common in the woods (*Fig. 388*). They have an underground stem which sends up leaves that have a finely divided vegetative portion and a spore-bearing portion that much resembles clusters of small grapes.

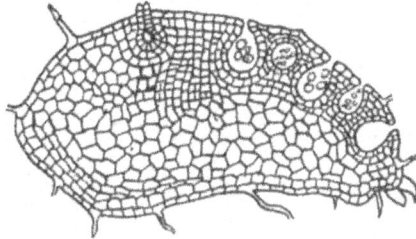

FIG. 389. — A section through the tuber-like gametophyte of Botrychium, showing one archegonium and a number of antheridia in the upper surface. × about 10.

It is, however, in their gametophyte generation that they differ most from True Ferns. Their gametophytes are tuberous sub-terranean structures bearing the sex organs on the upper surface, and associated with the gametophytes there is always an endophytic Fungus (*Fig. 389*).

Equisetales (Horsetails)

In ancient times, as shown by their fossils in coal and other kinds of rock, the Equisetales were very abundant, but the only surviving group is the Horsetails. Their slender stems, often called Joint Grass, are common in meadows, in moist places in the woods and along roadsides. There are about 25 species of Equisetum. There is *Equisetum palustre* common in swamps, *Equisetum pratense* and *Equisetum arvense* common in meadows and fields, and so on. Those growing in meadows and fields are often troublesome weeds. They are widely distributed over North America and also occur on other continents. They range in height from a few inches to several feet. It is reported that one form in the West Indies and Chili sometimes reaches a height of 40 feet, but in our region 3 or 4 feet is a good height. The Equisetums are also called *Scouring Rushes* because their stems contain silica which is used in making scouring powders.

Sporophyte. — The sporophyte consists of a horizontal, much branched, underground stem from which two kinds of aërial branches or shoots arise (*Fig. 390*). One kind of shoot bears spores and is called a fertile shoot, while the other kind does only vegetative work and is called a sterile shoot. Both kinds of

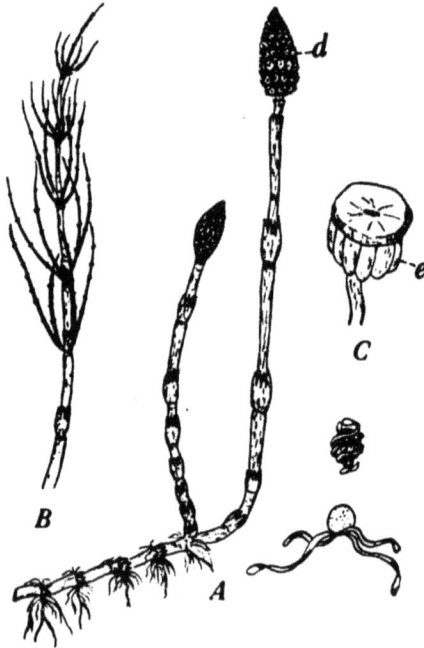

FIG. 390. — *Equisetum arvense.* A, a portion of the underground stem with two fertile or spore-bearing shoots, each of which bears a strobilus (*d*) (× ½). B, a portion of a sterile or vegetative shoot (× ½). C, a sporophore, showing the stalk and umbrella-like top on the under surface of which are the sporangia (*e*) (× 6). Below, at the right, are shown spores, one with elaters coiled about the spore and the other with elaters uncoiled (× about 15).

shoots are formed under the ground in the fall in most Equisetums and are thus ready to elongate and appear above ground early in the spring. On both kinds of shoots the leaves are mere scales, which are so joined as to form a sheath at each node. The sterile shoots produce whorls of slender branches at the nodes and are so finely branched as to resemble a horse's tail — whence the name Horsetails. The food is made by the green cortex of the aërial shoots in the epidermis of which are stomata through which carbon dioxide and oxygen reach the cortex.

The fertile branch commonly appears first in the spring, and in some common forms of Equisetum bears no side branches, thus having only whorls of scale-like leaves at the nodes. At the apex of the fertile branch is borne the *strobilus* (plural *strobili*) which is so named because of its resemblance to a cone such as occurs in Pines (*A, Fig. 390*). The strobilus consists of a central axis (the prolongation of the axis of the branch) to which are attached the stalked shield-shaped structures or *sporangiophores*, so named because they bear sporangia (*C, Fig. 390*). Some regard the sporangiophores as modified leaves and, therefore, call them *sporophylls*, which means spore-bearing leaves, but until their relation to leaves is definitely determined, sporangiophore is the safer term. Under the shield-shaped top of the sporangiophores are borne the sporangia, ranging from five to ten in number on each sporangiophore. The spores are provided with ribbon-like appendages, called *elaters*, which become entangled and thus cause the spores to fall in clumps. The spores, although alike in size, are physiologically different, for some of them produce only male while others produce only female gametophytes. In some species of Equisetum the fertile branch dies after the spores are shed, but in others the strobilus falls off and the branch continues to elongate, becomes green, and makes food during the remainder of the growing season.

There are two notable features presented by the sporophytes of the Equisetums. One is the differentiation of the aërial portion of the stem into sterile and fertile shoots. The second is the aggregation of sporogenous tissue into a strobilus. The sterile branch is a means by which sporangia can be elevated, so that the spores are in a good position to be scattered. The strobilus is supposed to be the forerunner of the flower, which likewise is a structure consisting essentially of aggregates of sporogenous tissue, for the pollen grains are spores, and also in the ovules there are spores developed.

Gametophytes. — In the Equisetums the gametophytes are much more reduced than in the True Ferns (*Fig. 391*). They are so small that one needs a lens to identify them. Unless conditions are very favorable, they are not able to survive out of doors, and consequently the Equisetums are propagated principally vegetatively.   The gametophytes are small, green, ribbon-like bodies and lie flat on the surface of the substratum.   The male gametophyte is the smaller and is one cell in thickness.   It bears the antheridia on the tips of the lobes or on the margin.   The female gametophyte

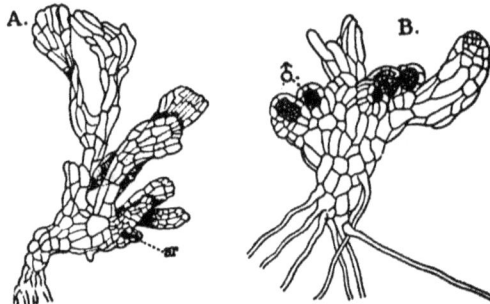

FIG. 391. — The gametophytes of Equisetum arvense.   A, female gameto-phyte, showing one archegonium (ar) (× about 20).   B, male gametophyte with four antheridia shown (♂) (× about 40).

forms a cushion, a number of cells in thickness, on the upper sur-face of which the archegonia are borne.

The multiciliate sperms, after being set free from neighboring male gametophytes, swim to the archegonia and down their necks to the eggs.   The fertilized egg begins to develop immediately and continues until a new sporophyte is formed, and the life cycle is thus completed.

Lycopodiales (Club Mosses)

About one-eighth of the living Pteridophytes are Club Mosses. They are commonly divided into four groups — *Lycopodium Phylloglossum, Selaginella*, and *Isoetes* — but a study of the Lycopodiums and the Selaginellas will serve to give a general notion of the Club Mosses.

The Club Mosses, although not Mosses at all, get their name from their Moss-like stem and their club-shaped appearance due to the large terminal strobili which some have.

Lycopodium. — There are several hundred species of Lycopo-diums, and they are widely distributed, occurring in both hemi-spheres and from the torrid to the frigid zones.   They prefer shady places and some are aquatic.

Sporophyte. — The sporophytes vary considerably in the different species, but consist of a stem simple or branched, bearing numerous small leaves (*Fig. 392*). In numerous species common in temperate America the stems trail over the ground. These species are often used for decorations at Christmas time and are called Ground Pines, probably from the appearance of their foliage, although they are not Pines at all.

One of the notable features of the sporophyte has to do with a suggestion as to the origin of the strobilus. In the simplest forms all leaves are alike and sporangia occur in the axils of the leaves on most any part of the stem. These leaves do the vegetative work and in addition are sporophylls in so far as they bear sporangia. In the more advanced sporophytes of Lycopodium only certain leaves bear sporangia, and these leaves differ considerably in form as well as in function from the other leaves. They are located at the top of the stem, forming the close aggregation or strobilus. In such forms it is obvious that there are two distinct kinds of leaves — sporophylls and vegetative leaves. In intermediate forms one can find sporophytes in which the leaves are

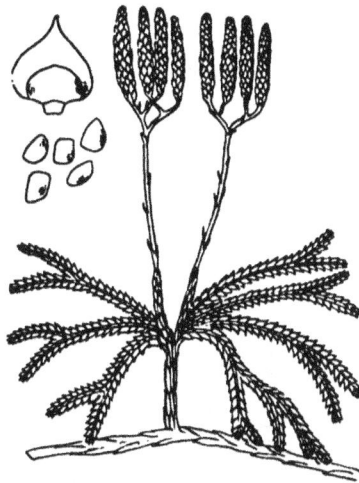

Fig. 392. — *Lycopodium complanatum*, showing vegetative branches and clusters of terminal strobili (× ⅓). At the left of the strobili is an enlarged view of a sporophyll showing the sporangium. Below the sporophyll are shown some spores highly magnified. Redrawn from Britton & Brown.

all alike but some bear sporangia while some do not, and often leaves bearing rudimentary sporangia can be found. These facts have suggested that all leaves were at first spore-bearing and that foliage leaves are sterilized sporophylls. According to this theory, the simplest condition is one in which all leaves bear sporangia, and the differentiation of foliage leaves and sporophylls came about by sterilizing the leaves from below until the spore-bearing leaves were finally limited to the top of the stem.

The strobilus, therefore, arose as a result of differentiating the leaves in function and aggregating the sporophylls. Differing in function, sporophylls and vegetative leaves would come to differ in form. One can see considerable advantage in this to the plant. It permits a large amount of leaf tissue to be devoted entirely to the manufacture of food, while the sporophylls, since they are not depended upon for food, can be much crowded, and as a result many spores can be produced on a small region. In scattering the spores there is also an advantage in having the sporophylls, at the top of the stem.

Gametophyte. — When the spores fall to the ground and germinate, they develop fleshy gametophytes consisting usually of a tuberous subterranean portion from which small, aërial, green lobes arise on which the sex organs are produced. Within

Fig. 393. — The sporophyte of a Selaginella. After J. M. Coulter.

the tissues of the gametophyte there lives a filamentous Fungus, and thus it is seen that the gametophyte resembles the gametophyte of Botrychium in a number of ways.

The fertilized egg begins to develop immediately after fertilization, and the young sporophyte is soon formed and the life cycle thus completed.

.. Selaginella. — The Selaginellas, known as Little Club Mosses. are widely distributed over the world and are common in conservatories where they are grown under the benches, in pots, and in hanging baskets for their decorative effect.

Sporophyte. — The sporophytes are delicate plants with leafy much branched stems (*Fig. 393*). The strobili occur on the ends of the branches, and the sporophylls somewhat resemble the foliage leaves, but are usually smaller and more compact (*Fig. 394*).

One notable feature is that there are two kinds of spores produced. In Bryophytes, True Ferns, Horsetails, and Lycopo-

FIG. 394. — The vegetative and spore-bearing structures of the sporophyte of Selaginella. *A*, a shoot of Selaginella, showing the stem, vegetative leaves, and the strobili (*st*) at the ends of the branches (× 2). *B*, a microsporophyll, showing the microsporangium (*m*) which has opened to allow the microspores to escape (× about 10). At the right of the microsporophyll are shown two microspores (*s*) (× 50). *C*, megasporophyll with megasporangium (*me*) open, thus exposing the four megaspores and permitting the microspores to come in contact with the megaspores. Below the megasporophyll are shown two megaspores (*n*) (× about 20). *D*, lengthwise section through a portion of a shoot, showing the position of the two kinds of sporangia in relation to the leaves, and also the relative sizes of the two kinds of spores (× 15). Partly from Dodel-Port and partly from nature.

diums the spores are alike as to size, although in some cases they
differ in the kinds of gametophytes produced.   Other Pteridophytes differentiated spore-bearing and vegetative tissues, but
the Selaginellas have differentiated spores both in size and function. The larger spores, which are many times larger than the
smaller ones, produce only female, while the smaller ones produce
only male gametophytes. The two kinds of spores are borne
in separate sporangia which also differ in size. The prefixes,
micro, meaning little, and *mega* or *macro*, meaning large, are used
to designate these spores and also the sporangia and sporophylls
which bear them. Thus we speak of *microspores* and *megaspores*,
microsporangia and *megasporangia*, and *microsporophylls* and *megasporophylls* (*B* and *C*, *Fig. 394*).

This habit of producing two kinds of spores in regard to size is
called *heterospory* (meaning different spores), while the habit of
producing spores alike in size is called *homospory* (meaning same
spores). The introduction of heterospory by Selaginella is a
significant feature because all Seed Plants are heterosporous. In
Seed Plants the pollen grains are microspores and within the
ovules occur the megaspores.

Gametophytes. — The second notable feature which Selaginella presents is that the gametophytes are so much reduced that
they develop within the spores, where food and protection are
provided. Thus in Selaginella there are no green independent
gametophytes as we have been used to in other Pteridophytes
and in Bryophytes, but the gametophyte now lives on the sporophyte just as the sporophyte of the Bryophytes lives on the
gametophyte. This, also, is a feature that is characteristic of
Seed Plants.

The *male gametophyte* is extremely simple, consisting of one
vegetative cell and a simple antheridium containing only a few
sperms, each of which has two slender cilia (*C*, *Fig. 395*). In
developing, the male gametophyte breaks the spore wall, so that
a crack is produced through which the sperms escape.

The megaspores germinate and form the female gametophytes
while still in the sporangium, and this is a third feature that is
characteristic of Seed Plants. The female gametophyte is much
larger than the male gametophyte (*A* and *B*, *Fig. 395*). Its much
larger size is permitted by the greater size of the megaspore and
is also necessary because the female gametophyte must support

the young sporophyte until it becomes self-supporting. The
female gametophyte therefore consists of many cells when mature
and bears a number of archegonia on the portion exposed by the
opening forced in the spore wall by the expansion of the gametophyte.

Previous to fertilization, the male gametophytes, each still,
except for a small slit-like opening, encased in the wall of the

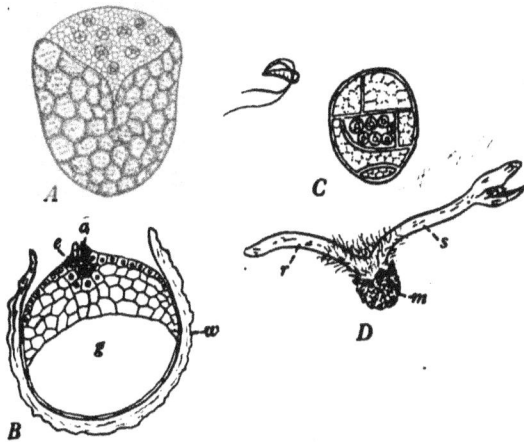

FIG. 395. — The gametophytes and young sporophyte of Selaginella. A,
a megaspore containing a female gametophyte with the portion bearing the
archegonia exposed by the slit-like opening in the spore wall (× 100). B,
section through a megaspore, showing the spore wall (w) and female gametophyte (g) with one archegonium (a) with neck and egg (e) visible (× 100).
C, a section through an antheridium, showing the small prothallial cell at the
base and the wall cells which enclose the sperms within, one of which is shown
fully mature at the left (× 500). D, a young sporophyte with stem at s and
root at r and foot extending into the gametophyte which is still enclosed in
the spore wall (m). From Atkinson and nature.

microspore, fall out or are blown out of the microsporangia, which
open when the spores are mature, and fall or are carried by the
wind to the megasporangia where the female gametophytes are
developing. Here the sperms escape, and reach the archegonia,
which are accessible through the slit-like openings in the walls of
the megasporangia and megaspores. The fertilized egg develops
immediately into a sporophyte. Often the female gametophyte
remains in the megasporangium until the weight of the young
sporophyte tumbles it out. After the young sporophyte becomes

established in the soil and reaches maturity, strobili are produced, and thus the life cycle is completed. Thus besides having an independent complex sporophyte, the Selaginellas protect their gametophytes and this is an additional adjustment to the land habit.

Summary of Pteridophytes. — They present a number of features characteristic of Seed Plants. They have an independent sporophyte with well developed roots, stems, and leaves, which in general have the same tissues that are characteristic of these organs in Seed Plants. The second important feature is the differentiation of vegetative and spore-bearing tissues. This gave rise to the strobilus which is regarded as the forerunner of the flower. The third important feature is the introduction of heterospory and the production of gametophytes within the spore wall. Heterospory and dependent gametophytes made the origin of the seed possible. The fourth feature is the retention of the female gametophyte within the megasporangium during fertilization. This also is a seed-like feature.

CHAPTER XVIII

SPERMATOPHYTES (SEED PLANTS)

Gymnosperms (seed not enclosed)

Spermatophytes or Seed Plants constitute the fourth large division of plants. They are the most highly developed plants, and, therefore, in them we find the final achievement of plant evolution. Their distinguishing feature is the seed, although they have other notable features not found in the groups previously studied. The notable features of Pteridophytes, such as sporophylls, strobili, heterospory, dependent gametophytes that are developed within the spore wall, and the retention of the megaspore in the megasporangium, are retained by the Spermatophytes and to these they have added new features. Because of the seed, lumber, fibers, and numerous other products obtained from them, the Spermatophytes surpass all other divisions of plants in economic importance. They are also very numerous, and on account of the large size of their sporophytes they are our most conspicuous plants.

The Spermatophytes are divided into two groups, — the *Gymnosperms* and *Angiosperms*. As the names suggest, the Gymnosperms bear their seeds exposed while Angiosperms bear them enclosed, but the two groups differ also in other features as will be noted later.

The Gymnosperms are more primitive than the Angiosperms and are, therefore, more like the Pteridophytes, the group from which Seed Plants are supposed to have originated. The groups of Gymnosperms most like Pteridophytes are now extinct and hence are known only by their fossils. Some of these extinct forms resembled Ferns so much that they are called *Pteridosperms*, a term which means " Ferns with seeds." Thus Gymnosperms connect more closely with the Pteridophytes than the latter group does with the Bryophytes. The Gymnosperms still in existence are divided into a number of groups, but a study of the Cycads and Pines will give a notion of the general features characteristic of Gymnosperms.

Cycads

Of the Gymnosperms now in existence, the Cycads bear most resemblance to the Ferns. In leaf and stem characters, some of them could easily be mistaken for Ferns (*Fig. 396*). There are nearly one hundred species of Cycads. They are tropical plants but are grown nearly everywhere in greenhouses. One of the

FIG. 396. — A Cycad, showing the finely divided leaves and the short thick trunk with its rough covering of leaf bases. After J. M. Coulter.

forms (*Cycas revoluta*) common in cultivation is often labeled "Sago Palm" because its leaves resemble those of some of the Palms.

Sporophyte. — The sporophyte has a tuberous or columnar stem at the top of which are borne the large, much branched, fern-like leaves. The stems are covered by the leaf-bases which remain after the leaves fall. In some Cycads, where the stem is subterranean, the plant is small, but in others with columnar stems, the plant may reach a height of 50 feet or more.

Strobili. — The strobili are borne near the apex of the stem of which they are really branches, and are of two kinds — *staminate* and *ovulate*. The staminate strobili are simply microstrobili, that is, strobili in which only microsporophylls and microsporangia are produced. The name, however, suggests the likeness of the microsporophylls to the stamens of Flowering Plants. The ovulate strobili are strobili in which only megasporophylls and megasporangia occur. The term ovulate suggests the likeness of the megasporangium to the ovule of Flowering Plants. The megasporangia are now called ovules because they remain closed, so that the female gametophyte is at no time exposed.

It is obvious that the Cycads have carried the differentiation of structures farther than the Selaginellas have. In Cycads, not

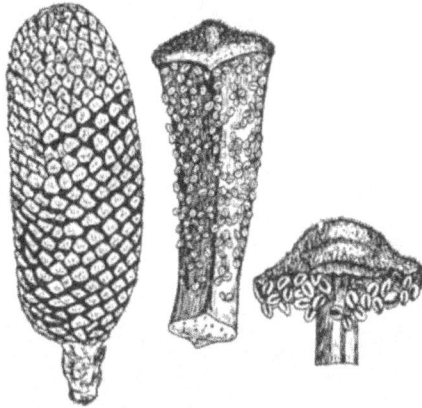

FIG. 397. — Staminate strobilus and microsporophylls in Cycads. At the left, a staminate strobilus of a Cycad (*Dioon*); at the right, microsporophylls from two different Cycads, showing difference in shape, and the way the sporangia are borne. After Chamberlain and Richard.

only spores, sporangia, and sporophylls are differentiated, but there is also a differentiation of strobili.

The strobili of Cycads are much larger than those of Selaginella or Lycopodium, and the sporophylls are usually very different from the foliage leaves. In some Cycads the strobili are a foot or more in length and several inches in diameter.

In the *staminate strobili*, the sporophylls are closely crowded and practically have no resemblance to foliage leaves. They vary considerably in shape in different Cycads, but have an outer, expanded, sterile portion and bear the microsporangia, usually grouped in sori, on their under surface (*Fig. 397*).

The *ovulate strobili* are often much larger than the staminate strobili. The megasporophylls are usually closely crowded, and when they are short and fleshy, they fit together like the kernels on an ear of Corn. The ovules are borne separately near the base of the megasporophyll and as shown in *Figure 398*. In some Cycads each megasporophyll bears only two ovules, while in others, as *Figure 398* shows, a larger number may be present. In some Cycads the megasporophylls are much branched like foliage leaves, and the sporangia appear to be transformed lower branches or pinnae. Megasporophylls of this type suggest the relationship of sporophylls to foliage leaves.

The young *megasporangium* or ovule contains four megaspores, which are enclosed by two distinct coverings of sterile tissue. The inner covering is the *nucellus*, which surrounds and encloses

Fɪɢ. 398. — Ovulate strobilus and megasporophylls in Cycads. At the left, an ovulate strobilus; at the right, two types of megasporophylls, showing the ovules (*o*).

the megaspores, and the outer one is the *integument*, which grows up from the base of the ovule and forms a covering over the nucellus. The integument is a protection for the nucellus, and, when the ovule develops into a seed, it is transformed into a seed coat. At the outer end of the megasporangium where the integument closes over the nucellus, a small opening or micropyle is left which leads into a cavity, called the *pollen chamber*, into which a beak-like portion of the nucellus projects (*Fig. 399*).

Female Gametophyte. — Only one of the four megaspores in the megasporangium develops. The other three disappear and all of the space and food is therefore given over to the development of one gametophyte. The megaspore germinates in the sporangium as in Selaginella, but a new feature of the Cycads is that the megasporangium does not open to allow the megaspore to be exposed, and therefore the female gametophyte remains permanently enclosed in the sporangium. The developing female gametophyte uses most of the nucellus for food and thereby makes room for itself. When the gametophyte is mature the

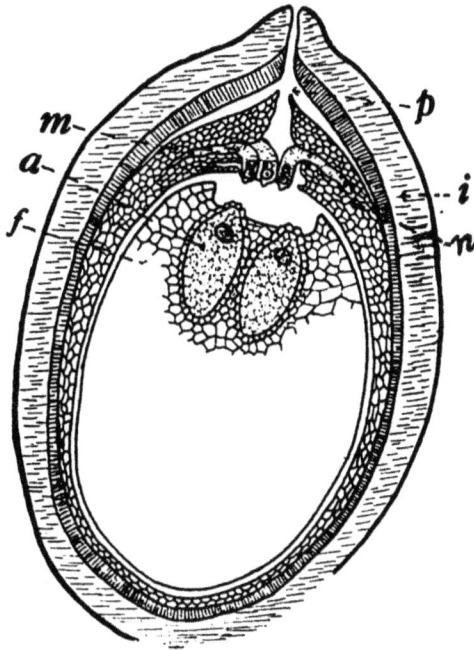

FIG. 399. — Section through a Cycad ovule containing a mature gameto-phyte. *f*, female gametophyte with two archegonia (*a*) shown; *m*, micro-spores developing tubes, and male gametophytes; *n*, nucellus; *i*, integument; *p*, pollen chamber into which the micropyle shown just above opens. Re-drawn from Webber.

nucellus is so nearly used up that it is reduced to a thin layer, except at the micropylar end where a beak-like portion remains. A female gametophyte when fully formed consists of a large num-ber of cells, most of which form a nutritive tissue for the devel-oping sporophyte and are therefore spoken of as endosperm, although the endosperm of Cycads is not the same in origin as the endosperm of Angiosperms. The archegonia, usually several in number, are produced at the micropylar end, and have much shorter necks and are simpler in other ways than the archegonia of Pteridophytes. The eggs are large and the most conspicuous part of the archegonia. A section through an ovule ready for fertilization looks like the one shown in *Figure 399*.

Male Gametophyte. — The microspores or pollen grains, as they may now be called since they have to be transferred to the ovule before they can function, usually contain three-celled gametophytes at the time of their shedding, and in this condition they reach the megasporangium, pass through the micropyle, and reach the pollen chamber, where they are in contact with the beak of the nucellus. In this position the three-celled gametophyte, which consists of a vegetative, generative, and tube cell, completes its development. The miscrospore develops tubes which branch and penetrate the beak of the nucellus in various directions, and function as absorptive structures. Finally, the beak of the nucellus breaks down and thereby a passage way to the archegonia is provided. Meanwhile the generative cell enters one of the pollen tubes and passes farther into the pollen chamber where it divides, forming a stalk cell and a body cell, the latter of which forms the sperms, usually two in number. The sperms bear a large number of cilia, and after escaping from the pollen tube they swim through the watery solution present in the chamber and thereby reach the archegonia and finally the eggs.

Thus, when the male gametophyte is mature, it consists of only four cells besides the sperms, and there is no structure formed that resembles an antheridium. In addition to the absence of an antheridium, it should also be noted that pollination and the growth of tubes are other new features which occur in connection with the male gametophytes of Cycads. It is obvious that the introduction of pollination and the growth of pollen tubes must accompany the permanent enclosing of the female gametophyte in the megasporangium.

Seed. — The seed is another new feature of the Cycads. After fertilization, a young sporophyte (*embryo*) is developed and is pushed well down into the nutritive tissue of the gametophyte by a filament of cells (*suspensor*). During fertilization and the development of the embryo, the ovule continues to grow and the integument becomes pulpy, while the outer region of the remaining portion of the nucellus hardens, so that the seed when mature resembles some of the stone fruits, such as the Plum, although it is a seed and not a fruit.

It is obvious that a seed is simply a transformed megasporangium. In the Cycads a seed is a megasporangium which has its outer portions modified for protection and contains within a female gametophyte bearing a young sporophyte. Thus the reduction of the female gametophyte through the Pteridophytes and finally its retention in the megasporangium in the Cycads so that the young sporophyte also develops within the megasporangium were important steps in the evolution of the seed.

Although the Cycads resemble Ferns in having swimming sperms, and in having leaves and stems that are Fern-like, they contrast with them in such new features as differentiation of strobili, simpler gametophytes, pollination, growth of pollen tubes, and the seed.

Pines (Pinaceae)

The Pines are a subdivision of the Pine family (*Pinaceae*). In addition to the Pines, the Pine family includes the Spruces, Firs, Hemlocks, Larches, Cedars, Redwood, Cypress, and others. The Pine family is an

Fig. 400. — Pine sporophytes. After Miss Hayden.

exceedingly important one because it includes a large proportion of the trees from which lumber is obtained. The Pine family belongs to the order of Conifers (*Coniferales*), so named because of the cones which they bear. Not all of them, however, bear dry cones like the Pines, for some have fleshy fruit-like structures, as the berry-like structures of the Junipers illustrate. All of the representatives of the Pine family are interesting, but a study of their life history will be limited to that of the Pine.

Sporophyte. — The sporophytes of the Pines are mostly large and in some cases are of huge dimensions. Some species of Pine attain a height of 150 feet or more. It is characteristic of Pine trees to have a main trunk and comparatively small lateral branches. The main branches are usually in clusters, and in some Pines, unless closely inspected, one might mistake the branches to be in whorls. There is a gradual reduction in length of branches from below upward, so that trees grown in the open have a conical shape (*Fig. 400.*)

The needle-like leaves are usually borne in groups or fascicles of two, three, or five leaves according to the species. The duration of leaves varies according to the species and conditions, but Pines shed only a part of their leaves at a time and hence are always green.

Strobili. — The strobili, as in the Cycads, are of two kinds — staminate and ovulate (*Fig. 401*). The staminate and ovulate strobili occur separately, on the same trees, or on different trees.

FIG. 401. — A branch of a Pine, showing an ovulate strobilus at *a* and a cluster of staminate strobili at *b*.

The *staminate strobili* or cones (*Fig. 402*) are produced in clusters and in the Northern states may be seen in May or early June. They vary in size in different species, sometimes attaining a length of half an inch or more, but in many species they are much smaller. They expand from the buds in a few days, soon shed their pollen and disappear, usually persisting only a few weeks. A microstrobilus is, in reality, a modified branch consisting of a main axis bearing scale-like microsporophylls or stamens, which are arranged spirally and closely crowded. On

the back or lower side of the microsporophylls are the microsporangia, usually two, and each contains numerous microspores.
Nearly opposite each other on the microspore are two air-sacs
whereby the spores are easily carried by the wind. When the
spores are mature, the microsporangia or pollen sacs open by
longitudinal slits, and the pollen shatters out, often like small

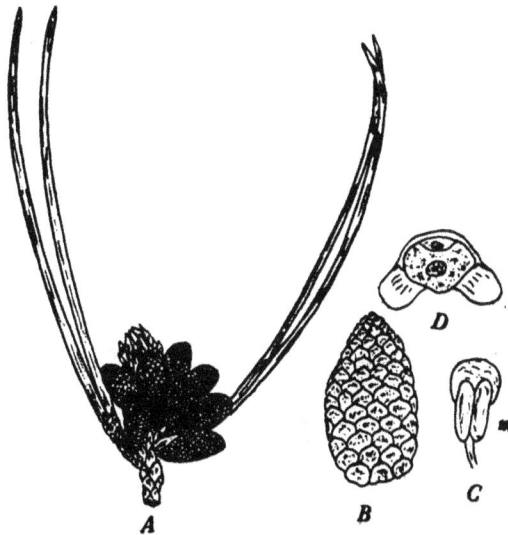

Fig. 402. The staminate structures of the Pine. *A*, cluster of staminate
strobili (× about ⅓). *B*, a staminate strobilus enlarged, showing the arrangement of the microsporophylls. *C*, a microsporophyll, showing the two
sporangia (*m*); *D*, microspore showing the two wings and two cells of the male
gametophyte.

clouds of dust. The wind carries the pollen about, and some
reaches the ovulate strobili, but much the larger part of it is
wasted. Sometimes pollen accumulates on walks under Pines
that are shedding their pollen until the walks look as if they had
been sprinkled with finely powdered sulphur.

The *ovulate strobili* or cones appear near the tips of the new
growths in early spring. Usually they are smaller when they
first appear than the staminate cones, but they persist and, after
a growth of two seasons, become the conspicuous scaly cones so
familiar on or about pine trees. Sometimes several occur to-

gether, but they do not form close clusters as the staminate cones do.

The *scales* of the ovulate cones are considered too complex to be called sporophylls, for each scale consists of an ovuliferous scale (ovule-bearing scale) and a bract, the two being partly united. Some morphologists think that the ovuliferous scale itself represents two sporophylls fused together. The megasporangia or

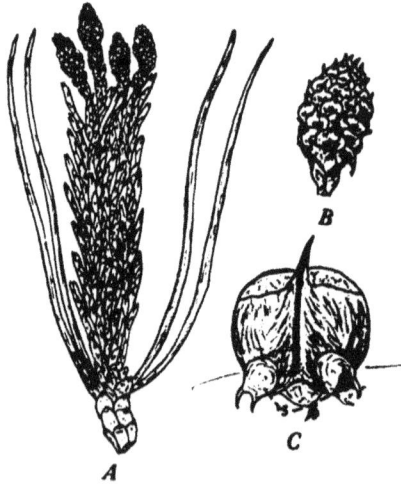

Fig. 403. — The ovulate structures of the Pine. *A*, branch bearing four ovulate strobili, *B*, ovulate strobilus, showing the arrangement of scales (× about 2); *C*, a view of the inner or upper side of a scale, showing the two sporangia (*s*).

ovules, two in number, are borne on the upper side and at the base of the ovuliferous scale (*Fig. 403*). The scales are spirally arranged and closely crowded, but during pollination they spread apart, and the pollen can slide in between them and reach the ovules. After pollination the scales close together again, and the cone is made water-tight by a secretion of resin. After pollination the cone also changes from the vertical to the nodding position.

The *ovules* consist of an integument and a nucellus, and deeply buried within the nucellus the four megaspores occur. The ovules are arranged one on each side of the median line of the scale, with the micropyles pointing downward. The integument extends beyond the nucellus, and its free margin flares open, thus forming an open micropyle that leads into the pollen chamber.

Female Gametophyte. — Although four megaspores are formed in the megasporangium, only one of them develops a gametophyte, the others being destroyed and used for food by the one that develops. During the first season the surviving megaspore enlarges and becomes multinucleate. With the megaspore in this

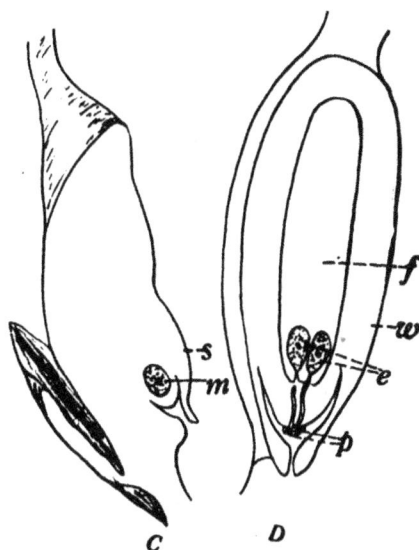

FIG. 404. — Development of the ovule and pollen tubes in the Pine. *C*, section through an ovuliferous scale, showing the bract behind and a section of an ovule (*s*) on its inner face, the megaspore being shown at *m*; *D*, an ovule with female gametophyte (*f*) mature, showing eggs at *e*, ovule wall consisting of nucellus and integument at *w*, and pollen grains growing tubes through the nucellus at (*p*).

condition the ovule passes the winter. Early next spring growth is resumed, and by about the first of June of the second season the gametophyte is complete, consisting of 250 or more cells and bearing a number of archegonia (usually two to five) at the micropylar end (*Fig. 404.*) The eggs are usually ready for fertilization about the first of June of the second season. While the female gametophyte is developing, the male gametophyte is completing its development in the pollen chamber and the pollen tube is eating its way through the nucellus to the female gametophyte.

Male Gametophyte. — The male gametophyte forms within the pollen grain and its tube. At the time of pollination the male gametophyte commonly consists of four cells — two *prothallial* or *vegetative cells*, a *generative cell*, and a *tube cell*. At least one of the prothallial cells usually disintegrates and disappears early in the development of the gametophyte. This is the condition of the male gametophyte when the pollen is carried to the ovulate cone. Upon reaching the ovulate cones the pollen grains fall down to the base of the scales in the region of the ovules, and

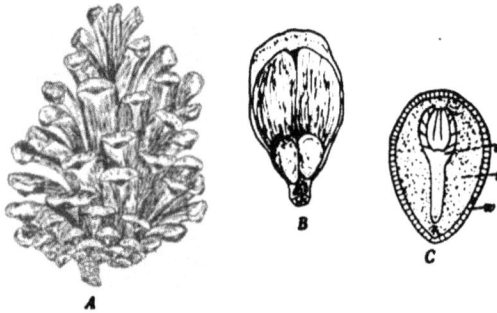

FIG. 405. — Seed structures of the Pine. *A*, a mature ovulate strobilus with scales spread apart to allow the seeds to escape. *B*, a view of the inner side of a scale, showing the two seeds when mature. The wings of the seeds are a part of the scale and did not develop from the ovule. *C*, section through a pine seed, showing the female gametophyte (*g*), embryo (*e*), and seed coat (*w*).

some lodge at the mouth of the micropyles, where they are caught in a drop of a mucilaginous secretion and drawn in close to the tip of the nucellus. In this position the pollen grains begin to develop tubes, which by means of an enzyme dissolve the nucellar tissue, using it as food and at the same time making a way for themselves. Cold weather finally checks the growth of the pollen tubes, and the male gametophytes now rest over winter. Early the next spring the pollen tube resumes its growth toward the archegonia, and the generative cell passes into the pollen tube and divides, forming two cells, one of which divides and forms the two sperms which now have the pollen tube as a passageway to the archegonia. The sperms reach the archegonia about the middle of June of the second season and fertilization soon follows. In addition to its simplicity the notable features of the male gametophyte are that the sperms have no cilia and that they are conducted to the archegonia by the pollen tube.

Seed. — The fertilized egg at first forms tiers of cells, which constitute a long filament, called a *suspensor,* at the end of which the embryo develops deeply imbedded in the nutritive tissue of the female gametophyte. When mature the embryo is still surrounded by much gametophytic tissue called endosperm.

While the embryo or the young sporophyte is developing, the ovule and the entire cone continue to enlarge. The integument is transformed into a seed coat, and when mature the seed sepa-

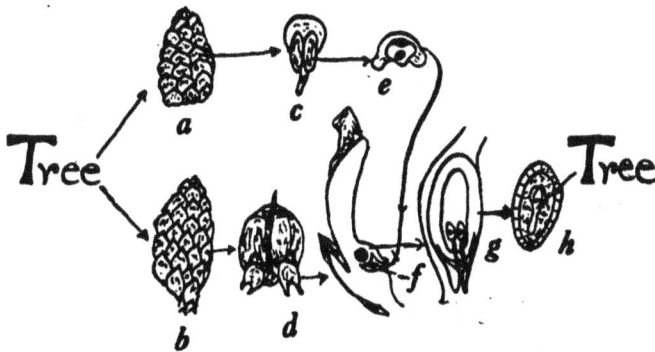

FIG. 406. — Diagram of the life cycle of the Pine. Starting with the tree at the left, the two kinds of strobili are shown at *a* and *b*, the two kinds of sporophylls and their sporangia at *c* and *d*, the two kinds of spores at *e* and *f*, the gametophytes at *g*, the mature seed at *h*, from the embryo of which a new tree develops.

rates from the ovulate scale with a long membraneous wing, which enables the seed to float in the air (*Fig. 405.*) Pine seeds, although usually smaller, are similar in general structure to the seeds of Cycads. They contain a female gametophyte bearing a young sporophyte and a protective covering composed of the integument and the nucellus, the latter persisting as a membrane about the gametophyte or endosperm.

The scales of the ovulate strobilus continue their development until the seeds are mature and remain tightly closed so that the seeds are well protected. After the cone is mature, the scales dry and spread apart and the seeds fall out.   Although the seeds are protected between the scales, they are not enclosed as the seeds of a Bean or an Apple are.   They are on the outside of the structure which bears them, — whence the name Gymnosperms.

The seeds are dispersed by the wind and usually do not germinate until the next spring after dispersal.   In germination the axis (hypocotyl) of the sporophyte elongates, forming an arch and drawing the cotyledons out of the ground, and at the same time the tap-root at the lower end of the hypocotyl becomes established in the soil.   By the straightening of the hypocotyl the green cotyledons are lifted into the air and sunlight, and the sporophyte soon becomes independent of the seed.   After a number of years of growth, it begins to bear strobili, thus completing the life cycle of the Pine as shown in *Figure 406.*

In summarizing it should be noted that the Pines have two kinds of strobili, reduced gametophytes, pollination, and pollen tubes, features which were pointed out as the notable ones of the Cycads.   But in contrast with the Cycads the Pines have more massive sporophytes with leaves bearing no resemblance to those of Ferns, and also the Pines have abandoned swimming sperms and conduct the sperms to the eggs through pollen tubes.

In pines the cones mature the second fall after pollination, but in some genera of the pine family, as the Spruces illustrate, sexual reproduction proceeds more rapidly. although similar in nature, and the cones mature the fall following pollination.

CHAPTER XIX

SPERMATOPHYTES (Continued)

Angiosperms (Seeds Enclosed)

General Characteristics. — The Angiosperms are the most highly evolved group of the plant kingdom, being the most perfectly adapted to terrestrial conditions. They also surpass all other groups in economic importance, for they include the large majority of our cultivated plants. Our dependence upon the grains and fruits and upon forage, root, and tuber crops attests the economic importance of the Angiosperms. The Angiosperms probably have more species than any other group of plants and show more variations. Approximately 125,000 species are known. They form the most conspicuous part of our vegetation, for not only most of our cultivated plants but nearly all weeds are Angiosperms. The origin of the Angiosperms is not known, but they probably arose from some Fern-like plants as the Gymnosperms did. The Angiosperms, as the name suggests, are characterized by having their seeds enclosed. The enclosure is the ovary, which is one of the notable features of Angiosperms. Another notable feature is the flower, which is regarded as a special type of strobilus. They also differ from the Gymnosperms in having more reduced gametophytes. Both male and female gametophytes consist of only a few cells and have lost all traces of sex organs. Since the gametophytes are microscopical, most people are acquainted with only the sporophytes of Angiosperms. In character of roots, stems, leaves, flowers, seeds, and fruits, there are numerous variations in Angiosperms, but, since Part I of this book is devoted chiefly to these variations, the discussion will now be limited to the characteristic features of the group and to such features as characterize the families of most economic importance.

The Flower. — The flower (*Fig. 407*), consisting of a perianth (calyx and corolla), stamens, and one or more pistils, is a structure characteristic of Angiosperms. The stamens are microsporophylls and the pistils are megasporophylls. A typical flower is, therefore, essentially an association of sporophylls surrounded by a perianth, and, in so far as a flower is an association of sporophylls, it does not differ fundamentally from a strobilus. In passing from the simplest Angiosperms, where there are flowers that have no perianth, to those Angiosperms having typical flowers, all gradations between a typical strobilis and a typical flower can be found. It is, therefore, impossible to define a' flower so as to include the flowers of all Angiosperms and at the same time separate the flower from the strobilus. The flowers of Angiosperms and the strobili of the Gymnosperms and Pteridophytes differ in the character of their sporophylls more than in any other feature.

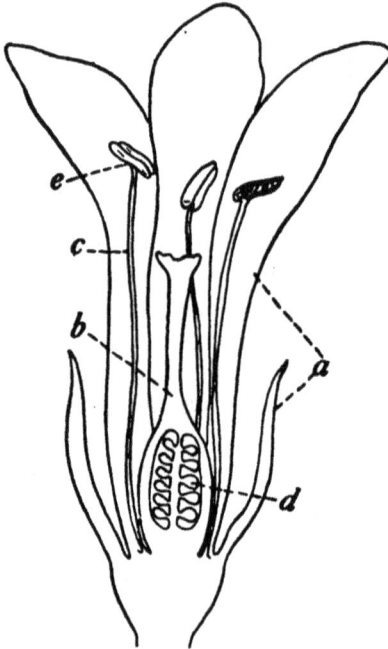

Fig. 407. — The floral structures of a typical flower. The floral structures comprise a perianth (a) composed of calyx and corolla, a number of microsporophylls or stamens each consisting of anther (e) and filament (c), and a pistil (b) composed of one or more megasporophylls with the megasporangia or ovules (d) enclosed in an ovary.

Perianth. — The perianth, usually consisting of both sepals and petals, not only protects the sporophylls during their development but also serves in pollination, which in Angiosperms is done largely by insects. At the base of the perianth occur nectar glands, which are further adaptations to insect pollination. The perianth seems to have arisen in two ways. In some cases there is evidence that the parts of the perianth are modified sporophylls, while in other cases they are apparently modified foliage leaves.

Stamen. — The stamen (microsporophyll) has its pollen sacs (microsporangia), usually four in number, joined into the structure called anther. The pollen grains (microspores) are numerous in each sac and are formed before the flower opens. Like the spores of Gymnosperms, Pteridophytes, and Bryophytes, they are formed by special cells known as mother cells of which there are many in each pollen sac as shown at *A* in *Figure 408*. These mother cells also divide by the reduction division, that is, by the kind of cell division in which the daughter nuclei get only half the sporophytic number of chromosomes. The mother cells

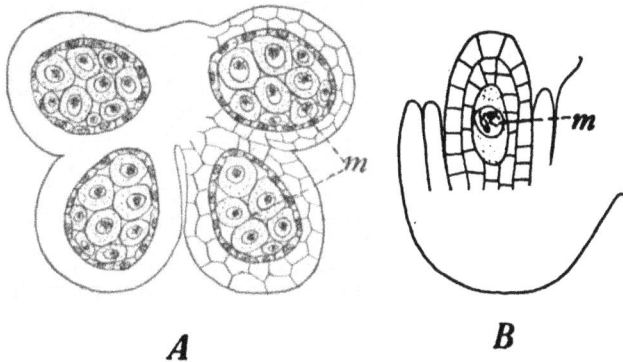

A   **B**

FIG. 408. — The spore mother cells of Angiosperms. *A*, cross section of a young anther, showing the microspore mother cells (*m*). *B*, section through an ovule, showing the megaspore mother cell (*m*). Both are highly magnified.

are formed and undergo the reduction division while the flowers are still small buds. Immediately following the division of the mother cell, the daughter nuclei resulting from this division divide and consequently there are four spores or pollen grains formed from each mother cell. The four spores constituting the progeny of a mother cell are called a *tetrad*. The cells of the tetrad commonly cling together for a short time after they are formed, but soon separate and each becomes a pollen grain. The pollen grains are in reality the one-celled stages of the male gametophytes, since they have the reduced or gametophytic number of chromosomes. Usually before the pollen grain leaves the anther its nucleus divides, forming a tube and generative nucleus. In this condition the pollen grain is carried to the stigma where the male gametophyte completes its development. The history of the pollen is shown in the upper diagram of *Figure 409.*

The Pistil. — A pistil consists of one or more megasporophylls (carpels). The megasporophyll is usually organized into an

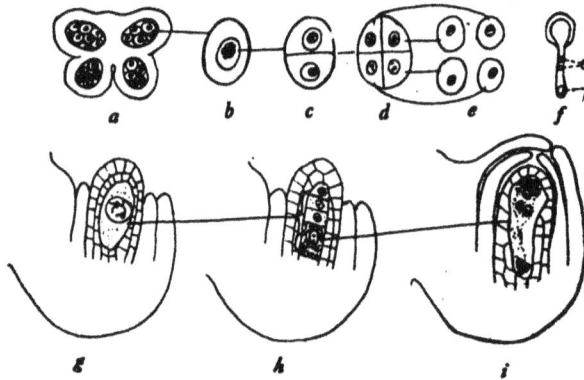

FIG. 409. — The formation of the spores and gametophytes in Angiosperms. The upper diagram shows the origin of the pollen grains and male gametophytes. *a*, cross section of a young anther, showing the mother cells; *b*, a mother cell beginning to divide; *c*, the first division of the mother cell completed; *d*, the second division of the mother cell completed, resulting in a tetrad of daughter cells; *e*, cells of the tetrad separated and fully formed pollen grains; *f*, pollen grain with male gametophyte developed, showing tube nucleus at *t*, and sperms at *s*.

The lower diagram shows the formation of megaspores and female gametophyte. *g*, section through an ovule, showing the megaspore mother cell with chromatin in a thread in preparation for the reduction division; *h*, a section through an ovule, showing the four megaspores resulting from the two successive divisions of the megaspore mother cell; *i*, section through an ovule showing the mature female gametophyte which is formed by the surviving megaspore.

ovary, style, and stigma. In compound pistils, where a number of carpels are present, the ovaries are usually joined, thus forming a compound ovary, and often the styles and sometimes the stigmas are also joined.

The *ovary*, which is the enclosure for the megasporangia or ovules, is one of the notable features of Angiosperms. With the ovules enclosed the pollen cannot come in contact with the ovules as it does in Gymnosperms, so the stigma, another characteristic structure of the Angiosperms, had to be introduced. That the ovary gives the Angiosperms a special economic importance is attested by the fact that our fruits are either ripened ovaries or ripened ovaries plus closely related parts. Within the ovary occur the cavities or locules in which are borne the megasporangia or ovules, varying in number and also in the way they are attached in different Angiosperms.

The *ovule* is generally borne on a stalk (funiculus), and the chief structure of the ovule is the nucellus, which in most Angiosperms is enclosed by two integuments, an inner and an outer one. As in Gymnosperms, the integuments do not completely close over the top of the nucellus, but leave a small opening (micropyle).

Usually the ovule curves as it develops and the micropyle is brought around to near the base of the ovule. This position of the micropyle is a favorable one for the entrance of the pollen tube. There are terms used to indicate the amount of curving ovules undergo in their development. Ovules that remain straight are *orthotropous*. Those that double clear back upon themselves are *anatropous*. Those turning only part way back upon themselves are *campylotropous*. Within the nucellus is formed the megaspore mother cell (*B, Fig. 408*), which also divides by two successive divisions in one of which the number of chromosomes is reduced to the gametophytic number. A megaspore, therefore, produces four megaspores, each of which is comparable to a pollen grain. Although the megaspores are formed while the flowers are mere buds, they are formed later than the pollen grains. As in the Gymnosperms, in most Angiosperms only one of the megaspores develops into a gametophyte, although among Monocotyledons, there are cases in which more than one or all of the megaspores apparently take part in forming the one gametophyte. The lower diagram in *Figure 409* gives the usual history of the megaspores.

The *female gametophyte* is very much reduced, consisting of only a few nuclei and naked cells in a small mass of cytoplasm. In most Angiosperms the female gametophyte is developed in the following way. The megaspore first enlarges by digesting and using the other three megaspores and the adjoining cells of the nucellus as food. Then as the megaspore further enlarges the nucleus divides, and the daughter nuclei pass to opposite ends of the embryo sac which is the term now applied to the region enclosed within the cell membrane of the germinating megaspore. In this position nuclear division follows until there are four nuclei at each end. The megaspore has now become the female gametophyte consisting of eight nuclei, four at the micropylar and four at the opposite end, known as the chalazal or antipodal end of the embryo sac. After the stage with eight nuclei is reached, then the organization of the female gametophyte begins as shown in *Figure 410*. A nucleus called polar nucleus from each end of the embryo sac moves toward the center of the sac until the two come in contact. Sometimes they fuse soon after coming in contact to form the primary endosperm nucleus, but often they remain in contact until fertilization and then fuse at the same time they fuse with the sperm to form the endosperm nucleus. The three nuclei and adjacent cytoplasm at the micropylar end are organized into three naked cells, the inner one being the egg and the other two the synergids. The three nuclei at the antipodal end and known as antipodals usually disappear early, but in some Angiosperms they

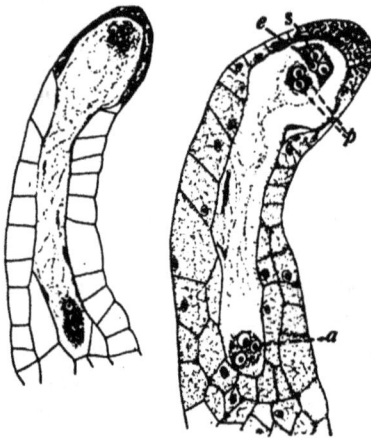

Fig. 410. — Organization of the female gametophyte in Red Clover. At the left, a section through the nucellus, showing eight nuclei of the female gametophyte with four nuclei at each end of the embryo sac. At the right, the gametophyte fully organized, showing the antipodals at *a*, the polars at *p*, the egg at *e*, and the synergids at *s*.

become organized with the adjacent cytoplasm into cells that seem to have an absorptive function. The female gametophyte is now organized and ready for fertilization. When compared with the female gametophyte of the Pine, its remarkable reduction in number of cells, the absence of archegonia, and the formation of a nucleus for providing endosperm are notable features.

Male Gametophyte and Fertilization. — On the stigma the pollen grain develops a tube which by means of enzymes eats its way through the stigma, style, and ovule into the embryo sac.

The pollen tube lives as a parasite on the structures through which it passes, using their tissues as food for growth and making a passageway for itself at the same time. The growth of the pollen tube is directed by the tube nucleus which maintains a position near the end of the tube. Soon after the pollen tube is well started, the generative nucleus passes from the pollen grain into the tube and later divides, forming two sperms which are carried along with the contents of the tube to the embryo sac. The male gametophyte, consisting of tube nucleus and two sperms, is now complete. In some plants, however, the formation of the sperms occurs before the development of the tube is begun.

When the tube reaches the embryo sac and comes in contact with its contents, the membrane enclosing the tube is destroyed, and the tube nucleus, sperms, and other contents of the tube flow into the embryo sac. The contents of the embryo sac apparently destroy the tube nucleus, for it soon disappears, while the sperms apparently thrive. Since there are no cell walls in the embryo sac, the sperms are free to move about. As to how they are moved is not known, for they have no cilia, but one very soon reaches the nucleus of the egg and the other the polar nuclei or the primary endosperm nucleus, with which they come in contact and fuse. Since there are two fusions, one with the egg nucleus and the other with the polar nuclei or the primary endosperm nucleus, there are two fertilizations or *double fertilization*, and this also is a notable

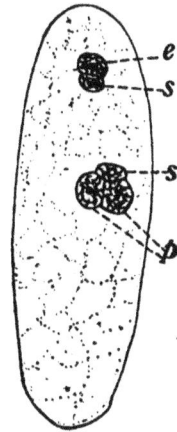

FIG. 411. — An embryo sac of a Lily, showing double fertilization. At the upper end of the sac the egg (*e*) and a sperm (*s*) are shown fusing, and near the center of the sac the second sperm (*s*) is shown fusing with the two polar nuclei (*p*).

feature of Angiosperms (*Fig. 411*). Of course fertilization is difficult to follow and has been seen in only a comparatively few Angiosperms. It is therefore possible that many times the second sperm does not fuse with the polars or the primary endosperm nucleus, but double fertilization has been found so generally in the Angiosperms whose fertilization has been studied that it is believed to be quite universal among Angiosperm. In connection with double fertilization it should be noted that the endosperm nucleus contains the contents of three nuclei, since it is a product of a triple fusion, involving a sperm and the two polar nuclei.

Embryo. — The first cells produced by the division of the fertilized egg form a filament which pushes down into the embryo sac. This filament is called the *proembryo.* The terminal cell of the proembryo develops the embryo, while the remainder of the filament remains as a stalk called *suspensor.* After the termi-

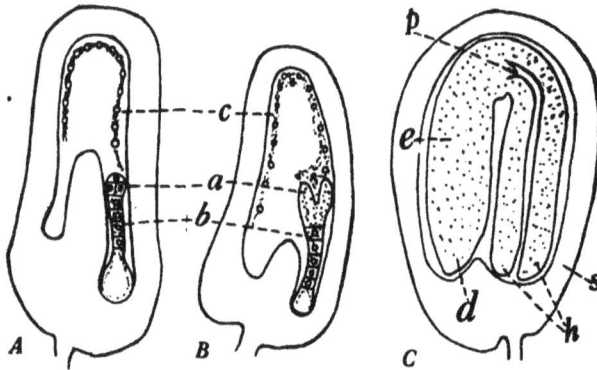

FIG. 412. — Development of the embryo and endosperm in the Shepherd's Purse. *A*, section through ovule with embryo and endosperm in early stage of development, showing the proembryo which consists of the suspensor (*b*), and the terminal three-celled embryo (*a*), and also showing the endosperm (*c*), as a chain of free nuclei around the wall of the embryo sac. *B*, the same as *A*, excepting that the proembryo and endosperm are more developed. *C*, section through a mature seed showing the seed coat (*s*), and the mature embryo with cotyledons at *h*, plumule at *p*, hypocotyl at *e*, and radicle at *d*.

nal cell divides a number of times, the parts of the embryo begin to be differentiated. In Dicotyledons two lobes appear at the end farthest from the micropyle and these become the two cotyledons characteristic of dicotyledonous Angiosperms. Between the cotyledons the plumule is formed, while the axis of the embryo below the cotyledons is differentiated into the hypocotyl, which is the main part of the axis, and the radicle at its lower end (*Fig. 412*).

The embryos of monocotyledonous Angiosperms have a radicle, hypocotyl, plumule, but only one cotyledon. They also differ from the embryos of Dicotyledons in the relative positions of the cotyledon and plumule. Although the cotyledon apparently arises laterally, it soon becomes terminal and the plumule appears to develop on the side of the embryo (*Fig. 413*).

Parthenogenesis. — Parthenogenesis, which is the development of an embryo from a supposedly unfertilized egg, occurs in a number of Angiosperms. In the Dandelion (*Taraxacum*), Meadow Rue (*Thalictrum*), Everlasting (*Antennaria*), A p p l e s, Pears, Quinces, and a few other plants parthenogenesis is known to occur. In cases which have been investigated cytologically, it has been found that the mother cell in the ovule omits the reduction division, and, therefore, the cell which occupies the position of an egg has the sporophytic number of chromosomes and fertilization is not necessary. Since parthenogenetic plants show no results of crossing in the offspring when cross-pollinated, parthenogenesis may be a source of disappointment to the plant breeder.

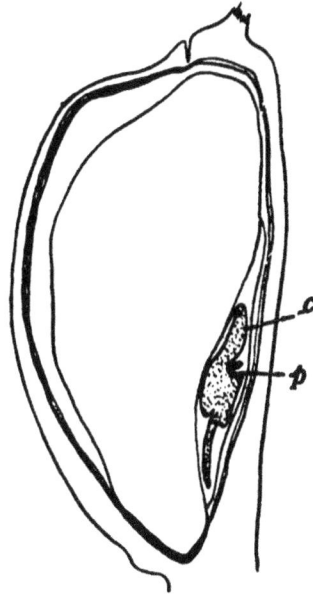

FIG. 413. — A monocotyledonous embryo as typified by that of Corn. The cotyledon (c) appears terminal and the plumule (p) as arising from the side of the embryo.

Parthenocarpy. — Parthenocarpy is the development of fruit without fertilization and is quite common among Angiosperms. Bananas, seedless Oranges, and seedless Currants are familiar examples of parthenocarpic plants. Sometimes Apples develop without seeds, and some varieties of Cucumbers develop fruits without pollination.

Polyembryony. — In a few Angiosperms, of which one of the Onions (*Allium*) is a notable example, a number of embryos may be developed in the same embryo sac or around it. The synergids and antipodals have been known to develop embryos, and sometimes some of the cells of the nucellus around the embryo sac develop like buds and form embryos, in which case, of course, there is no fertilization. Polyembryony may also be a source of annoyance to plant breeders, for if plants that are used in crossing develop polyembryonous seeds, the offspring arising from these seeds may develop from embryos that were formed by the budding of the nucellus, in which case the embryos have only the characteristics of the mother plant. For example, in crossing different strains of Tobacco, in some cases the plants arising from the seeds obtained by crossing are not hybrids but like the mother plant. Some think this may be due to parthenogenesis and others attribute it to polyembryony.

Endosperm. — While the embryo is developing, the endosperm nucleus is dividing and its accompanying cytoplasm is increasing. The free nuclei at first form in a chain around the wall and then multiply towards the center. Cell walls are finally formed and in these cells food is stored. In some Angiosperms the endosperm is taken up by the embryo almost as rapidly as formed and stored in the cotyledons, while in other Angiosperms most of the endosperm remains outside of the embryo until the seed germinates.

Since the endosperm nucleus contains the contents of a sperm, the character of the endosperm of a seed is often determined by the sperm. Thus, as in case of Corn where the endosperm remains outside of the embryo, the color and other characteristics of the endosperm are often like the pollen parent and not at all like those of the mother parent. This feature called xenia has already been referred to. In some seeds, in addition to the formation of endosperm, the portion of the nucellus remaining becomes stored with food and forms what is known as perisperm.

Seed Coat. — As the embryo and endosperm develop, the ovule enlarges rapidly, and at the same time the embryo sac destroys much or all of the nucellus and frequently a part or all of the inner integument. Consequently the seed coat consists chiefly of the outer integument, which is usually very much modified for protection.

It is obvious that the seeds of Angiosperms differ considerably from the seeds of Gymnosperms, for the female gametophyte of Angiosperms is soon destroyed after fertilization by the developing embryo and endosperm, and consequently there is no gametophytic tissue in the seeds of Angiosperms comparable to that in the seeds of Gymnosperms. The endosperm in the seeds of Gymnosperms is simply the portion of the gametophyte that

FIG. 414. — The life cycle of Angiosperms illustrated by the life cycle of Red Clover. At the left in the line above, a branch of Red Clover with heads of flowers (× ½); next, a vertical section through a flower, showing the floral structures; at the right, a section of an anther, a pollen grain, and a pollen grain with tube and male gametophyte developed. At the left in the line below, an ovule with female gametophyte mature and pollen tubes entering through the micropyle; next, embryo and endosperm forming; next, seed mature from the embryo of which the new plant at the right develops.

remains, but in Angiosperms the endosperm develops after the gametophyte is formed and from a nucleus formed by the fusion of three other nuclei, one of which came from the male gametophyte.

Notable Features of Angiosperms. — In contrast to Gymnosperms, the Angiosperms have the flower; a megasporophyll consisting of an ovary, in which the megasporangia are enclosed, and of a stigma to receive the pollen; more reduced gametophytes; and endosperm nucleus and double fertilization. The life cycle of an Angiosperm is shown in *Figure 414.*

CHAPTER XX

CLASSIFICATION OF ANGIOSPERMS AND SOME OF THEIR FAMILIES OF MOST ECONOMIC IMPORTANCE

Classification. — The Angiosperms are so numerous and vary so widely that their classification is not at all settled. Ray, a noted English botanist (1628–1705), divided the Angiosperms into two sub-classes — Monocotyledons and Dicotyledons — on the basis of the number of cotyledons. There are also other features which are used in distinguishing these two groups, such as the number of floral structures composing the flower, the venation of the leaves, the arrangement of the vascular bundles in the stem, and the presence or absence of cambium. Thus leaves with parallel veins, the parts of the flower in threes or sixes, the scattered arrangement of vascular bundles in the stem, and closed vascular bundles are characteristic of Monocotyledons, while leaves with net-veins, floral parts in fours or fives, vascular bundles arranged in a circle so as to enclose the pith, and indefinite growth by means of a cambium are characteristic of Dicotyledons. As to whether the Monocotyledons arose from the Dicotyledons, or the Dictyledons from the Monocotyledons is a question that botanists are not able to answer satisfactorily. However, recent studies of the young embryos of some of the Monocotyledons show that there are two cotyledons present, one of which is very rudimentary. This discovery with other structural and historical features has given rise to the view that the monocotyledonous condition arose from the dicotyledonous condition through the suppression of one of the cotyledons. This means that the growth which first becomes evident at the top of the developing embryo as two points, each of which develops into a cotyledon in Dicotyledons, became concentrated into the development of only one point which consequently develops the single large cotyledon characteristic of Monocotyledons.

Upon differences which pertain chiefly to the flowers, the Monocotyledons and Dicotyledons are subdivided into many groups.

The Monocotyledons are subdivided into 8 or 10 orders which are in turn subdivided into about 42 families. The families are subdivided into many genera and the genera into species of which there are about 25,000.

The Dicotyledons, of which there are more than 100,000 species, include most of the Angiosperms, being more than four times as numerous as the Monocotyledons. The Dicotyledons are divided into two large subdivisions — the Archichlamydeae and the Sympetalae.

The Archichlamydeae have a corolla of separate petals or no corolla at all. They include about 180 families and 61,000 species of Dicotyledons. They are grouped into two classes, one of which has apetalous flowers, that is, flowers without petals, and the other of which has polypetalous flowers, that is, flowers with petals present and free from each other.

The Sympetalae include those Dicotyledons in which the petals are more or less united. There are about 50 families and 42,000 species of the Sympetalae.

In arranging the orders and families taxonomists have endeavored to follow an evolutionary sequence. The rank of an order or family depends chiefly upon the organization of its flowers. Flowers most like a typical strobilus, that is, resembling most the strobili of Gymnosperms, are regarded as the simplest of flowers. Thus a flower without any perianth is simpler than one with a perianth. Also a flower with parts arranged spirally, thus having parts arranged like the sporophylls in a strobilus, is considered simpler than one with parts having a cyclic arrangement. Again flowers having petals joined or carpels united are considered more advanced than flowers in which these parts are separate. Thus the Sympetalae, since they have united petals, are considered more advanced than the Archichlamydeae which have separate petals or no petals at all. In respect to these evolutionary tendencies the orders and families of both Dicotyledons and Monocotyledons form an ascending series.

Most of the families of the Angiosperms have some species of economic importance, but some families are much more notable than others for their species related to man's welfare.

The species may concern us because they are useful for food, fibers, lumber, medicine, etc., or because they are weeds which hinder the growth of cultivated plants, poison live stock, or do damage in other ways.

Beginning with one of the lower families of the Dicotyledons, a number of families of Angiosperms having species of considerable economic importance are discussed in the following pages.

FIG. 415. — The flowers of a Willow. Above, at the left, a staminate catkin, and below, at the left, a staminate flower, showing the bract and stamens; above, at the right, a pistillate catkin, and below, at the right, a pistillate flower, showing the bract and pistil. After Burns and Otis.

Archichlamydeae

Apetalae

Willow Family (Salicaceae). — This family, although it is not the lowest family of the Dicotyledons, stands well toward the bottom of the series. To this family belong the Willows and Poplars. The flowers are unisexual and simple in type. The plants are dioecious and bear their apetalous flowers in scaly spikes or catkins (*Fig. 415*). A flower consists of a pistil or of a number of stamens borne in the axil of a small scale or bract.

The Weeping Willow, so named because of its drooping branches, is cultivated for its beauty. The growing of Basket Willows for sprouts, which are woven into baskets, chairs, and other articles, is an industry of considerable importance. Willows are easily propagated, taking root readily when transplanted or from cuttings. They grow especially well near water and are often planted along river banks where they prevent the cutting away of the banks by floods. A number of the Poplars, such as the Aspens, Balm of Gilead, and Cottonwood, are cultivated for shade. The Cottonwood grows to be a very large tree and is of some value for lumber. Both Willows and Poplars are used in making medicinal charcoal, and a number of substances, such as salicin, populin, tannin, and a volatile oil are obtained from their bark.

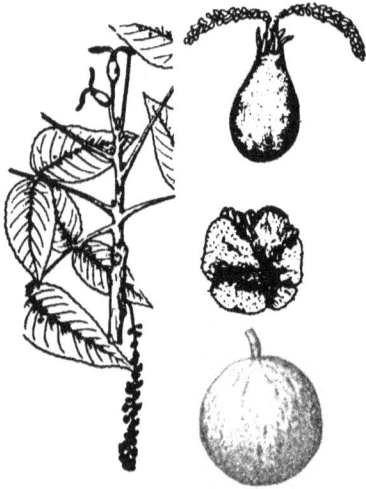

FIG. 416.—The flowers and fruit of the Black Walnut. At the left, a branch bearing a catkin of staminate flowers below and two pistillate flowers above (×½). At the right, above, a pistillate flower, showing the pistil enclosed in bracts which form the husk of the fruit; next, below, a staminate flower, showing the bracts and the stamens; at the bottom, a fruit (×½). After Burns and Otis.

Walnut Family (Juglandaceae). — This family comprises the Walnuts and Hickories. The Walnuts and Hickories are monoecious, and their flowers are generally apetalous, although in some cases the pistillate flowers have petals The staminate flowers are borne in catkins, while the pistillate flowers are borne singly or in small clusters (*Fig. 416*).

The White Walnut (*Juglans cinerea*), called Butternut, and the Black Walnut (*Juglans nigra*) are the most common Walnuts in the United States. The European Walnut (*Juglans regia*), notable for its delicately flavored nuts, is grown in California and the Southern States, and some other species occur in certain parts of the United States.

The nuts are rich in oil, which is expressed and used as food and in painting. The nuts are common on the market and are of considerable importance as food. The wood of the White and Black Walnut is much used for furniture and cabinet work. The wood of the Black Walnut is probably the most valuable wood of the North American forest. It is a durable wood, takes a fine polish, and is much sought for furniture, gunstocks, and for cabinet work.

There are a number of species of Hickories, and the Pecans and several other species bear nuts having considerable value for food. Hickory wood is very tough, and on account of its strength, elasticity, and lightness, it is the best wood for spokes of buggy and wagon wheels and for ax handles. It is also the best wood for fuel.

Fig. 417. — The flowers and fruit of the Cherry Birch. At the left, above, a flowering branchlet bearing two staminate catkins at the left and one pistillate catkin at the right ($\times \frac{1}{2}$); at the right, above, a pistillate flower and just below a staminate flower; at the left, below, a pistillate catkin in fruit and at the right, below, a single fruit. After Burns and Otis.

Birch Family (Betulaceae). — To this family belong the Birches, Hazelnuts, Ironwoods, and Alders. They are trees or shrubs and, except in rare cases, are monoecious with the staminate flowers borne in catkins, and the pistillate flowers borne in clusters, in spikes, or scaly catkins (*Fig. 417*). The fruit is a one-seeded nut, which in the Hazel is of some value for food. The Birches, of which there are many species, are the most important genera in this family. They are much used for shade and ornamental trees, and the wood is used for furniture, barrel hoops, shoe pegs,

spools, and paper pulp. The bark of the Paper Birch was employed by the Indians for canoes, baskets, cups, and for sheathing wigwams.

Beech and Oak Family (Fagaceae). — This family includes the Beeches, Chestnuts, and Oaks.

The plants of this family are monoecious trees or shrubs with staminate flowers in catkins or clusters, and pistillate flowers solitary or slightly clustered (*Fig. 418*). The fruit is a one-seeded nut partly or entirely enclosed by a covering called cupule, which is formed by bracts that develop at the base of the ovary and grow up over it.

The nuts of the Chestnut are common on the market and are of considerable value for food. Beech nuts contain much oil and are a good feed for hogs. From the Oaks, of which there are a large number of species, a large proportion of our hardwood is obtained. The beautiful figures which Oak lumber can be made to show make it a valuable wood for furniture, inside finishing of buildings, and for cabinet work. Beech wood is very hard and is used considerably for hardwood floors and in the manufacture of furniture. Chestnut wood is soft but durable and is used for fences and buildings. The bark of Oak and Chestnut trees is rich in tannin and at one time was the source of tannin for tanning hides. From the Cork Oak the cork of commerce is obtained (*Fig. 419*).

FIG. 418. — The flowers and fruit of the Red Oak. Above, a flowering branchlet bearing a cluster of staminate catkins below and solitary pistillate flowers above ($\times \frac{1}{2}$); at the right, above, a pistillate flower, and just below, a staminate flower; at the bottom, a mature fruit, showing the matured ovary and the cupule (natural size). After Burns and Otis.

FIG. 419. — Stripping cork from the Cork Oak. After Lecomte.

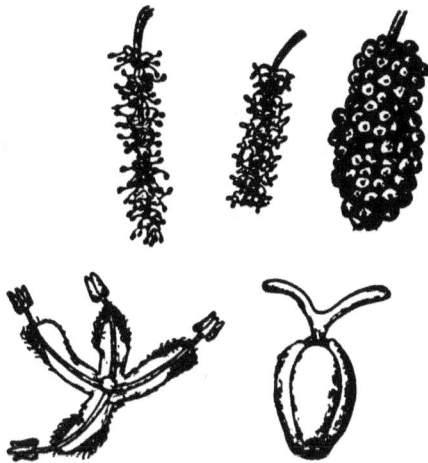

FIG. 420. — The flowers and fruit of the Red Mulberry. Above, from left to right, a spike of staminate flowers, a spike of pistillate flowers, and a pistillate spike in fruit (natural size); at the bottom, a staminate and pistillate flower much enlarged. After Burns and Otis.

Elm Family (Urticaceae). — The Elm family includes about 1500 species of herbs, shrubs, and trees. Besides the Elms this family includes the Mulberries, Figs, Hemps, Hops, Nettles, tropical Bread Fruits and a number of others less important.

The apetalous flowers are mostly unisexual. The flowers are usually borne in loose or catkin-like clusters (*Fig. 420*). In the Fig the flowers are produced in hollow receptacles, which with the ovaries within form the well-known fleshy fruits of the Fig (*Fig. 421*). The fruits in this family vary much in size, form, and texture. In the Elms the fruits are winged and depend upon the wind for dissemination.

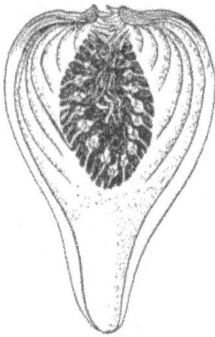

The Elms are very popular shade trees, and their wood is used for flooring, hubs, barrels, sills, posts, and railroad ties. The multiple fleshy fruits of the Mulberries are edible, and the leaves of Mulberries constitute the food for silkworms. The Hemps are well-known fiber plants, and the Hop Vine is extensively grown for its fruits, which are used in brewing beer and at one time were used in making bread. The Rubber Plant, so common in greenhouses and homes, belongs to this family and is one of a number of plants that yield the invaluable rubber from their milky juice.

FIG. 421. — Pistillate flowers of the Fig, showing the flowers borne in a hollow receptacle.

Buckwheat Family (Polygonaceae). — The plants of this family are mostly herbs, distinguished by their swollen nodes, sheathing stipules, and simple flowers in clusters (*Fig. 422*). The Smartweeds and Knotweeds, which are extremely common around gardens and in waste places, are well-known plants of this family. The fruit, in most cases, is an achene which is usually angled and sometimes winged. In case of Buckwheat, which is an important cereal crop, the starchy achene is ground into flour. Some of them, as the Rhubarb and Sorrel, contain acid in the leaves or stem. The family includes a number of weeds of which the Docks, Field or Sheep Sorrel (*Fig. 423*), Black Bindweed, Climbing False Buckwheat, and the Smartweeds are common ones.

FIG. 422. — A Smartweed (*Polygonum Muhlenbergii*), one of the trouble-some weeds, showing the sheathed nodes and terminal spikes of flowers (× ⅓), and also showing a flower and a fruit much enlarged. This plant has both underground and aërial stems.

FIG. 423.—Field or Sheep Sorrel (*Rumex Acetosella*), showing the underground and aërial stems, the halberd-shaped leaves, and terminal spikes of flowers. × ⅓.

Goosefoot Family (Chenopodiaceae). — This family contains many plants, chiefly herbs and most of which are weeds. The

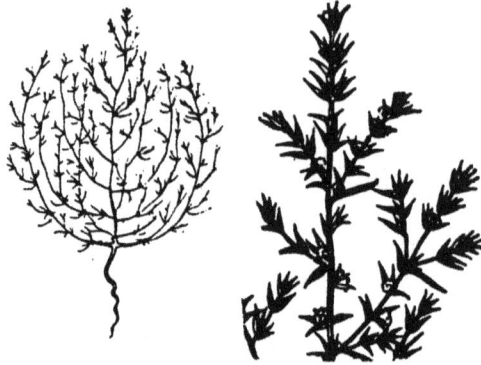

FIG. 424. — Russian Thistle (*Salsola Kali*, var. *tenuifolia*). At the left, an entire plant, showing the tap-root and character of the stem ($\times \frac{1}{15}$); at the right, a portion of a plant, showing the leaves and flowers about natural size. Modified from Oswald and from Beal.

flowers are small and usually greenish. The Spinach and Beets are well-known pot herbs of this family, and also from Beets most of our sugar is now obtained. Among the many that are classed as weeds, the Russian Thistle (*Fig. 424*) is the most noted one.

Belonging to the same order is the Amaranth family, which contains some ornamental plants and a number of common weeds. Of those that are ornamental, the Cockscomb, Prince's Feather, and Bachelor's Button, grown in gardens for their highly colored flower clusters, are common ones. The Pigweed, and Tumbleweed (*Fig. 425*), common in gardens, truck patches, and waste places, are the most troublesome weeds of this family.

FIG. 425. — The Tumble Weed (*Amaranthus graecizans*), showing the general character of the plant. $\times \frac{1}{8}$.

Pink Family (Caryophyllaceae). — This family contains many species, which are chiefly herbs of the temperate regions. The

plants are like those of the preceding families in character of
the ovary and seeds but differ from them in having a perianth
differentiated into a showy corolla
and a large calyx (*Fig. 426*). They
are regarded as a transition group
between the Apetalae and Polypetalae. Among them are some
garden favorites, such as the Carnations, Pinks, Sweet Williams, and
Lychnis, and also some weeds of ·
which the Chickweeds, Corn Cockle,
Cow-herb, and Bouncing Bet are
common ones.

Fig. 426. — A portion of a
plant of Corn˙ Cockle (*Agro-
stemma Githago*) (×⅓). The
flowers have a perianth consisting of a calyx and showy corolla.
Modified from Beal.

Polypetalae

As previously stated the Polypetalae have petals and the petals
are generally separate. The colored
corolla is usually distinct from the
green calyx, and the flowers are pollinated chiefly by insects. Among
the lower families of the Polypeta-
lae, as the Buttercups (*Ranunculaceae*) illustrate, the flower usually has numerous stamens and a number
of separate pistils. The calyx and corolla
are also attached below the stamens and
pistils or, in other words, the flowers are
hypogynous. In passing to the more advanced families of the Polypetalae, the
number of stamens and carpels become
more definite, and assume the cyclic arrangement. There is also a tendency for
the carpels to join and a tendency of the
flower toward epigyny in the higher
families.

Fig. 427. — A flower
of a Buttercup, showing
the many stamens and
pistils.   ×2.

Crowfoot or Buttercup Family (*Ranunculaceae*). — This family includes numer-
ous species, mostly herbs, having in common separate petals,
and separate sepals. The stamens and commonly the carpels

are numerous, but indefinite in number and separate (*Fig. 427*).
A few of the well-known plants of this family are the Anemone,
Clematis, Larkspur, Columbine, Hepatica, Marsh Marigold, and
Peony. The Wolfsbane or Aconite, which contains the virulent
poison aconite, and the Golden Seal, which yields the drug hydras-
tis, are medicinal plants of considerable importance. Belonging

Fig. 428. — American-grown Camphor trees. From Yearbook, U. S.
Dept. Agr.

to other families grouped in the same order with the Buttercups,
are the Magnolias, trees and shrubs noted for their large flowers
and including the Tulip tree, a noted timber tree. Also the
Barberries, the tropical Nutmeg tree, and the Laurels belong
to the same order. The Laurels include such plants as the Sassafras, Cinnamon and Camphor tree (*Fig. 428*).

Mustard Family (*Cruciferae*). — The flowers of this family
generally have four sepals, four petals, and six stamens. The

pistil forms a pod known as the *silique*. The four petals, when opened out, suggest the Greek cross, — whence the name Cruciferae (*Fig. 429*).

To this family belong such useful plants as the Cabbage, Turnip, Kohlrabi, Brussels Sprouts, and Rape.

A number of plants of this family, such as Peppergrass, Shepherd's Purse, White and Black Mustard, Tumbling Mustard, Indian Mustard, and Charlock are weeds. Their seeds

· FIG. 429. — The character of the plant, flowers, and fruit of the Black Mustard (*Brassica nigra*). At the right, a plant in flower ($\times \frac{1}{10}$), and a mature pod about natural size; at the left, above, a flower, and below, an open pod. After Vasey and Nature.

FIG. 430. — One of the Poppies, showing the character of the flowers and pod. After Lecomte.

are troublesome impurities in commercial seeds, and the seeds of some are poisonous.

Associated with the Mustard family is the Poppy family (Papaveraceae), characterized by a milky juice and represented by Bloodroot, common in the woods, and by the California Poppy from the juice of which opium is obtained (*Fig. 430*).

Rose Family (*Rosaceae*). — To this family belong about 2000 species of herbs, shrubs, and trees. In most plants of this family, there is an indefinite number of stamens and one to many separate carpels. The flowers of Strawberries and Blackberries, for example, have many stamens and many separate pistils, and the number of each is indefinite, while in the Apple there are generally five united carpels, and in the Peach, Plum, Cherry, and Almond the number of carpels has settled down to one. There is also a noticeable tendency toward epigyny, for perigyny, which is common in the family, is a step toward epigyny (*Fig. 431*). The Rose family is the family of fruits. It includes Apples, Pears, Peaches, Plums, Apricots, Cherries,

FIG. 431. — Some flowers of the Rose family. At the left, a Strawberry flower, which has many stamens and pistils and is hypogynous; next, a flower of an Agrimony, and, at the extreme right, a Pear flower, both of which are perigynous and have few pistils with ovaries joined.

Quinces, Strawberries, Blackberries, Raspberries, and some others. No one can estimate what this family contributes to the welfare of mankind.

Some, like the Roses, Spireas, and Hawthornes, are important ornamental plants. Some of them, as the Cinquefoils or Five-fingers and the Agrimonies, are weeds. The Five-fingers grow in fields and crowd out other plants, while the Agrimonies grow in pastures, and their spiny fruits get in the wool and hair of live stock.

Closely related to the Rose family is the Saxifrage family (*Saxifragaceae*), the family to which the Gooseberry, Currant, Syringa, and Hydrangea belong.

Pea Family (*Leguminosae*). — The Pea family, which includes about 7000 species of herbs, shrubs, and trees, is the largest group of the Archichlamydeae. The flowers are hypogynous or somewhat perigynous, and the parts of the calyx and corolla are generally in fives. The stamens are usually 10, and 9 or all of them are joined. The petals are often irregular, as those of the Beans and Peas illustrate, and also show a tendency to unite (*Fig. 432*). In the uniting of some of the petals, the plants of the Pea family suggest those of the Sympetalae which is considered the most advanced group of Dicotyledons. Also irregularity in the shape or size of sepals or petals is considered an advanced feature. The pistil consists of one carpel and becomes the one-celled fruit called *legume*, which is characteristic of the family.

The Beans, Peas, Peanuts, Soy Beans, Cow-peas, Clovers, Alfalfas, and Vetches make this family a noted one. The value of Beans, Peanuts, and Peas as food for man, and of the others mentioned for forage and the improvement of the soil are well known to the student. The Peanut is peculiar in that it forces its pods underground to ripen. Although Peanuts are not so important for food as Beans and Peas, several millions of bushels of them are grown in the United States per year. From some of the leguminous plants medicinal substances, dyestuffs, gum arabic, licorice, logwood, copal varnish, and other useful substances are obtained. Some of the leguminous trees, as the Black Locust, Honey Locust, and a number of trees in the tropics and sub-tropics, furnish fine cabinet woods.

FIG. 432. — Flowers and fruit of the Common Locust (*Robinia Pseudo-Acacia*). At the right, a raceme of flowers, showing the irregular corollas ($\times \frac{1}{2}$); at the left, above, a flower with a portion of corolla removed to show the diadelphous stamens; at the left, below, a mature pod or legume ($\times \frac{1}{2}$). After Burns and Otis.

Thirty or more leguminous plants are classed as weeds. Some, like the Loco-weeds and some of the Lupines, are poisonous to live stock and cause considerable trouble in pastures in the Western states. Some, like the Rabbit-foot Clover, are very hairy and when eaten by stock, the hairs often collect in balls and clog the intestines. In the Tick Trefoils, of which there are many species, the fruits are commonly spiny and are troublesome to wool-growers.

Spurge Family (*Euphorbiaceae*). — The Spurge family contains many species, many of which are tropical. The flowers are commonly small, hypogynous, and unisexual. The perianth is usually simple and sometimes absent. The stamens range from one to many, and the pistil is composed of three united carpels (*Fig. 433*). The plants usually contain a milky juice, which in many species is poisonous. A few of them are common weeds, usually growing prostrate in gardens and truck patches.

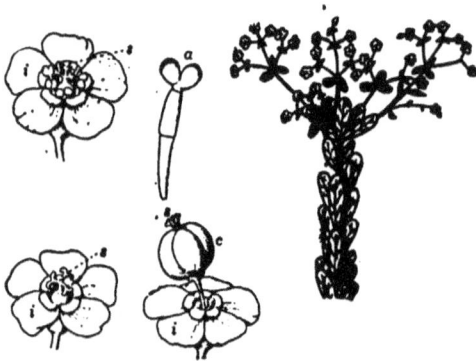

FIG. 433. — Flowers and fruit of the Flowering Spurge (*Euphorbia corollata*). At the right, a portion of a plant in flower; above, at the left, a flower cluster consisting of one pistillate flower and a number of staminate flowers enclosed by an involucre (*i*) bearing appendages resembling petals; at the right of the flower cluster, a single staminate flower with anther at *a*; below, at the left, a flower cluster with staminate flowers removed to show the pistillate flower; below, at the right, a pistillate flower in fruit, showing the ovary (*c*), the stigma (*s*), and the involucre (*i*). In part after Bergen and Caldwell.

FIG. 434. — The Hevea tree, one of the plants from the milk-juice of which India rubber is obtained. After Lecomte.

The Castor Bean, from which castor oil is obtained, is one of the large species of our region. Some are trees, as for example the Hevea tree (*Fig. 434*) of South America from which India rubber is obtained. Tapioca is obtained from the Cassava plant, a plant of the Spurge family and native of Brazil. A number are useful for medicine, and some, as the Castor Bean, Poinsetta, and some others, are ornamental plants.

Between the Pea family and the Spurge family is usually placed the Flax family (*Linaceae*) to which the cultivated Flax belongs, and the Rue family (*Rutacea*), the family of citrous fruits, such as Oranges, Lemons, Tangerines, Grapefruit, and others.

Maple Family (*Aceraceae*). — This family is composed chiefly of the Maples, valuable trees for shade, lumber, and yielding a sweet sap from which maple syrup and sugar are obtained. Closely related to the Maples are the Buckeyes which are also important shade trees.

Mallow Family (*Malvaceae*). — This family is a notable one chiefly because it includes the Cotton plant (*Fig. 435*). The

FIG. 435. — A Cotton Plant, showing the general character of the plant. × about $\frac{1}{10}$. After Orton.

flowers have five sepals and five petals. The stamens are numerous and united, and the pistil is composed of a number of carpels united at the base. The sepals are also partly united (*Fig. 9*).

Cotton surpasses all other plants of the family in value. To this family also belongs the Theobroma Cacao, a small tree which yields cocoa and chocolate. The Shrubby Althaea and Hollyhock are of some importance as ornamental plants, while the Indian Mallow (*Albutilon Theophrasti*), Flower-of-an-hour (*Hibiscus Trionum*), and a few others are more or less troublesome weeds.

Parsley Family (*Umbelliferae*). — The Parsley family comprises about 1300 species. The small epigynous flowers are borne in umbels, — whence the name of the family (*Fig. 436*). The stamens and parts of the calyx and corolla are five. The pistil consists of two partly united carpels which separate in the fruit. Carrots, Parsnips, Celery, and Fennel are members of this family.

FIG. 436. — Flowers and fruit of the Wild Carrot (*Daucus Carota*). At the left, a portion of a plant bearing umbels of flowers and fruit; at the right, flowers and a fruit much enlarged to show their structure.

This family also contains some bad weeds. The poison Hemlock (*Conium maculatum*) and Water Hemlock (*Cituta maculata*) are two very poisonous plants, which often grow in pastures where livestock eat them and are killed. The Wild Carrot (*Fig. 437*) is troublesome in pastures, meadows, and grain fields where it crowds out other plants.

FIG. 437. — A meadow taken by the Wild Carrot.

Sympetalae

Among the fifty or more families of the Sympetalae, there are some families of considerable economic importance. As previously stated, the Sympetalae are characterized by a gamopetalous corolla. Also the ovaries are commonly inferior. Their flowers are commonly showy and insect pollinated.

Heath Family (*Ericaceae*). — The plants of the Heath family are mostly shrubs, and they are distributed from the polar regions to the

Fig. 438. — One of the Bindweeds (*Convolvulus sepium*), showing the corolla composed of united petals.

Fig. 439. — Alfalfa Dodder twining about an Alfalfa plant and drawing nourishment from it by means of parasitic roots (× ½). Below, at the right, also a fruit, called capsule, of the Dodder is shown much enlarged.

tropical forests. The flowers are usually regular, and both calyx and corolla are 4–5 lobed. The stamens are as many or twice as many as the lobes of the calyx or corolla, and the flowers are hypogynous or perigynous.

Some, as the Cranberries, Blueberries, and Huckleberries, produce berries that are valuable fruits. The Heath family also includes some highly prized ornamental shrubs, such as the Rho-

FIG. 440. — A portion of a Tomato plant bearing flowers and fruits, and also a flower enlarged to show the structure of the flower.

FIG. 441. — A portion of a Jimson Weed bearing flowers and fruit. Both sepals and petals are joined most of their length.

dodendrons and Heathers. The Trailing Arbutus (*Epigaea*), which is the favorite spring flower wherever it grows, and the Madrona, one of the most beautiful trees of the Pacific coast, belong to this family.

Sweet Potato Family (*Convolvulaceae*). — The plants of this family are chiefly trailing or twining herbs. Their flowers, as those of the Morning Glory illustrate, are often quite showy. They have five stamens, and their calyx and corolla are composed of five parts (*Fig. 438*). There is usually one pistil with two or three locules in the ovary.

The Sweet Potato is of considerable value for food and is quite extensively grown in a number of states. A number of plants of this family are weeds, of which the Morning Glory (*Ipomoea*), Bindweeds, and Dodders (*Fig. 439*) are the chief ones. The Morning Glory and Bindweeds twine around cultivated plants, cutting off the light and often breaking them down. The Bindweeds are extremely hard to eradicate because of their spreading roots and rootstocks which propagate the plants very rapidly. The Dodders are parasitic plants and do much damage in Clover, Alfalfa, and Flax fields, where they twine about the plants and grow their roots into their stems and rob them of their food.

Nightshade Family (*Solonaceae*). — This family is the one to which the Irish Potato, Tomato, and Tobacco belong. Some authors give the number of species as about 1700. Both the five sepals and five petals are more or less joined (*Fig. 440*). The stamens are five and usually inserted on the corolla. The Irish Potato (*Solanum tuberosum*) is probably the most important plant of this group and Tobacco (*Nicotiana Tabacum*) next. Some years the potato crop in the United States is more than 300,000,000 bushels. New York is the chief potato growing state, although many potatoes are grown in Michigan, Wisconsin, and Pennsylvania.

The Tomato (*Lycopersicum esculentum*), when first introduced from tropical America as an ornamental plant, was considered poisonous, but now its fruits are important vegetables.

FIG. 442. — A portion of the Horse Nettle, showing flowers and fruits and the spiny character of the plant (× ½). After Dewey.

In some of the Southern states, as Kentucky, North Carolina, and Virginia, Tobacco is one of the leading agricultural products, while in many other states it is grown in considerable quantities. Some other cultivated plants of this family are the **Egg** Plant, Cayenne Pepper, Petunia, and Belladonna.

To this family belong a number of weeds, some of which are quite troublesome. The Black Nightshade (*Solanum nigrum*) **and** Jimson Weed (*Datura Stramonium*) (*Fig. 441*) are common

weeds that are poisonous. The Horse Nettle (*Solanum caro-linense*) (*Fig. 442*) is troublesome on account of its spiny stems, and it has a deep rootstock, which is difficult to eradicate. Another troublesome weed of this family is the Buffalo Bur (*Solanum rostratum*) (*Fig. 443*), which has spiny fruits that catch into the wool and hair of livestock.

The Madder Family (*Rubiaceae*). — This is one of the largest families of the Dicotyledons. There are more than 4000 species belonging to this family, but the majority of them are tropical. They include herbs, shrubs, and trees. Their flowers are epigynous, and the stamens and lobes of the calyx and corolla are the same in number (usually 4–5).

The Coffee tree (*Fig. 444*), which is grown extensively in Brazil, Arabia, and Java, is the most important plant of the family. The fruit (*Fig. 445*) of the Coffee tree

FIG. 443. — A plant of the Buffalo Bur bearing flowers and fruits, showing the character of the plant ($\times \frac{1}{10}$); and a single flower, showing the prickly calyx and gamopetalous corolla. After Dewey.

is a cherry-like drupe containing two seeds, and these seeds are the coffee of commerce. The Cinchona tree, growing wild in the Andes and cultivated in India, furnishes Cinchona bark from which quinine is made.

Gourd Family (*Cucurbitaceae*). — This family includes the Gourds, Pumpkins, Squashes, Melons, and Cucumbers. The flowers are epigynous, and the plants are monoecious or dioecious (*Fig. 6*). The stamens are usually more or less united. In our region there are only a few species of this family and none of much importance except those mentioned above.

Composite Family (*Compositae*). — This is an immense family and is of world-wide distribution. It is the highest group of Dicotyledons. The most conspicuous character of the family is the grouping of the flowers into a compact head, which is surrounded by bracts forming the structure called involucre (*Fig. 446*). The flowers are epigynous, the corolla is usually tubular or strap-shaped, and the five stamens are inserted on the corolla and usually have their anthers united in a tube around the style. The calyx is often a tuft of hairs (*pappus*). They have developed very effective means of disseminating their seeds. In many, as the Dandelion and Thistles illustrate, the pappus forms a parachute-like arrangement, which enables the fruit to be easily transported by

FIG. 444. — A Coffee tree in fruit.
After Lecomte.

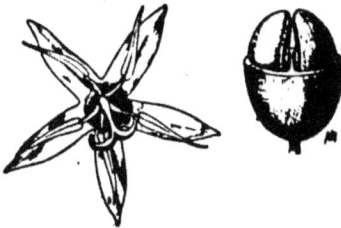

FIG. 445. — Flower, fruit, and seeds of the Coffee. At the left, a flower, and at the right, a fruit with the upper portion of the ovary removed to show the two seeds. After Karsten.

the wind. In others, as the Burdock, Cocklebur, and Spanish Needles illustrate, the fruits have hooks or spines, which catch onto passing animals.

Although the family is a large one, it contains only a few food plants, of which Lettuce, Chicory, Oyster plant, the Globe Artichoke, and Jerusalem Artichoke are the chief ones. Some, as Arnica, Boneset, Camomile, Dandelion, Tansy, and Wormwood, are used some for Medicine, and from the seeds of the Sunflower oil is extracted.

The family includes a number of ornamental plants, of which the Cornflower (also called Bachelor's Button), Marguerite, China Aster, Chrysanthemum, Cosmos, Dahlia, and English Daisy are familiar ones.

In number of weeds which it includes this family surpasses all others. About one hundred plants of this family are classed

FIG. 446. — The Marguerite, one of the Composites, showing the flowers grouped into a compact head and surrounded by an involucre. In this composite a head contains two kinds of flowers — ligulate flowers, one of which is shown at the left, and tubular flowers, one of which is shown at the right of the heads. After Lecomte.

FIG. 447. — Canada Thistle, showing a horizontal root and an aërial stem in flower ($\times \frac{1}{2}$), and also showing single fruits or achenes, one of which is shown without pappus and slightly enlarged.

as weeds, although not many of them are bad weeds. The Canada Thistle (*Fig. 447*) is probably the worst weed of the family. It spreads rapidly by spreading roots or rootstocks and soon takes possession of pastures and meadows and gives considerable trouble in cultivated ground. On account of the spreading underground structures which propagate readily when cut into pieces, the plant is exceedingly hard to eradicate. Some of the other Thistles are also quite troublesome in some regions.

Some other well-known weeds of the family are the Cockle-burs, Ragweeds, Ironweeds, Spanish Needles, Wild Lettuce, and Beggar-ticks.

Monocotyledons

Among Monocotyledons about 25,000 species are recognized, which are distributed among 42 families. They are less than one-fourth as numerous as the Dicotyledons. As previously stated, Monocotyledons differ from Dicotyledons in having flowers with parts usually in threes or sixes, leaves with parallel veins except in rare cases, and vascular bundles with the scattered arrangement. The Monocotyledons contain a few families of economic importance and one family that surpasses all other groups of Angiosperms in number of valuable food plants.

Cat-tail Family (*Typhaceae*). — This family is mentioned because it includes the simplest of the Monocotyledons. They are aquatic plants, growing in groups in swamps and wet places. Some get as high as one's head, and in the late summer and fall, when their inflorescences resembling a cat's tail are well formed, they are conspicuous plants (*Fig. 448*). The flowers are monoecious and have neither calyx nor corolla (*Fig. 449*). The pistil is composed of one carpel containing one locule and only one ovule. The staminate flowers are

FIG. 448. — The common Cat-tail (*Thypha latifolia*), showing the terminal spikes of flowers consisting of staminate flowers above and pistillate flowers below (×¼).

borne at the top and the pistillate flowers below on the spike. The pistil is supported by a stalk or stipe which develops hairs that become the brown down of the fruit. The stamens are attached directly to the axis of the spike and are intermixed with hairs. As to whether the simple flowers of the Cat-tails are primitive or are reduced forms of more complex flowers is not known.

Grass Family (*Gramineae*). — The Grasses constitute one of the largest families of Angiosperms and are widely distributed over the earth. The many valuable plants, such as Corn, Wheat, Oats, Barley, Rye, Rice, Millet, Sugar Cane, Sorghum, Blue-Grass, Timothy, and others that are included, make the Grass family the most important family of Angiosperms. Except the Bamboos, which are shrubs or trees, the Grasses are herbaceous. Some have unisexual (*Fig. 14, 16*), while others have bisexual flowers (*Fig. 18*), and the flowers are commonly arranged in spikes or panicles. Their chief characteristics are that their essential reproductive organs are enclosed in bracts and that they have a nut-like fruit called a grain or cariopsis.

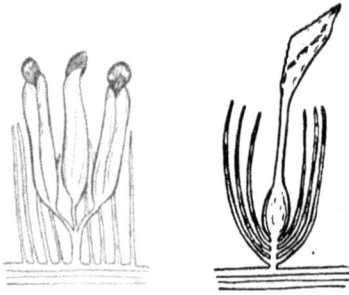

FIG. 449. — The flowers of the common Cat-tail. At the left, a staminate flower; at the right, a pistillate flower.

FIG. 450. — Sugar Cane. After Lecomte.

Besides the grains upon which mankind depends so much for food and the Sugar Cane (*Fig. 450*), which is grown extensively in the Southern states, West Indies, Hawaii, and Java for sugar and molasses, there are the meadow and pasture Grasses which are highly important to man. The Grasses most valuable for hay are Timothy and Redtop, while the Kentucky Blue Grass, Bermuda Grass, Brome Grass, Meadow Fescue, and Rye Grass are some of the Grasses useful for pasture.

A large number of the Grasses are weeds, of which the Sand Bur, Foxtails, Chess, Wild Oats, Quack Grass, and Darnel are some of the worst ones. In the Southern states Johnson Grass, although useful for hay and pasture, is regarded as a weed

FIG. 451. — A group of Date Palms.

because it spreads so rapidly by rootstocks to regions where it is not wanted and is so hard to eradicate. Quack Grass, which spreads by rootstocks, is a bad weed in some of the Northern states. The Wild Oats is troublesome in grain fields, and grain containing the seeds of Wild Oats in considerable quantities is usually docked. The seeds of Darnel are poisonous and, when ground with Wheat, make the flour unwholesome, for which reason Darnel is a bad weed.

Palm Family (*Palmaceae*). — This is about the only family of Monocotyledons that contains trees. Nearly all of the family are tropical or subtropical, but they are quite extensively grown in greenhouses everywhere.   The flowers have three sepals, three petals, three to six stamens, and a pistil commonly of three united carpels.   The flowers are borne on a spadix and enclosed in a spathe.   The fruit is sometimes a berry, as in the Date, or nut-like, as in the Coconut.   A number of the palms are valuable plants in the region where they grow. The Date Palm (*Fig. 451*) yields the dates of the market. The Coconut Palm yields the Coconuts of the market and is probably one of the most useful Palms to the natives, furnishing food, clothing, utensils of all kinds, building materials, etc.   The Sago Palms yield Sago, which is prepared by washing

FIG. 452. — A portion of a Lily in flower and also a single flower, showing the perianth consisting of six similar parts.   After Lecomte.

out the starch from the stems.   A tree 15 years old will sometimes yield 800 lbs. of starch.   The Oil Palm of West Africa yields a fruit from which palm oil is obtained.

Lily Family (*Liliaceae*). — The Lilies have a perianth of six parts and six stamens (*Fig. 452*).   The pistil usually consists of three united carpels.   Their flowers are often showy, and many of them, as the true Lilies, Hyacinths, Star of Bethlehem, Tulip, Day Lily, and Lily of the Valley, are ornamental plants.   The Onion and Asparagus are common articles of food.   Some, as the Aloe, Smilax, Colchicum, and Veratrum, yield valuable medicines.

FIG.   453. — A   Century Plant, one of the Agaves, showing the thick leaves and shape of the plant ($\times \frac{1}{12}$).

One, called New Zealand Flax, is a valuable fiber plant.   In another family closely related to the Lily family are the Agaves, of which the Century Plant (*Fig. 453*) is a familiar

one in our region. The Agaves are very important plants in
Mexico where the natives obtain from them pulque, a fermented
drink, mescal, a distilled drink resembling rum, and various
fibers as sisal hemp and henequen.

In connection with families noted for fibers and not previously referred to, there is the Linden family of the Dicotyledons from which Jute is obtained and the
Banana-like plant of the Banana family
from the leaf stalks of which Manila hemp
is obtained.

Orchid Family (*Orchidaceae*). — This
family includes the most highly developed
Monocotyledons, and if the Monocotyledons are higher than the Dicotyledons,
then the plants of this family are the most
highly developed of the plant kingdom.
In the Orchids the flowers are highly
specialized, often very showy, and present
interesting mechanisms to secure cross-
pollination. The family includes numerous species and nearly one-fourth of the
Monocotyledons. The most highly specialized ones are tropical and occur only
in greenhouses in the temperate regions.

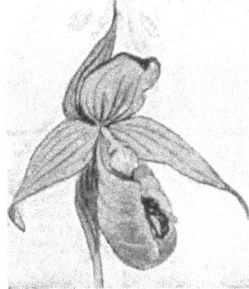

Fig. 454. — A flower of
an Orchid (*Cypripedium*),
showing the irregularity
among the parts of the
perianth, and an insect
entering the pouch-like
structure of the corolla.
After Gibson.

The flowers are epigynous and show extreme irregularity
(*Fig. 454*). One of the petals called the lip varies much in shape
and is usually very different from the other petals. The one
or two stamens join with the style of the pistil to form the column.
In most cases the pollen sticks together, forming masses called
pollinia, and it is in these masses that the pollen is carried from
one flower to another by insects.

CHAPTER XXI

ECOLOGICAL CLASSIFICATION OF PLANTS

Nature of Ecology

It is common observation that certain kinds of plants live only in certain places. Thus regions distinct in type, such as ponds, bogs, shady ravines, dry hillsides, etc., have distinct types of vegetation. The plants in ponds and bogs are adjusted to much water, in shady ravines to shade and moist air, and on dry exposed hillsides the plants are adjusted to hot sunshine and dry soil. Certain kinds of plants are therefore adjusted to a certain environment which is known as their habitat. In order to thrive, a plant must be able to compete with other plants and endure the hardships which the environment imposes upon it. It must be adjusted to the range of temperature, amount of light and moisture, conditions of the soil, surrounding plants and animals, etc. Plant Ecology is the science which treats of the adjustments and distribution of plants in relation to the various environmental factors. Throughout the preceding chapters Ecology has been touched upon repeatedly, for the adjustment of leaves and stems to light, the storage of food in tubers and seeds for the next generation, the adjustments of flowers to various kinds of pollination, the parasitic and saprophytic habits, the adjustments for living in the water or air, etc., really belong to Ecology. In the classification of plants phylogenetically, which is emphasized in the previous chapters of Part II, the basis of classification is kinship, but in classifying plants ecologically the basis is adjustment to environment, and plants varying widely in their phylogenetic relationships occur together in the same ecological class. For example, Thallophytes, Bryophytes, Pteridophytes, and Spermatophytes occur together in some ecological classes of water plants.

Many of the problems of Agriculture have to do with the securing of strains or varieties of crop plants better adjusted

to a particular environment. We are constantly striving to
find the Apples, Pears, and other fruits best adjusted to the
environmental factors of different regions. One of the objects
in the breeding of Citrous fruits has been to procure varieties
less sensitive to cold, so that Citrous fruits can be grown farther
north and consequently over a larger area. Much time and
energy has been spent in obtaining strains of Cotton resistant
to the insect pests and other unfavorable environmental factors
of the Southern states. In the Northern states, where the
growing season is short, one of the problems in connection with
the raising of Corn is to secure varieties that can mature before
frost. The securing of drought resistant plants for dry regions,
of plants resistant to the diseases prevalent in the different
agricultural regions, of pasture Grasses best adapted to a given
region, of trees adapted to grow in a given region for shade or on
a given area that is to be reforested are some of the many other
agricultural problems that have to do with adjustment of plants
to their environment and hence are ecological.

Ecological Factors

The various environmental features to which plants and animals must adjust themselves are called ecological factors. The
chief ecological factors are water, heat, light, soil, wind, and
associated plants or animals.

Water. — This is one of the most important ecological factors.
The amount of water to which various plants are adjusted varies
from complete submergence to perpetual drought. Most Algae
live completely submerged in water, while Cacti are adjusted
to the drought of deserts. Most crop plants require a medium
amount of water in the soil, and an excess or lack of water retards their growth. But among crop plants there is also much
variation in the amount of water necessary for living. For
example, the Sorghums are more resistant to drought than
Corn, while some varieties of Rice require flooding.

Warmth. — All kinds of plants are adjusted to certain ranges
of temperature. For example, Wheat and Oats require less
warmth than Corn, and hence can be grown farther north.
There are great zones of plants corresponding to the great
zones of temperature. Thus the arctic, temperate, and tropi-

cal zones are distinguished by their kinds of plants as well as by their difference in temperature. When the temperature is extremely low, as in the polar ice regions, or extremely hot, as in some deserts, very few or no plants at all are able to live. Even on the same area, as in a woods or a field, if the plants are not disturbed, one can observe the effect of the heat factor in the succession of plants through the growing season, the spring plants being very different from the summer and autumn plants. To secure crop plants adapted to the temperatures of the different agricultural regions is also one of the problems of Agriculture.

Light. — Not all plants in an association can receive the same amount of light, and some plants are so adjusted that they can live in the shade. They are known as shade plants, and the Ferns, common in the woods, are examples of such plants. But even in an association of herbaceous plants, as in a field of weeds, many small plants grow among and in the shade of the taller ones. Some plants, like the Pumpkins and Melons which grow well along with Corn, have a very large leaf surface which may compensate for the lack of light. Plants climb other plants or walls, grow tall erect stems, and adjust themselves to neighboring plants in various other ways in order to obtain sufficient light.

Soil. — The soil in regard to its chemical and physical properties determines largely the kinds of plants that can grow in a given region. Thus the plants on a sandy beach or sand dune differ from those on a clay or loam soil. The chemical elements of a soil and its power to retain water both have a determining effect upon the growth of plants. Some plants, like Alfalfa and some of the Clovers, are more sensitive than the grains to acids in the soil. Some weeds, like the Sheep Sorrel, grow best in an acid soil. Some plants require more potash, nitrates, or some other element than other plants. Even water plants are somewhat dependent upon the soil, for the minerals in a pond or lake are carried in from the soil. One of the chief problems of Agriculture consists in putting the soil in a suitable condition for plants and in choosing plants adapted to the different types of soil.

Wind. — The wind tends to dry out plants by increasing their transpiration, while at the same time it is an important agent in pollination and dissemination of fruits and seeds. In regions where there are strong prevailing winds only such plants as are adapted to regulate transpiration can grow. Most of our early flowering plants, as the Pines, Oaks, Beeches, and Poplars, are pollinated by the wind, and some of our crop plants, as Corn illustrates, depend largely upon the wind for pollination. For the wide dissemination of the fruits and seeds of many of the common weeds and of some cultivated plants, and also for the spreading of some fungous diseases the wind is responsible.

Associated Plants and Animals. — A plant must compete with surrounding plants and often with animals for existence. It is common observation that most crop plants will not do well under the shade of trees. The trees cut off the light and make the soil too dry for the crop plants. On the other hand, there are plants which require shade and hence grow best in the woods. In some cases plants are benefited while in other cases they are injured through the association of their roots with the roots of other kinds of plants. For example, when Corn and Clover are grown together, experiments indicate that Corn does better than when it is grown alone. One experimenter grew Oats, Barley, Buckwheat, Wheat, and Flax in pots with and without the underground shoots of Canada Thistle and found all except Buckwheat to grow better with the Canada Thistle than alone. He repeated the experiment, using a young Elm tree instead of the Canada Thistle, and found that all grew more poorly with the Elm tree than alone. In Jutland it is found that Spruce trees grow well on waste areas if their roots can associate with those of the Mountain Pine. If there are no Mountain Pines present, the Spruces will not grow. If the Pines are present but are cut before the Spruces get well started, the Spruces die or make a poor growth. No doubt much injury to crops caused by weeds is due to the antagonistic effects of their root systems. The association of certain kinds of nitrogen-fixing Bacteria with the roots of legumes and of parasitic plants with their hosts are familiar examples of a very intimate relation of the life processes of one plant with those of another. In competing for light, as previously pointed out, plants must adjust themselves to each other in various ways. Climbing plants, in securing a better position in reference to light for themselves, frequently injure the plant which they climb. For example, Morning

Glories and Bindweeds cut off the light and break plants down, and Grape vines often injure the trees over which they spread.

In a number of ways plants are adjusted to animals. The presence of thorns, stinging hairs, and bitter juices may protect plants against destruction by animals. Insect pollination is a notable example of the dependence of plants upon animals. The flowers of some plants are so adjusted that they require insects and often certain species of insects to pollinate them. Thus bees are required to cross-pollinate Red Clover, and Sweet Clover and Alfalfa, although they do not require cross-pollination, require insects which can trip their flowers, so that the pollen can get on the stigma. It is also recognized that bees are essential to good pollination in orchards. Orchids and Yuccas are two of the most notable examples of plants which have flowers so constructed that only certain types of insects can pollinate them. In such cases it is obvious that propagation by seeds depends upon the presence of the insects which are required to pollinate the flowers. For securing the dissemination of their seeds, plants are adjusted to animals in a number of ways, but chiefly by developing hooked or spiny fruits or seeds which cling to the coats of animals.

The above factors with minor ones largely determine the modifications and distribution of plants. These factors work together and not singly, and the combinations of factors are numerous. According to their adjustment to the ecological factors, plants fall into groups or classes known as societies. Thus all plants adjusted to a water habitat belong to a hydrophytic society and are called Hydrophytes, while those adjusted to a drought habitat belong to a xerophytic society and are known as Xerophytes.

Ecological Societies

Since the ecological factors and their combinations vary widely, there are many different habitats and hence many ecological societies. With reference to the water factor plants are grouped into Hydrophytic, Mesophytic, and Xerophytic societies.

Hydrophytic Societies. — These are the societies of water plants called Hydrophytes and include plants which live submerged, standing in the water, or floating on the surface of the water. As previously stated, they include plants from various phylogenetic groups. Many are Thallophytes, as the Algae illustrate, while some, like the Pond Lilies, Duckweeds, Pondweeds, Eelgrass, and others, are Angiosperms. Not only representatives of the lowest and highest divisions of the Plant Kingdom, but also some Bryophytes and Pteridophytes are included in these societies.

The hydrophytes are adapted in various ways to living in the water. In the Algae the unicellular and filamentous bodies with all cells thin-walled afford the maximum amount of surface for absorbing gases and minerals from the water and for absorbing the light that reaches them. The more massive Algae are commonly so anchored that they are aërated through wave action, and many are provided with floats or air chambers whereby they float near the surface where there are more gases and light than at greater depths. The more complex Hydrophytes, such as the Seed Plants, that live chiefly submerged in the water have a thin-walled epidermis, so that all parts of the plant can absorb, and water-conducting tissues are feebly developed. Since they depend upon the buoyant power of the water for support, the root system is commonly reduced or even wanting, and their mechanical tissues are not so well developed as those of Seed Plants that live on land. Usually such plants collapse when taken out of the water. Some, like the Pond Lilies, raise their leaves to the surface of the water where they receive good light, while others, as the Pondweeds and Eelgrass illustrate, are wholly submerged and are able to get along with the little light that reaches them. The submerged forms even bear their flowers under water. Among the Hydrophytic societies there are the free-swimming, pondweed, and swamp societies.

The *free-swimming societies* are made up of such plants as the Diatoms, Algae, Duckweeds, and other plants which float in stagnant or slow-moving water.

In the *pondweed societies* the plants are anchored, but their bodies are submerged or floating (*Fig. 455*). To this society belong the Water Lilies, Pondweeds, Water Ferns, Marine Algae, some fresh-water Algae, and some species of Mosses.

Swamp societies consist of water plants which have leaf-bearing stems reaching above the surface of the water. Some typical plants of swamp societies are the Sagittarias, Bulrushes, Cat-tails, Rushes, Sedges, and Reedgrasses, which form fringes around ponds and lakes (*Figs. 456* and *457*). Some trees, such as Willows, Poplars, Birches, and Alders, are common in swamp societies. In a swamp of the bog type, Sphagnum Moss, Orchids, and some trees, such as the Tamarack, Pine, and Hemlock, are characteristic plants.

Aside from Rice, which is a Hydrophyte during a part of its

Fig. 455. — A pond in which are growing Water Lilies, plants typical of a Pond-weed society. After C. M. King.

development, the hydrophytic societies are not noted for plants important economically.

Mesophytic Societies. — The mesophytic societies comprise the common vegetation. They require a medium amount of moisture and a fertile soil. To these societies belong our cultivated plants, weeds, and deciduous forests. The mesophytic condition is the arable condition and is the normal or optimum condition for plants. If a hydrophytic area is to be cultivated, it must be drained and made mesophytic.

FIG. 456. — A swamp society consisting chiefly of Sagittarias and Sedges.
After C. M. King.

FIG. 457. — A swamp society in which Cat-tails are dominant.
After C. M. King.

Mesophytes, in contrast to Hydrophytes, are exposed much more to the drying effect of the air and consequently are better protected against transpiration.   They need better root systems for absorption and anchorage and also have better developed conductive and mechanical tissues.   There are many types of mesophytic societies.

Meadows and *prairies* are mesophytic societies in which trees are absent, and the dominant plants are, therefore, grasses and other herbaceous plants (*Fig. 458*).   The most important of

Fig. 458. — A prairie, a mesophytic society in which trees are absent.

the woody mesophytic societies are the *deciduous forests* composed of Maples, Beeches, Oaks, Tulips, Elms, Walnuts, and other valuable trees (*Fig. 459*).   In such forests grow also characteristic societies of herbaceous plants.   The *thicket*, composed of small woody plants, such as Willows, Birches, Alders, Hazel bushes, etc., is another woody mesophytic society.   The most remarkable of the mesophytic societies are the *rainy tropical forests*, where, due to a heavy rainfall and great heat, vegetation reaches its climax, and gigantic jungles are developed, composed of trees of various heights, shrubs of all sizes, tall and low herbs, all bound together in a great tangle by vines and covered by numerous epiphytes.

FIG. 459. — A deciduous forest, a mesophytic society consisting of Basswood, Birches, Elms, Maples, and Oaks, under which grow many herbaceous plants. After C. M. King.

Xerophytic Societies. — These are the societies adapted to drought. Among xerophytic plants there are various adaptations to drought, such as sunken stomata, hairy epidermis, reduction of leaf surface, deep tap-roots, reservoirs within the leaves or other parts of the plant for holding water, edgewise position or rolling of leaves, bridging over the period of drought in the form of seeds or subterranean structures, etc.

Among the xerophytic societies are the *rock societies*, composed chiefly of Lichens (*Fig. 460*) and Mosses which grow on dry and exposed rocks; *desert* and *dry plain* societies (*Fig. 461*) where such plants as Cacti, Sage Brush, Agaves, and Yuccas dominate; *xerophytic thickets*, composed of a dense mass of bushes and represented by the *chaparral* of the Southwest; and the *xerophytic forests*, in which Pines, Spruces, and Firs, adapted to mountain slopes and gravel ridges, occur.

In Asia, Africa, and North America, there is much land that is xerophytic. Much of the Southwestern part of the United States is xerophytic. One of the important problems in Agriculture is to bring xerophytic areas into cultivation. This may be done by making these areas mesophytic through irrigation or by securing crop plants through selection or breeding that are drought resistant, that is, able to grow under xerophytic conditions.

FIG. 460. — A xerophytic society, consisting of Lichens growing on a bare rock. After Bailey.

Plant Succession

One society of plants commonly prepares the way for another. For example, the Lichens and Mosses, growing on bare rocks, disintegrate the rocks and form soil in which other plants can get a start (*Fig. 460*). Ponds and lakes are gradually filled up

FIG. 461 — A desert xerophytic society consisting chiefly of Sage Brush and Yuccas. After R. G. Kirby.

through the growth of pond societies until they are transformed into swamps, in which the Pond Lilies, Pondweeds, Eelgrass, and other representatives of pond societies are replaced by Rushes, Sedges, Sagittaraes, Cat-tails, Reeds, True Flags, and other representatives of swamp societies. Through the growth of the swamp societies, the swamp is finally so filled up that it is transformed into a mesophytic area, and the plants of the swamp societies are succeeded by Mesophytes (*Figs. 462* and *463*). It is obvious that the hydrophytic societies have been exceedingly important factors in transforming lakes, ponds, and old river beds into tillable land, and the fertile soil of such

FIG. 462. — A succession of plant societies, showing transition from hydrophytic to mesophytic societies. The successive societies are as follows: Pond Lily Society, Sedge Society at the margin of the pond and grading into a Swamp Grass Society further back, a shrub society still further back, and finally in the background a mesophytic forest society. From Coulter, photo. by Lewis.

areas is largely due to the humus added through the decay of the hydrophytic societies. On sand dunes, beaches, ground cleared and allowed to grow up again, and most everywhere one can observe plant succession. On sand dunes around the Great Lakes, for example, Poplars are succeeded by Pines, which are in turn succeeded by Oaks and other deciduous trees.

Studies of successions and societies give us very useful information as to what plants can be successfully grown on a given area.   There are instances, as in case of some of the wild lands of the West, where a study of the societies of wild plants has suggested the kind of crop plants best adapted to the conditions.   It is quite probable that more extended studies in Ecology in connection with soil analyses will reveal such a close

Fig. 463. — A lake which is being rapidly filled up by the accumulation of vegetable matter. Swamp societies consisting of clumps of Rushes, Sedges, and Sagittarias are most conspicuous about the water. Further back are swamp Grasses grading into mesophytic Grasses, and finally on the ridge, as shown by the corn field and trees, a typical mesophytic condition prevails. After C. M. King.

association of plant societies and the chemical and physical characteristics of soils that the chemical and physical differences of soils on different farms or in different parts of the same farm may be quite accurately judged by observing the societies of weeds and other wild plants.   In reforesting a given area it is very essential to take into consideration the plant societies adapted to the region.   For example, it would be unwise to plant Pines on bare sand dunes, or Maples where Black Oaks, which grow in much drier situations than Maples, prevail.

CHAPTER XXII

EVOLUTION

Meaning and Theories of Evolution

Meaning of Evolution. — Throughout the preceding discussion of plant groups evolution was assumed. It was assumed that the more complex forms of plants have come from the simpler ones by gradual changes which involved the modification of structures and the introduction of new structures. It was also assumed that some simpler plants are reduced forms of more complex plants. Hence evolution, which is usually forward, that is, leading to more advanced forms, may be backward, leading to simpler forms. According to the theory of evolution, the organisms which first inhabited the earth were extremely simple, and the various forms of plants and animals which we now have are their modified descendants.

The evidences of evolution in both plants and animals are obtained by studying the structure, development, and behavior of living forms, and the structure of ancient forms preserved as fossils. Evolution takes place too slowly to be observed or demonstrated, and hence our conclusions about it are only inferences.

There are two kinds of evolution — *organic* and *inorganic.* Organic evolution is confined to living things including animals as well as plants. However, inorganic things are also constantly changing, and hence evolution applies to all nature and not merely to living things. The physical features of the earth are constantly changing. Mountains are being worn down, while there are other regions where the land is becoming more elevated. Areas that are now land were seas or a part of the ocean at one time. A study of fossil plants shows that climates have changed, so that regions once tropical now have a temperate or arctic climate. Rivers and valleys are constantly changing and thus altering the landscape. Also the planets, like our own earth, and even the stars, are changing externally and internally.

Again, the phenomenon of radioactivity teaches us that the atoms composing one chemical substance are transformed into those of another, and thus chemical substances are built up by the process of evolution. There seems to be but one thing that is constant and that is constant change.

Evolution and the Doctrine of Special Creation. — The theory of evolution is directly opposed to the " Doctrine of Special Creation." The " Doctrine of Special Creation " is based upon a literal interpretation of the account of creation given in the Bible and, therefore, assumes that all things were created at the beginning of the world. According to the " Doctrine of Special Creation " plants, animals, mountains, oceans, planets, and stars were created in the beginning by the Creator and have remained constant in all fundamental features until the present time. This means that Angiosperms and all other groups of plants, however simple or complex, did not come from simpler forms, but were made in the beginning and, therefore, have been in existence practically ever since the world began. It is thus seen that the " Doctrine of Special Creation " is not at all in harmony with the theory of evolution, for the latter theory assumes that in the early history of the world there were only very simple organisms, and that from them through changes involving many millions of years the complex forms have been derived.

Although a few believed in evolution even as far back as the Greek philosophers, the " Doctrine of Special Creation " prevailed until comparatively a short time ago. During the last 150 years, the theory of evolution has gradually gained favor, and, since Charles Darwin's time, it has gained such supremacy that it is now a fundamental conception not only in botany and zoölogy but also in such subjects as history, philosophy, sociology, and theology.

Theories in Regard to Evolution. — The most difficult thing about evolution is its explanation. One can trace connections between the higher and lower forms, but to explain just in what way one form arose from another is not at all easy. Scientists are all convinced of the reality of evolution, but the forces or factors which bring about evolution are still under discussion.

Earliest Theories. — Perhaps the oldest explanation of evolution was that of Erasmus Darwin, Goethe of Germany, and a few others of their time. According to the explanation of these early scientists, plants and animals are changed by their environment, and these changes are then inherited by the offspring and retained as long as the environment remains constant. For example, according to this explanation, a plant, originally smooth but having been induced to become hairy through exposure to a drier climate, will impart the hairy feature to the offspring, which will maintain the modification until the environment so changes that hairiness is lost. In this way the origin of new characters and new species was explained. This assumes of course that a change in any part of the plant is recorded in the sperms and eggs of the plant and, therefore, transmitted to the progeny.

Lamarck's Explanation. — Lamarck, a noted French naturalist whose views were published first in 1801 and in an enlarged form in 1809, offered the explanation which he called " Appetency," meaning desire. His explanation was based upon the observation that the organs of men and other animals are enlarged and strengthened by use and particularly by conscious use. For example, it is common observation that one's muscles enlarge and become stronger with proper use, while, on the other hand, with lack of use they decrease in size and strength. Long continued disuse may even result in the loss of an organ.

There are three ideas involved in Lamarck's explanation. *First*, his explanation assumes that the environment of animals and plants has been constantly changing, so that they have been constantly subjected to changes in temperature, moisture, light, nutrition, etc. *Second*, he believed that all living things have come from preëxisting forms as a result of changes which were responses to changes in the environment that made a new mode of life necessary. Thus the neck of the giraffe lengthened as a result of the animal's effort to reach leaves on high branches. Also the form of the body of reptiles, such as snakes, which glide over the ground and conceal themselves in the Grass, is due to the mode of life which these animals have adopted. By repeated efforts of the animal to elongate in order to pass through small spaces, the body became extremely elongated and very narrow, and since long legs would raise the body too high from the ground and short legs would not move them rapidly enough, legs, vestiges of which are still in their plan of organization, were finally lost and another means of transportation was

evolved. Although Lamarck's explanation, as based upon the
use and disuse of organs, applies particularly to animals, he also
offered an explanation for evolution in plants.   In case of plants,
in which there is no conscious effort as in animals, he assumed
that changes in the environment affect the body of a plant
directly and induce modifications which may become sufficiently
pronounced to characterize a new species.   Since species are
the units of all other groupings of plants or animals, the origin
of new species results in the origin of new genera, new families,
new orders, and so on.   It is, therefore, obvious that accounting
for the origin of species accounts for the origin of all those
differences upon which the various groupings of organisms are
based.

Third, Lamarck believed that whatever changes a plant or
animal made in the form, structure, or function of its body
were inherited by the offspring.   To the succeeding generation
each generation transmits what it inherited and whatever additional modifications it may take on.   In this way modifications
which are only slight at first may become more pronounced in
succeeding generations, if the conditions remain constant, until
finally plants or animals so different from their ancestors as to
form new species may arise.   He did not claim that all individuals taking on new modifications survive but only those possessing changes that fit them most perfectly to their environment.

Lamarck's explanation is unsatisfactory in a number of ways.
In the first place both observations and experiments furnish
much evidence that the effects of use and disuse are seldom, if
at all, inheritable and hence have no permanency such as the
characters of species have.   If the effects of use and disuse are
not transmitted, the hypothesis that the effects of use and disuse may accumulate from generation to generation also lacks
support.   Also, in case of plants, more recent investigations show
that modifications that are direct responses to the environment
are not generally, if at all, inheritable.   In the second place his
explanation does not account for the desire of the animal to
change its habits, but simply assumes that animals change in
their desires, and that such changes are also transmitted.

Darwin's Explanation. — Although Charles Darwin (*Fig. 464*)
was neither the first to believe in evolution nor the first to

attempt to explain it, his arguments for evolution were much more convincing than those of his predecessors, and his explanation was so well based upon facts and so well organized that it was widely accepted. His book, the *Origin of Species*, published in 1859, in which he set forth his argument for evolution and its explanation, was based upon 20 years of careful observat:on, experiments, and thought, and is one of the greatest books ever published. To this book is largely due the acceptance of the doctrine of evolution as based upon natural selection, and modern biology is said to date from this book. The two fundamental conceptions of this book are: (1) that the process of creation is evolution; and (2) that the process of evolution is based upon natural selection.

Fig. 464. — Charles Darwin, the noted scientist, to whose work the establishment of the theory of evolution by natural selection is chiefly due.

Natural Selection. — According to Darwin's theory of natural selection, the individuals of the plant and animal world are involved in continuous competition in nature, and only those best adapted to their surroundings survive. Thus through the destruction of those individuals not able to survive in the struggle for existence, a selective process, which permits only certain individuals out of a large number to live and propagate, is thereby established. Darwin's theory of natural selection involves five fundamental conceptions, — *variation, inheritance, fitness for environment, struggle for existence,* and *survival of the fittest.*

Variation. — Variation is the fundamental fact in Darwin's theory of natural selection. By variations is meant the deviations of organisms from a type chosen as a standard of compari-

son.   Thus if one should select a certain height, a certain number of flowers per plant, etc., as typical of a given species and as
standards of comparison, deviations of individuals from these
standards are variations.   Darwin was a careful student of

FIG. 465. — Heads of Timothy selected from a field of Timothy to
show variation in form and size of heads.   After Clark.

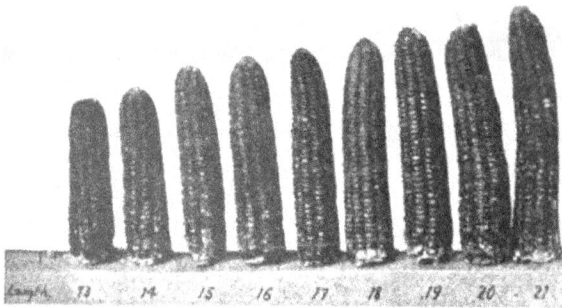

FIG. 466. — Variation in length of ears selected from a field of Black
Mexican Sweet Corn.   After East.

variations and observed that variations in structure and function are so common that no two individual organisms are exactly alike.   In a field of grain or in a group of any of the cultivated or wild plants no two individuals can be found that are
exactly alike (*Figs. 465* and *466*).   They differ in height, shape,

number of leaves or flowers, time of maturing, character of root system, etc. The individuals of a group of organisms not only differ from each other, but they also differ just as strikingly from their parents. Even the organs of the same plant, such as leaves, vary widely (*Fig. 467*). Many of the variations are conspicuous, while others are discovered only through close inspection. Some variations better adjust the individual to its

FIG. 467. — A number of Mulberry leaves selected from the same tree to show variation in form.

surroundings, others are detrimental, and some are neither useful nor detrimental. Darwin's idea was that variations, which are innumerable and various in kind, afford ample material upon which natural selection can work. Why plants and animals vary, Darwin did not attempt to explain.

Inheritance. — Although it is common observation that offspring and parents differ, it is also common observation that there are always some fundamental resemblances. Thus the offspring of a given variety of Corn are the same in variety as

the parent and not of another kind, although there may be much
difference in size of plants, length of ears, size and shape of kernels, etc. In spite of variations there is inheritance which is
an imparting of something by the parents to the offspring,
which as a result develop some of the parental features. Darwin also thought that not only the resemblances to parents, but
also whatever variations the offspring may have are inheritable.
Assuming that variations are transmitted to succeeding generations in which they may become more pronounced, he could
explain the origin of new characters and new species. If a
variation is such as to better adapt individuals to their environment, those individuals in which the variation is most
pronounced have a better opportunity to survive and propagate
in greater numbers than individuals in which the variation is
less pronounced. Thus through many successive generations in
which the individuals with the variation most pronounced are
more favored than other individuals, the variation is intensified
by natural selection and eventually becomes a character of a new
species. Darwin drew this conclusion from some of his experiments as well as from general observations of plants and animals
under domestication. He observed that through selection both
plants and animals changed much under domestication. Starting
with wild forms of plants, he was able by selecting the variants
from the progeny for a number of generations to obtain individuals differing strikingly from the original wild forms. He
found that continuous selection gradually built up the selected
character until the desired result was obtained. He concluded
that in nature such a selective process was brought about by
the competition among individuals for existence; but, while
any character might be built up by artificial selection, only those
which enable the individual to withstand competition are built
up in nature.

Fitness for Environment. — It is common observation that
different kinds of plants and animals require different conditions under which to live. As pointed out in the discussion of
Ecology, some plants and animals live submerged in the water,
but most plants and animals can live only on land. The Cacti
are so constructed that they can endure the drought of the
desert, but Corn, Wheat, and most plants require a medium
amount of moisture. Again some plants which are well pro-

tected by hairs, like the Mullein, can thrive in the open on dry hillsides, while there are other plants that can grow only in the shade or moist ravines. The polar bear is adjusted to live where the climate is cold, while the elephant is adjusted to a tropical climate. Colored people can live better than white people under the tropical sun because of the black pigment in their skin. There are countless ways in which plants and animals show adjustments to particular kinds of environment, and according to Darwin these adjustments are largely the results of natural selection.

Struggle for Existence. — That there is an immense struggle for existence in which vast numbers of both plants and animals perish is easily demonstrated. The number of seeds produced by a plant and the number of offspring that mature are commonly very different. For example, one plant of the Russian Thistle, one of the common weeds, produces from 20,000 to 200,000 seeds. Taking 25,000 seeds to a plant as a moderate estimate, the offspring of one plant would number 15,625,000,-000,000 in the third generation, if all the seeds grew. Allowing one square foot per plant, the plants of the third generation would cover more than 500,000 square miles. At this rate of multiplication, there would be no room in the United States for anything else in a few years. But the number of plants that develop is exceedingly small in comparison with the number of seeds produced. Many of the seeds are destroyed before they germinate, but many plants start that do not complete their development. Many are killed by insects, and many are crowded out by more vigorous individuals. On an area three feet long and two feet wide which had been dug and cleared so that the seedlings were not choked by other plants, Darwin found that out of a total of 357 seedlings no less than 295 were destroyed by slugs and insects. He also measured off a small area of turf which had long been mown and allowed the plants to grow. Out of the 20 species of plants growing on this small plot of turf nine species, some of which were fully grown, were crowded out by the more vigorous species and perished. The same process of elimination is going on among animals. Even in case of the elephant, which is a very slow breeder, Darwin showed that the progeny of a single pair would number 19,000,000 in less than 800 years, if all survived. But since the number of elephants in the world remains practically the same, many must perish for every one that survives.

Survival of the Fittest. — If only a few of the vast number of living things which come into the world survive, then the question as to what individuals survive arises. Darwin's answer is that the survivors are those individuals having those variations which adjust them most perfectly to their surroundings. Thus a vigorous growing plant will soon get out of the shade of its neighbors and will also get a larger proportion of the water and mineral substances of the soil. It will therefore succeed in crowding out the less vigorous plants around it. Also the plant that succeeds in developing the best protective structures against drought, heat, bright sunshine, or animals will have an advantage over the less fortunate ones, and will therefore survive while the others perish. The better adaptation may be in the production of more seeds, in better methods of disseminating the seeds, or in numerous other ways. Among animals the strongest, fleetest, most cunning, or best equipped for fighting are the fittest and survive to the expense of those not so well equipped for the struggle. To this process of natural selection Herbert Spencer applied the phrase " survival of the fittest." It is obvious, however, that this process in nature is more a rejection of the unfit than a selection of the fit, and it has been suggested that " natural rejection " would be a more appropriate phrase for the process than " natural selection." The rejection of the unfit makes room for the fit to live and perpetuate their variations through offspring.

Although the variations which are useful may be slight at first, through successive generations of selection Darwin assumed that they become more marked and finally new characters are established and thus new species formed. Of course there are many variations which are neither of advantage nor of disadvantage to the individual. According to Darwin only those variations that are of advantage or disadvantage to the individual are affected by natural selection.

Objections to Darwinism. — Darwin's theory aroused bitter antagonism among theologians because they thought it eliminated God from the plan of Creation. Darwin was even accused of teaching that man descended from monkeys. But Darwin's theory neither eliminates God nor does it teach that man descended from monkeys, and theologians gradually came to see that a plan in which the multitudinous forms are evolved is just as noble a conception of God as the " Doctrine of Special Creation."

The scientists offered a number of objections, some of which later investigations have answered. They said that, if evolution by natural selection is now in progress, one should be able to see one species forming from another, but such has never been observed. The absence of forms connecting two related species, and the presence of many apparently useless characters among both plants and animals they said were not accounted for. Again, according to geologists and astronomers, the world has not been in existence long enough for the present forms to be evolved by natural selection. The discovery of mutations enables us to answer the above objections as will be noted later.

A number of questions in regard to his theory remain to be answered satisfactorily and are receiving much attention at the present time.

First, as was stated under Lamarck's explanation of evolution, there is much evidence that acquired characters, that is, characters which an individual does not get from its parents but takes on during its lifetime, are seldom if at all inherited. This strikes at Darwin's assumption that useful variations are finally established as characters through inheritance and selection.

Second, it is claimed that by the selection of slight variations new species cannot be formed. The individuals of a species can be changed, but they can never be changed so much as to form a new species. In support of this objection, it is claimed that through centuries of artificial selection, plant and animal breeders have not been able to produce new species.

Third, although the theory assumes that variations are selected because of their advantage to the individual, it also assumes that useful variations may be built up through the selection of variations which are so slight at first that they give the individuals having them no advantage over individuals lacking them. Also the causes of variations Darwin left to his successors to explain, and variations are still a subject of much investigation and discussion.

Experimental Evolution

The early students of science studied plants and animals simply by observing them in the field. They made no effort to control the conditions under which the plants or animals were growing. But one can see that, in order to draw definite conclusions in regard to the inheritable factors in plants, the ancestry of the plants must be known, their pollination controlled so as to know definitely the parents of the progeny, and the various factors that affect the growth of the plants must be taken into account. Likewise, in the study of animals in reference to problems of evolution it is essential to control their breeding and often the conditions to which they are exposed. The early scientists had poorly equipped laboratories or none at all, and science then was chiefly a description of nature and was called "Natural History." Darwin and a few of his contemporaries put considerable emphasis on the experimental method, but since Darwin's time the experimental method has been especially emphasized with the result that rapid strides have been made in interpreting and explaining facts.

FIG. 468. — Hugo De Vries, whose mutation theory is one of the most important contributions to the study of evolution since Darwin's time. He has also made valuable contributions to our knowledge of osmosis.

Hugo De Vries. — Hugo De Vries (*Fig. 468*), director of the Botanic Garden in Amsterdam, Holland, was among the first to apply the experimental method to the study of evolution. Starting with seed selected from plants which he thought were pure, that is, not mixed with another variety, he grew a large number of generations, which, by carefully preventing cross-pollination, were kept pure to the parent type. In order to make accurate comparisons and thereby detect variations from the parents, such as the dropping of parental characters or the taking on of new ones, he not only kept careful records but also preserved specimens of each generation. At the same time he also carefully observed plants in the field, and, when one was found that showed extraordinary features, the experimental method was applied to it. He was especially interested in variations, and his most notable contribution is on this subject. He demonstrated by his painstaking work that there are two kinds of variations — *continuous* or *fluctuating* and *discontinuous* or *saltative* variations. Discontinuous variations are also called *mutations* and are those extreme variations which suddenly arise and remain fixed, that is, they are transmitted to succeeding generations.

Nature of Continuous Variation. — Continuous variations are the most common kind of variations. They are simply the fluctuations that individuals show in size, shape, color, and other characters. Thus red flowers vary in degree of redness, leaves vary in shape and size, seeds vary in number per pod as well as in shape and size, plants differ in height, shape, method of branching, and so on. Continuous variations are chiefly due . to differences in the environment, such as differences in sunlight, food and water supply, temperature, and influences exerted by one organism upon another. According to the work of De Vries and other investigators, they are not inheritable and, therefore, are constantly changing with the conditions that cause them. They fluctuate around a mean or average which remains practically constant, and, above or below this average, the individuals varying gradually grow less in number as variability departs more and more from the average until a limit in each direction is reached. Continuous variations follow the law of Quetelet, the Belgian anthropologist, who found that variability follows the law of probability. Small divergences from the average are numerous, while larger ones are less numerous, and the larger the less numerous they are. If, for example, a bushel or any quantity of ears of Corn are separated into piles according to length, there will be one length which will include the greatest number and, above or below this length, which is known as the average, the piles will decrease in size as the length of ears in each pile are greater or less than the average. This is well illustrated in *Figure 469* in which 82 ears of Corn with extreme lengths 4.5 and 9 inches are arranged in 10 piles according to size. The same fact is illustrated in *Figure*

470, in which case beans are assorted according to size. Of course where size is the variation considered, the space occupied by each class of individuals will vary more than the number of individuals in each class, for the smaller individuals occupy less

FIG. 469. — Quetelet's law of continuous or fluctuating variability, demonstrated by arranging 82 ears of Corn in piles according to size. The ears were taken from unselected material from a field of Corn. The length and number of ears in each pile are given in figures below. Notice that the piles decrease each way from the pile (highest pile) containing the ears of average length, decreasing accordingly as the length of ears in each pile is greater or less than the average length. After Blakeslee.

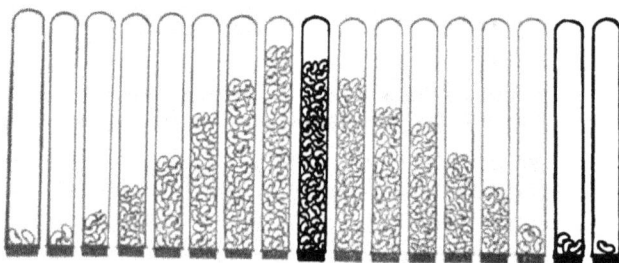

FIG. 470. — A demonstration of Quetelet's law of continuous variation in the size of the seeds of a Common Bean. The seeds are grouped with reference to length. The longest column contains those of average length and the columns to the right or left of it are shorter accordingly as the length of Beans in each column are greater or less than the average length. Redrawn from De Vries.

space than the larger ones. All kinds of continuous variations, such as number of flowers per plant, number of seeds per pod, weight of seeds, height of plant, size and shape of leaves, etc., distribute themselves around an average in the same general way as illustrated by size in case of Beans and ears of Corn.

When a number of generations of offspring are considered, the continuous variations in each generation tend to fluctuate around an average that is common for all the generations. Consequently the selection of continuous variations seldom improves the average, and, if any improvement is obtained in this way, it is soon lost when selection is discontinued. The average yield of sugar in Sugar Beets has been improved and is maintained by selecting for seed the plants having the highest sugar content, but the improvement is lost when selection is discontinued. Johannsen has demonstrated that, if one starts with a pure line, that is, with the offspring of a single individual produced by self-fertilization, and keeps the generations pure by preventing cross-pollination, the average of a fluctuating continuous variation cannot be increased. He clearly demonstrated this with Beans, which self-pollinate and hence remain pure. He attempted to increase the average size of the seeds by selecting the largest seeds of each generation of a certain variety of Beans for planting. He continued this for a number of generations, but obtained no increase in the average size of the seeds. Similar results have been obtained by other investigators in attempting to intensify certain desirable variations in Wheat, Oats, and in pure lines of other plants. For example, an effort to increase the yield in a strain of Oats by selecting each year the best yielding plants for seed gave practically no increase in yield after a number of years of selection.

Discontinuous Variations or Mutations. — That there are two kinds of variations was observed by Darwin and others before and after him, but De Vries was the first to show the importance of discontinuous variations in evolution. He formulated the theory that discontinuous variations and not continuous variations furnish the material for natural selection. Discontinuous variations differ from continuous variations in that they arise suddenly, are usually of marked character, and breed true, that is, they are passed on to the offspring. Discontinuous variations De Vries called *mutations*. A plant that gives rise to mutations is said to *mutate*, and a plant arising by mutation is called a *mutant*. De Vries's theory of evolution is known as the *mutation theory*, and its fundamental conception is that species are formed by the selection of mutations and not by the selection of continuous variations.

We now believe that our cultivated plants afford many examples of mutations. Strawberries without runners have suddenly arisen among plants with runners and have bred true from
seed.   The Beseler Oats, a beardless variety, originated from a few
plants found in a field of bearded Oats.   Also a number of choice
new varieties of Wheat started from one or a few plants which

FIG. 471. — The Wild Cabbage and some of the forms that are supposed to
be mutants of the Wild Cabbage. A, Wild Cabbage; B, Kohlrabi; C, Cauliflower; D, Cabbage; E, Welsh or Savoy Cabbage; F, Brussels Sprouts.
After Smalian.

suddenly appeared differing in characters from the other plants
of the field. The Cauliflower and Kohlrabi (*Fig. 471*) were
raised from isolated monstrosities of the wild Cabbage (*Brassica
oleracea*). Green Roses, green Dahlias, seedless Oranges, seedless Bananas, and varieties of the Boston Fern with finely divided
leaves are other examples of mutations. Sometimes a bud may
mutate, giving rise to a bud sport. In this way the Nectarine,
which has a fruit resembling that of the Peach but lacking

the fuzz of a peach, sometimes arises as a branch of the Peach tree.

Mutation in the Evening Primrose. — The Evening Primrose is especially noted because it has furnished much of the material upon which the mutation theory is founded. One of the difficulties in finding mutations is that any given species does not mutate all of the time but only at occasional periods. In 1886 De Vries began to search for species that were in the mutating period. The American Evening Primrose (*Oenothera Lamarckiana*) (*Fig. 472*), also known as Lamarck's Evening Primrose, proved to be the species for which he was searching. He found a large number of plants of this species growing in an abandoned potato field at Hilversum, near Amsterdam. Among them he found some unknown and very distinct forms which apparently had come from seeds of the normal American Evening Primrose. Seeds were secured from the normal plants, and cultures were begun in the Botanical Garden at the

FIG. 472. — Lamarck's Evening Primrose (*Oenothera Lamarckiana*), a mutating species. After De Vries.

University of Amsterdam. From the first sowing he obtained another new form. Through a series of pedigree cultures involving a number of generations, quite a number of distinct forms were obtained. Some of these distinctly new forms appeared repeatedly in the cultures, while others appeared only once, but they all bred true, thus producing offspring like themselves. These new forms did not arise gradually but appeared suddenly and were so distinct from the American Evening Primrose, their parent, as to be called new species.

The mutations involved various kinds of characters. One of the new forms, *Oenothera brevistylis*, had, among other distinctive characters, a much shorter style than the *Oenothera Lamarckiana*. Another new form, *Oenothera laevifolia*, had smooth leaves and much prettier foliage than the parent type, and its petals were not notched. One of the finest and rarest of the mutants was the *Oenothera gigas* (*Fig. 473*), which was stronger, bigger, and more heavily built than the parent. Others of the new forms differed from the parent in other characters.

As to what a new form is, can be determined only by breeding it and its parents in pedigree cultures. A new form may result from crossing between two parents with different characters and, therefore, be a hybrid. The new form may be due to the fact that the parent is a hybrid or descendant of a hybrid and consequently does not breed true, thus producing offspring different from the parent type. If the parents are pure, and the new form is not a hybrid, it must be a mutant or a fluctuating variant. If it breeds true, it is a mutant; otherwise, it is a fluctuating variant.

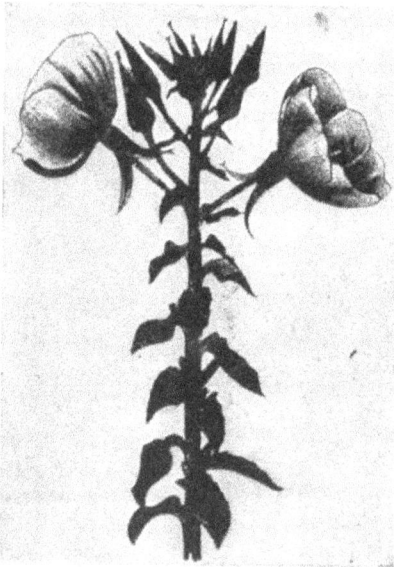

FIG. 473. — The Giant Evening Primrose (*Oenothera gigas*), one of the mutants from Lamarck's Evening Primrose. After De Vries.

By growing the parents of the new forms in pedigree cultures for a number of generations, he found that they bred true, except for the new forms which occasionally appeared, and concluded that the parents were pure. Since the parents of the new forms were carefully pollinated artificially, so as to prevent crossing between parents differing in characters, the new forms were not the result of hybridizing. They were either mutants or fluctuating variants and, when the test of breeding true was applied, they proved to be mutants. Thus De Vries had obtained mutations under experimental conditions and was ready to announce the mutation theory.

The Mutation Theory and Darwinism. — The mutation theory does not disturb the theory of evolution by natural selection, but holds a different view as to the material upon which natural selection works. According to Darwinism, most all kinds of variations are inheritable, and even though slight at first, they can become intensified through generations of selection and finally become distinct characters of new species. According to the mutation theory, only mutations are inheritable, and they are not built up through generations of selection, but arise suddenly, in full force, and breed true thereafter. Thus according to the mutation theory, new species arise at one bound, and all that natural selection has to do is to determine whether they survive or perish. If the mutation is such that the new species is well adapted to its surroundings, then, according to the law of the survival of the fittest, it will survive; otherwise, it will likely perish.

The mutation theory explains a number of the early objections to the theory of natural selection. It accounts for the fact that species have so many characters which are apparently of no value in fitting the individual to live. It is obvious that a species may have characters of no importance as well as useful ones, if new characters arise at a bound in full force, and their presence does not depend upon their having met the test of fitting the species to live through generations of selection. The mutation theory accounts for the absence of intermediate forms or so-called connecting links between species. Evolution by mutations requires less time than evolution by the natural selection of fluctuations, and in this way the theory answers the objection to the lack of time.

Causes of Variations. — There are various causes which have to do with bringing about variations in both plants and animals, many of which are not understood. Numerous variations are due directly to differences in food supply, climatic conditions, and other external factors to which the individual is exposed. Thus a plant well situated in reference to light, so that its leaves can make carbohydrates abundantly, is likely to be larger than a plant that is shaded. Likewise, the amount of soil moisture and mineral matter available, the amount of transpiration to which the plant is exposed, the temperature of the soil and atmosphere, and the velocity of winds, and the amount of competition with other plants are also common environmental factors that cause variations. Variations which are responses to variations in the environment are seldom, if at all, inheritable and hence are fluctuating variations. Fluctuating variations in individuals may be due also to fluctuating variations in parents. Thus, if a parent plant is poorly nourished, its seeds may be poorly developed and produce offspring that vary from the ordinary type in size and vigor.

Fluctuating variations also arise as a result of sex. Plants produced by vegetative propagation are often less vigorous than those grown from seed. The fusion of a sperm and an egg in fertilization often results in a rejuvenating effect which is manifested in a more vigorous offspring. The relationship of the sperm and egg involved in fertilization has an important bearing upon the variations in the offspring. For example, in Corn the offspring resulting from self-fertilization is not nearly so vigorous as offspring resulting from a fertilization in which the sperm and egg come from different parents, although the parents are the same in type. In addition to fluctuating variations and mutations, there are those numerous differences among individuals due to heredity, such as occur in the offspring when parents differing in variety or species are crossed. In connection with these differences due to heredity, some fluctuating variations, such as variations in size and vigor, commonly occur.

Mutations are apparently caused by changes within the individual, and, although environmental factors may have much to do with bringing them about, they are not direct responses to variations in the environment. Usually they involve the entire constitution of the individual, the gametes as well as vegetative structures, while fluctuating variations usually involve only vegetative structures.

Somatoplasm and Germ-plasm. — Weismann, a German biologist, and his followers hold the theory that a plant or animal consists of two kinds of protoplasms, which act more or less independently of each other. The protoplasm of which sperms and eggs are formed they call *germ-plasm*, while all protoplasm that does not have to do directly with forming sex cells is called *somatoplasm*. Thus the protoplasm of all vegetative structures of plants, such as leaves, roots, and stems, is somatoplasm. Even the parts of a flower, excepting the protoplasm immediately involved in the production of sex cells, is somatoplasm. According to Weismannism, the characters of a species are determined by certain units or factors within the germ-plasm and the germ-plasm remains practically the same from generation to generation in respect to the factors contained, although the factors may change in reference to each other. He holds that changes in the somatoplasm, such as those variations in leaves, roots, and stems that occur in response to environmental influences, are not imparted to the germ-plasm and consequently are not inheritable. This theory that the germ-plasm remains practically the same throughout generations is known as the continuity of the germ-plasm. Since modifications in the somatoplasm leave no trace of themselves in the germ-plasm, it is obvious that, according to Weismann's view, characters cannot be acquired. This means that any trait which an individual does not inherit but acquires during its life time in response to environment is not transmitted to the offspring. Thus, if a parent acquires great skill as a musician, mathematician, or in other lines, the children of this parent inherit none of this acquired ability. Also, in case of plants, the particular modifications which individuals take on during their life time disappear with the individuals.

In accounting for the inheritable changes occurring in individuals and generations, Weismann tells us that the units or factors in the germ-plasm are changing in relation to each other, and these changes account for the origin of new characters. Some units may become stronger and others weaker, and they may combine in various ways. Such changes may be induced by external conditions, such as poor nourishment, drought, competition, etc., but the character resulting therefrom may be of any kind, and hence only by chance is it of such a nature as to adjust the individual to its environment. For example, the changes induced in the units of germ-plasm by an environmental factor, such as drought, may result in a change in the color of the flower, length of style, arrangement of leaves, etc. Thus the character resulting from the change induced by the environment may show no adaptive connection whatever with the external influence inducing the change. Another cause of changes among the units in the germ-plasm Weismann attributes to interactions upon each other of different units brought together through fertilization.

According to Weismann's theory of the constitution of organisms, fluctuating variations are due to changes only in the somatoplasm, while mutations are due to shifts among the factors in the germ-plasm. Mutations arise as a result of changes within the individual, while fluctuating variations usually arise in response to influences external to the individual. Although the external influences causing fluctuating variations may at the same time so indirectly influence the germ-plasm as to cause mutations, the fluctuating variations themselves involve only the somatoplasm, and hence are not recorded in the germ-plasm. For example, a lack of moisture may cause such fluctuating variations as a reduction in size of leaves, fruit, and in number of flowers produced per plant, and at the same time induce such changes in the germ-plasm that a mutation in color of flowers, length of style, etc., may appear in the offspring, but the fluctuating variations disappear with the vegetative structures involved.

Weismann's theories have not been sufficiently demonstrated, and there are some objections to them. Although the evidence seems to be against the inheritance of acquired characters, this question is not yet settled.

CHAPTER XXIII

HEREDITY

General Features of Heredity

Nature of Heredity. — The constancy of species of plants and animals through successive generations depends upon the fact that the individuals of each generation are fundamentally like their parents. Thus the offspring of Sweet Corn have the characters of Sweet Corn, and the offspring of Flint Corn have the characters of Flint Corn. Even when parents differing in one or more fundamental characters are crossed, the characters of both parents will appear somewhere in future generations. The transmission from parent to offspring of similarities in structure and function is heredity. But heredity means more than the transmission of similarities. In the study of variations it was learned that no two individuals are alike, and hence offspring, although fundamentally similar and like their parents, always have individual differences. · Thus every plant or animal, besides resembling its parents, brothers, and sisters, has its own peculiar features which give it individuality. In a field of a given variety of Corn, although the plants have the characters of the parent variety, they differ in height of stalk, length and shape of ear, depth of kernel, time of maturing, and in many other ways. Most of these differences are fluctuating variations, while some may be due to something inherited. In the study of heredity not only the resemblances but also the differences must be accounted for. Heredity means the transmission of fundamental resemblances with differences in detail.

The Physical Basis of Heredity. — It is obvious that parents do not actually transmit characters to the offspring, but transmit something that causes the characters to appear in the offspring. For example, a red flowered Sweet Pea does not transmit a red color to the flowers of its offspring, but transmits something through the sperm and egg that causes a red color to appear in the flowers of its progeny. The exact nature of the factors or substances which are responsible for the appearance of characters is not well understood, but it is quite evident that they are protoplasmic substances. That they are protoplasmic substances is probably more easily demonstrated in the lower than in the higher organisms. In the reproduction of simple one-celled plants, like Pleurococcus, the plotoplasm of the parent divides, and each half of the parent becomes a new individual. The parent thus disappears in the formation of new individuals or progeny, which are at first merely segments of the parent. The new individuals, as they develop to normal size, develop in full the features characteristic of the parent. They separate soon after they are formed, develop a lobed chloroplast, enlarge and thicken their walls with cellulose, and retain a globular form. These are the constant characteristics by which we know Pleurococcus, despite the fact that there are numerous other ways the plant might develop. It might, for example, form a filament like that of Spirogyra, develop ribbon-like chloroplasts, and enclose itself in a woody wall. The characters of Pleurococcus are the results of the way the protoplasm works, for the protoplasm forms the chloroplasts, the cell walls, and is responsible for the separation and shape of the cells. It is obvious that the characters of this simple plant are what they are and are constant because the protoplasm has a disposition to work only in certain ways and retains this particular disposition as it passes from generation to generation.

In higher plants and animals the parent does not divide and each half go to form a new individual, but only a small part of the parent, a sperm and an egg, are transmitted to the offspring. Hence the sperm and egg must contain all of the protoplasmic constituents necessary for producing in the offspring the characters of the parents. But the sperm consists almost entirely of a nucleus, and hence it is believed that the material upon which the development of characters depends is within the nucleus, and occurs in connection with the chromatin, which, in the form of chromosomes, behaves in such a regular way during cell division as to suggest a definite relation to heredity. These protoplasmic constituents upon which the development of characters depends, Weismann called *determinants,* and some other biologists call them *genes.*

Active and Latent Genes. — Not all of the genes inherited manifest themselves, for many lie dormant and consequently cause no corresponding characters to develop. Sometimes they lie dormant for a generation or more and then become active. On this account offspring may have ancestral characters which the parents did not have. Certain genes for male characters are always latent in females. Thus a mother may transmit to her son genes for a beard like her father's, although she develops no beard herself. It is obvious that one cannot accurately judge the constitution of a plant or animal by the characters present, for judgment based upon external appearances takes no account of the latent genes. Further breeding is necessary to determine these. Latent genes becoming active is, therefore, one of the reasons why offspring differ from their parents.

Importance of the Study of Heredity. — The study of heredity occupies an important position among the sciences. The study of heredity has for its aim the discovery of the laws of heredity, and a knowledge of these laws is essential in many lines of work. The improvement of our crop plants and domestic animals through breeding depends upon the laws of heredity. The science of sociology and all sciences dealing with the physical, moral, and spiritual welfare of humanity are more or less concerned with the laws of heredity. Even in the realm of medicine the laws of heredity are taken into account.

Experimental Study of Heredity

Need of Experimental Study. — In the discussion of evolution it was shown that the application of the experimental method to the study of evolution has added much to our knowledge of this subject. We had no definite knowledge of the kinds of variations and their relation to natural selection until they were studied by the experimental method. In the study of heredity the experimental method is as essential as in the study of evolution. Heredity is so apparent in both plants and animals that we are all convinced of its reality. That children resemble their parents in habits, disposition, color of eyes and hair, and other features are so noticeable that they are matters of common observations. Casual observations, however, fall short of giving us a knowledge of the laws of heredity. The discovery of the laws of heredity requires carefully planned and systematic work. One must obtain a more or less accurate knowledge of the history of the parents, control the breeding so as to know the exact parents of the offspring, carefully study each individual of the offspring so as to discover the hereditary relationship between parents and offspring and between the different individuals of the offspring. One must also take into account the conditions which affect the plants or animals of the experiment. Carefully recorded facts obtained by experimental study involving a number of generations and various kinds of plants and animals afford a basis for conclusions concerning the laws of heredity. The experimental study of heredity as just described is known as *genetics*, a subject in its infancy but one of the most popular and most promising of the sciences.

Biometry. — Before the experimental method of studying heredity came into common use, the statistical method was employed. The investigators who study heredity by the statistical method of recording data are called biometricians. Instead of dealing with the variations of single individuals, they deal with the average variations of a mass of individuals or populations. It is a method of discovering how masses of individuals behave through a series of generations, and not a method of discovering how individuals behave. For example, they determine whether or not the average yield, average height, or average weight of a population is remaining constant or shifting, and such information is often valuable. By keeping a record of the average yield per acre of different strains of Wheat for a number of years, the strain yielding best can be determined. By such records one can also detemine whether or not newly introduced strains or varieties hold up in yield.

The biometricians formulated some laws of heredity. Francis Galton, who was one of the foremost of the biometricians, formulated a law of heredity and announced it in 1897. This law states that to the total heritage of the offspring the parents on an average contribute $\frac{1}{2}$, the grandparents $\frac{1}{4}$, and the great grandparents $\frac{1}{8}$, and so on, the total heritage being taken as unity.

The objection to the method employed by the biometricians is that it does not pay enough attention to the variations of individuals. A mass of individuals, such as a field of Wheat or Corn grown from the purest market seed, is a mixture of individuals differing in heritage, and not much can be determined concerning the laws of heredity from such a mixture. The average means nothing unless the individuals measured or counted are alike in their heritage, and the only way to be sure that the individuals of a mass or population are homogeneous in constitution is to pedigree them, that is, grow them all from a common stock. The importance of pedigree cultures is well shown in Mendel's work.

Gregor Mendel. — Gregor Mendel (1822–1884) (*Fig. 474*), was an Austrian monk and abbott in the monastery of Brünn, where he conducted his experiments in the Cloister Garden. He loved plants and loved to experiment with them. Although he studied heredity only as a pastime, his laws of heredity and his experimental method of investigating them are two of the most important contributions ever made to biological science.

Mendel's success was due to the clearness with which he thought out the problem. He knew the works of other investigators of heredity, and attributed their failure to reach definite conclusions to a want of precise and continued analysis. To obtain

Fig. 474. — Gregor Mendel, whose theory of inheritance is the most important contribution ever made to our knowledge of heredity.

definite results he saw that it was necessary to start with pure material, to consider each character separately, and to keep the different generations distinctly separate. He also realized that the progeny of each individual must be recorded separately. Such ideas were new in Mendel's time, but he felt certain that experiments carried on in this systematic way would give regular results and lead to definite conclusions.

Mendel saw that most could be accomplished by crossing plants of different varieties or species and observing the be-

havior of the hybrid offspring in successive generations. His plan was to cross plants differing in one or a few outstanding characters, such as the color of flowers, height of plant, color and shape of seeds, etc., and determine the laws governing the appearance of these characters in the hybrid offspring.

Material Chosen. — Mendel used great care in the selection of the plants to be used in the experiment, for he realized that the success of any experiment depends upon the choice of the most suitable material. After careful consideration he chose the Edible or Garden Pea as the chief plant with which to work. The Garden Pea proved to be the most suitable plant because: (1) it matures in a short time; (2) varieties in cultivation are distinguished by striking characters recognizable without trouble; (3) the plants are self-fertilized, and hence plants chosen for parents would be pure, that is, they would have no hybrid blood in them, and the hybrids and their offspring would not be disturbed by crossing in the successive generations.

Mendel's Experiments. — Mendel investigated pairs of characters separately and in relation to each other, and extended his investigations to include many pairs of characters, in order to see if all appeared in the successive generations of offspring according to the same law. His method of procedure may be shown by describing his experiments with tall and dwarf Peas. A tall Pea, having a height of 6–7 feet was crossed with a dwarf Pea, having a height $\frac{3}{4}$ to $1\frac{1}{2}$ feet. By means of forceps or other instruments and before the flowers were open, the anthers were removed from the flowers of the plant selected as the mother plant, and pollen from the pollen parent was applied to the stigma. The hybrid seeds developed by the mother plant as a result of the crossing were carefully collected. These cross-bred seeds were planted and produced the first hybrid generation of plants, known as the F_1 generation in our modern terminology. The height of each individual of this generation was carefully noted, and each individual was compared with the parents in respect to tallness or dwarfness. The individuals of this generation were allowed to self-fertilize, and the seeds of each individual were collected and planted separately. From these seeds he grew the second generation or F_2 generation according to modern terminology. The individuals of the progeny of each of the F_1 plants were carefully compared with their parents and grandparents in respect to tallness and dwarfness and the facts carefully recorded. The individuals of the F_2 generation were allowed to self-fertilize, and from the seeds obtained the F_3 generation was grown, and the individuals in this generation were studied in the same careful way as those of the previous generations. Throughout a number of generations the behavior of tallness and dwarfness was carefully recorded. In this way he studied many pairs of characters such as: (1) shape of pod (whether simply inflated or deeply constricted between the seeds); (2) color of unripe pod (whether green or yellow); (3) distribution of flowers on the stem (whether distributed along the axis of the plant or bunched at the top); (4) color of cotyledons (whether yellow or green); (5) shape of seeds (whether round or wrinkled); and (6) color of seed coat (whether gray or brown, with or without violet spots, or white).

Mendel's Discoveries. — Mendel found that in most cases the different pairs of characters investigated behaved in the same way and appeared in a regular way in the successive generations. Furthermore, it made no difference as to which variety was used as the mother parent. In case of tallness and dwarfness, all the plants of the first or F_1 generation were tall. They were all like the tall parent. In the second or F_2 generation there were both tall and dwarf plants, but there were three times as many tall plants as dwarf ones, the talls and the dwarfs thus occurring in the ratio of 3 : 1. · The offspring of the dwarfs were all dwarfs in the third or F_3 generation and in all succeeding generations. The dwarfs, therefore, were pure for dwarfness, that is, they had no factors or genes for tallness in them. One out of every three tall plants also bred true and, therefore, proved to be pure for tallness, but two out of every three tall ones gave three times as many tall ones as dwarfs or a ratio of 3 : 1, thus being apparently the same in constitution as each of the individuals of the F_1 generation. They evidently contained factors or genes for both tallness and dwarfness. The dwarfs and one-third of the tall ones of the F_3 progeny bred true, while two-thirds of the tall ones again bred as in the previous generation, giving the ratio 3 : 1, and two-thirds of the tall ones being impure. This proved to be a constant way of behaving throughout generations. The character of the individuals of the different generations are shown in *Figure 475*. Thus by the further breed-

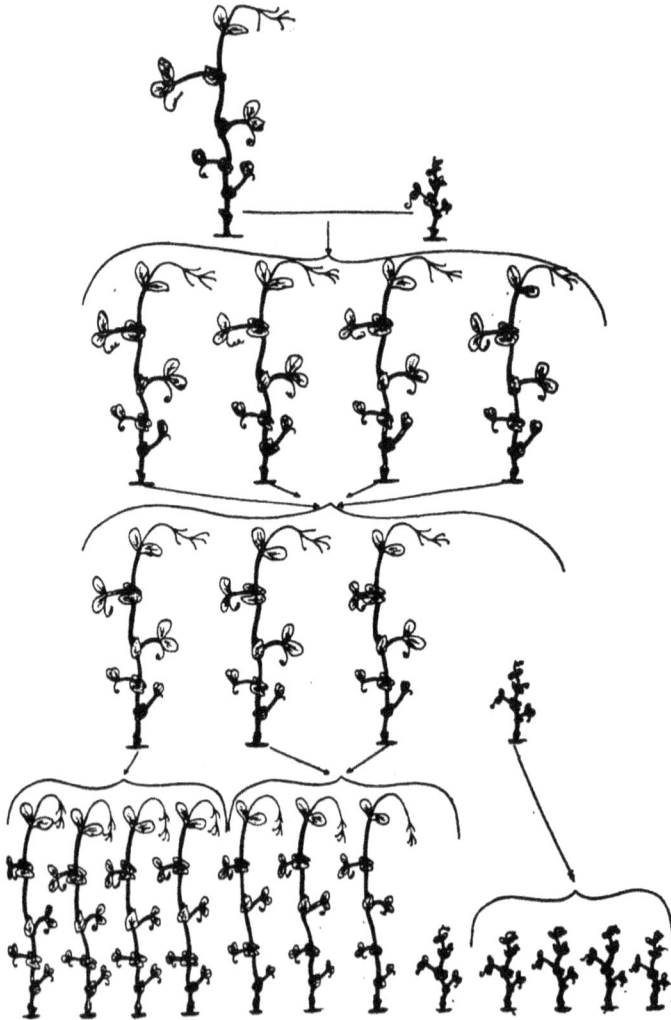

Fig. 475. — A diagram illustrating Mendel's discovery concerning the inheritance of tallness and dwarfness in the Garden Pea. At the top are the parents of the cross, the tall variety at the left and the dwarf variety at the right. In the line immediately below is the first (F_1) generation, all plants of which are tall and thus like the tall parent, and each of which upon being self-fertilized produced a progeny (F_2 generation) consisting of tall and dwarf plants in the ratio of 3 : 1, as shown in the third line. As shown in the lower line (F_3 generation), the dwarfs and one-third of talls of the F_2 generation bred true, that is, they produced progeny like themselves, while two-thirds of the tall ones produced a progeny consisting of tall and dwarf plants in the ratio of 3 : 1.

ing of the second hybrid generation, it was found that although the talls and dwarfs appeared in the ratio of 3 : 1, there were in reality three kinds of plants, pure talls, impure talls, and pure dwarfs, occurring in the ratio 1 : 2 : 1, and that the impure talls always produced three kinds of plants in the same ratio of 1 : 2 : 1.

Law of Dominance. — It is obvious that tallness dominated dwarfness in the hybrid Peas, and this accounts for the fact that all of the first generation were tall, although all of them had genes for dwarfness as well as for tallness in them. It also explains why the impure tall ones in succeeding generations were tall, although they had genes for dwarfness in them. In extending his investigations to other pairs of characters, Mendel found that smooth-

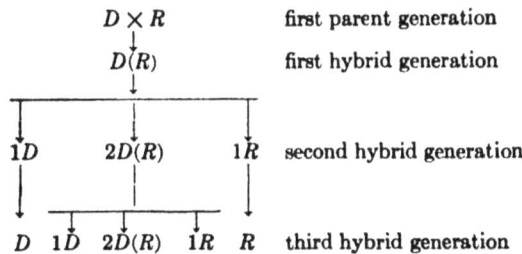

$$D \times R \qquad \text{first parent generation}$$
$$D(R) \qquad \text{first hybrid generation}$$

$$1D \qquad 2D(R) \qquad 1R \qquad \text{second hybrid generation}$$

$$D \quad 1D \quad 2D(R) \quad 1R \quad R \qquad \text{third hybrid generation}$$

Fig. 476. — Diagram illustrating the constitution of the individuals of the first, second, and third hybrid generation with reference to dominant (D) and recessive characters (R).

ness of seeds dominated wrinkledness, yellow color of cotyledons dominated green, and so on. Such pairs of contrasting characters are called *allelomorphs*, and the one dominating is known as the *dominant* and the other as the *recessive* character. Mendel's law of dominance may be stated as follows: When pairs of contrasting characters are combined in a cross, one character behaves as a dominant while the other behaves as a recessive. Representing the dominant character by D and the recessive by R, the behavior of dominant and recessive characters are as shown in the diagram in *Figure 476*.

Segregation and Purity of Gametes. — Since the pure tall and pure dwarf plants of the second generation and succeeding generations showed no tendency to produce anything but pure. tall or pure dwarf plants, they evidently had no genes or parts of genes for the contrasting characters. The genes for contrasting characters must have separated as units, and in the separation no straggling part of a gene was left associated with the gene for the contrasting character. To this complete separation of genes and consequently contrasting characters the term segregation was applied.

The complete segregation of characters also implies a purity of gametes. The constitution of an individual depends upon what the sperm and egg introduced into the fertilized egg from which the individual developed. Thus, if a plant is pure for tallness, the sperm and egg involved in the fertilization resulting in the production of this plant could not have contained genes for dwarfness. Of the two kinds of genes, they contained only those for tallness. The same is true in case of dwarfness or any other one of a pair of contrasting characters. This really means that in a fertilization resulting in the production of a plant pure for a character both the sperm and egg have genes for the same contrasting character, and that an individual pure in respect to a character, therefore, is one that has inherited from both parents genes for the same character. In other words, a plant pure for a character is one that receives a double dose of genes for this character. On the other hand, plants, like the impure tall ones, have received genes for the dominant character from one' parent and genes for the recessive character from the other parent, and hence they have only a single dose of genes for either of the characters. Such a plant we now speak of as being *heterozygous*, while plants having a double dose of genes and hence pure for a character are regarded as *homozygous*. Since plants pure for a character breed true, their gametes must be alike in respect to genes contained. The descendants of a homozygous parent propagated entirely by self-fertilization are of course pure and constitute what is known as a pure line.

After tracing the behavior of single pairs of characters through successive generations, he took up the study of two or more pairs of contrasting characters, the aim being to determine how pairs of contrasting characters behave in respect to each other. For example, he crossed Peas characterized by smooth yellow seeds with Peas characterized by wrinkled green seeds. In this case he was dealing with two pairs of characters, smooth and wrinkled, and yellow and green, with smooth and yellow as dominants. He found that each pair of contrasting characters behaved independently of each other, but all possible combinations of them could be obtained. The F_2 generation of seeds contained smooth and yellow, wrinkled and yellow, smooth and green, and wrinkled and green seeds, and each kind of seeds occurred in a definite proportion of about 9 smooth and yellow: 3 wrinkled and yellow: 3 smooth and green: 1 wrinkled and green. The wrinkled green seeds were pure recessives and bred true, and 1 out of 9 of the smooth yellow seeds was a pure dominant and thus bred true. All of the other seeds were not pure and various combinations again occurred in their offspring. The combinations and the number of individuals in each combination that occurred in the F_2 generation were in accord with mathematical laws governing combinations. Representing the dominants, smooth and yellow, by large S and large Y, and the recessives, wrinkled and green, by small w and small g, the combinations of S and w are $SS + 2\,Sw + ww$, and the combinations of Y and g are $YY + 2\,Yg + gg$. These combinations are simply the pure dominants, impure dominants, and recessives in the ratio of $1 : 2 : 1$ which occurs when a pair of contrasting characters is considered separately.   Now $(SS + 2\,Sw + ww)$ $(YY + 2\,Yg + gg) = SSYY + 2\,SYYw + YYww + 2\,YgSS + 4\,YSwg + 2\,Ygww + SSgg + 2\,ggSw + ggww$, which are the different combinations and the relative numbers of individuals in each combination obtained when two pairs of contrasting characters were considered in relation to each other.   Since the dominants obscure the recessives, the apparent combinations with the relative number of individuals in each are 9 dominants, 3 individuals with dominant yellow and recessive wrinkled, 3 individuals with dominant smooth and recessive green, and 1 individual with recessive wrinkled and green. The individuals having the constitution $YYSS$, as represented in above formula, are pure dominants, the individuals having the constitution $wwgg$ are pure recessive, while the others are not pure.   Thus the laws of mathematics afford a way of expressing what Mendel discovered concerning the behavior of characters in inheritance.

He crossed Peas having smooth yellow seeds and gray-brown seed coats with Peas having wrinkled green seeds with white seed coats, thus employing three pairs of contrasting characters. He found also in this case that the pairs of contrasting characters behaved independently of each other, and that the combinations in the F_2 generation were of many kinds. The combinations in this case also agreed quite well with the mathematical laws of combination, when a large number of the F_2 individuals were taken into account. The kinds of combinations and their proportions follow quite well the general algebraic formula $(a + b)^n$, in which n represents the number of characters involved. Thus $(a + b)^2$ expanded gives $a^2 + 2\,ab + b^2$ which is in accord with the $1 : 2 : 1$ ratio, the ratio expressing the inheritance of two contrasting characters. The formula $(a + b)^4$ gives the combinations when plants are crossed that have two pairs of contrasting characters. Of course the results obtained scarcely ever exactly agree with the mathematical formula, and the more individuals taken into account, the closer the agreement.

As a result of his work with a number of pairs of characters, Mendel showed that by means of repeated artificial fertilization, the constant characters of different varieties of plants may be obtained in all of the associations which are possible according to the mathematical laws of combination. This means that, by crossing in a certain way, the desirable characters of different varieties may be brought together, and thereby plants of a more desirable type produced.

Mendel's Law. — Mendel's discoveries and conclusions concerning the way parental characters appear in hybrids and their offspring constitute Mendel's law, and his discoveries may be summarized as follows: (1) characters are of two kinds, dominant and recessive; (2) characters do not blend but behave as units and separate completely from one another; (3) gametes are, therefore, pure, never containing genes for both of a pair of contrasting characters; (4) the offspring of a hybrid consist of dominants and recessives in the ratio of three dominants to one recessive, and the recessives and one-third of the dominants breed true, while two-thirds of the dominants breed as hybrids, producing offspring consisting of dominants and recessives and again in the ratio $3 : 1$; (5) when any number of pairs of characters are considered, each pair behaves independently, and all combinations of characters according to the mathematical laws of combination can be obtained.

After eight years of work, Mendel published an account of his remarkable discoveries, but unfortunately his publication remained unnoticed until 1900, thirty-five years after its publication and sixteen years after Mendel's death. In 1900 his paper was discovered simultaneously by three students of genetics, Correns, De Vries, and Tschermak, who recognized its importance. Since that time Mendel's law has formed the basis of all work in genetics.

The Value of Mendel's Discoveries. — Mendel's discoveries have completely revised our methods of investigating and ideas concerning heredity. *First,* Mendel's discoveries have impressed upon us the value of pedigree cultures in investigating problems of heredity. *Second,* they afford us laws concerning the appearance of characters in the offspring, whereby we know what to expect and can thereby interpret results which were previously a medley and not understandable. *Third,* knowing how characters behave in the offspring when plants or animals are crossed, we can start in our crossing work with definite results to be obtained in mind and also plan a definite method of procedure to obtain the desired results. *Fourth,* owing to the discovery of the segregation of characters, we now know that, in the second generation of hybrids, individuals that are perfectly pure occur in definite proportions and that purity of plants and animals in respect to a character does not depend upon a long series of selections as was formerly the notion. *Fifth,* the law of dominance explains why plants or animals impure in respect to a character may appear just as pure as pure individuals. *Sixth,* knowing that some characters are recessive and are entirely obscured by the contrasting dominant characters, we can now explain the appearance in the offspring of a character which did not appear in the parents or even for generations back, and in this way account for many of the variations in offspring, such as talented offspring of mediocre parents, blue-eyed children of brown-eyed parents, bad sons of pious preachers, rust-resistant plants of plants susceptible to rust, and so on. *Seventh,* Mendel's discovery that pairs of contrasting characters behave independently of each other but may be combined in various ways makes it possible for us to improve plants and animals by breeding them in such a way as to bring the desirable characters of different varieties together in one individual.

Investigations since Mendel. — Since the discovery of Mendel's paper, numerous investigators have been applying and

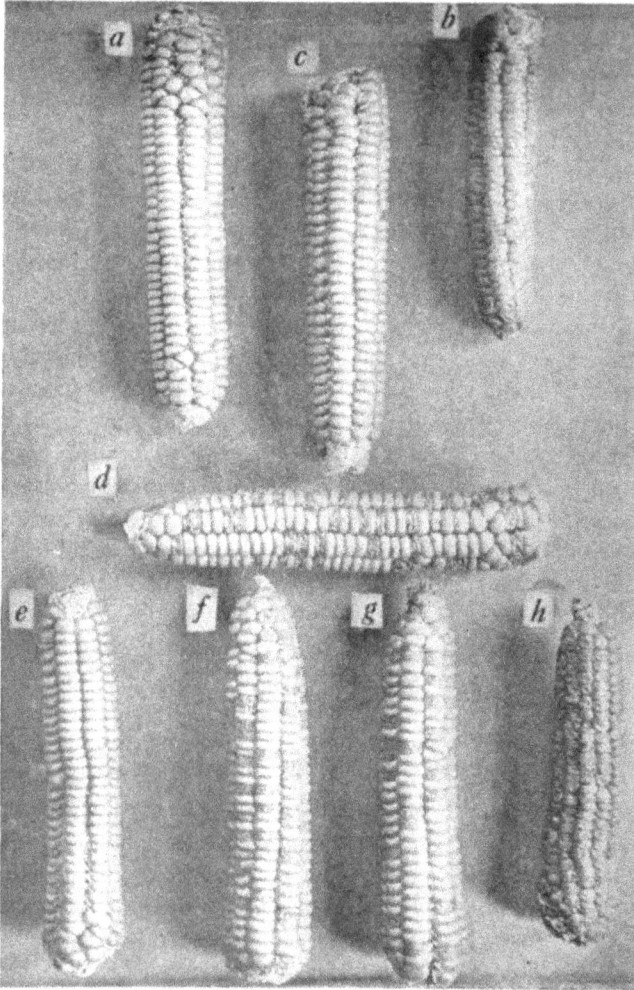

Fig. 477. — Mendelism demonstrated in the inheritance of starchy and non-starchy endosperm in Corn. In the top row, the ear *c* shows the immediate result obtained when the starchy parent (*a*) and non-starchy parent (*b*) are crossed. It is evident that starchness is completely dominant. *d*, an ear with F_2 kernels resulting from the cross, showing segregation of starchiness and non-starchiness. Lower row, ears of plants grown from kernels of *d*. *e*, *f*, and *g*, result from planting starchy seeds. One ear out of the three is pure starchy. *h*, result from planting non-starchy kernels, showing that the non-starchy kernels were pure for the recessive character. After East.

testing out Mendelism.   In both plants and animals numerous
pairs of characters have been found to behave in accordance
with Mendelism.   In plants alone more than 100 pairs of characters of various kinds have been found to behave according
to the Mendelian conception.   Among plants, color and shape of

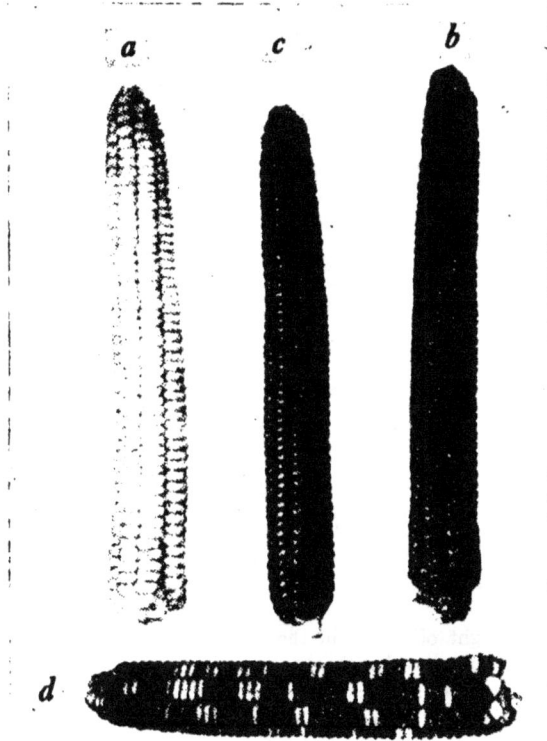

FIG. 478. — Mendelism demonstrated in the inheritance of color in the
endosperm of Corn.   c, ear bearing the F_1 kernels of the cross between a
(white endosperm) and b (yellow endosperm), showing dominance of yellow.
d, ear bearing F_2 kernels of the cross, showing segregation of color.   After East.

flowers; color, shape, size, and quality of fruit and seeds (*Figs.*
477 and *478*); time required to mature; resistance to disease,
drought, and cold; and many others have been found to follow
Mendel's law.   Among live stock Mendelism applies to numerous
characters, such as the presence or absence of horns in cattle, the
color of the hair in cattle and horses, the character of the comb

and feathers in chickens, etc. In man many characters, among which are insanity and susceptibility to tuberculosis, are known to behave according to Mendel's law, and Eugenics, which has to do with applying the laws of heredity in a way to produce a healthier and a more efficient race of men, has its chief support in Mendelism.

Mendel's discoveries have already enabled us to make some notable achievements in the way of improving plants and animals. By working according to the Mendelian conception, many desirable varieties of the cereals, much more desirable

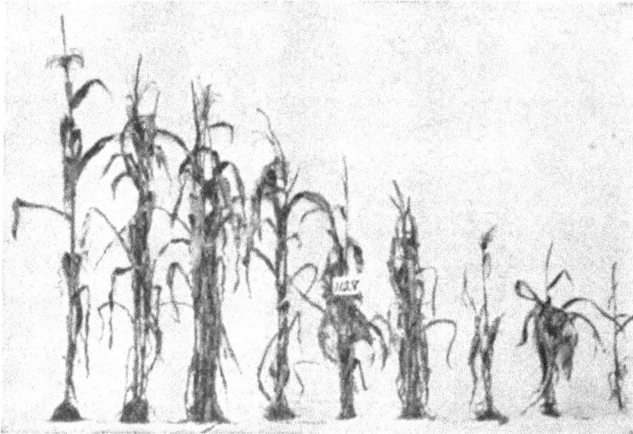

Fig. 479. — Height of plants in the F_2 generation of 'Tom Thumb Pop Corn (a dwarf Corn) crossed with Missouri Dent (a large Corn). The plant at the extreme right is similar in height to the dwarf parent, while the one at the extreme left is similar in height to the Missouri Dent. After Emerson and East.

ornamental plants, and various kinds of better fruits have been developed.

Of course in the extended investigations in Genetics since 1900, many situations have arisen that Mendel did not meet Cases have arisen in which the Mendelian behavior can be explained better by assuming that pairs of contrasting characters are due to the presence and absence of certain factors and not to dominant and recessive factors. According to the latter hypothesis, the tallness of the tall variety of Peas is due to the presence of a factor for tallness, while dwarfness in the dwarf variety is

due to the absence of the factor for tallness. Since the presence
and absence hypothesis explains more cases than the dominant
and recessive hypothesis, it has been generally accepted.

Again Mendel worked chiefly with qualitative characters, which
have been found to behave differently from most quantitative
characters, such as size and weight. For example, in crossing large
and small varieties of Corn, the individuals of the first hybrid gen-

Fig. 480. — Inheritance of length of ears in Corn. The ears P_1 are ears
of the parent plants (Tom Thumb Pop Corn at the left and Purple Flint Corn
at the right) chosen to represent the average length of ears of parents. Notice
that the ear of the F_1 generation is intermediate in length between the parental ears, while in the F_2 generation, as shown by the ears at the left and right
of the F_1 ear, the length of ears range from that of Tom Thumb Pop to that
of Purple Flint. After East.

eration are intermediate in size between the parents, the size of
neither parent dominating, and in the second hybrid generation
the individuals are of various sizes, ranging from that of the
smaller to that of the larger parent (Figs. 479, 480 and 481).
At first such cases were considered striking exceptions to Mendel's law. However, a more careful study has led to the view
that quantitative characters do mendelize but commonly depend
upon so many independent factors, each of which is responsible

for a part of the character, that, although they do segregate and combine according to Mendelism, they form so many kinds of combinations and thus so many kinds of individuals occur in the second generation of hybrids that it is difficult to detect Mendelian ratios.   For example, in the case of crossing the tall and small varieties of Corn, it is assumed that the tall variety has a number

Fig. 481. — Inheritance of size and beards in Wheat. Parent types (Turkey × Bluestem at the left and a hybrid No. 143 at the right) and between the parent types the F_1 generation of the Cross.   In the F_1 generation the heads are somewhat intermediate in size and have short beards. After Gaines.

of factors for size that are not present in the small variety.   Let us suppose the large variety has four extra factors for size that are not present in the small variety.   These factors may be represented by A, B, C, and D.   Since the tall variety is pure for its height, its extra height over the small variety is due to the presence of $AABBCCDD$, and the corresponding constitution of the small variety is $aabbccdd$, in which the small letters represent the absence of the extra factors for size. If the tall variety is 32 inches taller than the small variety, each of the factors A, B, C, and D represents 4 inches in height. Now the gametes of the tall variety have $ABCD$ in them, while the corresponding constitution of the gametes of the small variety is $abcd$, and the fertilized eggs and first generation of hybrids resulting from the cross between these two varieties have the formula $AaBbCcDd$. Now since each factor for height represented by the large letters is responsible for 4 inches of height, the individuals of the first generation of hybrids should be 16 inches taller than the small variety but 16 inches shorter than the tall variety. They are intermediate in height between the two parents. The hybrids form gametes having the constitution $ABCD$, $aBCD$, $abCD$, $abcD$, $abcd$, $AbCD$ and so on, involving all the combinations that can be made with the four pairs of letters. In fertilization all possible combinations of the various kinds of gametes can take place, and consequently individuals of eight various sizes can occur in the second generation of hybrids. Thus, if a gamete with a constitution $abcd$ unites with a gamete with the constitution $abcD$, the resulting offspring has the constitution $aabbccdD$ and should be 4 inches higher than the smaller variety of the parent generation. If a gamete with the constitution $ABCD$ unites with a gamete having the constitution $abCD$, the resulting offspring, which has the factors $aAbBCCDD$, should be 24 inches higher than the smaller variety or 8 inches lower than the taller variety of the parent generations. It is, therefore, obvious that due to the various kinds of combinations that may occur among the gametes, individuals of various sizes may occur in the second hybrid generation.

Another peculiar situation which has been discovered among both plants and animals may be illustrated by the behavior of color in the Andalusian fowl. These fowls are what fanciers call blue, but when they are bred together the offspring consist of black, blue, and white fowls, and the proportion is according to the Mendelian ratio 1 : 2 : 1. The black and white fowls breed true, but the blues breed as before. When black and white fowls are crossed, blue fowls are obtained. The blue is therefore a result of a heterozygous condition in which the factor for black is combined with a factor for white. In this case the hybrids may be regarded as having a different character from that of either parent. A similar situation has been discovered in connection with the breeding of Sweet Peas. Certain white-flowered varieties of Sweet Peas when crossed produce red-flowered offspring. There are still a number of other situations that Mendel did meet in his experiments.

To more recent investigators we are also indebted for some present conceptions of the inheritable constitution of organisms. Johannsen of Copenhagen, Denmark, who is responsible for the pure line theory, has done much to establish the theory that inheritance is due to the reappearance of the same organization of protoplasm with reference to genes or character units in successive generations and not to the transmission of external characters. The sum total of all the genes in a gamete or fertilized egg Johannsen calls a *genotype*, while an organism considered as to its appearance he calls a *phenotype*. Organisms may be alike genotypically, that is, alike as to genes but be very different phenotypically. For example, two Corn plants may be exactly alike in their genes for size, yield, etc., but due to a difference in environment differ greatly in these features. On the other hand, organisms may be different genotypically but be very similar phenotypically.

Segregation and the Reduction Division. — As previously stated, the purity of gametes and the segregation of characters depend upon the separation of the genes for contrasting characters. A plant that is a hybrid for tallness and dwarfness can not have gametes pure for tallness and dwarfness, unless the genes for these contrasting characters are separated so as to appear in different cells. The reduction division, which always precedes the formation of gametes in both plants and animals, affords a mechanism by which genes may be segregated. The constant occurrence of the reduction division and also the fact that it is the division in which chromosomes are separated, suggest that it has some vital connection with heredity.

It is generally believed that the genes are associated with the chromatin of the nucleus and are, therefore, distributed with the chromosomes to new cells during cell division. The chromatin of a plant or animal consists of the chromatin contributed by each of its parents. At each cell division this chromatin is organized into a definite number of chromosomes, and there is considerable evidence that the chromatin of each of the parents of the plant or animal whose cell is dividing organizes separately into chromosomes, thus one-half of the number of chromosomes being composed of father chromatin and the other half being composed of mother chromatin. This means that the chromosomes contributed to the offspring by each of the parents maintain their individuality in the offspring. In vegetative cell division each chromosome splits longitudinally, and to each new nucleus there is contributed a half of each chromosome. It is obvious

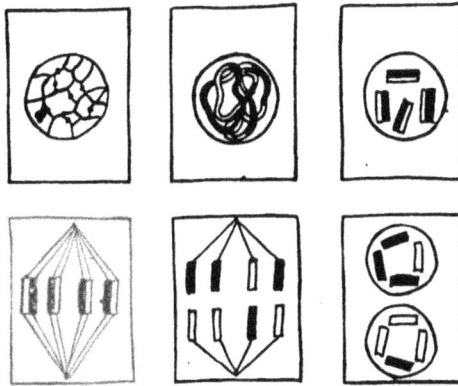

Fig. 482. — A diagram illustrating the behavior of chromatin in the reduction division. For convenience the chromatin contributed by the father of the plant, the division of whose cell the diagram illustrates, is shown black and the chromatin contributed by the mother plant is shown white. In the upper line, organization of the chromosomes and their pairing, each pair consisting of one father and one mother chromosome; in the lower line, the distribution of the chromosomes in the formation of the daughter nuclei. In this case one of the daughter nuclei receives one father and three mother chromosomes, while the other daughter nucleus receives one mother and three father chromosomes, but this is only one of a number of ways of distributing the chromosomes.

that the vegetative cell division tends to distribute the chromatin from both parents equally to the new nuclei. But in the reduction division, as shown in *Figure 482*, whole chromosomes and not halves are contributed to each new nucleus, and consequently the new nuclei resulting from the reduction division receive only half as many chromosomes as the mother cell contained. In the reduction division the chromosomes contributed to the daughter nuclei may be only those of the mother parent or only those of the father parent, in which case the daughter nuclei receive only the genes of one of the parents. On the other hand, the daughter nuclei may receive chromosomes of both parents and in different proportions in different divisions. Again cytological studies of the reduction division show that there is a pairing of chromosomes previous to their separation, and there is evidence that each pair consists of a father and a mother chromosome. Now, if we assume that chromosomes pairing carry genes for contrasting characters, then the separation and distribution of the members of each pair to different daughter nuclei should result in the segregation of genes for contrasting characters and in the production of pure gametes. The trouble with this assumption is that a plant or animal has so many more pairs of contrasting characters than chromosomes, that it is difficult to explain the numerous combinations that occur when many pairs of contrasting characters are taken into account. Despite the fact that there are some things about segregation we are unable to explain by the mechanism of reduction division, it is generally believed that the two phenomena are vitally related.

The Mendelian Ratio and the Combinations of Gametes. — It is possible to account for the Mendelian ratio $1 : 2 : 1$ by taking into account the probable combinations that may occur among gametes during fertilization. A hybrid forms two kinds of gametes equal in number in respect to a pair of contrasting characters. One kind of sperms and eggs may be represented by A and the other by B. Now the probable combinations between the two kinds of sperms and two kinds of eggs in the self-fertilization of a hybrid are represented by $\begin{smallmatrix} A \\ A \end{smallmatrix} \times \begin{smallmatrix} B \\ B \end{smallmatrix}$. There are two chances for A and B to unite to one chance for A to unite with A or B to unite with B. The probable combinations and their ratios are, therefore, $AA : 2AB : BB$ or $1 : 2 : 1$. If the factors represented by either A or B are dominant, then $3 : 1$ is the ratio of the dominant to the recessive offspring.

CHAPTER XXIV

PLANT BREEDING

Plant breeding has to do with the improvement of old plants and the securing of new ones. Many and various are the aims of plant breeding. The object may be to improve the yield, increase the resistance to drought or disease, shorten the period of development, or secure strains or varieties with new characters. The two important methods used are selection and hybridization.

In connection with plant breeding, the discoveries of De Vries and Mendel have proven to be of inestimable value. The discoveries of De Vries have resulted in a better understanding of the nature of variations and has enabled us to improve plants by selection much more efficiently. The introduction of Mendel's methods of investigation and his discoveries concerning the behavior of characters in hybrid offspring afford a scientific foundation to the improvement of plants by hybridization. As a result of Mendel's contributions, we now know much more about how to proceed, what to expect, and how to interpret the results obtained in hybridizing.

Selection. — Selection takes advantage of variations. Variations, as previously noted, are not only due to differences in gametes and their combinations in fertilization, but also to differences in temperature, moisture, soil conditions, and other environmental factors. But only those variations due to factors which can be transmitted by the gametes are inheritable through the seed. A Corn plant may be larger or bear larger ears than the ordinary type because of especially favorable conditions. It may stand alone in the hill, thus having all of the water and mineral supply to itself, or it may be growing on ground more heavily fertilized. This increased size, due to external conditions and not to any special factors in the cells of the plant, is not transmitted to the offspring, and the embryos in the kernels of this especially favored plant may have inherited no more for size than the embryos developed by a much smaller plant which has grown in less favorable conditions. To compare plants as to what is really in their cells, the conditions under which the plants were grown must be considered. It is for this reason that it is much better to select seed Corn from the field than to select it from the crib; for by the first method the conditions under which the plants developed can be considered and their genetic constitution better estimated.

In addition to Johannsen's investigations of inheritance in Beans and a number of other plants, there are many other experiments that tend to establish the fact that little is gained by selections in pure lines, unless mutations happen to occur. For example, as previously cited a long series of selections in a pure line of Oats to increase the yield secured no results. Likewise selections in pure lines of Wheat to intensity and fix a desirable variation have given no results. In each generation plants having the desirable variation were selected for seed, but selections carried on this way for a number of generations did not increase the average of the variation.

In vegetative propagation, where the progeny does not develop from seed but grows from vegetative structures taken from the parent, some variations, such as bud sports, that are often not inheritable through seed can be perpetuated. Such is true in such plants as Strawberries, which are propagated by runners, and in fruit trees, which are propagated by grafting. But modifications that are simply responses to some peculiarity in the environment are not perpetuated even by vegetative propagation.

Although selection often fails to produce the desired results, nevertheless, selection is one of the chief means of improving plants. A mass of plants, such as a field of grain, is a mixture of individuals most of which are heterozygous for one or more

Fig. 483. — Heads of Wheat, showing improvement in size as a result of a five-year selection in which the plants bearing the largest heads were selected each year for seed. Redrawn from De Vries.

characters. By selecting, through a number of generations, the most desirable individuals for seed, eventually individuals that are homozygous and breed true to the desirable character may be secured, and a better race of plants thereby established. Mutations also afford considerable opportunity to improve plants by selection. In case individuals appear that are more desirable due to a mutation, a more desirable race of individuals is immediately secured by selecting and propagating these mutants. Through selection, races of plants much more desirable than the ordinary types from which the plants were selected have been produced. Grains, forage crops, Strawberries, Blackberries, Melons, fruit trees, etc., have been improved by selecting and propagating those plants having more desirable features than the ordinary types. In this way plants have been improved in yield (*Figs. 483* and *484*), ability to resist drought and disease, length of period

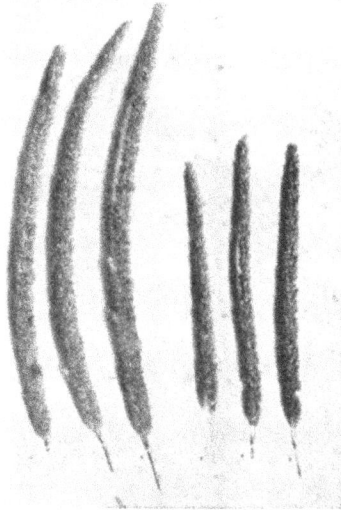

Fig. 484.—Heads of Timothy, showing improvement by selection. After Hays.

required for maturing (*Fig. 485*), and many other ways. There are two methods used in improving plants by selection, the *mass culture* and *pedigree culture.*

Mass Culture. — This is the oldest method of plant breeding. This method employs large masses or fields of plants, known as mass cultures, from which to select. For example, in applying this method to the breeding of small grains, the plant breeder, desiring to produce a better yielding race, goes through the field and selects those plants with heads having the largest number of grains. From the next year's crop grown from the seed of the plants selected the previous year, the best yielding plants are again selected for seed, and year after year he continues to select until a race more or less constant for high yield is obtained.

This method of selection is productive of good results, but has some disadvantages. It requires much time and labor as well as the use of much ground. Since each crop is grown from seed furnished by many plants selected the previous year, the progeny of many plants are involved and the yield of a crop

Fig. 485. — Dakota Amber Sargo, a strain that matures much earlier and is more drought-resistant than the South Dakota No. 341 from which this new strain was produced by selection. After Dillman.

is the average yield of the descendants of many plants varying in capacity and heritage for high yield. Many of the plants in the selection are likely to be heterozygous for the character and consequently will not breed true. Races obtained by this method of selection usually lose their desirable features unless selection is continued.

Pedigree Culture. — The value of pedigree cultures was well demonstrated by De Vries and Mendel. In the method of selection by pedigree cultures, a single plant is selected, and from its progeny, which are carefully guarded, the best individuals are selected. After continuing the selection for a few generations, a race with a certain standard and steadiness is obtained. The race obtained by this method of selection is the progeny of a single individual, and its desirable features are more stable than in most races secured by mass selection. This method also requires less labor and usually less time than the method of mass culture. After the race is secured by pedigree culture, it is usually tested in mass culture to see how it behaves when grown in masses under ordinary field conditions.

Selection of Mutants. — Many valuable races of plants have been discovered accidentally and apparently have arisen suddenly. The Fultz Wheat comes from a few plants which were accidentally discovered growing in a field of Lancaster Red. These few plants, which were smoother and had more beautiful heads than the Lancaster Red, were saved for seed, and from these seeds the well-known and valuable race of Fultz Wheat originated. The Gold Coin Wheat was accidentally found growing in a field of Mediterranean Wheat. There are a number of varieties of Wheat, Oats, Barley, and Rye which apparently originated in a similar way.

Many or all of the different cultivated varieties of Dewberries were accidentally found growing wild and were selected because they showed some desirable features not possessed by the ordinary type of wild Dewberries. Some may be hybrids, while others are most likely mutants.

In woody plants, such as fruit trees, the selection of vegetative mutations known as bud sports, in which a branch may produce a type of fruit different from the fruit produced by other branches, often leads to the establishment of new varieties. By propagating these special branches by grafting, a different type of tree may be obtained. The Nectarine has already been mentioned as arising in this way, and there still are other examples among Peaches, Apples, and other fruits. Greening Apples often have branches bearing Russet Apples, and Russet Apples often have branches bearing Greening Apples. There are, therefore, many instances in which selection has not only resulted in the securing of better grains, vegetables, fruits, and ornamental plants, but also in new types.

Hybridization. — The advantage of hybridization is that by crossing one can combine in the offspring the different desirable features of the two plants used in the cross. Since Mendel's discoveries have furnished principles that make it possible to interpret the behavior of hybrids, one can proceed with considerable certainty. As to just how the factors introduced by the sperm and egg will manifest themselves in the offspring resulting from a cross is not known until the offspring appear. The characters, whether they blend or behave as dominants and recessives, are identified only by observations of the hybrid generations. The hybrid may be like one parent in some features and like the other parent in other features, or in size and some other characters it may be intermediate between the two parents. According to Mendel's law, we can expect three kinds of individuals in the F_2 generation when one pair of contrasting characters is considered, and that the pure dominants and pure recessives will breed true whether one or many pairs of characters are taken into account. The pure dominants and pure recessives can be identified by further breeding, and if they prove to be more desirable than the varieties used in the cross, then by propagating them a more desirable race or variety is established. In case one wishes to bring together in one individual a number of desirable characters, some of which are present in one variety and some in another, the breeding process to obtain the individuals pure for these characters is complex, as was shown in the discussion of Mendelism, and the more factors involved, the more complex is the process. But Mendel's law points the way of procedure, and it is possible for the patient plant breeder to so manipulate the breeding through a number of generations as to finally obtain a combination of the desirable characters in an individual that will breed true. The desired individual having been secured, the new race or variety is practically established. Much has been accomplished in improving plants through hybridization. For example, in this way a much more desirable race of Wheat has been obtained in England. One variety of English Wheat, yielding well but producing a poor grade of flour, was crossed with a variety of Canadian Wheat, which produces a good grade of flour but does not yield so well in the English climate as the English variety. The plant breeder finally succeeded in getting a race having the desirable features of producing good flour and yielding well in the English climate By crossing Wheat, having some desirable qualities but susceptible to Rust, with Wheat, immune to Rust but less desirable in other features, a type of Wheat having the Rust resistance of one parent and the desirable features of the other has been obtained. Cotton producing longer and better lint has been obtained by crossing the Sea Island Cotton with the Upland Cottons. There are many instances in which more desirable races have been secured through hybridization.

Fig. 486. — The effect of three degrees of relationship in breeding Corn. Nos. 3 and 4 are pure strains from seed-stock inbred for three years. No. 2 is from a close-fertilized seed-stock, the plants each year being fertilized with pollen from sister plants grown from the same ear. No. 1 is from seed-stock that has been cross-fertilized for three years. After Montgomery.

The greatest advantage arising from hybridization is among plants propagated by vegetative methods, as by tubers, bulbs, cuttings, layering, grafting, etc.; for in these cases the progeny is simply a continuation of the hybrid individual and not the result of the fusion of gametes. Many berries, vegetables, fruit trees, and ornamental plants are hybrids. By crossing different kinds of Strawberries, hybrids more desirable than either of the parents have been obtained, and since they propagate by runners, the hybrid type is maintained generation after generation. Blackberries, which are propagated vegetatively, have been improved by hybridization. By crossing the cultivated Blackberry, which has a large black fruit, with a small wild Blackberry, having a whitish or cream colored fruit, a Blackberry having a fruit large in size and light in color has been obtained. Many

FIG. 487. — Results of inbreeding and crossing on the size of ears in Corn. Outer ears, result of inbreeding one generation; middle ear, result in the first generation of crossing these inbred generations. After East.

of the best Plums and other fruit trees are hybrids, and the hybrid characters are retained by propagating the trees by grafting and budding. Hybrids are also common among Roses, Carnations, and other ornamental plants.

Crossing and Vigor of Offspring. — Crossing usually results in increased vigor, while self-fertilization commonly results in the loss of vigor in the offspring. Hybrids are usually more vigorous than their parents. Corn grown from seed resulting from self-fertilization shows much loss in vigor and consequently does not yield so well (*Figs. 486* and *487*). The difference in yield between plants resulting from crossing and plants resulting from self-fertilization often amounts to several bushels per acre.

FIG. 488. — Increase in size of fruits in Cucumbers as a result of crossing. *a* and *c* show size of fruits borne by the parents and *b*, the size of fruits borne by the first generation of the cross. After Halsted.

Darwin found that Cabbage plants obtained by crossing were nearly three times the weight of those obtained by self-fertilization. In Buckwheat Darwin obtained plants much taller and about one-fifth better in yield by crossing. In Lettuce, Beets, Pumpkins, Squashes, Tomatoes, and many other plants (*Fig. 488*), it has been shown that crossing produces more vigorous offspring.

INDEX

(The numbers with stars refer to the pages on which the illustrations are given.)